CW00469399

Where to watch birds in

Africa

THE *WHERE TO WATCH BIRDS* SERIES

Where to watch birds in Africa
Nigel Wheatley

Where to watch birds in Bedfordshire, Berkshire, Buckinghamshire, Hertfordshire and Oxfordshire
Brian Clews, Andrew Heryet and Paul Trodd

Where to watch birds in Cumbria, Lancashire and Cheshire
Jonathan Guest and Malcolm Hutcheson

Where to watch birds in Devon and Cornwall
David Norman and Vic Tucker

Where to watch birds in Dorset, Hampshire and the Isle of Wight
George Green and Martin Cade

Where to Watch Birds in East Anglia
Peter and Margaret Clarke

Where to watch birds in France
Ligue Française pour la Protection des Oiseaux

Where to watch birds in Ireland
Clive Hutchinson

Where to watch birds in Italy
Lega Italiana Protezione Uccelli

Where to watch birds in Kent, Surrey and Sussex
Don Taylor, Jeffrey Wheatley and Tony Prater

Where to watch birds in Scotland
Mike Madders and Julia Welstead

Where to watch birds Somerset, Avon, Gloucestershire and Wiltshire
Ken Hall and John Govett

Where to watch birds in South America
Nigel Wheatley

Where to watch birds in Southern Spain
Ernest Garcia and Andrew Paterson

Where to watch birds in Wales
David Saunders

Where to watch birds in the West Midlands
Graham Harrison and Jack Sankey

Where to watch birds in Yorkshire and North Humberside
John Mather

Where to watch birds in

Africa

Nigel Wheatley

Christopher Helm
A & C Black · London

Christopher Helm (Publishers) Ltd, a subsidiary of
A & C Black Ltd, 35 Bedford Row, London WC1R 4JH

ISBN 0-7136-4013-8

A CIP catalogue record for this book is available
from the British Library

Printed and bound by Biddles Limited, Guildford,
Surrey in Great Britain

CONTENTS

ACKNOWLEDGEMENTS

It would have been impossible to write this book without the help of numerous birders who have not just travelled to Africa to see the wonderful birds, but have been unselfish enough to record their experiences for the benefit of others. These people have made their information generally available and, to me, are some of the heroes of the birding world.

I would like to express my heartfelt thanks to the following birders and organisations who have kindly allowed me either to use the information contained within their reports, papers, books, brochures and letters, and/or covered some country accounts in honest red ink: John Ash, Dylan Aspinwall, Zul Bhatia, BirdLife International, Birdquest, Pierre Bulens, Mike Catsis, 'Chief' (Nick Cobb), Peter Colston, Cygnus, John Day, Dirk de Moes, Ron Demey, Bob Dowsett, John Edge, John Elgood, Lincoln Fishpool, Ghana Wildlife Society, Chris Gibbins, Gary Grant, Clive Green, Nodlaig Guinan, Tom Gullick, Tom Heijnen, Henk Hendriks, John Hollyer, Rob Hopkinson, Hauke Kahl, Steve Keen, Guy Kirwan, John Leefe, Bob Medland, Heimo Mikkola, Chris Petrow, Barry Reed, Gerry Richards, Iain Robertson, Dave Sargeant, Herbert and Christa Schels, Ian Sinclair, 'Spotter' (John Mason), Terry Stevenson, Barry Stidolph, Sunbird, Gavin and Val Thomson, Don Turner, Alan Tye, Nick Wall, Frank Walsh, Jerry Warne, Geoff and Hilary Welch, Roger Wilkinson, Eddie Williams, Mark Wotham, Barry Wright, and Jan Zwaaneveld. Naturally, many thanks also go to the many birders who accompanied these people in the field, helped to find the birds, and no doubt contributed their own information.

In particular I would like to express special thanks to Nick Gardner, Jon Hornbuckle and Richard Webb, who have not only provided a lot of information but, along with Alun Hatfield, offered plenty of encouragement.

I have spoken to many other people on the telephone or in the field about minor but important matters, whom I may have unwittingly omitted from the above list. I sincerely hope these people will accept my profuse apologies if I have failed to acknowledge their help in this edition, and hope they will let me know before the next.

It has to be said that there are some birders, including a few with a wealth of experience in Africa, who have *never* written any trip reports; or, if they have done so, have not made their information generally available. Fortunately such people are few and far between, and sharing information comes naturally to the vast majority of birders.

When I started writing the book it seemed as though every bird had at least three different names. This major headache was cured by James Clements, to whom I am very grateful for giving me permission to use his *Check List* as the baseline for this book.

Finally, writing a book of this nature is, for the most part, an obsessive labour of love, and the writer can all too easily forget the other aspects of his or her life, except birds of course; and so I must give special thanks to Georgie Malpass, since she has soothed the many headaches encountered *en route* to the final version, and insisted on me taking the odd break.

INTRODUCTION

My parents delighted me when, for Christmas 1975, they gave me *The Dictionary of Birds in Colour*, illustrated with numerous superb photographs. There was one photograph, which is credited to A Weaving, that particularly stood out. It was of a sunlit Lilac-breasted Roller perched atop a dead snag. A birder for just nine months, I had barely stepped outside Gloucestershire in search of birds nor imagined there could have been any bird so exotic. That Lilac-breasted Roller conjured up all sorts of fantastic birding images in my mind. For many years I dreamt of seeing one of those fabulous birds. I cut out the photograph and put it on my wall as a stimulus to fulfil my dream.

In 1987 my dream came true. I saw my first Lilac-breasted Roller perched on a telegraph pole by the side of Lake Naivasha, Kenya, and it was every bit as exotic and exciting as I had imagined. I saw 630 species during the following three months in Africa, including many, many more Lilac-breasted Rollers, and every one was still a beauty.

However, I have to admit that my beloved roller was overshadowed by a few even more exciting birds and marvellous moments in Africa, not least my first Blue-headed and White-throated Bee-eaters in Kakamega, west Kenya; my first sight of the Masai Mara, which seen from an escarpment to the west, looked like it took up the rest of the world; and looking at a tiny orange ball of fluff with two huge yellow eyes, otherwise known as the Sokoke Scops-Owl, lit up in a torchbeam in the pitch black Arabuko–Sokoke Forest. It was Lake Naivasha though that I remember the best. Its shores were generously sprinkled with shorebirds and its surrounding acacias abounding with passerines, making it my kind of paradise. Two weeks there in March 1988 culminated on the 15th when, during an eight-hour walk, I saw 175 species, including many of those spectacular birds for which Africa is renowned. Secretary-bird, African Fish-Eagle, Blacksmith Plover, Superb Starling, and yes, Lilac-breasted Roller, to name a few. I can see the photograph of the Lilac-breasted Roller as I write. It was once a catalyst. It is now a powerful reminder of great birding days in Africa.

When birders contemplate where they would like to go birding in the world, it is only natural for Africa to seep in to their thoughts. If it sticks, a multitude of questions usually spring to mind. The first question usually concerns the whereabouts of certain species. Where is the best place to see Ostrich, Goliath Heron, Shoebill, Saddle-billed Stork, African Fish-Eagle, Bateleur, Secretary-bird, Kori Bustard, Crab Plover, coursers, Egyptian Plover, Blacksmith Plover, Great Blue Turaco, trogons, kingfishers, all those fantastic bee-eaters, rollers, hornbills, bushshrikes, batises, oxpeckers, rock-jumpers, rockfowl and sunbirds such as Golden-winged? Birders thinking about returning to the continent will wonder about the whereabouts of more obscure species such as rare guineafowl, francolins, Congo Peacock, flufftails, fishing-owls, honeyguides, pittas, broadbills, ground-thrushes, and even greenbuls, cisticolas, and larks. If Madagascar is on their mind, there are mesites, ground-rollers, asities and vangas to ponder over.

Once the birds have been decided upon, further questions need answering. Which country is best? When is the best time to go? Where are the best sites? How easy is it to get from site to site? How long will I need to spend at each one? What other species are there at these sites? Which birds should I concentrate on? Are there any endemics? How many species am I likely to see? The list goes on.

Such questions need careful consideration if the proposed birding trip is going to be enjoyable. Without months of painstaking preparation a trip may not be anywhere near as exciting as it could be.

This book's aim is to help answer the questions birders ask themselves before venturing to Africa for the first, or fortieth, time. It is not meant to direct you to every site and bird in the minutest detail, but to be *a guiding light*. There can be no substitute for an up-to-date report. I urge readers to seek these reports out (see p. 413) once they have decided on their destination, and to write their own reports on their return.

Birders are notoriously hard to please, so writing this book has been all-consuming. I began by compiling a list of sites and the species recorded at them, from every imaginable source. Birders reports were the major goldmine and without the generous permission of the writers (see Acknowledgements) this book would not exist. Whilst compiling the site lists I realised that English bird names are a problem. I decided I needed a list of species as the baseline for names used and for the taxonomic order of the species lists for each site. I chose *Birds of the World: A Check List*, by James Clements (Fourth Edition 1991, together with Supplements 1 and 2), simply because the names and taxonomic order used seemed the most logical.

The names of birds in this check list are spelt in 'American'. For example, 'coloured' is spelt 'colored' and 'grey' is spelt 'gray'. Although the 'English' names of New World birds should be spelt in the American way I have written them in English in this edition.

Many of the names used by James for species restricted to southern Africa are different from those used in field guides to that region, so a table comparing the two has been included (p. 417).

Using databases such as reports most, if not all, of the best birding sites, spectacular and endemic species, as well as those birds hard to see beyond the continent's boundaries, have been included, albeit in varying levels of detail.

The result is over 200 main sites, listed in the Contents, over 100 maps, endemic and near-endemic species-lists (at the end of each country account) where appropriate, and a species index (p. 419).

After much consideration the book has taken the following shape. Countries are treated alphabetically. Details for each country are dealt with as follows:

The **Country Introduction** includes:

A brief **summary** of the features discussed below.
Size, in relation to England and Texas.
Getting around, where the infrastructure of the country is discussed.
Accommodation and food.
Health and safety, although general advice is given, it is best to check the latest immunisation requirements (immunisation against yellow fever may be compulsory, not just recommended) and per-

sonal safety precautions before planning your trip.
Climate and timing, where the best times to visit are given (summarised in the Calendar, p. 412).
Habitats.
Conservation.
An overview of the **bird families** represented within the country (see Figure 1, below).
The total number of **bird species** recorded in the country, followed by a short list of non-endemic specialities and spectacular species, which is intended to give a brief taste of what to expect (rarely seen species are not usually included in this brief list).
The total number of **endemic species** and near-endemic species, followed by a short list of the most spectacular birds in this category.
Expectations, where an idea of how many species to expect is given.

Some of these sections may be missing for the less well known countries, and the details given are intended to be as brief as possible. There seems little point here in repeating the vast amount of information now available in travel guides, and it makes much more sense to save room for more information on the birds and birding in this book.

FIGURE 1: BIRD FAMILIES IN AFRICA

The 17 families listed below in bold type are endemic to the Afrotropical region, which includes sub-Saharan Africa and its related islands. The ten families listed below in bold capitals are endemic to the African mainland, the five families listed in bold, small type are endemic to the Malagasy region (Madagascar and the Comoros), and the two families listed in bold, small, italic type are endemic to the African mainland, south Arabia and Madagascar (in the case of Hamerkop), or the African mainland and south Arabia (in the case of guineafowls).

OSTRICH
Grebes
Penguins
Albatrosses
Shearwaters and petrels
Storm-Petrels
Diving-Petrels (Common Diving-Petrel)
Tropicbirds
Frigatebirds
Gannets and boobies
Cormorants
Anhingas (African Darter)
Pelicans
Waterfowl
Flamingos
Herons and egrets
SHOEBILL
Hamerkop
Ibis and spoonbills
Storks
Osprey
Hawks, eagles and kites
SECRETARY-BIRD
Falcons
Guineafowl
Francolins, partridges and quails
Buttonquails
Rails
Sungrebes (African Finfoot)

Mesites
Cranes
Bustards
Jacanas
Painted-snipes (Greater Painted-snipe)
Snipes and sandpipers
Crab Plover
Thick-knees
Oystercatchers
Stilts and avocets
Coursers and pratincoles
Plovers and lapwings
Gulls and terns
Skuas and jaegers
Skimmers (African Skimmer)
Auks
Divers
Sandgrouse
Pigeons and doves
Parrots
MOUSEBIRDS
TURACOS
Cuckoos
Coucals
Barn-Owls
Owls
Nightjars
Swifts
Trogons
Kingfishers
Bee-eaters
Rollers
Ground-Rollers
Cuckoo-Roller
Hoopoes
WOODHOOPOES
Hornbills
GROUND-HORNBILLS
AFRICAN BARBETS
Honeyguides
Woodpeckers
Pittas
Broadbills
Asities
Paradise-Flycatchers
Drongos
Corvids
Orioles
Cuckoo-shrikes
Shrikes
Bushshrikes
Vangas
Dippers (White-throated Dipper)
Thrushes
Starlings
Old World flycatchers (akalats, robin-chats, scrub-robins, wheatears etc.)
Nuthatches
Treecreepers
Wrens (Winter Wren)
Swallows
Kinglets('crests)
Bulbuls
White-eyes
Cisticolas
Warblers
Babblers
ROCKFOWLS
Tits
Penduline-Tits
Larks
Old World sparrows
Waxbills
Wagtails and pipits
Accentors
Weavers
SUGARBIRDS
Sunbirds
Finches
Buntings

Total = 108

On each country map the **sites** are numbered along a more or less logical route through the country or in 'bunches', and discussed in that order under each country account. Naturally, different birders will prefer their own routes, but I felt this was a better method than dealing with the sites alphabetically because birders intending to visit just one region of a country will find all the sites in that region dealt with in the same section of the book.

Sites are dealt with as follows:

The **site name** usually refers to the actual site. However, if it is nameless, or it involves a number of birding spots which are in close proximity, the best city, town, village, lodge or road name from which to explore the site, however remote, is used.

The **site introduction** gives its general location within the relevant country before describing its size, main physical characteristics, habitat make-up and avifauna, including the number of species recorded (if known) and particular reference to endemic and speciality species best looked for at that site. It is *important* to remember here that specialities of the given site are mentioned in the introduction and do not include all the birds listed under the section headed **Specialities** in the list for that site (see full explanation below).

The site's altitude (where known) is also given, in metres and feet. Both measurements are given since some birders prefer metres and some prefer feet, whereas km readings only are given for distances because most birders now have a grasp of kilometres. For those that do not, remember that one mile equals 1.6093, or roughly 1.6 kilometres.

Restrictions on access, if there are any, are also given in the site introduction. Such a negative start is designed to eliminate the extreme disappointment of discovering the site is inaccessible to all but the most well-prepared and adventurous *after* reading about the wealth of avian riches present at the site. It is *imperative* to check the situation in some countries with the relevant authorities before even considering a visit.

The **species lists** for the site follow the introduction and include:

Endemics: Species found only in the country in which the site is located (not species endemic to the site). Some species listed here may occur only at one or two sites within the country so it is important to make a special effort to see them. Such species are mentioned in the site introduction. Others are more widespread but *still* endemic to the relevant country.

Specialities: Species which have (1) Restricted ranges which cross country boundaries. (2) Wider distributions throughout Africa but are generally scarce, rare or threatened. (3) Rarely been mentioned in the literature consulted in preparing this book.

It is important to remember here that the species listed under **Specialities** are *not* specialities of the site (such species are mentioned in the site introduction). In southern African countries (Namibia, Botswana, Zimbabwe and South Africa) birds listed under specialities are *not* southern African endemics, they are species with more restricted ranges than that. Most occur only in two of the four countries or in small areas which cross more than two country boundaries.

Some species listed under **Specialities** may be very rare at the given site. Nevertheless they *still* fit the criteria given above and merit the 'status' of speciality as far as this book is concerned.

Others: Species that are well distributed but uncommon, spectacular or especially sought after for a variety of reasons.

Some species are specialities in one country but not another so they may appear under **Specialities** for one country and **Others** for another. Some species may appear under **Specialities** for one country and **Others** for another because they are more likely to be seen at the site where they are listed under **Specialities** and are difficult to see at sites where they are listed under **Others**.

At the end of the bird lists there is also a list of **Other Wildlife** which includes mammals, reptiles, amphibians, fish, insects etc., listed in alphabetical order.

The lists, particularly the **Others** section, are not comprehensive and many more species may have been recorded at the given site. Such species are common and likely to be seen at many sites in that region of the country or throughout a large part of Africa. Abundant, widespread, but no less spectacular species, which are not normally listed, include African Fish-Eagle, Long-crested Eagle, African Jacana, Crowned Lapwing, Malachite, Grey-headed and Woodland Kingfishers, Rufous-crowned and Broad-billed Rollers, Sulphur-breasted and Grey-headed Bushshrikes and Scarlet-chested Sunbird. By restricting the numbers of species listed under **Others** I have hoped to avoid repetition.

No one, not even the most experienced observer, is likely to see all the species listed under each site in a single visit, or even over a period of a few days or, in some cases, during a prolonged stay of weeks or more. This is because a number of African species, especially those found in forest, apart from being extremely shy, are very thin on the ground.

Within these lists, species marked with an asterisk (*) have been listed as threatened, conservation dependent, data deficient or near-threatened (by BirdLife International/IUCN in *Birds to Watch 2: The World List of Threatened Birds*. Collar, N *et al.* 1994). It is important to report any records of these species, and those described as rare in the text, to BirdLife International, Wellbrook Court, Girton Road, Cambridge CB3 0NA, UK. The BirdLife book deals in detail with all threatened species so birders interested in the rarest species, many of which are some of Africa's most spectacular, should seriously consider scrutinising it as part of their pre-trip planning and research.

After the bird lists, directions to the site from the nearest large city, town or village, or previous site, are given in the **Access** section. Then the best trails, birding 'spots' and birds are dealt with. Most distances are given to the nearest km because speedometers and tyres vary so much, and directions are usually described as points of the compass rather than left or right so as not to cause confusion if travelling from a different direction from that dealt with. These directions are aimed at birders with cars. However, it is important to note that in most countries buses and bush taxis go virtually anywhere there is habitation and will drop the passenger off at birding sites on request.

If the detail under this section seems scant this is usually because one or more severely endangered species are present at that site.

I have decided not to repeat the vast amount of information regarding means of public transport given in reports or compete with the extensive detail presented in the various guide books. These can be used by birders requiring them.

Where access is limited or permission required this is stated and a contact address given, sometimes in the **Additional Information** section at the end of each country account.

Under **Accommodation** I have included the names of hotels and other forms of accommodation recommended by birders for their safety, economy, comfort, position and, especially, opportunities for birding. I have not listed all types of accommodation available at every site since it would be foolish to waste so much space on repeating all the information to be found in the general guide books.

Hotels and other accommodation are graded as follows: (A) = Over £10/$15 (usually a long way over); (B) = £5 to £10/$7.5 to $15; (C) = Under £5/$7.5 (all prices per person per night).

In a few cases these price codes have been used to indicate other costs, such as boat hire and guide fees.

Under each main site other nearby spots worth visiting are also mentioned. These usually offer another chance to see species already listed under the main sites but, in some cases, include sites, especially new ones, where information is scant and some pioneer spirit is required. African veterans may wish to find out more about such sites (and send me the details for inclusion in the next edition).

At the end of each country account there is an **Additional Information** section which includes lists of **Books and Papers** for further research and field use, and **Addresses** to contact for more information or advanced booking of permits, accommodation etc.

Finally, each country account ends, where relevant, with a list of **Endemic Species** and the best sites to look for them. There may be no specific sites for some species. This is the time to leave this guide in the car, put your exploring boots on, and set out to find these little known birds. If successful, please send the details to me for inclusion in the next edition (see Request, p. 411).

Lists of **Near-endemic** species are also given where appropriate. The species listed here have restricted ranges which cross two or three country boundaries. Birders with a particular interest in the endemics and near-endemics may wish to plan their trip around these sections, especially if many of the near-endemics are difficult to get to or see in the neighbouring countries and a return trip is unlikely.

It is important to remember that this book is not an up-to-the-minute trip report. Some sites will have changed when you get there, some may not even be there. For example, some sites are accessible only on tracks which have been built by logging and mining companies, and whilst these enable birders to get to the remaining habitat, they also act as a catalyst for new settlements (See Conservation, p. 29).

Still, a little uncertainty is what makes birding so fascinating. It would be a poor pastime if every bird was lined up by an 'x' on the map, or at a 'km reading'. Exploration is exciting, and if you arrive at a site to find the marsh on the map has vanished, set out to find another one. There is immense satisfaction to be gained from finding your own birds, although a little guidance is often appreciated.

I hope this book offers that guidance, and helps you to find and enjoy the fabulous birds of Africa.

INTRODUCTION TO BIRDING IN AFRICA

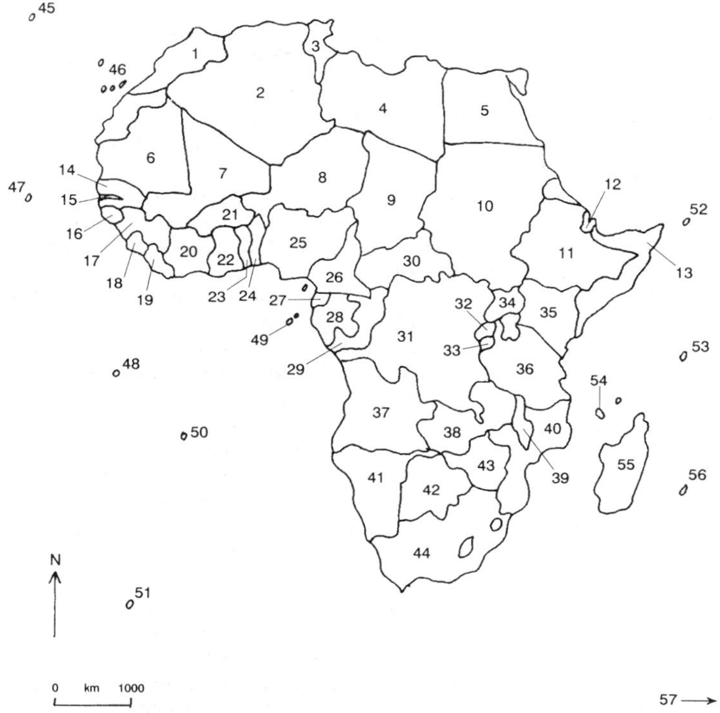

1 Morocco
2 Algeria
3 Tunisia
4 Libya
5 Egypt
6 Mauritania
7 Mali
8 Niger
9 Chad
10 Sudan
11 Ethiopia
12 Djibouti
13 Somalia
14 Senegal
15 Gambia
16 Guinea Bissau
17 Guinea Conakry
18 Sierra Leone
19 Liberia
20 Côte D'Ivoire
21 Burkina Faso
22 Ghana
23 Togo
24 Benin
25 Nigeria
26 Cameroon
27 Equatorial Guinea
28 Gabon
29 Congo
30 Central African Republic
31 Zaïre
32 Rwanda
33 Burundi
34 Uganda
35 Kenya
36 Tanzania
37 Angola
38 Zambia
39 Malawi
40 Mozambique
41 Namibia
42 Botswana
43 Zimbabwe
44 South Africa (including Swaziland and Lesotho)
45 Azores
46 Canary Islands (and Madeira)
47 Cape Verde Islands
48 Ascension Island
49 São Tomé and Principe
50 St Helena
51 Tristan da Cunha Islands
52 Socotra
53 Seychelles
54 Comoros
55 Madagascar
56 Mauritius and Réunion
57 Amsterdam Island

Over 2,300 species have been recorded in Africa, 770 fewer than South America, but some 400 more than the Orient.

Based on *Birds of the World: A Check List* by James Clements, a total of 2,313 species have been recorded in Africa. Nearly 500 of these species also occur outside the continent, mainly in Eurasia (around 185 breed in the Palearctic and winter in Africa), leaving 1,767 species which are totally endemic to Africa and its satellite islands, including Madagascar. Over 1,500 species (1,528) are confined to the African mainland. Clements lists some 9,700 species for the world; Africa supports nearly a quarter (24%) of this total.

FIGURE 2: SPECIES LISTS OF THE WORLD'S AVIFAUNAL REGIONS (approximate figures)

Region	List	% of world total	% of African total
SOUTH AMERICA	3,083	32	133
AFRICA	2,313	24	-
ORIENT	1,900	20	82
PALEARCTIC	950	10	41
AUSTRALASIA	900	9	39
NEARCTIC	800	8	35

Habitat Diversity

Not surprisingly for such a huge land mass, which is crossed by the equator, Africa supports a tremendous variety of habitats, despite the fact that much of the northern half of the continent is taken up by the Sahara Desert.

The many coastal lagoons and slopes of shrubby maquis which line Africa's northern coast soon give way to the massive Sahara Desert (1500 km from north to south) separating the northern Palearctic part of Africa from the southern Afrotropical zone. The southern edge of the world's biggest desert is fringed with a narrow belt of semi-arid scrub known as the Sahel, an important wintering ground for many Palearctic passerines. South of the Sahel is savanna. This is dry in the north (Sudan savanna), and moist in the south (Guinea savanna). These savannas comprise grassland and deciduous woodland, often present in a park-like pattern, and support many birds such as bee-eaters and rollers. A number of large rivers, the Niger for instance, flow through these savannas, and when seasonally flooded they form important wintering grounds for Palearctic waterfowl and shorebirds, as well as numerous African birds.

In northeast and East Africa the highlands of Ethiopia, Kenya, Tanzania and Malawi, rising to 5894 m (19,337 ft) at mighty Mount Kilimanjaro, support montane forest and grassland, which in turn supports many restricted-range species. The Great Rift Valley, a massive rip in the planet's crust, extends from the Red Sea coast of Ethiopia to Tanzania, and the string of freshwater and soda lakes that lie in it support a multitude of birds, particularly plovers. These wetlands are often surrounded by bird-rich acacia savanna.

AFRICA: MAIN PHYSICAL FEATURES AND HABITATS

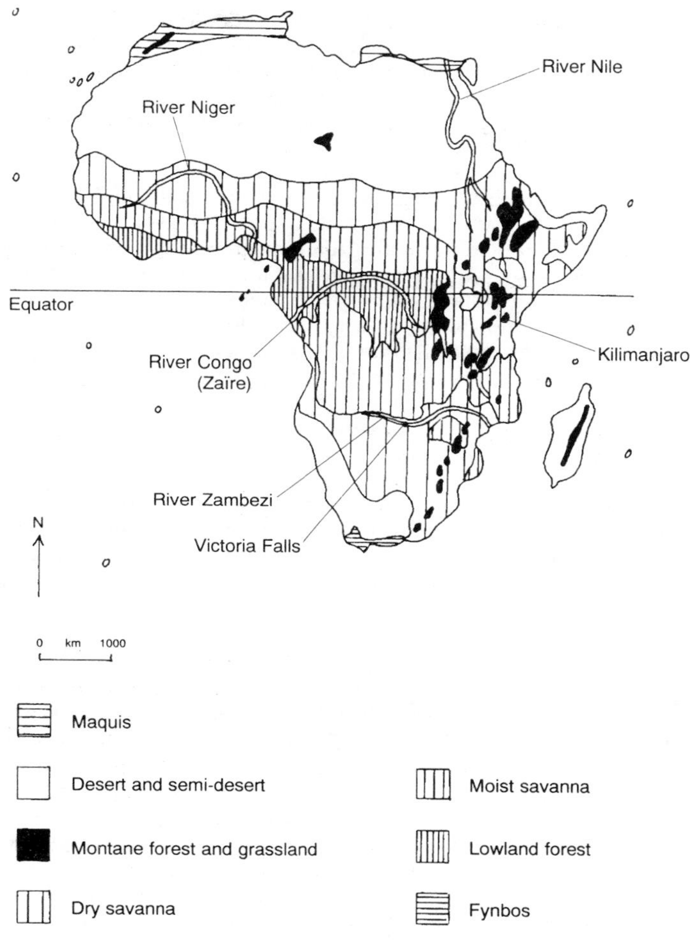

In far West Africa little lowland rainforest remains, but that which still exists, in pockets from Guinea-Bissau to Ghana (once a whole block and known as the Upper Guinea forest) supports a distinct avifauna. East of the Dahomey Gap, where savanna reaches the coast in Togo and Benin, a huge expanse of lowland rainforest, second only in size to Amazonia, stretches from Nigeria to east Zaïre, and remains a very rich area for birds. The unique Congo Peacock* is one of many species restricted to this forest. On the Nigeria/Cameroon border mountains rise from the sea, reaching 4070 m (13,353 ft) at Mount Cameroon, and the montane forest and grassland remaining on their slopes also supports an endemic avifauna. More mountains are present in east Zaïre on the borders with Uganda, Rwanda and Burundi. These 'Mountains of the Moon' form the Albertine Rift, which rises to 3475 m (11,401 ft) at Mount Mohi in Zaïre, yet another important refuge for birds in Africa.

South of the great forests of the Congo Basin lies a broad belt of moist savanna, which stretches across the continent to east Tanzania. South of the Zambezi river the savanna becomes more arid, giving way to the Kalahari and Namib Deserts in the southwest, and a narrow band of coastal forest in the southeast. The southern extremity of the continent, known as the Cape, is subtropical, and the coastal hills here support a shrubby habitat known as fynbos, which is very similar to Mediterranean maquis at the other end of the continent.

The cold Benguela Current flows northwards past the Cape of Good Hope at the southern tip of Africa, along the west coasts of South Africa and Namibia, providing a rich feeding ground for many seabirds. Africa's eastern seas are also rich in seabirds, many of which breed on the islands in the Indian Ocean. These islands form their own zoogeographical zone known as Malagasy, and they support many endemic landbirds. This is especially true of Madagascar, where the unique wet and dry forest supports a highly endemic avifauna.

Country Lists

Three African countries boast lists in excess of 1,000 species: Zaïre, Kenya and Tanzania, but it is Uganda's avifauna which is, arguably, the most impressive considering the country's size. Despite being less than half the size of Kenya, its list has only 86 fewer species. There is less avian diversity in West Africa, but Cameroon, which is a little smaller than Kenya, has a list which has only 200 fewer species. South Africa's list (790) is only 84 short of Cameroon's.

FIGURE 3: TOP TEN COUNTRY SPECIES LISTS (approximate figures) (see Figure 4)

	Country	Species
1	ZAÏRE	1,094
2	KENYA	1,078
3	TANZANIA	1,038
4	UGANDA	992
5	SUDAN	938
6	ANGOLA	909
7	CAMEROON	874
8	NIGERIA	862
9	ETHIOPIA	836
10	SOUTH AFRICA	790

Although Kenya has an impressive list in African terms, it falls some way short of some South American countries. For example, Ecuador, which also straddles the equator, supports nearly 500 more species, despite being only half Kenya's size. Kenya's lack of extensive lowland rainforest and lofty peaks, with their associated temperate forest, accounts for much of this difference. Africa's largest lists are also surpassed by India's list of 1,300, although this huge country is 1.4 times the size of Zaïre and 5.6 times larger than Kenya. China too has a larger list (1,195) than Kenya or Zaïre, but it is so vast it hardly merits comparison.

FIGURE 4: COUNTRIES WITH OVER 750 SPECIES (See Figure 3)

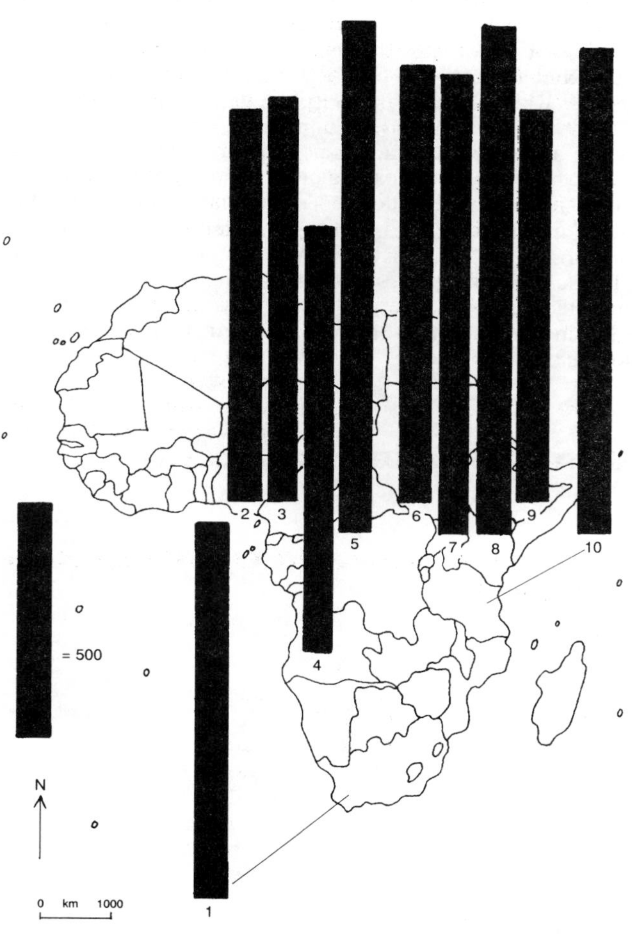

1	SOUTH AFRICA	6	SUDAN
2	NIGERIA	7	UGANDA
3	CAMEROON	8	KENYA
4	ANGOLA	9	ETHIOPIA
5	ZAÏRE	10	TANZANIA

Three countries from Africa, South America and Asia, which lie just north of the equator and support large areas of lowland rainforest, are worthy of comparison. Cameroon's list of 874 compares favourably with similar-sized Thailand's 915 and Venezuela's 1,360 since this South American country is nearly twice as large.

Site Lists

Surprisingly Kenya does not boast the largest site list in Africa. This honour goes to Ruwenzori NP in Uganda, which has a total 535 species. It is closely followed by the similar Akagera NP in Rwanda (this park may no longer exist), which lies nearby, and the huge Kruger NP in South Africa.

There are a lot of sites in Kenya with lists above 400, but Lake Naivasha and its environs has breached the 450 mark. Away from Kenya, sites with lists over 400 include Awash NP in Ethiopia, Hwange NP in Zimbabwe, Lochinvar in Zambia, the Okavango Delta area in Botswana, and the almost adjacent Mkuzi and Ndumu NPs in South Africa. All these sites are mixtures of savanna, wetland and gallery forest. Only one site where rainforest is dominant has a list of 400: the massive Ituri Forest in east Zaïre. Although impressive, this forest's list pales in comparison to Tambopata, a rainforest reserve in Peru, which, arguably, supports the greatest concentration of species in the world: its list currently stands at 587.

Birders in search of huge trip lists in Africa should read the Uganda and Kenya chapters first.

FIGURE 5: THE TOP TEN SITE LISTS IN AFRICA (approximate figures)

Site	List
RUWENZORI NP (Uganda)	535
AKAGERA NP (Rwanda)	500+
KRUGER NP (South Africa)	500
LAKE NAIVASHA (Kenya)	450+
AWASH NP (Ethiopia), HWANGE NP (Zimbabwe), ITURI FOREST (Zaire), LAKE BARINGO (Kenya), LAKE NAKURU (Kenya), LOCHINVAR (Zambia), MKUZI NP (South Africa), NAIROBI NP (Kenya), NDUMU NP (South Africa), OKAVANGO (Botswana)	400+

Trip and Day Lists

Owing to the habitat diversity and the ease with which birds may be seen it is possible to record 730 species in three weeks in Kenya, and in November 1991 a 25-day tour led by Brian Finch recorded an amazing 797 species, the African bird tour record. In South America the richest places for birds tend to include lowland rainforest so birds are harder to find than in Kenya where such forest is limited in extent.

Elsewhere in Africa it is still possible to record around 450 in three weeks in Uganda and Cameroon, whilst Steve Keen managed almost 600 in Cameroon during a ten-week trip. Three- to four-week trips to

Côte D'Ivoire, Ethiopia, and Tanzania may produce around 400 species, whilst a recent four-week trip to Gabon produced over 350. A month in Namibia and Zimbabwe may also see the 300 mark well beaten, whilst two to three weeks may produce a maximum of 300 in Gambia, 220 in Morocco and 130 in Egypt.

Family Diversity

Africa supports 108 families of birds, ten more than the Orient, and 16 more than South America. Of the 17 families endemic to Africa, ten are represented only in sub-Saharan, mainland Africa: Ostrich, Shoebill*, Secretary-bird, mousebirds, turacos, woodhoopoes, ground-hornbills, African barbets, rockfowl and sugarbirds; two more are present on the sub-Saharan mainland as well as in south Arabia and Madagascar: Hamerkop and guineafowls; five are confined to the Malagasy region: mesites, ground-rollers, Cuckoo-Roller, asities and vangas, three of which are confined to Madagascar (Cuckoo-Roller and Blue Vanga also occur on the Comoros) (see Figure 1, p. 14).

Birders interested in seeing a wide cross-section of Africa's unique bird families have a choice of ten countries, all of which boast ten of the seventeen endemic Afrotropical families. Of these, Cameroon and Nigeria lack Shoebill* and the two sugarbirds, whilst the Central African Republic, Ethiopia, Sudan, Tanzania and Uganda have no rockfowl or sugarbirds. Mozambique, South Africa and Zimbabwe all lack Shoebill* and rockfowl.

Botswana, Kenya, Namibia and Senegal fall one short of the magic ten because they do not support Shoebill*, rockfowl or sugarbirds. Both Zaïre and Zambia do support Shoebill*, but they still only support nine endemic Afrotropical families because they both lack Ostrich, as well as rockfowl and sugarbirds.

There are several countries with eight endemic Afrotropical families, including Côte D'Ivoire, Malawi, and Rwanda, whilst those with seven include Gabon and Gambia. There are no endemic Afrotropical families on the Seychelles or Mauritius.

Endemic Species

Regions of the world with concentrations of restricted-range birds have been identified as Endemic Bird Areas (EBAs) in BirdLife International's *Putting Biodiversity on the Map*. Out of the world total of 221 EBAs, Africa has 37, 18 fewer than South America. Half (18) of Africa's EBAs are concentrated on the Atlantic and Indian Ocean islands, with five on Madagascar alone (see Figure 6 below).

FIGURE 6: AFRICAN ENDEMIC BIRD AREAS (37)

CANARY ISLANDS and MADEIRA
CAPE VERDE ISLANDS
UPPER GUINEA FORESTS
NIGERIA/CAMEROON
NIGERIA/CAMEROON/GABON
PRINCIPE
SÃO TOMÉ

ANGOLA
TRISTAN DE CUNHA and GOUGH ISLANDS
SOCOTRA
SOMALIA (Northeast)
SOMALIA (Central coast)
ETHIOPIA (Central)
ETHIOPIA (South)
UGANDA/ZAÏRE
ALBERTINE RIFT
KENYA/TANZANIA (Mountains)
KENYA/TANZANIA (Masai Mara/Serengeti)
KENYA/TANZANIA (Coastal forest)
EASTERN ARC MOUNTAINS (Tanzania, Mozambique and Malawi)
ZIMBABWE/MOZAMBIQUE (Mountains)
ZAMBEZI (Zambia, Botswana and Zimbabwe)
SOUTH AFRICA/MOZAMBIQUE (Coastal forest)
SOUTH AFRICA (Montane grassland in and around Lesotho)
SOUTH AFRICA (Cape)
SEYCHELLES
ALDABRA
COMOROS
MAYOTTE
MADAGASCAR (Western dry forest)
MADAGASCAR (Western coast)
MADAGASCAR (Central)
MADAGASCAR (East)
MADAGASCAR (South)
RÉUNION
MAURITIUS
RODRIGUEZ

FIGURE 7: COUNTRY ENDEMIC LISTS (See Figure 8)

1	MADAGASCAR	102
2	SOUTH AFRICA	34
3	ETHIOPIA	30
4	SÃO TOMÉ and PRINCIPE	25
5	TANZANIA	20
6	ZAÏRE	18
7	COMOROS	16
8	ANGOLA	15
9	SEYCHELLES	11
10	SOMALIA	10
11	CANARY ISLANDS, MADEIRA ISLANDS and AZORES	9
12	CAMEROON	7
	MAURITIUS	7
14	KENYA	6
	SOCOTRA	6
	TRISTAN DE CUNHA and GOUGH ISLANDS	6
17	RÉUNION	5
18	CAPE VERDE ISLANDS	4

2: Aldabra, Equatorial Guinea, Nigeria, Rodriguez, Sudan and Uganda
1: Algeria, Amsterdam Island, Ascension Island, Djibouti, Liberia, Mali, Namibia, St Helena, Southern Arc Islands and Zambia

FIGURE 8: COUNTRIES AND ISLANDS WITH OVER TEN ENDEMICS (See Figure 7)

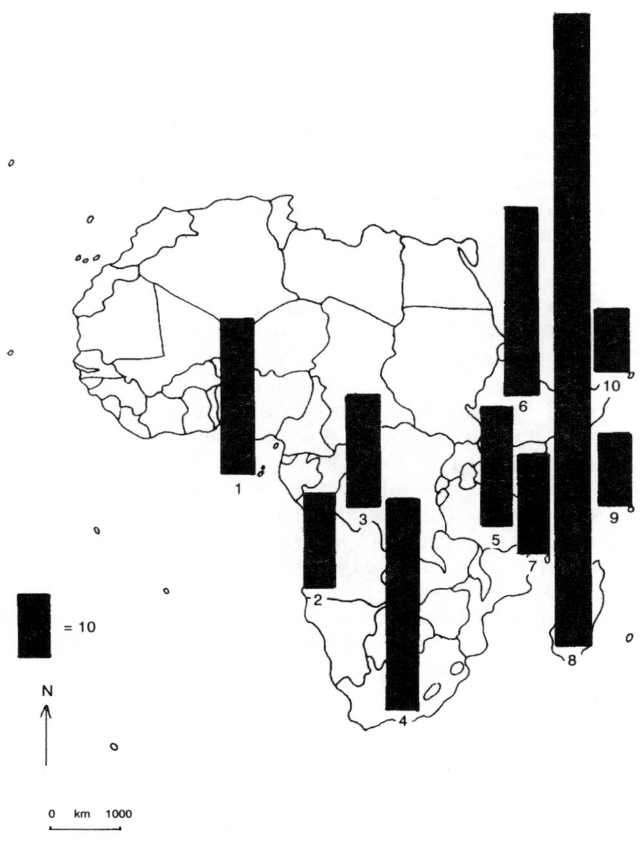

1	SÃO TOMÉ and PRINCIPE	6	ETHIOPIA
2	ANGOLA	7	COMOROS
3	ZAÏRE	8	MADAGASCAR
4	SOUTH AFRICA	9	SEYCHELLES
5	TANZANIA	10	SOMALIA

EBA distribution is reflected in country endemics lists. With just over 100 unique species, Madagascar is by far the richest African country for endemics. Its total of 102 compares favourably with Peru's 104, but is well below the Philippines' total of 185.

South Africa supports more endemics than any other mainland country, with a total of 34 unique species, closely followed by Ethiopia with 30. The tiny Atlantic archipelago of São Tomé and Principe, like the Galápagos Islands, supports 25 unique species, seven more than the whole of Zaïre. Tanzania on 20 and Angola on 15 come next. The three remaining countries and archipelagos with ten or more endemics are the Comoros (16), the Seychelles (11) and Somalia (10), whilst Cameroon supports only seven, and Kenya just six.

It is possible to see many of the Madagascar endemics on a four- to six-week trip, and high percentages are also possible in Ethiopia, South Africa, São Tomé and Principe, Comoros, Seychelles and Cameroon. However, it would be virtually impossible to see all of the endemics in Zaïre, Angola and Somalia, even on very prolonged trips, thanks to the travel situation, and the remoteness and inaccessibility of many of the species. It would be possible to see most of Kenya's endemics on a short trip, but only with concentrated effort.

Exploration

A lot of birders have seen over 1,000 species in Africa, some over 1,250 and a select few over 1,500. The man who has seen more birds in Africa than anyone else is Tom Gullick who, having visited 21 countries over the period of 14 years, had amassed a staggering total of 1,950 by November 1994, an incredible 85% of the African avifauna. There are only three countries where he is likely to see more than ten new birds: Angola, Somalia and Zaïre, all of which are politically unstable and currently unsafe to visit (except extreme east Zaïre). Birders who have seen over 1,500 African species will now be researching the little-known species which occur in off-the-beaten-track places such as Zambia's borders with Angola and Zaïre and, should the travel situation improve, Ethiopia's borders with Somalia.

Birders in search of virtually unknown species need not look far for places to explore. Painstaking research into old records, habitat preferences, present-day distribution of those habitats, and an eye for the areas which are opening up, may result in some very interesting discoveries. As recently as June 1991, Thomas Lehmberg and Lars Dinesen found a new species of partridge (provisionally called Udzungwa Forest-partridge*) in the Udzungwa Mountains of Tanzania.

In fact, some 15 new species have been discovered in Africa since 1980 by the keenest researchers and birders determined to get to out-of-the-way localities, some of which are actually just off the beaten track. It is not impossible for an adventurous birder to find the great rarities of Africa and, who knows, maybe a new cisticola, or even a turaco.

CONSERVATION

During the 1980s, 17% of Africa's lowland rainforest was destroyed. Over 90% of the original forest in Côte D'Ivoire and Nigeria has gone, and the Côte D'Ivoire forests are expected to be completely logged out by the end of the century. Only 20% of Madagascar's unique forest remains. The Dodo is extinct. What will be next? 322 species, 14% of the African avifauna, are considered to be threatened or near-threatened. Their habitats are disappearing fast and their prospects are grim.

The loss and degradation of habitat throughout the world is primarily linked to an ever expanding human population. In Africa, the human being is booming, and their demands for the 'comforts' of a developed society are putting an immense strain on the continent's natural resources.

With the forests from Nigeria west virtually logged out, European logging companies, encouraged by the World Bank, are moving into central Africa, and are poised to destroy the vast forests of the Congo Basin, in countries such as Cameroon, Congo, Gabon, Zaïre and the Central African Republic. Forest is also felled for mining, oil production, agriculture and domestic firewood. Where reforestation is taking place it usually involves re-planting with inappropriate non-native trees, such as fast-growing *Eucalyptus* species. These alien trees support few of the birds which are endemic to Africa. They *are* good for honeyeaters, but these birds are endemic to Australasia.

Burgeoning populations force local people, quite understandably, to seek new land away from the long-established agricultural areas, in order to survive. This slash-and-burn way of life, coupled with the planting of cash-crops to repay debt, has a particularly disastrous effect in tropical forest where tree removal and inappropriate land-use, including the use of chemicals, lead to soil degradation, erosion and poor water quality. Some bird species have adapted and will adapt, especially open-country birds which naturally do better when trees are felled, but some of these species suffer in turn from hunting and the loss of specific grass species to preferred agricultural crops.

Away from the forests, in the huge areas of semi-desert and savanna that once covered much of Africa, overgrazing may be accelerating desertification and, in some areas, the Sahara is expanding by as much as twenty metres every year. Much of the adjacent, semi-arid Sahel, home to a number of specialist species and an important wintering ground for many Palearctic migrants, is currently suffering from overgrazing, and the harmful effects of too many cattle have been enhanced by the droughts of recent decades. Huge areas of the Sahel and the savannas to the south are also burnt annually to encourage the early growth of grasses to feed domesticated animals. Cattle displace the natural herbivores, prevent the growth of shrubs and trees, and decrease the value of the habitat to birds.

Even Africa's wonderful wetlands, including such natural wonders as the Okavango Delta in Botswana are under serious threat, mainly from siltation, reclamation and irrigation schemes.

The only long-term solution to these massive problems is to curb human population growth. However, stemming population growth seems impossible, and indeed undesirable, to some governments. Smaller initiatives such as integrating local needs with sustainable use of the natural habitat, through such schemes as ecotourism, need to be implemented. Ecotourism has the potential to boost many African economies. For example, the annual value of wildlife to the Tanzanian economy is currently estimated at $US 108 million. If the Tanzanian government continues to promote and expand ecotourism this figure is expected to rise to $US 500 million by 1999.

Some governments have catered for those tourists interested in Africa's wild animals for many years, but providing specifically for birders is a relatively recent phenomenon. The examples set by BirdLife International at such sites as Mount Kupé in Cameroon need to be encouraged and established elsewhere. Bird tourism is one of the few hopes left for the birds and other animals in Africa.

I hope this book, in its own small way, will help to convince governments that by encouraging bird tourism to their countries the sustainable use of their natural resources, especially birds and their habitats, is the logical solution to the long-term economic and social problems associated with human population growth.

GENERAL TIPS

Any birding guide should include tips on how to see the most birds, how to see them well, how to get the most out of a birding trip and, most importantly of all, how to enjoy the experience. The following tips are by no means comprehensive, and they are little more than a mish-mash of points resulting from personal experience and birding tales shared between friends. However, they may help maximise the enjoyment of a birding trip to Africa.

Most birders know that, apart from plenty of pre-trip research, walking quietly and slowly together with patient stalking using vegetation usually results in the best birding, but it is surprisingly easy to forget these basic field skills, especially in the frenzy that comes from being in a place full of new and exciting birds.

Early morning is usually the best time for birding anywhere in the world and Africa is no exception, especially in the savanna zones where it can be extremely hot at high noon. The middle of the day is a good time to move from one site to another or, if this is not appropriate, to take a siesta before a late afternoon sorty, the evening owl and nightjar search, and the appropriate celebration of another great day in the field. Fanatical birders will argue that it is still possible to see plenty of birds around midday, especially where there is some shade or water, and the hours of darkness are the best time to move from site to site. Travelling at night can be dangerous on Africa's bad roads and tracks, and this activity is not allowed in many national parks, but where it is possible, overnight drives will help to keep accommodation costs down and may produce a few unexpected birds such as coursers, and mammals. Whilst a couple of night drives may be fun, being constantly tired may impair your enjoyment of the whole trip.

It is also worth remembering that owing to the poor roads and tracks, long drives in Africa can be very time-consuming and tiring, even in daylight hours. It is not possible to bird on foot in many places south of the Sahara owing to the presence of large predators, and although sitting in a vehicle for hours can be very frustrating, they do act as excellent mobile hides. However, driving off-piste not only destroys the habitat, it can result in getting stuck, especially in sandy and wet areas. Digging the vehicle out 'in the bush' can be an unnerving experience.

Many birds, including Turacos, hornbills and barbets are attracted to fruiting trees. Whilst such trees may seem devoid of life as the birds feed quietly, they can slowly come alive, and standing next to one for a few hours may be more productive than frantic wandering.

Flocks of feeding birds, known as 'bird waves' in some circles, are a feature of African forest and savanna woodland, and they can move through an area of trees very quickly. Once a wave is located it is worth sticking with the birds as long as possible, even after it seems like they have all passed, because the stragglers often turn out to be especially interesting species.

Rain and mist is prevalent in most lowland and montane forest, especially in West and Central Africa, but this rarely seems to affect bird activity, so it is worth carrying on birding in such conditions. Air- and water-tight binoculars, as well as an umbrella, are essential in these wet forests.

Whilst altitude sickness is not a major problem in Africa, it is worth remembering the following: most people can travel up to 3000 m (9843 ft) in a short time, and manage 4500 m (14,764 ft) after a night at 3000 m. Going straight to 4500 m can be very dangerous. One in three people who attempt this usually end up with a severe headache or, even worse, feel dizzy and begin to vomit. If that person then turns blue or coughs up pink mucus they should descend immediately to below 3000 m, where a quick recovery is normal. High-altitude health problems can be alleviated by eating lightly, taking it easy, using maximum sun-block, and keeping warm when the sun goes down.

It is worth taking an altimeter if you are unsure of the terrain you are visiting or if the only information you have on a certain species is the altitude at which it has been recorded. Vehicles may be a problem at high altitudes. If you have difficulty starting your engine in the early mornings try pouring petrol directly into the carburetter.

Using tapes of bird calls and songs to lure skulkers out into the open helps to confirm identification, but this devious birding method is *not* appropriate for use with threatened species, if any species at all. It distracts birds from feeding and causes them undue excitement. If you can not see the bird which you hear it is frustrating, but surely there is more joy to be gained from seeing the bird after a long and hard stalk than standing by a tape recorder waiting for the unfortunate creature to come and peck at it.

GLOSSARY

2WD: Two-wheel-drive vehicle.
4WD: Four-wheel-drive vehicle.
FR: Forest Reserve.
Fynbos: This incredibly rich habitat (more plant species per square metre than any other habitat in the world) is confined to extreme South Africa, where it forms shrublands reminiscent of Mediterranean maquis. It supports few bird species, but many of these are endemic.
Gallery forest/woodland: Waterside (riparian) forest and woodland, usually where forested areas merge into more open areas such as savanna, alongside watercourses.
Karoo: This semi-desert shrub and grassland, present in southwest Africa, supports many endemic bird species.
Coastal forest: This rich forest type occurs from southern Somalia south through Kenya and Tanzania along the coastal plain to far South Africa.
Lowland forest: Rainforest present from Sierra Leone to Ghana in West Africa (**Upper Guinea**), and from southern Nigeria to the Congo Basin in Central Africa (**Lower Guinea**).
Maquis: The northern equivalent of fynbos, maquis consists of shrublands dominated by heath, broom, rosemary and sage. It is present along the North African coast in Morocco, Algeria, Tunisia, Libya and Egypt.
Montane forest: This forest type occurs on mountain slopes in West Africa (mostly on the Nigeria/Cameroon border), in East Africa from Ethiopia south through Kenya, Tanzania and eastern Zimbabwe to the Knysna area of far South Africa (where it is actually present near sea level), and in Central Africa along the Albertine Rift, which runs through Uganda, eastern Zaïre, Rwanda and Burundi. Such forest is often misty owing to high humidity and low temperatures, and has a broken canopy which allows a lush understorey to develop, unlike lowland forest.
NP: National Park
NR: Nature Reserve
Pan: A natural depression, usually found in arid areas, which when full forms shallow lakes attracting numerous birds.
Sahel: The Sahel stretches across northern Africa in a narrow belt below the Sahara. It is characterised by areas of flat-topped trees (mostly acacia) and sparse, arid grassland.
Savanna: Much of low-lying Africa is savanna. In northwestern and northern Africa the dry acacia woodland of the **Sudan savanna** lies south of the Sahel, whilst moist *Isoberlinia* (doka) woodland characterises **Guinea savanna**, south of the Sudan savanna. In eastern and southern Africa there are three major types of savanna: (1) Widely spaced, scrubby, dry acacia woodland. (2) Tall, broadleaved, moist miombo (*Brachystegia*) woodland. (3) Mopane woodland, which usually occurs in isolated stands. Such wooded areas are often interspersed with grassland which, in effect, forms part of the savanna.
Secondary: This term usually refers to forested areas which have regenerated after clearance, albeit usually in fragments alongside the newly established land-use.

MAPS

Birders, understandably, are more interested in finding birds rather than noting distances and directions when in the field, so although every effort has been made to make the maps in this book as precise as possible, they may not be entirely accurate, at least in terms of the exact scale and compass points.

The main purpose of the maps is to facilitate birding at the sites so more often than not 'direction-pointers' such as rivers and buildings, and on-site detail such as trails, have been exaggerated and are not drawn to scale.

Each country account begins with a map of the country with the main sites numbered, and there are also some maps of regions within countries to show how 'bunches' of sites are distributed. These are intended to aid birders in their production of trip routes and itineraries during the planning stage.

It is important to remember that Africa is a fast changing continent so trails may have become tracks, tracks may have become roads, buildings may have been knocked down, buildings may have been put up, marshes, lakes and rivers may have dried up, rivers may have changed course, signs may have fallen down, habitats may have been totally destroyed, and some sites may no longer exist by the time you come to use these maps. Remember, this book is a guiding light, not a substitute for up-to-the-minute information.

The map symbols used are as follows:

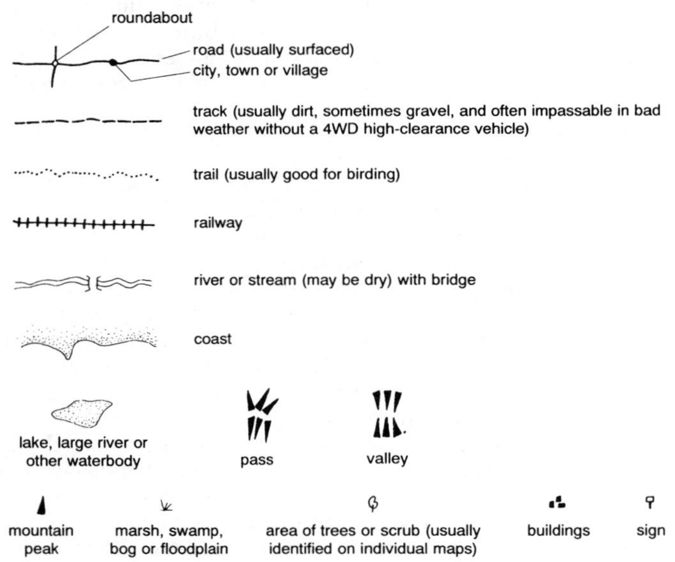

ALGERIA

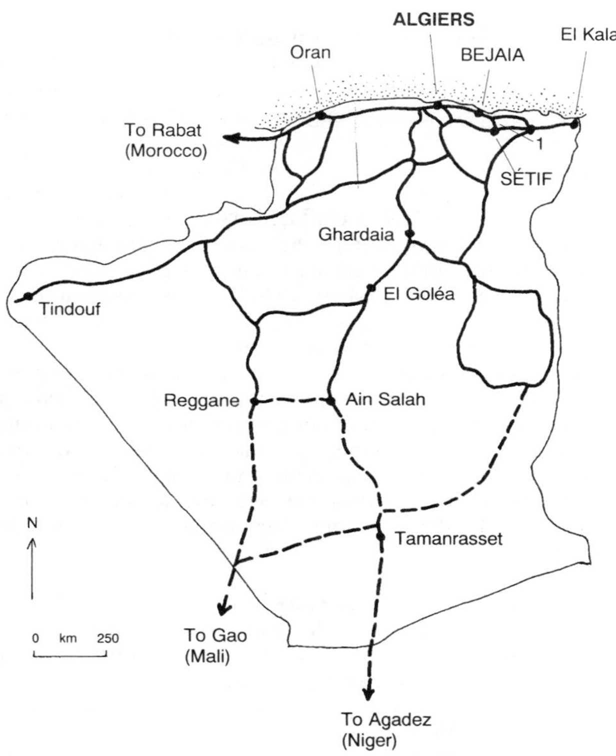

1 Djebel Babor

INTRODUCTION

Summary

In early 1995 the activities of Islamic fundamentalists persuaded most travellers and many expatriate workers to leave Algeria. If political stability is restored birders may find it surprisingly easy to see this country's major avian attraction, the endemic Algerian Nuthatch*.

Size

At 2,381,741 sq km Algeria is Africa's second largest country (after Sudan). It is 18 times larger than England and 3.5 times the size of Texas.

Getting Around

Getting around is not difficult. Getting *in* is the problem. Once customs have been negotiated, a basic knowledge of French is almost essential since very few people speak English. There are extensive, but often fully booked, internal air and long-distance bus networks. The roads in the north, including those into the mountains, are excellent, although often blocked by snow in winter (Nov–Apr); those in the south, especially those traversing the Sahara, can be tricky without 4WD.

Accommodation and Food

Accommodation in Algeria is cheap, but often difficult to find in summer, and the cheapest, the bathhouses, are for men only. There are plenty of campsites, especially along the Saharan routes in the south. The staple diet seems to be couscous (cracked wheat) with meat or fish, and vegetables.

Health and Safety

Immunisation against hepatitis, typhoid, polio and yellow fever is recommended, as are precautions against malaria.

Contact the Foreign Office for latest details on visiting Algeria.

Climate and Timing

Northern Algeria has a Mediterranean-like climate, but it is much hotter and more humid during the dry summer months, which last from May to October. In the south it is almost always incredibly hot. The northern rainy season lasts from November to April, when deep snow in the mountains usually means many roads become impassable, and sites for Algerian Nuthatches* inaccessible. The best time to visit, especially if you want to look for the endemic Algerian Nuthatch*, is May to September.

Habitats

The northern mountains, known as the Saharan Tell, run east-west parallel to the Mediterranean coast, and are separated from the narrow Saharan Atlas, to the south, by the wide Hauts Plateau. Oak, cedar and fir forests remain on the slopes of some summits of the Saharan Tell. South of the Saharan Atlas lies the semi-desert of the Grand Erg, and south of here, the Sahara. Together, these vast semi-deserts and deserts make up 75% of the country.

Conservation

Algeria's endemic bird, the Algerian Nuthatch*, seems safe as long as the montane forest it inhabits remains intact.

Seven threatened and three near-threatened species occur in Algeria.

Bird Families

Two families are particularly well represented in Algeria: sandgrouse and larks.

Bird Species

By 1981, 382 species had been recorded in Algeria, over 70 fewer than in Morocco, and only 30 more than Tunisia. Non-endemic specialities and spectacular species include White-headed Duck*, Marbled Teal*, Houbara Bustard, Marmora's Warbler, and Red-billed Firefinch, here at its only locality within the Western Palearctic.

Endemics and Near-endemics

The sole endemic, Algerian Nuthatch*, which was only discovered in

1975, is confined to montane forest in northeast Algeria. Near-endemics include Levaillant's Woodpecker, Moussier's Redstart and Tristram's Warbler.

Access

Algeria's star avian attraction, the endemic Algerian Nuthatch*, was discovered in 1975 at **Djebel Babor** (2004 m (6575 ft)), an eight-hour, 225-km drive (car-hire available in Algiers) east from Algiers via Bejaia. From Bejaia head southeast via Kherrata towards Sétif, and turn east 12 km south of Kherrata (46 km north of Sétif), just south of the village of Tizi-n'bechar. After the tarmac ends take the first gravel track left to the top of Djebel Babor where the nuthatch occurs in the remaining 13 sq km of cedar forest, especially around the summit. There are thought to be approximately 80 pairs here. The best time to visit is May to September since the track may be blocked by deep snow between November and April. Barbary Partridge and Levaillant's Woodpecker also occur here.

DJEBEL BABOR

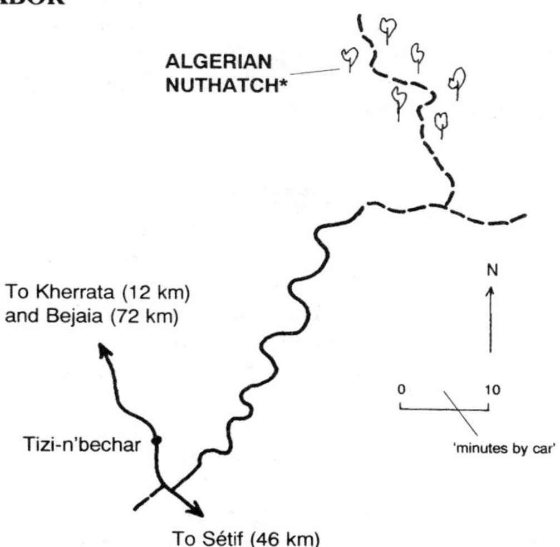

Algerian Nuthatch* also occurs in the Guerrouch (Taza NP), Tamentout and Djimla Forests, all of which are in the Petite Kabylie region, within 30 km of each other and Djebel Babor.

The coastal lagoons around the town of **El Kala** in extreme northeast Algeria form a national park (HQ at Lac Tonga), which supports many waterfowl in winter, including White-headed Duck* and Marbled Teal*, as well as Long-legged Buzzard, Purple Swamphen and Marmora's Warbler.

A number of people drive south through the desert of Algeria to Niger, via **Tamanrasset**. Roadside birds along this route include Brown-necked Raven, White-tailed, Black and Mourning Wheatears,

Pale Crag-Martin, Tristram's Warbler, Fulvous Chatterer, Bar-tailed and Desert Larks, Greater Hoopoe-Lark, Desert Sparrow, Red-billed Firefinch (Tamanrasset), Trumpeter Finch and House Bunting.

A SELECTION OF SPECIES OCCURRING IN ALGERIA

Many of these are only summer visitors and occur either in the northern mountains or the Grand Erg semi-desert belt further south.

White Stork, Bonelli's Eagle, Eleonora's (north coast) and Barbary Falcons, Small Buttonquail, Houbara Bustard, Cream-coloured Courser, Audouin's Gull*, Pin-tailed, Spotted, Black-bellied, Crowned and Lichtenstein's (southeast) Sandgrouse, Red-necked and Egyptian Nightjars, Black-crowned Tchagra, Spotless Starling, Moussier's Redstart, Red-rumped Wheatear, Streaked Scrub-Warbler, Thick-billed, Lesser Short-toed, Dupont's and Temminck's Larks, Alpine Accentor, and Crimson-winged Finch (northeast).

ADDITIONAL INFORMATION

Papers

Mise a Jour de L'avifaune Algerienne (A Checklist). Ledant, J-P *et al.* 1981. *Le Gerfaut* 71:295–398.

ENDEMICS (1)

Algerian Nuthatch*	Northeast: Djebel Babor

Near-endemics

Levaillant's Woodpecker, Moussier's Redstart, Tristram's Warbler.

ANGOLA

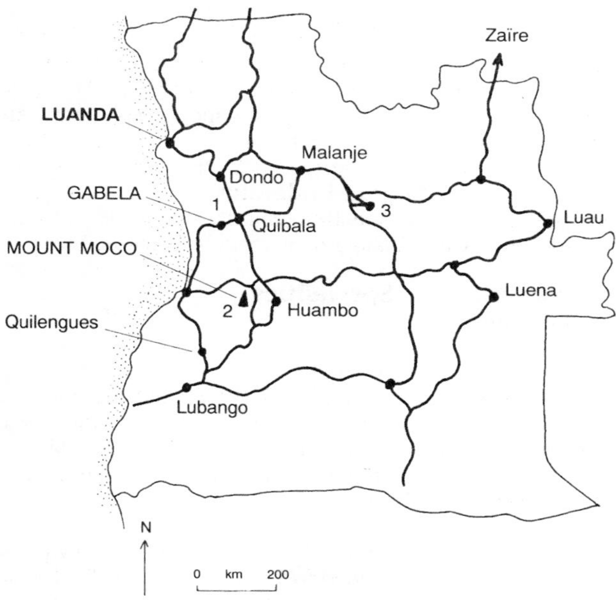

1 Amboim
2 Bailundu Highlands
3 Kangandala NP

INTRODUCTION

Angola boasts a fine selection of birds, including plenty of endemics and near-endemics. However, the lengthy civil war devastated the country and it is depressing to think what toll has probably been taken of the habitats and birds in the process. Thirteen threatened and 12 near-threatened species occur in Angola. Gaining entry to this huge country (at 1,246,700 sq km, nearly ten times the size of England and twice the size of Texas) is very difficult and travel inside once there is virtually impossible, although political problems seemed to be at a low ebb in early 1995. This is unfortunate because ornithological surveys carried out before the war revealed an impressively diverse avifauna. A total of 909 species have been recorded in Angola, including 15 endemics and many near-endemics which are otherwise found only in Zaïre, Zambia and southern Africa. Of the ten families endemic to mainland Africa, three are not represented in Angola: Shoebill*, rockfowl and sugarbirds. Well represented families include bee-eaters, hornbills, barbets, and bushshrikes. Non-endemic specialities and spectacular species include Babbling Starling, White-headed Robin-Chat*, Laura's Wood-Warbler, Black-chinned Weaver*, and Bocage's Sunbird.

AMBOIM

Remnant forest along the west Angolan escarpment, from Dondo south to Quilengues, used to support some very special species, many of which occur only here.

Angola Endemics

Grey-striped Francolin*, Gabela Bushshrike*, Angola Helmetshrike*, White-fronted Wattle-eye*, Gabela Akalat*, Pulitzer's Longbill*.

Specialities

Monteiro's Bushshrike*.

Access

The best forest used to be just north of Gabela, although most of the species listed above have been recorded from Mumbondo, Assango, Conda, Dondo, Amboim, Gabela and Vila Nova do Seles. Monteiro's Bushshrike*, recently rediscovered on Mount Kupé, Cameroon, has not been recorded here since 1954.

The endemic Swierstra's Francolin*, as well as two little known species, Boulton's Batis and Black-chinned Weaver*, occur in the **Bailundu Highlands**, inland from the Angola escarpment. Remnant forest patches may still be present on Mount Moco, Mount Soque (accessible from Galanga to the west), and the Mombolo Plateau, but it is more likely that very little forest now remains, having been cleared to provide timber and fuel.

The forest northeast of Duque de Braganca in north Angola is also important for birds such as White-headed Robin-Chat*, a species which occurs only in north Angola and south Zaïre.

Miombo woodland covers much of the rest of Angola, and **Kangandala NP** (600 sq km), southeast of Malanje, and the area around **N'gola**, a village near Caluquembo, support Pale-billed Hornbill, Anchieta's Barbet, Souza's Shrike, Sharp-tailed Glossy-Starling, Spotted Creeper, Piping Cisticola, Red-capped Crombec, Miombo Tit and Miombo Sunbird, whilst the N'gola area also supports Miombo Rock-Thrush, Babbling Starling, Chestnut-backed Sparrow-Weaver and Black-eared Seedeater.

A SELECTION OF NON-ENDEMIC SPECIES RECORDED IN ANGOLA

Ostrich, Crowned Cormorant*, White-backed Duck, African Pygmy-goose, Hartlaub's Duck, Rufous-bellied Heron, White-crested Bittern, Hamerkop, Spot-breasted Ibis, Congo Serpent-Eagle, Long-tailed Hawk, Secretary-bird, Black and Plumed Guineafowl, Finsch's, Orange River and Hartlaub's Francolins, Red-chested, Chestnut-headed and Streaky-breasted Flufftails, Nkulengu Rail, African Finfoot, Wattled Crane*, Ludwig's and Ruppell's Bustards, Lesser Jacana, African Oystercatcher*, Grey Pratincole, Forbes' Plover, Damara Tern*, African Skimmer, Namaqua, Yellow-throated and Burchell's Sandgrouse, Grey, Brown-necked and Red-fronted Parrots, Black-billed and Great Blue Turacos, Dusky Long-tailed and Olive Long-tailed Cuckoos, Gabon and Coppery-tailed Coucals, Fraser's and Akun Eagle-Owls, Pel's and Vermiculated Fishing-Owls, Bradfield's Swift, Narina and Bar-tailed Trogons, White-bellied, Chocolate-backed and Brown-hooded Kingfishers, Black, Blue-breasted, Black-headed and Rosy Bee-eaters, Racket-tailed and Blue-throated Rollers, Pale-billed Hornbill, Anchieta's, Miombo, Pied and Black-backed Barbets, Rufous-sided Broadbill, African Pitta, Blue Cuckoo-shrike, Souza's and White-tailed Shrikes, Red-eyed Puffback, Grey-green Bushshrike, Angola Batis, Black-necked Wattle-eye, Short-toed and Miombo Rock-Thrushes, Orange Ground-Thrush, Sharp-tailed Glossy-Starling, Babbling Starling, Boehm's Flycatcher, Bocage's Akalat, Grey-winged Robin-Chat, Rufous-tailed Palm-Thrush, Miombo and Kalahari Scrub-Robins, Herero* and Karoo Chats, Congo Moorchat, Brazza's Martin, Black-and-rufous and Pearl-breasted Swallows, Cabanis' and Pale-olive Greenbuls, Black-collared Bulbul, Bubbling, Chirping, Slender-tailed, Cloud and Cloud-scraping Cisticolas, Damara Rock-jumper, Black-necked Eremomela, Laura's Wood-Warbler, Thrush and Bare-cheeked Babblers, Angola, Dusky, and Gray's Larks, Woodhouse's Antpecker, Red-faced Crimson-wing, Dusky Twinspot, Brown and Jameson's Firefinches, Black-tailed, Cinderella*, Black-headed and Black-cheeked Waxbills, Locustfinch, Fuelleborn's and Grimwood's* Longclaws, Bush Pipit, Black-chinned*, Bocage's and Bar-winged Weavers, Golden-backed Bishop*, Anchieta's, Violet-tailed, Bannerman's, Oustalet's, and Bocage's Sunbirds.

ADDITIONAL INFORMATION

Books and Papers

Ornitologia de Angola. Pinto, A. 1983.
The Avifauna of Angolan Miombo Woodlands. Dean, W. 1988. *Tauraco* 1:99–104.

ENDEMICS (13)

Grey-striped Francolin*	West/central: Amboim
Swierstra's Francolin*	West/central: Bailundu Highlands
Red-crested Turaco	West: woodland and savanna
Orange-breasted Bushshrike*	Northwest: rainforest
Gabela Bushshrike*	West/central: Amboim
Angola Helmetshrike*	West/central: Amboim
White-fronted Wattle-eye*	West/central: Amboim
Angola Slaty-Flycatcher	West: mountains
Gabela Akalat*	West/central: Amboim
Angola Cave-Chat*	West: rocky gorges
Hartert's Camaroptera	West: forest

Pulitzer's Longbill*	West/central: Amboim
Montane Double-collared Sunbird	Central: highlands

(Monteiro's Bushshrike*: no records since 1954 from the western escarpment of Angola, but recently (1992) rediscovered on Mount Kupé, Cameroon.)

ANGOLA AND CABINDA (2)

Red-backed Mousebird	Throughout: savanna
Loanda Swift	Coast: northwest Angola

Near-endemics (Central, North and East)

Miombo Barbet, Perrin's Bushshrike, Boulton's and Angola Batises, Babbling Starling, Bocage's Akalat, White-headed Robin-Chat*, Rufous-tailed Palm-Thrush, Brazza's Martin, Black-and-rufous Swallow, Pale-olive Greenbul, Lepe, Bubbling and Slender-tailed Cisticolas, Salvadori's Eremomela, Angola Lark, Grimwood's Longclaw*, Black-chinned*, Bocage's and Bar-winged Weavers, Golden-backed Bishop*, Bocage's Sunbird.

Near-endemics (South)

Crowned Cormorant*, Hartlaub's Francolin, Ludwig's and Ruppell's Bustards, African Oystercatcher*, Rueppell's Parrot, Rosy-faced Lovebird, White-backed Mousebird, Bradfield's Swift, Monteiro's Hornbill, White-tailed Shrike, Short-toed Rock-Thrush, Pale-winged Starling, Chat Flycatcher, Herero Chat*, Mountain Wheatear, Tractrac Chat, Red-headed Cisticola, Damara Rock-jumper, Bare-cheeked Babbler, Bradfield's, Long-billed, Gray's and Stark's Larks, Cinderella Waxbill*, Dusky Sunbird, White-throated Canary.

BENIN

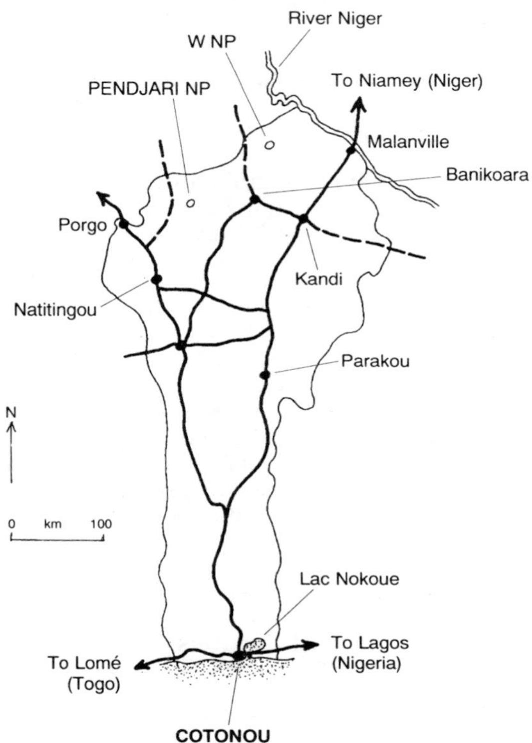

Summary

Little is known about this small country, which lies between the Upper Guinea forest to the west and the Lower Guinea forest to the east in the savanna of what is known as the Dahomey Gap. There are few, if any, species here which cannot be seen more easily elsewhere.

Size

At 112,622 sq km, Benin is nearly the same size as England, and one sixth the size of Texas.

Getting Around

Up to the mid 1990s, tourism was not encouraged, but Benin is likely to become more accessible in the future. Apart from along the coast and on the main north-south Malanville–Cotonou route, the roads are bad and there are often numerous road-blocks. The railway system is worse, and the internal air network almost non-existent. However, bush taxis reach almost every habitation, given time.

Accommodation and Food

Camping is illegal and it is compulsory to stay in basic, relatively expensive hotels. Rice is the staple diet away from Cotonou, and beer is widely available.

Health and Safety

Immunisation against cholera, hepatitis, polio, typhoid and yellow fever is recommended, as are precautions against malaria.

Climate and Timing

In the constantly humid south the dry season lasts from December to March (although August can also be dry); in the north it is dry from November to May.

Habitats

The short, lagoon-lined coast gives way to plantations (mainly coffee and oil palm) and intensive farming inland. The south of the country is particularly densely populated, but in the north there is a lot more lightly wooded savanna. In the northwest there is small mountain range known as the Atakora. There is very little lowland rainforest in Benin, the country being part of the Dahomey Gap, where the sub-Saharan savanna reaches the coast between the Upper Guinea forest of Ghana to the west and the Lower Guinea forest of Nigeria to the east.

Conservation

One threatened and two near-threatened species occur in Benin.

Bird Families

Of the ten families endemic to the African mainland six are represented in Benin. Ostrich is a notable absentee.

Bird Species

Only 423 species have been recorded in Benin, one of the lowest totals for a sub-Saharan mainland country, and a reflection of its small size and almost complete lack of lowland rainforest. Non-endemic specialities and spectacular species include Egyptian Plover, Grey Pratincole and Rosy Bee-eater.

Endemics

There are no endemics and few near-endemics, although Brown-cheeked Hornbill* and Chestnut-bellied Helmetshrike, two species restricted to the coastal countries from Nigeria westwards, are present.

A SELECTION OF SPECIES RECORDED IN BENIN

African Pygmy-goose, Hamerkop, Scissor-tailed Kite, Secretary-bird, Fox Kestrel, White-throated Francolin, Quail-plover, African Crake, African Finfoot, Egyptian Plover, Rock and Grey Pratincoles, African Skimmer, Bruce's Green-Pigeon, Senegal Parrot, Guinea and Violet Turacos, Western Grey Plantain-eater, Black Coucal, Pel's Fishing-Owl, African

Wood-Owl, Narina Trogon, Shining Blue and Blue-breasted Kingfishers, Red-throated, Swallow-tailed, and Rosy Bee-eaters, Abyssinian and Blue-bellied Rollers, White-crested, Piping and Brown-cheeked* Hornbills, Bearded Barbet, Fire-bellied Woodpecker, African Blue-Flycatcher, Piapiac, Chestnut-bellied Helmetshrike, Bronze-tailed Glossy-Starling, White-throated Blue, Pied-winged and Preuss' Swallows, Grey-headed Bristlebill, Siffling Cisticola, Oriole Warbler, Grey Longbill, Blackcap, Brown and Capuchin Babblers, Chestnut-backed Sparrow-Lark, Sun Lark, Gray's Malimbe, Buff-throated and Olive-bellied Sunbirds, Brown-rumped Bunting.

Access

Although the coastal areas west of the capital, Cotonou, may be worth exploring, more is known about the north of the country where the W and Pendjari NPs lie. **W NP**, parts of which also lie in Burkino Faso and Niger (see p. 273), supports some excellent birds as well as elephant. Whilst the national park is easy to visit in Niger, it forms a remote part of Benin, and access is restricted by the lack of tracks. However, with a 4WD it is possible to visit part of the park from Keremou, near Banikoara. The lightly wooded savanna of **Pendjari NP** (2750 sq km), part of which also lies in Burkina Faso, supports species associated with Guinea savanna, such as Abyssinian Roller, as well as buffalo, elephant and lion. This park is open from mid December to May, and accessible from Porgo where there is a camp. It is also possible to stay in the park, at the Hotel de la Pendjari, or to camp.

ADDITIONAL INFORMATION

Books and Papers

The Birds of Pendjari NP. Green and Sayer. 1979. *Malimbus* 1:14–28.
Distributional Notes on the Birds of Benin. Holyoak, D and Seddon, M. 1989. *Malimbus* 11:128–134.

Near-endemics (Upper Guinea to Nigeria)

Brown-cheeked Hornbill*, Chestnut-bellied Helmetshrike.

BOTSWANA

1 Okavango Delta
2 Chobe NP
3 Gaborone

INTRODUCTION

Summary

This sparsely populated, wild country is famous for the Okavango, a vast inland delta surrounded by the Kalahari Desert. This waterbird paradise supports such gems as Slaty Egret*, but it is a very expensive place to visit. Fortunately for budget birders, all of the Okavango area specialities can be seen elsewhere, especially in neighbouring Namibia.

Size

At 581,730 sq km, Botswana is 4.5 times larger than England, and slightly smaller than Texas.

Getting Around

Roads are rare in Botswana. The only way into the Okavango is via expensive charter flights from Maun, itself accessible by air from the capital, Gaborone, as well as neighbouring countries. Irregular buses run on some routes, mainly in the east, but to see the best of the country a 4WD is recommended.

Accommodation and Food

Accommodation in Botswana is expensive and sparse away from the few main towns and the Okavango. Within the Okavango there are a number of places to stay, mainly tented camps, but all of them are expensive. A tent is a must for budget travellers, although campsites tend to have very basic facilities. Food is basic beyond the Okavango and towns.

Health and Safety

Immunisation against hepatitis, polio, rabies, typhoid and yellow fever is recommended. Mosquitoes abound in the Okavango and all precautions against malaria are a must.

Climate and Timing

The water levels in the Okavango usually reach their peak from May to August. At this time the delta may be fully flooded, but the surrounding plains are usually dry so many birds and mammals are concentrated in the Okavango area. Therefore October, when the waters have receded somewhat, is the best time to visit, because from November onwards, when the rains begin in the surrounding plains, the birds and mammals usually disperse.

Habitats

Rivers in the Angolan uplands swollen by rain flow not to the sea, but into the Kalahari Desert in northern Botswana, forming, for a few months a year, a vast inland delta known as the Okavango. Semi-desert and scrub make up much of the rest of the country.

Conservation

Nearly 20% of Botswana lies within national parks. However, the Okavango, most of which does not lie in a 'protected' area, remains under threat. The eradication of the tsetse fly (1944 to 1964) involved killing 60,000 large (wild) mammals and all trees in a huge area (9000 sq km) southeast of the Okavango. Once this initial step was complete, chemicals, most of which are banned outside the third world, were used to finish off the fly. The fly was eliminated from this area so that farmers could raise their cattle without fear of disease. Domestic animals are more important than money in Botswana, and they need water, water which is only reliably present in Botswana in the Okavango. Various drainage and irrigation schemes have been put forward to address this problem, hence even the Okavango, one of Africa's wildest places, is not safe.

Five threatened and four near-threatened species occur in Botswana.

Bird Families

Of the ten families endemic to the African mainland seven are represented in Botswana. Well represented families include herons and larks.

Bird Species

Botswana is a land-locked and relatively uniform country, so only 550 species have been recorded, nearly 200 fewer than Zambia, and 100 fewer than Zimbabwe, two neighbouring countries which are also land-locked, but more ecologically diverse. Non-endemic specialities and spectacular species include Rufous-bellied Heron, Cape Griffon*, Wattled Crane*, Lesser Jacana, Pel's Fishing-Owl, Southern Carmine Bee-eater and Bradfield's Hornbill.

Endemics

No species are endemic to Botswana, but near-endemics include Okavango area specialities such as Slaty Egret*, Gabon Boubou and Brown Firefinch, and a few species shared only with Namibia, South Africa and Zimbabwe.

Expectations

Keen birders may see 320 species during a two-week visit.

OKAVANGO DELTA

The Okavango Delta, one of the world's natural wonders, is a geological quirk. Rain-swollen rivers, which originate in the Angolan uplands, do not flow into the sea but into the Kalahari Desert in north Botswana, forming a vast wetland wilderness where waterbirds abound. Over 400 species have been recorded in the delta where, apart from the seemingly endless channels lined with reeds and papyrus, there is also mopane woodland and acacia savanna.

Unfortunately, it is very expensive to get the best out of the Okavango in Botswana so many birders choose to visit the far northwest corner, via Namibia, where access is much cheaper and all the specialities, including Slaty Egret* and Pel's Fishing-Owl, can be seen.

Specialities

Slaty Egret*, Wattled Crane*, Lesser Jacana, Coppery-tailed Coucal, Bradfield's Hornbill, Gabon Boubou, Chirping Cisticola, Angola Babbler, Southern Pied-Babbler, Brown Firefinch.

Others

African Darter, Pink-backed Pelican, White-backed and Comb Ducks, African Pygmy-goose, Hottentot Teal, Black, Goliath and Rufous-bellied Herons, White-backed Night-Heron, Hamerkop, Hadada Ibis, African Openbill, Woolly-necked and Saddle-billed Storks, Bat Hawk, African Fish-Eagle, Lappet-faced Vulture, Banded Snake-Eagle, Wahlberg's Eagle, Dickinson's Kestrel, African and Black Crakes, Long-toed Lapwing, African Skimmer (Aug–Nov), Meyer's Parrot, Black Coucal, Verreaux's Eagle-Owl, Pel's Fishing-Owl, African Barred Owlet, Fiery-necked Nightjar, Woodland Kingfisher, Little and Southern Carmine Bee-eaters, Lilac-breasted and Rufous-crowned Rollers, Southern Ground-Hornbill, Black-collared and Crested Barbets, Black Cuckoo-shrike, White Helmetshrike, Burchell's Glossy-Starling, Grey Tit-Flycatcher, White-headed Black-Chat, African Bush-Warbler, Greater Swamp-Warbler, Rufous-naped Lark, Buffy Pipit, Southern Brown-throated Weaver, Fan-tailed Widowbird.

Other Wildlife

Buffalo, Burchell's zebra, bush baby, cheetah, civet, elephant, giraffe, hippo, honey badger, hunting dog, impala, large spotted genet, leopard, lion, red lechwe, roan, sable, sitatunga, spotted hyena, spring hare, tsessebe, wild cat, wildebeest.

Accommodation: Delta edge near Maun: Crocodile Camp. In the delta: Xakanaxa (White-backed Duck, Slaty Egret*, Lesser Jacana, Grey Tit-Flycatcher); Mombo tented camp (Slaty Egret*, Wattled Crane*, woodland, mammals); Jedibe tented camp (Pel's Fishing-Owl). Northwest delta edge: Xaro (A) (camping (C)) (White-backed Night-Heron, Pel's Fishing-Owl); Shakawe fishing camp (A) (camping (C)), near the Namibian border.

The African Fish-Eagle is a familiar sight in the Okavango and throughout much of Africa. Its wild, yodelling calls are one of the most evocative sounds of the continent

CHOBE NATIONAL PARK

The grassy floodplains, mopane woodland and bush alongside the Chobe river in this big park (11,700 sq km) east of the Okavango, support a similar avifauna to that found in the virtually adjacent Hwange NP in Zimbabwe (p. 401).

The roads are often in a bad condition here so a 4WD is recommended.

Specialities

Slaty Egret*, Wattled Crane*, Bradfield's Hornbill, Southern Pied-Babbler, Brown Firefinch.

Others

Ostrich, Rufous-bellied Heron, Hamerkop, African Openbill, Saddle-billed Stork, Bat Hawk, Martial Eagle, Secretary-bird, Red-billed Francolin, Small Buttonquail, Kori, Red-crested and White-quilled

Bustards, Greater Painted-snipe, Water and Spotted Thick-knees, Double-banded Courser, Rock Pratincole (Nov–Mar), Caspian (Nov–Mar) and Blacksmith Plovers, African Skimmer (Nov–Mar), Burchell's Sandgrouse, Pied Cuckoo, African Scops-Owl, Verreaux's Eagle-Owl, African Barred Owlet, Fiery-necked Nightjar, Half-collared Kingfisher, Southern Carmine Bee-eater, Lilac-breasted Roller, Crimson-breasted Gonolek, Yellow-billed Oxpecker, Mariqua Flycatcher, Winding Cisticola, Eurasian River Warbler (Nov–Mar), Sabota Lark, Rosy-throated Longclaw, Scaly Weaver.

Other Wildlife

Bat-eared fox, buffalo, elephant, giraffe, greater kudu, hippo, hunting dog, impala, leopard, lion, meerkat, puku, red lechwe, spotted hyena, tsessebe, waterbuck, wild cat.

Access

Chobe NP is situated in northeast Botswana and is accessible from Maun or Kasane, itself accessible from the excellent road from Victoria Falls on the Zambia/Zimbabwe border. In the dry season (Apr–Oct) it is possible to drive in a 2WD for at least 50 km along the Chobe river from Kasane. Such a drive is likely to produce many birds, including Half-collared Kingfisher. Rock Pratincole is present from November to March. The **Kasane FR** (Eurasian River Warbler (Nov–Mar)) and the Serondella area are also worth a look if time allows. Boat trips along the Chobe river can be arranged at Chobe Chilwero and Chobe Safari Lodges within the park. Bradfield's Hornbill occurs near Lloyd's tented camp at Savuti in the park's southwest corner.

Accommodation: Chobe Chilwero Lodge (A); Lloyd's tented camp (A); Serondella campsite (C) (beware of baboons); Chobe Safari Lodge (B) (camping (C)).

Chobe NP lies next to **Moremi NP** in the eastern Okavango. This national park is renowned for its animals, especially roan, sable and hunting dog, rather than its birds, although these include Slaty Egret*.

Nxai Pan NP, on the edge of the arid Kalahari, east of Maun, may reward adventurous birders. Stanley Bustard and Sabota and Dusky Larks occur here. One hundred and thirty-five km east of Maun on the Nata road turn north on to the 35-km sandy entrance track (4WD recommended). Chestnut-banded Plover and a variety of larks occur at **Makgadikgadi Pans**, when wet, also east of Maun. Nata Lodge, 10 km south of Nata and 190 km northwest of Francistown off the road to Kasane, is 10 km east of Sowa Pan. It is possible to camp (C), stay in a permanent tent (B) or a rondavel (A) here. A new reserve, **Nata Sanctuary**, protects part of the Sowa Pan, a waterbird paradise during the wet season, especially December to March.

White-backed Duck (Nov–Mar) occurs at the Phakalane Sewage Works, 8 km north of **Gaborone**, Botswana's capital, situated in the southeast corner of the country. Contact the Botswana Bird Club for the latest access details, although some ponds are visible from outside the perimeter fence. Verreaux's Eagle, Natal Francolin, Pied Barbet, Short-toed Rock-Thrush, and Mocking Cliff-Chat occur on Kgale Hill, a bushy kopje just south of Gaborone. Cape Griffon*, Red-crested and White-quilled Bustards, Black Cuckoo, Short-toed Rock-Thrush, Mocking Cliff-

Chat, and Short-clawed Lark* all occur in the Otse area, 50 km south of Gaborone on the Lobatse road. The bustards and Short-clawed Lark occur in the grassland west of Mogobane Dam, reached by turning west 42 km south of Gaborone. There is a Cape Griffon* colony (Apr–Oct) on Mannyelenong Hill, reached by turning east some 46 km south of Gaborone.

ADDITIONAL INFORMATION

Books and Papers

The Birds of Botswana. Newman, K. 1991. HarperCollins.
The Botswana Bird Atlas (1980–1990). Published by the Botswana Bird Club.

Addresses

Please send records to The Botswana Bird Club, PO Box 71, Gaborone, which publishes the bi-annual *Babbler* journal.

Department of Wildlife and National Parks, PO Box 131, Gaborone (tel: 371405).

Near-endemics (Okavango area)

Slaty Egret*, Coppery-tailed Coucal, Angola Babbler, Brown Firefinch.

Near-endemics (Central)

Latakoo Lark.

Near-endemics (South and West)

Clapper Lark, Black-eared Sparrow-Lark, Pink-billed Lark.

Near-endemics (South)

South African Shelduck, Transvaal Rock-Thrush, Rufous-eared and Fairy Warblers, Damara Canary.

BURKINA FASO

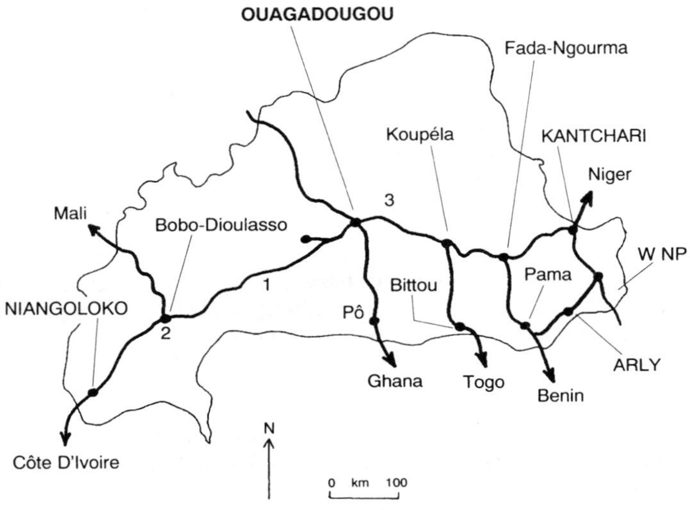

1 Niangoloko–Kantchari road
2 La Guinquette
3 Kaya

INTRODUCTION

Summary

Burkina Faso is a very poor, overpopulated and overgrazed country. However, the people are extremely friendly and the birds include a number of the arid savanna specialities such as Sudan Golden-Sparrow.

Size

At 274,200 sq km, Burkina Faso is twice the size of England, and less than half the size of Texas.

Getting Around

There are few good roads and these are often dotted with endless but friendly military checkpoints. The ubiquitous bush taxis reach most places.

Accommodation and Food

Accommodation is sparse but quite cheap. However, it is not as cheap as camping, which is allowed anywhere away from towns. The people live on rice, millet and fish, and so do most travellers.

Health and Safety

Immunisation against hepatitis, polio, typhoid and yellow fever is recommended. Also take precautions against malaria, and beware of bilharzia and river blindness.

Throughout the third world, the poorest people tend to be the friendliest, and this is certainly the case in Burkina Faso.

Climate and Timing

Normally the dry season lasts from November to April, and the sandy Harmattan wind, which originates in the Sahara, often blows hard during these months. The coolest months are January and February so this is the best time to visit. During the normal rainy season (Jun–Oct), only the main west-east road from Niangoloko to Kantchari is passable with a 2WD.

Habitats

Burkina Faso lies in a very flat part of the world, although there are some wooded hills in the Banfora region in the extreme southwest. Otherwise this is a country of semi-arid, overgrazed wooded savanna and, in the Sahel of the far north, arid acacia scrub.

Conservation

Overpopulation and overgrazing, which exacerbate desertification, have badly degraded the savanna and Sahelian habitats.

One threatened and one near-threatened species occur in Burkina Faso.

Bird Families

Of the ten families endemic to the African mainland, six are represented in Burkina Faso.

Bird Species

Because Burkina Faso is land-locked and has no lowland rainforest, only 453 species have been recorded, nearly 300 fewer than neighbouring Ghana, a coastal, forested country. Non-endemic specialities and spectacular species include Scissor-tailed Kite, Lesser Jacana, Black and Red-throated Bee-eaters, Blue-bellied Roller, Little Grey Woodpecker, Chestnut-bellied Starling, Sudan Golden-Sparrow and Brown-rumped Bunting.

Endemics

There are no endemics or near-endemics, although a number of arid-savanna specialities are present.

NIANGOLOKO–KANTCHARI ROAD

This road runs west-east across the centre of Burkina Faso, from the Côte D'Ivoire to Niger. Although many of the species recorded alongside this road are widespread in Africa, they do include localised birds such as Lesser Jacana and Orange Weaver.

Others

African Darter, African Pygmy-goose, Hamerkop, Hadada Ibis, Scissor-tailed Kite, Palm-nut Vulture, Bateleur, Gabar Goshawk, Grasshopper and Red-necked Buzzards, Allen's Gallinule, Lesser Moorhen, Stanley and White-bellied Bustards, Lesser Jacana, Senegal and Spotted Thick-knees, Bronze-winged and Temminck's Coursers, Black-headed Lapwing, Four-banded Sandgrouse, Vinaceous Dove, Bruce's Green-Pigeon, Senegal Parrot, Violet Turaco, Western Grey Plantain-eater, Pied, Levaillant's and African Cuckoos, Black Coucal, White-faced Scops-Owl, Standard-winged Nightjar, Mottled Spinetail, Woodland Kingfisher, Red-throated, Green and Northern Carmine Bee-eaters, Abyssinian and Blue-bellied Rollers, Black Scimitar-bill, Yellow-fronted Tinkerbird, Vieillot's and Bearded Barbets, Fine-spotted Woodpecker, African Blue-Flycatcher, Piapiac, Red-shouldered Cuckoo-shrike, Yellow-billed Shrike, Common Gonolek, Many-coloured Bushshrike, White Helmetshrike, Senegal Batis, Red-winged Starling, Yellow-billed Oxpecker, Heuglin's Wheatear, Red-chested, Rufous-chested and Mosque Swallows, Croaking and Rufous Cisticolas, Sun Lark, Lavender and Black-rumped Waxbills, Broad-tailed Paradise-Whydah, Orange Weaver, Yellow-crowned, Black-winged and Orange Bishops, Pygmy and Beautiful Sunbirds, White-rumped Seedeater, Brown-rumped Bunting.

Access

Lesser Jacana and Orange Weaver have been recorded around Lac Tingrela and the 'Cascades', near Banfora. Just east of Ouagadougou, where the main road from Niger enters the city, there used to be some good woodland where Green Bee-eater, Common Gonolek and White Helmetshrike may still occur.

LA GUINQUETTE

La Guinquette is a freshwater spring surrounded by the Kou Forest, 20 km from Bobo-Dioulasso.

Others

Dwarf Bittern, Palm-nut Vulture, Black Crake, Senegal Parrot, Violet Turaco, Western Grey Plantain-eater, Senegal Coucal, Black Bee-eater, White Helmetshrike, White-crowned Robin-Chat, Oriole Warbler, Vitelline Masked-Weaver, Black-faced Firefinch.

Access

Turn south off the main Niangoloko–Kantchari road 18 km southwest of Bobo-Dioulasso. Bird the forest around the springs and the surrounding farmland. The springs are used by the local people as a swimming pool, especially at weekends, so midweek is best for birding.

KAYA

Kaya lies near the Sahel in north Burkina Faso; some of the species here are not found further south, along the Niangoloko–Kantchari road.

These include Little Grey Woodpecker, Chestnut-bellied Starling and Sudan Golden-Sparrow.

Specialities

Sudan Golden-Sparrow.

Others

Wahlberg's Eagle, Grey Kestrel, Bruce's Green-Pigeon, Black-headed Lapwing, Abyssinian Roller, Green Bee-eater, Black Scimitar-bill, Yellow-fronted Tinkerbird, Little Grey Woodpecker, Chestnut-bellied Starling, Black Scrub-Robin, Chestnut-backed Sparrow-Lark, Black-rumped Waxbill, Beautiful Sunbird, Brown-rumped Bunting.

Access

Kaya is 100 km northeast of Ouagadougou. Bird the surrounds of Lac de Dem, 15 km north of the town.

Part of **W NP** (p. 273), which stretches into Niger and Benin, is in Burkina Faso. The Ministère de l'Environment et du Tourisme in Ouagadougou organises trips to **d'Arly NP**, which is contiguous with W NP and probably supports similar birds. Two other sites may repay a visit: **Pô NP** and **Nazinga Reserve**, which are both accessible from Pô, south of Ouagadougou on the road to Ghana.

ADDITIONAL INFORMATION

Books and Papers

Distributional Notes on the Birds of Burkina Faso. Holyoak, D and Seddon, M. *Bull.* B.O.C. 1989: 109:205–216.

Addresses

West African Ornithological Society (WAOS), see Useful Addresses, p. 413.

BURUNDI

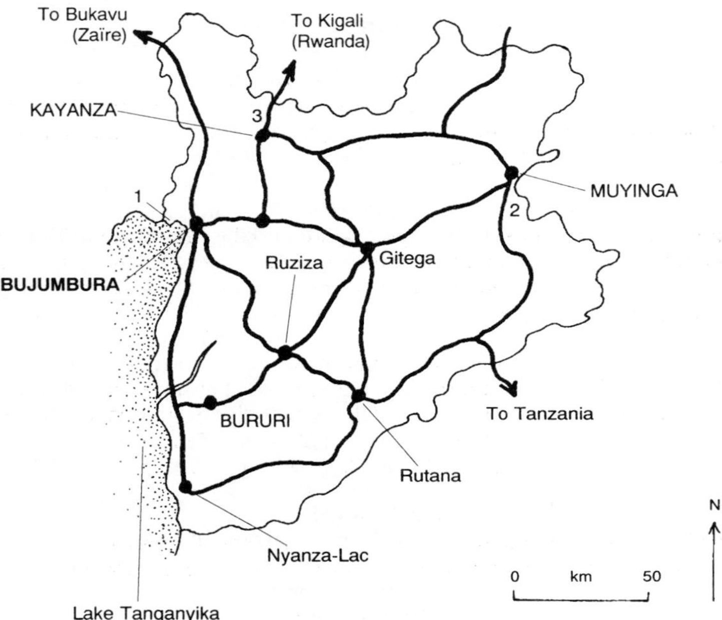

1 Ruzizi Delta
2 Ruvuvu NP
3 Kibira NP

INTRODUCTION

Summary

Periodical political problems withstanding, Burundi is a fine country for birding, where a good selection of Central African specialities, including 18 of the 43 Albertine Rift endemics and papyrus-dwellers such as Papyrus Gonolek*, can be seen in a small area.

Size

At 27,834 sq km, Burundi is a tiny country which is just one fifth the size of England and 4% the size of Texas.

Getting Around

The roads are good by African standards and plenty of modern buses run along them. There are no regular internal flights.

Accommodation and Food

Outside the capital, Bujumbura, there are missions, auberges and even lodges. The food is good and includes sandwiches and omelettes.

Health and Safety

Immunisation against hepatitis, polio, typhoid and yellow fever is recommended, as are precautions against malaria.

Climate and Timing

This is a wet country and only December and January could be described as dry months, although August is not too bad. It is hot and humid around Lake Tanganyika all year round.

Habitats

Burundi is a highland country, lying between 762 m (2500 ft) and 2286 m (7500 ft), with much montane forest, although marshes, which include the inland delta formed by the Ruzizi river, and savanna also make up a fair portion of the land.

Conservation

Burundi is one of the most densely populated countries in the world and yet there are few big towns. The people, mostly farmers, had up to the 1990s made little serious impact on the natural environment.

Five threatened and six near-threatened species occur in Burundi.

Bird Families

Only five of the ten families endemic to the African mainland are represented in Burundi. Both Ostrich and Secretary-bird are absent.

Bird Species

Despite its small size and land-locked position, 596 species have been recorded in Burundi. Although this total is 70 fewer than similar Rwanda, the list is increasing at a steady rate, and may eventually match that of its northern neighbour. Non-endemic specialities and spectacular species include Madagascar Pond-Heron*, Blue-breasted Bee-eater, Red-faced Barbet*, Papyrus Gonolek*, Collared Palm-Thrush, Kungwe Apalis* and Papyrus Yellow Warbler*.

Endemics

There are no endemics, but 18 of the 43 Albertine Rift endemics are present, including Archer's Robin-Chat and Regal Sunbird.

Bat Hawk and Palm-nut Vulture occur in and around the capital, **Bujumbura**, and Chirping Cisticola has recently been recorded in the marsh 200 m south of the golf course.

RUZIZI DELTA

This delta, near Bujumbura, supports such localised species as Madagascar Pond-Heron*, Blue-breasted Bee-eater and Chirping Cisticola.

Specialities

Collared Palm-Thrush, Chirping Cisticola, Red-chested Sunbird.

Others

Black and Goliath Herons, Madagascar Pond-Heron*, Rufous-bellied Heron, Hamerkop, Hadada Ibis, African Openbill, Saddle-billed Stork, Palm-nut Vulture, African Goshawk, Grey Kestrel, Black-rumped Buttonquail, Black Crake, Grey Crowned-Crane, Black-bellied Bustard, Water and Spotted Thick-knees, Bronze-winged and Temminck's Coursers, Three-banded and White-fronted Plovers, Long-toed and Senegal Lapwings, African Skimmer, Blue-naped Mousebird, Red-chested Cuckoo, Black Coucal, Woodland Kingfisher, Little, Blue-breasted, Madagascar and Northern Carmine Bee-eaters, Lilac-breasted Roller, Grey-backed Fiscal, Brown-crowned Tchagra, Spotted Morning-Thrush, Banded Martin, Angola Swallow, Red-faced, Trilling, and Croaking Cisticolas, Greater and Lesser Swamp-Warblers, Red-faced Crombec, Red-billed Quailfinch, Slender-billed Weaver, Holub's Golden-Weaver, Black-headed and Grosbeak Weavers. (Grey Pratincole, Forbes' Plover and Brown-chested Lapwing have all been recorded here in the past.)

Other Wildlife

Hippo, Nile crocodile.

Access

The delta lies next to Lake Tanganyika, west of Bujumbura, alongside the road to Uvira in Zaïre. There is a small reserve here, which is sign-posted.

RUVUVU NATIONAL PARK

The savanna, pools, wooded hills, and gallery forest alongside the Ruvuvu river in this park in east Burundi, support some localised species such as Red-faced Barbet* and four papyrus specialities including the rare Papyrus Yellow Warbler*.

Specialities

Ring-necked Francolin, Red-faced* and Black-backed Barbets, Papyrus Gonolek*, Grey-winged Robin-Chat, Brown-backed Scrub-Robin, Tabora Cisticola, White-winged Scrub-Warbler, Papyrus Yellow Warbler*, White-collared Oliveback, Papyrus Canary.

Others

African Darter, White-backed Duck, African Pygmy-goose, Black Heron, Madagascar Pond-Heron*, Rufous-bellied Heron, White-backed Night-Heron, Dwarf Bittern, Woolly-necked and Saddle-billed Storks, White-headed Vulture, Banded Snake-Eagle, Little Sparrowhawk, Wahlberg's and Martial Eagles, African Finfoot, Stanley Bustard, Bronze-winged Courser, Rock Pratincole, Meyer's Parrot, Red-headed Lovebird, Purple-crested and Ross's Turacos, Eastern Grey Plantain-eater, Yellowbill, Blue-headed Coucal, Marsh Owl, Black-shouldered Nightjar, Swamp, Square-tailed and Pennant-winged Nightjars, Mottled and African

Swifts, Blue-breasted Bee-eater, Lilac-breasted Roller, Yellow-fronted Tinkerbird, Spot-flanked, Black-collared and Double-toothed Barbets, Green-backed Woodpecker, Black Cuckoo-shrike, Marsh Tchagra, White Helmetshrike, Yellow-billed Oxpecker, Familiar and Sooty Chats, White-headed Black-Chat, Red-capped and Snowy-crowned Robin-Chats, Banded Martin, Grey-rumped Swallow, White-headed Sawwing, Yellow-throated Greenbul, Siffling Cisticola, Grey Apalis, Grey-capped Warbler, Grey Wren-Warbler, Yellow-bellied Hyliota, Fawn-breasted Waxbill, Yellow-throated Longclaw, Vieillot's Black Weaver, Yellow Bishop, Fan-tailed and White-winged Widowbirds, Copper and Mariqua Sunbirds, Black-faced Canary, Cabanis' Bunting.

Other Wildlife

Blue monkey, buffalo, bush duiker, hippo, red colobus, reedbuck, sitatunga, waterbuck.

Access

This park is situated near the Tanzanian border, south of Muyinga.

Accommodation: Muyinga; Ruvuvu Safari Camp; Camping (take food).

KIBIRA NATIONAL PARK

Situated in northwest Burundi near Kayanza, the montane forest in this park is contiguous with the Nyungwe Forest in Rwanda (p. 284), and together they constitute one of the largest remaining tracts of montane forest in Africa. The 170 sq km of forest in Kibira NP support a fine selection of the Albertine Rift endemics including Regal Sunbird, as well as other localised species such as Kungwe Apalis*.

Specialities

Ruwenzori Turaco, Ruwenzori Nightjar, Western Green-Tinkerbird, White-tailed Blue-Flycatcher, Mountain Boubou, Doherty's and Lagden's* Bushshrikes, Ruwenzori Batis, Red-throated Alethe, Archer's Robin-Chat, Chubb's Cisticola, Black-faced and Kungwe* Apalises, Grauer's Scrub-Warbler*, White-browed Crombec, Red-faced Woodland-Warbler, Stripe-breasted Tit, Dusky and Shelley's* Crimson-wings, Strange Weaver, Blue-headed, Regal and Purple-breasted Sunbirds.

Others

African Black Duck, Black Goshawk, Mountain Buzzard, Ayre's Hawk-Eagle, African Snipe, African and Bronze-naped Pigeons, Lemon Dove, Black-billed and Great Blue Turacos, Black, Barred Long-tailed and African Emerald Cuckoos, Scarce and Horus Swifts, Narina and Bar-tailed Trogons, Cinnamon-chested Bee-eater, White-headed Woodhoopoe, Black-and-white-casqued Hornbill, Yellow-billed Barbet, Tullberg's, Elliot's and Olive Woodpeckers, White-tailed Crested-Flycatcher, Black-tailed Oriole, Mackinnon's Shrike, Many-coloured Bushshrike, Brown-chested Alethe, Waller's, Slender-billed and Sharpe's Starlings, White-starred Robin, Equatorial Akalat, Shelley's, Mountain and Placid Greenbuls, White-chinned and Black-faced

Prinias, Black-throated, Chestnut-throated and Grey Apalises, Mountain Warbler, Abyssinian Hill-Babbler, Grey-headed Negrofinch, Red-faced Crimson-wing, Yellow-bellied and Black-headed Waxbills, Black-and-white Mannikin, Mountain Wagtail, Black-billed and Brown-capped Weavers, Olive, Northern Double-collared, Bronze and Malachite Sunbirds, Streaky and Thick-billed Seedeaters.

(Since this NP is contiguous with Nyungwe Forest in Rwanda (p. 284), a number of species which have been recorded there, but not in Kibira, may well be found here in the future.)

Other Wildlife

Chimpanzee, L'Hoest's monkey, mona monkey.

Access

Bird roads and trails.

Accommodation: Kayanza; Auberge de Kayanza (B).

Bar-tailed Trogon, Cinnamon-chested Bee-eater, White-tailed Blue-Flycatcher, Black-tailed Oriole, Ruwenzori Batis, Red-throated Alethe, Collared Apalis, and Ruwenzori Hill-Babbler have been recorded in **Bururi Forest**, near the town of Bururi in south Burundi.

ADDITIONAL INFORMATION

Addresses

Please send all records to Dr Jean Pierre Vande Weghe, BP 2900 Bujumbura.

Near-endemics (Albertine Rift)

Ruwenzori Turaco, Ruwenzori Nightjar, Ruwenzori Batis, Red-throated Alethe, Yellow-eyed Black-Flycatcher, Archer's Robin-Chat, Black-faced Apalis, Grauer's* and White-winged Scrub-Warblers, Red-faced Woodland-Warbler, Stripe-breasted Tit, Dusky and Shelley's* Crimson-wings, Strange Weaver, Grey-headed, Blue-headed, Regal and Purple-breasted Sunbirds.

CAMEROON

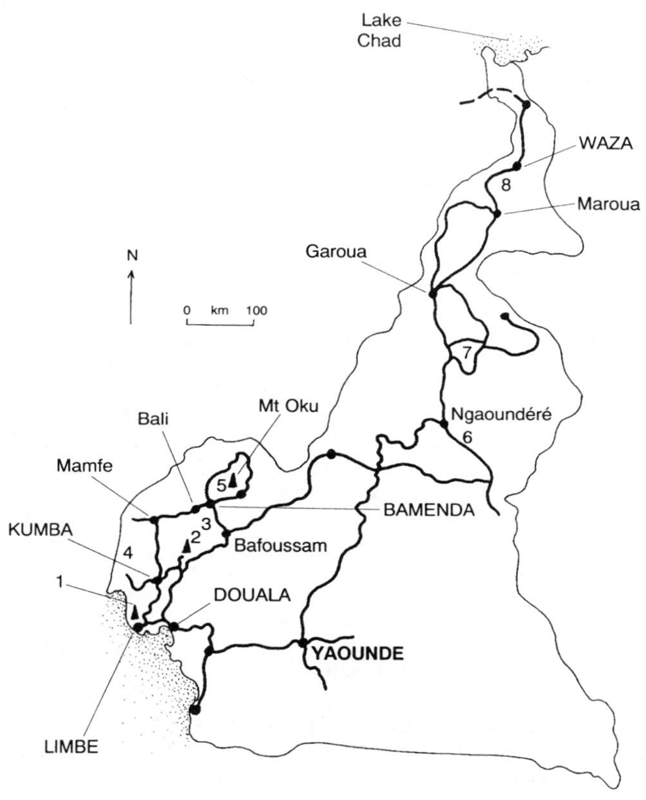

1 Limbe and Mount Cameroon
2 Mount Kupé
3 Bakossi Mountains
4 Korup NP
5 Bamenda Highlands
6 Ngaoundaba Ranch
7 Benoue NP
8 Waza NP

INTRODUCTION

Summary

Cameroon is the most accessible country in West-Central Africa and a top birding destination. Most of the speciality species, including the seven endemics, are concentrated in the forests of the south where there are a number of sites accessible by road and a fairly good selection of accommodation.

Size

At 475,442 sq km, Cameroon is nearly four times the size of England, and one third the size of Texas.

Getting Around

Although car-hire (4WD recommended) is very expensive, the cheap and efficient bush taxis, which may take the form of cars, land-rovers or buses, cover much of the country. There are also express buses between all major towns. The major roads in the north are fine, but in the south some are in a very poor state, and during the heavy rains (Jun–Oct) many are impassable. On some roads a toll has to be paid and on others there are police checkpoints (always carry your passport). There is a good, fairly priced internal air network.

Accommodation and Food

Western standard hotels are rare outside the major towns, but there are plenty of alternatives, including cheap auberges. Camping is the cheapest way to bird, at least in the north, but there are no 'official' campsites. Local food, heavily influenced by the French, can also be expensive. Guinness is a popular tipple in Cameroon, but drinking palm wine seems to be a national pastime.

Health and Safety

Immunisation against hepatitis, meningitis, polio, typhoid and yellow fever is recommended. Malaria is rife, especially in the south, and bilharzia is also present.

Walk the streets of Douala at night with care, and beware of trouble day and night in the Douala harbour area.

Climate and Timing

The southern dry season, December to March, is the best time to visit, although a number of species, such as weavers, are not in breeding plumage at this time, especially in the north. The lowlands are generally hot and humid, but it can be very chilly in the highlands at night.

Habitats

Cameroon's impressive bird species list (at least 874) reflects the great diversity of habitats present within the country. In the north, Cameroon's borders encompass part of the southern Sahel, a land of savanna, bush and seasonal marshes, whilst in the south there is lowland and montane forest, centred on Mounts Oku, Kupé and Cameroon. In between, lies the wooded savanna of the Benoue lowlands and the Adamawa Plateau.

Conservation

The forest of Cameroon, including that within so-called 'protected areas', is under threat from agriculture, logging and hunting (50% lost in last few decades). Even the forest on Mount Kupé, where BirdLife International are promoting ecotourism and making strenuous efforts to involve the local people in the sustainable use of their local natural resources, is not sacrosanct.

Fourteen threatened and 16 near-threatened species occur in Cameroon.

Bird Families

Of the ten families endemic to the African mainland eight are represented in Cameroon. Only Shoebill* and sugarbirds are absent. Well represented families include guineafowl, turacos, kingfishers, hornbills, bushshrikes, sunbirds and weavers.

Bird Species

Cameroon's list is growing steadily, with a few species being added almost every year, mainly in the north. Even so, the 1981 total of 874 is still the seventh highest for an African country. Non-endemic specialities and spectacular species include Long-tailed Hawk, Black Guineafowl, Quail-plover, Arabian Bustard, Lesser Jacana, Egyptian Plover, Grey Pratincole, Bare-cheeked Trogon, White-bellied and Chocolate-backed Kingfishers, Rufous-sided Broadbill, Chestnut-bellied Starling, and Sudan Golden-Sparrow.

Endemics

Only six mainland countries have more endemics than Cameroon. The seven species unique to this country include Bannerman's Turaco*, Mount Kupé Bushshrike* and Banded Wattle-eye*, whilst Monteiro's Bushshrike* is known elsewhere only from very old Angolan records. There are also plenty of near-endemics, most of which are shared with Gabon, Fernando Po and southeast Nigeria. These include Yellow-breasted Boubou, Green-breasted Bushshrike*, Black-capped Woodland-Warbler, Grey-necked Rockfowl*, Fernando Po Oliveback, Bannerman's Weaver*, and Ursula's Sunbird*.

Expectations

Well prepared, keen birders may see 300 species during a two-week trip to the south, or over 450 in three weeks, if both the north and south are visited.

The coastal lowlands with mudflats, scrub and mangroves, surrounding **Douala**, in west Cameroon, support White-fronted Plover, Royal Tern, Grey Parrot, Shining Blue Kingfisher, Spotted Greenbul, and Mouse-brown and Carmelite Sunbirds. Good birding spots near Douala include the mangroves and mudflats of the Wouri river, just out of town on the Limbe road, and La Digue, on the coast at the southern end of the harbour.

Accommodation: Douala: Sawa Hotel (A); Hotel Ibis (A); Hotel de l'Air (B); Catholic Procure (Franceville Street) (C).

LIMBE and MOUNT CAMEROON

The isolated Mount Cameroon, an active volcano, rises spectacularly from the sea on the west coast, to form the highest peak in West Africa (4070 m (13,353 ft)). Forest once covered the slopes up to 2500 m (8202 ft), but much of the lower altitude forest has been lost to cultivation. However, the remaining forest and montane grassland still supports three endemics, two of which are confined to this single mountain: Cameroon Francolin* and Cameroon Speirops*.

Cameroon Endemics

Cameroon Francolin*, Cameroon Speirops*, Brown-backed Cisticola, Cameroon Pipit, Bates' Weaver*.

Specialities

Cameroon Pigeon, Western Green-Tinkerbird, Green-breasted Bushshrike*, Yellow-breasted Boubou, Mountain Robin-Chat, Mountain Sawwing*, Cameroon Mountain* and Grey-headed* Greenbuls, Green Longtail, Cameroon Scrub-Warbler, White-tailed Warbler, Yellow Longbill, Black-capped Woodland-Warbler, Fernando Po Oliveback, Cameroon and Ursula's* Sunbirds.

Others

Western Reef-Egret, Palm-nut Vulture, Red-chested Goshawk, Cassin's and Crowned Hawk-Eagles, Scaly Francolin, Nkulengu Rail, Royal Tern, Lemon Dove, Grey Parrot, Guinea, Yellow-billed and Great Blue Turacos, Levaillant's and African Emerald Cuckoos, Blue-headed Coucal, Fraser's Eagle-Owl, Sabine's Spinetail, Bates' Swift, Shining Blue, White-bellied, Dwarf and Chocolate-backed Kingfishers, Yellow-casqued Hornbill*, Naked-faced and Yellow-spotted Barbets, Spotted Honeyguide, Tullberg's, Gabon and Elliot's Woodpeckers, White-bellied Crested-Flycatcher, Black-winged Oriole, Petit's Cuckoo-shrike, Mackinnon's Shrike, Chestnut and White-spotted Wattle-eyes, Rufous Flycatcher-Thrush, White-tailed Ant-Thrush, Narrow-tailed and Waller's Starlings, Dusky-blue Flycatcher, Yellow-whiskered Bulbul, Swamp, Xavier's, Eastern Bearded and White-bearded Greenbuls, Chattering Cisticola, Banded Prinia, Grey Apalis, Blackcap and Grey-chested Illadopsises, Woodhouse's Antpecker, Chestnut-breasted and Pale-fronted Negrofinches, Red-faced Crimson-wing, Western Bluebill, Slender-billed, Black-billed and Brown-capped Weavers, Gray's Malimbe, Little Green and Carmelite Sunbirds, Thick-billed Seedeater, Oriole Finch. (Grey-necked Rockfowl* has also been recorded.)

Other Wildlife

Mona monkey, Preuss' and russet-eared guenons.

Access

Mount Cameroon is normally accessible from two places: (1) 70 km west of Douala a track leads up the mountain from **Buea** (1000 m (3281 ft)), to 2000 m (6562 ft), where the forest ends and montane grassland (Cameroon Pipit) begins. Visitors to Mount Cameroon are required to obtain a permit from the Tourism Office in Buea. The permit fee includes the services of a guide. (2) From **Mapanja** (870 m (2854 ft)), a village just above Limbe, where various trails are worth exploring. Guides should be hired in the village as it is easy to get lost. A small gift (of whisky) should be offered to the Chief in Mapanja to obtain his permission to enter tribal lands.

Shining Blue and White-bellied Kingfishers, Western Bluebill and Carmelite Sunbirds occur in and around **Limbe**, on the Atlantic coast. The botanical gardens are a particularly good spot. Western Reef-Egret occurs along the palm-fringed, mainly black lava beaches, and there is a good lagoon worth checking behind Mile Six Beach, west along the coast road to Batoke. The **Mabeta Moliwe Reserve**, a small area of lowland rainforest and mangrove, 13 km east of Limbe alongside the road to Mabeta, may also be worth a visit, but a guide is recommended. It is possible to arrange guides at the botanical gardens in Limbe.

Accommodation: Buea: Flats Hotel (A/B) and Mountain Hotel (B). Mapanja: ask for permission to stay in a village house on giving the Chief a small gift (he likes whisky). Limbe: Tabai Park (Miramar) Hotel (B); Atlantic Beach Hotel.

Grey Pratincole and White-headed Lapwing occur on the Mungo river, and Blue-breasted Bee-eater in the farmland around Loum, *en route* from Douala to Mount Kupé.

Congo Serpent-Eagle, African Finfoot, Yellow-billed Turaco, Yellowbill, Cassin's Spinetail, Shining Blue Kingfisher, Bristle-nosed Barbet, Large-billed Puffback, White-throated Blue Swallow, and Bates' Sunbird have been recorded on and around **Lake Barombi Mbo**, a crater lake just outside Kumba. However, the forest has been badly degraded in recent years, especially during the early 1990s, as Kumba has expanded. The trackside forest in the 'canyon' (cliffs on both sides) just before the lake and the path to the right on reaching the lake used to be good birding spots, whilst dugout canoes can be hired to look for African Finfoot.

Accommodation: Kumba: Hotel Meme Pilot (B).

MOUNT KUPÉ

This isolated mountain (2064 m (6772 ft)) supports 25 sq km of primary montane forest, where over 320 species have been recorded including some of Africa's rarest birds, not least Mount Kupé* and Monteiro's* Bushshrikes. The Mount Kupé Bushshrike* was seen for the first time in 36 years in 1989, and Monteiro's Bushshrike* was rediscovered in 1992, the first sighting since 1954 in Angola and 1894 on Mount Cameroon.

All three African trogons, eight kingfishers, seven honeyguides, including Zenker's, 21 greenbuls and 17 sunbirds help to make up Mount Kupé's impressive list, whilst particularly interesting species include White-naped Pigeon*, Black Bee-eater, Black-necked Wattle-eye, Crossley's Ground-Thrush, Alexander's Akalat and Grey-necked Rockfowl*.

BirdLife International established a conservation and development project here in 1991, with the support of the local people.

Cameroon Endemics

Mount Kupé Bushshrike*.

Specialities

Cameroon and White-naped* Pigeons, Sjostedt's Owlet, Bare-cheeked Trogon, Western Green-Tinkerbird, Zenker's Honeyguide, Grey-headed Broadbill, Mountain Boubou, Green-breasted* and Monteiro's* Bushshrikes, Black-necked Wattle-eye, Crossley's Ground-Thrush*, Alexander's Akalat, Mountain and White-bellied Robin-Chats, Forest Swallow, Cameroon Mountain* and Grey-headed* Greenbuls, Green Longtail, White-tailed Warbler, Yellow Longbill, Black-capped

Woodland-Warbler, White-throated Mountain-Babbler*, Grey-necked Rockfowl*, Fernando Po Oliveback, Cameroon and Ursula's* Sunbirds.

Others

Red-chested Goshawk, Cassin's and Crowned Hawk-Eagles, Scaly Francolin, White-spotted Flufftail, Black, Olive Long-tailed and African Emerald Cuckoos, Yellowbill, Guinea, Yellow-billed and Great Blue Turacos, Fraser's Eagle-Owl, Black-shouldered Nightjar, Sabine's Spinetail, Bates' Swift, Narina and Bar-tailed Trogons, White-bellied, Dwarf and Chocolate-backed Kingfishers, Black and White-throated Bee-eaters, White-crested and Black-casqued Hornbills, Speckled Tinkerbird, Yellow-spotted and Yellow-billed Barbets, Thick-billed and Cassin's Honeyguides, African Piculet, Green-backed, Tullberg's, Gabon, Golden-crowned and Elliot's Woodpeckers, Chestnut-capped Flycatcher, White-bellied Crested-Flycatcher, Shining and Velvet-mantled Drongos, Blue and Petit's Cuckoo-shrikes, Grey-green, Many-coloured and Fiery-breasted Bushshrikes, African and Black-and-white Shrike-flycatchers, Black-headed Batis, Chestnut, White-spotted and Yellow-bellied Wattle-eyes, Rufous Flycatcher-Thrush, White-tailed Ant-Thrush, Brown-chested and Fire-crested Alethes, Little Grey and Yellow-footed Flycatchers, Square-tailed Sawwing, Cameroon Olive-Greenbul, Red-tailed Greenbul, Banded Prinia, Black-capped and Black-throated Apalises, Olive-green Camaroptera, Rufous-crowned Eremomela, Green Crombec, Grey Longbill, Green Hylia, Violet-backed Hyliota, Grey-chested Illadopsis, Tit-hylia, Woodhouse's Antpecker, White-breasted, Chestnut-breasted and Pale-fronted Negrofinches, Green-backed Twinspot, Mountain Wagtail, Crested and Red-headed Malimbes, Scarlet-tufted and Bates' Sunbirds. (There have also been records of Sandy Scops-Owl, Green-breasted Pitta and Bates' Weaver*.)

Other Wildlife

Chimpanzee (rare), crowned monkey, cusimanse, drill (rare), greater white-nosed monkey, mona monkey, russet-eared guenon.

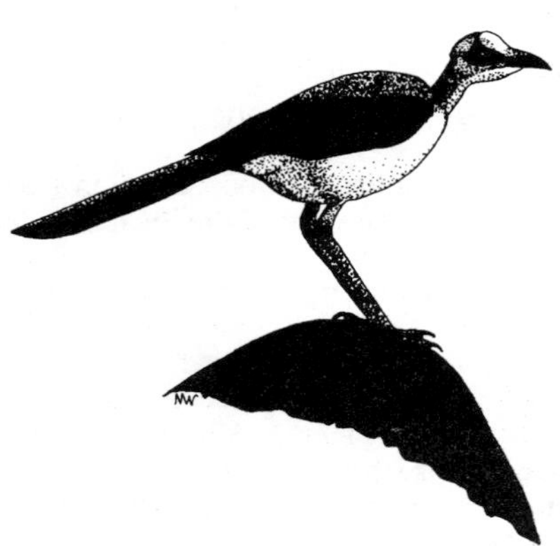

Mount Kupé is one of the few easily accessible sites in Africa where Grey-necked Rockfowl occurs, but visiting this mountain is one thing, seeing the rare rock-fowl is another.*

Access

The base for birding Mount Kupé, the village of **Nyasoso**, is three to four hours by car from Douala (4WD recommended Jun–Oct), and up to six hours by bush taxi, via Loum and Tombel. Bird around the village (850 m (2789 ft)) and the forest above where there are three major trails, complete with altitude markers. They are: (1) The **Nature Trail**, a short loop which begins at the south end of the school campus, where Bates' Swift, Grey-headed Broadbill, Forest Swallow, Green Longtail, Violet-backed Hyliota and Grey-necked Rockfowl* (rare amongst the large boulders and caves at the top of the loop) occur. (2) The **Shrike Trail**, which begins at the right-hand side of the pink building at the far side of the school campus, behind the dam, and is good for Mount Kupé Bushshrike* (1100 m (3609 ft) to 1400 m (4593 ft)), as well as tro-

MOUNT KUPÉ

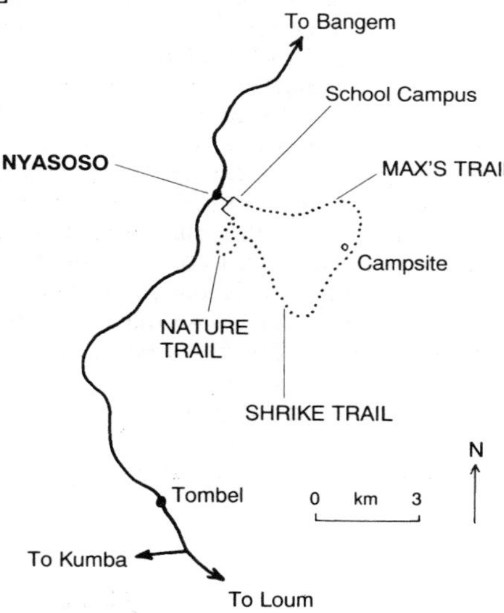

gons, White-bellied and Chocolate-backed Kingfishers, and Crossley's Ground-Thrush* (higher up). (3) **Max's Trail**, which starts at the project leader's cottage, 1–2 km through bush (excellent for birding, with Black Bee-eater at the forest edge) from the village. This is a good trail for Bare-cheeked Trogon, Zenker's Honeyguide (1170 m (3839 ft)), Mount Kupé* (sometimes), Green-breasted* and Monteiro's* (both above 1300 m (4265 ft)) Bushshrikes, Black-necked Wattle-eye, Black-headed Batis, White-throated Mountain-Babbler* and Woodhouse's Antpecker. The areas around 1050 m (3445 ft) (mixed species flocks) and 1550 m (5085 ft) (Crossley's Ground-Thrush*, White-throated Mountain-Babbler*) are particularly good spots. This trail eventually reaches the mountain summit. Both Shrike and Max's Trails can be hard to find, and the local guides, who can be arranged at the HQ, are recommended, at least for the first time.

Accommodation: To book in advance contact WWF Cameroon, BP 2417, PMB 1 Bonanjo, Douala (tel/fax: 237 432171). It is possible to stay in the Guesthouse (C) or with local families, and there are campsites (without facilities) on Shrike and Max's Trails (arrange use in village). Tombel: Alson's Guesthouse.

Most Mount Kupé specialities also occur in the **Bakossi Mountains**, where there is ten times as much forest. The number of birders who have penetrated this remote area can be counted on the fingers of one hand, but the site may become more accessible in the future. At present, birding here involves asking village chiefs permission to stay in their remote villages, and rewarding their hospitality with a small gift (money (C) is preferred). A guide is recommended (B per day). Ask at Nyasoso or in the village of Edib. It is possible to access the forests here via: (1) Ngomboko, a village 10 km north of Nyasoso. From here it is 3 km to Baseng where, after fording the river, it is possible to walk (5 km) to Edib, and on (2 km) to Lake Edib, Masaka (5 km) and Nyali; the Edib–Lake Edib (and around)–Masaka section is particularly good: Congo Serpent-Eagle and many of the Mount Kupé specialities have been recorded here. (2) The village of Nyandung, which is 3 km from Masaka, and linked to the Kumba–Mamfe road by a track.

The near-endemic Bannerman's Weaver* occurs at **Mount Manenguba** (2411 m (7910 ft)), near the town of Bangem, north of Mount Kupé, as well as Cameroon Pigeon, African Grass-Owl, Bates' Swift (over Lake Manenguba at dawn), Blue-breasted Bee-eater, Yellow-breasted Boubou, Preuss' Swallow, Cameroon Mountain Greenbul*, Cameroon Pipit and Fernando Po Oliveback. A 4WD is needed to reach Bangem (3 hours from Nyasoso), where a track leads off right towards the mountain, ending at the rim of a crater lake.

BAKOSSI MOUNTAINS

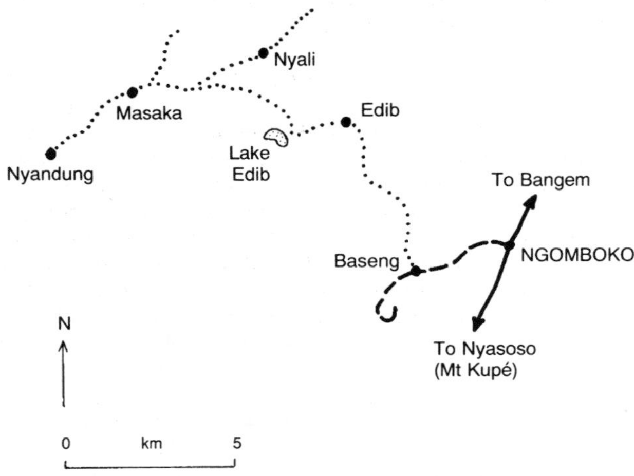

KORUP NATIONAL PARK

This extensive park (837 sq km) in Southwest Cameroon, adjacent to the Nigerian border, protects an area of species-rich, moist lowland evergreen forest. Plant diversity is possibly the richest in Africa and it also supports seven species of threatened mammals and an impressive list of lowland forest birds, which includes species such as Long-tailed Hawk, Black Guineafowl, Blue-headed Bee-eater, Black-eared and Grey Ground-Thrushes, Kemp's Longbill and Grey-necked Rockfowl*.

Specialities

Hartlaub's Duck, Black Guineafowl, Sjostedt's Owlet, Brown Nightjar, Black Spinetail, Rufous-sided Broadbill, Black-eared and Grey Ground-Thrushes, Kemp's Longbill, Grey-necked Rockfowl*, Rachel's Malimbe.

Others

White-crested Bittern, Long-tailed Hawk, Cassin's Hawk-Eagle, Crested Guineafowl, Forest Francolin, Nkulengu Rail, Rock Pratincole, Afep Pigeon, Levaillant's and African Emerald Cuckoos, Black-throated Coucal, Great Blue Turaco, White-bellied and Chocolate-backed Kingfishers, Blue-headed Bee-eater, Forest Woodhoopoe, White-crested, Red-billed Dwarf, White-thighed and Yellow-casqued* Hornbills, Spotted and Willcock's Honeyguides, African Piculet, Gabon, Fire-bellied, Golden-crowned and Elliot's Woodpeckers, Chestnut-capped Flycatcher, Blue-headed Crested-Flycatcher, Blue Cuckoo-shrike, Sooty Boubou, Many-coloured Bushshrike, White-spotted and Yellow-bellied Wattle-eyes, White-browed Forest-Flycatcher, Forest Robin, White-throated Blue Swallow, Xavier's, Red-tailed and White-bearded Greenbuls, Lemon-bellied Crombec, Grey Longbill, Brown Illadopsis, Black-headed Waxbill, Yellow-mantled and Maxwell's Black Weavers, Black-throated, Gray's and Crested Malimbes, Johanna's Sunbird.

Other Wildlife

Chimpanzee, collared mangabey, drill, elephant, greater white-nosed monkey, Preuss' red colobus, Preuss' and russet-eared guenons.

Access

There are two HQs for Korup NP, run by WWF, at Mundemba in the south and at Nguti in the north. **Mundemba** is six hours by rough road from Kumba. This road passes through some excellent forest, especially 30 km before Mundemba. Once at Mundemba, permits and a compulsory guide must be arranged before continuing to the park. These minor delays can be swiftly overcome at the office in Mundemba, 1 km before the Iyaz Hotel, around which Bates' Swift has been recorded. Hartlaub's Duck has been recorded on roadside pools south of Mundemba. Rock Pratincole and several species of hornbills occur on and over the Mana river, which is crossed by a suspension bridge at the entrance to the park, 10 km from Mundemba (lifts available from project workers). There are a number of trails, one of which leads 10 km to Chimpanzee Camp. There is a Grey-necked Rockfowl* colony (Apr–Nov) halfway along this trail. It is also possible to arrange boat trips (at Mundemba) to the coastal mangroves near Bula Bridge, where African Finfoot has been recorded.

Blue Cuckoo-shrike and Many-coloured Bushshrike occur along the the road to the radio mast from **Nguti**, a town 20 km north of Manyemen, which is on the Kumba–Mamfe road. The WWF in Nguti may help to arrange a visit to the small village of **Baro**, 30 km to the west. Long-tailed Hawk, Black Spinetail, Chocolate-backed Kingfisher, Blue-headed Bee-eater, Willcock's Honeyguide and Kemp's Longbill all occur near Baro, in a little visited area with great potential. WWF are planning to open up this area to visitors not prepared to camp for their birds. Once at Baro, bird the access road (Long-tailed Hawk and Golden-crowned Woodpecker), the track to Korup NP (Kemp's Longbill), reached by turning left in the village, heading towards the church and following the track around to the right after 1 km, and the forest within the park, reached via a rope-bridge over the river (Blue-headed Crested-Flycatcher, Kemp's Longbill). It is 15 km from the park entrance to a research station where it is possible to camp (porters available in Baro).

Accommodation: Mundemba: Iyaz Hotel (B). Korup NP: camping (take own supplies). Nguti: Safariland Hotel (C). Baro: camping (take own supplies).

BAMENDA HIGHLANDS

The remnant montane and riverine forest on the slopes of Mount Oku (3011 m (9879 ft)), the second highest mountain in West Africa, and around Bali, support three highly localised endemics: Bannerman's Turaco*, Banded Wattle-eye* and Bamenda Apalis*, as well the near-endemic Bannerman's Weaver*.

Cameroon Endemics

Bannerman's Turaco*, Banded Wattle-eye*, Bamenda Apalis*.

Specialities

Western Green-Tinkerbird, Yellow-breasted and Mountain Boubous, Green-breasted Bushshrike*, Mountain Robin-Chat, Forest Swallow, Cameroon Mountain Greenbul*, Green Longtail, Bannerman's Weaver*, Cameroon Sunbird.

Others

Black Goshawk, Cassin's Hawk-Eagle, African Cuckoo, Bar-tailed Trogon, Blue-breasted and White-throated Bee-eaters, White-headed Woodhoopoe, Cassin's Honeyguide, Green-backed, Tullberg's and Elliot's Woodpeckers, White-bellied Crested-Flycatcher, Black-winged Oriole, Waller's Starling, Fanti Sawwing, Cameroon Olive-Greenbul, Black-collared, Black-throated and Grey Apalises, Cinnamon Bracken-Warbler, African Yellow Warbler, White-bellied Tit, Mountain Wagtail, Red-faced Crimson-wing, Black-necked and Brown-capped Weavers, Green-throated and Orange-tufted Sunbirds, Thick-billed Seedeater, Oriole Finch.

Access

For Mount Oku head from Bamenda to Kumbo (also known as Banso) and the village of **Elak**, where the Kilum Mountain Forest Project HQ

The endemic Banded Wattle-eye, which is considered by some authorities to be a race of Black-necked Wattle-eye, occurs in the Bamenda Highlands*

(run by BirdLife) is situated. Green Longtail has been recorded in the tiny patch of forest alongside the HQ, Forest Swallow breeds here and Oriole Finch occurs in the village. On the opposite side of the road to the HQ there is a trail which leads through farmland (45 minutes) to the forest, which begins at 2200 m (7218 ft). This trail splits, just after the school, (the gentle KA Trail (right) and the steeper KD Trail (left)) before reaching the forest. The KD Trail has been best in the past. Bannerman's Turaco*, Banded Wattle-eye* and Bannerman's Weaver* all occur here, and may be found more easily with the assistance of a local guide (Ernest is recommended, and so is a tip).

Bamenda Apalis* occurs near **Bali Safari Lodge**, close to Bamenda. Bird the woodland 200 m along the road (towards Bamenda) from the lodge.

Accommodation: Elak: Guesthouse. Bali: Safari Lodge. Bamenda: Mondial Hotel (B).

Bannerman's Turaco*, Banded Wattle-eye* and Bannerman's Weaver* are easier to see at the **Bafut–Nguemba FR** near Bamenda. Turn east off the N6 18 km south of the Mondial Hotel in Bamenda (33 km north of Mbouda) and bird beyond the barrier which is reached after 3 km, concentrating on the forested gullies amongst the eucalypt plantations.

NGAOUNDABA RANCH

Much of the Adamawa Plateau in north Cameroon has been turned over to grazing land, but some open woodland, savanna and a crater lake surrounded by remnant patches of gallery forest still exist at this ranch, supporting the endemic Bamenda Apalis*, and an assortment of more widespread but scarce species, including White-collared Starling, Red-winged Grey Warbler and Thrush Babbler.

Cameroon Endemics

Bamenda Apalis*.

Specialities

Schlegel's Francolin, Adamawa Turtle-Dove, White-crested Turaco, White-collared Starling, Grey-winged Robin-Chat, Red-winged Grey Warbler, Thrush Babbler, Red-faced Pytilia, Marsh Widowbird, Violet-tailed Sunbird.

Others

Red-necked Buzzard, White-spotted Flufftail, Kaffir Rail, Temminck's Courser, Red-headed Lovebird, Speckled Mousebird, Ross' Turaco, Levaillant's Cuckoo, White-faced Scops-Owl, Verreaux's Eagle-Owl, Blue-breasted Kingfisher, Red-throated Bee-eater, Abyssinian Ground-Hornbill, Yellow-fronted Tinkerbird, Double-toothed Barbet, Brown-backed Woodpecker, Piapiac, Red-shouldered Cuckoo-shrike, Yellow-billed Shrike, White Helmetshrike, Purple, Lesser Blue-eared and Splendid Glossy-Starlings, Violet-backed Starling, Pale Flycatcher, Snowy-crowned and White-crowned Robin-Chats, Heuglin's Wheatear, Sooty Chat, Spotted Creeper, Yellow-throated Greenbul, White-chinned Prinia, Oriole Warbler, Blackcap Illadopsis, Flappet and Sun Larks, Grey-headed Oliveback, Brown and Dybowski's Twinspots, Bar-breasted Firefinch, Black-crowned Waxbill, Long-tailed Paradise-Whydah, Compact and Red-headed Weavers, Yellow-crowned Bishop, Yellow-shouldered Widowbird, Pygmy and Splendid Sunbirds.

Access

Ngaoundaba Ranch is 40 km southeast of Ngaoundéré, just off the Meiganga road. Bird the 'garden' between the ranch buildings and the lake (Red-winged Grey Warbler), the lake edge and the surrounding savanna.

Accommodation: Ngaoundaba Ranch (B).

White-backed Duck, African Pygmy-goose, Lesser Moorhen, Lesser Jacana and Marsh Widowbird have been recorded on the large **Dang Lake**, just north of Ngaoundere near the university, alongside the road north to Garoua.

BENOUE NATIONAL PARK

This park lies in the Guinea savanna belt, some 100 km north of Ngaoundere and 150 km south of Garoua in north Cameroon. The low rocky hills covered with dry, open woodland support an avifauna similar to that of Gambia, although Grey Pratincole is one species which occurs here but not in Gambia.

It is only possible to visit this park with a vehicle. However, the surrounding areas, accessible via bush taxi, may be equally productive (beware of lions).

Specialities

Grey Pratincole, Adamawa Turtle-Dove.

Others

White-backed Night-Heron, Hamerkop, Bat Hawk, Red-necked Buzzard, Martial Eagle, Grey Kestrel, White-throated Francolin, Stone Partridge, Stanley Bustard, Senegal Thick-knee, Bronze-winged Courser, Egyptian and Three-banded Plovers, White-headed Lapwing, Bruce's Green-Pigeon, Senegal Parrot, Violet Turaco, Narina Trogon, Red-throated and White-throated Bee-eaters, Rufous-crowned Roller, Vieillot's and Bearded Barbets, Fine-spotted Woodpecker, African Blue-Flycatcher, Piapiac, White-breasted Cuckoo-shrike, Black-headed Gonolek, White Helmetshrike, Purple and Bronze-tailed Glossy-Starlings, Gambaga Flycatcher, White-fronted Black-Chat, Spotted Creeper, Preuss' Swallow, Croaking and Rufous Cisticolas, Yellow-bellied Hyliota, Grey-headed Oliveback, Orange-cheeked Waxbill, Bar-breasted, Black-bellied and Black-faced Firefinches, Chestnut-crowned Sparrow-Weaver, Western Violet-backed and Green-headed Sunbirds, Cabanis' Bunting.

Other Wildlife

Black-and-white colobus, buffalo, eland, hartebeest, hippo, lion, Nile crocodile, waterbuck, kob.

Access

The two national park entrances are at the towns of Mayo Alim and Banda. The tracks from both towns lead to the Campement du Bufflé Noir, which is situated on the banks of the Benoue river, and is the best birding area within the park. Bronze-winged Courser has been recorded on the track 3–4 km before the campement. Outside the park, the Guidjiba–Tchollire–Lakatolore area to the east is worth exploring, especially: (1) Hippo Point (head east from Guidjiba towards Tapare and turn south after 24 km, just before the Benoue river), where Grey Pratincole as well as hippo occur, and White-backed Night-Heron has been recorded. (2) The streamside 1 km north of Lakatolore village, 10 km north of Tchollire, where Narina Trogon has been recorded.

Accommodation: NP: Campement du Bufflé Noir (A). To book in advance contact Provincial Tourism Service, BP 50, Garoua (tel: 271020). There are several other campements. Tchollire.

Egyptian Plover, Grey Pratincole and White-headed Lapwing occur on the Benoue river, which is crossed by the Ngaoundere–Garoua road, just south of **Garoua**. Bird north or south of the bridge (not from the bridge itself - the police may arrest you), or hire a boat from a local fisherman.

The barren, rugged **Mandara Mountains** near Maroua southwest of Waza NP, support Scissor-tailed Kite, Senegal Parrot, Common Gonolek and Lavender Waxbill. Bird the small river at Mayo Louti, crossed by the only bridge between Rumsiki and Mokolo.

Accommodation: Rumsiki.

WAZA NATIONAL PARK

This large national park (1700 sq km) in far north Cameroon, some 300 km north of Garoua, supports acacia savanna, seasonal marshes and grassland dotted with inselbergs. Masses of waterbirds are usually present here during September, and the best time to visit is March when the waters have usually receded and the birds are more concentrated. However, the best birds at Waza are not waterbirds, and include Scissor-tailed Kite, Quail-plover, Arabian Bustard and Sennar Penduline-Tit.

The park is open from mid November to mid June only, and it is only possible to enter with a vehicle and in the company of a guide, although birding by bush-taxi may be equally good outside.

Specialities

Arabian Bustard, Niam-Niam Parrot, Red-pate Cisticola, River Prinia*, Sennar Penduline-Tit, Sudan Golden-Sparrow.

Others

Ostrich, White-backed Duck, Hadada Ibis, Saddle-billed Stork, Scissor-tailed Kite (Jan–Mar), White-headed Vulture, Bateleur, Gabar Goshawk, Grasshopper Buzzard, Secretary-bird, Fox Kestrel, Clapperton's Francolin, Quail-plover, Lesser Moorhen, Black Crowned-Crane, Stanley and White-bellied Bustards, Greater Painted-snipe, Spotted Thick-knee, Black-headed Lapwing, Chestnut-bellied and Four-banded Sandgrouse, African Collared-Dove, Bruce's Green-Pigeon, Western Grey Plantain-eater, Long-tailed Nightjar, Green and Northern Carmine Bee-eaters, Abyssinian Roller, Black Scimitar-bill, Abyssinian Ground-Hornbill, Little Grey Woodpecker, Masked Shrike (Nov–Mar), Chestnut-bellied Starling, Yellow-billed Oxpecker, Black Scrub-Robin, Heuglin's Wheatear, Northern Anteater-Chat, Ethiopian Swallow, Chestnut-backed Sparrow-Lark, Black-rumped Waxbill, Long-tailed Paradise-Whydah, Speckle-fronted and Little Weavers, Pygmy and Beautiful Sunbirds, White-rumped Seedeater.

Other Wildlife

Buffalo, elephant, giraffe, kob, lion, patas monkey, red-fronted gazelle, roan, topi.

Access

It is possible to fly from Douala to Maroua, the nearest large town. The park entrance is just south of Waza village. Permits and guides (Buccard Bana is recommended) are compulsory and can be arranged at the park entrance. Bird the tracks inside the park, the roadside fields and quarry (turn west at the radio mast) just north of Waza, the roadside fields (usually wet Nov–Mar) north of Ndiguina (20 km north of Waza), and the roadside pools and fields south of Waza to Mora (beware of elephants and lions). Sennar Penduline-Tit occurs around the pools 1–8 km south of Waza, and Quail-plover occurs in the roadside fields some 30 km south of Waza and 10 km north of Mora, in wispy grass areas amongst the crops.

Accommodation: Campement de Waza (A). To book in advance contact Provincial Tourism Service, BP 50, Garoua (tel: 271020). Mora: Auberge le Podoko (C); camping (ask for permission).

Lake Chad and its environs, 150 km north of Waza, may well reward the adventurous, but this area is currently considered unsafe for travellers owing to the presence of bandits and continuing border disputes.

Grey Pratincole and African Skimmer occur on the River Sanaga, one hour by road east of Douala on the N3 to **Yaounde**. Turn right just before the bridge on to a track which runs alongside the river after 10 km or so. Pel's and Vermiculated Fishing-Owls occur at **Ndibi**, near Akonolinga, two hours by road east of Yaounde. From Akonolinga it is best to hire a pirogue to Ndibi, although it is also accessible via dirt tracks. The dry season (Jan–May) is the best time to visit. Bird the south bank of the Nyong river below Ndibi, accessible via a track.

Accommodation: Ndibi: camping only.

A large Grey-necked Rockfowl* colony has recently been discovered in **Dja Reserve** (5400 sq km), which lies in a big meander of the Dja river in south Cameroon. The lowland rainforest and swamps within this reserve are likely to support lots more exciting species including Bob-tailed Weaver. However, very few birders have been to this remote area.

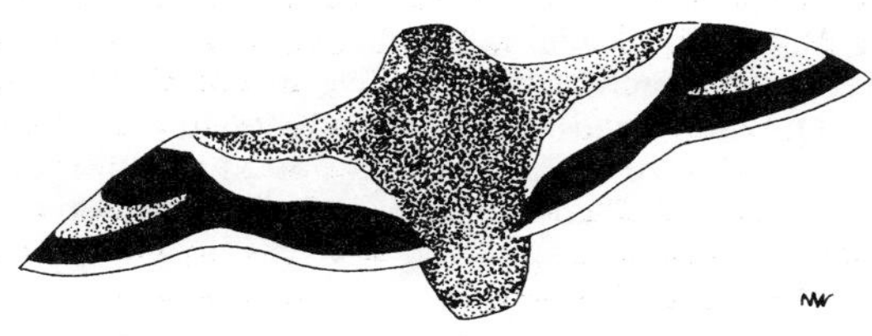

The Quail-plover is found throughout the savanna south of the Sahara, but the Waza area in north Cameroon is one of the few easily accessible sites where this odd buttonquail is seen with any regularity

ADDITIONAL INFORMATION

Books and Papers

The Birds of Cameroon: An Annotated Check-list. Lovette, M. 1981. *Verhandl. Kon. Acad. Wetensch. Lett. Schone Kunst. Belge.* 43:163.
Cameroon (trip report), September 16th to December 3rd 1992. Steve Keen. Contact 9 Parnham Close, New Milton, Hants. BH25 5XB, UK.
Cameroon, 27 December 1994 to 18 January 1995. A trip report by Richard Webb and Chris Gibbins, available via the ABC.

Addresses

For information on access and accommodation contact The Park Advisor, Korup Project, WWF Cameroon, BP 2417, PMB 1 Bonanjo, Douala (tel/fax: 237 432171).

ENDEMICS (7)

Cameroon Francolin*	West: Mount Cameroon
Bannerman's Turaco*	Northwest: Bamenda Highlands
Mount Kupé Bushshrike*	West: Mount Kupé
Banded Wattle-eye*	Northwest: Bamenda Highlands
Cameroon Speirops*	West: Mount Cameroon
Bamenda Apalis*	Northwest/north: Bamenda Highlands and Ngaoundaba Ranch
Bates' Weaver*	West: Mount Cameroon, Mount Kupé
(Monteiro's Bushshrike*)	West: Mount Kupé; also one 1894 record from Mount Cameroon (and Angola, where not recorded since 1954)

Near-endemics

Cameroon Pigeon, Bates' Swift, Yellow-breasted Boubou, Green-breasted Bushshrike*, Mountain Robin-Chat, Mountain Sawwing*, Cameroon Mountain Greenbul*, Cameroon Olive-Greenbul, Grey-headed Greenbul*, Green Longtail, Ja River Scrub-Warbler*, Cameroon Scrub-Warbler, White-tailed Warbler, Black-capped Woodland-Warbler, White-throated Mountain-Babbler*, Fernando Po Oliveback, Bannerman's Weaver*, Cameroon and Ursula's* Sunbirds.

CANARY ISLANDS, MADEIRA ISLANDS AND THE AZORES

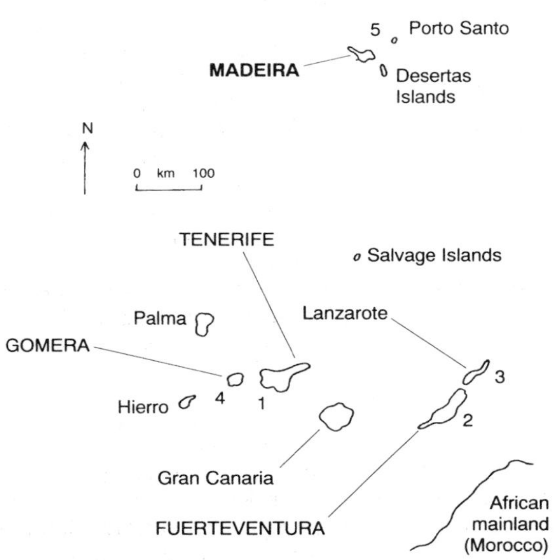

1 Tenerife
2 Fuerteventura
3 Lanzarote
4 Gomera
5 Madeira Islands

INTRODUCTION

Summary

The popular tourist destinations of the Canary and Madeira Islands support a handful of endemic landbirds and some rare seabirds, most of which can be seen with some ease thanks to modern infrastructure. The Azores have no endemics, but they support important numbers of breeding seabirds and attract North American vagrants.

Size

These three archipelagos comprise small islands, of which Fuerteventura in the Canary Islands is the longest (110 km).

Getting Around

Good roads, tracks and paths make travelling around most of the main islands very easy. Car-hire is available on the main Canary Islands and Madeira.

Accommodation and Food

Most islands, especially the main Canary Islands, offer a wide choice of accommodation, from cheap tourist hotels to traditional spanish pensions. The food is equally varied.

Health and Safety

Immunisation against yellow fever is recommended for visitors to the Madeira Islands. Otherwise, this is a hassle-free part of visiting the Azores and Canary Islands.

Climate and Timing

May to August, when the seabirds are breeding, is the best time to visit these islands. On the Canary Islands, the climate is warm all year round, although not always sunny. Tenerife, for example, is a mountainous island which is often cloud-covered.

Habitats

The Canary Islands are volcanic in origin and vast areas of barren, solidified lava dominate much of the landscape. The western Canary Islands are wet and well-vegetated, whilst those in the east are dry and desert-like. Remnant patches of native laurel forest survive in the remote, misty mountains of the western Canary Islands and on the otherwise, barren and rugged Madeira Islands, whilst pine forests are also present on the Canary Islands.

Conservation

Seven threatened and near-threatened species occur on these islands.

Bird Families

No endemic Afrotropical families are represented, and the avifauna, apart from the endemics and near-endemics, is akin to that of Europe.

Bird Species

Over 315 species have been recorded on the Canary Islands and the list is growing fast thanks to American vagrants and strays from the African mainland. Non-endemic specialities and spectacular species on the Canary Islands include Bulwer's Petrel, Barbary Falcon, Barbary Partridge, Houbara Bustard, Cream-coloured Courser and Lesser Short-toed Lark, whilst on the Madeira Islands such species include Cape Verde Island Petrel*. A potential new species, currently a race of Eurasian Bullfinch, is present on The Azores.

Endemics

Five species are found only on the Canary Islands: Bolle's* and Laurel* Pigeons, Canary Islands Chat*, Canary Islands Kinglet and Canary Islands Finch*. All of these may be found on just two islands, Tenerife and Fuerteventura. Three more species are shared with only Madeira and The Azores: Madeira Petrel*, Berthelot's Pipit and Island Canary. A further species, which occurs only elsewhere on Madeira and in Morocco, is Plain Swift.

The Madeira Islands boast one endemic, the Trocaz Pigeon*, and the near-endemic Madeira* and Cape Verde Island* Petrels.

Expectations

Seventy species in a week is a good total on the Canary Islands, so long as both Tenerife and Fuerteventura are visited, whilst only 40 are likely during the same period on the Madeira Islands.

TENERIFE

This 80-km long island, rising to 3718 m (12,198 ft) at the active volcano, Pico de Teide, is the best base. It is an island of black lava fields, pine forest, small remnant patches of laurel forest and semi-desert scrub, surrounded by mainly rocky, grey and black beaches. The north is rather damp and cultivated, whilst the south, in contrast, is dry and barren.

Four of the five Canary Island endemics, as well as Plain Swift, Berthelot's Pipit and Island Canary, occur on Tenerife.

Canary Islands Endemics

Bolle's* and Laurel* Pigeons, Canary Islands Kinglet, Canary Islands Finch*.

Specialities

Bulwer's Petrel, Plain Swift, Berthelot's Pipit, Island Canary.

Others

Cory's and Little Shearwaters, Barbary Falcon, Barbary Partridge, Eurasian Thick-knee, Pallid Swift, Northern Shrike, Sardinian and Spectacled Warblers, Lesser Short-toed Lark, Spanish Sparrow, Rock Petronia, Trumpeter Finch.

Access

Canary Islands Kinglet and Canary Islands Finch* occur at the **Las Lajas Recreation Area**, 9 km north of Villaflor along the Santiago del Teide road. North of Santiago del Teide is **Erjos**. Turn west here on to a

winding track and scan the laurel forest below, to the right, after 5 km (where there is a rock with a metal cross on it) for Bolle's* and Laurel* Pigeons.

Seawatching can be good from Punta de la Rasca, southeast of Los Christianos and reached by turning south off the Los Christianos–Santa Cruz road towards Las Galletas. Turn south to **El Fraile** before Las Galletas, and bird from the lighthouse south of here. The best way to see seabirds, however, is to take the regular **Tenerife–Gomera Ferry**; Bulwer's Petrel, Cory's and Little Shearwaters, and European Storm-Petrel are all possible. White-faced (Aug) and Band-rumped Storm-Petrels and Red-billed Tropicbird (Mar/May/Aug) are rarities.

Although most birders visit the Canary Islands to see the endemic landbirds, seabirds such as Bulwer's Petrel are also a major attraction.

FUERTEVENTURA

This barren, sandy island is 110 km long and up to 25 km wide. The inland desert is surrounded by white beaches. This is the only island where Canary Island Chat* occurs, and it is one of the best sites in the world for Houbara Bustard.

Canary Islands Endemics

Canary Islands Chat*.

Specialities

Houbara Bustard, Plain Swift, Berthelot's Pipit.

Others

Egyptian Vulture, Eleonora's and Barbary Falcons, Barbary Partridge, Eurasian Thick-knee, Cream-coloured Courser, Black-bellied Sandgrouse, Pallid Swift, Northern Shrike, Spectacled Warbler, Lesser Short-toed Lark, Spanish Sparrow, Trumpeter Finch.

Access

A good place to look for Canary Islands Chat* is the **Barranco de Rio Cabras** (dry river bed) on the inland side of the road 1 km north of the airport, although it also occurs around the Las Penitas Reservoir and between Betancuria and Pajara. Houbara Bustard occurs on the **Cotillo Plain** northwest of La Oliva, alongside other desert species. Bird the El Cotillo–Tindaya Track. The surrounds of Los Molinos Reservoir, reached by turning left just before the town of Los Molinos, is another good site for Houbara Bustard, and Marbled Teal* has been recorded on the reservoir.

Houbara Bustard may also still occur on **Lanzarote**, a small, arid island north of Fuerteventura. Eleonora's and Barbary Falcons, Barbary Partridge, Eurasian Thick-knee, Cream-coloured Courser, Spectacled Warbler, Lesser Short-toed Lark, Spanish Sparrow, Berthelot's Pipit and Trumpeter Finch do occur on this island. The best place for Houbara Bustard used to be north of **Playa Blanca** and west of **Teguise**. Eleonora's and Barbary Falcons have been recorded around **Mirador Del Rio** at the northeast tip of the island.

The mountainous island of **Gomera**, southwest of Tenerife, still supports a relatively substantial area of laurel forest where both endemic pigeons occur, as well as Plain Swift, Canary Islands Kinglet, Berthelot's Pipit and Island Canary. Both pigeons occur in the **Alto Garajonay NP** near El Cedro.

The **Salvage Islands** (which belong to Madeira), 190 km north of Tenerife, support large colonies of Bulwer's Petrel and Cory's and Little Shearwaters, whilst White-faced Storm-Petrel has been recorded on the crossing from the Canary Islands. Making such a crossing normally involves chartering a yacht.

FUERTEVENTURA

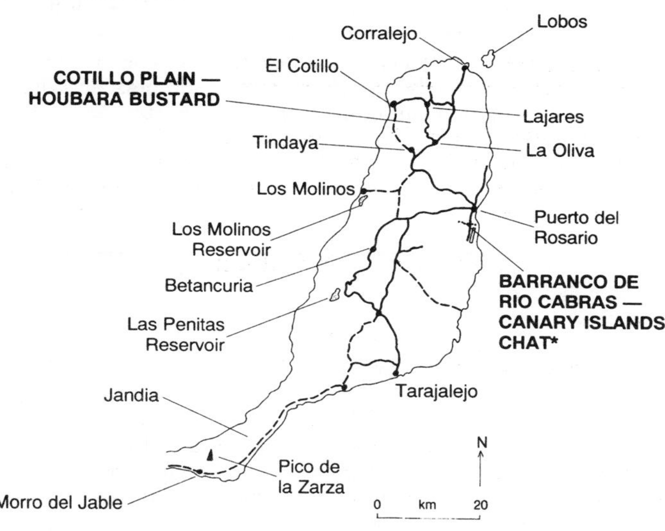

MADEIRA ISLANDS

These rugged, volcanic islands lie north of the Canary Islands. The main island of Madeira is well-vegetated with misty laurel forests which support the endemic Trocaz Pigeon*. Apart from the pigeon, the major attractions are the two *Pterodroma* petrels, Madeira* and Cape Verde Island* Petrels, both of which can be seen from the mainland or on boat trips. There is plenty of cheap accommodation on the main island and cars can be hired.

Madeira Islands Endemics

Trocaz Pigeon*.

Specialities

Madeira*, Cape Verde Island* and Bulwer's Petrels, Plain Swift, Berthelot's Pipit, Island Canary.

Others

Cory's and Little Shearwaters, Spectacled Warbler, Firecrest, Spanish Sparrow, Rock Petronia.

Access

The best place to look for Trocaz Pigeon* is **Balcoes**, north of the capital, Funchal. There are a number of places along the levada (a narrow path alongside an irrigation channel), which leads off the Funchal–Cruzinhas road, where it is possible to scan the laurel forest, although low cloud can be a problem. Island Canary is present in Funchal.

There are only 20–30 pairs of Madeira Petrel* in the world, and they breed in the highlands of Madeira Island. Some 150–200 pairs of Cape Verde Island Petrel* breed on Bugio, one of the three **Desertas Islands**, which lie 30 km southeast of Funchal. These islands have been designated as a Nature Park, and the park's offical vessel, the *Boa Tarde*, travels to Deserta Grande, the largest of the three islands, once a week. A tourist boat, the *Pirata Azul*, also makes the trip (to look for the rare monk seal), albeit irregularly. Try Reid's Hotel for information on these crossings. If no boats are available to make the crossing, which offers the best chance of seeing the petrels, they may still be seen from the eastern headlands of the main island, especially **Ponta das Gaivotas** (July and August).

THE AZORES

This archipelago of nine islands in the north Atlantic, due west of Portugal, hosts some important seabird colonies, including over 50% of the Western Palearctic population of Roseate Terns, Cape Verde Island* and Bulwer's Petrels, Cory's and Little Shearwaters and Band-rumped Storm-Petrel; but there are few landbirds save Island Canary and a race of Eurasian Bullfinch (in the laurel forests of the mountains in east São Miguel, eg. Pico da Vara). The islands also attract North American vagrants, especially shorebirds in mid September. The best site for these is the disused coastal quarry just south of the harbour at Praia da Vitoria (known locally as Cabo da Praia) on Terceira Island.

AZORES

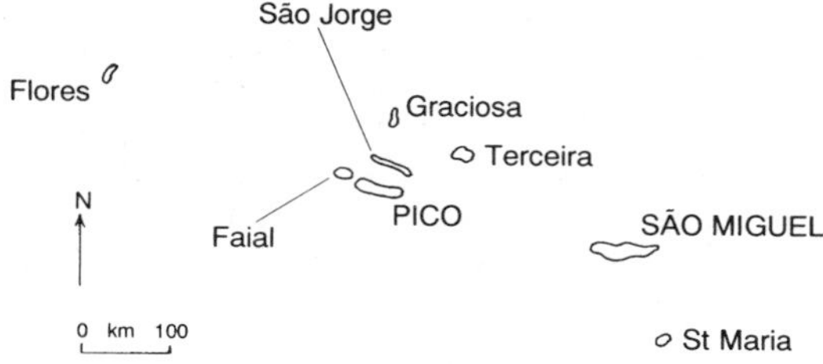

ADDITIONAL INFORMATION

Books and Papers

The Birds of Britain and Europe with North Africa and the Middle East. Heinzel, H *et al.* HarperCollins.
Birds of the Canary Islands. Emmerson, K and Martin, A. In prep. BOU.

Addresses

Please send records to Tony Clarke, Republica Dominica No. 61, Barrio de Fatima, 38500 Guimar, Tenerife, and/or Juan Antonio Lorenzo, La Laguna University, Tenerife.
Portuguese National Tourist Office, 22–25a Sackville Street, London W1X 1DE, UK (tel: 0171 4941441, fax: 0171 4941868).

ENDEMICS (9)

CANARY ISLANDS (5)

Bolle's Pigeon*	Tenerife and Gomera
Laurel Pigeon*	Tenerife and Gomera
Canary Islands Chat*	Fuerteventura
Canary Islands Kinglet	Tenerife and Gomera
Canary Islands Finch*	Tenerife and Gran Canaria

(The Canary Island Oystercatcher* has not been seen since 1968 (one flying over Puerto del la Cruz, Tenerife) despite extensive searches, and is probably extinct, although a 'black oystercatcher' was seen just south of Dakar, Senegal in 1970, and two were seen on the coast near the Senegal/Guinea Bissau border in 1975.)

CANARY ISLANDS and MADEIRA (2)

Madeira Petrel*	Rare around the Canary Islands
Berthelot's Pipit	Most of the Canary Islands

CANARY ISLANDS, MADEIRA and THE AZORES (1)

Island Canary	Canary Islands: Tenerife and Gomera

MADEIRA (1)

Trocaz Pigeon*

Near-endemics

Cape Verde Island Petrel*, Plain Swift.

CAPE VERDE ISLANDS

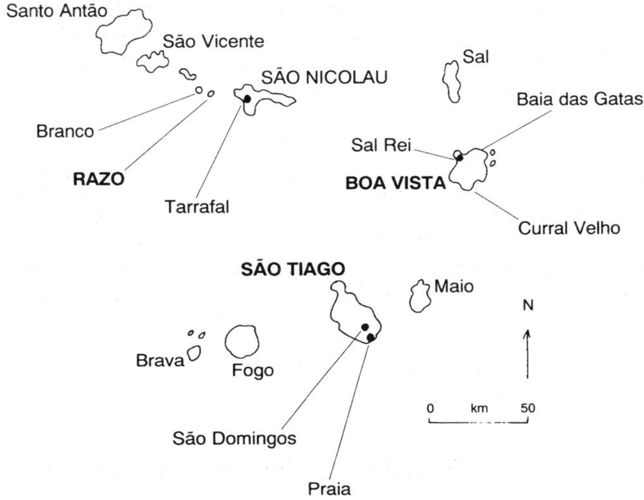

The remote Cape Verde Islands, 500 km west of Senegal, support four endemics and some important seabird colonies. Most of the archipelago is accessible via an excellent internal air network and some boat services, but there are few roads on the islands themselves. A basic grasp of Portuguese helps, particularly in arranging boats with the friendly islanders. The two main islands, São Tiago and São Nicolau, have good accommodation. Immunisation against hepatitis, polio, typhoid and yellow fever is recommended. Birders travelling beyond São Tiago would be wise to take precautions against malaria too. It is hot and dry all year round, but the coolest months (Feb–Apr) coincide with the seabird breeding season, so this is the best time to visit. Three threatened species occur on the Cape Verde Islands. One hundred and forty-three species have been recorded including Bulwer's Petrel, White-faced and Band-rumped Storm-Petrels, Red-billed Tropicbird and Cream-coloured Courser. Four species are endemic, and one, Cape Verde Island Petrel*, is near-endemic.

Access

São Tiago is a stark island of flat-topped volcanoes, where the roads are made from black lava. It supports three of the archipelago's four endemics: Alexander's Swift, Cape Verde Swamp-Warbler* (São Domingos Valley), and Cape Verde Sparrow, as well as Red-billed Tropicbird, Cream-coloured Courser, Grey-headed Kingfisher, Brown-necked Raven, Spectacled Warbler, Black-crowned Sparrow-Lark, Bar-tailed Lark, Spanish Sparrow and Common Waxbill.

Accommodation: Praia: pensions (B) and hotels.

The fourth Cape Verde endemic, Razo Skylark*, occurs only on **Razo**, a tiny (7 sq km), desolate, uninhabited island, accessible from São Nicolau. There are believed to be just 250 of these very confiding birds left. Razo also supports Red-billed Tropicbird (south coast), Brown Booby, and Cape Verde Sparrow. The nearest settlement is Tarrafal on the island of São Nicolau, where it is possible to hire a fishing boat for the 25-km trip to Razo from the El Faust Pousada. Cape Verde Island Petrel* is possible on the crossing.

Accommodation: El Faust Pousada (B).

Boa Vista island supports White-faced Storm-Petrel (Ilheu dos Passaros, off Baia das Gatas on the east coast), Magnificent Frigatebird (around the offshore islet of Curral Velho, off the south coast), Cream-coloured Courser, Black-crowned Sparrow-Lark, Bar-tailed Lark, and Greater Hoopoe-Lark. Jeeps are available for hire to reach the south and east coasts.

Accommodation: Sal Rei: Club Marlin.

ADDITIONAL INFORMATION

Books and Papers

The Birds of the Cape Verde Islands. Hazevoet, C. In prep. BOU.
The Cape Verde Islands (Birding Guide). Noeske, A and Pfu tzke, S. 1994. *Birding World* 7:152–160.

Addresses

Please send all records to Dr C Hazevoet, Institut voor Systematiek en Populatiebioliogie (Zoologisch Museum), Mauritskade 61, Postbus 94766, 1090 GT Amsterdam, The Netherlands.

ENDEMICS (4)

Alexander's Swift	São Tiago
Cape Verde Swamp-Warbler*	São Tiago, Brava and São Nicolau
Razo Skylark*	Razo
Cape Verde Sparrow	São Tiago and Razo

Near-endemics

Cape Verde Island Petrel* (also possible on Madeira).

CENTRAL AFRICAN REPUBLIC

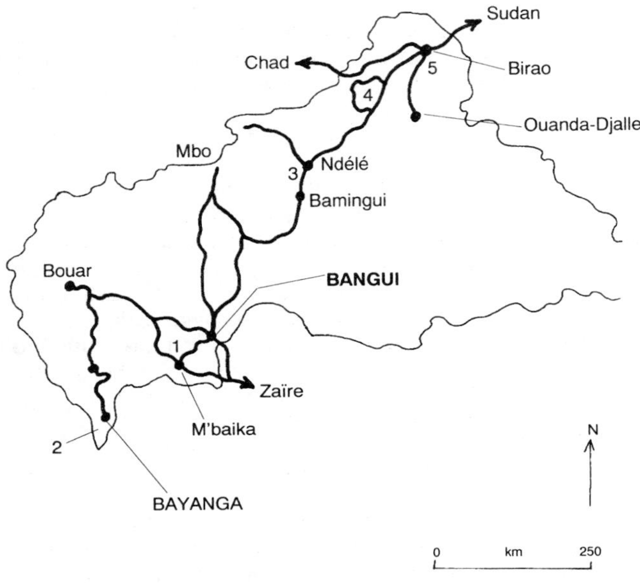

1 Lobaye Prefecture
2 Haute Sangha Prefecture
3 Bamingui–Bangoran NP
4 Manovo–Gounda–Saint Floris NP
5 Birao

INTRODUCTION

Summary

If the Central African Republic had something resembling an infrastructure, it would undoubtedly be a very popular birding destination. Unfortunately, this is a very poor country where ecotourism is not encouraged, and its great selection of little known birds remains inaccessible to all but the most adventurous.

Size

At 622,984 sq km, the Central African Republic is nearly five times larger than England, and only slightly smaller than Texas.

Getting Around

The roads in the extreme west, near the capital Bangui, are quite good, but for the most part they are much, much worse. Buses are cheap and there are some internal flights, including one between Bangui and Birao, in the far north. A basic knowledge of French is a great aid to getting around.

Accommodation and Food

There is virtually no accommodation in the top birding areas, so a full expedition would be necessary to get the best out of the Central African Republic.

Health and Safety

Immunisation against hepatitis, meningitis, polio, typhoid and yellow fever is recommended, whilst the usual precautions against malaria are a must.

Walk the streets of Bangui with great care, especially at night.

Climate and Timing

The best time to visit the Central African Republic is the dry season, which lasts from December to March in the southwest, and slightly longer in the northeast.

Habitats

The Central African Republic is basically a 'plain-on-a-plateau', lying at an average height of 600 m (1969 ft), with highlands in the far west, rising to 1360 m (4462 ft), and the far east, rising to 1300 m (4265 ft). Tropical rainforest is present in the southwest, at the northern edge of the Congo Basin, but most of the country is covered in savanna, wooded in the south, grassy in the north (at the southern edge of the Sahel).

Conservation

The northern savanna is being degraded by overgrazing and desertification, the sparsely populated east suffers heavily from poaching, with organised gangs from Sudan taking a heavy toll of wildlife many tourists would pay handsomely to see, and yet, the major problem in the Central African Republic is the increase in the amount of logging. The forests of Central Africa are under an even greater threat now that those west of Cameroon have been virtually wiped out.

Two threatened and one near-threatened species occur in the Central African Republic.

Bird Families

Eight of the ten families endemic to the African mainland are represented in the Central African Republic. Only rockfowl and sugarbirds are absent. Well represented families include guineafowl, bee-eaters and honeyguides.

Bird Species

A total of 622 species have been recorded in the land-locked Central African Republic, 200 fewer than in neighbouring Cameroon. Non-endemic specialities and spectacular species include Shoebill*, Long-tailed Hawk, Schlegel's Francolin, Egyptian Plover, Grey Pratincole, Forbes' Plover, Brown-chested Lapwing, Niam-Niam Parrot, Black-collared Lovebird, Chocolate-backed Kingfisher, Blue-headed and Black-headed Bee-eaters, African and Green-breasted Pittas, Dusky Babbler and Woodhouse's Antpecker.

Endemics

There are no endemics, but a few near-endemics and localised species are present in the Central African Republic.

The country's capital, **Bangui**, lies near the lowland rainforest of the Congo Basin in the southwest, so there are some excellent birds in its vicinity including Yellow-throated Nicator and Black-headed Batis. Other species recorded include Blue-breasted Kingfisher, Speckle-breasted Woodpecker, Marsh Tchagra, Sooty Boubou, Chestnut Wattle-eye, Petit's Sawwing, Grey, Plain, Yellow-throated, Yellow-necked and White-throated Greenbuls, Green Crombec, Green Hylia, Pale-fronted Negrofinch, Grey-headed Oliveback, Black-bellied Seedcracker, Brown and Dybowski's Twinspots, Compact Weaver and Red-collared Widowbird.

LOBAYE PREFECTURE

The remnant lowland forest north of the town of M'baika in the region of the country known as the Lobaye Prefecture, approximately 100 km southwest of Bangui, supports some great birds, not least the very rarely reported Green-breasted Pitta.

Specialities

Hartlaub's Duck, Spot-breasted Ibis, Plumed Guineafowl, Heuglin's Francolin, Egyptian Plover, Niam-Niam Parrot, Black-collared Lovebird, Yellow-throated Cuckoo, Bare-cheeked Trogon, Rosy Bee-eater, Black-breasted Barbet, African and Green-breasted Pittas, Rufous-sided Broadbill, Grey Ground-Thrush, Grey-throated Tit-Flycatcher, Brown-backed Scrub-Robin, Red-winged Grey Warbler, Red-faced Pytilia, Yellow-capped Weaver.

Others

African Darter, African Pygmy-goose, White-backed Night-Heron, White-crested and Dwarf Bitterns, Hamerkop, Olive Ibis, African Cuckoo-Falcon, Bat Hawk, Congo Serpent-Eagle, Red-chested Goshawk, Chestnut-flanked and Red-thighed Sparrowhawks, Long-tailed Hawk, Forest Francolin, Black-rumped Buttonquail, Nkulengu Rail, African and Black Crakes, Allen's Gallinule, Lesser Moorhen, African Finfoot, Black Crowned-Crane, Rock Pratincole, Afep Pigeon, Grey Parrot, Guinea, Black-billed, White-crested and Great Blue Turacos, Dusky Long-tailed and African Emerald Cuckoos, Yellowbill, Blue-headed Coucal, Fraser's and Akun Eagle-Owls, Pel's and Vermiculated Fishing-Owls, African Wood-Owl, Rufous-cheeked (Apr–Oct), Swamp, Plain, Standard-winged and Pennant-winged Nightjars, Cassin's Spinetail, Narina Trogon, Dwarf and Blue-breasted Kingfishers, Blue-breasted and White-throated Bee-eaters, Abyssinian, Blue-bellied and Blue-throated Rollers, Forest Woodhoopoe, White-crested, Black Dwarf, Red-billed Dwarf and White-thighed Hornbills, Bristle-nosed, Yellow-spotted and Yellow-billed Barbets, Spotted, Willcock's and Lyre-tailed Honeyguides, African Piculet, Speckle-breasted, Gabon and Golden-crowned Woodpeckers, African Broadbill, Chestnut-capped Flycatcher, Dusky and Blue-headed Crested-Flycatchers, Shining and Velvet-mantled Drongos, Black-winged Oriole, Blue Cuckoo-shrike, Luehder's, Many-coloured and Fiery-breasted Bushshrikes, Chestnut and White-spotted Wattle-eyes, Red-tailed Ant-Thrush, Fire-crested Alethe, Purple-headed and Splendid Glossy-Starlings, Red-billed Oxpecker, White-browed Forest-Flycatcher,

Olivaceous, Little Grey, Yellow-footed and Dusky-blue Flycatchers, Forest Robin, White-throated Blue Swallow, Petit's Sawwing, Plain, Slender-billed, Golden, Spotted, Yellow-throated, and White-throated Greenbuls, Yellow-throated Nicator, Red-faced and Whistling Cisticolas, Gosling's Apalis, Yellow-browed Camaroptera, Oriole Warbler, African Yellow Warbler, Lemon-bellied Crombec, Grey Longbill, Capuchin Babbler, Sun Lark, Woodhouse's Antpecker, White-breasted, Chestnut-breasted and Pale-fronted Negrofinches, Grey-headed Oliveback, Black-bellied Seedcracker, Brown and Dybowski's Twinspots, Black-bellied and Black-faced Firefinches, Magpie Mannikin, Red-collared Widowbird, Mountain Wagtail, Orange, Preuss' and Compact Weavers, Red-crowned, Black-throated, Red-bellied, Crested and Red-headed Malimbes, Cardinal Quelea, Little Green and Olive-bellied Sunbirds.

Accommodation: M'baika.

HAUTE SANGHA PREFECTURE

This site incorporates the contiguous Dzanga–Ndoki NP (1220 sq km) and the Dzanga–Sangha Rainforest Reserve (3359 sq km) in southwest Central African Republic, at the northern end of the Congo Basin. Over 250 species have been recorded in the rainforest, swamp forest, savanna and marshes here, including Black and Plumed Guineafowl, Black-collared Lovebird and Black-headed Bee-eater.

This is a remote area where Bai-aka pygmies still live, and a full expedition would be needed to see most of the good birds. It is very wet here in September and October, but usually dry from December to February.

Specialities

Black and Plumed Guineafowl, Egyptian Plover (Nov–Apr), Grey Pratincole (Dec–Apr), Forbes' Plover, Black-collared Lovebird, Gabon Coucal, Brown Nightjar, Black-headed Bee-eater.

Others

White-crested and Dwarf Bitterns, Hamerkop, Palm-nut Vulture, Chestnut-flanked and Red-thighed Sparrowhawks, Black Goshawk, Long-tailed Hawk, Crowned Hawk-Eagle, Forest Francolin, Nkulengu Rail, Black Crake, African Finfoot, Rock Pratincole, White-headed Lapwing (Nov–Jun), Afep Pigeon, Grey Parrot, Guinea and Great Blue Turacos, Dusky Long-tailed Cuckoo, Yellowbill, Fraser's Eagle-Owl, African Wood-Owl, Plain (Dec–Mar) and Standard-winged (Dec–Mar) Nightjars, Sabine's and Cassin's Spinetails, Narina Trogon, Shining Blue, White-bellied, Dwarf and Chocolate-backed Kingfishers, Black, Blue-headed, Blue-breasted and White-throated Bee-eaters, Blue-throated Roller, White-headed Woodhoopoe, White-crested, Black Dwarf, Red-billed Dwarf and White-thighed Hornbills, Speckled Tinkerbird, Yellow-billed Barbet, Lyre-tailed Honeyguide, African Piculet, Green-backed, Speckle-breasted and Golden-crowned Woodpeckers, Chestnut-capped Flycatcher, Dusky and Blue-headed Crested-Flycatchers, Shining Drongo, Piapiac, Black-winged Oriole, Blue Cuckoo-shrike, Large-billed Puffback, Sooty Boubou, Chestnut Wattle-eye, Purple-headed and Splendid Glossy-Starlings, Yellow-billed Oxpecker, Olivaceous, Yellow-footed, Dusky-blue and Cassin's Flycatchers, White-throated Blue Swallow, Spotted Greenbul, Chattering Cisticola, Banded Prinia, Blackcap Illadopsis, Dusky Tit, White-breasted Negrofinch, Black-headed Waxbill, Orange and Compact Weavers, Gray's, Crested and Red-headed Malimbes, Black-winged Bishop, Olive-bellied Sunbird.

Other Wildlife

Buffalo, chimpanzee, elephant, leopard, golden cat, gorilla.

Access

This site lies south of Berberati and Nola in the extreme southwest corner of the country. The main track south from Nola goes to Bayanga, from where good birding lies to the east and south. Forbes' Plover occurs on the airfield and farmland around Bayanga, Hartlaub's Duck, Forbes' Plover and Black-headed Bee-eater occur at Dzanga (where there is a watchtower), and Grey Pratincole occurs on the Sangha river.

HAUTE SANGHA PREFECTURE

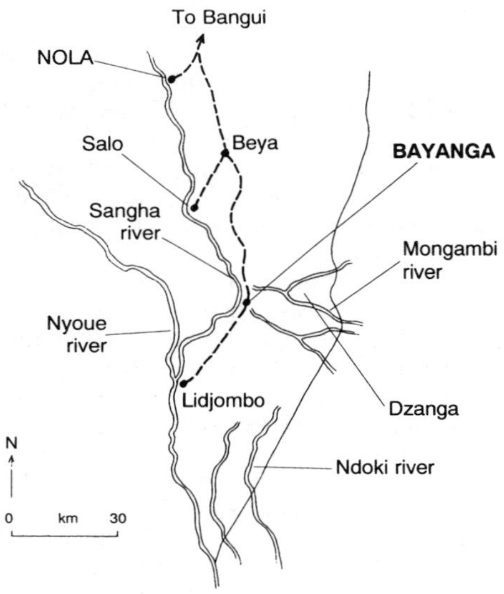

BAMINGUI–BANGORAN NATIONAL PARK

This huge, remote park in the north of the country, supports a more or less typical savanna avifauna, with specialities such as Schlegel's Francolin and Forbes' Plover.

Specialities

Schlegel's and Heuglin's Francolins, Lesser Jacana, Forbes' Plover.

Others

African Darter, Comb Duck, African Pygmy-goose, Goliath Heron, Hamerkop, Saddle-billed Stork, Palm-nut and White-headed Vultures, Bateleur, Black Goshawk, Grasshopper Buzzard, Martial Eagle, Secretary-bird, Black Crake, Black Crowned-Crane, Stanley Bustard, Senegal and Spotted Thick-knees, White-headed Lapwing, Four-banded Sandgrouse, Bruce's Green-Pigeon, Red-headed Lovebird, White-faced Scops-Owl, Pel's Fishing-Owl, African Wood-Owl, Standard-winged and Pennant-winged Nightjars, Blue-breasted Kingfisher, White-fronted and Swallow-tailed Bee-eaters, Blue-bellied Roller, Black Scimitar-bill, Abyssinian Ground-Hornbill, Bearded Barbet, Fine-spotted and Green-backed Woodpeckers, African Blue-Flycatcher, Common Gonolek, Purple Glossy-Starling, Black Scrub-Robin, Familiar Chat, White-fronted Black-Chat, White-winged Black-Tit, Black-faced Firefinch, Orange-cheeked and Black-rumped Waxbills, Yellow-throated Longclaw, Pygmy Sunbird.

Access

The park lies to the west of the Bamingui–Ndélé road.

Accommodation: Bamingui.

MANOVO–GOUNDA–SAINT FLORIS NATIONAL PARK

The wooded savanna, marshes and gallery forest in this national park, which is situated in the far north of the country, support a fine selection of species, not least Shoebill*, Brown-chested Lapwing, Black-headed Bee-eater and Dusky Babbler.

Specialities

Shoebill*, Ring-necked and Heuglin's Francolins, Egyptian and Forbes' Plovers, Brown-chested Lapwing, Niam-Niam Parrot, Bates' Swift, Black-headed Bee-eater, Black-breasted Barbet, Emin's Shrike, White-collared Starling, Congo Moorchat, Foxy Cisticola, Red-winged Grey Warbler, Dusky Babbler.

Others

Ostrich, African Darter, African Pygmy-goose, Dwarf Bittern, Goliath Heron, Hamerkop, Saddle-billed Stork, Bat Hawk, White-headed Vulture, Banded Snake-Eagle, Bateleur, Black Goshawk, Grasshopper Buzzard, Wahlberg's, Verreaux's and Martial Eagles, Secretary-bird, Pygmy Falcon, Clapperton's Francolin, Harlequin Quail, Quail-plover, Grey-throated and Kaffir Rails, Black Crake, Black Crowned-Crane, Stanley Bustard, Senegal and Spotted Thick-knees, Bronze-winged and Temminck's Coursers, Black-headed and White-headed Lapwings, Chestnut-bellied and Four-banded Sandgrouse, Bruce's Green-Pigeon, Meyer's Parrot, Red-headed Lovebird, Guinea, White-crested, Violet and Ross's Turacos, Pied Cuckoo, White-faced Scops-Owl, Verreaux's Eagle-Owl, Pel's Fishing-Owl, Standard-winged and Pennant-winged Nightjars, Narina Trogon, White-bellied, Dwarf and Blue-breasted Kingfishers, White-fronted, Swallow-tailed, Green and Northern Carmine Bee-eaters, Abyssinian and Blue-bellied Rollers, Black

Scimitar-bill, Crowned Hornbill, Abyssinian Ground-Hornbill, Fine-spotted Woodpecker, African Blue-Flycatcher, Piapiac, Pink-footed Puffback, Common and Black-headed Gonoleks, Grey-green and Many-coloured Bushshrikes, White Helmetshrike, Black-headed Batis, Purple Glossy-Starling, Yellow-billed Oxpecker, Blue-shouldered Robin-Chat, Sooty Chat, White-fronted Black-Chat, Spotted Creeper, Fanti Sawwing, Gosling's Apalis, White-winged Black-Tit, Grey-headed Oliveback, Variable Indigobird, Yellow-throated Longclaw, Lesser Masked Weaver, Fan-tailed Widowbird, Pygmy Sunbird, Cabanis' Bunting.

BIRAO

Situated in the far northeast of the country, the town of Birao lies on the Vakaga Plain, which is flooded during the wet season (Jun–Sep), with marshes and pools usually remaining into January at least. On the slightly higher ground, wooded savanna supports species typical of the sub-Saharan zone, as well as Grey-headed Batis.

Specialities

Heuglin's Francolin, Egyptian Plover, Black-breasted Barbet, Grey-headed Batis.

Others

African Pygmy-goose, Dwarf Bittern, Hamerkop, African Cuckoo-Falcon, Scissor-tailed Kite, Bateleur, Grasshopper Buzzard, Fox and Grey Kestrels, Clapperton's Francolin, Stone Partridge, Lesser Moorhen, Black Crowned-Crane, Stanley Bustard, Bronze-winged Courser, Bruce's Green-Pigeon, Western Grey Plantain-eater, Pied and Levaillant's Cuckoos, Standard-winged Nightjar, Mottled Swift, Red-throated, Little, Swallow-tailed, White-throated and Green Bee-eaters, Abyssinian Roller, Black Scimitar-bill, Abyssinian Ground-Hornbill, Yellow-fronted Tinkerbird, White-headed Barbet, Piapiac, Red-shouldered Cuckoo-shrike, White Helmetshrike, Purple Glossy-Starling, Yellow-billed Oxpecker, Northern Anteater-Chat, Red-winged Pytilia, Slender-billed Weaver, Vitelline Masked-Weaver, Yellow-crowned Bishop, Copper Sunbird, Golden-breasted Bunting.

Access

There are a few tracks from which to explore this area.

ADDITIONAL INFORMATION

Books and Papers

Birds of the Central African Republic. Carroll, R. *Malimbus* 10:177–200. 1988.

The Avifauna of Dzanga–Ndoki NP and Dzanga–Sangha Rainforest Reserve. Green, A and Carroll, R. *Malimbus* 13:49–66. 1991.

Near-endemic

Heuglin's Francolin (also occurs in Zaïre and southwest Sudan).

CHAD

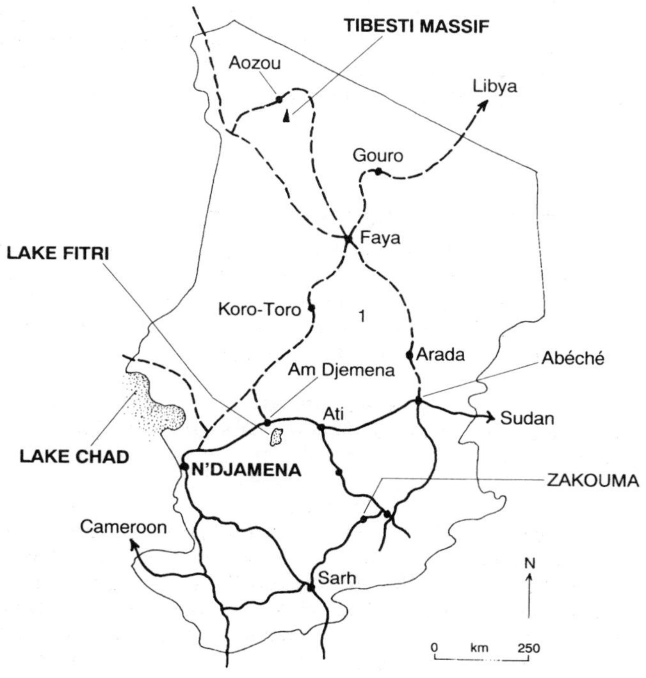

1 Ouadi Rime–Ouadi Achim Reserve

INTRODUCTION

Summary

Chad was explored extensively by ornithologists from the 1950s to the 1970s, but since the Libyans invaded the north in 1980, very few birders have visited this remote country. The poor infrastructure makes birding extremely difficult. However, there are few species occurring in Chad which can not be seen in more accessible parts of the continent.

Size

Chad is a big country, covering 1,284,000 sq km. It is ten times larger than England, and nearly twice the size of Texas.

Getting Around

There are few paved roads and most roads and tracks are usually impassable during the normal wet season (Jun–Oct). There is little if any public transport and a very limited internal air network.

Accomodation and Food

Accommodation is virtually non-existent and food very difficult to come by away from the capital N'Djamena.

Health and Safety

Immunisation against hepatitis, meningitis, polio, typhoid and yellow fever is recommended, as are precautions against malaria.

Climate and Timing

The best time to visit is during the dry season, which usually lasts from November to May, though such 'seasons' have been very unpredictable in Chad during recent years.

Habitats

Chad encompasses three major habitat zones: seasonally flooded Guinea savanna in the south, Sahel in the centre and Saharan desert in the north. Although mainly a flat country, the remote Tibesti Massif in the northwest rises to almost 3500 m (11,483 ft).

Conservation

Rainfall has decreased by 20%–40% since the 1960s, a serious shortfall which led to the diminution of Lake Chad (not full since 1975) and the complete drying out of Lake Fitri in 1984. These two lakes were formerly of immense importance to wintering Palearctic migrants, especially waterfowl and shorebirds.

Three threatened and five near-threatened species occur in Chad.

Bird Families

Of the ten families endemic to the African mainland seven are represented in Chad. Well represented families include larks and buntings.

Bird Species

A total of 532 species have been recorded in land-locked Chad, on a par with Niger, its similar neighbour. Non-endemic specialities and spectacular species include Schlegel's Francolin, Arabian Bustard, Lesser Jacana, Egyptian Plover, Grey Pratincole, Niam-Niam Parrot, Golden Nightjar, Chestnut-bellied Starling, Cricket Longtail, Kordofan and Rusty Larks and Sudan Golden-Sparrow.

Endemics

There are no endemics, but near-endemics include River Prinia* and many arid-savanna specialities are also present.

OUADI RIME–OUADI ACHIM RESERVE

This huge 'reserve' (78,000 sq km) covers most of central Chad. The desert and Sahel habitats such as wooded wadis, wet season (Jun–Oct) pools, and sparsely wooded steppe, support such species as Quail-plover and Rusty Lark.

Specialities

Rusty Lark, Sudan Golden-Sparrow.

Others

Quail-plover, Blue-naped Mousebird, White-faced Scops-Owl, White-throated and Green Bee-eaters, Abyssinian Roller, Abyssinian Ground-Hornbill (May–Oct), Vieillot's and Yellow-breasted Barbets, Little Grey Woodpecker, Masked Shrike (Oct–Mar), Black-crowned Tchagra, Long-tailed Glossy-Starling, Chestnut-bellied Starling, Black Scrub-Robin, White-tailed and Heuglin's Wheatears, Ethiopian Swallow, Desert Cisticola, Fulvous Chatterer, Brown Babbler, Sennar Penduline-Tit, Chestnut-backed Sparrow-Lark, Bar-tailed and Desert Larks, Greater Hoopoe-Lark, Desert Sparrow, Vitelline Masked-Weaver, White-rumped Seedeater, House Bunting.

Other Wildlife

Aardvark, dorca gazelle.

Access

These species have been recorded in the area between Faya, Koro-Toro and Arada.

A SELECTED LIST OF SPECIES RECORDED IN CHAD

Ostrich, African Darter, African Pygmy-goose, Dwarf Bittern, Hamerkop, Saddle-billed Stork, Scissor-tailed Kite, Secretary-bird, Schlegel's and Clapperton's Francolins, African Finfoot, Demoiselle Crane, Black Crowned-Crane, Arabian Bustard (Batha and d'Ouaddai prefectures), Lesser Jacana, Egyptian Plover, Bronze-winged Courser, Grey Pratincole, African Skimmer, Spotted and Crowned Sandgrouse, Adamawa Turtle-Dove, Niam-Niam Parrot, White-crested Turaco, Golden Nightjar, Red-throated, Swallow-tailed and Northern Carmine Bee-eaters, Blue-bellied Roller, White-headed, Black-breasted and Yellow-breasted Barbets, Speckle-breasted Woodpecker, Grey-headed Batis, Brown-tailed Chat, Dorst's Cisticola, River Prinia*, Cricket Longtail, Rueppell's Warbler, Yellow Penduline-Tit, White-tailed and Kordofan Larks, Greater Hoopoe-Lark, Dunn's and Sun Larks, Rufous Sparrow, Jameson's and Black-faced Firefinches, Pale-winged Indigobird, Togo Paradise-Whydah, Brown-rumped Bunting.

ADDITIONAL INFORMATION

Books and Papers

Observations sur la Presence et l'Abondance des Oiseaux au Tchad. de Boer, W and Legoupil, F. 1992. *Malimbus* 15:17–24.
The Birds of the Ouadi Rime–Ouadi Achim Faunal Reserve. Newby, J. 1980. *Malimbus* 2:29–49.
Synthese de l'Avifaune du Massif Montagneux du Tibesti. Simon, P. 1965. *Le Gerfaut* 55:26–71.

Near-endemics

Dorst's Cisticola, River Prinia*.

COMOROS AND MAYOTTE

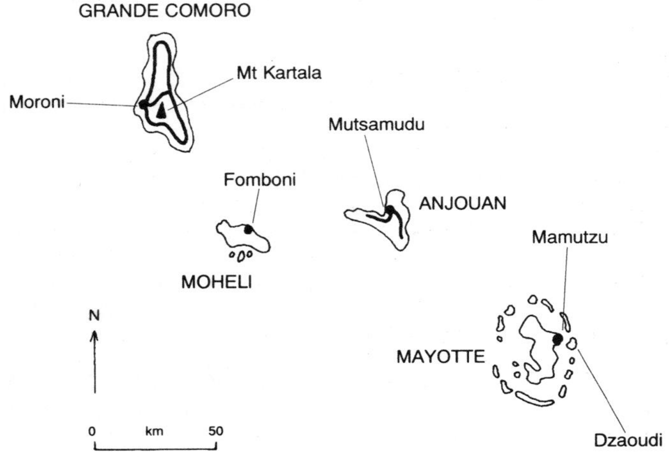

This lovely archipelago, lying between Mozambique and Madagascar, supports an impressive 16 endemics, most of which are not too difficult to see so long as the four main islands are visited.

Contact (in French) the tourist agency, Comores Tours, at BP 974, Moroni, Grande Comoro, before visiting and, once there, basic French greatly assists in getting around. Small boats connect the four main islands, all of which boast endemic species and good accommodation. Immunisation against hepatitis, polio and typhoid is recommended, as are precautions against malaria. The best time to visit is the dry season which lasts from May to October. Seven threatened and four near-threatened species occur on the Comoros and Mayotte. Two of the five families endemic to the islands offshore from East Africa are represented, in the form of Cuckoo-Roller and Blue Vanga. Ninety-nine species have been recorded, 120 fewer than on the Seychelles, but on a par with Mauritius. Non-endemic specialities and spectacular species include White-tailed Tropicbird and Masked Booby. The 16 endemics include two scops-owls, two drongos, two white-eyes, three brush-warblers and three sunbirds. Two species present occur elsewhere only on the nearby island of Aldabra, and a further 14 are restricted to the Comoros, Aldabra and Madagascar. These include Diademed Kingfisher; another near-endemic is Réunion Harrier*. In total, 35 of the 175 Malagasy endemics occur on the Comoros.

Five species occur only on the 65 km-long island of **Grand Comoro**: Comoro Scops-Owl*, Comoro Drongo*, Grand Comoro Flycatcher*, Comoro White-eye* and Grand Comoro Brush-Warbler. These five species (Comoro White-eye* above 1800 m (5906 ft)), as well as Comoro Thrush, Comoro Bulbul, and Humblot's Sunbird all occur on the slopes of **Mount Kartala**, the active volcano (2461 m (8074 ft)) which dominates the island. Transport can be arranged in Moroni, the 'capital', to Bomboni or Niambadjou, from where it is possible to walk to the crater forest. Comoro Blue-Pigeon and Red-headed Fody, both of which also occur on Aldabra, also occur here. It is also possible to explore Mount Kartala from Kurani, where guides are available to escort visitors to the very top (at a price).

Three species are restricted to **Anjouan**: Anjouan Scops-Owl*, which was rediscovered in 1992, Anjouan Brush-Warbler and Anjouan Sunbird.

Moheli Brush-Warbler* occurs only on **Moheli**, along with Madagascar Green-Pigeon, Comoro Thrush, Blue Vanga, Comoro Bulbul and Humblot's Sunbird.

Three species occur only on **Mayotte**, which is still a French colony: Mayotte Drongo*, Mayotte White-eye and Mayotte Sunbird.

ADDITIONAL INFORMATION

Books and Papers

Les Oiseaux des Comores. Annales Serie-in-8 Sciences Zoologiques No. 255. Louette, M. 1988. Musée Royale de L'Afrique Centrale Tervuren, Belgium (contains some illustrations and maps).

Addresses

Please send records to Dr M Louette, Musée Royale de L'Afrique Centrale, B-3080 Tervuren, Belgium.

ENDEMICS (16)

Comoro Pigeon*	All islands
Anjouan Scops-Owl*	Anjouan
Comoro Scops-Owl*	Grand Comoro
Comoro Drongo*	Grand Comoro
Mayotte Drongo*	Mayotte
Comoro Thrush	Grand Comoro, Anjouan and Moheli
Grand Comoro Flycatcher*	Grand Comoro
Comoro Bulbul	Grand Comoro and Moheli
Mayotte White-eye	Mayotte
Comoro White-eye*	Grand Comoro
Grand Comoro Brush-Warbler	Grand Comoro
Moheli Brush-Warbler*	Moheli
Anjouan Brush-Warbler	Anjouan
Humblot's Sunbird	Grand Comoro and Moheli
Anjouan Sunbird	Anjouan
Mayotte Sunbird	Mayotte

Near-endemics

Comoros and Aldabra
Comoro Blue-Pigeon, Red-headed Fody.

Comoros, Aldabra and Madagascar
Madagascar Bulbul, Madagascar White-eye.

Comoros and Madagascar
Frances' Goshawk, Madagascar Green-Pigeon (Moheli), Vasa Parrot, Madagascar Spinetail, Madagascar Swift, Diademed Kingfisher, Cuckoo-Roller, Madagascar Paradise-Flycatcher, Crested Drongo (Anjouan), Madagascar Cuckoo-shrike, Blue Vanga (Grand Comoro and Moheli), Madagascar Sunbird.

Comoros, Madagascar and Seychelles
Black Parrot.

Comoros, Madagascar, Seychelles and Aldabra
Madagascar Turtle-Dove.

Comoros, Madagascar and Réunion
Réunion Harrier*.

CONGO

INTRODUCTION

Summary

Although Congo's avifauna is similar to that of its more accessible neighbours, Cameroon and Gabon, some scarce species, such as White-crested Bittern and Vermiculated Fishing-Owl, seem to be easier to see here. Based in good accommodation at Pointe Noire on the west coast, it is possible to drive into the interior forest (with a 4WD) and look for such birds.

Size

At 342,000 sq km, Congo is 2.6 times the size of England, and half the size of Texas.

Getting Around

There are no good roads beyond the capital, Brazzaville, only tracks, and most of these are impassable during the wet season (Oct–May). A railway connects Brazzaville with Pointe Noire, but the service is unreliable.

Accommodation and Food

Accommodation is expensive in Brazzaville and Pointe Noire.

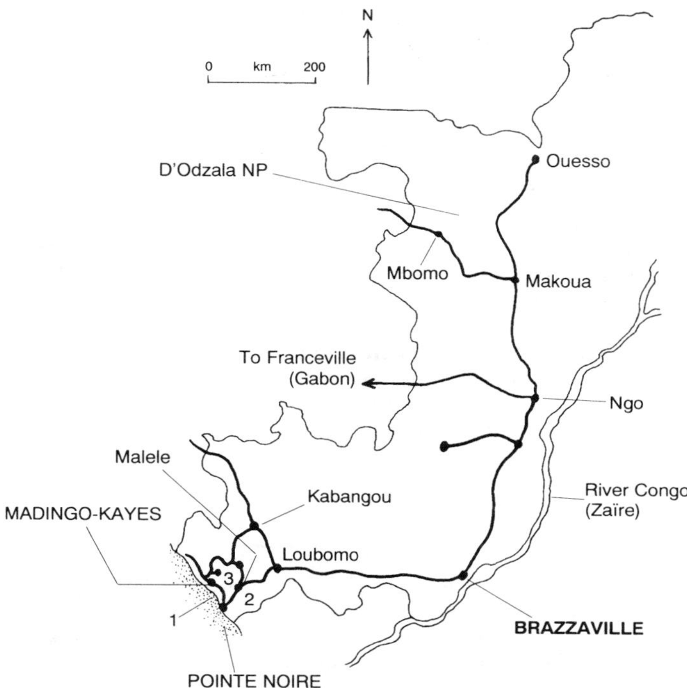

1 Congo Coast
2 Pointe Noire–Sounda road
3 Koubotchi Forest

Health and Safety

Immunisation against hepatitis, polio, typhoid and yellow fever is recommended, as are precautions against malaria.

Climate and Timing

The very long wet season lasts from October to May, so the best time to visit is July and August.

Habitats

The grassland of the narrow, dry coastal plain soon gives way to forested plateaux and highlands. Lowland rainforest still covers large stretches of the land, especially in the north.

Conservation

As is the case with most central African countries, the forest of Congo is under serious threat from logging companies; logging has depleted the forest west of Cameroon, and now threatens the remaining forest in the Congo Basin.

Three threatened and one near-threatened species occur in Congo.

Bird Families

Three only of the ten families endemic to the African mainland are represented in Congo. Ostrich, Shoebill*, Secretary-bird, woodhoopoes, ground-hornbills, rockfowl and sugarbirds are all absent. Well represented families include guineafowl, weavers and sunbirds.

Bird Species

A total of 569 species have been recorded in Congo, 100 fewer than Gabon, but the real total is probably much higher. Non-endemic specialities and spectacular species include Damara Tern*, Long-tailed Hawk, Streaky-breasted Flufftail, Yellow-throated Cuckoo, Black-headed and Rosy Bee-eaters and Rufous-sided Broadbill.

Endemics

There are no endemics, but near-endemics include Perrin's Bushshrike, Rufous-tailed Palm-Thrush, African River-Martin and Pale-billed Firefinch.

CONGO COAST

The 100-km stretch of road between Pointe Noire and Madingo-Kayes on Congo's southwest coast passes through coastal scrub, lowland forest patches and estuaries which support Vermiculated Fishing-Owl, African River-Martin and Pale-billed Firefinch.

Specialities

Damara Tern* (Aug–Dec), Vermiculated Fishing-Owl, Perrin's Bushshrike, African River-Martin (Sep–Nov), Forest Swallow, Black-collared Bulbul, Pale-billed Firefinch, Violet-tailed Sunbird.

Others

Harlequin Quail, Black-rumped Buttonquail, White-spotted Flufftail, Striped Crake, White-fronted Plover, White-headed Lapwing, Royal Tern, Black Coucal, Horus Swift, Rufous-necked Wryneck, African Piculet, Golden-crowned Woodpecker, Petit's Cuckoo-shrike, Snowy-crowned Robin-Chat, White-throated Blue and Red-throated Swallows, Yellow-throated and Yellow-necked Greenbuls, Buff-throated Apalis, Rufous-crowned Eremomela, Grosbeak Weaver, Yellow-crowned Bishop, Reichenbach's, Blue-throated Brown and Orange-tufted Sunbirds.

Access

Damara Tern* and Perrin's Bushsrike have been recorded at **Pointe Indienne**, 15 km north of Pointe Noire, as well as Harlequin Quail, Black-rumped Buttonquail, Black Coucal, Vermiculated Fishing-Owl and Reichenbach's Sunbird. The surrounds of **Diosso**, 20 km north of Pointe Noire, support species such as Perrin's Bushshrike (around the Musée de Diosso), Black-collared Bulbul (Diosso golf course) and Pale-billed Firefinch. Just outside Diosso town, White-headed Lapwing, Horus Swift, Forest Swallow (in dead trees alongside road to the River Noubi), and Yellow-throated Greenbul occur at the **Gorges de Diosso**. Damara Tern* and African River-Martin have been recorded around the estuary at **Bas-Kouilou**, 5 km south of Madingo-Kayes. African River-Martin has also been recorded on passage (Sep–Nov) at **Lac Fonie**, near Bas-Kouilou, whilst Reichenbach's Sunbird occurs around the lake.

POINTE NOIRE–SOUNDA ROAD

Mayumbe Forest lies alongside the road to Sounda, 120 km inland from Pointe Noire *en route* to Kabangou. This forest supports Yellow-throated Cuckoo and Congo Serpent-Eagle.

Specialities

Yellow-throated Cuckoo.

Others

Congo Serpent-Eagle, White-spotted Flufftail, Guinea Turaco, Thick-billed, Black and Olive Long-tailed Cuckoos, Blue-headed Coucal, Fraser's Eagle-Owl, Dwarf Kingfisher, Black and Little Bee-eaters, Blue-throated Roller, Naked-faced and Bristle-nosed Barbets, Cassin's Honeyguide, Western Black-headed Oriole, Blue Cuckoo-shrike, Black-and-white Shrike-flycatcher, Angola Batis, Narrow-tailed Starling, White-throated Blue Swallow, Golden Greenbul, Violet-backed Hyliota, Brown Twinspot, Western Bluebill, Little Green and Superb Sunbirds.

Access

Bird alongside the roads to **Mango Tandou**, **Malele** and **Sounda**.

KOUBOTCHI FOREST

Black-headed Bee-eater occurs on the edge of this forest, approximately 20 km inland from the coastal town of Madingo-Kayes.

Specialities

Black-headed Bee-eater.

Others

White-bellied and Black-bellied Bustards, Senegal Lapwing, Afep Pigeon, Great Blue Turaco, Olive Long-tailed Cuckoo, Mottled Spinetail, Black, Little and Blue-breasted Bee-eaters, White-crested and Black Dwarf Hornbills, Gabon Woodpecker, Rufous-sided Broadbill, Blue-headed Crested-Flycatcher, Blue Cuckoo-shrike, Large-billed Puffback, Chestnut Wattle-eye, Rufous Flycatcher-Thrush, White-tailed Ant-thrush, Olivaceous Flycatcher, Icterine and Red-tailed Greenbuls, Lemon-bellied Crombec, Yellow and Grey Longbills, Woodhouse's Antpecker, Yellow-mantled Weaver, Gray's Malimbe.

Access

Madingo-Kayes is approximately 100 km north of Pointe Noire.

Black-headed Bee-eater also occurs around **Menengue**, where other species present include Long-tailed Hawk, African Wood-Owl, Swamp

Nightjar, White-thighed Hornbill, Golden-crowned Woodpecker, Blue Cuckoo-shrike, Olivaceous Flycatcher, Red-capped Robin-Chat, Leaflove, Rufous-crowned Eremomela, Chestnut-breasted and Pale-fronted Negrofinches, Western Bluebill, Brown Twinspot and Johanna's Sunbird.

Black-headed Bee-eater and Gabon Helmetshrike occur at the edge of the forest at **Bena**. Other species here include White-spotted Flufftail, Black Bee-eater, Black-casqued Hornbill, Rufous-sided Broadbill, Large-billed Puffback, Rufous Flycatcher-Thrush, Honeyguide Greenbul, Yellow-browed Carmaroptera, Pale-breasted Illadopsis, and Red-bellied Malimbe.

A SELECTED LIST OF SPECIES RECORDED IN SOUTHWEST CONGO

White-crested Bittern, Streaky-breasted Flufftail (Tchissanga and Mpinde), Nkulengu (Mayombe) and Grey-throated Rails, African Finfoot (River Nanga), Grey Parrot, Yellow-billed Turaco, African Emerald Cuckoo, Gabon Coucal, Maned Owl, Bates' Nightjar, White-fronted and Rosy Bee-eaters, Green-backed Woodpecker, Rufous-tailed Palm-Thrush, Sooty Chat, Spotted, Swamp and Icterine Greenbuls, Bubbling Cisticola (Djeno), Long-legged Pipit, Yellow-shouldered Widowbird, Carmelite Sunbird.

ADDITIONAL INFORMATION

Books and Papers

Additions and Corrections to the Avifauna of Congo. Dowsett-Lemaire, F, Dowsett, R and Bulens, P. 1993. *Malimbus* 15:68–80.
The Avifauna of the Kouilou Basin in Congo. Dowsett-Lemaire, F and Dowsett, R. 1991. *Tauraco Research Report* 4:189–239.
The Status of Seabirds off the Coast of Congo. Dowsett, R and Simpson, R. 1991. *Tauraco Research Report* 4:241–250.
Liste Preliminaire des Oiseaux du Congo. Dowsett, R and Dowsett-Lemaire, F. 1989. *Tauraco Research Report* 2:29–51.

Addresses

Please send all records to Mr R Dowsett, c/o Projet ECOFAC, BP 62 Brazzaville.

Near-endemics

Perrin's Bushshrike, Angola Batis, Rufous-tailed Palm-Thrush, African River-Martin, Congo and Brazza's Martins, Sjostedt's and Pale-olive Greenbuls, Bubbling Cisticola, Pale-billed Firefinch, Black-chinned* and Bob-tailed Weavers, Congo Sunbird.

CÔTE D'IVOIRE

1 Grand Bassam
2 Orstom (lirsda)
3 Yapo
4 Lamto
5 Maraoué NP
6 Tai Forest NP
7 Mount Tonkoui
8 Comoe NP

INTRODUCTION

Summary

The Côte D'Ivoire is a popular holiday destination for the French, who also have a strong presence within the country. Consequently it is one of Africa's most developed countries. Although most of the spectacular species present are widespread, and can be seen elsewhere in West Africa, the Côte D'Ivoire is the most accessible country in which to look for the Upper Guinea endemics: 14 of the 16 species confined to the region between Guinea-Bissau and Ghana have been recorded here.

Size

At 322,463 sq km, the Côte D'Ivoire is 2.5 times larger than England, and half the size of Texas.

Getting Around

This country boasts one of the best road systems in Africa, but car-hire is very expensive. Fortunately for budget travellers there is a good bus network.

Accommodation and Food

The accommodation and food in Côte D'Ivoire are both good, but expensive.

Health and Safety

Immunisation against hepatitis, meningitis, polio, typhoid and yellow fever is recommended. It is also wise to take all precautions against malaria, and to beware of tsetse flies in the northern savannas, especially in Comoe NP.

Climate and Timing

There are two wet seasons in the south. The long rains last from April to July and the short rains from October to November. In the north, the rainy season lasts from May to November, and during this time Comoe NP is usually closed. It is dry throughout the country from December to March and this is the best time to visit, although the Harmattan wind from the Sahara often blows hard across the north at this time. It is hot and humid all year round near the coast.

Habitats

This is a mainly flat country which rises to only 1189 m (3901 ft) at Mount Tonkoui in the far west. Palm-fringed beaches, lagoons and mangroves line the southern Gulf of Guinea coast. Some remnant 'Upper Guinea' rainforest patches remain in the southern half of the country, whilst to the north lies the Guinea savanna where many *Borassus* palms grow and gallery forest lines the rivers. During December and January vast stretches of the grassy savanna are burnt in an attempt to improve grazing and these areas often attract many birds. Arid bush country and wooded savanna are present on the plateau in the far north.

Conservation

Not much longer than fifty years ago much of the southern half of this country was covered in lowland rainforest. However, selective logging, the spread of agriculture and the construction of new roads, which act as catalysts for new settlements, have left but a few remnant patches, some of which have been designated as 'reserves'.

Eleven threatened and eight near-threatened species occur in Côte D'Ivoire.

Bird Families

Of the ten families endemic to the African mainland six are represented in Côte D'Ivoire. Ostrich, Shoebill*, mousebirds and sugarbirds are absent. Well represented families include kingfishers, woodhoopoes, bulbuls and sunbirds.

Bird Species

An impressive 694 species have been recorded in Côte D'Ivoire, just 30 fewer than its eastern neighbour, Ghana. Non-endemic specialities and spectacular species include Long-tailed Hawk, African Finfoot,

Egyptian and Forbes' Plovers, Black-collared Lovebird, Yellow-throated Cuckoo, Chocolate-backed Kingfisher, Black and Blue-headed Bee-eaters, Red-cheeked Wattle-eye and Jameson's Antpecker.

Endemics

There are no endemics, but 14 of the 16 Upper Guinea endemics are present, including White-breasted Guineafowl*, Rufous Fishing-Owl*, Ghana Cuckoo-shrike*, Iris Glossy-Starling, Liberian Black-Flycatcher*, White-necked Rockfowl* and Ballman's Malimbe*. Only Turati's Bushshrike* and Liberian Greenbul* are missing.

Expectations

Well prepared and keen birders may see 350 species during a three-week trip or 400 over the period of four weeks, so long as both the north and the south are visited.

The coastal resort of **Grand Bassam**, 43 km southeast of Abidjan, lies at the mouth of the River Comoe on the Gulf of Guinea coast. Lagoons and scrub here support Black Coucal, Orange Weaver, and Mouse-brown, Reichenbach's and Carmelite Sunbirds. Head east out of Abidjan on the main road past the airport. Just before Grand Bassam turn right, cross Lagune Ebrie, and turn right at the T junction. After 2.5 km, bird alongside the lagoon close to the road. Birding east of Grand Bassam may also be productive.

Black Bee-eater has been recorded in **Banco NP** (30 sq km), just 3 km from Abidjan, the capital, on the road to Orstom and Dabou west of the city.

The stunning Blue-breasted Kingfisher is likely to be seen at a number of sites in Côte D'Ivoire

ORSTOM (IIRSDA)

This French agricultural research station, some 20 km west of Abidjan, overlooks the Lagune Ebrie, and is surrounded by a small patch of remnant rainforest. The star attraction here is Tit-Hylia, which may even be seen from the balcony of the resthouse, although Forbes' Plover, Black Coucal, Black Bee-eater and Reichenbach's Sunbird have also been recorded.

Specialities

Forbes' Plover (Nov–Mar), Tit-hylia.

Others

Bat Hawk, Palm-nut Vulture, Chestnut-flanked Sparrowhawk, Black Goshawk, White-spotted Flufftail, Nkulengu Rail, African and Black Crakes, African Finfoot, Greater Painted-snipe, Levaillant's Cuckoo, Yellowbill, Black Coucal, Fraser's Eagle-Owl, Plain Nightjar, Black and White-throated Bee-eaters, White-headed Woodhoopoe, White-crested and African Pied Hornbills, Speckled Tinkerbird, Hairy-breasted Barbet, Cassin's Honeyguide, Melancholy and Fire-bellied Woodpeckers, White-tailed Ant-Thrush, Splendid Glossy-Starling, White-throated Blue Swallow, Fanti Sawwing, Simple Greenbul, Grey-headed Bristlebill, Whistling and Siffling Cisticolas, Chestnut-breasted Negrofinch, Crimson Seedcracker, Orange-cheeked Waxbill, Magpie Mannikin, Red-vented and Red-headed Malimbes, Yellow-shouldered Widowbird, Little Green, Reichenbach's, Blue-throated Brown, Buff-throated, Olive-bellied, Tiny and Copper Sunbirds.

Access

Orstom lies just south of the Dabou road (signposted on a rock). Bird the area around the resthouse, particularly from the balcony (White-headed Woodhoopoe, Tit-hylia, malimbes and sunbirds), the lagoon (Nkulengu Rail), and the surrounding farmland (Forbes' Plover).

Accommodation: Resthouse (B). It is best to book in advance. Write (in French) to The Director, IIRDSA, BP 51, Abidjan 01.

Rice paddies and lily-ponds around **Dabou**, 25 km west of Orstom, support Dwarf Bittern, Allen's Gallinule, Greater Painted-snipe, Black Coucal and Crimson Seedcracker.

YAPO

The forest in this reserve, just 40 km north of Abidjan, has been selectively logged in the past and most of what remains is secondary growth. However, there are plenty of good birds here including the rare Black-collared Lovebird, West African Batis and Yellow-bearded Greenbul*.

Specialities

Black-collared Lovebird, Chestnut-bellied Helmetshrike, West African Batis, Finsch's Flycatcher-Thrush, Ussher's Flycatcher, Yellow-bearded Greenbul*, Sharpe's Apalis, Jameson's Antpecker.

Others

African Pygmy-goose, Ayre's Hawk-Eagle, Ahanta Francolin, White-spotted Flufftail, Grey-throated Rail, Bronze-naped Pigeon, Yellow-billed Turaco, Yellowbill, Black-throated Coucal, Cassin's Spinetail, White-bellied and Dwarf Kingfishers, Black, Blue-headed and White-throated Bee-eaters, Blue-throated Roller, White-crested and Piping Hornbills, Naked-faced Barbet, Speckled and Yellow-throated Tinkerbirds, Yellow-spotted and Hairy-breasted Barbets, Cassin's Honeyguide, Melancholy and Fire-bellied Woodpeckers, Rufous-sided Broadbill, Shining Drongo, Western Black-headed Oriole, Large-billed Puffback, African Shrike-flycatcher, Chestnut and Yellow-bellied Wattle-eyes, Brown-chested and White-tailed Alethes, African Forest-Flycatcher, Olivaceous and Dusky-blue Flycatchers, Square-tailed Sawwing, Little, Grey, Ansorge's, Slender-billed, Honeyguide, Spotted, Icterine, Western Bearded and Red-tailed Greenbuls, Black-capped Apalis, Yellow-browed Camaroptera, Rufous-crowned Eremomela, Green and Lemon-bellied Crombecs, Grey Longbill, Green Hylia, Pale-breasted and Brown Illadopsises, Western Bluebill, Gray's, Crested and Red-headed Malimbes, Scarlet-tufted, Bates', Olive-bellied and Johanna's Sunbirds.

Access

Approximately 25 km north of Abidjan take the left fork towards Agboville. The entrance to the forest is on the right-hand side 15 km beyond this fork. From the Forestry Office a track leads east past a village. There are several trails worth exploring from this main track. Black-collared Lovebird occurs in the palms opposite the generator (usually at dawn).

Accommodation: Forestry Offices. Agboville.

A number of the species listed above also occur at the **Plantation de L'Abie**, which is reached by taking the right fork approximately 25 km north of Abidjan (instead of the left to Yapo). The plantation is on the east side of the road 35 km beyond the fork, *en route* to Agou.

LAMTO

Lamto should be penned in the itinerary of anyone planning a visit to Côte D'Ivoire. Here, 180 km north of Abidjan, there is an ecological research station and nature reserve (2500 ha) situated on the eastern bank of the Bandama river. The mixture of Guinea savanna and Upper Guinea forest with rocky outcrops supports such species as White-necked Rockfowl*, although some birders believe the bird (or birds) present here are vagrants since there is no known colony actually on the reserve. In fact, there are only two known White-necked Rockfowl* colonies in Côte D'Ivoire. One of them was situated in a forest near Lamto but, depressingly, this forest has recently been felled and replaced with a banana plantation. However, White-necked Rockfowl* was recorded at Lamto after this forest was destroyed, and Lamto probably remains the most accessible place in Africa to see this rare and elusive species. Lamto is also one of the best sites in Africa to see African Finfoot and Rufous Fishing-Owl*, although the owl is still a great rarity.

Specialities

Spot-breasted Ibis, Rufous Fishing-Owl*, Chestnut Owlet, Red-cheeked Wattle-eye, Finsch's Flycatcher-Thrush, Rufous-winged Illadopsis*, White-necked Rockfowl*.

Others

White-backed Night-Heron, White-crested Bittern, Olive Ibis, African Cuckoo-Falcon, Wahlberg's Eagle, Cassin's Hawk-Eagle, African Crake, African Finfoot, Senegal Thick-knee, Rock Pratincole, White-headed Lapwing, Brown-necked and Senegal Parrots, Guinea and Great Blue Turacos, Pel's Fishing-Owl, African Wood-Owl, Plain, Long-tailed and Standard-winged Nightjars, Mottled Spinetail, Shining Blue and Blue-breasted Kingfishers, Black Bee-eater, Blue-bellied Roller, White-headed Woodhoopoe, White-crested and Black Dwarf Hornbills, Naked-faced and Hairy-breasted Barbets, Fire-bellied Woodpecker, Chestnut-capped Flycatcher, Velvet-mantled Drongo, Black-winged Oriole, Purple-throated Cuckoo-shrike, White Helmetshrike, Chestnut Wattle-eye, White-tailed Ant-Thrush, Chestnut-winged Starling, White-browed Forest-Flycatcher, Cassin's Flycatcher, Forest Scrub-Robin, White-throated Greenbul, Lemon-bellied Crombec, Grey Longbill, Puvel's Illadopsis, Capuchin Babbler, Green-headed Sunbird.

Access

Turn off the main Abidjan–Yamoussoukro road 2 km south of Aheremou. Bird the 15 km entrance track (Standard-winged Nightjar), the forest halfway along (Black Bee-eater), the savanna beyond (African Crake and Blue-bellied Roller), the gardens on the right 500 m before the Resthouse turn-off (African Wood-Owl), the riverine forest beyond the Resthouse (White-necked Rockfowl*), the river viewpoint beyond here (White-backed Night-Heron, White-crested Bittern, Rock Pratincole, Pel's and Rufous* Fishing-Owls), the water pump area at the end of the main track (White-crested Bittern, Spot-breasted Ibis, and the fishing-owls), best at dusk, and the riverine forest to the left. Black Bee-eater also occurs in patches of dry forest in the savanna around Lamto.

LAMTO

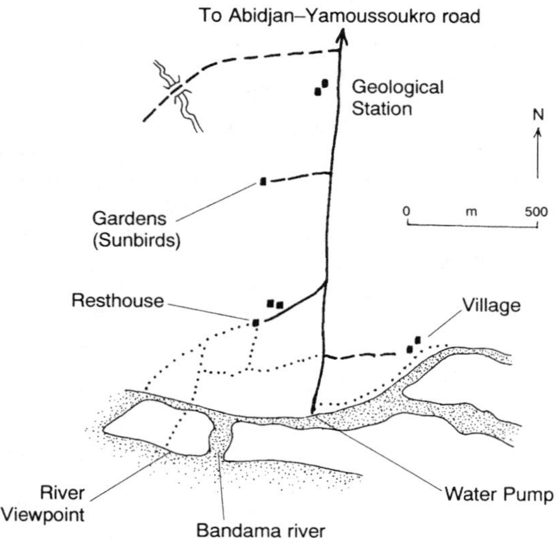

Accommodation: Resthouse (C). To book in advance write (in French) to The Director, Station Ecologique de Lamto, BP 28, N'Douci.

White-throated Blue Swallow may be seen from **Bonzi Bridge**, 26 km east of Bouafle on the Yamoussoukro–Bouafle road.

Lamto is the most accessible site in Africa for the bizarre White-necked Rockfowl, a species which occurs only between Sierra Leone and Ghana*

MARAOUÉ NATIONAL PARK

Situated alongside the River Bandama Rouge near Kossou in south-central Côte D'Ivoire, the savanna-covered rolling hills and gallery forest of Maraoue NP (1000 sq km), support the rare and beautiful Iris Glossy-Starling.

Specialities

Brown-cheeked Hornbill*, Iris Glossy-Starling.

Others

Palm-nut Vulture, Crested Guineafowl, Ahanta Francolin, White-headed Lapwing, Great Blue Turaco, Black-throated Coucal, Blue-breasted Kingfisher, White-throated Bee-eater, Red-billed Dwarf and Black-casqued Hornbills, White-throated Blue-Swallow, Rufous-rumped and Sun Larks, Broad-tailed Paradise-Whydah, Western Violet-backed Sunbird.

Access

The park entrance is at Goazra village, on the Bouafle–Daloa road. Iris Glossy-Starling is especially attracted to burnt savanna in December and January. There are plenty of good tracks worth exploring here.

Accommodation: Bouafle. Camping (ask permission in village at entrance to park):

Black Crake and White-headed Lapwing may be seen from **Delaya Bridge**, on the Daloa–Duekoue road.

TAI FOREST NATIONAL PARK

Tai Forest (3300 sq km), in west Côte D'Ivoire near the Liberian border, is one of the most important forests in the Upper Guinea region, and a must for birders visiting the country. It is the largest surviving area of 'protected' lowland rainforest in Africa west of Nigeria, and supports 11 of the 16 Upper Guinea endemics including White-breasted Guineafowl*, Ghana Cuckoo-shrike*, Liberian Black-Flycatcher* and Yellow-bearded Greenbul*. Other species include Yellow-throated Cuckoo, Long-tailed Hawk, Chocolate-backed Kingfisher and Black Bee-eater.

Specialities

White-breasted Guineafowl*, Yellow-throated Cuckoo, Rufous Fishing-Owl*, Black Spinetail, Brown-cheeked Hornbill*, Little Green Woodpecker, Ghana Cuckoo-shrike*, Chestnut-bellied Helmetshrike, Grey Ground-Thrush, Copper-tailed Glossy-Starling*, Liberian Black-Flycatcher*, Yellow-bearded Greenbul*, Sierra Leone Prinia*, Sharpe's Apalis, Black-capped Rufous Warbler*, Rufous-winged Illadopsis*.

Others

Palm-nut Vulture, Congo Serpent-Eagle, Black Goshawk, Long-tailed Hawk, Crowned Hawk-Eagle, Crested Guineafowl, Forest Francolin, African Finfoot, Rock Pratincole, Afep Pigeon, Grey Parrot, Yellow-billed and Great Blue Turacos, Black Cuckoo, Dusky Long-tailed Cuckoo, African Emerald Cuckoo, Black-throated Coucal, Akun Eagle-Owl, Sabine's and Cassin's Spinetails, Narina Trogon, Shining Blue, White-bellied, Dwarf and Chocolate-backed Kingfishers, Black, Blue-headed and White-throated Bee-eaters, Blue-throated Roller, White-headed and Forest Woodhoopoes, Black Dwarf, Red-billed Dwarf,

The more colourful western race of Black Bee-eater occurs in Tai Forest and on the slopes of Mount Tonkoui

Black-casqued and Yellow-casqued* Hornbills, Bristle-nosed and Yellow-spotted Barbets, Lyre-tailed Honeyguide, Melancholy and Fire-bellied Woodpeckers, Black-winged Oriole, Blue and Purple-throated Cuckoo-shrikes, Large-billed Puffback, Fiery-breasted Bushshrike, White-tailed Ant-Thrush, Brown-chested and White-tailed Alethes, Chestnut-winged Starling, African Forest-Flycatcher, Cassin's Flycatcher, Forest Robin, Lowland Akalat, Honeyguide, Spotted, Baumann's* and Icterine Greenbuls, Yellow-browed Camaroptera, Green and Lemon-bellied Crombecs, Kemp's Longbill, Violet-backed Hyliota, Blackcap and Pale-breasted Illadopsises, White-breasted Negrofinch, Magpie Mannikin, Red-vented, Gray's and Red-headed Malimbes, Blue-throated Brown and Johanna's Sunbirds.

(Two more Upper Guinea endemics, Liberian Greenbul* and Ballman's Malimbe*, occur just across the border in adjacent Liberia and may well be found in Tai Forest in the future. Ballman's Malimbe* has been recorded in Côte D'Ivoire, but outside the Tai NP boundaries. In addition, an undescribed species, provisionally called 'Pygmy Oxpecker', was glimpsed in Tai Forest in the 1970s, but has not been seen since.)

Other Wildlife

Chimpanzee, collared mangabey, diana monkey, Jentink's duiker, lesser white-nosed monkey, mona monkey, olive colobus, pygmy hippo, red colobus, western black-and-white colobus.

Access

The forest is best approached from the town of Tai, southwest of Daloa, via Guiglo. Tai town is 86 km south of Guiglo on a pretty rough track (Ahanta Francolin, Black Bee-eater). The track into the forest leads east from Pauleoula village, 8.5 km south of the police post on the south side

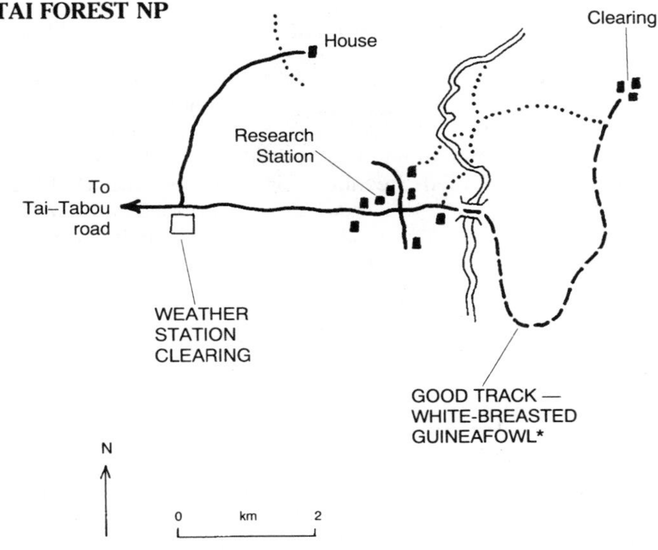

of Tai town. From here take the left fork after 2 km. Bird the weather station clearing 6.7 km along here (Ghana Cuckoo-shrike* and Liberian Black-Flycatcher*), 3 km before the Research Station, and the trails and tracks east of the Research Station, where walking quietly should turn up the rare but noisy White-breasted Guineafowl*, and scanning high dead branches may reveal the rare Liberian Black-Flycatcher*, which catches insects in nuthatch fashion.

The Cavally river, which runs along the Liberian border, is also worth birding (African Finfoot and Rock Pratincole). To reach this river park 4.3 km south of the Tai town police post and walk down the track on the west side of the road, bearing left at the fork.

Accommodation: Research Station (C). To book in advance write (in French) to Institut d'Ecologie Tropicale, BP 109, Abidjan.

MOUNT TONKOUI

The forest on the upper slopes of this inselberg, at 1189 m (3901 ft) the highest peak in the country, supports Black Bee-eater and Sharpe's Apalis.

Specialities

Sharpe's Apalis.

Others

African Emerald Cuckoo, Akun Eagle-Owl, Plain and Long-tailed Nightjars, Black Bee-eater, White-crested Hornbill, Naked-faced Barbet, Yellow-throated Tinkerbird, Melancholy Woodpecker, Red-shouldered Cuckoo-shrike, White-tailed Ant-Thrush, White-tailed Alethe, White-throated Greenbul, Lemon-bellied Crombec, Crested Malimbe.

Access

Bird the track northwest from Man which leads 32 km to the summit.

Part of **Mount Nimba** (p. 201) crosses the Côte D'Ivoire border. Rare species recorded there, which may occur in the Côte D'Ivoire section, include Rufous Fishing-Owl*, Yellow-footed Honeyguide*, Ghana Cuckoo-shrike*, Copper-tailed Glossy-Starling*, Liberian Black-Flycatcher*, Yellow-bearded Greenbul*, Sierra Leone Prinia*, Black-capped Rufous Warbler*, Rufous-winged Illadopsis*, and White-necked Rockfowl*. The road from Danane, west of Man, to Nzerekore in Guinea Conakry, runs close to this inselberg, and birders may be rewarded by exploring the area from Yeale. It is necessary to contact the Forest Warden first.

COMOE NATIONAL PARK

This park in northeast Côte D'Ivoire, is one of the biggest in West Africa (11,500 sq km). The savanna and gallery forest, together with the River Comoe, which crosses the park, support Egyptian and Forbes' Plovers, Emin's Shrike, Spotted Creeper and Brown-rumped Bunting.

A 4WD is recommended for those who intend to explore this park fully. Beware of tsetse flies.

Specialities

Egyptian and Forbes' Plovers, Emin's Shrike.

Others

Goliath Heron, Hamerkop, Saddle-billed Stork, African Cuckoo-Falcon, White-headed Vulture, Brown Snake-Eagle, Bateleur, Gabar Goshawk, Ayres' Hawk-Eagle, Martial Eagle, Stone Partridge, African Finfoot, Stanley and Black-bellied Bustards, Senegal Thick-knee, Temminck's Courser, White-headed Lapwing, Four-banded Sandgrouse, Vinaceous Dove, Bruce's Green-Pigeon, Senegal Parrot, Guinea and Violet Turacos, African Cuckoo, Shining Blue and Blue-breasted Kingfishers, Red-throated, Swallow-tailed and Northern Carmine Bee-eaters, Abyssinian and Blue-bellied Rollers, Black Scimitar-bill, Abyssinian Ground-Hornbill, Yellow-fronted Tinkerbird, Vieillot's and Double-toothed Barbets, Fine-spotted Woodpecker, African Blue-Flycatcher, White-breasted Cuckoo-shrike, Yellow-billed Shrike, Common Gonolek, Senegal Batis, Bronze-tailed Glossy-Starling, Pale and Gambaga Flycatchers, Snowy-crowned and White-crowned Robin-Chats, White-fronted Black-Chat, Spotted Creeper, Pied-winged and Preuss'

COMOE NP (WEST)

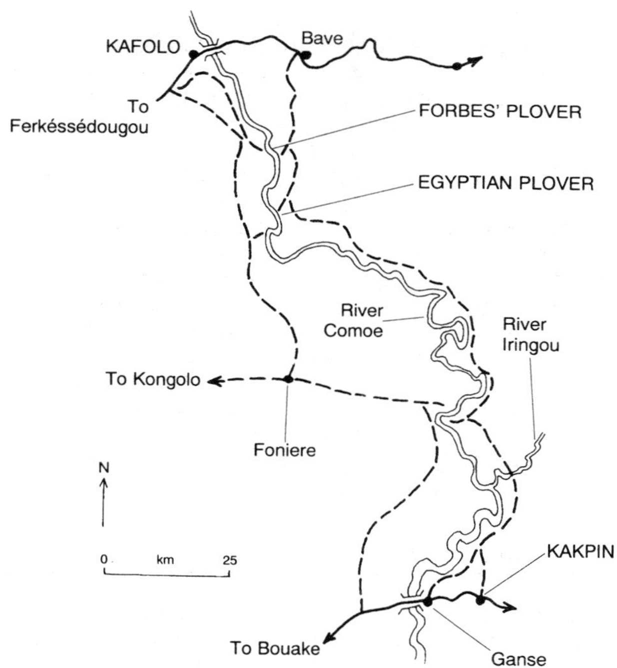

Swallows, Red-pate Cisticola, Oriole Warbler, Yellow-bellied Hyliota, Yellow Penduline-Tit, Flappet, Rufous-rumped and Sun Larks, Bar-breasted, Black-bellied and Black-faced Firefinches, Lavender Waxbill, African Quailfinch, Red-headed Weaver, Beautiful Sunbird, Brown-rumped and Cabanis' Buntings.

Other Wildlife

Buffalo, elephant, green monkey, hartebeeste, hippo, kob, lion, olive baboon, oribi, patas monkey, red-flanked duiker, waterbuck.

Access

The southern gateways, Ganse and Kakpin, are 180 km northeast of Bouake. Bird the tracks north from here, either side of the River Iringou. Specialities of the northern part of the park include Emin's Shrike, Rufous-rumped Lark and Brown-rumped Bunting. The northern entrance track starts 8 km southwest of Kafolo and leads to the River Comoe, where Egyptian and Forbes' Plovers occur.

Accommodation: Ganse: Comoe Sogetel (A+). Kakpin: Safari Camp (B). Kafolo: Comoe Safari Lodge (A+).

African Pygmy-goose, African Crake, Allen's Gallinule, Lesser Moorhen, Northern Carmine Bee-eater and Abyssinian Roller all occur at the **Lokpoho Marshes**, a few km west of Ferkéssédougou on the Odienné road.

ADDITIONAL INFORMATION

Books and Papers

The Birds of Ivory Coast. Thiollay, J. 1985. *Malimbus* 7:1–59.

Addresses

West African Ornithological Society (WAOS); see Useful Addresses, p. 413.

Near-endemics (Upper Guinea)

White-breasted Guineafowl*, Rufous Fishing-Owl*, Little Green Woodpecker, Ghana Cuckoo-shrike*, Iris and Copper-tailed* Glossy-Starlings, Liberian Black-Flycatcher*, Yellow-bearded Greenbul*, Sierra Leone Prinia*, Sharpe's Apalis, Black-capped Rufous Warbler*, Rufous-winged Illadopsis*, White-necked Rockfowl*, Ballman's Malimbe*.

Near-endemics (Upper Guinea and Nigeria)

Brown-cheeked Hornbill*, Chestnut-bellied Helmetshrike, Finsch's Flycatcher-Thrush.

DJIBOUTI

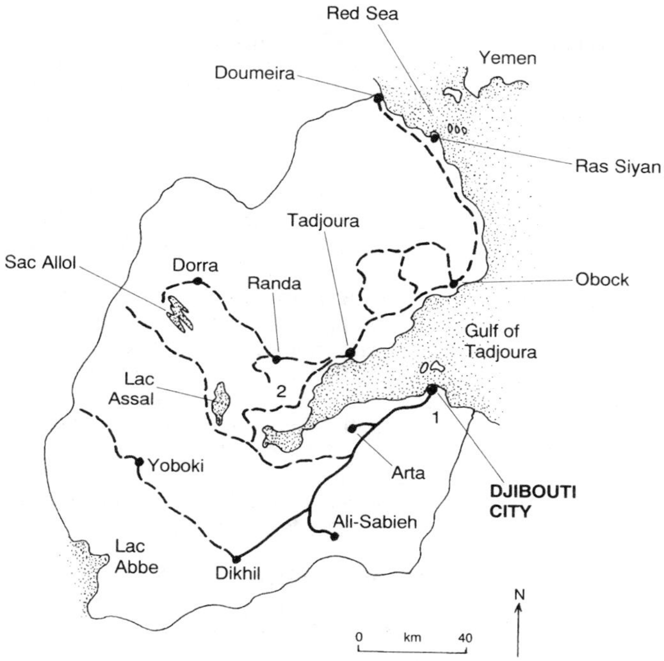

1 Djibouti City
2 Fôret du Day NP

INTRODUCTION

Summary

Few birders have ventured to Djibouti, and those who do in the future will need an expensive 4WD to see the endemic francolin, the selection of northeast African specialities, and the impressive autumn raptor passage. That is, if the small civil war does not prevent entry to or exit from the capital.

Size

At 22,000 sq km this tiny country is one sixth the size of England, and only a fraction the size of Texas.

Getting Around

An extremely expensive 4WD is essential to get around most of Djibouti.

Accommodation and Food

Accommodation is expensive and sparse away from the capital.

Health and Safety

Immunisation against hepatitis, polio, typhoid and yellow fever is recommended, as are precautions against malaria.

Climate and Timing

This is a hot country, especially from May to September. Birders intending to bird extensively in Djibouti would do well to visit the country in the autumn (around September), to coincide with the often impressive raptor passage.

Habitats

Most of Djibouti is sparsely inhabited, poorly vegetated, volcanic desert, although there is some juniper woodland on the Goda and Mabla Massifs north of the Gulf of Tadjoura, and a few saline lakes.

Conservation

Djibouti's forest continues to disappear, owing to overgrazing, clearance, the demand for firewood, army manoeuvres and development. In the recent civil war, the Fôret du Day, the stronghold of the endemic Djibouti Francolin*, was even being used by troops for 'cover'.

Three threatened and one near-threatened species occur in Djibouti.

Bird Families

Only three of the ten families endemic to the African mainland are represented in Djibouti: Ostrich, mousebirds and barbets.

Bird Species

An impressive 342 species have been recorded in tiny Djibouti. Non-endemic specialities and spectacular species include Arabian Bustard, Crab Plover, White-eyed Gull*, Grey-headed Batis, Botta's Wheatear, White-breasted White-eye, Red-faced Apalis, Arabian Golden-Sparrow, Rueppell's Weaver and Shining Sunbird.

Endemics

Surprisingly for such a small country there is an endemic species, the Djibouti Francolin*, approximately 1,500 of which are thought to remain. Somali Starling is a near-endemic.

DJIBOUTI CITY

Restricted-range species such as Arabian Golden-Sparrow can be seen within easy reach of the country's capital, which lies on the south shore of the Gulf of Tadjoura.

Specialities

White-eyed Gull*, Arabian Golden-Sparrow, Rueppell's Weaver.

Others

Greater Flamingo, Western Reef-Egret, Goliath Heron, Abdim's Stork, Crab Plover, Sooty Gull, Chestnut-bellied Sandgrouse, Laughing and Namaqua Doves, Blue-cheeked Bee-eater, House Crow, White-throated

Robin (passage), Graceful Prinia, Black-crowned Sparrow-Lark, Greater Hoopoe-Lark, Pale Rockfinch.

Access

Bird L'Escale Harbour (White-eyed Gull*), the mudflats and scrub between the airport and the prison (Crab Plover, Arabian Golden-Sparrow), market gardens at Ambouli Wadi (White-throated Robin), west of the city on the Arta road, the Dorale road (Arabian Golden Sparrow), which leads north through acacia scrub to the coast, beyond Ambouli and, if desperate for more, the rubbish dump 11 km west of the city on the road to Arta (Abdim's Stork and Chestnut-bellied Sandgrouse).

The village of **Arta**, 40 km west of the city, lies on a hill surrounded by scrub which, along with the village gardens, supports Rosy-patched Bushshrike and Shining Sunbird. The hill is quite a good vantage point and acts as a convenient raptor migration watchpoint during passage periods. The scrubby wadi 10 km west of Arta, north of the road, supports Nubian Nightjar, Yellow-breasted Barbet, Blackstart and Red-faced Apalis.

Arabian Bustard occurs in the **Dorra** desert region of west Djibouti, along with Chestnut-bellied and Lichtenstein's Sandgrouse, Yellow-breasted Barbet, Black Scrub-Robin, Red-faced Apalis, Red Sea Warbler, Black-crowned Sparrow-Lark and Desert Lark.

Wetlands are few and far between in Dijibouti, but include **Lac Abbe** in the southwest and **Sac Allol** in the northwest, both of which are saline. Kittlitz's and Spur-winged Plovers breed at both of these sites, which are also important refuelling stations for migrant and wintering flamingos, herons and shorebirds.

FÔRET DU DAY NATIONAL PARK

This small park (14 sq km) in the Goda Massif (1783 m (5850 ft)) on the northern side of the Gulf of Tadjoura, supports juniper woodland where the endemic Djibouti Francolin* and near-endemic Somali Starling occur.

A 4WD is recommended to explore this area.

Djibouti Endemics

Djibouti Francolin*.

Specialities

Hemprich's Hornbill, Grey-headed Batis, Somali Starling, Botta's Wheatear, White-breasted White-eye.

Others

Verreaux's and Bonelli's Eagles, African Hawk-Eagle, Bruce's Green Pigeon, African Scops-Owl, Black-throated Barbet, African Paradise-Flycatcher, Tropical Boubou, Violet-backed Starling, Red-billed Oxpecker, Rock Martin, Brown Woodland-Warbler, Shining Sunbird.

Access

The shy and little-known Djibouti Francolin* occurs above 700 m (2297 ft). Good places to look for it are Garrab, Adonta and Hambocka in the Fôret du Day region, and the gardens and wadis at **Dittilou** and **Bankouale**.

Obock, at the northeast corner of the Gulf of Tadjoura, is accessible from Tadjoura (Fan-tailed Raven, Rueppell's Weaver) by track or from Djibouti City by ferry. White-eyed* and Sooty Gulls occur here. East and north of Obock, Crab Plover and Spotted Sandgrouse occur around the Ras Bir Lighthouse, Spotted Sandgrouse around Godoria, and Sooty Falcon has been recorded at **Ras Siyan** hill (140 m (459 ft)), a major raptor migration viewpoint (see below).

The **Bab-el-Mandeb Straits** are an important crossing point for migrants, especially raptors moving between Africa and Arabia in autumn. Nearly 250,000 raptors have been counted moving between the two areas during the autumn, mainly Common Buzzards and Steppe Eagles, but with 24 other species as well. Movements take place along a 30-km coastal stretch and at very low altitude (usually around 60 m). Unfortunately, the two best places to observe this remarkable phenomenon are both remote, windy, and very hot, and it is necessary to take all supplies in a 4WD to **Doumeira** and **Ras Siyan**, which are both situated in far northeast Dijibouti. However, the rewards are eye-level views of birds close enough to hear the wind rushing through their outstretched primaries. Northern Shrike, Black-crowned Sparrow-Lark and Greater Hoopoe-Lark also occur here, and seawatching may turn up Audubon's Shearwater, Red-billed Tropicbird, Brown Booby, Crab Plover (over 5,000 were seen flying south in autumn 1987) and Great Crested-Tern.

ADDITIONAL INFORMATION

Books and Papers

Birding in Djibouti. Welch, G and Welch, H. 1991. *Dutch Birding* 13:161–167.

The Autumn Migration of Raptors and Other Soaring Birds Across the Bab-el-Mandeb Straits. Welch, G and Welch, H. 1988. *Sandgrouse* 10:26–50.

Birds Seen on an Expedition to Djibouti. Welch, G and Welch, H. 1984. *Sandgrouse* 6:1–23.

Catalogue Commente des Oiseaux de Djibouti. Laurent, A. 1990. Djibouti Office Nat. Tourisme.

Addresses

Please send all records to Geoff Welch, Minsmere Reserve, Westleton Saxmundham, Suffolk, IP17 3BY, UK.

ENDEMICS (1)

Djibouti Francolin*	North: Fôret Du Day NP and Mablas

Near-endemics

Somali Starling.

EQUATORIAL GUINEA

Equatorial Guinea includes the island of Fernando Po (also known as Bioko), the island of Annobon (also known as Pagalu) and a small part of the African mainland, known as Mbini or Rio Muni. None are easy to get to. Fernando Po and Annobon both support single endemic species.

The Gulf of Guinea island known as **Fernando Po** (2000 sq km) is rugged and volcanic. It is dominated by Mount Malabo, which rises out of the sea to 3008 m (9867 ft). There are some good roads on this island, where forest remains on the slopes of Mount Malabo and in the southwest lowlands, although much has been lost to coffee, banana and palm plantations. One hundred and eighty-six species have been recorded including White-tailed Tropicbird, Buff-spotted Flufftail, African Finfoot, Great Blue Turaco, Bar-tailed Trogon, Chocolate-backed Kingfisher, Blue-headed Bee-eater, Grey-headed Broadbill, Green-tailed Bristlebill* and Grey-necked Rockfowl* (southwest). The sole endemic, Fernando Po Speirops*, occurs in 'lichen forest' and heathland (above 1900 m (6234 ft)) on Pico de Santa Isabel. Near-endemics include Fernando Po Batis, Black-necked Wattle-eye, Mountain Sawwing*, Green Longtail, Cameroon Scrub-Warbler, White-tailed Warbler, Black-capped Woodland-Warbler, Fernando Po Oliveback and Cameroon and Ursula's* Sunbirds.

The mainland part of Equatorial Guinea is a mixture of coffee plantations and forest, but mostly forest. Over 270 species have been recorded here, including Hartlaub's Duck, Spot-breasted Ibis, Congo Serpent-Eagle, Long-tailed Hawk, Grey Parrot, Yellow-billed and Great Blue Turacos, Maned Owl, Sjostedt's Owlet, Bare-cheeked Trogon, White-bellied and Chocolate-backed Kingfishers, Black, Blue-headed and Rosy Bee-eaters, Blue-throated Roller, White-crested and Black-casqued Hornbills, Zenker's Honeyguide, Grey-headed Broadbill, Black-necked Wattle-eye, Lowland Akalat, Rufous-tailed Palm-Thrush, Yellow-footed and Tessman's Flycatchers, Yellow-necked Greenbul, Grey-necked Rockfowl* and Red-crowned Malimbe. Mount Alen NP is probably the best birding area.

The remote island of **Annobon** (17 sq km), south of São Tomé, supports the endemic Annobon White-eye*, as well as São Tomé Pigeon, which also occurs on São Tomé and Principe, White-tailed Tropicbird and Brown and Black Noddies.

ENDEMICS (2)

Fernando Po Speirops*	Fernando Po: Pico de Santa Isabel
Annobon White-eye*	Annobon: throughout

Near-endemics (occur also in Cameroon and Nigeria)

Fernando Po Batis, Mountain Sawwing*, Green Longtail, Cameroon Scrub-Warbler, White-tailed Warbler, Black-capped Woodland-Warbler, Fernando Po Oliveback, Cameroon and Ursula's* Sunbirds.

EGYPT

INTRODUCTION

Summary

Egypt is a popular destination for birders interested in adding a few species, which are more African than European, to their Western Palearctic lists. However, it is also a good country in which to see many of the Red Sea specialities. Together with the amazing archaeology, a birding trip to Egypt can be a rewarding experience, but be prepared for a certain amount of hassle.

Size

At 1,001,449 sq km, Egypt is nearly eight times larger than England, and 1.5 times the size of Texas.

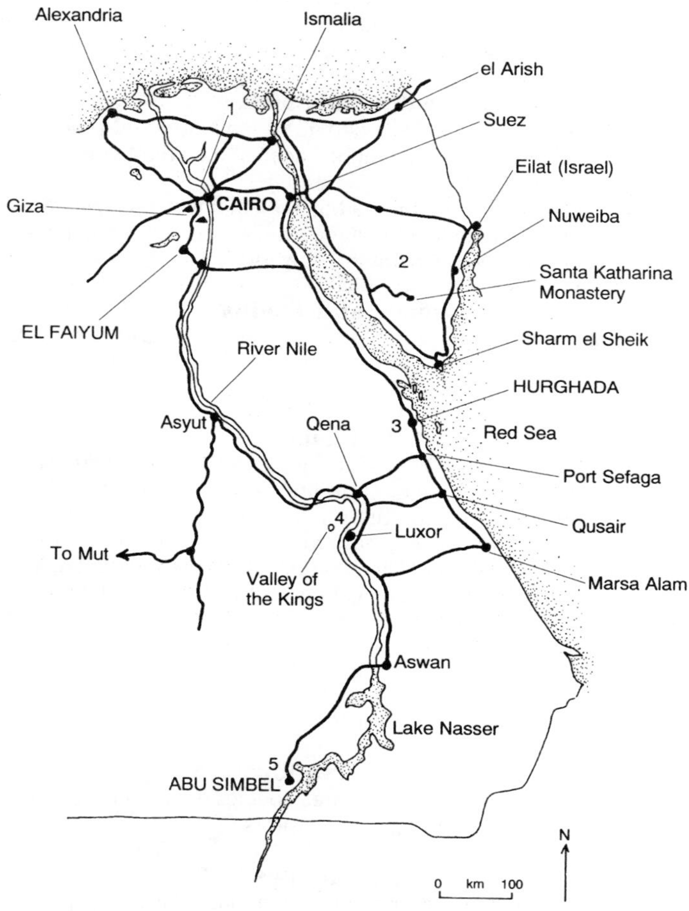

1 Cairo
2 Sinai
3 Hurghada
4 Luxor
5 Abu Simbel

Getting Around

The bus, mini-bus, taxi and train networks are cheap and relatively efficient, although timetables are not rigid and the trains are often overcrowded. It is wise to reserve seats on air-conditioned buses and in the first-class train compartments in advance. Although a little more expensive, cars with drivers are also an excellent, cheap way to see the Egyptian archaeology and avifauna. Boat cruises along the Nile are much more expensive and not the best way to see the birds, especially the sought after species. There is also a good internal air network.

Accommodation and Food

The whole range of accommodation exists virtually everywhere. Beans, kebabs and houmous dominate the out-of-town menus.

Health and Safety

Immunisation against hepatitis, polio, rabies, typhoid and yellow fever are recommended, as are precautions against malaria if you intend to visit the Nile Delta.

Off the beaten track, and this is a big track in Egypt, the Egyptians are honest and friendly people, but where tourists are abundant, there are plenty of people ready to exploit the unwary.

Climate and Timing

Egypt is hot and dry throughout the year. The best times to visit are April to May and September to October, when it is slightly cooler and migrant species are moving through.

Habitats

Over 95% of the 53 million Egyptians live alongside the 1000-km River Nile. The great river is the country's lifeline and its heavily cultivated hinterland forms a lush green ribbon in the stark brown desert, which runs north–south through the eastern half of the country, down to Aswan. North of Cairo, the Nile fans out to form a huge delta. To the west of the Nile there is a huge expanse of remote desert with a few oases. To the east is a narrower strip of desert, coastal hills and a coastal plain alongside the Red Sea, which is dotted with numerous coral islands. The barren Sinai Peninsula, adjacent to Israel and the wider Middle East, lies at the northern end of the Red Sea, and is separated from the rest of the country by the Suez Canal.

Conservation

Ten threatened and six near-threatened species occur in Egypt, most of which are non-breeding and passage visitors.

Bird Families

Only one of the ten families endemic to mainland Africa is represented in Egypt: Ostrich is occasionally reported from the extreme southeast, an area normally out of bounds to visiting birders.

Bird Species

A total of 421 species have been recorded in Egypt, 40 fewer than Morocco. Non-endemic specialities and spectacular species include Sooty Falcon, Sand Partridge, Greater Painted-snipe, Senegal Thick-knee, Cream-coloured Courser, White-tailed Lapwing, Sooty Gull, White-cheeked Tern, Pharaoh Eagle-Owl, Egyptian Nightjar, White-throated Kingfisher, Hooded Wheatear and Pale Rosefinch.

Endemics

There are no endemics, but a good selection of Red Sea specialities, such as White-eyed Gull* and Nile Valley Sunbird, are present.

Expectations

It is possible to see 100 to 130 species on a two- or three-week trip.

CAIRO

Egypt's frenetic capital, in the northeast corner of the country, lies close to some excellent birding sites. Pharaoh Eagle-Owl and Nile Valley Sunbird may be seen close to the city itself, whereas other species such as Egyptian Nightjar occur a little further afield.

Specialities

Pharaoh Eagle-Owl, Nile Valley Sunbird (Nov–Feb).

Others

Greater Painted-snipe, Senegal Thick-knee, Cream-coloured Courser, Kittlitz's Plover, Laughing Dove, Senegal Coucal, Egyptian Nightjar, Pallid Swift, White-throated Kingfisher, Green and Blue-cheeked (May–Sep) Bee-eaters, Brown-necked Raven, Mourning (May–Sep), Red-tailed (Nov–Mar) and Isabelline Wheatears, Graceful Prinia, Greater Hoopoe-Lark. (Streaked Weaver and Red Avadavat also occur here, but they have been introduced).

Access

Nile Valley Sunbird occurs sparingly between November and February within this heavily polluted city. Good places to look for it are the grounds of the Gezira Sports Club and Cairo Zoo. Green Bee-eater also occurs at these sites.

It is worth visiting the **Giza Pyramids**, a few km west of Cairo, the Sphinx, the Sakkarah (Saqqara) Pyramid, and Cairo Museum where the Tutankhamen exhibition is housed. Pharaoh Eagle-Owl occurs on the Step Pyramid at Sakkarah, along with Laughing Dove, Pallid Swift, Green Bee-eater, Brown-necked Raven, Mourning, Red-tailed and Isabelline Wheatears and Greater Hoopoe-Lark. Egyptian Nightjar has been recorded 1 km and beyond, northwest of Abu Sir pyramids, along with Cream-coloured Courser.

Gabel Asfar, on the city outskirts near the international airport, may still support Greater Painted-snipe, Senegal Thick-knee, Kittlitz's Plover, Senegal Coucal, White-throated Kingfisher, Green and Blue-cheeked Bee-eaters and Graceful Prinia, despite the fact that the sewage pools here were destroyed in 1994–95. Head east past the airport on the road to Ismalia. Two and a half km beyond the airport take the road north, signposted to 'El Khanka-Bilbeis Road' (this may involve a 'U' turn a little further ahead on the main Cairo–Ismalia road). Follow the El Khanka road for 5.5 km past the sand dunes to the first fork. Take the left fork here, signposted to 'Abu Zebal–El Khanka Road', and the next left fork to the police station. At the police station either: (1) Continue straight on to the canal and bird the track to the right which runs alongside the eastern side of the canal, a good area for White-throated Kingfisher; or (2) Turn left and then take the second track to the left. Two and a half km along here on the left there used to be some pools.

Accommodation: Cairo: Fontanna Hotel (C)(rooftop pool).

Saline pools at **Wadi Natrun**, northwest of Cairo, approximately halfway between Cairo and Alexandria, support Kittlitz's Plover and, in summer, Blue-cheeked Bee-eater. The pools are 1–2 km south of the main road and visible from surrounding tracks.

GABEL ASFAR

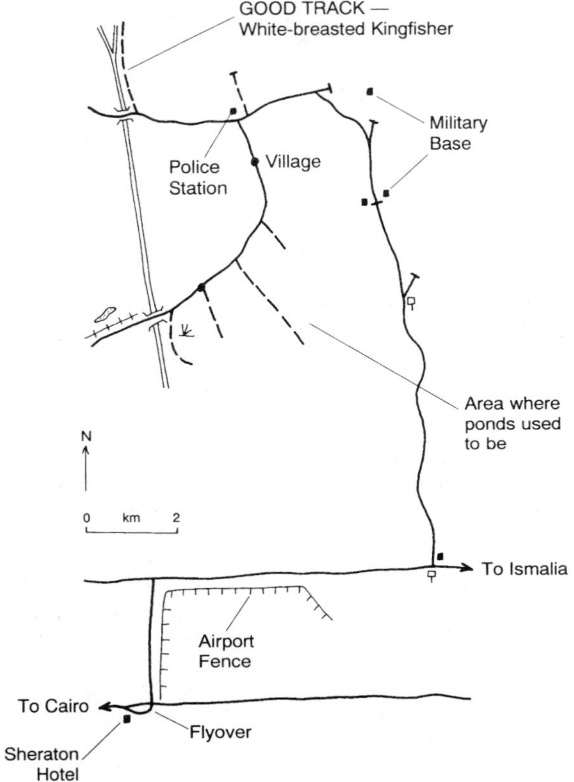

Little Crake (spring), Senegal Thick-knee (breeding on rooftops), Spur-winged Plover, Great Black-headed and Slender-billed Gulls, Laughing Dove, Senegal Coucal, European (autumn) and Green Bee-eaters, Graceful Prinia, and Clamorous Reed-Warbler, occur at the huge oasis of **el Faiyum**,110 km southwest of Cairo. During the autumn many shorebirds are attracted to Lake Qarun, which lies at the northern end of the oasis, and these sometimes include White-tailed Lapwing. The area around Ducks Island Hotel has been the most productive in the past.

Raptor passage near **Suez**, a town at the southern end of the Suez Canal, 135 km east of Cairo, can be spectacular, especially in autumn, and species may include Levant Sparrowhawk, Long-legged Buzzard, Lesser Spotted, Greater Spotted* and Imperial* Eagles and Eleonora's Falcon. The best place to look for raptors is from the cafe just south of the Ain Sukhna Hotel, a few km south of Suez. View the ridge opposite. To the north of Suez try the road which goes past the army camp. White-eyed Gull* and House Crow occur in Suez itself.

SINAI

This barren triangular extension of Egypt, at the northern end of the Red Sea, supports some excellent species, notably Pale Rosefinch.

Specialities

Sooty Falcon, Sand Partridge, White-eyed Gull*, Hume's Owl, Fan-tailed Raven, Tristram's Starling, Hooded Wheatear, Blackstart, Dunn's Lark, Palestine Sunbird, Desert Finch, Pale Rosefinch.

Others

Western Reef-Egret, Striated Heron, Chukar, Sooty Gull, Bridled Tern, Crowned and Lichtenstein's Sandgrouse, Namaqua Dove, Green Bee-eater, Brown-necked Raven, Masked Shrike (spring), Bluethroat (spring), White-tailed and Mourning Wheatears, Pale Crag-Martin, White-spectacled Bulbul, Streaked Scrub-Warbler, Rueppell's Warbler (spring), Bar-tailed and Desert Larks, Greater Hoopoe-Lark, Lesser Short-toed Lark, Trumpeter Finch, House Bunting.

Access

Hooded and Mourning Wheatears, Blackstart and Streaked Scrub-Warbler occur around 'The Springs of Moses', a small oasis *en route* from Suez to Santa Katharina, which is also good for migrants. Pale Rosefinch occurs around the **Santa Katharina Monastery**, 450 km from Cairo (315 km south of Suez), along with Tristram's Starling, whilst the monastery gardens are good for migrants. Pale Rosefinch is frequently recorded at the roadside near the barrier on the way up to the monastery, but Hume's Owl is rare in the chasms to the right of the road before the barrier. Namaqua Dove, Fan-tailed Raven, Blackstart and Palestine Sunbird occur around **Nuweiba** on the Gulf of Aqaba in east Sinai. The elegant Sooty Falcon occurs at the southern tip of Sinai, around **Sharm el Sheik**. The falcons breed on offshore islets but visit the Sewage Works pools on the mainland to hunt migrating birds, usually towards dusk. Crowned and Lichtenstein's Sandgrouse are also possible here. Head north out of town and turn east on to track just north of electricity pylons towards the sea. The snorkelling off Sharm el Sheik/Ras Muhammad is some of the best in the world.

The **Zaranik Protected Area**, a beach at the eastern edge of Lake Bardawil, on the north coast of Sinai is a good place for autumn migrants (mid August to early October). Dunn's Lark and Desert Finch have recently been recorded in northern Sinai, south of el Arish.

Accommodation: Santa Katharina. Nuweiba. Sharm el Sheik.

The **Sharm el Sheik-Hurghada Ferry** trip (4–6 hours) offers the chance to see Red-billed Tropicbird (rare) and Bridled Tern, both of which breed on the coral islands at the mouth of the Gulf of Suez.

HURGHADA

Situated on Egypt's Red Sea coast opposite the tip of Sinai and close to offshore coral islets, this booming resort area is best visited in spring or autumn. In September summering Sooty Falcons and White-cheeked Terns are still present, and northern migrants are moving through on their way south.

Specialities

White-eyed Gull*, White-cheeked Tern (May–Sep).

Others

Brown Booby, Western Reef-Egret, Sooty (May–Sep) and Barbary Falcons, Sooty, Great Black-headed (spring) and Slender-billed (winter) Gulls, Great Crested-Tern, Bridled Tern (Jun–Sep), Crowned Sandgrouse, Brown-necked Raven, Masked Shrike (spring), Thrush Nightingale, Bluethroat (spring), Cretzschmar's Bunting (spring).

Access

The sprinkling of town and hotel/tourist village gardens act as powerful migrant magnets in the spring and autumn, and scouring these tiny oases for birds during May or September can produce some great birding. Sooty Falcon is often recorded over Hurghada town towards dusk, and a good vantage point from which to look for these birds, with a beer to hand if required, is the Arabia Hotel pier. It is possible to take boat trips (B) from the Marine Sports Club, or to arrange special charters into the Red Sea, where birding and snorkelling can be excellent. Red-billed Tropicbird is seen on the odd occasion from Hurghada.

Accommodation: A wide selection of hotels (cheapest in town) and a Youth Hostel (near Gifton Tourist Village).

Sand Partridge, Cream-coloured Courser, Spotted and Crowned Sandgrouse, Brown-necked Raven, Hooded Wheatear, Bar-tailed and Desert Larks and Trumpeter Finch all occur in the Eastern Desert, which is traversed by the Hurghada–Qena–Luxor road, via Port Sefaga or Qusair. Crowned Sandgrouse visit waterholes at Bir Beida, 10 km west of Qusair, to drink and bathe at dawn.

Hurghada is a good site to catch up with the striking White-eyed Gull, a species whose range is centred on the Red Sea*

Goliath Heron, Sooty Falcon and Crab Plover have been recorded in the mangrove-lined lagoons south of Marsa Alam *en route* to Berenice in southeast Egypt. Try walking east 108 km south of Marsa Alam.

LUXOR

Famed for some of Egypt's most impressive archaeological sites, including the Valley of the Kings and the Colossi of Memnon, Luxor in east/central Egypt is also a good birding area, with possible species including White-tailed Lapwing and Nile Valley Sunbird.

Specialities

White-tailed Lapwing, Hooded Wheatear, Nile Valley Sunbird.

Others

Purple Swamphen, Senegal Thick-knee, Spur-winged Plover, Green Bee-eater, White-tailed and Mourning Wheatears, Pale Crag-Martin, Moustached Warbler, Clamorous Reed-Warbler, Trumpeter Finch.

Access

The west bank of the Nile, between the main hotel area and the temples, is good for common species. White-tailed Lapwing and Nile Valley Sunbird (hotel grounds) occur on Crocodile Island, 4km south (upriver) of Luxor. The Valley of the Kings is a good place to see Hooded Wheatear and Trumpeter Finch, so long as you are there before the crowds.

Accommodation: Mina Palace Hotel (C).

Nile Valley Sunbird also occurs in the parks and gardens of **Aswan**, near the Aswan Dams (White-tailed Wheatear and Pale Crag-Martin), at the northern end of Lake Nasser, and around the Temple of Philae. It is possible to hire a boat (felucca) here to explore Elephantine (where the roof of the Oberoi Hotel is a good spot for Barbary Falcon) and Kitchener Islands where 'waterbirds' abound.

Lappet-faced Vulture, Cream-coloured Courser, Spotted and Crowned Sandgrouse, and Greater Hoopoe-Lark occur alongside (or on) the road south from Aswan to Abu Simbel.

ABU SIMBEL

Situated in far south Egypt near the border with Sudan on the western shores of Lake Nasser, the Abu Simbel area attracts a number of species which are rare this far north, including Long-tailed Cormorant, Pink-backed Pelican, Goliath Heron, Yellow-billed Stork, African Skimmer, African Collared-Dove and African Pied Wagtail. These birds, in turn, attract Western Palearctic listers in search of species virtually impossible to see elsewhere within this particular zoogeographical zone.

Specialities

Sooty Falcon, Pharaoh Eagle-Owl, Cyprus Wheatear (Nov–Mar).

Others

Long-tailed Cormorant, Pink-backed Pelican, Goliath Heron, Yellow-billed Stork, Pallid Harrier, Senegal Thick-knee, Kittlitz's and Spur-winged Plovers, African Skimmer, Spotted Sandgrouse, African Collared-Dove, Blue-cheeked Bee-eater, Brown-necked Raven, White-tailed and Isabelline Wheatears, Pale Crag-Martin, Graceful Prinia, African Pied Wagtail.

Other Wildlife

Horned viper, Nile crocodile.

Access

Most of the interesting species here occur on Lake Nasser. The best part of this lake seems to be north of the temple (it is possible to hire a felucca in the village to explore the lake itself),just north of the airport. Take the 4-km track from the airport fence to the lake. The nearby farmland is good for migrants, as are the grounds of the Nefatari Hotel. White-tailed Wheatear and Pale Crag-Martin occur around the two famous temples of Ramses II. Beware of horned vipers.

Accommodation: Nefatari Hotel (B).

ADDITIONAL INFORMATION

Books and Papers

Birds of the Middle East and North Africa. Hollom, P *et al.* 1988. Poyser.
Birds of Egypt. Goodman, S and Meininger, P (eds). 1989. Oxford University Press.

Addresses

Please send all records to Sherif Baha el Din, 4 Ismail El Mazni Street, Apt. 8, Heliopolis, Cairo.

Black Skimmers appear with some regularity at Abu Simbel, at the north of their range and within the Western Palearctic

ETHIOPIA (AND ERITREA)

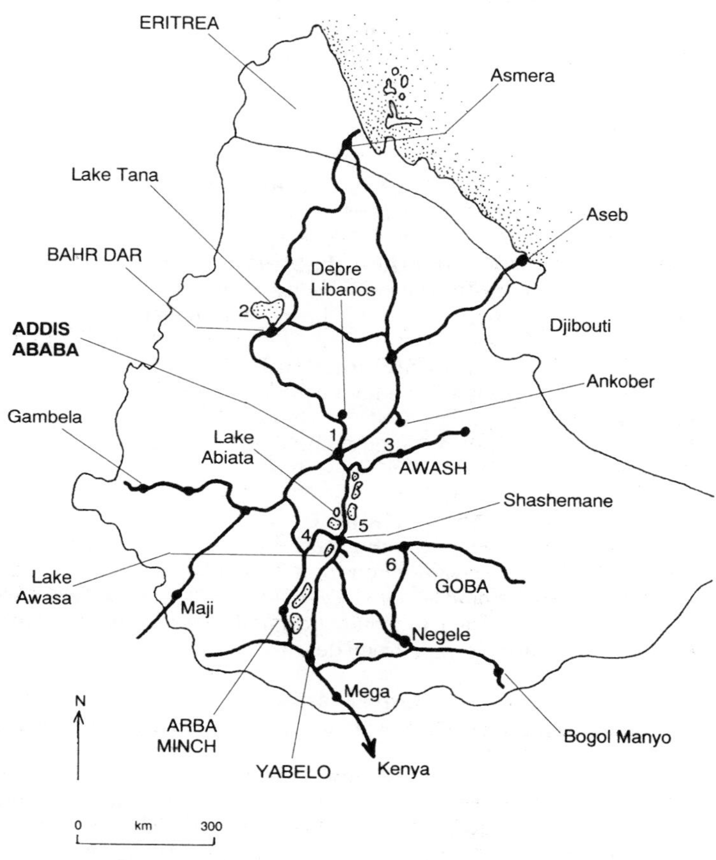

1 Addis Ababa
2 Lake Tana
3 Awash NP
4 Eithiopia's Great Rift Valley
5 Wondo Genet
6 Bale Mountains NP
7 Negele–Yabelo Area

INTRODUCTION

Summary

Ethiopia is not the famine-stricken and war-torn country most people imagine. On the contrary, it is, on the whole, stable and friendly, with a good infrastructure. Although it holds fewer species than Kenya, there are 30 endemics, 20 of which are fairly easy to see, fewer tourists and, owing to the absence of dangerous animals, it is possible to bird on foot in many places.

Size

At 1,023,500 sq km, Ethiopia is nearly ten times larger than England, and nearly twice the size of Texas.

Getting Around

Many of the roads are in poor condition and getting around without a 4WD can be very time consuming. There are extensive internal flight and bus networks but tourists are not allowed on the Addis Ababa–Djibouti train.

Accommodation and Food

A variety of food is available in most places, including pasta.

Health and Safety

Immunisation against hepatitis, meningitis, polio, typhoid and yellow fever is recommended, as are precautions against malaria.

Climate and Timing

Owing to the dominance of the high central plateau, Ethiopia is more temperate than tropical despite its proximity to the equator. The main rains usually fall in July and August, and November to February is the best time to visit.

Habitats

Part of the Great Rift Valley, with its large freshwater and saline lakes surrounded by acacia savanna, runs north to south through the central highlands. These highlands rise to 4620 m (15,015 ft) and support montane forest, juniper woodland and grassland. East of the highlands much of the country is remote semi-desert.

Conservation

Nineteen threatened and five near-threatened species occur in Ethiopia.

Bird Families

Eight of the ten families endemic to the African mainland are represented in Ethiopia. Only rockfowl and sugarbirds are absent. Well represented families include falcons, francolins, bustards and larks.

Bird Species

Ethiopia has one of the top ten lists in Africa. A total of 836 species have been recorded, 240 fewer than Kenya. Non-endemic specialities and spectacular species include Arabian Bustard, Black-winged Lapwing, Yellow-throated Sandgrouse, Blue-breasted Bee-eater and Abyssinian Roller.

Endemics

Ethiopia boasts the second highest number of endemic species for a mainland African country (two less than South Africa). The 30 species which occur only here include such wonderful birds as the bold Rouget's Rail*, Spot-breasted Lapwing, Prince Ruspoli's Turaco*, the unique Stresemann's Bush-Crow* and Abyssinian Catbird. There are also plenty of near-endemics, which are mainly shared with Somalia and Kenya, and they include Heuglin's Bustard and White-cheeked Turaco.

Expectations

It is possible to see 350 to 400 species in two to three weeks, including over 20 endemics.

ADDIS ABABA

Ethiopia's capital lies at 2440 m (8005 ft) in the central highlands west of the Great Rift Valley, and is the gateway to all the sites. Within and around the city it is possible to see at least eight endemics and plenty of other good birds.

Ethiopia Endemics

Blue-winged Goose, Wattled Ibis, Rouget's Rail*, White-collared Pigeon, Thick-billed Raven, Abyssinian Slaty-Flycatcher, Abyssinian Longclaw*, Abyssinian Siskin.

Specialities

Erckel's Francolin, Black-winged Lapwing, Botta's Wheatear, White-breasted White-eye, Swainson's Sparrow, Brown-rumped Seedeater.

Others

Black Goshawk, Dusky Turtle-Dove, Speckled Mousebird, Nyanza Swift, Blue-breasted Bee-eater, Groundscraper Thrush, Moorland Chat, Yellow-spotted Petronia, Yellow-bellied Waxbill, Baglafecht Weaver, Yellow Bishop, Tacazze Sunbird, Streaky Seedeater.

Access

Good birding sites within the city include the grounds of the Ghion Hotel (Wattled Ibis, Blue-breasted Bee-eater) and the British Embassy, but it is probably best to head straight for **Gefersa Reservoir**, 30 km away. The reservoir and its environs support Blue-winged Goose, Wattled Ibis, Rouget's Rail*, Abyssinian Longclaw* and Abyssinian Siskin, as well as Erckel's Francolin, Botta's Wheatear and Swainson's Sparrow. The area around the airport, to the southeast of the city, is also good (Wattled Ibis, Rouget's Rail*, Abyssinian Longclaw*), but birding here is not really safe.

Accommodation: Ghion Hotel (A) (good birding).

The heavily grazed, seasonally wet highland grasslands of the **Sululta Plains**, 31 km north of Addis Ababa, support most of those species present at Gefersa Reservoir, as well as Black-winged Lapwing.

Sixty km north of Addis Ababa, the arid Blue Nile gorges of **Debre Libanos** support seven endemics: Black-winged Lovebird, Banded Barbet, Dark-headed Oriole, White-billed Starling, Rueppell's Chat, White-winged Cliff-Chat and White-backed Black-Tit, as well as Lammergeier, Verreaux's Eagle, the localized Erckel's Francolin, White-cheeked Turaco and Little Rock-Thrush. Bird the area around the monastery and along the roadside by the edge of the gorge. The handsome endemic Gelada baboon also occurs here.

LAKE TANA

This huge (350 sq km) papyrus-fringed freshwater lake in northwest Ethiopia is the largest high-altitude lake in Africa. A few endemics occur here, but the real attraction is the waterbirds.

Ethiopia Endemics

White-collared Pigeon, Yellow-fronted Parrot, Black-winged Lovebird, Abyssinian Woodpecker, Dark-headed Oriole.

Specialities

White-cheeked Turaco, Botta's Wheatear, White-breasted White-eye.

Others

African Darter, African Pygmy-goose, Goliath Heron, Hamerkop, African Openbill, Abdim's Stork, Black Crowned-Crane, Black Crake, Senegal Thick-knee, Three-banded Plover, Great Black-headed Gull (Dec–Mar), Lemon Dove, Bruce's Green-Pigeon, Eastern Grey Plantain-eater, Half-collared Kingfisher, Blue-breasted and Northern Carmine Bee-eaters, Silvery-cheeked Hornbill, Abyssinian Ground-Hornbill, Yellow-fronted Tinkerbird, Black-billed and Double-toothed Barbets, Brown-backed Woodpecker, Grey-backed Fiscal, Red-winged and Slender-billed Starlings, Lesser Blue-eared Glossy-Starling, Red-billed Oxpecker, Rueppell's Robin-Chat, Lesser Swamp-Warbler, Bush Petronia, Eastern Paradise-Whydah, Black-headed Weaver, Yellow-crowned and Black-winged Bishops, Yellow-shouldered Widowbird.

Other Wildlife

Hippo.

Access

Bahr Dar, on the southern shores of Lake Tana, is accessible by air from Addis Ababa. Bird the grounds of Lake Tana and Ghion Hotels (White-cheeked Turaco, Abyssinian Woodpecker), and along the lake shore. It is also possible to take a boat trip (one hour each way) to the monasteries on Ura Kidane Mihert and Kebrane Gabriel Islands (African Pygmy-goose). The **Tississat Falls** (70 m (230 ft)), 35 km south of Bahr Dar, are also worth birding. The falls are a 45-minute walk from the village. They help form a luxuriant subtropical forest oasis in the midst of arid gorges, which supports Yellow-fronted Parrot, White-cheeked Turaco and Blue-breasted Bee-eater.

Accommodation: Lake Tana Hotel (A); Ghion Hotel (A)/Camping (C).

Northeast of Addis Ababa, near the old village of **Ankober**, perched on top of the Ankober escarpment, it is possible to see the very localised endemic Ankober Serin*, which was only described in 1976. Search the terraced, rocky hillsides 3 km west of Ankober, alongside the Debre Berhan–Ankober road. This species also occurs at Gosh Meda, north of Debre Berhan.

South of Addis Ababa there is a crater lake near **Debre Zeit**, which supports African Darter, Maccoa Duck, Hottentot Teal, and Southern Pochard, whilst Bruce's Green-Pigeon, Little Rock-Thrush, the endemic

White-winged Cliff-Chat, Grosbeak Weaver and Mariqua Sunbird occur on the surrounding slopes.

AWASH NATIONAL PARK

This park, four hours drive east of Addis Ababa, lies in the rolling acacia savanna of the Great Rift Valley. Over 400 species have been recorded including Arabian Bustard, Grey-headed Batis, Somali Starling and Rueppell's Weaver. One major attraction of Awash NP is the chance to bird on foot in the African bush.

Specialities

Arabian Bustard, Three-banded Courser, Somali Fiscal, Grey-headed Batis, Somali Starling, Sombre Chat, Gillett's Lark, Mouse-coloured Penduline-Tit, Rueppell's Weaver, Shining Sunbird.

Others

Ostrich, Scissor-tailed Kite, Brown Snake-Eagle, Bateleur, Gabar Goshawk, Martial Eagle, Secretary-bird, Pygmy and Sooty (Dec–Apr) Falcons, Crested Francolin, Kori, Buff-crested, White-bellied and Hartlaub's Bustards, Three-banded Plover, Black-headed and Crowned Lapwings, Chestnut-bellied and Lichtenstein's Sandgrouse, Bruce's Green-Pigeon, Orange-bellied Parrot, Blue-naped Mousebird, White-bellied Go-away-bird, Eastern Grey Plantain-eater, Donaldson-Smith's, Slender-tailed and Standard-winged Nightjars, Little, Madagascar and Northern Carmine Bee-eaters, Abyssinian and Lilac-breasted Rollers, Black-billed Woodhoopoe, Abyssinian Ground-Hornbill, Red-fronted Tinkerbird, Black-billed and Yellow-breasted Barbets, White-rumped Shrike, Rosy-patched Bushshrike, White Helmetshrike, Rueppell's Glossy-Starling, Superb Starling, Red-billed Oxpecker, Brown-tailed Chat, Blackstart, Ethiopian Swallow, Ashy Cisticola, Grey Wren-Warbler, Buff-bellied Warbler, Yellow-bellied Eremomela, Rufous Chatterer, Red-winged and Fawn-coloured Larks, Chestnut-backed Sparrow-Lark, Purple Grenadier, Crimson-rumped Waxbill, Cut-throat, Southern Yellow-rumped Seedeater, Somali Bunting.

(Unidentified 'cliff swallows' seen in Awash NP in 1988 and 1993 could have been Red Sea Swallows*, South African Swallow, or a new species.)

Other Wildlife

Beisa Oryx, greater kudu, hartebeest, lesser kudu, Salt's dikdik, Soemmering's gazelle.

Access

This national park is some 200 km east of Addis Ababa. Bird Awash River Falls, where it is possible to walk upstream through the excellent fig-filled gallery forest, and the hot springs surrounded by palms at Filoha, 42 km from Kereyo. A park guard (armed) is essential if visiting the Filoha area.

Accommodation: Kereyo Lodge (caravans) (B/C); camping (C).

ETHIOPIA'S GREAT RIFT VALLEY

South of Debre Zeit, a long line of large lakes surrounded by acacia savanna support a fine selection of birds, including Yellow-throated Sandgrouse, Shelley's Starling, the endemic Brown Sawwing, Swainson's Sparrow, and Salvadori's Weaver.

Ethiopia Endemics

Black-winged Lovebird, Banded Barbet, Brown Sawwing.

Specialities

Black-winged Lapwing, Yellow-throated Sandgrouse, Grey-headed Batis, Abyssinian Ground-Thrush, Shelley's Starling, White-rumped Babbler, Somali and Swainson's Sparrows, Salvadori's Weaver.

Others

African Darter, White-backed and Maccoa Ducks, African Pygmy-goose, Hottentot Teal, Southern Pochard, Greater and Lesser* Flamingos, Black and Goliath Herons, Hamerkop, Saddle-billed Stork, Gabar Goshawk, Pygmy Falcon, Grey Kestrel, Lanner Falcon, Scaly and Clapperton's Francolins, Black Crake, Common Crane, Black Crowned-Crane, African Snipe, Senegal and Spotted Thick-knees, Temminck's Courser, Chestnut-bellied Sandgrouse, Bruce's Green-Pigeon, Orange-bellied Parrot, Blue-naped Mousebird, Bare-faced and White-bellied Go-away-birds, Blue-headed Coucal, Mottled Swift, Woodland Kingfisher, Little, Blue-breasted and Northern Carmine Bee-eaters, Abyssinian and Lilac-breasted Rollers, Black Scimitar-bill, Von der Decken's and Hemprich's Hornbills, Abyssinian Ground-Hornbill, Red-fronted, Black-billed and Double-toothed Barbets, Rufous-necked Wryneck, Black Cuckoo-shrike, Grey-backed Fiscal, Masked (Nov–Mar) and White-rumped Shrikes, Slate-coloured Boubou, Rueppell's Glossy-Starling, Superb Starling, Red-billed Oxpecker, White-browed and Red-capped Robin-Chats, Schalow's Wheatear, Spotted Creeper, Banded Martin, Rattling and Stout Cisticolas, Buff-bellied Warbler, Crimson-rumped and Black-cheeked Waxbills, Little and Red-headed Weavers, Kenya Violet-backed, Pygmy and Beautiful Sunbirds.

(Unidentified 'cliff swallows' have been recorded at Lake Langano in recent years).

Each lake supports a slightly different selection of species, according to its salinity, but Lakes Abiata and Awasa boast the greatest variety. At **Lake Koka** bird from the causeway across northwestern end. Black Scimitar-bill occurs around **Lake Zwai** and Blue-breasted Bee-eater, Banded Barbet, Grey-headed Batis and Abyssinian Ground-Thrush around **Lake Langano** (40 km north of Shashemane), which is bordered by a steep escarpment worth exploring on one side. **Wondo Genet** is near here (see below). Both flamingos (in high numbers), Clapperton's Francolin, Yellow-throated Sandgrouse, Black-winged Lapwing, Von der Decken's Hornbill and Red-fronted Barbet occur on and around **Lake Abiata NP**, a saline lake surrounded by some dry grassland, Senegal Thick-knee occurs at **Lake Shala**, a deep, fishless lake, and White-backed Duck, African Pygmy-goose, Saddle-billed Stork, Black Crowned-Crane, White-rumped Babbler and Spotted Creeper occur on and around freshwater **Lake Awasa**. The nearby **Black River**

Forest supports Red-capped Robin-Chat. South towards Arba Minch, coffee plantations give way to arid scrubland then a forested escarpment, overlooking **Lakes Abaya** and **Chamo**, where Shelley's Starling occurs. Spotted Thick-knee, Somali Sparrow, Black-cheeked Waxbill and Kenya Violet-backed Sunbird occur around Lake Abaya, and Salvadori's Weaver around the shallow, papyrus-fringed Lake Chamo. Lammergeier has been recorded rarely on the **Arba Minch** escarpment.

Accommodation: Lake Langano. Lake Awassa.

WONDO GENET

This forested hill-resort (1900 m (6234 ft)) near Shashemane on the eastern slopes of the Great Rift Valley supports a fine selection of endemics, including Yellow-fronted Parrot, Abyssinian Slaty-Flycatcher and Brown Sawwing.

Ethiopia Endemics

Wattled Ibis, Yellow-fronted Parrot, Black-winged Lovebird, Banded Barbet, Abyssinian Woodpecker, Thick-billed Raven, Dark-headed Oriole, Abyssinian Slaty-Flycatcher, White-winged Cliff-Chat, Brown Sawwing.

Specialities

White-cheeked Turaco, Abyssinian Ground-Thrush, White-breasted White-eye, White-rumped Babbler, Brown-rumped Seedeater.

Others

African Black-Duck, Ayres' Hawk-Eagle, Crowned Hawk-Eagle, Lemon Dove, Blue-headed Coucal, Half-collared Kingfisher, Crowned, Hemprich's and Silvery-cheeked Hornbills, Double-toothed Barbet, Cassin's Honeyguide, Rueppell's Robin-Chat, Spotted Creeper, Abyssinian Hill-Babbler, Green-backed Twinspot, Abyssinian Crimson-wing, Yellow-bellied Waxbill, Black-and-white Mannikin, Mountain Wagtail, Grosbeak Weaver, Tacazze Sunbird.

Other Wildlife

Eastern Black-and-white Colobus.

Access

Turn east on to a track immediately south of Shashemane. Wondo Genet is 17 km along here, past the Forestry College. Bird around the Wabe Shebelle Hotel and the hot springs (100 m away).

Accommodation: Wondo Genet; Wabe Shebelle Hotel (B)/camping (with permission) in grounds.

BALE MOUNTAINS NATIONAL PARK

The often grey, cold and wet Bale Mountains NP (22,000 sq km) lies east of the Great Rift Valley, between Adaba and Goba. The juniper and

Hagenia woodland on the western slopes, high-altitude heathland and eastern foothill forest within this NP support a wide selection of Ethiopia's endemic species. The star attraction of the Bale Mountains is the endemic shorebird, Spot-breasted Lapwing, but the endemics, White-billed Starling and Abyssinian Catbird, are also present. Moorland Francolin, Wattled Crane* and Black-winged Lapwing complete the impressive avifauna.

Ethiopia Endemics

Blue-winged Goose, Wattled Ibis, Rouget's Rail*, Spot-breasted Lapwing, Black-winged Lovebird, Abyssinian Woodpecker, Thick-billed Raven, White-billed Starling, Abyssinian Catbird, White-backed Black-Tit, Abyssinian Longclaw*, Abyssinian Siskin.

Specialities

Moorland and Chestnut-naped Francolins, Wattled Crane*, Black-winged Lapwing, White-cheeked Turaco, Abyssinian Owl, Abyssinian Ground-Thrush, Botta's Wheatear.

Others

Ruddy Shelduck, African Black-Duck, Lammergeier, Rufous-chested Sparrowhawk, Mountain Buzzard, Ayres' Hawk-Eagle, Verreaux's Eagle, African Snipe, Montane Nightjar, Groundscraper Thrush, Slender-billed Starling, Moorland Chat, Grey-rumped Swallow, Cinnamon Bracken-Warbler, Brown Woodland-Warbler, Yellow Bishop, Tacazze and Malachite Sunbirds, Streaky Seedeater.

Other Wildlife

Abyssinian hare, Grimm's duiker, klipspringer, Menelik's bushbuck, mountain nyala, olive baboon, simien jackal.

Access

Take the track east immediately north of Shashemane towards Goba. This track climbs through open grassland then juniper woodland to marshy heathland, a day's trip with birding stops. Dinsho is some 170 km from Shashemane. Here, the *Hagenia* and juniper woodland sup-

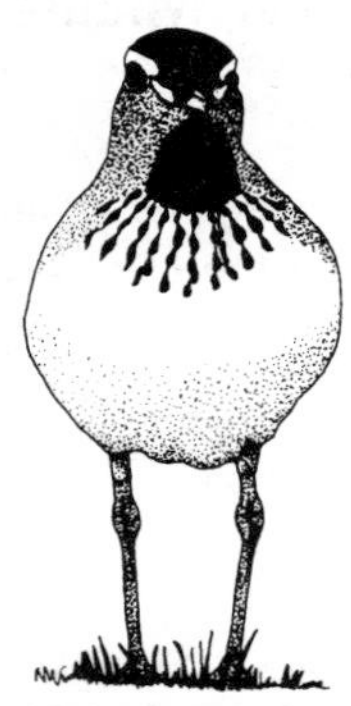

The superb Spot-breasted Lapwing, an Ethiopian endemic, is usually fairly easy to find in Bale Mountains NP

The unique Stresemann's Bush-Crow occurs only in southern Ethiopia, where it is highly localised but quite common, especially around Yabelo*

ports Abyssinian Catbird, Abyssinian Ground-Thrush and White-backed Black-Tit. There is also a 15-km trail to a waterfall, which passes through heathland where Moorland Francolin and Rouget's Rail* occur. From Dinsho head east 47 km to Goba. From here the highest road in Africa crosses the Sanetti Plateau (4000 m (13,123 ft)) where Wattled Crane* (65 km east of Dinsho) and Spot-breasted Lapwing occur, before descending to the Harrena Forest.

Accommodation: camping (C). Take food and petrol (especially east of Dinsho). Goba: Goba Ras Hotel (B).

From Goba in the Bale Mountains it is possible to travel south to the **Negele–Yabelo Area** where some of Ethiopia's most enigmatic endemics occur. In Sidamo Province, at the Genale river *en route* south to **Negele**, dry wadis support the spectacular endemic Prince Ruspoli's Turaco*. Try the area 12 km north of Wadera on the Negele–Kibre Mengist road. The rare Sidamo Lark* has been recorded on the Negele Plains, and the little known Degodi Lark* has been recorded in the dry thorn scrub either side of the road, 11 km east of **Bogol Manyo** in extreme southeast Ethiopia. Prince Ruspoli's Turaco* also occurs south of Negele, along with the unique endemic Stresemann's Bush-Crow* and rare endemic White-tailed Swallow*, which may be found along the Wachille–Yabelo track. The Yabelo–Arero road is also worth exploring. Recent surveys have revealed that Stresemann's Bush-Crow*, although highly localised, is quite common north and east of **Yabelo**. Vulturine Guineafowl, Violet Woodhoopoe, Red-fronted Barbet, Taita Fiscal, Three-streaked Tchagra, Banded Warbler, Short-tailed Lark, Shelley's, the rare White-crowned and Golden-breasted Starlings, Black-cheeked Waxbill, White-bellied Canary and Somali Bunting also occur in the area. Both the bush-crow and White-tailed Swallow*, as well as White-crowned Starling, also occur alongside the Yabelo–Mega–Moyale road, just north of the Kenyan border. From Mega it is possible to travel back north to Addis Ababa via the Great Rift Valley.

Accommodation: Mega, Yabelo, Negele: small hotels ('African' standard).

Ethiopian Sawwing, known from the **Maji** area, may be found there by the avid endemic hunter, or in the nearby but remote Omo NP, situated in southwest Ethiopia.

ERITREA

A total of 537 species have been recorded in Eritrea, at the northern tip of Ethiopia extending along the Red Sea coast from Sudan to Djibouti, including the rare Blue Sawwing.

ADDITIONAL INFORMATION

Addresses

The Ethiopian Wildlife and Natural History Society, Box 60074, Addis Ababa, publishes *Walia*, an annual journal.

Please send all Ethiopian records to Dr John Ash, Paysanne, Godshill Wood, Fordingbridge, Hampshire, UK, and/or John Atkins, FCO (Addis Ababa), King Charles Street, London SW1A 2AH, UK.

Please send all Eritrean records to Dr Chris Hillman, Assistant Head of Research, Ministry of Marine Resources, Box 923, Asmara, Eritrea.

ENDEMICS (30)

Blue-winged Goose	Central: Addis Ababa and Bale Mountains NP
Wattled Ibis	Central: widespread
Harwood's Francolin*	Central: Jemmu Valley, northwest of Addis Ababa
Rouget's Rail*	Central: Addis Ababa and Bale Mountains NP
Spot-breasted Lapwing	Central: Bale Mountains NP
White-collared Pigeon	Central/north: Addis Ababa and Lake Tana
Yellow-fronted Parrot	Central/north: Lake Tana and Wondo Genet
Black-winged Lovebird	Widespread
Prince Ruspoli's Turaco*	South: Negele
Banded Barbet	Central: widespread
Abyssinian Woodpecker	Widespread
Stresemann's Bush-Crow*	South: Yabelo
Thick-billed Raven	Central: widespread
Dark-headed Oriole	Widespread
White-billed Starling	Central: Debre Libanos and Bale Mountains NP
Abyssinian Slaty-Flycatcher	Central: Addis Ababa and Wondo Genet
Rueppell's Chat	Central: Debre Libanos
White-winged Cliff-Chat	Central: widespread
White-tailed Swallow*	South: Yabelo
Blue Sawwing	North: Eritrea
Brown Sawwing	Central: Wondo Genet
Abyssinian Catbird	Central: Bale Mountains NP
White-backed Black-Tit	Central: Debre Libanos and Bale Mountains NP
Degodi Lark*	Southeast: Bogol Manyo

Sidamo Lark*	South: Negele
Erlanger's Lark	Central: highlands
Lineated Pytilia	Central: highlands
Abyssinian Longclaw*	Central: Addis Ababa and Bale Mountains NP
Abyssinian Siskin	Central: Addis Ababa and Bale Mountains NP
Ankober Serin*	Central: Ankober

Near-endemics (Central)
Moorland, Erckel's and Chestnut-naped Francolins, White-cheeked Turaco, Black-billed Woodhoopoe, Moorland Chat, Broad-ringed White-eye, White-rumped Babbler, Somali and Swainson's Sparrows, Salvadori's Weaver, Brown-rumped Seedeater.

Near-endemics (South and East)
Heuglin's Bustard, White-winged Collared Dove*, Red-naped Bushshrike, Boran Cisticola, Brown-tailed Apalis, Somali Crombec, Scaly Chatterer, Scaly Babbler, Friedmann's*, Collared, Gillett's and Masked Larks, Donaldson-Smith's Sparrow-Weaver, Abyssinian Grosbeak-Canary.

Near-endemics (East)
Little Brown Bustard*, Somali Bee-eater, Somali Wheatear, Sombre Chat*, Short-billed Crombec*, Abyssinian and Blanford's Larks.

Near-endemics (West)
Cretzschmar's Babbler, Black-throated Firefinch, Abyssinian Waxbill.

GABON

INTRODUCTION

Summary
Gabon would undoubtedly be a major world birding destination if getting there and getting around was less expensive, and the infrastructure was more modern away from the main towns. Ecotourism is almost unheard of in this country where stunning birds abound and mammals such as chimpanzee and gorilla are still quite widespread.

Size
At 267,667 sq km Gabon is almost exactly twice the size of England and less than one third the size of Texas.

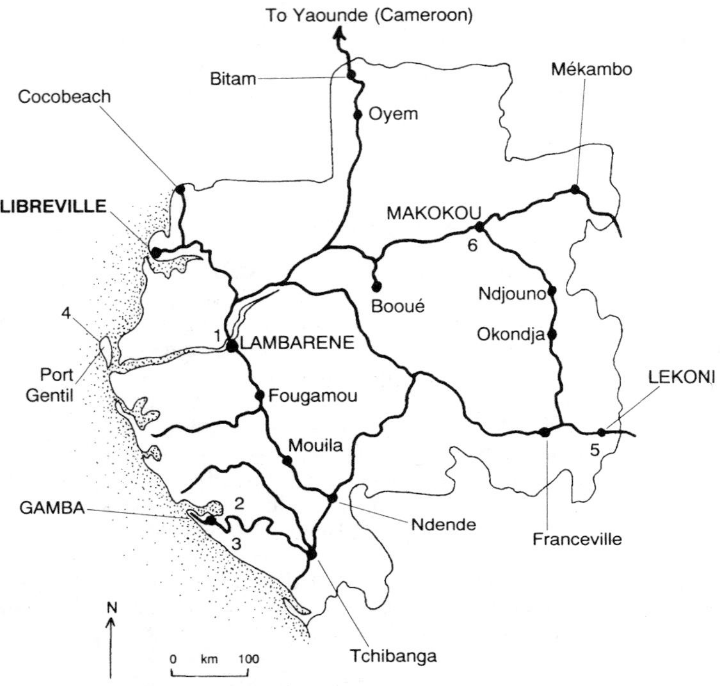

1	Lambarene	4	Port Gentil
2	Tondou and Pont Brulé Forests	5	Lekoni
3	Colas and Nyanga	6	Makokou

Getting Around

There are few good roads in Gabon and these are mainly restricted to the west of the country. Car-hire and public transport, including the internal air and long-distance bus networks, are very expensive, but bush taxis are cheaper. The Libreville–Franceville railway is also cheap but it does not connect with the major birding sites. A basic knowledge of French greatly assists travel in Gabon.

Accommodation and Food

Most hotels are prohibitively expensive to budget birders, but there are a few missions. Accommodation does not exist in some birding areas, but camping is possible anywhere (with the local village chief's permission). Such permission is usually granted without any problems, although local hunters may take offence if they are not informed.

Health and Safety

Immunisation against hepatitis, polio, typhoid and yellow fever is recommended, as are all precautions against malaria.

Gabon is one of Africa's safest countries, but beware of hunters when camping.

Climate and Timing

This is a hot and humid tropical country. The short and often wet 'dry season' lasts from June to September, and there is also a short 'dry' spell in mid December. The true rainy season lasts from October to May, with November and March to April being particularly wet. August to September is the best time to visit, late September if African River-Martin is crucial.

Habitats

Gabon's intricately indented coastline of mangrove-lined lagoons and estuaries soon gives way inland to plateaux and highlands, rising to 1500 m (4921 ft). Most of the country is still covered by rainforest, although this gives way to savanna and miombo woodland in the southeast.

Conservation

Gabon's three national parks, L'Okanda, Wonga-Wongue and Petit Loango are difficult to reach. Birders normally follow logging companies' roads and tracks to reach more inaccessible areas.

Four threatened and five near-threatened species occur in Gabon.

Bird Families

Five only of the ten families endemic to mainland Africa are represented in Gabon. Ostrich, Shoebill*, Secretary-bird, ground-hornbills and sugarbirds are all absent. Well represented families include bee-eaters, bushshrikes, swallows and greenbuls.

Bird Species

A total of 670 species have been recorded in Gabon, 200 fewer than its northern neighbour, Cameroon. Non-endemic specialities and spectacular species include Long-tailed Hawk, Grey Pratincole, Forbes' Plover, Damara Tern*, Vermiculated Fishing-Owl, Bare-cheeked Trogon, Chocolate-backed Kingfisher, Black-headed and Rosy Bee-eaters and Woodhouse's Antpecker.

Endemics

There are no endemics, and few near-endemics, but these include Angola Batis, Rufous-tailed Palm-Thrush, African River-Martin, Pale-olive Greenbul, Bubbling Cisticola, Salvadori's Eremomela, Grey-necked Rockfowl* and Black-chinned* and Loango* Weavers.

Expectations

It is possible to see 350 species on a three-week trip which covers most of the country.

Mangroves and scrub close to Gabon's modern capital city, **Libreville**, support White-crested Bittern, Chattering Cisticola, Black-bellied Seedcracker, Long-legged Pipit, and the very local Loango Weaver*, whilst Damara Tern* has been seen in Libreville Bay (July).

LAMBARENE

This town in west/central Gabon is situated on an island in the River Ogooué, and was made famous by Albert Schweitzer, who built a hospital nearby. Grey Pratincole, White-headed Lapwing and Rosy Bee-eater breed on the exposed sandbanks of the river during the dry season (Jun–Sep), whilst other species include White-crested Bittern.

Specialities

Spot-breasted Ibis, Grey Pratincole, Rosy Bee-eater, Violet-tailed Sunbird.

Others

African Darter, Goliath Heron, White-backed Night-Heron, White-crested Bittern, Hamerkop, Olive Ibis, African Cuckoo-Falcon, Ayres' Hawk-Eagle, Black Crake, African Finfoot, Rock Pratincole, White-fronted Plover, White-headed Lapwing, African Skimmer, Grey Parrot, Black and Blue-headed Coucals, Yellow-billed Turaco, Sabine's and Cassin's Spinetails, Shining Blue Kingfisher, Blue-breasted Bee-eater, Cassin's Honeyguide, Purple-throated Cuckoo-shrike, Chestnut Wattle-eye, Chestnut-capped Flycatcher, Rufous Flycatcher-Thrush, Splendid Glossy-Starling, White-throated Blue and Red-throated Swallows, Swamp Greenbul, Chattering Cisticola, Olive-green Camaroptera, Rufous-crowned Eremomela, Green Hylia, Pale-fronted Negrofinch, Black-bellied Seedcracker, Orange-cheeked Waxbill, Red-billed Quailfinch, Magpie Mannikin, Orange Weaver, Gray's and Red-headed Malimbes, Scarlet-tufted, Little Green, Bates', Carmelite and Johanna's Sunbirds.

Other Wildlife

Hippo, white-collared mangabey.

LAMBARENE

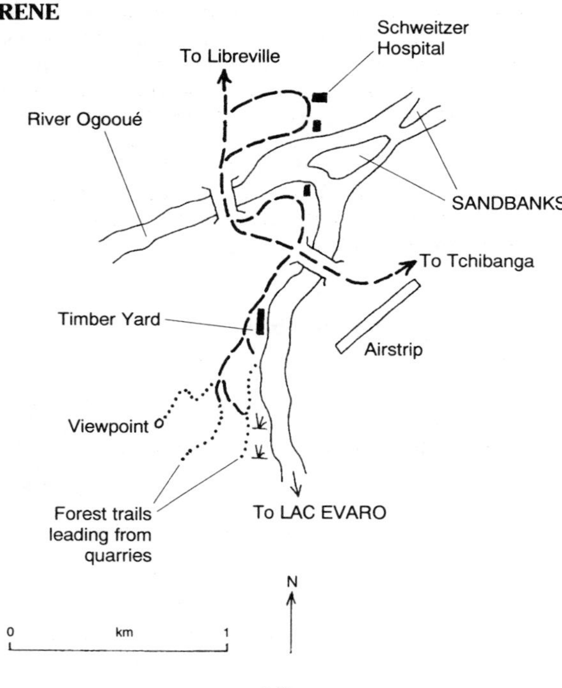

Delightful Grey Pratincoles may be seen hawking insects over the river at Lambarene

Access

The river is viewable from the town. The forest surrounding the quarries south of town is worth birding if time allows. It is also possible to hire a pirogue, at considerable expense, to travel three hours downstream to the remote island resort of Lac Evaro, where White-backed Night-Heron and White-crested Bittern both occur.

Accommodation: Lambarene: Two missions (C). Lac Evaro: Chalets.

Over 380 species have been recorded in the area surrounding the small settlement of **Gamba** in southwest Gabon, including African River-Martin, which breeds in the coastal savanna from mid September to mid November. This species can be hard to find since birds often feed high overhead. However, at other times they will perch on wires like many other swallows. Rosy Bee-eater may be seen at the airport or from the quay in town. It is possible to fly to Gamba from Libreville, and to hire a vehicle once there (write well in advance to EGCA, Location des Voitures, Gamba (tel: 558321)). There is no accommodation but camping is allowed in the nearby forests, which are discussed below, along with the other nearby sites of Colas and Nyanga.

TONDOU and PONT BRULÉ FORESTS

The lowland rainforest near Gamba supports a fine selection of species hard to see elsewhere in Africa, including Long-tailed Hawk, Black and Plumed Guineafowl, Black-headed Bee-eater, Gabon Helmetshrike and African River-Martin.

Specialities

Hartlaub's Duck, Black and Plumed Guineafowl, Gabon Coucal, Sandy Scops-Owl, Maned Owl, Sjostedt's Owlet, Bates' Nightjar, Black-headed and Rosy Bee-eaters, Rufous-sided Broadbill, Gabon Helmetshrike, African River-Martin (mid Sept to mid Nov), Sjostedt's Greenbul, Green-tailed Bristlebill*.

Others

Olive Ibis, Congo Serpent-Eagle, Long-tailed Hawk, Crowned Hawk-Eagle, Forest Francolin, White-spotted Flufftail, Nkulengu Rail, Grey Parrot, Yellow-billed and Great Blue Turacos, Black and African Emerald Cuckoos, Yellowbill, Akun Eagle-Owl, Pel's Fishing-Owl, African Wood-Owl, Marsh Owl, Swamp Nightjar, Shining Blue, White-bellied, Dwarf and Chocolate-backed Kingfishers, Black Bee-eater, Blue-throated Roller, White-crested, Red-billed Dwarf and Piping Hornbills, Naked-faced Barbet, Speckled Tinkerbird, Spotted and Lyre-tailed Honeyguides, Golden-crowned Woodpecker, Chestnut-capped Flycatcher, Blue Cuckoo-shrike, Large-billed Puffback, Chestnut and Yellow-bellied Wattle-eyes, Rufous Flycatcher-Thrush, Brown-chested and Fire-crested Alethes, Purple-headed and Splendid Glossy-Starlings, White-browed Forest-Flycatcher, Sooty, Olivaceous, Yellow-footed and Cassin's Flycatchers, Forest Robin, White-throated Blue Swallow, Yellow-whiskered Bulbul, Grey, Golden, Spotted and Swamp Greenbuls, Grey Longbill, Blackcap and Brown Illadopsises, Woodhouse's Antpecker, Chestnut-breasted and Pale-fronted Negrofinches, Red-billed Quailfinch, Mountain Wagtail, Yellow-mantled and Maxwell's Black Weavers, Black-throated, Red-bellied and Gray's Malimbes, Scarlet-tufted, Bates' and Johanna's Sunbirds.

Other Wildlife

Buffalo, chimpanzee, crowned guenon, elephant, greater white-nosed monkey.

GAMBA AREA

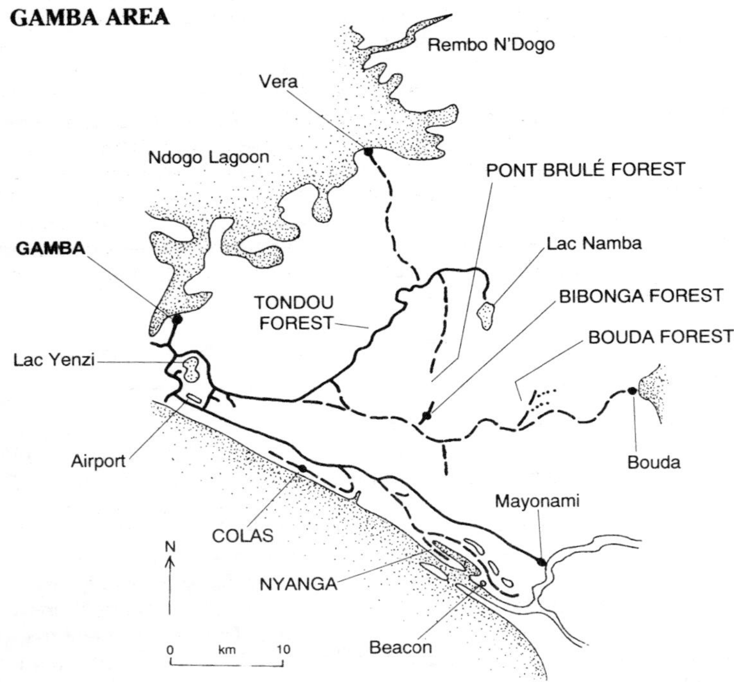

Access

Bird the forest around Tondou and Pont Brulé. From Gamba airport head south for 2.5 km then turn left. After 3 km turn right (keep left at Keleba village, 5 km from the airport) on to the Lac Namba road. Bird **Tondou Forest**, which lies along side this road, via the side-tracks and trails. Turn south 21 km from the airport to reach the forest at **Pont Brulé**. This track ends after 26 km at a small river. After 25 km there is a culvert where Pel's Fishing-Owl occurs. Elephant and buffalo tracks lead west 300 m from here to a small seasonal pool where Hartlaub's Duck and Olive Ibis occur. This area also supports Black Guineafowl, White-bellied, Dwarf and Chocolate-backed Kingfishers and Forest Robin. Beyond the Pont Brule turning the main track continues east and south through grassland to Lac Namba where Cassin's Flycatcher occurs.

Accommodation: There is a good area for camping at km 16 from Gamba airport (White-spotted Flufftail and Bates' Nightjar).

COLAS AND NYANGA

The coastal scrub and estuary south of Gamba, support Grey Pratincole and Loango Weaver*, whilst Damara Tern* occurs offshore.

Specialities

Hartlaub's Duck, Grey Pratincole (Nov–Mar), Forbes' Plover (Nov–May), Damara Tern* (May–Oct), Blue-breasted and Rosy Bee-eaters, Gabon Boubou, African River-Martin, Long-legged Pipit, Loango Weaver*, Violet-tailed Sunbird.

Others

African Darter, African Pygmy-goose, White-backed Night-Heron, White-crested Bittern, Hamerkop, African Finfoot, Water Thick-knee, White-fronted Plover, White-headed Lapwing (Oct–Apr), Royal Tern, African Skimmer (Jul–Nov), Grey Parrot, African Emerald Cuckoo, Blue-headed Coucal, Blue-breasted and Giant Kingfishers, Green-backed Woodpecker, White-browed Forest-Flycatcher, Snowy-crowned Robin-Chat, Green Crombec, Red-billed Quailfinch, Reichenbach's and Carmelite Sunbirds.

Other Wildlife

Red-capped mangabey.

Access

For Colas turn south 15 km southeast of Gamba Airport. Loango Weaver* occurs in the beach scrub here, and in the scrub north of the beach hut, 4 km north of **Colas**. It also occurs at **Nyanga**, reached by turning south 20 km southeast of the airport. From this junction it is 10 km to the coastal lagoon and a further 4 km to the beacon at the river mouth. Loango Weaver* occurs in the scrub south and east of the beacon. Otherwise, this species may be found in the spiny palms around the lagoon. Nyanga is also a good site for Grey Pratincole (Nov–Mar) and Damara Tern* (May–Oct). White-crested Bittern occurs around the inlet reached by turning west 17 km southeast of the airport. Hartlaub's

The lovely Rosy Bee-eater occurs at Gamba and a number of other sites in Gabon, the most accessible country in which to see this species

Duck, White-backed Night-Heron and Red-billed Quailfinch occur in the grassland and pools alongside the road south from the Nyanga turn-off to Mayonami.

There are a number of other good birding areas around **Gamba** These include: (1) The **River Rembo N'Dogo**, where boat trips are possible from Gamba (to Lac Kivoro, a few hours upstream) to look for White-backed Night-Heron and Vermiculated Fishing-Owl; ask about boats at Biffa's Boozer in Gamba. (2) **Yenzi Culvert**, alongside the airport–Gamba road, 4 km north of the airport, where White-backed Night-Heron, Vermiculated Fishing-Owl, Blue-breasted Bee-eater, Naked-faced Barbet and Red-billed Quailfinch have been recorded. (3) **Lac Yenzi**, where the surrounding degraded forest supports African Crake (Nov–Apr), Bristle-nosed Barbet, Purple-throated Cuckoo-shrike, Narrow-tailed Starling, Violet-backed Hyliota and Black-bellied Seedcracker. Five and a half km north of the airport on the road to Gamba turn east. Take the left fork after 200 m and the right fork after a further 100 m to reach the lake; bird this track and the other tracks leading off from the forks. (4) **Bibonga and Bouda Forests**, where Long-tailed Hawk, Black and Plumed Guineafowl, Sandy Scops-Owl, Chocolate-backed Kingfisher, Black-headed Bee-eater, Lyre-tailed Honeyguide and Pale-olive Greenbul (Bouda) occur. Take the right fork 8 km along the airport–Lac Namba road on to a track. Bibonga Forest is reached by turning left off this track, 17.5 km from the airport, and Bouda Forest is reached by turning left 25 km from the airport. East of the turning to Bouda Forest the track to Bouda village on the shores of Lake Cachimba passes through some open forest, a particularly good site for Black-headed Bee-eater. (5) **Sette Cama**, 35 km north of Gamba, via N'dogo Wharf, where Rufous-tailed Palm-Thrush occurs opposite the football pitch just south of the village. Beyond the village Loango Weaver* occurs at the edge of the lagoon by the Mission House. (6) **Vera**, a former hippy commune, reached by turning north 20 km along the airport–Lac Namba road. Spot-breasted Ibis has been recorded here and is best looked for at dusk.

Shell employees only are currently allowed in to the **Rabi** oilfield north of Gamba, although public roads do penetrate the surrounding area which is well forested. Hartlaub's Duck, Olive Ibis, Plumed Guineafowl, Bates' Nightjar, Bare-cheeked Trogon, Chocolate-backed Kingfisher,

Black, Black-headed and Rosy Bee-eaters, Lyre-tailed Honeyguide, Golden-crowned Woodpecker and Grey-throated Tit-Flycatcher have been recorded here. The best access is from the road north from Yombi, 20 km south of Fougamou, through Mandi and beyond.

Accommodation: Fougamou: Mission.

Permission to visit the **Moukalaba Reserve** must be obtained from the Forestry Department in Libreville. The reserve HQ is at Mourindi, two hours by bush taxi northwest of Tchibanga, which is accessible by air from Libreville. Bird the track northwest towards Mougouma which runs alongside the eastern boundary of the reserve. Black-backed Barbet, Black-headed Batis, and Brown Twinspot occur here. There are no tracks within the reserve, only a trail through tall savanna in which it is easy to get lost: a guide is needed. Black Scimitar-bill and Fiery-breasted Bushshrike, in swamp forest bordering the river, occur here. Other species recorded at Moukalaba include Black, Blue-breasted, Black-headed and Rosy Bee-eaters, Rufous-sided Broadbill and Lemon-bellied Crombec.

Accommodation: HQ chalets (take food).

Over 340 species have been recorded on Mandji Island, around **Port Gentil** on Gabon's west coast, including Forbes' Plover (Oct–May), White-headed Lapwing (Oct–Apr), Damara Tern* (May–Oct), African River-Martin (mid Sept to mid Nov) and Loango Weaver*. Both Damara Tern* and Loango Weaver* occur at **Cap Lopez**, 15 km north of the airport. There is a good beach for terns just before the Elf Oil terminal. Take the track leading west 800 m to the beach. Walk north from the beach to explore the scrub for Loango Weaver*. A number of rarities have been found at Cap Lopez and seawatching has produced some unusual seabirds including Black Noddy. Loango Weaver* also occurs at **Tchengue**, in the scrub around the oil-polluted pools 10 km south of Port Gentil.

Accommodation: Hotel Mandji (A+); Auberge du Forestier; Hotel Printemps.

Angola Swallow occurs alongside the road from the airport to **Franceville** in southeast Gabon. This town, accessible by air from Libreville, lies at the edge of savanna and miombo woodland, which is most accessible from Lekoni (below).

Accommodation: Lekoni Palace (A+) (Yellow-necked Greenbul, Black-faced Canary).

LEKONI

The extensive savanna and open miombo woodland on the edge of the Bateke Plateau near Lekoni, 100 km east of Franceville, supports a handful of restricted-range species including Finsch's Francolin, Angola Batis, Congo Moorchat, Black-collared Bulbul, Salvadori's Eremomela and

Black-chinned Weaver*. The range of species here is impressive, and 100 species in a day, including no less than eight bee-eaters, is possible.

Specialities

Finsch's Francolin, Black-headed and Rosy Bee-eaters, Black-backed Barbet, Gabon Boubou, Angola Batis, Congo Moorchat, Forest Swallow, Black-collared Bulbul, Bubbling Cisticola, Salvadori's Eremomela, Black-chinned Weaver*.

Others

Hamerkop, Palm-nut Vulture, Forest Francolin, Harlequin Quail, Black-rumped Buttonquail, African Crake, Stanley Bustard, Temminck's Courser, Senegal Lapwing, Red-headed Lovebird, Olive Long-tailed and African Emerald Cuckoos, Fiery-necked, Swamp, and Plain Nightjars, Horus Swift, Brown-hooded Kingfisher, Black, White-fronted, Blue-breasted and White-throated Bee-eaters, Lilac-breasted Roller, Black Scimitar-bill, Red-billed Dwarf Hornbill, Naked-faced, Grey-throated, Yellow-spotted, Black-collared and Double-toothed Barbets, Thick-billed Honeyguide, Rufous-necked Wryneck, Green-backed Woodpecker, African Broadbill, Petit's Cuckoo-shrike, Souza's Shrike, Red-eyed Puffback, Black-and-white Shrike-flycatcher, Black-headed Batis, Red-capped and White-crowned Robin-Chats, Sooty Chat, Banded Martin, Angola, Red-throated and South African Swallows, Square-tailed and Petit's Sawwings, Spotted, Simple and Yellow-throated Greenbuls, Chattering, Grey, Pectoral-patch and Cloud-scraping Cisticolas, White-chinned Prinia, Greencap Eremomela, Green Crombec, Yellow-bellied Hyliota, White-winged Black-Tit, Black-bellied Seedcracker, Fawn-breasted Waxbill, Red-billed Quailfinch, Black-and-white Mannikin, Yellow-throated Longclaw, Short-tailed Pipit, Vieillot's Black and Compact Weavers, Black-throated Malimbe, Black-winged Bishop, Yellow-shouldered and Marsh Widowbirds, Little Green, Green-headed, Green-throated and Copper Sunbirds, Black-faced Canary, Cabanis' Bunting.

Access

It is wise to wear long trousers in the savanna to avoid the attentions of the many blood-sucking flies. Bird: (1) The **Edjangoulou Track** north-east of Lekoni town. The small patch of forest on the right 4 km beyond the end of the paved road supports Olive Long-tailed Cuckoo, Angola Batis, Black-collared Bulbul, and Black-chinned Weaver*. (2) The **Canyons Track**, southeast of town. Finsch's Francolin (4.5 to 6 km from town), Black-backed Barbet, Petit's Cuckoo-shrike, Black-headed Batis (4.5 km to 6 km from town), Congo Moorchat, and White-winged Black-Tit occur along this track, and Petit's Sawwing at the canyon itself. Salvadori's Eremomela occurs near the lake towards the end of the track which leads east and south from the canyon. (3) The **Saye Track** which leads to the south side of the lake. Plain Nightjar occurs along the track and Souza's Shrike, Black-headed Apalis and Marsh Widowbird south of the lake.

Accommodation: Lekoni: Complex Touristique Hotel (A).

The **Franceville–Makokou road**, which may be impassable during the wet season (Nov–May), passes through some superb forest.

LEKONI

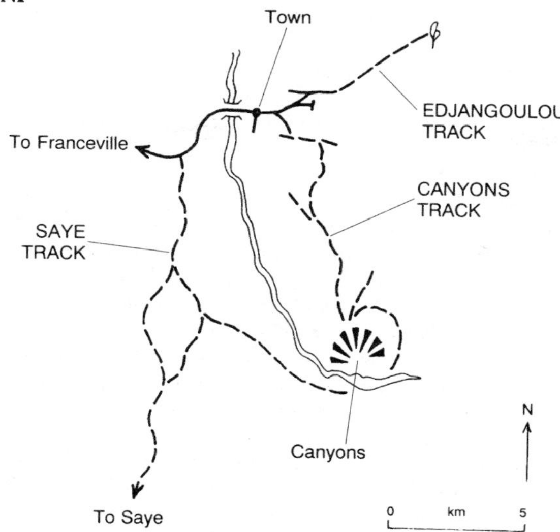

Between **Ndjouno** and **Zoolendé** is probably the best stretch, although the whole area supports Long-tailed Hawk, Gabon Coucal, Sandy Scops-Owl, Shelley's Eagle-Owl, Sjostedt's Owlet and Black-headed Bee-eater. There is a mission in **Okondja** where it is possible to stay (B) and where Blue-shouldered Robin-Chat and Crested Malimbe occur. All tracks leading from Okondja are worth exploring. Further on towards Makokou there is some good forest around the village of Zoolendé. Bare-cheeked Trogon, Least Honeyguide and Rachel's Malimbe have been recorded here.

MAKOKOU

This remote town in north Gabon, on the banks of the Ivindo river, lies in the richest area for birds in Africa. The forest here forms Africa's 'West Amazonia', although, in some birders minds, over 20 greenbuls make a poor substitute for at least as many antbirds. Still, there are many great birds to look for around Makokou and alongside the road east to Mekambo, including Black-collared Lovebird, Green-breasted Pitta, Gabon Helmetshrike, Black-eared and Grey Ground-Thrushes, African River-Martin and Grey-necked Rockfowl*.

Specialities

Hartlaub's Duck, Spot-breasted Ibis, Black and Plumed Guineafowls, Red-chested and Streaky-breasted Flufftails, Grey-throated Rail, Black-collared Lovebird, Yellow-throated Cuckoo, Gabon Coucal, Vermiculated Fishing-Owl, Sjostedt's Owlet, Brown Nightjar, Black Spinetail, Bare-cheeked Trogon, Zenker's Honeyguide, Green-breasted Pitta, Grey-headed and Rufous-sided Broadbills, Oriole Cuckoo-shrike, Gabon Helmetshrike, Black-eared and Grey Ground-

Thrushes, Grey-throated Tit-Flycatcher, African River-Martin, Forest Swallow, Sjostedt's Greenbul, Yellow-throated Nicator, Masked Apalis, Grey-necked Rockfowl*, Forest Penduline-Tit, Red-crowned and Rachel's Malimbes.

Others

Congo Serpent-Eagle, Red-chested and Black Goshawks, Cassin's and Crowned Hawk-Eagles, Forest and Scaly Francolins, White-spotted Flufftail, African and Black Crakes, Rock Pratincole, Afep Pigeon, Grey Parrot, Guinea, Yellow-billed and Great Blue Turacos, Black, Dusky Long-tailed, Olive Long-tailed and African Emerald Cuckoos, Yellowbill, Akun Eagle-Owl, Pel's Fishing-Owl, African Wood-Owl, Narina Trogon, Shining Blue, Dwarf and Chocolate-backed Kingfishers, Blue-headed and White-throated Bee-eaters, Blue-throated Roller, White-crested, Black Dwarf, Red-billed Dwarf, and White-thighed Hornbills, Naked-faced, Bristle-nosed and Grey-throated Barbets, Red-rumped and Yellow-throated Tinkerbirds, Yellow-spotted, Hairy-breasted and Yellow-billed Barbets, Willcock's and Lyre-tailed Honeyguides, African Piculet, Green-backed, Gabon and Golden-crowned Woodpeckers, Chestnut-capped Flycatcher, Dusky Crested-Flycatcher, Black-winged Oriole, Blue and Purple-throated Cuckoo-shrikes, Black-and-white Shrike-flycatcher, West African Batis, Chestnut, White-spotted and Yellow-bellied Wattle-eyes, Rufous Flycatcher-Thrush, Red-tailed and White-tailed Ant-Thrushes, Brown-chested and Fire-crested Alethes, African Forest-Flycatcher, Sooty, Olivaceous, Yellow-footed and Dusky-blue Flycatchers, Forest Robin, White-throated Blue Swallow, Square-tailed and Petit's Sawwings, Ansorge's, Honeyguide, Spotted, Yellow-necked, Icterine, Xavier's, Eastern Bearded and Red-tailed Greenbuls, Chattering Cisticola, White-chinned and Banded Prinias, Black-capped, Black-throated and Gosling's Apalises, Yellow-browed and Olive-green Camaropteras, Rufous-crowned Eremomela, Green and Lemon-bellied Crombecs, Yellow and Grey Longbills, Green Hylia, Blackcap and Brown Illadopsises, Dusky Tit, Woodhouse's Antpecker, White-breasted, Chestnut-breasted and Pale-fronted Negrofinches, Black-bellied Seedcracker, Western Bluebill, Black-crowned and Black-headed Waxbills, Black-and-white Mannikin, Forest and Preuss' Weavers, Black-throated, Red-bellied, Gray's, Crested and Red-headed Malimbes, Scarlet-tufted, Bates', Tiny and Johanna's Sunbirds.

Other Wildlife

Chimpanzee, Congo clawless otter, crowned guenon, gorilla, greater white-nosed monkey, grey-cheeked mangabey, moustached guenon, sitatunga, water chevrotain.

Access

Makokou is accessible by air and road (15 hours) from Libreville or, alternatively, via train (to Booué) and bush taxi (200 km).

Purple-throated Cuckoo-shrike, Dusky-blue Flycatcher and Preuss' Weaver have been recorded in the scrub around the mission in **Makokou**. Streaky-breasted Flufftail, Masked Apalis and Black-crowned Waxbill occur in the scrub around the old airfield. Gosling's Apalis has been recorded near Epassendje Bridge over the Liboumba river, east of town, and African River-Martin has been seen perched on the wires over the river.

MAKOKOU

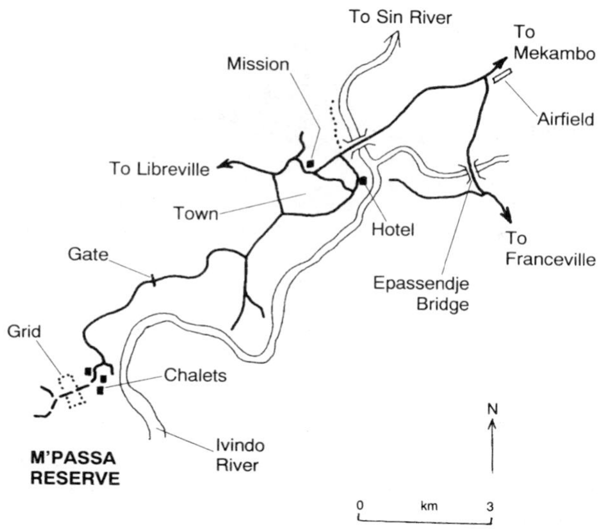

Local drivers with 4WD or taxis and personal vehicles are available for hire at the **M'Passa Reserve**, but all these options are expensive. From Makokou bird: (1) The 100 sq km M'Passa Reserve some 15 km south of town, where a grid network of overgrown trails allows limited access to the forest. The old Research Station chalets, which would make a great ecotourist's lodge, overlooking the Ivindo river, is a good place to stay. It is necessary to persuade the caretaker, a Mr Ngandaloa, who lives in Makokou near the hotel, to let you into the reserve and chalets, although officially a full written permit is required from the Forestry Department in Libreville. An incredible 362 species have been recorded within 2 km of the Research Station, including Black Guineafowl and Grey-throated Rail. (2) The 140-km **Makokou–Bokaboka road**, to the northeast of Makokou, along which Oriole Cuckoo-shrike occurs. The forest 100 km east of Makokou is a particularly good spot. (3) The **Bokaboka area** where there is a small Grey-necked Rockfowl* colony, This is a hard 1–2 hour hike from Bokaboka village and a guide is recommended. Bare-cheeked Trogon, Green-breasted Pitta and Black-throated Apalis have also been recorded in this area, along with chimpanzee.

There is also a Grey-necked Rockfowl* colony near **Belinga**, a remote village accessible only by pirogue (dug-out canoe) from Makokou, followed by a 15-km hike. The old road to Belinga, now unused owing to a collapsed bridge, is 40-km along the road to Bokaboka from Makokou. Rufous-sided Broadbill has been recorded along the 12-km stretch before the broken bridge. It is also possible to hire boats in Makokou to travel along the Ivindo river in search of Hartlaub's Duck, fish-owls, Grey-headed Broadbill, Oriole Cuckoo-shrike, Black-eared and Grey Ground-Thrushes, and African River-Martin.

The swamp forest alongside the **Sin river**, a tributary of the Ivindo, also supports Grey-headed Broadbill, Oriole Cuckoo-shrike, and Black-eared and Grey Ground-Thrushes. This is a beautiful but remote area

Makokou's many birds include White-spotted Wattle-eye

and visiting it necessitates a very expensive mini-expedition. Hire a pirogue not more than 8 m long, preferably 'skippered' by a guide who has been before, and take all provisions and camping gear. On such a trip Hartlaub's Duck, White-crested Bittern, Spot-breasted Ibis, Congo Serpent-Eagle, African Finfoot, Pel's and Vermiculated Fishing-Owls, Bare-cheeked Trogon, Black and Rosy Bee-eaters, Gabon Helmetshrike, Red-crowned Malimbe and Violet-tailed Sunbird are all possible.

Accommodation: Makokou: Ivindo Palace (no palace!) (A); Mission; M'Passa Research Station chalets (ask caretaker). Bokaboka: Camping in village only.

The 5000 sq km of forest and savanna in the **La Lope–Okanda Reserve**, near Booué in central Gabon, support a number of rare mammals including gorilla and mandrill, as well as Rosy Bee-eater (Nov–May) and Grey-necked Rockfowl*. The little known Ja River Scrub-Warbler* has been reported. This is one of the few sites accessible by train in Gabon, whilst bush taxis from Libreville take approximately seven hours. However, once there, a 4WD is necessary to bird the reserve thoroughly. Permission to visit is required from the Forestry Department in Libreville, although travel agents do run organised tours.

Accommodation: Case de Passage at HQ (A).

Although primary forest is hard to find in the heavily populated area of far north Gabon, some does still exist between plantations alongside the **Oyem–Bitam road**. Oyem is accessible by air from Libreville, and by road, although reaching it by bush taxi or 4WD would involve a full day on the road. White-backed Night-Heron, Bates' Swift, and Black-crowned Waxbill occur around the lake by the Novotel. Secondary forest alongside the tracks to Abameba and M'Bolonzok, both south and west of Oyem, supports Mackinnon's Shrike and Tit-hylia. Other birds in the Oyem area include Blue-throated Roller and Yellow-mantled Weaver.

Accommodation: Novotel Relais de M'Vett (A). Mission.

ADDITIONAL INFORMATION

Books and Papers

A Birders Guide to Gabon (privately published report). Sargeant, D. 1993. Available from D Sargeant, Ieplaan 179, 2565 LK Den Haag, Netherlands.

Gabon (Aug–Sep 1993) (privately published report). Webb, R. 1993. Available through ABC.

Les Oiseaux des Regions Forestieres du Nord-est du Gabon. Brosset, A and Erard, C. Societé Nationale de Protection de la Nature, Paris.

Addresses

Travel Agent: Mistral Voyages, Immeuble Diamant, BP 2106 Libreville (tel: 241 760421/22; fax: 747780).

Please send all records to Patrice Christy, BP 2240 Libreville, and/or D Sargeant (address above).

Near-endemics

Bates' Swift, Angola Batis, Rufous-tailed Palm-Thrush, African River-Martin, Pale-olive Greenbul, Ja River Scrub-Warbler*, Bubbling Cisticola, Salvadori's Eremomela, Black-chinned* and Loango* Weavers.

GAMBIA

INTRODUCTION

Summary

By mid 1995 Gambia appeared to be politically stable, after the bloodless coup of 1994, and the country looks set to become a very popular destination once again. Birders can expect a select band of spectacular species which includes bee-eaters, rollers and the fabulous Egyptian Plover, for the price of a package holiday.

Size

At just 10,689 sq km, Gambia is barely one tenth the size of England, a fraction of the size of Texas, and easily the smallest mainland African country. Although merely a sliver of land, this country is 400 km long and it takes seven hours to reach Egyptian Plover territory.

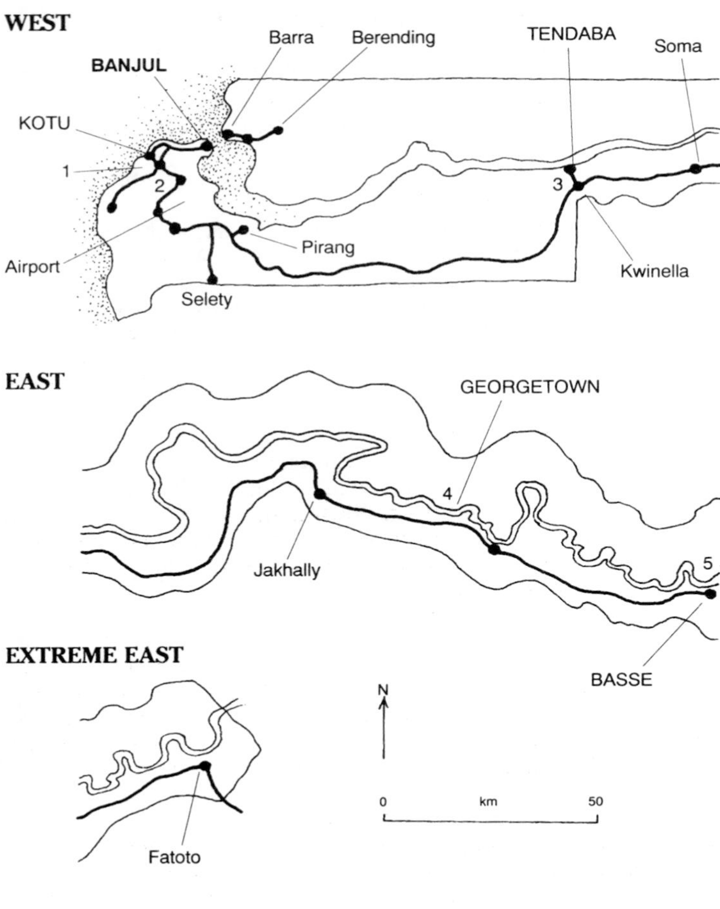

1 Kotu Creek
2 Abuko NR
3 Tendaba
4 Georgetown
5 Basse

Getting Around

Although 'tourist' taxis, available with drivers for the journey upriver to Basse, and car hire are very expensive, neither form of transport is a necessity in Gambia. Cheap buses cover the southern half of the country and reach all of the most important birding sites. Local bush taxis, which come in the form of estate-cars and mini-buses, and called 'tanker-tankers' by the Gambians, are even cheaper.

At Kotu, on the coast, visiting birders are soon tracked down by the Gambian 'bird-guides'. Some of these guides are excellent birders, but they charge extortionate prices for their services, which usually involve showing birders the species they will find for themselves, in time. If money is not a problem and time is, stand on Kotu Bridge and wait for the guide with the right answers to come along.

Accommodation and Food

Coastal Gambia has a wide range of package tourist hotels to choose from. Inland, there are less options, and at Basse the scant accommodation is basic to say the least. Those who like their food chilli-hot, and/or from the sea, will enjoy eating in Gambia, although budget birders will find eating out quite expensive.

Health and Safety

Immunisation against hepatitis, meningitis, polio, typhoid and yellow fever is recommended, as are precautions against malaria.

Although described as a friendly country, caution is necessary, particularly along the coast. Some Gambians tell visitors a guide is essential away from the hotels. If you do not wish to spend your trip to Gambia with a paid 'friend', it is wise to quickly inform potential companions that you have 'been there, done that, and already bought one', and you will be perfectly safe. Having said that, independent travellers have to beware of hassle when using bush taxis instead of tourist taxis at the coast. In such circumstances it is prudent to be polite but firm.

Climate and Timing

From October to June it is extremely hot and dry in Gambia, especially inland, although the nights can be cool. The Harmattan, a dry, dusty northeasterly wind from the Sahara, often blows hard during this dry season. The rainy season normally lasts from July to September, when it can be very wet and even hotter. November, when Palearctic migrants are passing through and some wet season visitors from the south are still present, is the best time to visit, although this may be a little early for Egyptian Plover. This species may not be present when water levels in the River Gambia are very high, usually at the end of the rainy season (Oct) in Guinea Conakry, the river's source.

Habitats

Gambia is a flat, heavily populated country, which lies either side of the lower River Gambia, and is dotted with numerous palms and baobabs. Where the land is not used for growing groundnuts or rice, there is some remnant savanna and gallery forest. At the coast and around the mouth of the River Gambia, there are mangrove-lined estuaries and many fine beaches.

Conservation

Much of Gambia, originally savanna and gallery forest, has been turned over to agriculture. Groundnuts recently superseded rice as the major crop when the authorities realised the irrigation of the paddies was drying up the River Gambia. There are a few reserves, but these are mostly very small and under pressure from the usual multitude of problems associated with high human population densities.

One threatened and two near-threatened species occur in Gambia.

Bird Families

Five of the ten families endemic to the African mainland are represented in Gambia. These include turacos and woodhoopoes, but Ostrich and mousebirds are absent.

Bird Species

Over 560 species have been recorded in Gambia, only 80 fewer than Senegal which is 17 times its size. Non-endemic specialities and spectacular species include Black Crowned-Crane, Senegal Thick-knee, Egyptian Plover, Blue-breasted Kingfisher, Red-throated and Swallow-tailed Bee-eaters, Abyssinian and Blue-bellied Rollers, Pied-winged Swallow and Oriole Warbler.

Endemics

There are no endemics or near-endemics, although a few arid-savanna specialities such as Chestnut-bellied Starling do occur.

Expectations

Zealous birders may see 240 species in two weeks between December and February, perhaps 280 in November.

KOTU CREEK

Kotu, on Gambia's Atlantic coast, is where most of the tourist hotels are situated. Fortunately for birders, these hotels lie next to the tidal Kotu Creek which is surrounded by mangrove, palm-dotted paddies, scrub, a small sewage farm, and a golf course with some stands of mature trees. It is possible to see over 100 species in a day within a 2 km radius of Kotu, and around 150 in a week, including Senegal Thick-knee, Swallow-tailed Bee-eater, Blue-bellied Roller and Oriole Warbler.

Others

White-faced Whistling-Duck, Western Reef-Egret, Black-headed Heron, White-backed Night-Heron, Palm-nut Vulture, African Harrier-Hawk, Lizard Buzzard, Grey Kestrel, Red-necked Falcon*, Double-spurred Francolin, Greater Painted-snipe, Senegal Thick-knee, Black-headed and Wattled Lapwings, Royal Tern, Vinaceous Dove, Senegal Parrot,

Blue-bellied Roller is likely to be one of the highlights of a trip to Gambia

Western Grey Plantain-eater, Levaillant's Cuckoo, African Scops-Owl, Pearl-spotted Owlet, Long-tailed and Standard-winged Nightjars, Malachite, Striped and Giant Kingfishers, Little and Swallow-tailed Bee-eaters, Abyssinian, Rufous-crowned, Blue-bellied and Broad-billed Rollers, Green Woodhoopoe, Red-billed Hornbill, Vieillot's and Bearded Barbets, Fine-spotted Woodpecker, Piapiac, Yellow-billed Shrike, Black-crowned Tchagra, Common Gonolek, Brown-throated Wattle-eye, Purple and Long-tailed Glossy-Starlings, Northern Black-Flycatcher, Snowy-crowned and White-crowned Robin-Chats, Red-chested Swallow, Singing Cisticola, Red-winged Prinia, Oriole Warbler, Blackcap and Brown Babblers, Lavender and Orange-cheeked Waxbills, African Silverbill, Bronze Mannikin, Village Indigobird, Yellow-throated Longclaw, Village Weaver, Splendid and Beautiful Sunbirds.

Other Wildlife

Gambian fruit-bat.

Access

The whole of the Kotu area is worthy of prolonged birding, especially the creek (White-backed Night-Heron roosting in large trees lining the north side, and Senegal Thick-knee), the golf course (White-crowned Robin-Chat and Oriole Warbler in and around the Bakotu Hotel), and the Sewage Farm (Greater Painted-snipe), for which there is a token entrance fee. Blue-bellied Rollers can be remarkably inconspicuous when they sit at the top of palm trunks, under the fronds, but at other times they perch openly and are stunningly obvious. White-crowned Robin-Chat occurs in the Senegambia Hotel grounds, behind the swimming pool.

KOTU CREEK

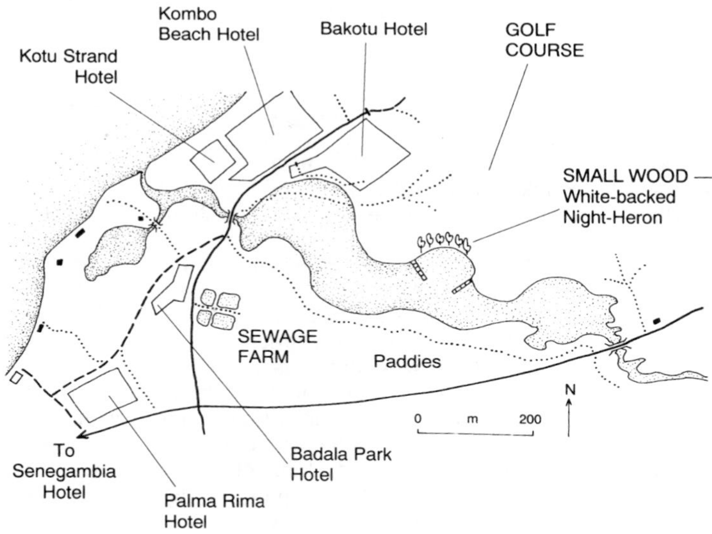

Accommodation: Bakotu (A); Kombo Beach (A); Senegambia (A). Atlantic Hotel (A — excellent birding in grounds and bird tours available).

There are a number of other sites worth birding at the coast. Mudflats and mangroves alongside the **Bund road** south of Banjul, support Greater Flamingo, Black Heron, Slender-billed Gull, and Royal Tern. **Cape Creek** is a good place for White-fronted Plover. Black Crowned-Crane has been recorded at **Camalou Corner**. Arid savanna, north of the River Gambia, around **Barra**, **Berending** and **Essau** (accessible by ferry from Banjul) supports Temminck's Courser, Bruce's Green-Pigeon, Chestnut-bellied Starling, Yellow-billed Oxpecker, Northern Anteater-Chat, Chestnut-backed Sparrow-Lark and Speckle-fronted Weaver.

BANJUL PENINSULA

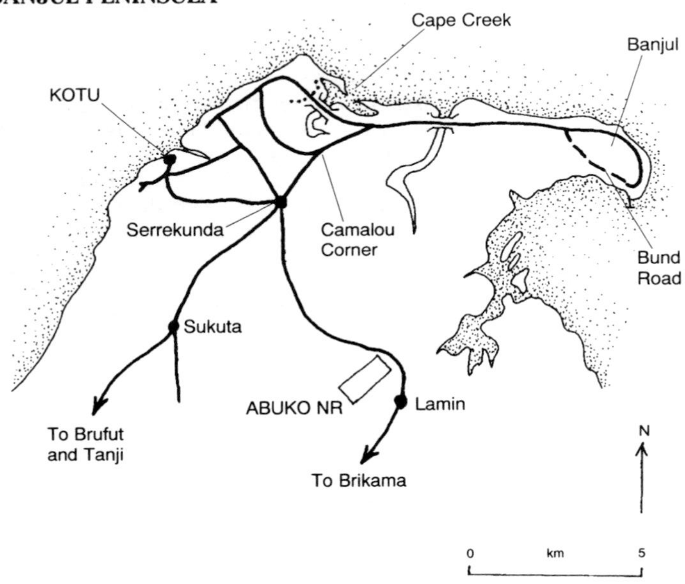

Woodland around the village of **Brufut**, south of Kotu, supports White-fronted Black-Chat, Fanti Sawwing and Red-faced Cisticola. More woodland and scrub alongside the road between Brufut and **Tanji**, further south, especially just north of Tanji, supports Siffling Cisticola. Some 300 species have been recorded at **Tanji Bird Reserve**, which was established to protect the estuary at Bald Cape and the Bijol Islands. For more information and details of how you can help to protect this reserve contact the Tanji Trust/Birders Group, c/o John Tyler, 154 Lightwoods Hill, Warley, West Midlands B67 5ED, UK.

Black Crowned-Crane and Brown-necked Parrot occur in the marshes and woodland north of **Pirang**, 12 km east of Brikama. The open woodland near **Selety**, on the Senegal border south of Brikama, supports Guinea Turaco, Black Scimitar-bill, Yellow-bellied Hyliota and White-shouldered Black-Tit, whilst Four-banded Sandgrouse drink from the pools near the border signs here, usually at dusk.

ABUKO NATURE RESERVE

Over 250 species have been recorded in this tiny reserve (73 ha) near Kotu. Here there are hides overlooking pools surrounded by gallery forest and savanna, where White-backed Night-Heron, Red-thighed Sparrowhawk, Ahanta Francolin, White-spotted Flufftail and Pied-winged Swallow occur.

Others

African Darter, Black Heron, Western Reef-Egret, White-backed Night-Heron, Hamerkop, African Harrier-Hawk, Lizard Buzzard, Red-thighed Sparrowhawk, Ahanta Francolin, Stone Partridge, White-spotted Flufftail, Black Crake, Senegal Parrot, Guinea and Violet Turacos, Western Grey Plantain-eater, Klaas' Cuckoo, White-faced Scops-Owl, Verreaux's Eagle-Owl, Mottled Spinetail, African Pygmy-Kingfisher, Giant Kingfisher, Little and Swallow-tailed Bee-eaters, African Pied Hornbill, Yellow-rumped Tinkerbird, Bearded Barbet, Spotted Honeyguide, Buff-spotted Woodpecker, Black-headed Paradise-Flycatcher, Red-shouldered Cuckoo-shrike, White Helmetshrike, Brown-throated Wattle-eye, Purple and Splendid Glossy-Starlings, Snowy-

ABUKO NR

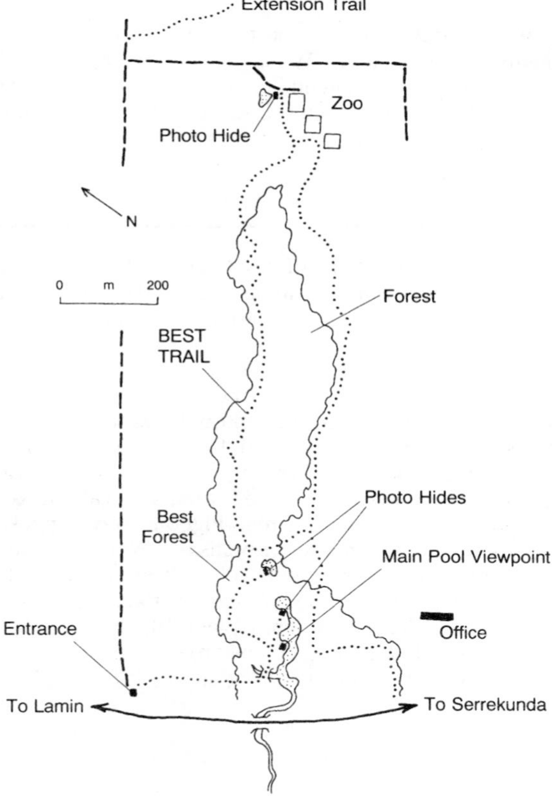

crowned and White-crowned Robin-Chats, Pied-winged Swallow, Fanti Sawwing, Little Greenbul, Leaf-love, Grey-headed Bristlebill, Yellow-breasted Apalis, Oriole Warbler, Green Hylia, Western Bluebill, Black-necked Weaver, Vitelline Masked-Weaver, Pygmy Sunbird.

Other Wildlife

Green vervet, Nile crocodile, red colobus, red patas monkey, sitatunga (introduced).

Access

The entrance ((B)) is on the south side of the main road to the airport, just south of Lamin. Bird the 3-km trail, especially the section which passes through the thickest part of the gallery forest (Guinea Turaco), just beyond the main pool (White-backed Night-Heron), and leave via the entrance, not the exit, if you wish to avoid the tourist stalls.

The paddies and scrub to the north of **Lamin** support Dark Chanting-Goshawk and White-faced Scops-Owl, whilst the drier fields around **Yundum**, to the south, support Temminck's Courser, Black Scimitar-bill, White-fronted Black-Chat, Pied-winged Swallow, Rufous Cisticola, Yellow Penduline-Tit, Little Weaver, Heuglin's Masked-Weaver, Black-winged Bishop and Yellow-shouldered Widowbird, whilst Bronze-winged Courser has also been recorded here.

The **Kemoto Hotel**, 75 km inland from Banjul, runs boat trips on the River Gambia. Goliath Heron, Woolly-necked Stork, African Fish-Eagle, African Finfoot, Bruce's Green-Pigeon, Brown-necked Parrot, Blue-breasted Kingfisher, Abyssinian Ground-Hornbill and Mouse-brown Sunbird occur in this area.

TENDABA

Situated on the southern bank of the River Gambia, 100 km inland, the mangrove-lined creeks and savanna around Tendaba Camp support Black Crowned-Crane, Brown-necked Parrot, African Blue-Flycatcher and Mouse-brown Sunbird.

Others

African Darter, Goliath Heron, Hamerkop, Hadada Ibis, Woolly-necked Stork, Scissor-tailed Kite, African Fish-Eagle, Palm-nut Vulture, Brown Snake-Eagle, Bateleur, Grasshopper Buzzard, Martial Eagle, Grey Kestrel, Black Crake, Black Crowned-Crane, Senegal Thick-knee, Four-banded Sandgrouse, Bruce's Green-Pigeon, Brown-necked Parrot, Mottled Spinetail, Blue-breasted Kingfisher, Northern Carmine Bee-eater, Abyssinian Ground-Hornbill, Yellow-fronted Tinkerbird, African Blue-Flycatcher, Red-shouldered Cuckoo-shrike, Grey Tit-Flycatcher, Mosque Swallow, White-shouldered Black-Tit, Black-rumped Waxbill, Cut-throat, Village Indigobird, Mouse-brown and Beautiful Sunbirds, Yellow-fronted Canary. African Finfoot and Pel's Fishing-Owl have also been recorded.

Other Wildlife

Clawless otter.

Access

Bird Kisi (African Blue-Flycatcher) and Tunku Bolons, the two creeks on the opposite side of the river, where African Finfoot and Pel's Fishing-Owl have been rarely recorded, the airstrip area, and the trails west of the camp. Tunku Bolon leads to Tunku village, where Scissor-tailed Kite has been recorded.

Accommodation: Camp (B) (basic).

TENDABA

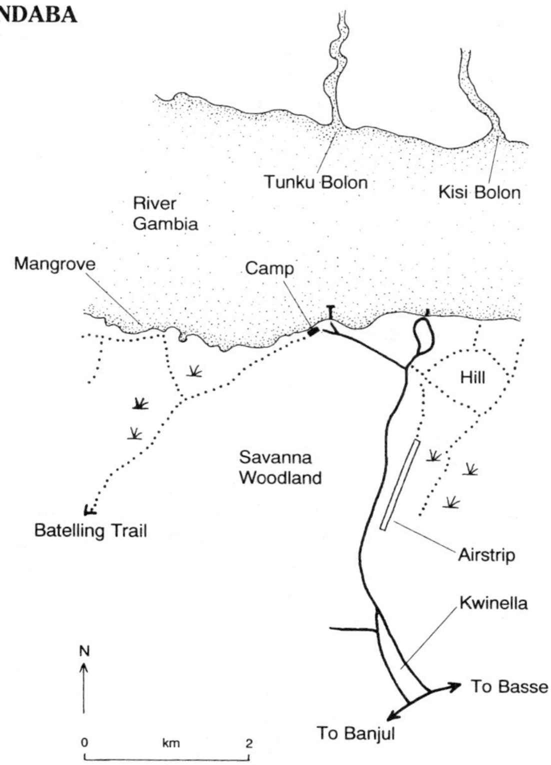

The fast disappearing marshes and savanna near **Jakhally**, north of the village of Madina 280 km east of Banjul on the road to Basse, may still support Black Heron, Bronze-winged Courser, Winding Cisticola, Oriole Warbler, Chestnut-backed Sparrow-Lark and Yellow-crowned Bishop.

GEORGETOWN

This town is situated on an island in the middle of the River Gambia, 300 km upstream from Banjul. From the nearby lodge it is possible to bird the river and the surrounding savanna, where Egyptian Plover, Red-throated Bee-eater and Bronze-tailed Glossy-Starling occur.

Others

Black and Goliath Herons, Hamerkop, Yellow-billed Stork, Banded Snake-Eagle, Bateleur, Grasshopper Buzzard, Stone Partridge, African Finfoot, Senegal Thick-knee, Egyptian Plover, Bronze-winged Courser, Four-banded Sandgrouse, Bruce's Green-Pigeon, African Pygmy-Kingfisher, Red-throated, White-throated and Northern Carmine Bee-eaters, Bronze-tailed Glossy-Starling, Yellow-billed Oxpecker, Swamp Flycatcher, White-crowned Robin-Chat, Yellow-throated Greenbul, Oriole Warbler, Orange-cheeked and Black-rumped Waxbills, Cut-throat. (Adamawa Turtle-Dove has also been recorded here.)

Access

Georgetown is accessible by boat from Sankule Kunda, directly opposite on the southern shore of the River Gambia, Walikunda, approximately 30 km downstream, and Kudang Tenda, approximately 100 km downstream. **Jang Jang Bureh Camp**, which lies on the north shore just outside Georgetown, is the best base. Oriole Warbler occurs here and boat trips are possible to a Red-throated Bee-eater colony at Bansang, some 25 km upstream. **Kuntaua Marsh**, on the north bank of the River Gambia near Georgetown, supports Black Crake, Green Bee-eater and Eastern Paradise-Whydah.

Accommodation: Jang Jang Bureh Camp (A) (no electricity).

BASSE

The small town of Basse, 374 km inland from Banjul, lies on the south bank of the River Gambia and is one of the best places to see Egyptian Plover in Africa. This fabulous species' supporting cast includes Great Snipe*, Blue-breasted Kingfisher and Red-throated Bee-eater.

Although widespread across northern Africa, Basse is one of the few reliable sites for Egyptian Plover. Seeing the 'crocodile bird' is a just reward for the effort involved in getting there

Specialities

Egyptian Plover.

Others

Hamerkop, Brown Snake-Eagle, Dark Chanting-Goshawk, Grasshopper Buzzard, Greater Painted-snipe, Great Snipe*, Senegal and Spotted Thick-knees, Four-banded Sandgrouse, Blue-breasted Kingfisher, Red-throated and Northern Carmine Bee-eaters, Abyssinian Roller, Black Scimitar-bill, Bearded Barbet, Yellow-billed Oxpecker, Winding Cisticola, Flappet Lark, Chestnut-backed Sparrow-Lark, African Quailfinch, Cut-throat, Yellow-throated Longclaw, Beautiful Sunbird.

Access

Basse is accessible by bus from Banjul. The normal bus takes seven hours and the 'express' about the same. Tourist taxi operators also offer round trips to Basse, but this is an outrageously expensive option for less than two people. It is worth a crew of four considering such transport though, because it enables birding *en route*. At Basse, it is possible to see Egyptian Plover in the small creek, to the left of the road to the jetty, on the jetty itself, or anywhere alongside the river. Hiring a boat may produce the best views. The boatmen know the 'crocodile bird' well, and should find them if they are present. The wet paddies and pools to the east of Basse support Great Snipe*.

BASSE

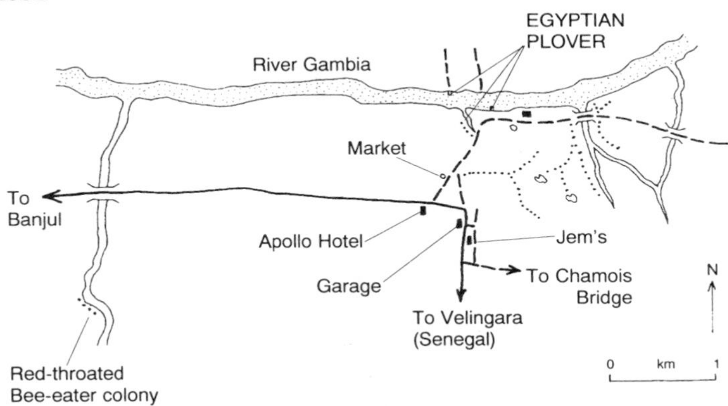

Accommodation: Jem's (B). The following are listed, but definitely not recommended: Basse Guesthouse (C); Plaza Hotel (C); Apollo Hotel (C).

Egyptian Plover, along with White-headed Lapwing, which is rarely recorded in Gambia, also occurs at **Gouloumbo Bridge**, beyond Basse, in Senegal, *en route* to Tambacounda.

ADDITIONAL INFORMATION

Books and Papers

A Birdwatcher's Guide to the Gambia. Ward, R. 1994. Prion.
A Field Guide to the Birds of The Gambia and Southern Senegal. Barlow, C *et al.* In prep. Pica Press.
Birds of The Gambia: an Annotated Check-list. 2nd edition. Gore, M. 1990. BOU.
Field Check-list for the Birds of Senegambia. Rumsey, S and Rodwell, S. 1992. The Wetland Trust.

Addresses

Please send all records to The Gambia Ornithological Society, Box 757, Banjul.

GHANA

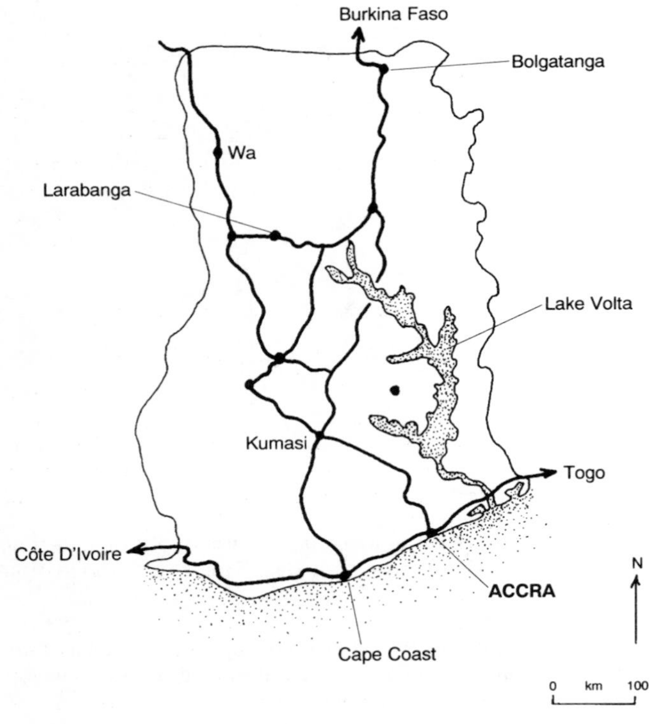

With tourism now being encouraged, Ghana deserves to be a popular birding destination. However, all of the Upper Guinea endemics present occur in neighbouring Côte D'Ivoire, whilst most of the more eastern species can be seen in Cameroon and Gabon.

At 238,537 sq km, Ghana is nearly twice the size of England, and a third the size of Texas. The infrastructure is well developed and good value by West African standards. The bus network is particularly sound. Immunisation against hepatitis, polio, typhoid and yellow fever is recommended, as are all precautions against malaria. November to March is the driest time of the year, although it is very humid in the south and very hot in the north throughout much of the year. Ghana is a low-lying country with many beaches, remnant lowland Upper Guinea rainforest, savanna, a small line of hills in the northeast, known as the Akwapim Range, and a huge man-made reservoir, Lake Volta.

Seven threatened and seven near-threatened species occur in Ghana. Seven of the ten families endemic to the African mainland are represented. An impressive 725 species have been recorded, 30 more than in adjacent Côte D'Ivoire. Non-endemic specialities and spectacular species include Long-tailed Hawk, Arabian Bustard, Egyptian and Forbes' Plovers, Black-collared Lovebird, Chocolate-backed Kingfisher, Rosy Bee-eater, Yellow-footed Honeyguide*, Red-cheeked Wattle-eye, and Jameson's Antpecker. Although there are no endemics, ten of the 16 Upper Guinea endemics have been recorded, including Rufous Fishing-Owl*, Ghana Cuckoo-shrike* and White-necked Rockfowl*.

Ghana's best birding areas include the remnant forest within **Ankasa Resource Reserve**, **Bia NP** and **Kakum NP**, the savanna within **Mole NP** and **Shai Hills Resource Reserve**, and wetlands such as **Keta**, **Muni**, **Sakumo** and **Songor Lagoons**, and the **Densu Delta**, all of which are important to Palearctic migrants.

Species recorded in Kakum NP include Hartlaub's Duck, White-breasted Guineafowl*, Black-collared Lovebird, Rosy Bee-eater, Brown-cheeked* and Yellow-casqued* Hornbills, Little Green Woodpecker, Rufous-sided Broadbill, Blue Cuckoo-shrike, Red-cheeked Wattle-eye, Finsch's Flycatcher-Thrush, Copper-tailed Glossy-Starling*, Ussher's Flycatcher, Green-tailed Bristlebill*, Yellow-bearded Greenbul*, Sharpe's Apalis and Kemp's Longbill.

A SELECTED LIST OF SPECIES RECORDED IN GHANA

African Darter, Hartlaub's Duck, African Pygmy-goose, White-backed Night-Heron, White-crested and Dwarf Bitterns, Hamerkop, Saddle-billed Stork, Olive and Spot-breasted Ibises, Scissor-tailed Kite, Congo Serpent-Eagle, Long-tailed Hawk, Secretary-bird, Forest, White-throated and Ahanta Francolins, Quail-plover, Nkulengu and Grey-throated Rails, Striped Crake, African Finfoot, Black Crowned-Crane, Arabian Bustard, Senegal Thick-knee, Egyptian Plover (Oct–Mar), Bronze-winged Courser, Rock Pratincole, Forbes' Plover, Damara Tern*, Afep Pigeon, Grey Parrot, Black-collared Lovebird, Guinea, Yellow-billed, Violet and Great Blue Turacos, Dusky Long-tailed and Olive Long-tailed Cuckoos, Black Coucal, Sandy Scops-Owl, Fraser's, Shelley's and Akun Eagle-Owls, Pel's and Rufous* Fishing-Owls, Maned Owl, Red-chested Owlet, Brown and Swamp Nightjars, Black Spinetail, Narina Trogon, White-bellied, Dwarf and Chocolate-backed Kingfishers, Black, Blue-headed,

Black-headed and Rosy (Oct–Mar) Bee-eaters, Abyssinian, Blue-bellied and Blue-throated Rollers, White-headed and Forest Woodhoopoes, White-crested, Brown-cheeked* and Yellow-casqued* Hornbills, Naked-faced and Bristle-nosed Barbets, Willcock's and Yellow-footed* Honeyguides, Little Green and Fire-bellied Woodpeckers, African Pitta, Rufous-sided Broadbill, Blue-headed Crested-Flycatcher, Blue and Ghana* Cuckoo-shrikes, Emin's Shrike, Chestnut-bellied Helmetshrike, West African Batis, Red-cheeked and Yellow-bellied Wattle-eyes, Finsch's Flycatcher-Thrush, Grey Ground-Thrush, Narrow-tailed and Chestnut-winged Starlings, Copper-tailed* and Bronze-tailed Glossy-Starlings, Ussher's, Olivaceous, Tessman's, and Cassin's Flycatchers, Forest Scrub-Robin, White-throated Blue, Pied-winged and Preuss' Swallows, Golden, Baumann's*, Western Bearded and Yellow-bearded* Greenbuls, Rufous and Black-necked Cisticolas, Sharpe's Apalis, Black-capped Rufous Warbler*, Kemp's Longbill, Violet-backed Hyliota, Rufous-winged Illadopsis*, Capuchin Babbler, White-necked Rockfowl*, Dusky Tit, Sun Lark, Jameson's Antpecker, Grey-headed Oliveback, Jambandu, Baka and Pale-winged Indigobirds, Togo Paradise-Whydah, Orange, Yellow-mantled, Maxwell's Black and Preuss' Weavers, Gray's Malimbe, Scarlet-tufted, Bates' and Buff-throated Sunbirds, Brown-rumped Bunting.

ADDITIONAL INFORMATION

Books and Papers

The Birds of Ghana (BOU Checklist No 9). Grimes, L. 1987. BOU.

Addresses

Ghana Wildlife Society, Box 13252, Accra (tel: 664697/8).

Near-endemics (Upper Guinea)

White-breasted Guineafowl*, Rufous Fishing-Owl*, Little Green Woodpecker, Ghana Cuckoo-shrike*, Copper-tailed Glossy-Starling*, Yellow-bearded Greenbul*, Sharpe's Apalis, Black-capped Rufous Warbler*, Rufous-winged Illadopsis*, White-necked Rockfowl*.

Near-endemics (Upper Guinea and Nigeria)

Brown-cheeked Hornbill*, Chestnut-bellied Helmetshrike, Finsch's Flycatcher-Thrush.

GUINEA BISSAU

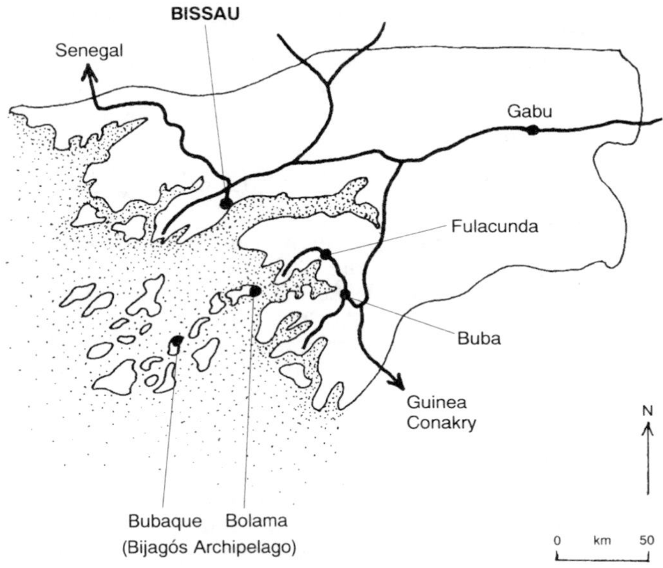

Only the important coastal wetlands of Guinea Bissau have been thoroughly explored by ornithologists in recent years, so very little is known about the landbirds, a situation not helped by the difficulties involved in getting around this very poor country.

Guinea Bissau is a tiny country (36,125 sq km), just a quarter of the size of England, and one twentieth the size of Texas. Getting around is very difficult and depends greatly on the state of the tides since ferries are virtually unavoidable. Accommodation is, at best, thin on the ground outside the capital Bissau and, where present, it is expensive. Camping is permitted, but there are no campsites. Food offers more value for money, although away from the main towns, rice is about all there is to eat. Immunisation against hepatitis, polio, typhoid and yellow fever is recommended, as are precautions against malaria. The local people are very poor, and as is usual in such circumstances, very friendly. Without doubt the best time to go is December to January. Otherwise it is incredibly humid and, from May to November, very very wet. Guinea Bissau's coast is a maze of mangrove-lined islands, bays, creeks and channels, whilst inland there is remnant lowland Upper Guinea rainforest and savanna. Conservation is non-existent, despite the importance of the coast to wintering Palearctic shorebirds, and the valuable Upper Guinea forest. No threatened and three near-threatened species occur in Guinea Bissau.

Six of the ten families endemic to the African mainland are represented. Only 319 species have been recorded in this little explored country, over 230 fewer than neighbouring Guinea Conakry. Non-endemic specialities and spectacular species include Egyptian and Forbes' Plovers. There are no endemics and only two Upper Guinea endemics, but these include the little known Turati's Bushshrike*.

Some forest remains on the islands of the **Bijagós Archipelago**, accessible from Bissau, and these islands may repay exploration, although accommodation is available only in Bubaque. Otherwise, camping is possible.

A SELECTED LIST OF SPECIES RECORDED IN GUINEA BISSAU

Red-billed Tropicbird, African Darter, African Pygmy-goose, Black and Goliath Herons, Hamerkop, Saddle-billed Stork, Secretary-bird, Ahanta Francolin, Black Crowned-Crane, Egyptian and Forbes' Plovers, White-headed Lapwing, Sabine's Gull, Grey and Brown-necked Parrots, Guinea, Violet and Great Blue Turacos, Black Coucal, White-bellied and Blue-breasted Kingfishers, Red-throated and Swallow-tailed Bee-eaters, Abyssinian, Blue-bellied and Blue-throated Rollers, Black Scimitar-bill, Piping and Yellow-casqued* Hornbills, Little Green Woodpecker, Piapiac, Turati's Bushshrike*, White-tailed Alethe, Bronze-tailed Glossy-Starling, White-browed Forest-Flycatcher, Preuss' Swallow, Grey-headed Bristlebill, Red-tailed Greenbul, Siffling and Black-necked Cisticolas, Puvel's Illadopsis, Capuchin Babbler, Grey-headed Oliveback, Crimson Seedcracker, Black-and-white Mannikin, Pale-winged Indigobird, Gray's Malimbe.

ADDITIONAL INFORMATION

Books and Papers

Ornithological Importance of the Coastal Wetlands of Guinea-Bissau. Altenburg, W *et al.* 1992. WIWO.

Near-endemics (Upper Guinea)

Little Green Woodpecker, Turati's Bushshrike*.

GUINEA CONAKRY

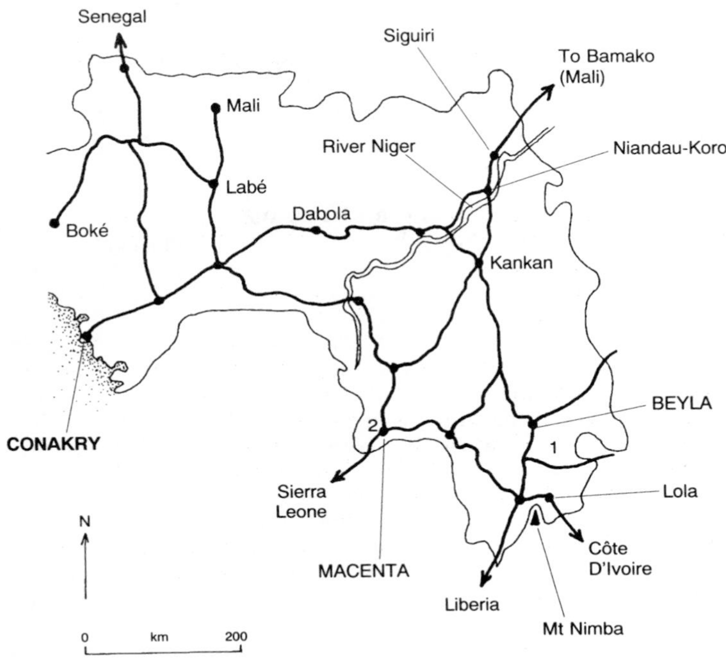

1 Beyla
2 Macenta

INTRODUCTION

Summary

Bumbling bureaucracy and a poor infrastructure have long deterred birders from visiting this country, but any improvements may encourage Upper Guinea endemic hunters to consider a visit since species such as White-necked Rockfowl* are not that difficult to find, at least in the few forests that remain.

Size

At 245,857 sq km, Guinea Conakry is nearly twice as large as England, and a third the size of Texas.

Getting Around

This is a hard country to get around owing to the poor roads. Buses and mini-buses are quite expensive and car-hire is *very* expensive. The internal air network could be improved. Beware of trouble in 'restricted military areas' such as Beyla.

Accommodation and Food

Accommodation and food, heavily influenced by the French, are both expensive in the capital, Conakry, but cheaper and more basic 'in the bush'.

Health and Safety

Immunisation against hepatitis, polio, typhoid and yellow fever is recommended, as are precautions against malaria. Also beware of bilharzia and avoid tap water.

The people are very friendly.

Climate and Timing

Although quite dry from November to May, Guinea Conakry is very wet for the rest of the year and, along the coast, it is hot and humid all year round.

Habitats

Guinea Conakry is quite mountainous by West African standards, although its most important habitat is lowland Upper Guinea rainforest, some of which remains in the extreme southeast. There is also some savanna and plenty of rivers which are wide and sandy in the north and rocky in the south.

Conservation

A continuing increase in rice cultivation and the number of coffee plantations threatens the remaining savanna and Upper Guinea forest.

Eleven threatened and five near-threatened species occur in Guinea Conakry.

Bird Families

Five of the ten families endemic to the African mainland are represented.

Bird Species

A total of 552 species have been recorded in Guinea Conakry, 140 fewer than its neighbour, Cote D'Ivoire. Non-endemic specialities and spectacular species include Long-tailed Hawk, Egyptian and Forbes' Plovers, Grey Pratincole, Black and Blue-headed Bee-eaters, Red-cheeked Wattle-eye and Jameson's Antpecker.

Endemics

There are no endemics, but ten of the 16 Upper Guinea endemics have been recorded, including Rufous Fishing-Owl*, Turati's Bushshrike* and White-necked Rockfowl*.

Ahanta Francolin, Yellow-casqued Hornbill and White-necked Rockfowl* occur in Kounounkan Forest, 90 km southeast of Conakry, near Moussayah. Sun Lark and African Quailfinch have been recorded around **Kankan**, in the savanna of east Guinea Conakry. Bird alongside the Milo river, upstream from the bridge in town. Red-throated Bee-eater has been recorded alongside the **Kankan–Bamako road**, north of Kankan to Mali, as well as Egyptian Plover, Grey Pratincole and White-headed Lapwing (at the Niger river crossing, Niandau-Koro), and Northern Carmine Bee-eater (at the Tinkisso river crossing, just south of Siguiri).

The remote, barely vegetated rolling hills and forested ravines south and east of **Beyla**, in southeast Guinea Conakry, support few species, but they include Hartlaub's Duck, African Finfoot, Rock Pratincole, Black Coucal and Blue-bellied Roller. This is a 'restricted military area' and care should be taken before entering seemingly sensitive areas.

MACENTA

This town lies in southeast Guinea Conakry, near savanna, wetlands and remnant Upper Guinea rainforest, most of which is present on the slopes of the Ziama Massif (1200 m (3937 ft)). Over 300 species have been recorded and the area is as rich as Gola Forest in Sierra Leone (p. 307) and Mount Nimba in Liberia (p. 201). As well as a fine selection of Upper Guinea endemics such as White-necked Rockfowl*, this is a good area for Hartlaub's Duck, Forbes' Plover and Blue-headed Bee-eater.

Specialities

Buff-spotted Flufftail, Forbes' Plover, Blue-headed Bee-eater, Little Green Woodpecker, Brown-cheeked Hornbill*, Ghana Cuckoo-shrike*, Red-cheeked Wattle-eye, Finsch's Flycatcher-Thrush, Lowland Akalat, Yellow-bearded Greenbul*, Sharpe's Apalis, Black-capped Rufous Warbler*, Kemp's Longbill, White-necked Rockfowl*, Jameson's Antpecker.

Others

Hartlaub's Duck, Hamerkop, Palm-nut Vulture, Congo Serpent-Eagle, Red-thighed Sparrowhawk, Black Goshawk, Long-tailed Hawk, Cassin's Hawk-Eagle, Forest and Ahanta Francolins, White-spotted Flufftail, African and Black Crakes, Allen's Gallinule, African Finfoot, Greater Painted-snipe, Afep Pigeon, Guinea, Yellow-billed and Great Blue Turacos, Black and African Emerald Cuckoos, Yellowbill, African Wood-Owl, Shining Blue, White-bellied and Blue-breasted Kingfishers, Black and White-throated Bee-eaters, Abyssinian (Feb–Mar) and Blue-throated Rollers, White-headed and Forest Woodhoopoes, White-crested, Black Dwarf, African Pied and Yellow-casqued* Hornbills, Naked-faced Barbet, Speckled and Yellow-throated Tinkerbirds, Yellow-spotted Barbet, Spotted, Thick-billed, Lyre-tailed and Cassin's Honeyguides, Melancholy and Fire-bellied Woodpeckers, Chestnut-capped Flycatcher, Blue-headed Crested-Flycatcher, Black-winged Oriole, Blue and Purple-throated Cuckoo-shrikes, Many-coloured and Fiery-breasted Bushshrikes, African and Black-and-white Shrike-flycatchers, White Helmetshrike, Chestnut and Yellow-bellied Wattle-eyes, White-tailed Ant-Thrush, Brown-chested and White-tailed Alethes, White-browed Forest-Flycatcher, Ussher's Flycatcher, Forest Robin, Snowy-crowned Robin-Chat, White-throated Blue Swallow, Square-tailed and Fanti Sawwings, Yellow-whiskered Bulbul, Honeyguide, Ansorge's, Swamp and Icterine Greenbuls, Grey-headed Bristlebill, Western Bearded Greenbul, Red-faced, Whistling and Siffling Cisticolas, Black-capped Apalis, Yellow-browed Camaroptera, Moustached Grass-Warbler, Rufous-crowned Eremomela, Green and Lemon-bellied Crombecs, Green Hylia, Violet-backed Hyliota, Pale-breasted and

Brown Illadopsises, Capuchin Babbler, Tit-hylia, White-breasted and Chestnut-breasted Negrofinches, Grey-headed Oliveback, Green-backed Twinspot, Crimson Seedcracker, Mountain Wagtail, Vieillot's Black and Yellow-mantled Weavers, Red-vented, Gray's, Crested and Red-headed Malimbes, Yellow-shouldered and Red-collared Widowbirds, Scarlet-tufted, Blue-throated Brown, Buff-throated, Copper and Splendid Sunbirds.

(White-breasted* and Crested Guineafowl have been reported by hunters, and a possible Ballman's Malimbe* has been recorded near Quinquina Post.)

Other Wildlife

Buffalo, elephant, pygmy hippo.

Access

This area is accessible via the Gueckedou–Seredou road. Bird the savanna north of Macenta, the wetlands and forested streams (Hartlaub's Duck) around Macenta, the remnant forest northwest of Pasima, the Macenta–Nzebela Ferry road, the Seredou Forest Research Centre area (Buff-spotted Flufftail), the Seredou area, and the Seredou–Quinquina Post track. White-necked Rockfowl* is rarely seen away from breeding sites at which it is present from July to January. It is known as 'Kouma Oni' by the local hunters who may act as guides.

In the far southeast of Guinea Conakry, near Nzerekore, the foothills of **Mount Nimba** (p. 201) stretch into the country. Rufous Fishing-Owl*, Yellow-footed Honeyguide*, Ghana Cuckoo-shrike*, Copper-tailed Glossy-Starling*, Liberian Black-Flycatcher*, Yellow-bearded Greenbul*, Sierra Leone Prinia*, Black-capped Rufous Warbler*, Rufous-winged Illadopsis* and White-necked Rockfowl* have all been recorded from Mount Nimba, most of which lies within Liberia.

ADDITIONAL INFORMATION

Books and Papers

Liste des Oiseaux de Guinée. Morel, G and Morel, M. 1988. *Malimbus* 10:143–176.

Annotated Bird List of Macenta Prefecture, Guinea. Halleux, D. 1994. *Malimbus*. 16:10–29

Addresses

West African Ornithological Society (WAOS); see p. 413.

Near-endemics (Upper Guinea)

Rufous Fishing-Owl*, Little Green Woodpecker, Turati's Bushshrike*, Iris and Copper-tailed* Glossy-Starlings, Yellow-bearded Greenbul*, Sierra Leone Prinia*, Sharpe's Apalis, Black-capped Rufous Warbler*, White-necked Rockfowl*.

Near-endemics (Upper Guinea and Nigeria)

Brown-cheeked Hornbill*, Chestnut-bellied Helmetshrike, Finsch's Flycatcher-Thrush.

KENYA

1	Lake Naivasha	6	Masai Mara	11	Tsavo NP
2	Lake Nakuru NP	7	Mount Kenya	12	Arabuko–Sokoke Forest
3	Lake Baringo	8	Samburu	13	Malindi
4	Lake Victoria	9	Marsabit NP		
5	Kakamega NR	10	Nairobi NP		

INTRODUCTION

Summary

Kenya is a birder's paradise. Habitats and birds change quickly here, and the amazing avifauna is ably supported by many mammals and dramatic landscapes. Surprisingly, after many years as one of world's major birding destinations, there is still no decent field guide (although at least two are in the pipeline). However, this is a minor drawback. Go now and prepare to be overwhelmed.

Size

At 582,646 sq km, Kenya is 4.5 times larger than England, and slightly smaller than Texas.

Getting Around

Public buses and matatus (bush taxis) are cheap and fairly wide-ranging. The efficient trains are also cheap and the major rail route crosses the middle of the country, stopping at Kisumu, Nakuru, Naivasha, Nairobi and Mombasa, all of which are close to major birding sites. There is also an excellent, relatively cheap internal air network. However, because the matatus do not reach all of the best birding sites, and birding on foot is not allowed in national parks and not recommended in many other areas, Kenya is one of those countries where it is worth forking out for personal transport. Even with a car though, do not expect an easy ride, for although Kenya is a modern country by African standards, many of the roads are in poor condition, and birding the country thoroughly by car will involve many hours on seemingly never-ending, corrugated, pot-holed and dusty tracks. Fortunately, the effort involved is more than worth it.

There is an entrance fee for most national parks where the gates are opened at 06.00 and closed at 18.00 or 18.30. Since virtually all lodges, shambas and campsites are inside the parks it is crucial to make the closing times, or face a night in the car in the bush.

Accommodation and Food

All national parks and other lodges are very expensive, although they serve fairly good value food to non-residents, usually birders in need of a decent meal after days in the bush. Budget birders are not encouraged in Kenya, and while most national park lodges have adjacent campsites, they are usually unfenced, completely devoid of facilities, including water, and positioned in rather unnerving locations. Having said that, camping is the ultimate way to experience Africa. Away from the major tourist areas food tends to be rather basic.

Health and Safety

Immunisation against hepatitis, meningitis, polio, rabies, typhoid and yellow fever is recommended, as are all precautions against malaria.

Most Kenyans are very friendly but some parts of 'Nairobbery' are not safe at night, and care should be taken anywhere in Kenya.

Kenya has many potentially dangerous animals. It is forbidden to leave your vehicle within the national parks except at designated areas. Buffalos, especially lone individuals, are particularly volatile, and it is wise never to get between a hippo and the water (these huge beasts feed in the campsite at Lake Baringo). Both buffalo and hippo have killed more people than lions, which along with elephants and rhinos, also have the right-of-way. If camping, beware especially of baboons. They can be very aggressive if tempted by stray food and have ripped open tents and even entered cars. Pitch tents in carefully chosen positions, such as near a tree, since any animal, or herd of animals, may stampede through an unfenced campsite.

Climate and Timing

The Kenyan climate is complex and unpredictable, owing to the varied topography and the country's position on the equator. Basically, it is hot and dry in January and February, hot and wet from March to May (especially on the coast), hot and dry again from June to October, and warm and wet in November and December. It can be very cold at night in the highlands, such as Mount Kenya. The peak time to visit is October to February when Palearctic migrants are present, or June to July when some southern African migrants occur, weavers and bishops are in breeding plumage, and Kakamega is at its liveliest.

Habitats

There is a great variety of habitats crammed between the country's borders and the capital Nairobi lies, more or less, at the centre of this complex commingle. It is situated at the southern end of the central highlands, which rise to 5199 m (17,057 ft) at snow-capped Mount Kenya. Lofty lobelias loom impressively out of this mountain's moorland, below which there is montane forest, although as one approaches Nairobi much of this has been replaced with plantations and rich farmland. North of Mount Kenya the montane forest quickly gives way to savanna and semi-desert at Samburu, Marsabit and beyond. The immense Great Rift Valley lies to the west of Nairobi. From the air, its savanna surrounded saline and freshwater lakes resemble a jewel-studded chain hanging across the country from north (Lake Turkana) to south (Lake Magadi). These shimmering jewels abound with birds. Beyond the Great Rift lies the papyrus-fringed Lake Victoria and, around Kakamega, an eastern extension of the lowland West African rainforest. To the south of Nairobi there are vast expanses of acacia savanna, crossed by gallery forest, especially in the Masai Mara, and dotted with marshes, especially in Amboseli NP. The word magnificent is often used out of context, but not in the case of Mount Kilimanjaro, which at 5894 m (19,337 ft) is the highest mountain in Africa. This vast volcano, complete with icing on top, dominates the scenery in southeast Kenya (although it lies in Tanzanian territory), all the way to the Indian Ocean coast where, inland from the fish-filled reefs, beaches and mangrove-fringed bays, there lies a narrow belt of coastal forest at Arabuko-Sokoke.

Conservation

Habitat destruction and degradation is taking place rapidly within Kenya, mainly as a result of an increasing human population. Few of Kenya's many visiting tourists realise that wetlands are being lost due to reclamation, irrigation, siltation, pollution and damming. Even much-visited Lake Nakuru, which lies in a national park, is being damaged by industrial waste and sewage from the nearby town. Savanna is also being degraded through overgrazing by domestic cattle, the increasing need for firewood and off-road driving by tourists. Forests, including those near Kakamega, are being depleted as more people need more land to grow more food.

One possible way forward would be to regulate and develop bird tourism as a means of generating local revenue. Kakamega is a prime example. Here, there is no charge to visiting birders and poor on-site accommodation, whilst the provision of a lodge, with an adjacent campsite, complete with the necessary facilities for those with less money in their pockets, would surely attract enough visitors to provide for the conservation of the forest and, perhaps, provide a valuable income for at least some of the local people.

Twenty-two threatened and 18 near-threatened species occur in Kenya.

Bird Families

Kenya is not one of the top-ten countries in Africa as far as family diversity is concerned. Seven of the ten families endemic to the African mainland are represented. Rockfowls and sugarbirds only are absent (a Shoebill*, believed to be the first for Kenya, was present in the Masai Mara and Amboseli in late 1994). Some families are very well represented indeed, and these include raptors, bustards, coursers, plovers, turacos, nightjars, kingfishers, bee-eaters, barbets, bushshrikes, starlings, larks and weavers.

Bird Species

Kenya has the second highest list for any African country. At 1,078 it is just 16 short of Zaïre's, a country four times the size. However, despite being over twice the size, Kenya's total is still only 86 higher than Uganda's and, in a worldwide context, nearly 500 short of Ecuador's, a country in a similar geographic position on the equator, but half its size. Non-endemic specialities and spectacular species include Vulturine Guineafowl, Crab Plover, Madagascar Pratincole, Black-winged Lapwing, Yellow-throated Sandgrouse, Blue-headed and Madagascar Bee-eaters, Green-headed Oriole, Jameson's Wattle-eye, Golden-breasted Starling and Golden Pipit.

Endemics

The six species unique to Kenya are Tana River* and Aberdare Cisticolas, Hinde's Pied-Babbler*, Williams' Lark*, Sharpe's Pipit* and Clarke's Weaver*.

Kenya's greatest ornithological attraction, apart from its variety, lies in its near-endemics, many of which are confined to northeast Africa and hard to see in other countries in which they are also present, such as Somalia and Ethiopia. These many specialities include Jackson's Francolin, Heuglin's Bustard, Hartlaub's Turaco, Sokoke Scops-Owl*, Somali Bee-eater, Papyrus Gonolek*, Turner's Eremomela*, Malindi* and Sokoke* Pipits, and Amani* and Golden-winged Sunbirds.

Expectations

Expect to see more birds than you could possibly imagine in Kenya. Some tour companies, geared to non-stop birding, notch up 600 species in two weeks and 700 in three. In November 1991 a Birdquest tour recorded an incredible 751 species (plus 70 mammals) over the period of four weeks, whilst another tour led by Brian Finch at the same time set the African record by notching up a staggering 797 in just 25 days. This compares favourably with the world tour record of 844, recorded over the period of 27 days, in Ecuador.

Independent, well-prepared birding zealots may see over 600 species in four weeks, so long as they cover the area between Nairobi, Samburu, Kakamega, Tsavo and the coast.

Kenya's modern capital, **Nairobi**, is only a day's drive away from some of the world's most wonderful wild places, not least the Great Rift Valley lakes, Samburu and the Masai Mara. Nairobi 'park' birds include Superb Starling, whilst Red-winged Starlings frequent the city centre tower blocks, one of the best sites for this species in Kenya. The grounds of the National Museum, itself worth at least a quick look, and surrounding scrub, support Cinnamon-chested Bee-eater, Brown-backed Woodpecker, Northern Pied-Babbler, Mountain Wagtail and Holub's Golden-Weaver.

Blacksmith Plover is one of many superb plovers widespread throughout Africa

NAIROBI NORTHWEST TO LAKE VICTORIA

White-backed and Maccoa Ducks occur on **Limuru Pond**, which lies alongside the A104, 30 km west of Nairobi *en route* to Lake Naivasha. The endemic Sharpe's Pipit* and Long-tailed Widowbird occur on the moorland of the **Kinangop Plateau**, north of Limuru. Turn north off the A104, 68 km west of Nairobi, across the flyover, towards Thika, on the C66. After 4 km keep your eyes peeled for the pipit in the roadside grassland. Continue along this road for another 16 km to reach **Kieni Forest** where Olive Ibis, Hartlaub's Turaco, Barred Long-tailed Cuckoo, Bar-tailed Trogon, Cinnamon-chested Bee-eater, Black-tailed Oriole, Black-fronted Bushshrike, Waller's and Abbott's* Starlings, Placid Greenbul, Broad-ringed White-eye and White-browed Crombec occur. There are a number of tracks into the forest along a 7 km-stretch here, after which it is 45 km to Thika. In addition, Purple-crested Turaco and Grey-olive Greenbul have been recorded at or near **Blue Posts River Lodge**.

LAKE NAIVASHA

This freshwater rift valley lake, 80 km northwest of Nairobi, is a superb site. The lake, lakeshore and surrounding acacias are brimming with birds. Over 450 species have been recorded on and around the lake and it is possible to see over 170 species in a day, on foot.

Specialities

Sharpe's Pied-Babbler, Golden-winged Sunbird (Dec–Mar).

Others

Southern Pochard, Greater and Lesser* Flamingos, Black and Goliath Herons, Saddle-billed Stork, Grey Crowned-Crane, African Snipe, Three-banded and Caspian Plovers (Nov–Mar), Long-toed Lapwing, Blacksmith Plover, Brown-hooded Kingfisher (vagrant), White-fronted Bee-eater, Lilac-breasted Roller, Red-fronted and White-headed Barbets, Wahlberg's Honeyguide, Red-winged and Superb Starlings, Grey Tit-Flycatcher, White-throated Robin (Nov–Mar), Northern Anteater-Chat, Banded Martin, Grey-rumped Swallow, Grey-capped Warbler, Lesser Swamp-Warbler, Arrow-marked Babbler, Chestnut Sparrow, Cape Wagtail, Purple Grenadier, Red-headed Weaver, White-winged Widowbird, Brimstone Canary.

Other Wildlife

Giraffe, hippo, waterbuck.

LAKE NAIVASHA

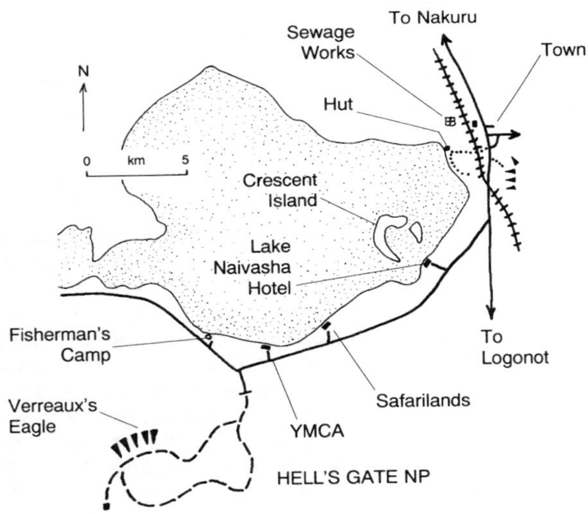

From Naivasha town head south, then bird: (1) The trail west which begins just after the last shop, before the railway line crosses the road, and leads to the northeastern shoreline (40 minutes on foot) (Cape Wagtail). (2) The small scarp to the east of the road just south of town (Red-fronted and White-headed Barbets), then along the road southwest that serves (3) The Lake Naivasha Hotel (Sharpe's Pied-Babbler in the grounds and Grey-capped Warbler near the jetty), on the edge of the lake opposite Crescent Island (boat-trips possible). (4) Safarilands Lodge, which has a good garden but poor views of the lake owing to papyrus. (5) The YMCA (Red-headed Weaver). (6) Fisherman's Camp, which has excellent grounds and lies next to a particularly productive part of the lake.

The escarpment to the northeast of Naivasha town supports Little Rock-Thrush, White-throated Robin (Nov–Mar), and Mocking Cliff-Chat. Bird the ravine and beyond, visible from the eastern edge of town. Verreaux's Eagle, Secretary-bird, Nyanza and Mottled Swifts and White-fronted Bee-eater occur in **Hell's Gate NP**, reached by turning southeast 5 km southwest of Safarilands.

Accommodation: Lake edge: Lake Naivasha Hotel (A+); Safarilands (A+); Fisherman's Camp — camping (C). Naivasha town: La Belle Inn (B).

Black Heron and African Skimmer have been recorded at **Lake Elmenteita** where, from the private Delamere Camp (owned and operated by East African Ornithological Safaris Ltd), it is possible to go on night-drives in search of nocturnal mammals, including aardvark and zorilla.

LAKE NAKURU NATIONAL PARK

'Lake Pink' would be a suitable alternative name for this saline lake, 160 km northwest of Nairobi, for it is often covered in hundreds of thousands of flamingos, and really does look pink from the top of Baboon Rocks. Over 400 species have been recorded on and around the lake, including Narina Trogon and Little Rock-Thrush.

Others

Maccoa Duck, Cape and Hottentot Teals, Southern Pochard, Greater and Lesser* Flamingos, Verreaux's and Long-crested Eagles,

LAKE NAKURU NP

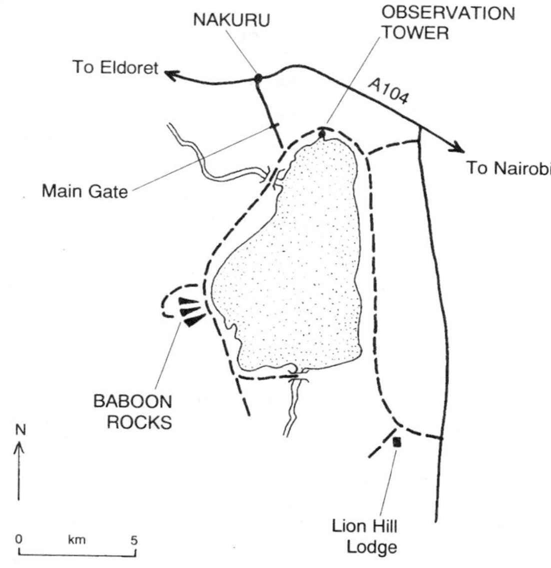

Hildebrandt's Francolin, Tambourine Dove, Blacksmith Plover, African and Horus Swifts, Narina Trogon, White-fronted Bee-eater, Southern Ground-Hornbill, Red-fronted Barbet, Rufous-necked Wryneck, Little Rock-Thrush, Mocking Cliff-Chat, Wailing Cisticola, Arrow-marked Babbler, Red-headed Weaver.

Other Wildlife

Bohor reedbuck, leopard, yellow-spotted hyrax.

Access

The park entrance is a few km south of Nakuru town. There is an observation tower at the north end of the lake. Tracks pass along the western and eastern shores, through excellent woodland, which is best at the southwest corner (Narina Trogon). Of the side-tracks, one leads to Baboon Rocks, where the sight of thousands of flamingos is spectacular. Mocking Cliff-Chat and Wailing Cisiticola occur here. The Lion Hill Lodge grounds are also well worth birding.

Accommodation: Lake surrounds: Lion Hill Lodge; campsite (C). Nakuru town: Mau View Lodge (C); Lake Nakuru Lodge (A).

LAKE BARINGO

This freshwater lake lies in a very hot, dry, dusty bowl, and is surrounded by acacia woodland. Over 400 species have been recorded here, including a handful of local specialities, most of which occur at the base of the nearby escarpment, and Three-banded Courser.

Specialities

Jackson's and Hemprich's Hornbills, Black-throated Barbet, Pygmy Batis, Bristle-crowned Starling, Brown-tailed Chat, Pale Prinia, Red-faced Apalis, Northern Masked-Weaver.

Others

Goliath Heron, Bat Hawk, Verreaux's Eagle, Greater Painted-snipe, Water Thick-knee, Three-banded Courser, Long-toed and Black-headed Lapwings, White-faced Scops-Owl, Spotted and Verreaux's Eagle-Owls, Slender-tailed Nightjar, African Pygmy-Kingfisher, White-throated and Madagascar (May–Sep) Bee-eaters, Red-fronted Tinkerbird, White-rumped Shrike, Magpie Starling, Spotted Morning-Thrush, Mocking Cliff-Chat, Grey Wren-Warbler, Mouse-coloured Penduline-Tit, Chestnut Sparrow, Green-winged Pytilia, Blue-capped Cordon-bleu, Black-cheeked Waxbill, Little, Black-headed and Golden-backed Weavers, Yellow-crowned and Orange Bishops, Beautiful Sunbird, White-bellied Canary.

Other Wildlife

Hippo, Nile crocodile.

Access

Lake Baringo is some 200 km north of Lake Nakuru. Bird around the Country Club, especially the adjacent campsite (Pygmy Batis), the (usually) dry river-bed a few hundred metres south of here (Three-banded

Courser), and the base of the escarpment to the west. The Country Club organise excellent guided birding walks, as well as boat-trips.

Accommodation: Lake Baringo Country Club (A+); campsite (C): this is a private campsite, so it is one of the best in Kenya, but beware of hippos; Island Camp (A).

The small town of **Kapedo**, 76 km north of Baringo on a very bad road (4WD recommended), lies near semi-desert. Species recorded include Quail-plover, Somali Fiscal, Magpie Starling, Somali Crombec and Chestnut-headed Sparrow-Lark. Another highly localised bird, Somali Sparrow, occurs in Kapedo itself, usually in the vicinity of the hospital.

Between Lake Baringo and Eldoret (Route C51), to the west, it is worth stopping at the observation lay-by halfway up the west side of the Kerio Valley. White-crested Turaco and Little Rock-Thrush have been seen from here.

Jackson's Hornbill is one of a number of northeast African specialities present around Lake Baringo

LAKE VICTORIA

The northeast corner of Lake Victoria lies in extreme southwest Kenya. Its papyrus fringes and adjacent marshes support some scarce specialists such as Papyrus Gonolek* and Papyrus Yellow Warbler*.

Specialities

Papyrus Gonolek*, Carruthers' Cisticola, Papyrus Yellow Warbler*, Red-chested Sunbird, Papyrus Canary.

Others

African Pygmy-goose, African Openbill, Allen's Gallinule, Lesser Moorhen, Swamp Flycatcher, Angola and Rufous-chested Swallows, Red-faced and Winding Cisticolas, Greater Swamp-Warbler, Brown Twinspot, Slender-billed and Black-headed Weavers, Black-winged Bishop, Copper Sunbird. (Rufous-bellied Heron has also been recorded here.)

Bird: (1) The pool, 2 km before Port Victoria on the road from **Siaport** (African Pygmy-goose, Copper Sunbird). (2) The lakeside at **Port Victoria**, near the Mulukoba Hotel (Swamp Flycatcher, Papyrus

Canary). (3) The pool known as 'Red Brick Dam', 2–3 km from Siaport towards Bumala which, when wet, is usually full of birds including African Pygmy-goose, Allen's Gallinule and Lesser Moorhen. The surrounding fields support Rufous-chested Swallow, Brown Twinspot and Copper Sunbird. At **Kisumu** Carruthers' Cisticola occurs at Hippo Point, but this species is very difficult to see in the dense papyrus. The road west to Usengi may also be productive.

Accommodation: Port Victoria. Kisumu.

KAKAMEGA NATURE RESERVE

Kakamega Forest, an eastern extension of the great Congo Basin rainforest, in extreme west Kenya, supports over 80 species which are not found elsewhere in Kenya. These include such spectacular birds as Great Blue Turaco and the fabulous Blue-headed Bee-eater. Although most are widespread in West Africa, some, such as Turner's Eremomela*, are rarities throughout their more westerly range.

Much of this forest has been lost and degraded since the 1970s through clearance, logging, grazing and use of timber for firewood, but what is left seems to teem with birds at times, although at other times it can appear to be lifeless. Patient birders who wait for the 'waves' will do best here.

Specialities

Blue-headed Bee-eater, Least Honeyguide, Jameson's and Yellow-bellied Wattle-eyes, Chapin's Flycatcher*, Toro Olive-Greenbul, Chubb's Cisticola, Black-faced Prinia, Turner's Eremomela*, White-browed Crombec, Uganda Wood-Warbler.

Others

Banded Snake-Eagle, Black Goshawk, Crested Guineafowl, White-spotted Flufftail, Grey Parrot, Black-billed and Great Blue Turacos, Black, African and African Emerald Cuckoos, Yellowbill, Bar-tailed Trogon, African Pygmy-Kingfisher, Cinnamon-chested and White-throated Bee-eaters, White-headed Woodhoopoe, Black-and-white-casqued Hornbill, Grey-throated Barbet, Yellow-rumped Tinkerbird, Yellow-spotted, Hairy-breasted and Yellow-billed Barbets, Thick-billed and Cassin's Honeyguides, Brown-eared and Golden-crowned Woodpeckers, African Broadbill, African Blue-Flycatcher, Black-headed Paradise-Flycatcher, Petit's and Purple-throated Cuckoo-shrikes, Mackinnon's Shrike, Pink-footed Puffback, Luehder's and Grey-green Bushshrikes, African Shrike-flycatcher, Chestnut Wattle-eye, White-tailed Ant-Thrush, Brown-chested Alethe, Stuhlmann's Starling, Equatorial Akalat, Blue-shouldered Robin-Chat, White-headed Sawwing, Shelley's, Ansorge's, Slender-billed, Honeyguide and Joyful Greenbuls, White-chinned Prinia, Buff-throated Apalis, Olive-green Camaroptera, Green Hylia, Yellow-bellied Hyliota, Grey-chested Illadopsis, Dusky Tit, White-breasted Negrofinch, Red-headed Bluebill, Black-crowned Waxbill, Mountain Wagtail, Black-billed, Vieillot's Black, Forest and Brown-capped Weavers, Red-headed Malimbe, Olive and Orange-tufted Sunbirds.

Other Wildlife

Chameleon, diademed guenon, eastern black-and-white colobus, giant forest squirrel, red-tailed monkey.

KAKAMEGA NR

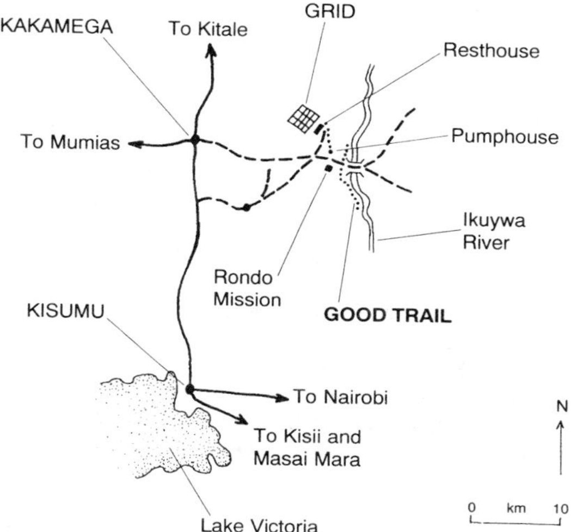

Access

To reach the forest head up the A1 north from Kisumu. After 38 km, 10 km before Kakamega town, turn east (just north of the Arap Moi Girls Secondary School) on to a track to Shinyala village, 7 km away. Take the right fork beyond here and after 5 km turn left to the resthouse in response to the 'Ministry of Natural Resources' sign. Bird the grid behind the resthouse (Brown-chested Alethe), the trail to the pumphouse (White-spotted Flufftail), the trackside forest *en route* to Ikuywa river, and the forest around the river-crossing, especially the trail heading south. The previous two resthouse caretakers have doubled as excellent guides.

Accommodation: Resthouse (C) (very basic); camping (C). Kakamega town: Golf Hotel (A); Franka Hotel (C). Rondo Mission in Forest (A).

Rock Pratincole occurs on the river at **Mumias**, west of Kakamega, the only known site in Kenya. This bird may be seen at the bridge, just beyond the town, or more reliably, behind the sugar factory, visible from the bridge. North of Mumias the small wooded valleys near Madende support Black-shouldered Nightjar and Speckle-breasted Woodpecker. A visit to this area can add some 30 species to the Kakamega leg of a trip to Kenya.

To the north of Kakamega, Ring-necked (very rare) and Jackson's Francolins have been recorded at **Mount Elgon**, west of Kitale. Fifteen

*One of Kakamega's star birds is the rare and little known gem, Turner's Eremomela**

km north of Kitale, lies **Saiwa Swamp NP** (turn east), where Ross's Turaco, Woodland Kingfisher, Double-toothed and Yellow-billed Barbets, African Blue-Flycatcher, Grey-winged and Snowy-crowned Robin-Chats, Black-throated Apalis, African Bush-Warbler and Marsh Widowbird occur. There are tree hides and trails through the forest which surrounds a marsh where the shy sitatunga antelope occurs.

Accommodation: Camping (C).

Spotted Creeper may be extinct in Kenya, but has occurred in the past alongside the road some 15 km north of the turning to Saiwa, south of Kapenguria. Further north still, the **Kongelai Escarpment** is another excellent site. Head west from Makutano which is on the Kitale–Turkana road (Route C46) and bird the trackside from 4 km onwards. White-crested Turaco, Spot-flanked Barbet, Yellow-billed Shrike, Violet-backed Starling, Silverbird and Chestnut-crowned Sparrow-Weaver have been recorded here.

NAIROBI SOUTHWEST TO MASAI MARA

The route in to the Masai Mara from the west via Kisii and Kilgoris, over the Lolgorien Escarpment, can be tortuous without a 4WD, especially if it rains. Although this route may look more direct on the map if you intend to visit the Masai after Kakamega or Lake Victoria, and it offers the chance for some good birding (White-crested Turaco), be prepared.

The A1-C13 route to the Masai Mara from Nairobi via Logonot and Narok is much smoother. The roadside plains 5–15 km beyond **Logonot Satellite Station** towards Narok, north of the Masai Mara, support Scissor-tailed Kite and Greater Kestrel, whilst Stanley Bustard occurs a few km south of Narok, 70 km north of the eastern entrance to Masai Mara.

MASAI MARA RESERVE

The massive Masai Mara, the Kenyan extension of the Serengeti in Tanzania, is a superb place for birds and mammals. Although mainly grassy savanna there are some acacia stands, excellent gallery forest along the Mara river, and a few marshes, where Rufous-bellied Heron, Schalow's Turaco, and the near-endemic Usambiro Barbet occur. The Masai is, arguably, at its best in September, when huge numbers of Burchell's zebras and wildebeest move in from the Serengeti.

Specialities

Yellow-throated Sandgrouse, Schalow's Turaco, Usambiro Barbet, Magpie Shrike, Hildebrandt's Starling, Silverbird, Familiar Chat, Trilling, Rock-loving and Tabora Cisticolas, Swahili Sparrow, Rosy-throated Longclaw.

Others

Ostrich, Rufous-bellied Heron, Saddle-billed Stork, White-headed Vulture, Brown Snake-Eagle, Bateleur, Secretary-bird, Greater and Grey Kestrels, Kori, White-bellied and Black-bellied Bustards, Temminck's Courser, Three-banded and Caspian (Nov–Mar) Plovers, Meyer's Parrot, Ross's Turaco, Bare-faced Go-away-bird, Pel's Fishing-Owl, African Wood-Owl, Slender-tailed Nightjar, Horus Swift, Narina Trogon, Woodland Kingfisher, Lilac-breasted Roller, Southern Ground-Hornbill, Spot-flanked and White-headed Barbets, Golden-tailed and Green-backed Woodpeckers, Black-backed Puffback, Red-billed Oxpecker, Capped Wheatear, Sooty Chat, Stout and Desert Cisticolas, Flappet Lark, Speckle-fronted and Speke's Weavers, Yellow-shouldered Widowbird, Mariqua Sunbird, Yellow-fronted Canary.

(The rare Grey-crested Helmetshrike*, which occurs only in southwest Kenya and northwest Tanzania, has also been recorded in and around the Masai Mara, and a Shoebill* was present in Sep–Nov 1994.)

Bateleurs pierce the sky above the Masai Mara

MASAI MARA

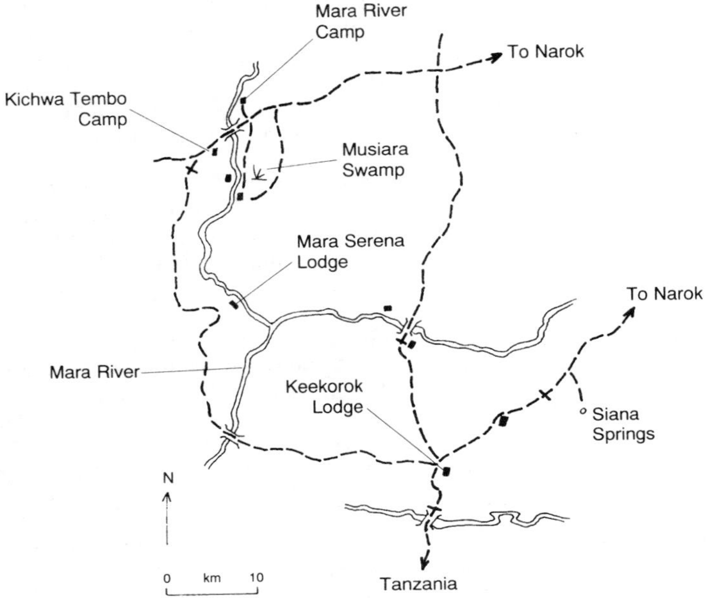

Other Wildlife

Banded mongoose, bat-eared fox, black rhino, black-backed jackal, buffalo, Burchell's zebra, cheetah, elephant, giraffe, Grant's gazelle, hartebeest, hippo, impala, Kirk's dik-dik, leopard, lion, spotted hyena, topi, wildebeest.

Access

Bird throughout the Masai Mara on the many tracks and, especially: (1) Kichwa Tembo Tented Camp where Schalow's Turaco, Narina Trogon and Black-backed Puffback occur within the fenced grounds, and Usambiro Barbet, Familiar Chat and Rock-loving Cisticola on the adjacent escarpment. (2) The plains above Mara River Camp. (3) Musiara Swamp (Rufous-bellied Heron). (4) The valley adjacent to Siana Springs Tented Camp where Magpie Shrike occurs. (5) The Keekorok Lodge grounds (White-headed Barbet). (6) The woodland reached by turning first right after leaving Keekorok (Schalow's Turaco).

Accommodation: Lodges: Mara Serena (A+)/campsite (C); Keekorok (A)/campsite(C); Kichwa Tembo Tented Camp (A+) (the best for birders); Mara River Camp; Siana Springs Tented Camp (just outside the reserve area); and a variety of others.

NAIROBI NORTH TO LAKE TURKANA

The bizarre Hinde's Pied-Babbler*, a Kenyan endemic, occurs near **Kianyaga** (also known as Kirinyaga). Head north from Nairobi on the A2. After 104 km turn east on to the C73. Approximately 20 km along here, just after a small town, turn north in response to the Kianyaga signpost. Ignore the next left and continue straight on for 10 km to the 'D.O.' (District Officer) signpost. Turn left here and left again after a few hundred metres. After another 150 m the road veers right. Park here and explore the steep valley below where the babblers, every one with different, even asymmetrical, plumages, occur.

The endemic Aberdare Cisticola occurs, aptly, in the **Aberdare** or **Nyandarua NP**, where **The Ark** (A+), a famous lodge, is situated. Olive Ibis, Ayres' Hawk-Eagle, Hartlaub's Turaco, Moustached Green-Tinkerbird, Doherty's Bushshrike, Broad-ringed White-eye, and White-browed Crombec occur around The Ark, where there is a canopy-walkway and floodlit waterhole (each room has an alarm to tell visitors there is something good at the waterhole!). Slender-billed Starling and Golden-winged Sunbird occur at **Nyahururu (Thomson's) Falls**, northwest of the Aberdares.

MOUNT KENYA

Snow-capped Mount Kenya (5199 m (17,057 ft)) is Africa's second highest mountain. The boggy grassland and montane forest below its peak support some superb birds, not least the near-endemic Jackson's Francolin, Hartlaub's Turaco and the fabulous Golden-winged Sunbird.

Specialities

Moorland and Jackson's Francolins, Hartlaub's Turaco, Moustached Green-Tinkerbird, Abyssinian Ground-Thrush, Kenrick's Starling, Moorland Chat, Broad-ringed White-eye, Hunter's Cisticola, Jackson's Widowbird, Tacazze, Golden-winged and Red-tufted Sunbirds.

Others

African Black-Duck, Olive Ibis, Mountain Buzzard, Crowned Hawk-Eagle, African Finfoot, Dusky Turtle-Dove, Montane Nightjar, Scarce Swift, Narina and Bar-tailed Trogons, Cinnamon-chested Bee-eater, White-headed Woodhoopoe, Silvery-cheeked Hornbill, Rufous-necked Wryneck, Tullberg's Woodpecker, Black-tailed Oriole, Grey Cuckoo-shrike, Stuhlmann's Starling, White-starred Robin, Rueppell's Robin-Chat, White-headed and Black Sawwings, Slender-billed and Mountain Greenbuls, Black-collared and Grey Apalises, Cinnamon Bracken-Warbler, Mountain Warbler, Brown Woodland-Warbler, Abyssinian Crimson-wing, Black-headed Waxbill, Mountain Wagtail, Long-tailed Widowbird, Green-headed, Eastern Double-collared, Bronze and Malachite Sunbirds, Streaky and Thick-billed Seedeaters, Oriole Finch.

Other Wildlife

Buffalo, bush pig, eastern black-and-white colobus, elephant, giant forest hog, leopard, Syke's monkey.

Access

Bird: (1) The **Naro Moru River Lodge**, 2 km from Naro Moru alongside the Nairobi–Nanyuki road, where African Finfoot, Hartlaub's Turaco, Grey Apalis and Golden-winged Sunbird occur. (2) The **Naro Moru Route**, which leads east from Naro Moru and ascends Mount Kenya to the Meteorological Station at 3048 m (10,000 ft). The riverine forest behind the Youth Hostel bandas (10 km from Naro Moru), supports Hartlaub's Turaco, the bamboo stands and ravines around the Meteorological Station, 26 km from Naro Moru, support Olive Ibis and Abyssinian Ground-Thrush, and the grassland and lobelias above the station support Jackson's Francolin and Red-tufted Sunbird. (3) **Mountain Lodge**, from the roof of which Hartlaub's Turaco, Narina and Bar-tailed Trogons, Kenrick's Starling, White-headed Sawwing, Grey Apalis, and Mountain Warbler may be seen.

Accommodation: Youth Hostel (B); Meteorological Station Bandas/camping (C) (chilly at night); Naro Moru River Lodge(A)/Bandas/camping (C); Mountain Lodge (A).

Boran Cisticola occurs in the acacia scrub around the fork in the road signposted 'Isiolo/Meru', north of Mount Kenya. The only known site in Kenya for Black-and-white Shrike-flycatcher is along the Meru fork, in and around the big fig tree to the left, at the bridge just before the forest starts.

Saddle-billed Stork, Scissor-tailed Kite, Palm-nut Vulture, Vulturine Guineafowl, White-headed Mousebird, Violet Woodhoopoe and Golden-breasted Starling occur in the 1800-sq-km **Meru NP**, approximately 250 km northeast of Nairobi.

Accommodation: Lodge; tented camp and campsites.

SAMBURU RESERVE

Samburu is situated at the southern edge of Kenya's wild northern semi-deserts, and is a great place for birds and mammals. The Samburu region comprises three separate reserves: Samburu, Buffalo Springs and Shaba, which protect arid acacia savanna, scrub and gallery forest alongside the Uaso Nyiro river. A number of northeast African specialities occur here, including Vulturine Guineafowl, Somali Bee-eater and Golden-breasted Starling, as well as the long-necked Gerenuk, the fine-striped Grevy's zebra and oryx.

Specialities

Vulturine Guineafowl, White-headed Mousebird, Yellow-vented Eremomela, Somali Bee-eater, Pygmy Batis, Bare-eyed Thrush, Fischer's and Golden-breasted Starlings, Pink-breasted Lark, Somali Tit, Parrot-billed Sparrow, Donaldson-Smith's Sparrow-Weaver, Golden Palm Weaver, Shining Sunbird (rare).

Others

Ostrich, Hamerkop, Brown Snake-Eagle, Bateleur, Eastern Chanting-Goshawk, Gabar Goshawk, Little Sparrowhawk, African Hawk-Eagle,

Martial Eagle, Pygmy Falcon, Crested Francolin, Kori and Buff-crested Bustards, Spotted Thick-knee, Three-banded and Cream-coloured Coursers, Three-banded Plover, Chestnut-bellied, Black-faced and Lichtenstein's Sandgrouse, Orange-bellied Parrot, White-bellied Go-away-bird, Slender-tailed Nightjar, White-throated Bee-eater, Lilac-breasted Roller, Abyssinian Scimitar-bill, Von der Decken's Hornbill, Red-and-yellow and D'Arnaud's Barbets, Nubian Woodpecker, Taita Fiscal, Slate-coloured Boubou, Rosy-patched Bushshrike, Yellow-billed Oxpecker, Northern Brownbul, Rattling Cisticola, Brown-headed Apalis, Yellow-bellied Eremomela, Rufous Chatterer, Fischer's Sparrow-Lark, Green-winged Pytilia, Golden Pipit, Black-capped Social-Weaver, Kenya Violet-backed and Mariqua Sunbirds, Somali Bunting.

Other Wildlife

Bat-eared fox, buffalo, cheetah, elephant, gerenuk, giraffe (reticulated), Grevy's zebra, Kirk's dik-dik, leopard, lesser kudu, lion, Nile crocodile, olive baboon, oryx, spotted hyena.

Access

Bird throughout, but beware of 4WD-only tracks which are too sandy for 2WD.

Accommodation: A variety of lodges and campsites.

Scissor-tailed Kite and Vulturine Guineafowl occur alongside the road north from Archer's Post, at the eastern edge of Samburu, to Marsabit. A 4WD is recommended for birding from Archer's Post northwards: this road is subject to 'Shiffa' trouble from time to time, hence it is often necessary to take an armed policeman or to drive in convoy. It is *always* necessary to inform the police at the Isiolo checkpoint if you wish to drive to Marsabit.

Samburu is one of the most accessible sites in Africa where Vulturine Guineafowl occur. This is a surprisingly attractive bird, thanks to its dazzling cobalt-blue neck plumes

MARSABIT NATURE RESERVE

Marsabit NR is a green highland island (1702 m (5584 ft)) amidst Kenyan's northern semi-desert. To the north lies the black lava Dida Galgalla Desert which supports the endemic William's Lark*, and a number of near-endemics, including Heuglin's Bustard, Somali Bee-eater, Masked Lark and Somali Sparrow.

Endemics

Williams' Lark*.

Specialities

Heuglin's Bustard, Nubian and Star-spotted Nightjars, Somali Bee-eater, Somali Fiscal, Ashy Cisticola, Red-faced Apalis, Somali Crombec, Masked and Short-tailed Larks, Somali Sparrow.

Others

White-backed and Maccoa Ducks, Greater Kestrel, Spotted Thick-knee, Bruce's Green-Pigeon, Freckled Nightjar, Brown-necked Raven, Pringle's Puffback, Desert Cisticola, Chestnut-headed Sparrow-Lark, Green-winged Pytilia, Black-cheeked Waxbill, Golden Pipit, Somali Bunting.

Other Wildlife

Elephant, greater kudu.

Access

Bird Marsabit NR which surrounds the town of Marsabit, and the surrounding area, especially the desert to the north (best beyond 30 km from town).

Accommodation: Marsabit Lodge.

The rare White-crowned Starling occurs at Turbi, north of Marsabit.

NAIROBI SOUTHEAST TO MOMBASA

NAIROBI NATIONAL PARK

In this small (110 sq km) but excellent park it is possible to see such extraordinary sights as Ostriches and giraffes on a grassy plain with distant skyscrapers as a backdrop. This is because Nairobi NP is just seven km from the centre of Kenya's capital. The park offers a great introduction to birding in East African acacia savanna and over 400 species have been recorded, including Northern Pied-Babbler, Red-throated Tit*, and Jackson's Widowbird*.

Specialities

Yellow-throated Sandgrouse, Long-tailed Fiscal, Northern Pied-Babbler, Red-throated Tit*, Short-tailed Lark, Jackson's Widowbird*, Pangani Longclaw.

Others

Ostrich, Hamerkop, Bateleur, Secretary-bird, Shelley's Francolin, African Finfoot, Grey Crowned-Crane, White-bellied and Hartlaub's Bustards, Blacksmith Plover, Red-chested Cuckoo, Marsh Owl, African Pygmy-Kingfisher, Little Bee-eater, Lilac-breasted Roller, White-headed Barbet, Superb Starling, Red-billed Oxpecker, Southern Black-Flycatcher, Red-backed Scrub-Robin, Yellow-breasted Apalis, Moustached Grass-Warbler, Buff-bellied Warbler, Red-faced Crombec, Banded Warbler, Rufous-naped Lark, Rufous Sparrow, Steel-blue Whydah, Yellow-throated Longclaw, Grey-headed Social-Weaver, Holub's Golden-Weaver, Red-collared Widowbird, Black-bellied Sunbird.

Other Wildlife

Black rhino (introduced), buffalo, Burchell's zebra, cheetah, eland, giraffe, Grant's gazelle, hartebeest, hippo, impala, olive baboon, steenbok, vervet monkey.

Access

The best birding area is around Hippo Pools where it is possible to bird on foot in the acacia woodland alongside the Athi river (Northern Pied-Babbler). African Finfoot has been recorded on the river near here, but it is very difficult to see this skulking species without leaving the official path.

The little known Athi Short-toed Lark has been recorded on the **Athi Plains**, as well as Greater Kestrel, Yellow-throated Sandgrouse, White-tailed and Short-tailed Larks and African Quailfinch. Turn off the Nairobi–Mombasa road in response to the 'Athi River/Namanga' signpost. Head straight through the town of Athi River and bird the roadside just south of town, especially any burnt areas, although 15 km further on, where the vegetation is more sparse, is the best place for Athi Short-toed Lark.

Lake Magadi, 130 km south of Nairobi, is the most reliable site in Kenya for the pretty Chestnut-banded Plover. This species is normally present on the salt pans either side of the road just before the town. 75 km south of Nairobi, *en route* to Lake Magadi, it is worth stopping at **Olorgasailie**, a national monument where Jameson's Firefinch, Blue-capped Cordonbleu, Crimson-rumped Waxbill, Cut-throat, Kenya Grosbeak-Canary and White-bellied Canary visit the small pond to drink and bathe.

The main route south from Nairobi leads to **Amboseli NP** where the savanna and swamps are overshadowed by colossal Kilimanjaro (5894 m (19,337 ft)), the highest peak in Africa. White-backed Duck, Double-banded Courser, Golden Pipit, Pangani Longclaw, and Taveta Golden-Weaver occur in Amboseli NP. It is possible to travel east from here to Tsavo NP through thick bush which supports White-headed Mousebird, Black-cheeked Waxbill and Kenya Grosbeak-Canary, although the track can be horrendous and this is potentially dangerous bandit-country.

The Nairobi–Mombasa road route to Tsavo NP is much smoother, and offers the chance to explore roadside areas for localised birds such as Rufous Short-toed Lark.

TSAVO EAST AND TSAVO WEST NATIONAL PARKS

The Nairobi–Mombasa road separates Tsavo West and Tsavo East, both of which support some excellent birds, including three potential new species, all of which are present on the Taita Hills in Tsavo West.

Specialities

Sombre Nightjar, Moustached Green-Tinkerbird, Black-throated Barbet, Fischer's and Golden-breasted Starlings, Grey-olive Greenbul, Basra Reed-Warbler* (Nov), Pink-breasted Lark, Pangani Longclaw.

Others

Ostrich, African Goshawk, Verreaux's Eagle, Secretary-bird, Pygmy Falcon, Shelley's Francolin, Quail-plover, Hartlaub's Bustard, Black-headed Lapwing, Black-faced Sandgrouse, African Scops-Owl, Donaldson-Smith's, Plain and Freckled Nightjars, Half-collared and Giant Kingfishers, Lilac-breasted Roller, Von der Decken's Hornbill, Southern Ground-Hornbill, Red-and-yellow and D'Arnaud's Barbets, White-necked Raven, Taita Fiscal, White-rumped Shrike, Three-streaked Tchagra, Rosy-patched Bushshrike, Thrush Nightingale (Nov), White-starred and White-throated (Nov) Robins, Stripe-cheeked Bulbul, Ashy Cisticola, Evergreen Forest, Eurasian River (Nov), Upcher's (Nov–Mar) and Olive-tree (Nov–Mar) Warblers, Yellow-throated Wood-Warbler, Flappet and Fawn-coloured Larks, Crimson-rumped Waxbill, Straw-tailed Whydah, Golden Pipit, Black-capped Social-Weaver, Golden-backed Weaver, White-winged Widowbird, Black-bellied Sunbird.

Other Wildlife

Buffalo, Burchell's zebra, cheetah, elephant, giraffe, impala, striped hyena.

Access

Birding throughout the Tsavo national parks is excellent, but particularly good spots in Tsavo West include: (1) Mzima Springs, 10 km from Kilaguni Lodge, one of the few areas where it is possible to bird on foot (Giant Kingfisher). (2) Ngulia Lodge, which is famous for its falls of Palearctic passerine migrants which, in November, may include White-throated Robin and Basra Reed-Warbler*. (3) Alongside the track between Ngulia and the Taita Hills where Half-collared Kingfisher and Grey-olive Greenbul have been recorded. (4) The Taita Hills (2228 m (7310 ft)) (outside the two parks), which support three potential new species: 'Taita Thrush', which does not respond to calls of Olive Thrush, 'Taita White-eye', currently considered by most taxonomists to be a form of Broad-ringed White-eye, and 'Taita Apalis', which does not respond to calls of Bar-throated Apalis. Bird the Ngaongao, Mbololo and Ronge forest patches which also support Moustached Green-Tinkerbird, White-starred Robin, Stripe-cheeked Bulbul, Evergreen Forest Warbler and Yellow-throated Wood-Warbler. Quail-plover has been recorded in the Kitani area.

TSAVO NP

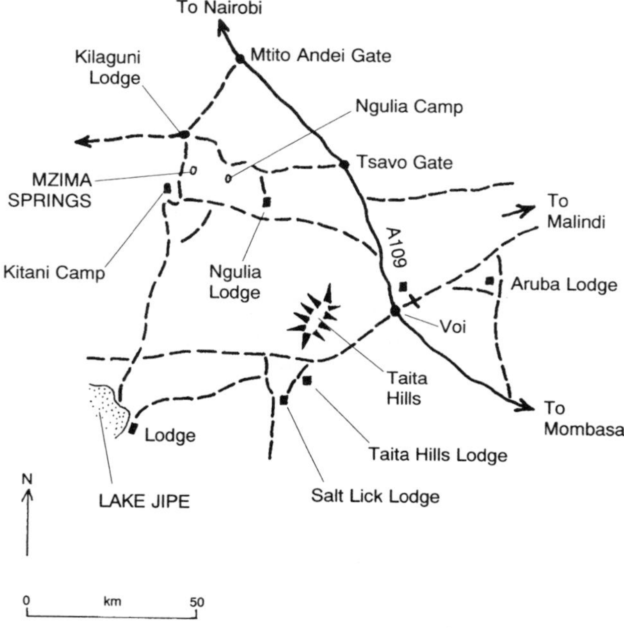

Accommodation: Kilaguni Lodge (A+) (floodlit waterhole) (bandas (B) nearby); Tsavo Safari Camp, Ngulia Lodge (A) (bandas); camping.

White-backed Duck, Black Heron, Water Thick-knee, Double-banded Courser, African Bush-Warbler, African Reed-Warbler and Taveta Golden-Weaver occur at Lake Jipe, south of Tsavo West. Buff-spotted Flufftail (rare), Narina Trogon, Red-capped Robin-Chat and Grey-olive Greenbul occur in groundwater forest near **Taveta**. Turn left just before the railway in Taveta coming from the direcion of Voi. After 1.5 km turn right at the crossroads. The forest is on the left 15 km along here.

Golden Palm Weaver and Purple-banded Sunbird occur in the grounds of Fort Jesus in **Mombasa**. There are a number of hotel complexes south of Mombasa where Black-collared and Brown-breasted Barbets, Golden Palm Weaver and Black-winged and Zanzibar Bishops occur (eg. in the gardens and surrounding scrub at Shelley Beach), whilst Mangrove Kingfisher occurs around Seafarer's and White-cheeked and Bridled Terns occur off Tiwi Beach.

Crested Guineafowl, Fischer's Turaco*, Yellowbill, Bat-like Spinetail, Narina Trogon, Green Barbet, African Green-Tinkerbird, Brown-breasted Barbet, Mombasa Woodpecker, Green-headed Oriole, Retz's and Chestnut-fronted Helmetshrikes, East Coast Akalat* (rare), Yellow-bellied Greenbul, Black-headed Apalis and Uluguru Violet-backed Sunbird occur in **Shimba Hills NP** (448 m (1470 ft)), near Kwale, south of Mombasa. Turn west off the A14 coast road just north of Tiwi. About halfway to Kwale there is a marshy valley where Peters' Twinspot and Black-winged Bishop occur. At Kwale village turn left and bird the roadside forest from here to the park entrance, a distance of 4 km. Brown-breasted Barbet occurs in the park, which is also the only known site in Kenya for the beautiful sable antelope.

Heading north from Mombasa, Brown-headed Parrot has been recorded around **Kilifi Creek**, along the road east to Mnarani Hotel just south of the creek, and east of the village just north of the creek.

ARABUKO–SOKOKE FOREST

This small coastal forest (372 sq km), near Malindi, supports some very rare birds, notably the endemic Clarke's Weaver*, and the near-endemics, Sokoke Scops-Owl*, Sokoke Pipit* and Amani Sunbird*. Over 230 species have been recorded, including many more species with restricted ranges. Birding in this forest can be very hard work, but the patient observer may see most of the specialities within a few days, as well as the bizarre golden-rumped elephant shrew.

Endemics

Clarke's Weaver* (Jul–Aug).

Specialities

Fischer's Turaco*, Thick-billed Cuckoo (Oct–Nov), Sokoke Scops-Owl*, Scheffler's Owlet, Forbes-Watson's Swift (Nov–Mar), Mangrove Kingfisher, Green Barbet, African Green-Tinkerbird, Pallid Honeyguide, Mombasa Woodpecker, African Pitta (Apr–Nov), Yellow Flycatcher, Short-tailed and Pale Batises, Spotted Ground-Thrush* (Feb–Nov), East Coast Akalat*, Bearded Scrub-Robin, Fischer's and Tiny Greenbuls, Scaly Babbler, Sokoke Pipit*, Plain-backed* and Amani* Sunbirds.

Others

African Cuckoo-Falcon (May–Nov), Fasciated Snake-Eagle*, African Goshawk, Crested Guineafowl, Allen's Gallinule, Greater Painted-snipe, Tambourine Dove, African Wood-Owl, Fiery-necked Nightjar, Mottled and Bat-like Spinetails, Narina Trogon, African Pygmy-Kingfisher, Madagascar and Northern Carmine Bee-eaters, Common Scimitar-bill, Crowned and Trumpeter Hornbills, Black-collared Barbet, Scaly-throated Honeyguide, Green-backed Woodpecker, African Crested-Flycatcher, Black Cuckoo-shrike, Black-backed Puffback, Four-coloured Bushshrike, Retz's and Chestnut-fronted Helmetshrikes, Red-tailed Ant-Thrush, Black-bellied Glossy-Starling, Red-capped Robin-Chat (Apr–Nov), Red-backed Scrub-Robin, Sombre, Yellow-throated and Yellow-bellied Greenbuls, Northern Brownbul, Black-headed Apalis, Rufous Chatterer, Green-backed and Peters' Twinspots, Black-and-white Mannikin, Forest Weaver, Olive and Mouse-coloured Sunbirds.

Other Wildlife

Aders' duiker, elephant, four-toed and golden-rumped elephant shrews, suni, Sykes' monkey, yellow baboon.

Access

Seeing the specialities is easier once some grasp of the three forest/woodland types has been obtained, since they determine the location of a number of species. These are: *Cynometra* (tangled red-soil), *Brachystegia* woodland (open, white-sand) and *Afzelia* (dense, evergreen). Sokoke Scops-Owl* and Four-coloured Bushshrike occur only in *Cynometra* forest, Pale Batis, Clarke's Weaver* and Amani Sunbird* occur only in *Brachystegia* woodland, and Fischer's Turaco*, African Green-Tinkerbird and East Coast Akalat* are rarely seen away from *Afzelia* forest.

There are a number of trails and tracks worth birding in Arabuko–Sokoke Forest. Before doing so however, it is essential to visit **Gede Forest Station**, to register as a visitor (thus helping to protect the site) and to arrange a guide to help look for the superb Sokoke Scops-Owl*. Guides may be unwilling to go, however, if there are elephant poachers about. The station is on the west side of the road, 1 km south of Gede village.

KENYA COAST

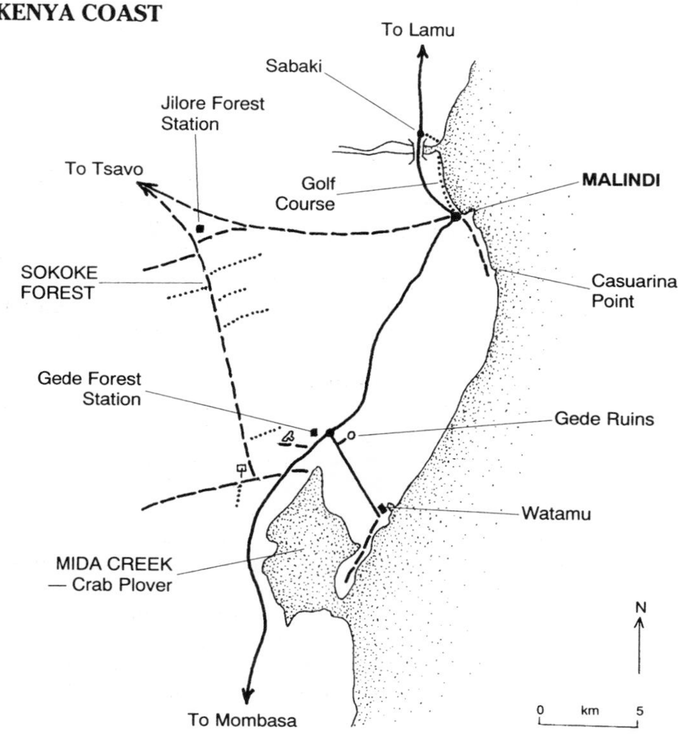

One km south of the Gede Forest Station, park at the roadside space and bird the two short **Gede Trails** through *Afzelia* forest, which lie to the west of the main Malindi–Mombasa road. Six km south of Gede Forest Station (0.5 km south of Mida village), turn west in response to the 'Jilore Forest Station' signpost, on to the **Mida** or **Nature Reserve Track**. Spotted Ground-Thrush* and East Coast Akalat* are seen with

Mida Creek is the most reliable place in Kenya to see the unique Crab Plover

some regularity along the first km of this track. After 1 km there is a fork. Along the left branch (straight on) bird the trail leading south through *Afzelia* forest, which begins after 1 km, and the *Brachystegia* woodland which begins after 2 km. Along the right branch (north) to Jilore Forest Station bird the trails to the east through *Afzelia* forest, then *Brachystegia* woodland and, after passing over a small rise, the trail to the west through *Cynometra* forest. When the water levels are right, Allen's Gallinule, Greater Painted-snipe and Madagascar and Northern Carmine Bee-eaters occur at Lake Jilore. Turn west, just beyond the Jilore Forest Station, on to the Malindi-Tsavo track. A good track leads south to the lake shore, 3 km west of the junction. Twenty-two km south of Gede Forest Station turn west on to the **Kararacha Track**, which passes through *Brachystegia* woodland where Spotted Ground-Thrush* and Sokoke Pipit* occur.

There are also tracks into the forest 40 km south of Malindi (25 km north of Kilifi Creek).

Fischer's Turaco*, Spotted Ground-Thrush* (Feb–Nov), Red-capped Robin-Chat (Apr–Nov), Bearded Scrub-Robin, and Scaly Babbler have been recorded at **Gede Ruins**, an old Arab settlement, signposted from the Watamu road, 1 km southeast of Gede village. African Pitta (Apr–Nov) is a rare visitor. Bird the trail between the 'Mosques on the Walls' at the eastern edge of the ruins (best at dawn). Few birders do well here and usually end up playing 'spot the bird' or looking for golden-rumped elephant shrew.

Crab Plover is one of many shorebirds which occur at **Mida Creek**, an intertidal lagoon east of Sokoke. This is also a good site for Mascarene Reef-Egret, Forbes-Watson's Swift (Nov–Mar) and Black-bellied Glossy-Starling. Head 25 km south out of Malindi, and turn east opposite the Mida Track into Arabuko–Sokoke Forest. Follow this track to the mangrove-fringed bay.

MALINDI

The small coastal town of Malindi is a good base from which to explore the town's seafront, where shorebirds, including White-fronted Plover, and terns, including Saunders', abound, and a number of nearby sites which support Madagascar Pratincole and Malindi Pipit*.

Specialities

Madagascar Pratincole (Apr–Sep), Scaly Babbler, Malindi Pipit*, Golden Palm Weaver, Sombre Greenbul, Fire-fronted and Zanzibar Bishops.

Others

African Pygmy-goose (May–Sep), Greater Flamingo, Madagascar Pond-Heron* (May–Sep), Dwarf Bittern (May–Sep), Woolly-necked Stork, African Crake, Crab Plover, Broad-billed Sandpiper, Water Thick-knee, White-fronted Plover, Sooty Gull, Great Crested-Tern, White-cheeked (Apr–Sep) and Saunders' Terns, African Skimmer (May–Sep), Yellowbill, Northern Carmine Bee-eater, Ethiopian Swallow, Rufous Chatterer, Black-and-white Mannikin, Grosbeak Weaver, Black-winged Bishop. Yellow-collared Lovebird (introduced/escape) also occurs here.

Access

The best birding sites are: (1) The old reef and mudflats at Malindi seafront (White-fronted Plover, Saunders' Tern). (2) The golf course just north of town, reached by turning right 1.5 km north of Malindi off the Lamu road, where the pools, which usually hold at least some water during the period May to September, have attracted African Pygmy-goose. (3) Casuarina Point, 5 km south of Malindi (Crab Plover). (4) **Sabaki River Mouth** 6 km north of Malindi. Head north out of Malindi on the Lamu Road and bird the trail east, which starts just north of the river bridge or, with more difficulty, the trail which runs along the southern edge of the estuary. Alternatively, it is possible to walk north to the estuary along the beach from Malindi, and back inland, via the golf course (allow at least four hours). Up to 400 Madagascar Pratincoles have been seen between April and September at the river mouth and on the pools in the dunes to the south. Bridled and Sooty Terns and Brown and Lesser Noddies are also possible off shore in this area.

Madagascar Pratincole also occurs at the saltpans on the east side of the road 27 km north of Malindi, but the star bird here is Malindi Pipit*, which occurs in the farmland between the road and the saltpans. Quail-plover (Aug), African Crake, Saunders' Tern and Madagascar Bee-eater have also been recorded here, but access is difficult. Malindi Pipit* also occurs around the saltpans at Karawa (3 km east of the main road), 70 km north of Malindi. Karawa is the type-locality for the endemic Tana River Cisiticola*, known from only six specimens taken in semi-arid bush. However, this species has never been relocated, despite extensive searching. Spotted Ground-Thrush* (Mar–Nov), East Coast Akalat*, White-winged Apalis* and Uluguru Violet-backed Sunbird (at Kitere) have been recorded in the **Lower Tana** riverine forests. Very few birders have explored these forests but the areas around Bura, upstream, and Kipini near the estuary, may reward those with time. Collared Lark has been recorded around Hola.

One of the non-birding highlights at Malindi is the stunning variety of fish which occur on the reefs in **Malindi Marine NP**. These fish have to be seen to be believed, and after an hour snorkelling in their company birding may suddenly seem like second best. Most hotels arrange trips to the reef, and low tide on a sunny day, when the water is clearest, is the best time to go.

Accommodation: A wide variety of accommodation is available in Malindi, and nearby.

ADDITIONAL INFORMATION

Books and Papers

A Bird Atlas of Kenya. Lewis, A and Pomeroy, D. 1989. AA Balkema, Rotterdam.
A Field Guide to the Birds of East Africa. Williams, J and Arlott, N. 1980. HarperCollins.
Check-list of the Birds of Kenya. Backhurst, G. 1986. EANHS.
A Field Guide to the Birds of Kenya and Northern Tanzania. Zimmerman, D, Turner, D and Pearson, D. In prep. (1996). Helm.
A Field Guide to the Birds of East Africa. Stevenson, T *et al.* In prep.

Addresses

The East African Natural History Society (EANHS), Box 44486 Nairobi, Kenya, publishes the *Scopus* journal.

The bi-annual *Kenya Birds* is published by the Dept of Ornithology, National Museums of Kenya, Box 40658, Nairobi, Kenya.

Please send interesting records to Don Turner, EANHS Ornithological Sub-committee, Box 48019 Nairobi.

ENDEMICS (6)

Tana River Cisticola*	East: Karawa, known from only six specimens
Aberdare Cisticola	Central: Aberdare Mountains NP
Hinde's Pied-Babbler*	Central: Kianyaga
Williams' Lark*	North: Marsabit (Dida Gigalla Desert)
Sharpe's Pipit*	Central: Kinangop Plateau
Clarke's Weaver*	East: Arabuko–Sokoke Forest

Near-endemics (North and East)

Chestnut-naped Francolin, Heuglin's Bustard, White-winged Collared Dove, White-headed Mousebird, Jackson's Hornbill, Somali Bee-eater, Black-billed Woodhoopoe, Red-naped Bushshrike, Boran Cisticola, Brown-tailed Apalis, Somali Crombec, Friedmann's*, Gillett's and Masked Larks, Somali and Swainson's Sparrows, Donaldson-Smith's Sparrow-Weaver, Salvadori's Weaver, Abyssinian Grosbeak-Canary.

Near-endemics (East)

Sokoke Scops-Owl*, Scheffler's Owlet, Fischer's Turaco*, Mombasa Woodpecker, Yellow Flycatcher, Long-tailed Fiscal, Short-tailed and Pale Batises, Fischer's Starling, East Coast Akalat*, Stripe-cheeked Bulbul, Fischer's and Tiny Greenbuls, Scaly Babbler, Collared Lark, Malindi* and Sokoke* Pipits, Golden Palm Weaver, Fire-fronted and

Zanzibar Bishops, Plain-backed*, Uluguru Violet-backed, and Amani* Sunbirds.

Near-endemics (Central and South/Southwest)

Moorland and Jackson's Francolins, Hartlaub's Turaco, Usambiro Barbet, Grey-crested Helmetshrike*, Kenrick's, Hildebrandt's (also east) and Abbott's* Starlings, Broad-ringed White-eye, Hunter's and Lynes' Cisticolas, Sharpe's and Northern Pied-Babblers, Red-throated Tit*, Buff-bellied Penduline-Tit, Athi Short-toed Lark, Swahili Sparrow, Pangani Longclaw, Taveta Golden-Weaver, Golden-winged Sunbird, Kenya Grosbeak-Canary.

Near-endemics (West and Central)

Papyrus Gonolek*, Doherty's Bushshrike, Chapin's Flycatcher*, Turner's Eremomela*, Papyrus Yellow Warbler*, White-browed Crombec, Uganda Wood-Warbler, Papyrus Canary.

Near-endemics (General)

Moorland Chat, Chubb's Cisticola, Scaly Chatterer, Jackson's Widowbird*.

LIBERIA

INTRODUCTION

Summary

The vicious civil war, which began in 1990 and was still going strong in mid 1995, has left Liberia out of bounds to most birders, which is unfortunate because 25% of the remaining Upper Guinea forest is in Liberia, along with all but two of the Upper Guinea endemics (14 out of 16).

Size

At 111,369 sq km, Liberia is nearly as large as England, but one sixth the size of Texas.

Getting Around

Cheap bush taxis reach most communities, but the roads are terrible, especially during the very wet rainy season (Apr–Nov). Missionary and mine company flights are the best mode of transport, but getting on to them requires some persuasion.

Accommodation and Food

Western standard accommodation may still exist in the capital, Monrovia, but both accommodation and food are basic beyond there.

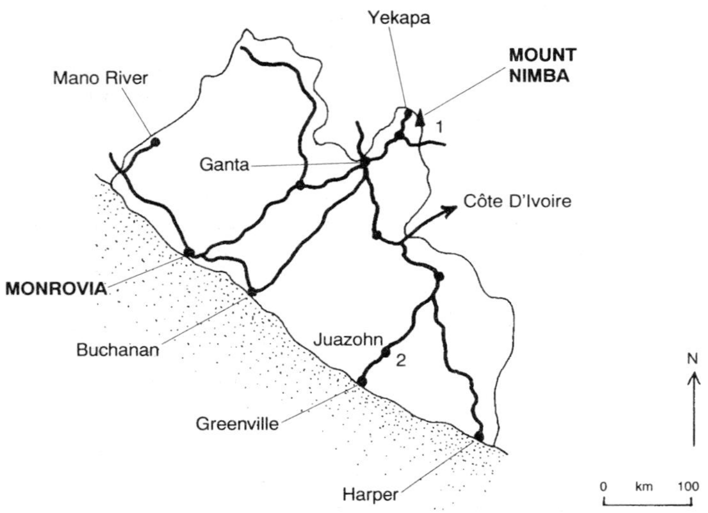

1 Mount Nimba
2 Sapo NP

Health and Safety

Immunisation against hepatitis, meningitis, polio, typhoid and yellow fever is recommended, as are precautions against malaria.

Climate and Timing

This is a very wet part of the world with the annual rains in Monrovia usually exceeding 5 m (16 ft). Water pours down virtually non-stop from April to November, so December to March is the best time to visit.

Habitats

Inland from the narrow coastal belt, large areas of lowland Upper Guinea rainforest still exist.

Conservation

Over 25% of the remaining Upper Guinea forest (12,000 sq km) is present in Liberia, but most of this is being logged, and the larger animals which inhabit the forest are still being hunted. Mining and its associated settlements are also a major cause for concern, especially on Mount Nimba.

Thirteen threatened and eight near-threatened species occur in Liberia.

Bird Families

Only four of the ten families endemic to the African mainland are represented. The notable absentees are those associated with savanna: Ostrich, Secretary-bird, mousebirds and ground-hornbills. Well represented families include cuckoos, kingfishers and honeyguides.

Bird Species

A total of 581 species have been recorded in Liberia, 40 fewer than adjacent Sierra Leone. Non-endemic specialities and spectacular species include Long-tailed Hawk, Forbes' Plover, Chocolate-backed Kingfisher, Blue-headed Bee-eater, Red-cheeked Wattle-eye and Jameson's Antpecker.

Endemics

There is one endemic, the recently described Liberian Greenbul*, and 14 of the 16 Upper Guinea endemics are present including White-breasted Guineafowl*, Rufous Fishing-Owl*, Ghana Cuckoo-shrike*, Liberian Black-Flycatcher*, White-necked Rockfowl* and Ballman's Malimbe*.

African Pygmy-goose, Western Reef-Egret, African and Black Crakes, Allen's Gallinule, Rock Pratincole (Mar–Jul), Blue-breasted Kingfisher and Orange Weaver have been recorded around **Buchanan**, a coastal iron-ore terminal, east of Monrovia.

Copper-tailed Glossy-Starling*, Yellow-bearded Greenbul*, Black-capped Rufous Warbler*, Rufous-winged Illadopsis* and Ballman's Malimbe* have been recorded in the **Lofa–Mano Forest** in west Liberia, near the border with Sierra Leone and Gola Forest (p. 307). Owing to its location close to the Gola Forest, White-breasted Guineafowl*, Rufous Fishing-Owl*, Ghana Cuckoo-shrike* and White-necked Rockfowl* are also probably present. This forest lies north of the town of Mano River, in a very remote area, and birding there would take on expedition proportions.

MOUNT NIMBA

The 40 km by 12 km Mount Nimba, in extreme north/central Liberia, used to rise to 1400 m (4593 ft), but its height has been reduced considerably since iron ore was discovered. However, despite the mining activities and the consequent loss of forest, many restricted-range, localised and Upper Guinea endemic species may still exist here, including the little known Yellow-footed Honeyguide*.

Specialities

Forbes' Plover (Jan–Feb), Sandy Scops-Owl, Rufous Fishing-Owl*, Red-chested Owlet, Blue-headed Bee-eater, Yellow-footed Honeyguide*, Little Green Woodpecker, Ghana Cuckoo-shrike*, Chestnut-bellied Helmetshrike, Red-cheeked Wattle-eye, Finsch's Flycatcher-Thrush, Grey Ground-Thrush, Copper-tailed Glossy-Starling*, Liberian Black-Flycatcher*, Yellow-bearded Greenbul*, Sierra Leone Prinia*, Sharpe's Apalis, Black-capped Rufous Warbler*, Rufous-winged Illadopsis*, White-necked Rockfowl*.

Others

White-crested Bittern, Bat Hawk, Palm-nut Vulture, Congo Serpent-Eagle, Long-tailed Hawk, Ayre's Hawk-Eagle, Forest and Ahanta Francolins, Black Crake, Guinea, Yellow-billed and Great Blue Turacos, African Emerald Cuckoo, Yellowbill, Sabine's Spinetail, Narina Trogon, White-bellied and Chocolate-backed Kingfishers, Black Bee-eater, Abyssinian and Blue-throated Rollers, White-headed and Forest

Woodhoopoes, White-crested, Piping and Yellow-casqued* Hornbills, Naked-faced Barbet, Speckled and Yellow-throated Tinkerbirds, Yellow-spotted Barbet, Willcock's and Lyre-tailed Honeyguides, Fire-bellied Woodpecker, Rufous-sided Broadbill, Chestnut-capped Flycatcher, Black-winged Oriole, Large-billed Puffback, Black-and-white Shrike-flycatcher, Chestnut Wattle-eye, White-tailed Alethe, Narrow-tailed Starling, African and White-browed Forest-Flycatchers, Ussher's Flycatcher, Square-tailed and Fanti Sawwings, Golden, Spotted, Swamp and Baumann's* Greenbuls, Whistling Cisticola, Black-capped Apalis, Yellow-browed Camaroptera, Rufous-crowned Eremomela, Kemp's Longbill, Capuchin Babbler, Tit-hylia, Jameson's Antpecker, Green-backed Twinspot, Magpie Mannikin, Mountain Wagtail, Maxwell's Black and Compact Weavers, Red-vented and Crested Malimbes, Blue-throated Brown, Buff-throated, Copper and Splendid Sunbirds.

Other Wildlife

Chimpanzee, golden cat.

Access

From Yekapa bird the whole area, especially the Seca Valley and the old mine road at Mount Graham.

The type-locality for the endemic Liberian Greenbul* is near Zwedru in **Grand Gedeh County**, east Liberia, near Tai Forest NP in Côte D'Ivoire (p. 110). White-breasted Guineafowl*, Ghana Cuckoo-shrike*, Copper-tailed Glossy-Starling*, Yellow-bearded Greenbul*, Black-capped Rufous Warbler*, Rufous-winged Illadopsis*, White-necked Rockfowl* and Ballman's Malimbe* also occur here.

SAPO NATIONAL PARK

Over 110 species have been recorded in the forest and swamps of this national park (1308 sq km), in southeast Liberia, including White-breasted Guineafowl*.

Specialities

White-breasted Guineafowl*, Ghana Cuckoo-shrike*, Copper-tailed Glossy-Starling*, Yellow-bearded Greenbul*, Black-capped Rufous Warbler*, Rufous-winged Illadopsis*, White-necked Rockfowl*, Ballman's Malimbe*.

(Rufous Fishing-Owl*, Yellow-footed Honeyguide*, Liberian Black-Flycatcher* and endemic Liberian Greenbul* may also be present.)

Other Wildlife

Bongo, chimpanzee, elephant, Jentink's duiker, pygmy hippo, yellow-backed duiker.

Access

It used to be possible to get into Sapo NP via canoe up the River Sinoe from Greenville (accessible by air from Monrovia) between January and March. Expensive trips were organised by the Peace Corps, who used to have an office in Monrovia.

ADDITIONAL INFORMATION

Books and Papers

The Birds of Liberia. Gatter, W. In prep. BOU.
The Birds of Mount Nimba. Colston, P and Curry-Lindahl, K. 1986. British Museum.
Bird Records from Liberia. Gore, M. 1994. *Malimbus.* 16:74–87.

Addresses

West African Ornithological Society (WAOS); see p. 413.

Please send all records to Dr W. Gatter, Buchsstrasse 20, D-73252 Lenningen 1, Germany.

ENDEMICS (1)

Liberian Greenbul*	East: Grand Gedeh County

Near-endemics (Upper Guinea)

White-breasted Guineafowl*, Rufous Fishing-Owl*, Little Green Woodpecker, Ghana Cuckoo-shrike*, Copper-tailed Glossy-Starling*, Liberian Black-Flycatcher*, Yellow-bearded Greenbul*, Sierra Leone Prinia*, Sharpe's Apalis, Black-capped Rufous Warbler*, Rufous-winged Illadopsis*, White-necked Rockfowl*, Ballman's Malimbe*.

Near-endemics (Upper Guinea and Nigeria)

Brown-cheeked Hornbill*, Chestnut-bellied Helmetshrike, Finsch's Flycatcher-Thrush.

LIBYA

Little visited and little known Libya has a similar avifauna to Morocco and Egypt, and fortunately there are no species here which cannot be seen with considerably more ease in one or other of the latter two countries.

At 1,759,540 sq km, this is a big country, nearly fourteen times larger than England, and over twice the size of Texas. The northern coastal road is well served by buses, but a 4WD is recommended for getting around the rest of the country. Accommodation and food are expensive. Immunisation against hepatitis, polio, typhoid and yellow fever is recommended. Except for the maquis on the north coast, Libya is virtually all desert; only 317 species have been recorded, 100 fewer than in neighbouring Egypt. Two of these species are threatened and three near-threatened. Non-endemic specialities and spectacular species include Houbara Bustard. There are no endemics but near-endemics include Moussier's Redstart and Tristram's Warbler, both of which are winter visitors to the northwest.

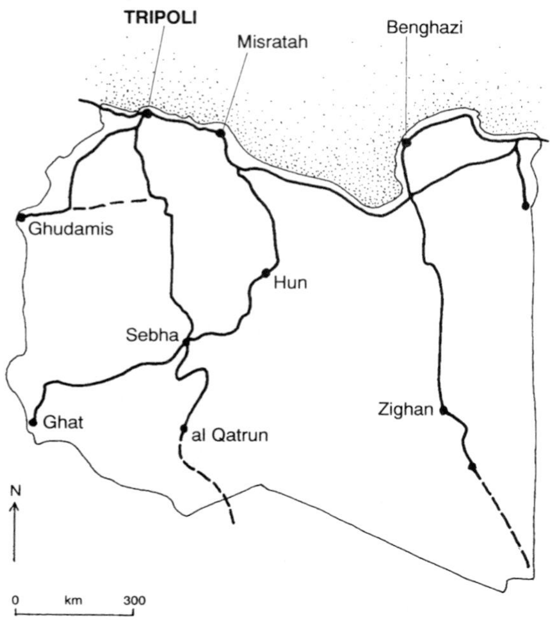

A SELECTION OF SPECIES RECORDED IN LIBYA

Sooty Falcon (southeast), Barbary Partridge (north), Houbara Bustard (north), Cream-coloured Courser (north), Pin-tailed, Spotted, Black-bellied and Crowned Sandgrouse, Laughing Dove, Brown-necked Raven, Moussier's Redstart (winter), White-tailed, Black, Mourning and Red-rumped Wheatears, Streaked Scrub-Warbler, Tristram's Warbler (winter), Fulvous Chatterer (northwest), Bar-tailed and Desert Larks, Greater Hoopoe-Lark, Thick-billed, Lesser Short-toed, Dupont's and Temminck's Larks, Desert Sparrow (southwest), House Bunting (northwest).

ADDITIONAL INFORMATION

Books and Papers

The Birds of Libya: An Annotated Checklist. Bundy, G. 1976. BOU.
Ornithological Survey of the Coast of Libya. July 1993. WIWO.

Near-endemics (also occur in Algeria, Tunisia and Morocco)

Moussier's Redstart, Tristram's Warbler.

MADAGASCAR

1 Ambanisana
2 Mahajanga
3 Lake Alaotra
4 Perinet
5 Ranomafana NP
6 Toliara
7 Berenty Reserve

INTRODUCTION

Summary

Madagascar is an island-continent with a very high degree of endemism. Although there are far less bird species here than in nearby mainland countries, half of the regularly breeding species are endemic. Although seeing most of these unique birds and the equally exciting lemurs can be time consuming or rather expensive, Madagascar is a 'must' for most of the keenest birders.

Size

This is a big island: 1600 km from north to south, and up to 550 km from west to east. At 587,041 sq km it is 4.5 times the size of England, and nearly as large as Texas.

Getting Around

Most of the roads are in poor condition, especially during the rains (Nov–Mar) making overland travel time consuming and, at times, impossible. Cheap long-distance taxis are available in some areas (eg. Antananarivo to Perinet and Ampijoroa), and the excellent internal air network is also cheap, especially when the airpass is used (book well in advance). There are also bush taxis and trains but these are slow, and delays owing to the poor roads are the norm. A basic knowledge of French is useful since few people speak English.

All national parks require entry permits (B), and for some sites (eg. Ampijoroa) these cannot be obtained at the entrances and must be arranged in advance, either by writing to the Service de la Protection de la Nature, Direction des Eaux et Fõrets (DET), BP 243, Antananarivo 101, or by visiting these offices on arrival in the capital, Antananarivo. Strict Nature Reserves (SNR) are normally accessible only to authorised research projects, perhaps a little unfair when ecotourists, many with the funds to help pay for the conservation of such reserves, are crying out to visit them.

Accommodation and Food

Beyond Antananarivo, most accommodation is quite basic, but good value. The food has strong French and oriental influences.

Health and Safety

Immunisation against hepatitis, polio, typhoid and yellow fever is recommended. Malaria is a major problem and all possible precautions should be taken. Sand flies can be a problem in coastal areas, and leeches abound in the damp eastern escarpment forests.

The islanders are very friendly.

Climate and Timing

Rain is possible all year round on the humid eastern escarpment, but elsewhere the rainy season usually lasts from November to March. The best time to visit Madagascar is September to November, during the austral spring, even though it may be wet on the eastern escarpment.

Habitats

The eastern escarpment supports remnant forest where most of the endemic birds are present. It rises to 2876 m (9436 ft) at Mount Maromokoto in the north, creating a rain-shadow over the interior plateau, much of which was once a vast grassland. Most of this habitat has since been turned over to rice-paddies. Near the west coast, lower down, there is dry, deciduous woodland and, in the southwest, in semi-desert terrain, unique *Didierea* thickets, characterised by thorny trees with cigar-shaped trunks. There are also coastal lagoons, lakes and marshes scattered throughout the island.

Conservation

The ten-foot-tall Elephant Bird, the largest bird to have existed, is extinct and, sadly, many more of Madagascar's endemics could follow. Eighty per cent of the forest has already been destroyed and now problems such as overgrazing, and the need for firewood for a rapidly expanding population look like making matters much worse. Despite an extensive network of 'protected' areas and some efforts to integrate conservation, ecotourism and local communities (eg. Ranomafana), the future for the unique birds of this island looks bleak.

Bird Families

Three families of birds are endemic to Madagascar: mesites, ground-rollers and asities, and two more, Cuckoo-Roller and vangas, are shared only with the Comoros. Only one other Afrotropical family is present, in the form of Hamerkop. Other well represented families include rails and cuckoos, within which lies the unique *Coua* genus.

Bird Species

Despite its size and subtropical location, Madagascar supports surprisingly few species. Only 256 species have been recorded, 60 fewer than the Canary Islands. Non-endemic specialities and spectacular species include Red-tailed and White-tailed Tropicbirds, Madagascar Pond-Heron*, Sooty Falcon, Crab Plover, Madagascar Pratincole and Madagascar Bee-eater.

Endemics

A remarkable 50% of the 200 regularly breeding species are totally endemic. An incredible 102 birds are found only here, and a further 23 Malagasy endemics are also present, making a total of 125 out of 175. Madagascar endemics include three mesites, nine couas, five ground-rollers, four asities and 13 vangas, whilst Malagasy endemics include Réunion Harrier*, Cuvier's Rail, Vasa Parrot, Diademed Kingfisher, Cuckoo-Roller and Blue Vanga.

Expectations

It is possible to see over 180 species on an expensive, non-stop four-week trip, or a cheaper and steadier six-week trip, including over 90 Madagascar and over 110 Malagasy endemics.

Madagascar Little Grebe*, Madagascar Pond-Heron*, Diademed Kingfisher and Madagascar Wagtail occur in the Tsimbazaza Botanic Gardens (where there is also a lake), near the centre of the capital, **Antananarivo**, and Meller's Duck*, Mascarene Reef-Egret, Madagascar Pond-Heron*, Réunion Harrier*, Cuvier's Rail and Diademed Kingfisher occur at **Lake Alarobia**, 15 minutes by road from the city centre, whilst other endemics present in the open areas around Madagascar's capital include Madagascar Munia and Red Fody. Malagasy endemics include Newton's Kestrel, Madagascar Coucal and Madagascar White-eye, whilst more widespread species include Madagascar Bee-eater and, from November to March, Eleonora's and Sooty Falcons.

Accommodation: Hotel Terminus (C); Hotel Mellis.

At the northern tip of Madagascar there are a few sites worth exploring if time is no problem. Crab Plover occurs at Ramena Beach, a resort 15 km east of Antsiranana (also known as Diego Suarez). **Montagne**

D'Ambre NP, 39 km south of Antsiranana, supports Madagascar Fish-Eagle*, Madagascar Pygmy-Kingfisher, Hook-billed Vanga, Forest Rock-Thrush*, Madagascar Munia and a number of other widespread endemics, as well as Brown and Crowned Lemurs. A permit, available from the DET in Antananarivo or Antsiranana, is required to visit this park. The forest at Ankarana (camping only) supports Madagascar Bee-eater and Hook-billed Vanga.

An integrated conservation and development project aims to create a 3000 sq km national park on the **Masoala Peninsula**, in northeast Madagascar, where Madagascar Serpent-Eagle* and Red-tailed Newtonia* have recently been recorded. Up until early 1994, this peninsula was virtually out-of-bounds to independent birders but, in late 1994, it was possible to visit the Ambanisana area (see below). Unfortunately, and much to the annoyance of the local people, efforts are still afoot to keep independent birders out of here in the future.

AMBANISANA

The area around Ambanisana on the Masoala Peninsula in northeast Madagascar supports a fine selection of rare Madagascar endemics, notably Scaly Ground-Roller*, Bernier's Vanga* and Helmetbird*, all three of which are virtually impossible to see elsewhere.

Madagascar Endemics

Henst's Goshawk*, Madagascar Wood Rail, Brown Mesite*, Red-breasted and Red-fronted Couas, Madagascar Hawk-Owl, Madagascar Long-eared Owl, Short-legged*, Scaly* and Pitta-like* Ground-Rollers, Velvet and Wattled Asities, Red-tailed, Rufous, Hook-billed, White-headed, Chabert and Bernier's* Vangas, Helmetbird*, Tylas, Coral-billed Nuthatch, Madagascar Starling, White-throated Oxylabes, Crossley's Babbler.

Specialities

Frances' Goshawk, Madagascar Pratincole, Vasa and Black Parrots, Madagascar Cuckoo-shrike, Blue Vanga.

Other Wildlife

Aye-aye, red-ruffed lemur.

Access

This superb site is accessible by boat from Maroantsetra. Boat-hire can be arranged at the Hotel Co-Co Beach or Hotel Tropical, and the trip takes 3–4 hours (otherwise it is a 2–3 day walk). There are many trails here (ask local people for directions) although one of the best is just behind where the boat docks.

Accommodation: Camping only (take all supplies).

Nearby Nosy Be island, also accessible by boat from Maroantsetra, is a popular resort. White-tailed Tropicbird, Brown Booby and Bridled and Sooty Terns breed on offshore islets here and are usually visible from the island.

MAHAJANGA

This coastal town in northwest Madagascar is the gateway to the Ampijoroa area, where the dry deciduous woodland and wetlands support many endemics including Madagascar Fish-Eagle*, White-breasted Mesite*, Coquerel's Coua, Schlegel's Asity* and Vam Dam's Vanga*, all of which are hard to see elsewhere.

It is necessary to obtain a permit in advance from DET in Antananarivo to visit Ampijoroa Forest Station.

Madagascar Endemics

Madagascar Little Grebe*, Madagascar Heron*, White-winged Ibis*, Madagascar Fish-Eagle*, Madagascar Harrier-Hawk, Madagascar Sparrowhawk*, Madagascar Buzzard, Madagascar Partridge, Madagascar Buttonquail, White-breasted Mesite*, Madagascar Jacana, Coquerel's, Red-capped and Crested Couas, Madagascar Pygmy-Kingfisher, Schlegel's Asity*, Rufous, Hook-billed, Van Dam's*, Sickle-billed, White-headed and Chabert Vangas, Common Newtonia, Sakalava Weaver, Red Fody.

Specialities

Frances' Goshawk, Cuvier's Rail, Vasa and Black Parrots, Madagascar Coucal, Madagascar Nightjar, Diademed Kingfisher, Cuckoo-Roller, Blue Vanga, Souimanga Sunbird.

Others

African Darter, White-backed Duck, African Pygmy-goose, Greater Flamingo, Black Heron, Madagascar Pond-Heron*, Sooty Falcon (Nov–Mar), Allen's Gallinule, Madagascar Bee-eater.

Other Wildlife

Avahi, brown lemur, common tenrek, lepilemur, mongoose lemur, Verreaux's sifaka.

Access

Mahajanga is accessible by air and road from Antananarivo. Ampijoroa Forest Station lies next to the Antananarivo–Mahajanga road, 462 km north of Antananarivo and 106 km south of Mahajanga. Between Ampijoroa and Mahajanga there are some good marshes, especially 17 km north of Ampijoroa, where Madagascar Heron*, Allen's Gallinule and Madagascar Jacana occur. White-breasted Mesite* and Van Dam's Vanga* occur in the forest behind Ampijoroa Forest Station. Schlegel's Asity* has been recorded 1.5 km north of the Forest Station (ask guides for details). Ampijoroa lies next to Ankarafantsika SNR, where the species found are similar.

Accommodation: Ampijoroa Forest Station/camping (no facilities).

The huge **Lake Alaotra**, 180 km northeast of Antananarivo, is famous for its endemic grebe and Madagascar Pochard*. The last positive sighting of Alaotra Grebe* was in 1985 (near Andreba), although a possible sighting was made in 1988. Unfortunately this species hybridises with Little Grebe, which has recently begun to breed on the lake, and 'pure' Alaotra Grebes* may now be extinct. A Madagascar Pochard* was acci-

Ampijoroa is a good place to see Sickle-billed Vanga, a bold bird which hops about on large, often rotten branches in search of its prey

dentally caught in a fisherman's net in 1991, the first positive record since 1960. The lake is best viewed from the villages of Ambatosoratra or Andreba on the southeast shore, or Anororo on the western side. Meller's Duck*, Madagascar Heron*, Réunion Harrier*, Madagascar Rail and Madagascar Snipe also occur around the lake.

Madagascar Pratincole (Nov–Mar) occurs on the Mangoro river, *en route* to Perinet, east of Antananarivo.

PERINET SPECIAL RESERVE

Situated on the eastern escarpment (900 m (2953 ft)), 150 km east of Antananarivo, the misty rainforest within this small reserve (810 ha) supports over 100 species, including 60 endemics, and a fine selection of lemurs. Furthermore, a potential new species, probably a *Sylvia* warbler, was discovered near here in 1992.

A number of the endemics here also occur at Ambanisana and Ranomafana, but this is the most reliable site for Rufous-headed Ground-Roller* and Ward's Flycatcher*.

A permit, available from DET in Antananarivo or at the entrance, is required to enter.

Madagascar Endemics

Madagascar Little Grebe*, White-winged Ibis*, Madagascar Buzzard, Madagascar Flufftail, Madagascar Wood Rail, Madagascar Rail, Brown Mesite*, Madagascar Blue-Pigeon, Red-breasted, Red-fronted and Blue Couas, Madagascar Long-eared Owl, Collared Nightjar, Madagascar Pygmy-Kingfisher, Short-legged* and Rufous-headed* Ground-Rollers, Velvet and Wattled Asities, Ward's Flycatcher*, Red-tailed, Hook-billed, Pollen's*, White-headed and Chabert Vangas, Tylas, Coral-billed Nuthatch, Madagascar Starling, Madagascar Magpie-Robin, Long-billed, Spectacled, Dusky* and Grey-crowned* Greenbuls, Madagascar Brush-Warbler, Rand's Warbler*, Dark and Common Newtonias, Common and Green Jeries, White-throated Oxylabes, Crossley's Babbler, Madagascar Munia, Madagascar Wagtail, Nelicourvi Weaver, Red and Forest Fodies.

Specialities

Frances' Goshawk, Newton's Kestrel, Cuvier's Rail, Vasa and Black Parrots, Madagascar Cuckoo, Madagascar Coucal, Malagasy Scops-Owl, Madagascar Nightjar, Madagascar Spinetail, Diademed Kingfisher, Cuckoo-Roller, Madagascar Paradise-Flycatcher, Crested Drongo, Madagascar Cuckoo-shrike, Blue Vanga, Mascarene Martin, Madagascar Bulbul, Madagascar White-eye, Madagascar Cisticola, Souimanga and Madagascar Sunbirds.

Other Wildlife

Brown lemur, eastern mouse lemur, greater dwarf lemur, grey bamboo (gentle) lemur, indri, russet mouse-lemur.

Access

This site is accessible by road and rail (to nearby Maromanga) from Antananarivo. The reserve entrance is 2 km down the road on the left from Andasibe. Local guides, most of whom are good birders, are recommended to help explore the maze of trails. Also bird the **Maromiza** area, where the potential new warbler was discovered, 10 km beyond the reserve entrance, and **Torotorofotsy Marsh**, some 15 km from Perinet, where Madagascar Rail and Madagascar Snipe occur in the marshes below the village. Madagascar Rail also occurs in the roadside marshes, 16 km from Andasibe on the road to Maromanga.

Accommodation: Andasibe: Hotel Feon' Ny Ala (B); Hotel de la Gare (C); Hotel Orchidee; camping.

RANOMAFANA NATIONAL PARK

Like Perinet this park, 445 km south of Antananarivo, is situated on the eastern escarpment, and the avifauna is very similar. However, the rainforest here is at a higher altitude, and endemics which are more reliably seen here and at nearby Vohiparara rather than at Perinet, include Small-billed Asity*, Grey-crowned Greenbul*, Wedge-tailed Jery* and Yellow-browed Oxylabes*. Nearly 100 species have been recorded, as well as the potential new *Sylvia* warbler.

A permit, available from the entrance gate, is required to visit, and guides are compulsory. Beware of the abundant leeches.

Madagascar Endemics

Meller's Duck*, White-winged Ibis*, Madagascar Harrier-Hawk, Henst's Goshawk*, Brown Mesite*, Madagascar Wood Rail, Madagascar Blue-Pigeon, Red-fronted, Crested and Blue Couas, Madagascar Long-eared Owl, Collared Nightjar, Madagascar Pygmy-Kingfisher, Short-legged*, Pitta-like* and Rufous-headed* Ground-Rollers, Velvet, Wattled and Small-billed* Asities, Ward's Flycatcher*, Red-tailed, Rufous, Hook-billed, Pollen's*, White-headed and Chabert Vangas, Tylas, Forest Rock-Thrush*, Long-billed, Spectacled, and Grey-crowned* Greenbuls, Brown Emu-tail*, Madagascar Swamp-Warbler, Rand's Warbler*, Dark and Common Newtonias, Common, Green, Stripe-throated and Wedge-tailed* Jeries, White-throated and Yellow-browed* Oxylabes, Crossley's Babbler, Madagascar Wagtail, Nelicourvi Weaver, Red and Forest Fodies.

Specialities

Réunion Harrier*, Frances' Goshawk, Madagascar Green-Pigeon, Vasa and Black Parrots, Madagascar Cuckoo, Malagasy Scops-Owl, Diademed Kingfisher, Cuckoo-Roller, Madagascar Paradise-Flycatcher, Blue Vanga, Souimanga and Madagascar Sunbirds.

Other Wildlife

Brown lemur, diademed sifaka, eastern mouse lemur, fossa, golden bamboo (gentle) lemur, greater dwarf lemur, red-bellied lemur, red-fronted lemur, ruffed lemur.

Access

This national park is 63 km northeast of Fianarantsoa and 5 km from Ranomafana village. Most compulsory guides are good birders and usually prove to be major assets on the maze of tracks. Also bird the **Vohiparara** area, approximately 13 km west of Ranomafana back towards Fianarantsoa. Small-billed Asity* and Short-legged* and Rufous-headed* Ground-Rollers occur here, as well as the potential new warbler (near the tourist routes sign). The remnant marsh and paddies 100 m north of the road and 0.5 km east of Vohiparara support Slender-billed Flufftail*, Madagascar Snipe and Grey Emu-tail, as well as Madagascar Flufftail and Greater Painted-snipe, whilst Meller's Duck* occurs on the river south of the road.

Accommodation: Station Thermale de Ranomafana (C); Hotely Ravinala (C).

The colourful Pitta-like Ground-Roller brightens up the misty forests of Ranomafana in Madagascar*

Réunion Harrier*, Madagascar Partridge and Madagascar Buttonquail all occur in roadside grassland between Fianarantsoa, near Ranomafana, and Toliara, on the southwest coast; a distance of 450 km. However, the two species to look for between Fianarantsoa and Toliara are Benson's Rock-Thrush* and Appert's Greenbul*. The rock-thrush occurs near **Ranohira**, 77 km southwest of Ihosy (a town 206 km south of Fianarantsoa and 245 km northeast of Toliara), in Isalo NP (obtain permit in Ranohira and bird the rocky plateau 4.5 km west of Ranohira), and at the 'oasis' 12 km south of Ranohira (take the 0.5-km track on the east side of the road opposite km post 97). Madagascar Partridge and Madagascar Lark also occur here. The very rare 'terrestrial' Appert's Greenbul* occurs in the dry **Zombitsy Forest** (permit required from office in Sakaraha), 18 km northeast of Sakaraha on the east side of the road 300 m north of km post 18. Madagascar Hawk-Owl and Giant Coua also occur here, and seeing these two species here would save a trip to Berenty in the far southeast. Other birds present in Zombitsy include Madagascar Paradise-Flycatcher, Red-tailed Vanga and Long-billed Greenbul.

TOLIARA

This coastal town in southwest Madagascar is surrounded by lagoons, mudflats, freshwater marshes and, most importantly, bizarre *Didierea* thickets. Couas are a speciality here (four possible), as well as Subdesert Mesite*, Madagascar Plover*, Long-tailed Ground-Roller* and Archbold's Newtonia.

Madagascar Endemics

Madagascar Harrier-Hawk, Madagascar Sparrowhawk*, Madagascar Buzzard, Barred Kestrel, Madagascar Buttonquail, Subdesert Mesite*, Madagascar Plover*, Madagascar Sandgrouse, Grey-headed Lovebird, Running, Red-capped, Crested and Verreaux's* Couas, Long-tailed Ground-Roller*, Red-tailed, Hook-billed, Lafresnaye's, Sickle-billed, White-headed and Chabert Vangas, Littoral Rock-Thrush, Thamnornis, Common and Archbold's Newtonias, Stripe-throated Jery, Madagascar Lark, Sakalava Weaver.

Specialities

Red-tailed Tropicbird, Frances' Goshawk, Vasa and Black Parrots, Madagascar Cuckoo, Madagascar Nightjar, Diademed Kingfisher, Madagascar Paradise-Flycatcher, Souimanga Sunbird.

Others

Crab Plover, Kittlitz's, Three-banded and White-fronted Plovers, Great Crested-Tern, Madagascar Bee-eater.

Access

The forest opposite Mora Mora Hotel, approximately 24 km north of Toliara *en route* to Ifaty, is the best area for Subdesert Mesite* and Long-tailed Ground-Roller*. These birds are best looked for at dawn with the local guides, Masindraka and Mosa (ask for them at the hotel). Madagascar Plover* occurs on the beach just south of Mora Mora Hotel, and on the salt pan opposite the airport hanger, some 7 km north-east of Toliara along the road to Sakaraha. A 1 km track leads to the salt pan.

The scrub alongside the road to Baie de St Augustin, at the mouth of the Onilahy river, 35 km south of Toliara, supports the highly localised Verreaux's Coua* and Littoral Rock-Thrush. The area around the Mangrove Hotel has been good in the past. The bay at St Augustin is worth checking for Madagascar Heron*, whilst conversing with the local people may reveal the best spots to look for Madagascar Sandgrouse. Littoral Rock-Thrush occurs behind the village of **Anakao**, accessible by boat, which can be arranged at the Mangrove Hotel or others (the village is an eight-hour trip by road). The Mangrove Hotel also arranges boat trips to **Nosy Be**, an island 4.5 km offshore, where Red-tailed Tropicbird breeds.

Accommodation: Mora Mora Hotel (C). Toliara: Hotel Plaza (B). Ifaty: Zahamotel; Bamboo Club. Anakao: Safari-Vezo Hotel (B).

The endangered Madagascar Plover retains a foothold in southeast Madagascar*

Madagascar Sandgrouse occurs alongside the 102-km **Ampanihy–Beloha** stretch of the Toliara–Talanaro road in south Madagascar.

Accommodation: Relais Ampanihy (C).

At the southern tip of Madagascar, Littoral Rock-Thrush occurs at **Faux Cap** (also known as Betauty), approximately 30 km south of Tsiombe, in the dunes where it is also possible to find eggshell fragments of the extinct Elephant Bird.

BERENTY RESERVE

This tiny (100 ha) area of private, remnant gallery forest in southeast Madagascar, on the banks of the Mandrare river, is surrounded by birdless sisal plantations. The ridiculously tame lemurs are the star attraction here, but there are also some good birds including Giant Coua, Malagasy Scops-Owl and Madagascar Hawk-Owl.

A permit, available from Le Galion and Le Dauphin hotels in Talanaro, is required to visit this reserve. Transport and accommodation can also be arranged at these hotels.

Madagascar Endemics

Madagascar Heron*, Madagascar Harrier-Hawk, Madagascar Sparrowhawk*, Madagascar Buzzard, Madagascar Buttonquail, Madagascar Sandgrouse, Grey-headed Lovebird, Running, Crested and Giant Couas, Madagascar Hawk-Owl, Hook-billed, Lafresnaye's, Sickle-billed and White-headed Vangas, Madagascar Magpie-Robin, Thamnornis, Common Newtonia, Common and Stripe-throated Jeries, Madagascar Lark, Madagascar Munia, Sakalava Weaver, Red Fody.

Specialities

Frances' Goshawk, Newton's Kestrel, Madagascar Green-Pigeon, Black Parrot, Malagasy Scops-Owl, Madagascar Nightjar, Madagascar Paradise-Flycatcher, Cuckoo-Roller, Souimanga Sunbird.

Other Wildlife

Brown lemur, lesser (western) mouse-lemur, Madagascar fruit-bat, ring-tailed lemur, Verreaux's sifaka, weasel lemur.

Access

Berenty is 80 km (through fairly good *Didierea* forest) from Talanaro (also known as Fort Dauphin) which is accessible by air from most major towns in Madagascar. Malagasy Scops-Owl and Madagascar Hawk-Owl both hunt around the main car park at night, and their day-time roosts are well known by the resident staff. Madagascar Sandgrouse occasionally drink at the Mandrare river at dawn and dusk.

Accommodation: Lodge (A+).

ADDITIONAL INFORMATION

Books and Papers

Guide to the Birds of Madagascar. Langrand, O. 1990. Yale University Press.
The Endemic Birds of Madagascar. Dee, T. 1986. BirdLife International.
A Birder's Guide to Travel in Madagascar. Gardner, N. 1992. Available from Nick Gardner, The Gannet, 37 Oaklands Avenue, Loughborough, Leics, LE11 3JF, UK.

Addresses

Please send all records to the Working Group on Birds in the Madagascar Region, via Olivier Langrand, WWFN Madagascar, BP 738, Antananarivo 101, Madagascar and/or Steve Goodman, Field Museum of Natural History, Roosevelt Road at Lake Shore Drive, Chicago, Illinois 60605, USA.

ENDEMICS (102)

Alaotra Grebe*	East/central: Lake Alaotra, possibly extinct, with the last positive sighting in 1985
Madagascar Little Grebe*	East/central: Tsimbazaza, Perinet

Madagascar (Bernier's) Teal*	West/north of Morondava: up to 95 were seen on Lac Bemamba, Lac Antsamaka, and in the general area near Masoarivi in 1993
Meller's Duck*	East/central: Lake Alarobia, Lake Alaotra, Torotorofotsy, Vohiparara
Madagascar Pochard*	East/central: Lake Alaotra: thought to be extinct until one was trapped accidentally by fishermen in 1991
Madagascar Heron*	Throughout: rare and local, Mahajanga–Ampijoroa road, St Augustin (near Toliara)
White-winged Ibis*	Throughout: rare and local, Montagne D'Ambre, Ampijoroa, Perinet, Ranomafana
Madagascar Cuckoo-Falcon	Throughout: scarce
Madagascar Fish-Eagle*	North/west: very rare and local, Montagne D'Ambre, Ampijoroa, Lac Bemamba
Madagascar Serpent-Eagle*	Northeast: very rare, Masoala peninsula
Madagascar Harrier-Hawk	Throughout
Madagascar Sparrowhawk*	Throughout
Henst's Goshawk*	Throughout: scarce, Ambanisana, Perinet, Ranomafana, North of Morondava
Madagascar Buzzard	Throughout
Barred Kestrel	Throughout but mainly west: rare, Toliara area, North of Morondava, Lake Alaotra
Madagascar Partridge	Throughout: Torotorofotsy, Fianarantsoa–Toliara road
Madagascar Buttonquail	Throughout
Madagascar Flufftail	East/central: Perinet, Ranomafana, Torotorofotsy, Vohiparara
Slender-billed Flufftail*	East/central: rare, Vohiparara
Madagascar Wood Rail	North/east/central: Ambanisana, Perinet, Ranomafana
Madagascar Rail	East/central: Lake Alaotra, Torotorofotsy
Sakalava Rail*	West: rare, Lac Bemamba and Lac Masama
White-breasted Mesite*	West: rare, Ampijoroa, North of Morondava
Brown Mesite*	North/east: rare, Ambanisana, Perinet, Ranomafana
Subdesert Mesite*	Southwest: rare, Toliara
Madagascar Jacana	West: Mahajanga–Ampijoroa road, north of Morondava
Madagascar Snipe	East/central: Lake Alaotra, Torotorofotsy, Vohiparara
Madagascar Plover*	Southwest: rare, Toliara
Madagascar Sandgrouse	West/south: Ampijoroa, North of Morondava, Ampanihy-Beloha Road, Berenty

Madagascar Blue-Pigeon	East
Grey-headed Lovebird	Throughout
Giant Coua	West/south: north of Morondava, Zombitsy, Berenty
Coquerel's Coua	West: Ampijoroa, north of Morondava
Red-breasted Coua	North/east: Iaraka, Ambanisana, Perinet
Red-fronted Coua	North/east: Ambanisana, Perinet
Running Coua	South
Red-capped Coua	West and south
Crested Coua	Throughout
Verreaux's Coua*	Southwest: Toliara
Blue Coua	East
Madagascar Red Owl*	East: one found as a pet in Andapa in 1993 was the second to be seen in the last 50 years, the other was at Perinet in 1973
Madagascar Hawk-Owl	North/south: Ambanisana, Ranohira, Zombitsy, Berenty
Madagascar Long-eared Owl	North/east/central: rare, Tsimbazaza, Ambanisana, Perinet, Ranomafana
Collared Nightjar	East/central and north: rare, Perinet, Ranomafana, Montagne D'Ambre
Madagascar Pygmy-Kingfisher	Throughout: Ampijoroa, Perinet, Ranomafana, Montagne D'Ambre
Short-legged Ground-Roller*	North/east/central: Ambanisana, Perinet, Vohiparara
Scaly Ground-Roller*	North/east: rare, Iaraka, Ambanisana, Andohahela
Pitta-like Ground-Roller*	North/east/central: Montagne D'Ambre, Ambanisana, Ranomafana
Rufous-headed Ground-Roller*	East/central: rare, Perinet, Vohiparara
Long-tailed Ground-Roller*	Southwest: Toliara
Velvet Asity	North/east/central: Ambanisana, Perinet, Ranomafana
Schlegel's Asity*	West: rare, Ampijoroa (and Namoroka SNR)
Wattled Asity	North/east/central: Ambanisana, Perinet, Ranomafana
Small-billed Asity*	East/central: rare, Vohiparara
Ward's Flycatcher*	East/central: Perinet
Red-tailed Vanga	Throughout: except southwest
Rufous Vanga	Throughout: except southwest
Hook-billed Vanga	West/north: Montagne D'Ambre, Ambanisana, Ampijoroa
Lafresnaye's Vanga	Southwest
Van Dam's Vanga*	West: rare, Ampijoroa
Pollen's Vanga*	East/central: rare, Perinet, Ranomafana
Sickle-billed Vanga	Northwest/west: Ampijoroa, Toliara
White-headed Vanga	Throughout
Chabert Vanga	Throughout

Bernier's Vanga*	North: Ambanisana
Helmetbird*	North: Ambanisana
Tylas	North/east/central: Ambanisana, Perinet, Ranomafana
Coral-billed Nuthatch	North/east/central: Ambanisana, Perinet
Forest Rock-Thrush*	North/east/central: Montagne D'Ambre, Ranomafana
Benson's Rock-Thrush*	South: Ranohira
Littoral Rock-Thrush	South: Anakao, Faux Cap
Madagascar Starling	Throughout
Madagascar Magpie-Robin	Throughout
Long-billed Greenbul	Throughout
Spectacled Greenbul	East
Appert's Greenbul*	South: very rare, Zombitsy
Dusky Greenbul*	North/east/central: Masoala Peninsula, Perinet
Grey-crowned Greenbul*	East/central: Perinet, Ranomafana
Brown Emu-tail*	East/central: rare, Ranomafana
Grey Emu-tail	East: marshes
Madagascar Brush-Warbler	Throughout
Thamnornis	Southwest
Madagascar Swamp-Warbler	Throughout
Rand's Warbler*	East: Perinet
Dark Newtonia	North/east: Montagne D'Ambre, Perinet, Ranomafana
Common Newtonia	Throughout
Archbold's Newtonia	Southwest: Toliara area
Red-tailed Newtonia*	Northeast and southeast: Masoala Peninsula, Ambatovaky Special Reserve, Andohahela SNR
Common Jery	Throughout
Green Jery	East/central: Perinet, Ranomafana
Stripe-throated Jery	Throughout
Wedge-tailed Jery*	East/central: Ranomafana
White-throated Oxylabes	North/east/central: Montagne D'Ambre, Ambanisana, Perinet, Ranomafana
Yellow-browed Oxylabes*	East/central: rare, Ranomafana
Crossley's Babbler	North/east/central, Ambanisana, Perinet, Ronomafana
Madagascar Lark	South
Madagascar Munia	Throughout
Madagascar Wagtail	Throughout
Nelicourvi Weaver	East/central/north
Sakalava Weaver	Throughout
Red Fody (introduced elsewhere)	Throughout
Forest Fody	East/central

(A potential new species, probably a *Sylvia* warbler, was discovered in 1992 in the Maromiza area near Perinet SR, in Ranomafana NP and at Vohiparara near Ranomafana in 1993. It has since been seen at most of these sites in 1994.)

Near-endemics

Madagascar and Comoros
Frances' Goshawk, Madagascar Green-Pigeon, Vasa Parrot, Madagascar Spinetail, Madagascar Swift, Diademed Kingfisher, Cuckoo-Roller, Madagascar Paradise-Flycatcher, Crested Drongo, Madagascar Cuckoo-shrike, Blue Vanga, Madagascar Sunbird.

Madagascar and Aldabra
Newton's Kestrel, Cuvier's Rail, Madagascar Coucal (and Assumption Island), Madagascar Nightjar, Madagascar Cisticola, Souimanga Sunbird.

Madagascar, Comoros and Aldabra
Madagascar Bulbul, Madagascar White-eye.

Madagascar, Comoros and Seychelles
Black Parrot.

Madagascar, Comoros, Seychelles and Aldabra
Madagascar Turtle-Dove.

Madagascar, Comoros and Pemba Island
Malagasy Scops-Owl.

Madagascar, Comoros and Réunion
Réunion Harrier*.

Madagascar, Réunion and Mauritius
Mascarene Martin (occasionally visits mainland Africa).

MALAWI

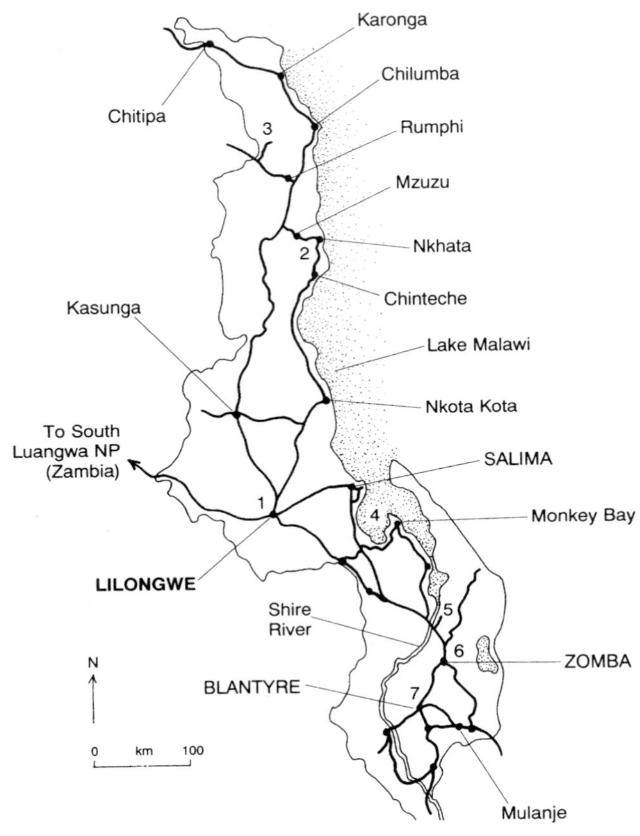

1 Lilongwe
2 Mzuzu–Nkhata Road
3 Nyika NP
4 Monkey Bay
5 Liwonde NP
6 Zomba
7 Blantyre

INTRODUCTION

Summary

With its relatively modern infrastructure, short distances, pleasant lake, fine landscapes and excellent avifauna, including plenty of birds which are hard to see elsewhere, one would expect Malawi to be a more popular birding destination than it is. Combined with a visit to part of adjacent Zambia, a trip to this part of Africa should produce a fine selection of birds and mammals.

Size

At 118,484 sq km, Malawi is a small country, just 900 km from north to south. It is slightly smaller than England, and one sixth the size of Texas.

Getting Around

Road conditions in Malawi vary, but are generally good by African standards. The north–south highway is surfaced all the way, but side roads and tracks may be impassable in the wet season (Dec–Feb), even with a 4WD. The bus network, which includes express buses, is quite extensive and cheap, but the few trains are slow and relatively expensive. There are a few internal flights. Steamers ply the waters of Lake Malawi.

It is possible to visit Zambia with relative ease from Malawi, but crossing the border can be slow process. Showing the essential health certificates (especially those for cholera and yellow fever) promptly may smooth the passage.

Accommodation and Food

There are plenty of cheap and clean, private and government (better) resthouses, and a sprinkling of fairly good campsites with some facilities. Most national parks have such resthouses, which are bookable in advance through the Department of National Parks and Wildlife. Good food is widely available except in the few remote locations.

Health and Safety

Immunisation against hepatitis, polio, rabies, typhoid and yellow fever is recommended, as are all precautions against malaria. Beware of bilharzia in shallow, reed-fringed sections of Lake Malawi.

The people of Malawi are friendly, although crime does exist in urban areas.

Climate and Timing

Malawi is dry, dusty and relatively cool from April to September, and hot and wet from October to March, with most of the rain falling from December to February. However, rain is possible at any time of the year in the highlands, where it is also much cooler, especially at night. The best time to visit is July and August, although many of Malawi's birds breed between October and December.

Habitats

The third largest lake in Africa, Lake Malawi, dominates the country, stretching 540 km from north to south and up to 75 km from west to east. Marshes, savanna and evergreen forest line its shores, giving way to miombo and mopane woodland to the west and south. The Shire river, which drains the south end of the lake has a wide, marshy floodplain. Montane forest and grassland are present on the Nyika Plateau (1372 m (4500 ft)) in the north, and near Blantyre in the south, where the mountains rise to 3001 m (9846 ft) at Mount Mulanje, the highest peak in southern Africa.

Conservation

The Malawi government seems keen to protect the country's natural resources. They have designated nine national parks, for which there are small entrance fees, and many forest reserves, which may help the nine threatened and eight near-threatened birds occurring in Malawi.

Bird Families

Six of the ten families endemic to the African mainland are represented in Malawi.

Bird Species

A total of 650 species have been recorded in this small, land-locked country, only 90 fewer than neighbouring Zambia which is six times the size. Non-endemic specialities and spectacular species include Wattled Crane*, Rufous-bellied Heron, Lesser Jacana, Pel's Fishing-Owl, Boehm's Bee-eater, Racket-tailed Roller, Green-headed Oriole, Collared Palm-Thrush, and Blue Swallow*.

Endemics

There are no endemic birds in Malawi. However, near-endemics include Malawi Batis, Cholo Alethe*, Babbling Starling, East Coast Akalat* and White-winged Apalis*.

Expectations

Keen birders may see 350 species during a two- to three-week trip.

LILONGWE

Over 200 species have been recorded in the Lilongwe Nature Sanctuary, which lies in the middle of the capital in central Malawi. The thick bush, gallery forest, bamboo thickets and woodland supports White-backed Night-Heron, and African Finfoot has also been recorded.

Others

White-backed Night-Heron, African and Black Goshawks, Hildebrandt's Francolin, African Finfoot, Livingstone's Turaco, White-faced Scops-Owl, Narina Trogon, African Broadbill, Terrestrial Brownbul, Peters' Twinspot, Blue-breasted Cordonbleu, Magpie Mannikin, Southern Masked-Weaver, Amethyst Sunbird.

Other Wildlife

Grey duiker, Nile crocodile.

Access

The Lilongwe Nature Sanctuary is just off Kenyatta Drive, between the old and the new towns. Lilongwe Golf Course, where it is possible to camp, and the adjacent river are also worth birding if time allows, but ask for permission first.

Accommodation: Lilongwe Hotel; Golden Peacock Resthouse; Lilongwe Golf Course campsite (C) (good birding and swimming pool).

Pale-billed Hornbill, Miombo Barbet, Green-backed Honeyguide, Stierling's Woodpecker*, White-tailed Blue-Flycatcher, Souza's Shrike, Miombo Rock-Thrush, Boehm's Flycatcher, Boulder Chat, Spotted Creeper, Stierling's Wren-Warbler, Southern Hyliota, Miombo Tit, Lesser Seedcracker, Olive-headed Weaver and Anchieta's and Shelley's

Sunbirds occur in the impressive expanse of miombo woodland at **Dzalanyama FR**, one hour south of Lilongwe.

Brown-headed Parrot, Purple-crested Turaco, Swallow-tailed Bee-eater, Pale-billed Hornbill, Lazy Cisticola, and Miombo Sunbird, as well as buffalo, elephant, four-toed elephant-shrew, greater kudu, hippo and roan occur in the rolling miombo woodland and seasonally flooded savanna in **Kasunga NP** (2000 sq km), north of Lilongwe. The entrance is 38 km west of Kasunga town. Cruise the tracks, which are passable from July to January, and bird on foot around Lifupa Lodge/campsite, on the shores of Lifupa Dam 14 km from the entrance. It is also possible to go on short walking safaris with guides.

Accommodation: Lifupa Lodge/campsite (rondavels (B); tents (C); camping (C)).

The dense tropical forest at the base of the escarpment which rises from the western shores of Lake Malawi supports a number of rare species, notably East Coast Akalat*. The best place to look for these birds is alongside the **Mzuzu–Nkhata road**, east of Mzuzu, and around Nkhata Bay, in north Malawi. Lemon and Tambourine Doves, Purple-crested Turaco, Yellowbill, Narina Trogon, Crowned Hornbill, Yellow-rumped Tinkerbird, Moustached Grass-Warbler and Olive Sunbird also occur here. To the south of Nkhata, **Chinteche**, next to an excellent beach, is also a good birding site. Hamerkop, Palm-nut Vulture, Dickinson's Kestrel, Black Crake, Red-faced Cisticola, Zebra Waxbill, Black-and-white Mannikin, Grosbeak Weaver, Red Bishop and Purple-banded Sunbird all occur here.

NYIKA NATIONAL PARK

The flower-filled rolling grassland, marshes and montane forest of Nyika NP, in north Malawi, support Wattled Crane*, Malawi Batis, Sharpe's Akalat and Blue Swallow*, as well as a number of other species which are hard to find elsewhere in Africa.

Specialities

Wattled Crane*, Moustached Green-Tinkerbird, Fuelleborn's Boubou, Malawi Batis, White-chested Alethe, Sharpe's Akalat, Olive-flanked Robin-Chat, Blue Swallow*, Sharpe's Greenbul, Black-lored and Churring* Cisticolas, Chapin's and Brown-headed Apalises, Evergreen Forest Warbler, Buff-shouldered Widowbird, Anchieta's Sunbird, Yellow-browed Seedeater.

Others

Red-winged Francolin, Stanley Bustard, African Pigeon, Dusky Turtle-Dove, Scarce Swift, Bar-tailed Trogon, Orange Ground-Thrush, Waller's and Slender-billed Starlings, Cape Robin-Chat, Angola Swallow, Mountain and Placid Greenbuls, Trilling and Lazy Cisticolas, Chestnut-throated Apalis, Mountain Warbler, Mountain Illadopsis, Rufous-naped Lark, Malachite Sunbird, Cape Canary, Oriole Finch.

Other Wildlife

Blue duiker, eland, klipspringer, leopard, oribi, porcupine, roan.

Access

The national park HQ is at Thazima Gate, 10 km northeast of the Rumphi–Katumbi road, 67 km northwest of Rumphi. From Thazima it is 60 km to Chelinda Camp, via the Zovo Chipolo Forest, where Bar-tailed Trogon and White-chested Alethe occur, and Chisanga Falls where Anchieta's Sunbird has been recorded. There are a number of trails worth exploring and birding on foot is allowed anywhere, both sides of the Malawi-Zambia border. There are no customs at the Zambian border here, but a small fee is payable at the Zambian Resthouse, 30 km northwest of the turning to Thazima Gate, just inside Zambia. Many of the specialities occur in Majanjire Forest on the Zambian side.

NYIKA NP

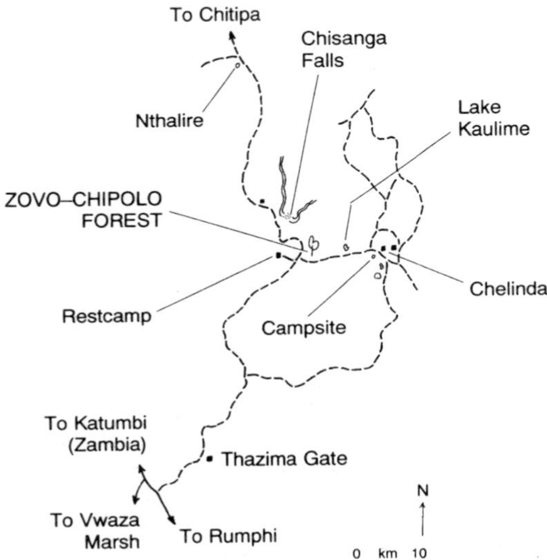

The rare Babbling Starling occurs at **Vwaza Marsh**, along with Chestnut-backed Sparrow-Weaver, another species rarely seen outside Angola and Zambia. This marsh can be reached by turning south, a few km west of the turning to Thazima.

Accommodation: Chelinda Camp (Rooms (C)/chalets (B)/camping (C) (take own food)); Zambian Resthouse (C).

The sandy beaches, rocky bays, woodland and marshes around **Senga Bay**, near Salima, east of Lilongwe in central Malawi, support African Pygmy-goose, Black and Rufous-bellied Herons, Dwarf Bittern, Black Crake, and Boehm's Bee-eater.

Accommodation: Livingstonia Beach Hotel (A)/campsite (C) (Pennant-winged Nightjar).

SENGA BAY

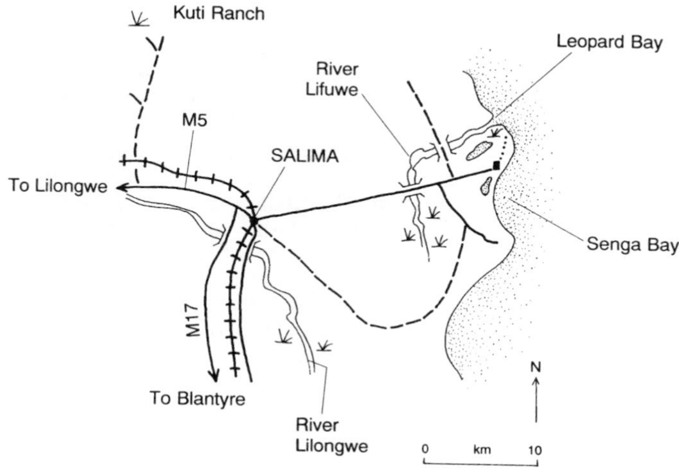

The shore and hills around **Monkey Bay**, south of Salima, support Dickinson's Kestrel, Freckled Nightjar, Swallow-tailed Bee-eater, Lilac-breasted Roller, Trumpeter Hornbill, Yellow-fronted Tinkerbird, Black-collared Barbet, Familiar Chat, Mosque Swallow and Striped Pipit. There are many brightly coloured, endemic fish in Lake Malawi, and **Cape Maclear**, 18 km north of Monkey Bay, is one of the best places to see them. Birding is also good here, especially at the aptly-named Otter Point. These two resorts are very popular, especially at weekends.

Accommodation: Golden Sands Holiday Resort (rondavels/campsite (C)).

LIWONDE NATIONAL PARK

The River Shire drains the southern end of Lake Malawi and winds its way south through Liwonde NP (548 sq km) forming, at times, a wide floodplain, with dense stands of reeds and pools. These wetlands, together with mopane woodland and palm savanna, have attracted over 300 species, including Lesser Jacana, Black-winged Lapwing, Boehm's Bee-eater, Racket-tailed Roller and Collared Palm-Thrush.

Specialities

Lesser Jacana, Black-winged Lapwing, Boehm's Bee-eater, Racket-tailed Roller, Livingstone's Flycatcher, Collared Palm-Thrush.

Others

African Darter, Rufous-bellied Heron, White-backed Night-Heron, Hamerkop, Saddle-billed Stork, Bat Hawk, Palm-nut Vulture, Wahlberg's Eagle, Dickinson's Kestrel, Crested Francolin, Black Crake, Long-toed Lapwing, Lilian's Lovebird, Red-faced Mousebird, African Cuckoo, Pel's Fishing-Owl, African Barred Owlet, Fiery-necked and

Square-tailed Nightjars, Brown-hooded Kingfisher, Little, Swallow-tailed and Southern Carmine Bee-eaters, Lilac-breasted Roller, Brown-breasted and Crested Barbets, Golden-tailed Woodpecker, White and Retz's Helmetshrikes, Southern Blue-eared Glossy-Starling, Red-billed Oxpecker, Red-backed Scrub-Robin, White-headed Black-Chat, Singing Cisticola, Yellow-breasted Apalis, African Bush-Warbler, Cape Crombec, Southern Black-Tit, Flappet Lark, Green-winged Pytilia, Jameson's Firefinch, Black-winged Bishop, White-breasted Sunbird.

Other Wildlife

Elephant, greater kudu, hippo, Nile crocodile, oribi, rusty-spotted genet, sable, spotted hyena, waterbuck.

Access

Turn east off the Lilongwe–Zomba road, 56 km north of Zomba. Birding is good around Mvuu Camp (Boehm's Bee-eater), on the banks of the Shire river, from where it is possible to hire boats with guides to look for White-backed Night-Heron and Pel's Fishing-Owl. For Racket-tailed Roller cruise through the mopane woodland and scour the mid stratum. Beware of elephants and tsetse flies.

Accommodation: Mvuu Camp rondavels/campsite; Kudya Lodge.

Check the grassland alongside the Liwonde–Zomba road for Buffy Pipit and Fan-tailed, Red-collared and Long-tailed Widowbirds. River gullies in the old town of **Zomba** in south Malawi, support the rare and beautiful White-winged Apalis*, as well as African Pigeon, Livingstone's Turaco, Olive Bushshrike, White-starred Robin, Placid Greenbul, Black-headed Apalis, Green-backed Twinspot and Red-faced Crimson-wing. The gullies alongside the top road in town are the best, and scanning the canopy may reveal the unobtrusive White-winged Apalis*.

From Zomba it is possible to drive up to the top of the the **Zomba Plateau** (1600 m (5250 ft)), where Black-rumped Buttonquail, Red-chested Flufftail, Black Cuckoo, Scarce Swift, Half-collared Kingfisher, African Yellow Warbler, Mountain Wagtail and Yellow Bishop occur. Bird around Chirigwe's Hole, the trail along the River Mulunguzi (Half-collared Kingfisher), around Mandala Falls, and the grounds of the Zomba Campsite and nearby Kuchawe Inn, both of which make convenient bases.

The big and beautiful Saddle-billed Stork, a widespread African bird, stalks the floodplain of the Shire river in Liwonde NP, Malawi

BLANTYRE

Amongst the numerous tea plantations on the Cholo Mountains to the south of Blantyre, remnant montane forest patches support some rare African species, including Green-headed Oriole, Spotted Ground-Thrush*, the near-endemic Cholo Alethe* and White-winged Apalis*.

Specialities

Green Barbet, Green-headed Oriole, Black-fronted Bushshrike, Malawi Batis, Spotted Ground-Thrush*, Cholo Alethe*, Olive-flanked Robin-Chat, Eastern Sawwing, Stripe-cheeked Bulbul, White-winged Apalis*, Evergreen Forest Warbler, Bertrand's Weaver.

Others

Crowned Hawk-Eagle, Delegorgue's Pigeon, African Emerald Cuckoo, Bar-tailed Trogon, White-eared Barbet, Scaly-throated Honeyguide, Olive Woodpecker, Orange Ground-Thrush, White-starred Robin, Red-capped Robin-Chat, Sombre Greenbul, Yellow-streaked Bulbul, Bar-throated and Black-headed Apalises, Yellow-throated Wood-Warbler, Green-backed Twinspot, Red-faced Crimson-wing, Forest Weaver.

Access

Delegorgue's Pigeon, Green Barbet, Green-headed Oriole, Spotted Ground-Thrush*, Cholo Alethe* (which attends ant swarms) and White-winged Apalis* occur on **Mount Cholo**, 30 km south of Blantyre. Ask permission at the Satema Tea Estate to bird the remnant forest above

BLANTYRE AREA

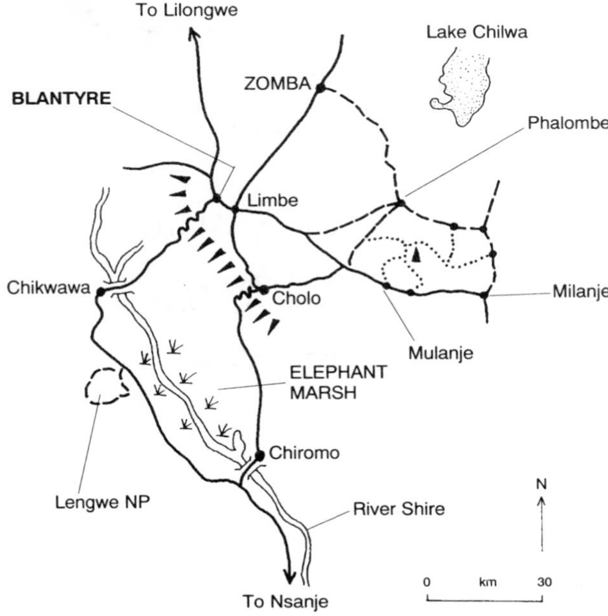

the estate. Lesser Jacana has been recorded on Coronation Dam near the city of Blantyre.

Narina Trogon, Pale Batis, Spotted Ground-Thrush* and Cholo Alethe* occur on **Mount Mulanje**. Birding this mountain involves a long trek from the Likhubula Forestry Office, 10 km from Mulanje, where the necessary arrangements can be made (porters are available). It is possible to hike to Chambe Hut, from where it is over ten hours to Sapitwa summit (3001 m (9846 ft)), and to descend via a different route.

Saddle-billed Stork, Boehm's (north of the camp) and Southern Carmine (Chikwawa) Bee-eaters and Livingstone's Flycatcher occur in **Lengwe NP**, 75 km southwest of Blantyre via Chikwawa. The park is signposted from the M8 between Blantyre and Chiromo. Here there are hides overlooking waterholes and, nearby, a huge wetland known as Elephant Marsh, which is accessible by boat. The park was established to protect the nyala, but buffalo, greater kudu and suni also occur. Beware of tsetse flies.

Accommodation: Chalets (take own food).

The fabulous White-winged Apalis, an elusive canopy-dwelling species, may be found in Zomba or on Mount Cholo near Blantyre*

ADDITIONAL INFORMATION

Books and Papers

Birds of Malawi: A Supplement to Newman's Birds of Southern Africa. Newman, K. *et al.* 1992. Southern.

Newman's Birds of Southern Africa. 1991 Update. Newman. K. 1992. HarperCollins.

Illustrated Guide to the Birds of Southern Africa. Sinclair, I *et al.* 1993. New Holland.

Addresses

Department of National Parks and Wildlife, PO Box 30131, Capital City, Lilongwe 3 (tel: 730 944).

The Wildlife Society of Malawi, Box 1429, Blantyre, publishes the biannual *Nyala*, c/o The Museums of Malawi, Box 30360, Blantyre.

Please send all records to Stewart Lane, PO Box 51147, Limbe.

Near-endemics (North)

Miombo Barbet, Stierling's Woodpecker*, Fuelleborn's Boubou, White-chested Alethe, Babbling Starling, Sharpe's Akalat, Olive-flanked Robin-Chat, Shelley's and Sharpe's Greenbuls, Black-lored and Churring* Cisticolas, Chapin's Apalis, Spot-throat, Lesser Seedcracker, Bertrand's and Olive-headed Weavers, Buff-shouldered Widowbird, Yellow-browed Seedeater.

Near-endemics (South)

Cholo Alethe*, White-winged Apalis*.

Near-endemics (General)

Malawi Batis.

MALI

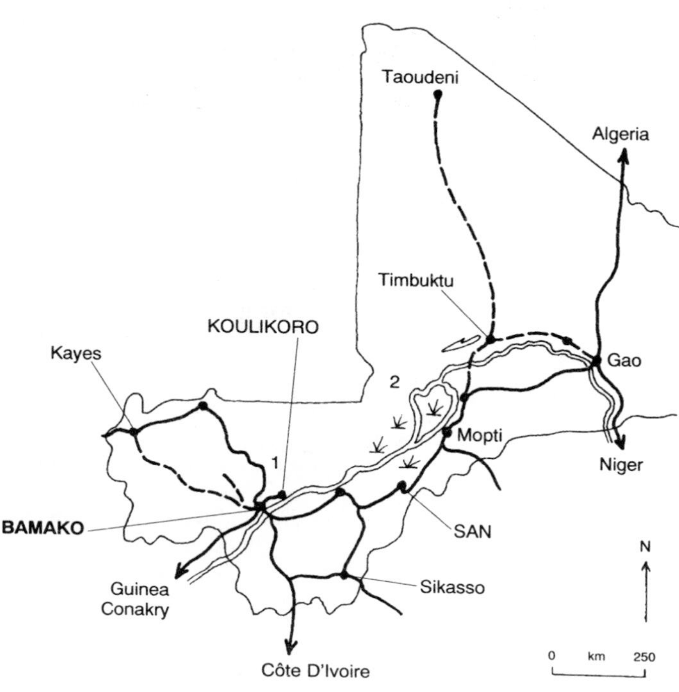

1 Bamako–Koulikoro Road
2 Niger Floodplain

INTRODUCTION

Summary

As well as the Niger floodplain, a very important wintering ground for migrant Palearctic waterfowl and shorebirds, Mali also supports a fine selection of spectacular African species such as Egyptian Plover, some arid-savanna specialities, and an endemic firefinch. Birders visiting Mali will find a good infrastructure for a West African country, but accommodation and travel is a little expensive.

Size

This is a big country. At 1,240,000 sq km, Mali is nearly ten times the size of England, and almost twice the size of Texas.

Getting Around

Apart from the Bamako–Mopti–Gao road, which runs across the south of the country, most of the other roads and tracks, especially in the northern desert, are bad. Most roads are also dotted with police checkpoints. Shared taxis (Taxis de Brousse) and trucks reach most settlements, but because these are far apart this is an expensive form of transport. When the River Niger is full, usually in August and September, it is possible to travel by boat between Kulikoro (near Bamako), Mopti, Timbuktu, and Gao, a distance of 1300 km. Internal flights exist but need to be booked well in advance.

Accommodation and Food

Accommodation is virtually limited to expensive, basic, Government-owned, campements, and the menus are dominated by rice and beef broth.

Health and Safety

Immunisation against hepatitis, meningitis, polio, typhoid and yellow fever is recommended, as are precautions against malaria. Also beware of bilharzia.

Climate and Timing

In the south the dry season lasts from November to February. February is the best time to visit the Niger floodplain because the birds are most concentrated then. Otherwise, prepare for very hot days and chilly nights, especially in the north.

Habitats

Mali is basically a flat country dominated by the Sahara desert in the north, and Sahel and savanna in the south. The River Niger flows west to east across the middle of the country and, in flood years, forms huge wetlands across its floodplain.

Conservation

Five threatened and seven near-threatened species occur in Mali.

Bird Families

Seven of the ten families endemic to the African mainland are represented in Mali, and well represented families include raptors and bustards.

Bird Species

A total of 655 species have been recorded in Mali, an impressive total for a land-locked country, and over 120 more than neighbouring Niger's. Non-endemic specialities and spectacular species include Scissor-tailed Kite, Nubian Bustard*, Egyptian Plover, Grey Pratincole, Red-throated Bee-eater, Abyssinian and Blue-bellied Rollers, Cricket Longtail and Sudan Golden-Sparrow.

Endemics

Mali has one endemic bird: Mali Firefinch* is fairly easy to see near the capital, Bamako.

Expectations

It is possible to see over 160 species during a two week trip.

BAMAKO–KOULIKORO ROAD

The 100-km road between the capital, Bamako, and Koulikoro, in south-west Mali, traverses the type-locality of the endemic Mali Firefinch*. It is also possible to see Egyptian Plover, Grey Pratincole, and Rock-loving Cisticola along this road.

Mali Endemics

Mali Firefinch*.

Specialities

Egyptian Plover, Grey Pratincole, Rock-loving Cisticola.

Others

Brown Snake-Eagle, Grasshopper Buzzard, Fox and Grey Kestrels, Double-spurred Francolin, Stone Partridge, Senegal Thick-knee, Four-banded Sandgrouse, Bruce's Green-Pigeon, Senegal Parrot, Violet Turaco, Red-throated, Swallow-tailed and Northern Carmine Bee-eaters, Blue-bellied Roller, Bearded Barbet, Fine-spotted, Golden-tailed and Brown-backed Woodpeckers, Yellow-billed Shrike, Common Gonolek, White Helmetshrike, Senegal Batis, Red-winged Starling, Purple Glossy-Starling, Familiar Chat, Mocking Cliff-Chat, Senegal Eremomela, Northern Crombec, Blackcap and Brown Babblers, Yellow-spotted Petronia, Bar-breasted Firefinch, Broad-tailed Paradise-Whydah, Speckle-fronted Weaver, Chestnut-crowned Sparrow-Weaver, Vitelline Masked-Weaver, Pygmy and Beautiful Sunbirds.

Access

Mali Firefinch* occurs in the rocky area behind the roadside forest, signposted 'Fôret Classée de Tienfala'. Rock-loving Cisticola has been recorded at Tienfala, at some distance from any rocks, and Egyptian Plover and Grey Pratincole occur on the river near Koulikoro.

Boucle du Baoule NP, a huge area of wooded savanna 100 km north-west of Bamako, may be worth exploring. The species here are probably similar to nearby Gambia (p. 153) and Senegal (p. 291).

Up to 75 Egyptian Plovers, in a single flock, have been recorded at **San Ferry**, near the Bamako–Mopti road. They occur, at least in January, on the River Bani, just west of San, along with Hamerkop, Scissor-tailed Kite, Grey Pratincole, Northern Carmine Bee-eater and Yellow-billed Oxpecker. To the north, Nubian Bustard, Cream-coloured Courser, Abyssinian Roller, Cricket Longtail and Sudan Golden-Sparrow have been recorded alongside the San–Gao road.

THE NIGER FLOODPLAIN

The Niger normally floods in August and September, creating a vast wetland in the middle of the Sahel. This floodplain is of immense importance to wintering Palearctic waterfowl, herons, ibises and shorebirds. Recent counts have revealed the presence of up to 500,000 Garganey, 200,000 Northern Pintail, 20,000 Glossy Ibises and 150,000 Ruff.

However, the Mali climate has been somewhat erratic in recent decades, and during the droughts of the 1970s and 1980s, both the birds and the native people found themselves struggling to survive.

Others

African Pygmy-goose, Black Heron, Hamerkop, Senegal Thick-knee, Egyptian and White-fronted Plovers, Marsh Owl.

Other Wildlife

Hippo.

Access

The best time to visit is February when the birds are concentrated on remaining waters. One way to see the birds is to take a boat trip along the Niger between Mopti and Timbuktu (accessible by air from Bamako), but this is only possible in 'normal' years.

The vegetated stream west of the road at **Loulouni**, 26 km south of Sikasso, in southeast Mali, supports Blue Quail, Black Crake, Violet Turaco, Shining Blue Kingfisher, African Blue-Flycatcher, White-crowned Robin-Chat, Oriole Warbler, Grey-headed Oliveback, Red-winged Pytilia, Dybowski's Twinspot and Black-faced Firefinch.

ADDITIONAL INFORMATION

Books and Papers

Liste Communitees des Oiseaux du Mali: Part 1, Non-passerines. Lamarche, B. 1980. *Malimbus* 2:121–158.

Liste Communitees des Oiseaux du Mali: Part 2, Passerines. Lamarche, B. 1981. *Malimbus* 3:73–102.

Addresses

West African Ornithological Society (WAOS); see p. 413.

ENDEMICS (1)

Mali Firefinch*	Southwest: Bamako–Koulikoro road

MAURITANIA

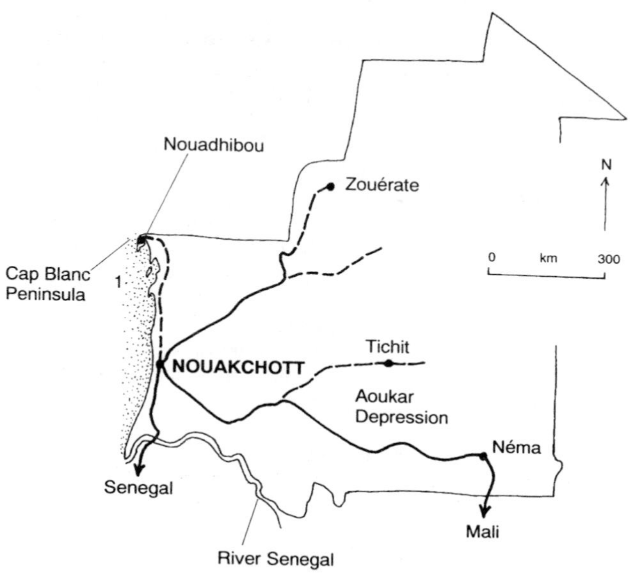

1 Banc D'Arguin NP

INTRODUCTION

Summary

Remote Mauritania is more renowned for its important numbers of wintering Palearctic shorebirds than its African avifauna. However, birders who overcome the problems of long distances, poor roads, virtually no accommodation and the desert sun, could see a fine selection of species, including some arid-savanna specialities.

Size

At 1,030,700 sq km, Mauritania is eight times larger than England, and 1.5 times the size of Texas.

Getting Around

Local transport in the form of shared cars is expensive, where it exists, and keen birders will need a 4WD and a compass for any serious exploration off the two main roads that cross the country. There are some internal flights.

Accommodation and Food

Cheap hotels are almost non-existent, but camping is possible. Rice with mutton, chicken, fish and even camel, make up most meals. Beer is illegal in public places so tea is the local tipple.

Health and Safety
Immunisation against hepatitis, polio, typhoid and yellow fever is recommended, as are precautions against malaria.

Climate and Timing
Mauritania is red-hot from April to October, and just very hot for the rest of the year, although December to February is slightly cooler and is the best time to visit. Rain is rare.

Habitats
Desolate desert dominates the terrain in Mauritania. It is, for the most part, a land of sand dunes and rocky crags, although there are estuaries on the western coast, and a narrow strip of the Sahel is present alongside the River Senegal on the southern border.

Conservation
Desertification and hunting are the two major conservation problems in Mauritania, where three threatened and six near-threatened species occur.

Bird Families
Seven of the ten families endemic to the African mainland are represented in Mauritania, and well represented families include bustards and larks.

Bird Species
A total of 541 species have been recorded in Mauritania, 80 more than Morocco, and 80 fewer than Mali. Non-endemic specialities and spectacular species include Scissor-tailed Kite, Nubian*, Arabian and Houbara Bustards, Egyptian Plover, Golden Nightjar, Chestnut-bellied Starling, Kordofan Lark and Sudan Golden-Sparrow.

Endemics
There are no endemics, but some arid-savanna specialities such as Cricket Longtail are present.

BANC D'ARGUIN NATIONAL PARK

Over two million shorebirds have been recorded at this internationally important wintering site for Palearctic migrants, on Mauritania's northwest coast. The lagoons, bays, mudflats, sandbanks and surrounding desert also support breeding pelicans and flamingos, and Sudan Golden-Sparrow.

Specialities
Sudan Golden-Sparrow.

Others
Wilson's Storm-Petrel, Great White Pelican, Greater Flamingo, Western Reef-Egret, Lanner Falcon, Cream-coloured Courser, Audouin's* (Nov–May), Grey-headed and Slender-billed Gulls, Royal and Bridled

(Apr–Oct) Terns, Brown-necked Raven, Bar-tailed Lark, Greater Hoopoe-Lark, Desert Sparrow.

Other Wildlife

Bottlenose dolphin, common jackal, dorcas gazelle, river dolphin.

Access

To arrange a visit contact the Ministre de la Pêche et de l'Économie Maritime, BP 137, Noukachott, or the National Park HQ in Nouadhibou (accessible by air from the capital, Nouakchott). Desert Sparrow has been recorded north of Tanoudert, and Sudan Golden-Sparrow occurs around Cansado.

A SELECTED LIST OF SPECIES RECORDED IN MAURITANIA

Bulwer's Petrel, White-faced and Band-rumped Storm-Petrels, African Darter, African Pygmy-goose, Dwarf Bittern, Hamerkop, Scissor-tailed Kite, Wahlberg's and Martial Eagles, Secretary-bird, Fox Kestrel, Barbary Partridge, Clapperton's Francolin, Stanley, Nubian*, Arabian and Houbara Bustards, Senegal and Spotted Thick-knees, Egyptian Plover, White-headed Lapwing, African Skimmer, Spotted and Crowned Sandgrouse, Bruce's Green-Pigeon, Senegal Parrot, Egyptian and Golden Nightjars, Red-throated and Northern Carmine Bee-eaters, Abyssinian Roller, Yellow-breasted Barbet, Little Grey Woodpecker, Piapiac, Common Gonolek, Senegal Batis, Chestnut-bellied Starling, Black Scrub-Robin, Desert Cisticola, Cricket Longtail, Yellow-bellied Eremomela, Sennar Penduline-Tit, Kordofan and Dunn's Larks, Brown-rumped Bunting.

ADDITIONAL INFORMATION

Books and Papers

Liste Commentée des Oiseaux de Mauritanie. Lamarche, B. 1988. (Privately published French text with brief English summary.)

Addresses

West African Ornithological Society (WAOS); see p. 413.

MAURITIUS, RÉUNION AND RODRIGUEZ

These three Indian Ocean islands, to the east of Madagascar, are all easily accessible, the best time to visit being October to March. A basic knowledge of French is useful in getting around. Immunisation against hepatitis, polio, typhoid and yellow fever is recommended, as are precautions against malaria, although this disease appears to be absent from Réunion.

Together these three islands support 20 of the 175 Malagasy endemics, 18 of which occur only here. One of the 18 'endemics', Barau's Petrel*, occurs around all three islands; three species occur on both Mauritius and Réunion, and 14 are present only on individual islands, with seven endemic to Mauritius, five endemic to Réunion and two endemic to Rodriquez.

MAURITIUS

This small volcanic island (2045 sq km), the haunt of the Dodo until around 1670, supports seven very rare endemics which, ironically, are fairly easy to see.

There are plenty of buses and taxis on Mauritius, although the latter are expensive, and a good range of accommodation, including cheap campsites and beach-bungalows.

Around 100 species have been recorded, including Madagascar Pratincole, Mascarene Martin and three species restricted to Mauritius and Réunion: Mascarene Swiftlet*, Mascarene Paradise-Flycatcher and Mascarene Grey White-eye. The remaining habitat on which most of the endemics depend is confined to the mountains of the southwest, and

Mauritius Kestrel is one of seven species which occur only on Mauritius*

MAURITIUS

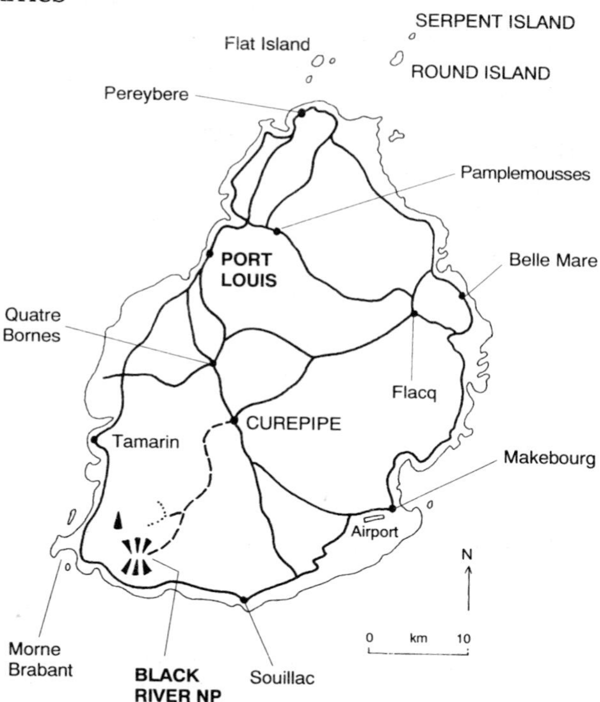

all the endemics may be seen there, mainly in **Black River NP**, near Black River village. Do not visit the Black River area without prior arrangement with the Mauritian Wildlife Appeal Fund (MWAF). The staff at the Captive Breeding Centre in Black River are doing their utmost to ensure the continued survival of the great rarities, Mauritius Kestrel*, Pink Pigeon* and Mauritius Parakeet*, and will assist visiting birders in return for a suitable donation. Their captive-release programmes have already met with some success. For example, there were just four wild Mauritius Kestrels* in 1973, today there are over 250 free-flying birds.

It is possible to visit **Serpent Island** and **Round Island**, off the north-east tip of Mauritius, by boat from Grand Baie. Red-tailed and White-tailed Tropicbirds, Masked Booby, Bridled Tern, some 250,000 pairs of Sooty Tern and Brown and Lesser Noddies breed on Serpent Island, and Herald Petrel and Wedge-tailed Shearwater breed on Round Island. Barau's Petrel* has been seen off Pointe aux Caves in February.

RÉUNION

Around 70 species have been recorded on this mountainous volcanic island, which rises to 2896 m (9501 ft). It is still a French colony and accommodation, apart from camping, is expensive. There is a good bus network and an amazing 600 km of trails, complete with hostels for overnight stays. To look for the four endemic landbirds (a cuckoo-shrike, a stonechat, a bulbul and a white-eye) head to the end of the steep track from St Denis to **La Brule** (one hour by car) at 1200 m (3937 ft). Walk and bird up from here for a few km, where Réunion Harrier*, Mascarene Swiftlet*, Mascarene Paradise-Flycatcher (more likely here than on Mauritius), Mascarene Martin and Mascarene Grey White-eye also occur. Another good site is the end of road RF20 (Plaine d'Affouches) where most of the endemics occur and an as yet undescribed scops-owl has been recorded.

The fifth Réunion endemic, the very rare and little known Mascarene Black Petrel*, may be seen whilst seawatching from the south coast, near the mouth of the St Etienne river, a few km west of St Pierre. Most of the previous sightings have been between October and March. This is also a good place to look for Barau's Petrel*, a species which usually appears in the late afternoon, *en route* to its breeding sites inland. Wedge-tailed and Audubon's Shearwaters are also possible. White-tailed Tropicbird occurs along the cliffs between St Denis and La Possession.

RÉUNION

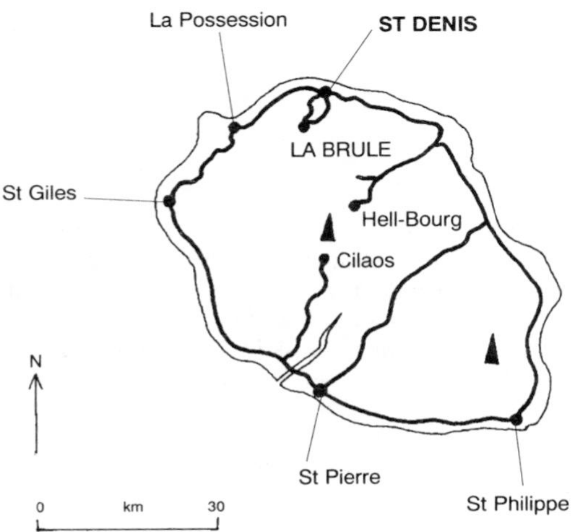

RODRIGUEZ

This small (10 km by 5 km), rather rugged and barren island, 650 km east of Mauritius, supports two endemics: Rodriguez Brush-Warbler* and Rodriquez Fody*, both of which maintain a toehold in the tiny remnants of native vegetation present amongst the mango plantations in the high northern valleys. Less than 30 species have been recorded here, but they include Barau's Petrel*, White-tailed Tropicbird and Common White-Tern.

RODRIGUEZ

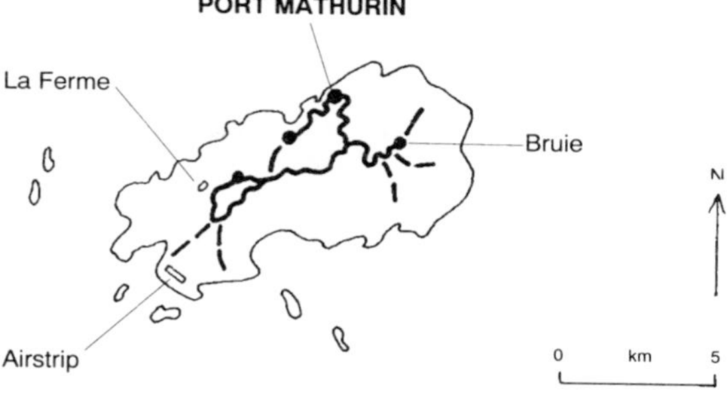

ADDITIONAL INFORMATION

Books and Papers

Birds of Mauritius. Michel, C. 1992. Rose Hill, Mauritius.
Oiseaux de la Réunion. Barre, N. and Barau, A. 1982. St Denis, Réunion.

Addresses

Please contact the Mauritian Wildlife Appeal Fund (MWAF), Tamarin, Mauritius, before visiting Mauritius and, after visiting, please send all Mauritius and Rodriguez records to the same address.

Please send Réunion records to The Societé Réunionnaise des Amis du Museum (Groupe Ornithologique)(SRAM), via Mme Sonia Ribes, Conservateur Museum d'Historie Naturelle, Rue Poivre, 97400 St Denis, Réunion (which publishes the *Borbonica* journal), and The Societé Réunionnaise d'Étude et de Protection de l'Environnement (SREPEN), BP 1109, 97482 St Denis, Réunion (which publishes *Info-Nature Île de la Réunion*).

ENDEMICS (14)

Mauritius (7)

Mauritius Kestrel*	Southwest: over 250 now present in the wild
Pink Pigeon*	Southwest: *c*50 birds now present in the wild
Mauritius Parakeet*	Southwest: *c*20 birds now present in the wild
Mauritius Cuckoo-shrike*	Southwest: over 200 pairs
Mauritius Bulbul*	Widespread: over 200 pairs
Mauritius Olive White-eye*	Southwest: *c*150 pairs
Mauritius Fody*	Southwest: over 80 pairs

Réunion (5)

Mascarene Black Petrel*	South: rarely seen offshore
Réunion Cuckoo-shrike*	Northwest

Réunion Stonechat	Northwest
Réunion Bulbul	Northwest
Réunion Olive White-eye	Northwest

(There is also an undescribed scops-owl on Réunion.)

Rodriguez (2)

Rodriguez Brush-Warbler*	North: 45–65 birds
Rodriguez Fody*	North: 350–450 birds

Mauritius and Réunion
Mascarene Swiftlet*, Mascarene Paradise-Flycatcher, Mascarene Grey White-eye.

Mauritius, Réunion and Rodriguez
Barau's Petrel*.

Near-endemics
Réunion Harrier*, Mascarene Martin.

MOROCCO

INTRODUCTION

Summary
Morocco boasts the richest avifauna north of the Sahara, the only known regular wintering site in the world for Slender-billed Curlew*, a regional field guide, a variety of superb landscapes, and an excellent infrastructure. All this makes it is a very popular birding destination.

Size
At 446,550 sq km, Morocco is over three times the size of England, and one third the size of Texas.

Getting Around
Most of the major roads are surfaced, although some of the best birding sites are accessible only on gravel tracks, especially in the south. There are plenty of cheap buses but they do not reach many of the birding sites, so this is a country where a personal vehicle is more or less a must for keen birders with little time to spare. In which case, it is wise to choose a car with good clearance and suspension, and to beware of reckless bus and taxi drivers.

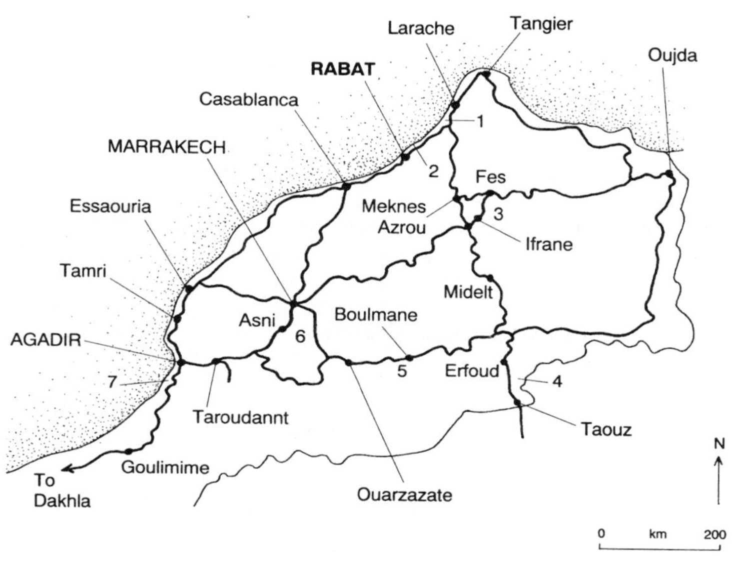

1 Merja Zerga NR
2 Sidi bou Ghaba NR
3 Ifrane
4 Merzouga
5 Boulmane
6 Oukaimeden
7 Sous Massa NP

Accommodation and Food

There is a great variety of accommodation, including campsites. On the whole it is basic, clean and cheap. The food, influenced by the French, is also cheap, especially the 'Tajine' casserole and couscous, but restaurants often close as early as 2000 hrs.

Health and Safety

Immunisation against polio, rabies and typhoid is recommended, as are precautions against malaria.

Most Moroccans are poor but, unlike most of the world's poorest people, who tend to be very friendly, they have been in touch with Europeans for a very long time, and they want what all westeners seem to have plenty of: money. They will do almost anything to get you to part with your precious cash, often in a very intimidating way, so prepare to be 'hassled to death' in some places.

Climate and Timing

Most of Morocco is hot, but it can be very cool at night in the high Atlas Mountains and the desert of the southeast. Whilst the months of April and May are a good time to visit because they coincide with the passage of northbound migrants, late November to mid February is the very best time to visit Morocco, because this is when the extremely rare Slender-billed Curlew* is usually present.

Habitats

Although it is a small country, Morocco has a diverse avifauna, thanks to the close proximity of coastal marshes, forested, snow-capped mountains, which rise to 4165 m (13,665 ft) at Mount Toubkal near Marrakech, and desert.

Conservation

Some of Morocco's habitats and birds are threatened by land-use pressures such as grazing, desertification, and hunting by Saudi Arabian falconers in search of bustards. However, some sites, especially coastal wetlands, are being managed sensitively, with the help of BirdLife International who have joined forces with the Moroccan Eaux et Fôret.

Eleven threatened and three near-threatened species occur in Morocco.

Bird Families

None of the families endemic to the African mainland are represented in Morocco. However, well represented families include 14 species of lark.

Bird Species

Over 460 species have been recorded in Morocco, 40 more than Egypt, and only 70 fewer than Gambia. Non-endemic specialities and spectacular species include Dark Chanting-Goshawk, Barbary Partridge, Double-spurred Francolin, Houbara Bustard, Slender-billed Curlew*, Pharaoh Eagle-Owl, Marsh Owl, Black-crowned Tchagra, Plain Martin, Fulvous Chatterer, Thick-billed Lark, Desert Sparrow and Crimson-winged Finch.

Endemics

There are no endemic birds, but the handful of near-endemics, which are easier to see here than in any other north African country, include Waldrapp*, Levaillant's Woodpecker, Moussier's Redstart and Tristram's Warbler.

Expectations

It is possible to see 200 species during a two-week winter trip, 230 over the same period in spring.

The sites discussed on the following pages are listed according to the following route: from Tangier, in the extreme north, to Agadir, in the south, via Larache, Rabat, Merja Zerga (Slender-billed Curlew*), Meknes, Ifrane, Midelt, al Rachidia (from where it is possible to travel to Erfoud and Merzouga in the Sahara), Boulmane, Ourazate, and Taroudannt. It is possible to fly into Tangier, drive to Agadir, and fly out from there, or vice versa, or drive between Tangier and Agadir along the coast.

White Stork and Spotless Starling breed at **Tangier** Airport. In winter, turn left off the P2 a few km south of the airport to bird the 25 km loop back to the P2 at Asilah. White Stork, Common Crane, Little* and Great* Bustards, and Calandra Lark occur along this loop, where the hill with radio masts acts as a fine viewing point over the flooded fields.

Pools and saltmarsh near Oued Loukkos, east of **Larache**, support wintering Marbled Teal*, Purple Swamphen and Little Bustard*, whilst Bluethroat (winter) and Moustached Warbler have been recorded in the reedy pools 7 km to the east.

MERJA ZERGA NATURE RESERVE

This large, internationally important wetland (7400 ha) near the small town of Moulay Bousselham on the Atlantic coast, 40 km south of Larache, is the only known regular wintering ground of Slender-billed Curlew*, one of the rarest species in the world.

Specialities

Slender-billed Curlew* (Nov to mid Feb), Marsh Owl.

Others

Marbled Teal*, Red-crested Pochard, Greater Flamingo, Glossy Ibis, Barbary Partridge, Common Crane (Nov–Mar), Little* (Nov–Mar) and Great* (Nov–Mar) Bustards, Eurasian Thick-knee, Audouin's Gull*, Caspian Tern, Spotless Starling, Moustached Warbler, Calandra Lark. (Plain Swift has also been recorded at Moulay Bousselham.)

Access

A Visitor Centre is planned, but for now, the first thing to do at Merja Zerga is to read the Bird Logbook at the Cafe Milano in Moulay Bousselham. This is also a good place to arrange a guide to help look for Slender-billed Curlew*. Without a guide the hassle at the actual site from local youths can be unbearable, and any vehicles may be unsafe.

MERJA ZERGA NR

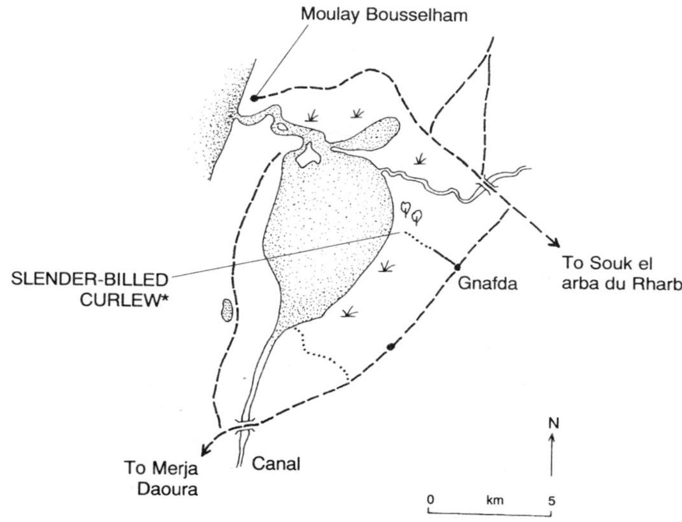

To look for Slender-billed Curlew*, turn south 10km east of Moulay Bousselham (signposted to 'Kenitra'). After passing over a slight rise on approaching the small village of Gnafda, turn west on to a track after the first couple of buildings, towards the lake. Scan the marshes from the end of this track for Slender-billed Curlew*, especially to the north around the isolated trees. This species usually associates with the vast Black-tailed Godwit and Eurasian Curlew flocks. If you do not have a guide pay the local hustlers (on return) to guard your vehicle, and hope its still in one piece when you return.

Moulay Bousselham campsite, just to the east of town, lies next to a Marsh Owl roost; Barbary Partridge also occurs here.

Accommodation: Moulay Bousselham: Laguna Hotel; campsite.

Morocco is the only country in the world where Slender-billed Curlew is seen on a regular basis*

Slender-billed Curlew numbers and dates, 1988–1995:*

Winter	Number	Arrival Date	Departure Date
1988–89	3	Nov 24	Feb 12
1989–90	3	Nov 26	Feb 17
1990–91	3	Oct 21	Feb 4
1991–92	2	Oct 23	Feb 2
1992–93	2	Nov 10	Feb 18
1993–94	2	Oct 29	Feb 11 at least
1994–95	1	Nov 2	Feb 6 at least

SIDI BOU GHABA NATURE RESERVE

This reserve, which was established by BirdLife International and Eaux et Fôret, lies very close to the town of Mehdiya Plage on the Atlantic coast, 30 km north of Rabat. The large lake here, surrounded by coastal juniper woodland, is of world importance to Marbled Teal* (up to 1,800 have been recorded in winter), and one of the best sites in Morocco for Marsh Owl.

Specialities

Marsh Owl.

Others

Marbled Teal*, Black-shouldered Kite, Red-knobbed Coot. (Slender-billed Curlew* has been recorded here in the past.)

Access

The reserve is easily accessible from the P2 road. There is a Visitor Centre on the eastern side of the lake, reached via a causeway, from which Marsh Owls are most often seen.

The cork oak royal forests of Sidi Bettache, southeast of Rabat, support Double-spurred Francolin, a difficult bird to find in Morocco (but much easier to see in sub-Saharan Africa). Turn off the Rabat–Casablanca road in response to signs to 'Temara'. In the town of Temara turn south to **Sidi Yahya des Ziaida**. Immediately south of Sidi Yahya turn west towards Sidi Bettache. After 10 km the road descends into a valley, which is the best area for the francolin and Barbary Partridge.

IFRANE

This cool hillside resort, 50 km south of Fes, lies in the Middle Atlas, east of Rabat. The mixed cedar and coniferous forest, and lake-dotted rocky terrain around Ifrane support Levaillant's Woodpecker and Moussier's Redstart.

Specialities

Levaillant's Woodpecker, Moussier's Redstart.

Others

Ruddy Shelduck, Marbled Teal*, Barbary Partridge, Red-knobbed Coot, Firecrest, Spotless Starling, Cirl Bunting. (Demoiselle Crane was recorded near here up until 1985.)

Access

Levaillant's Woodpecker occurs around Dayet Aaoua Lake, 20 km north of Ifrane. Turn east off the P24 on to the first road leading east, north of Ifrane. A road encircles the lake, and the southern slopes are best for Levaillant's Woodpecker. This species also occurs in the woods along the S309 east out of Ifrane, especially east of the turning to Mischliffen, and alongside the road south of Ifrane towards Azrou. Demoiselle Cranes used to be seen further east along the S309, around the junction with the P20.

The town of **Zeida**, 30 km north of Midelt (162 km south of Meknes on the P21), lies on a barren plateau, dotted with clumps of *Halfa* grass, where Dupont's Lark skulks. These birds are incredibly shy and it may be best to use a vehicle as a hide. Search the roadsides 4 km south of Zeida, and the track which leads west 3 km south of Zeida, signposted to 'Ait Illousen'. There is a quarry 1 km along this track where Cream-coloured Courser, Black-bellied Sandgrouse, Black and Red-rumped Wheatears, Thick-billed and Lesser Short-toed Larks, Rock Petronia and Trumpeter Finch occur.

Accommodation: Midelt (basic).

The road south of Midelt passes through the rugged, arid, low eastern end of the Atlas Mountains. Twenty-five km south of Midelt on the P21 there is a lay-by which may be worth a stop because the rocky slopes with scattered scrub to the west support Tristram's Warbler. This near-endemic also occurs around the 3 km post before the 'Tizi-n-Talhremt' pass, along with Crimson-winged Finch.

The town of **al Rachidia** lies just to the east of the intersection of the P21 and P32. Fulvous Chatterer occurs in the gully on the north side of the P32 just to the west of the intersection, as well as Desert Wheatear and Trumpeter Finch. The old rubbish dump, also north of the P32, closer to the intersection, supports Bar-tailed Lark.

Accommodation: Hotel Oasis.

The pleasant town of **Erfoud** is the gateway to the Erg Chebbi dune system near Merzouga (see below). It is possible to find a guide here (by sitting in a cafe with your binoculars and bird books on show) who may be willing, for a price, to help look for any remaining bustards in the surrounding desert. Going without a guide is not advisable as it is very easy to get lost or stuck (in deep sand) in the featureless desert landscape. Blue-cheeked Bee-eater (summer) occurs alongside the road south from Erfoud to Rissani, the most reliable site for this species in Morocco.

MERZOUGA

A number of desert specialities have been recorded around Merzouga, including Arabian and Houbara Bustards, Crowned Sandgrouse, Pharaoh Eagle-Owl, Egyptian Nightjar and Desert Sparrow, but few birders see more than three of these on a single trip. Permission from the military, easily obtained at the Taouz outpost, is required to enter the desert proper in search of bustards, and a tracker is recommended (falconers use spotter planes). Take great care not to cross the border into Algeria. Both Arabian and Houbara Bustards are very rare, if not extinct, around Merzouga now: Saudi Arabian falconers in December 1988 alone killed six Arabian and 120 Houbara Bustards.

Specialities

Arabian and Houbara Bustards, Spotted and Crowned Sandgrouse, Pharaoh Eagle-Owl, Egyptian Nightjar (Apr–Sep), Moussier's Redstart (Nov–Mar), Tristram's Warbler (Nov–Mar), Thick-billed Lark, Desert Sparrow.

Others

Ruddy Shelduck, Barbary Falcon, Cream-coloured Courser, Black-bellied Sandgrouse, Brown-necked Raven, White-tailed Wheatear, Streaked Scrub-Warbler, Desert and Spectacled Warblers, Fulvous Chatterer, Bar-tailed Lark, Greater Hoopoe-Lark, Temminck's Lark, Trumpeter Finch, House Bunting.

Access

Merzouga is 40 km south of Erfoud. Twenty-two km south of Erfoud where the road becomes a track there is a small oasis where Egyptian Nightjar (Apr–Sep), Moussier's Redstart (Nov–Mar), Tristram's Warbler (Nov–Mar), Fulvous Chatterer and Trumpeter Finch occur. To reach Merzouga to the south stay close to the telegraph poles. It is possible to sip mint tea in the cafes (eg. Cafe Yasmina) whilst watching Desert Sparrows at the dunes, along with tame White-tailed Wheatears, Bar-tailed Larks and Greater Hoopoe-Larks. The delightful sparrow also occurs at the Taouz outpost. Tristram's Warbler (Nov–Mar) occurs in the tamarisks along the track to the right, just south of the 'arch', south of Merzouga. The lake 2 km west of Merzouga is usually dry and, if so, may support Desert, Spectacled and Tristram's (Nov–Mar) Warblers and Thick-billed and Temminck's Larks (in 1990 and 1991 Kittlitz's Plover was recorded on this lake). Pharaoh Eagle-Owls perch on the dunes around Merzouga at dusk.

Accommodation: Cafe les Dunes Étoiles, 10 km north of Merzouga village (bustard guides available).

The easily missed, tiny hamlet of **Jorf** is approximately 30 km west of Erfoud. Two to three km west of Jorf there is a track south to a cultivated 'oasis' bordered by arid scrub and a sandy wadi, which is good for migrants. Ten km west of Jorf the road passes through scrubby desert where Houbara Bustard and Streaked Scrub-Warbler have been recorded.

The impressive **Gorge du Todra**, which is almost 300 m (984 ft) deep, is 14 km from Tinerhir, a town on the P32, 137 km west of al Rachidia and 53 km east of Boulmane. Bonelli's Eagle, Pallid Swift, Pale Crag-Martin and Tristram's Warbler occur here. The road to the gorge is well signposted, running east from the P32 just north of Tinerhir. Tristram's Warbler has been recorded in the scrub, 2.5 km up the gorge from the ford.

The stony desert between the Gorge du Todra and Boulmane supports most desert species including Mourning Wheatear.

BOULMANE

Several desert specialities occur near Boulmane, 480 km northeast of Agadir, including Houbara Bustard, Pharaoh Eagle-Owl and Thick-billed Lark (one of 13 species of lark recorded here).

Specialities

Houbara Bustard, Spotted and Crowned Sandgrouse, Pharaoh Eagle-Owl, Tristram's Warbler, Thick-billed and Dupont's Larks.

Others

Lanner Falcon, Cream-coloured Courser, Black-bellied Sandgrouse, European Bee-eater, Brown-necked Raven, Mourning and Red-rumped Wheatears, Bar-tailed, Desert and Lesser Short-toed Larks, Greater Hoopoe-Lark, Temminck's Lark, Trumpeter Finch.

Access

The **Tagdilt Track**, near Boulmane, is the most reliable site in Morocco for Thick-billed Lark, which is most numerous from November to March. The track passes through very arid, rolling country with scattered rocks and shallow wadis. One and a half km east of Boulmane town centre along the P32 turn south on to the track (just east of a service station on the north side of the P32). Both sides of the track are worth exploring and there is usually some water in the small fields to the west, 6 km along, which attracts most species, in time. A few km further east of Boulmane on the P32 there is another track leading south where Dupont's Lark has been recorded. These two tracks join to form a fine birding loop.

Accommodation: Boulmane: Auberge du Soleil Bleu (read the birders' logbook before venturing out) on eastern edge of town.

West of Boulmane the P32 traverses the Draa Valley, where Pale Crag-Martin occurs, and more desert where Thick-billed Lark has been recorded (a few km east of Ouarzazate).

Crimson-winged Finch occurs at the **Tizi-n-Tichka Pass** along the Ouarzazate–Marrakech road. Try the ridge to the north of the pass, a few hundred metres north of the shops, but the best site for this bird is Oukaimeden (see below).

OUKAIMEDEN

This small ski resort (2743 m (9000 ft)) in the High Atlas, 72 km south of Marrakech, is the best site for Crimson-winged Finch in Morocco.

Specialities

Levaillant's Woodpecker, Moussier's Redstart, Crimson-winged Finch.

Others

Lammergeier, Long-legged Buzzard, Golden Eagle, Barbary Falcon, Barbary Partridge, Yellow-billed Chough, White-throated Dipper, Black Wheatear, Pale Crag-Martin, Spectacled Warbler, Thekla and Horned Larks, Rock Petronia, Alpine Accentor, Rock Bunting.

Other Wildlife

Marmot.

Access

Oukaimeden is east of the Taroudannt–Marrakech road, near Asni. Crimson-winged Finch occurs around the resort and ski-lifts, and Black Wheatear around the radar station northeast of the village.

Accommodation: Hotel Chez Juju (B).

The P32 crosses the Aoulouz Gorge, a former breeding site for Waldrapp*, approximately 85 km northeast of Taroudannt. Barbary Falcon still occurs here, as well as Moussier's Redstart and Black Wheatear.

Small numbers of Dark Chanting-Goshawks winter in the **Sous Valley**, which is also good for migrants in spring. The section of the valley between Aoulouz and Taroudannt is the best area for Dark Chanting-Goshawk, a species which is only found away from sub-Saharan Africa (where it is much easier to see) in Morocco, and hence of great interest to Western Palearctic listers. Turn southeast 42 km west of Aoulouz (2 km west of Oulad Berrehil) to the village of Igoudar and take the left fork after the village to the hills, 3 km further on. These hills give a good view of the orange orchards over which the chanting-goshawk may be seen. Otherwise, look out for birds drifting over the P32 between Aoulouz and Taroudannt.

Four km southwest of red-walled **Taroudannt** (81 km east of Agadir) on the P32 there is a long causeway across the wide flood channel (usually dry) of the River Sous. A track leads west from the northern end of this causeway to: (1) An orange orchard which is good for migrants, and (2) The flood channel, which is a good site for Red-necked Nightjar (best looked for towards dusk when they begin to call).

A good selection of Morocco's best birds can be seen within 150 km of **Agadir**, a popular tourist resort in southwest Morocco, and an excellent base for birders who are unable to cover the whole country. Next to Agadir Airport is the mouth of the Sous river where Audouin's* and Slender-billed Gulls occur, along with Barbary Partridge and Red-necked Nightjar, which both occur around the Royal Palace. From Agadir head southeast on the P8. One km past the airport turn right in response to the 'Hotel Pyramid' sign to the estuary.

SOUS MASSA NATIONAL PARK

This park was established to protect 60 km of coast, from the Sous estuary in the north to the Massa estuary in the south, which is the world stronghold of Waldrapp*. There are believed to be only 50 wild pairs of these ibises left, and they all breed in just three colonies in or near this park.

The Massa estuary, at the southern end of the park, 60 km south of Agadir, is a good place to see Waldrapp*, as well as a fine range of other 'waterbirds', and even Plain Swift, which until recently was thought to be endemic to the Canary and Madeira Islands, is a possibility.

Specialities

Waldrapp*, Plain Swift, Moussier's Redstart.

Others

Ruddy Shelduck, Marbled Teal*, Greater Flamingo, Squacco Heron, Little Bittern, Glossy Ibis, Bonelli's Eagle, Lanner Falcon, Barbary Partridge, Common Crane, Little (Apr) and Baillon's (Apr) Crakes, Cream-coloured Courser, Audouin's* and Slender-billed Gulls, Royal Tern, Spotted and Black-bellied Sandgrouse, Laughing Dove, Pallid Swift, European Bee-eater, Black-crowned Tchagra, Spotless Starling, Bluethroat (winter), Rufous-tailed Scrub-Robin, Plain Martin, Moustached, Aquatic*, Orphean and Spectacled Warblers, Lesser Short-toed Lark, Spanish Sparrow, House Bunting. (Western Reef-Egret is a rare visitor.)

Other Wildlife

Egyptian mongoose, elephant shrew, jackal, leopard (rare), sand cat.

Access

Cream-coloured Courser has been recorded east of Massa village in the arid area between the P30 and Massa. To bird the estuary, take the turn-off signposted 'Massa 5' a few km south of Had Belfaa. The track runs alongside the north bank of the River Massa, where sandbanks, reedbeds, pools and scrub support Marbled Teal*, Waldrapp*, Spotted Sandgrouse, Black-crowned Tchagra and Plain Martin, whilst Audouin's Gulls* roost on the sandbanks at the river mouth. The track ends at Sidi R'bat beach resort, from where seawatching has produced Bulwer's Petrel.

Accommodation: Sidi R'bat beach resort/campsite complex.

The old market town of **Goulimime**, 180 km south of Agadir, is a tourist trap, but the surrounding stony hammada plains and scrubby wadis support Barbary Falcon, Cream-coloured Courser, Black-bellied and Crowned Sandgrouse, White-tailed, Black and Red-rumped Wheatears, Streaked Scrub-Warbler, Tristram's Warbler (Nov–Mar), Fulvous Chatterer, Bar-tailed and Desert Larks, Greater Hoopoe-Lark, Thick-billed, Lesser Short-toed and Temminck's Larks and Trumpeter Finch. Bird the roads east to Fask and south to Tan-Tan (120 km from Goulimime), and the Puerto Cansado area, where a lagoon supports many shorebirds during the winter (Slender-billed Curlew* has been recorded here). Streaked Scrub-Warbler occurs around the lagoon at Oued Chebeika.

Accommodation: Hotel Salem (B); camping.

The bay east of Dakhla (formerly in Western Sahara), 1300 km south of Agadir on a good road via Tan-Tan, supports Audouin's Gull and Royal Tern.

The colourful Moussier's Redstart, a northwest African endemic, is one of Morocco's star birds

Seawatching from **Cap Rhir**, 30 km north of Agadir on the P8, has revealed passing Madeira* and Bulwer's Petrels. The small town of **Tamri** on the Tinkert estuary, 55 km north of Agadir on the P8, is, with the Massa estuary, the most reliable site in Morocco for Waldrapp*. At dawn and dusk, when the birds are moving between feeding and roosting sites, they can be seen passing over the river mouth west of Tamri. Also check roadside fields. Plain Swift has also been recorded in this area.

The Island of Mogador, 1.6 km offshore from the town of **Essaouria** (192 km north of Agadir) on the Atlantic coast, is the best site in Morocco for Eleonora's Falcon (May–Oct). From the quay in town, it is possible to 'scope the island, where between 50 and 100 pairs breed, although the birds do occasionally visit the wadi 2 km south of town behind the beach, where Black-crowned Tchagra also occurs. Plain Swift has also been recorded in the Essaouria area.

Four to six Slender-billed Curlews* were reported from **Sidi Massa Oualidia**, an old traditional wintering site between Essaouria and Casablanca, in November 1993. Audouin's Gull* occurs on the lagoons and salt pans to the north of Oualidia and seawatching may be productive from Cap Beddouza to the south.

ADDITIONAL INFORMATION

Books and Papers

A Birdwatcher's Guide to Morocco. Bergier, P and Bergier, F. 1990. Prion.
Birds of Europe with North Africa and the Middle East. Jonsson, L. 1992. Helm.
Birds of the Middle East and North Africa. Hollom, P *et al.* 1988. Poyser.
The Birds of Morocco. Thevenot, M. *et al.* In prep. BOU.

Addresses

Groupe de Recherche pour la Protection des Oiseaux au Maroc (GREPOM), 12 rue Ottawa, Quartier Ocean, 10,000 Rabat.

Le Groupe d'Ornithologie du Maroc Centrale, Departement de Biologie, Faculte des Sciences de Meknes, BP 4010 Beni-M-hamed, 50003 Meknes. This group publishes the annual *Porphyrio*.

Please send all unusual records to the above organisations and Dr M Thevenot, Biogeographie et Écologie des Vertebres, EPHE case 94, Universite de Montpellier 2, F-34095 Montpellier Cedex 5, France.

Near-endemics

Waldrapp*, Slender-billed Curlew*, Plain Swift, Levaillant's Woodpecker, Moussier's Redstart, Tristram's Warbler.

(Waldrapp* is now present only as a feral species in Turkey, although recent winter records in Saudi Arabia and Yemen suggest an unknown breeding colony may exist somewhere in the Middle East.)

MOZAMBIQUE

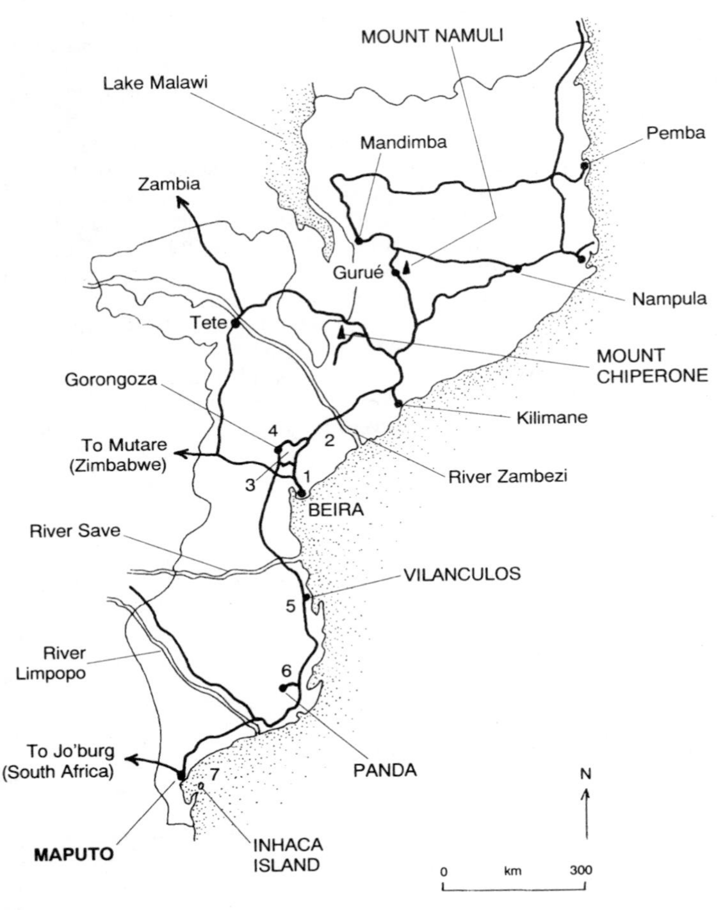

1 Beira to Tica
2 Dondo North
3 Gorongoza NP
4 Gorongoza Mountain
5 Vilanculos
6 Panda
7 Inhaca Island

Mozambique is well off the beaten birding track. A few birders did visit the southern half the country in the 1970s, revealing the presence of many near-endemics, most of which are easier to see in neighbouring countries. However, now the civil war has subsided somewhat adventurous birders may be tempted to return, and even venture to the north of the country, one of the few areas of Africa where it remains remotely possible to discover new species.

The infrastructure is poor, with virtually no accommodation and frequent food shortages. At 801,590 sq km, Mozambique is six times larger than England and a little larger than Texas. The dry season lasts from April to September, and it is hot, humid and wet, especially on the coast, from October to March. Mozambique has a long, mangrove-lined, indented coastline. The southern third of the country, south of the River Save, comprises a low-lying (under 200 m (656 ft)) sandy plain, where there are *Afzelia* forests, *Brachystegia* woodlands and palm savanna. North of the River Save the land rises towards the Zimbabwe border and here the mountain slopes support moist evergreen forest.

Eight of the ten families endemic to the African mainland are represented. Only Shoebill* and rockfowl are absent. A total of 690 species have been recorded in Mozambique, 350 fewer than Tanzania to the north, but only 100 fewer than South Africa, to the south. Non-endemic specialities and spectacular species include Lesser Jacana, Crab Plover, Mangrove Kingfisher, Boehm's Bee-eater, Racket-tailed Roller, African Pitta, Green-headed Oriole, Collared Palm-Thrush and Locustfinch. There are no endemics but plenty of near-endemics including Zululand Batis, Swynnerton's Robin*, White-winged* and Rudd's Apalises, Dapple-throat* and Gurney's Sugarbird.

BEIRA TO TICA

The road northwest from Beira on Mozambique's central east coast, to Tica, at the Pungwe river crossing, may still skirt remnant mangrove, gallery forest, *Brachystegia* woodland and marshes, which used to support Mangrove Kingfisher, Pale Batis, and East Coast Akalat*.

Specialities

Mangrove Kingfisher, Pale Batis, White-chested Alethe, East Coast Akalat*, Tiny Greenbul, Lesser Seedcracker.

Others

African Pygmy-goose, Fasciated Snake-Eagle*, African and Black Goshawks, Crested Francolin, Water Thick-knee, Long-toed Lapwing, African Skimmer, Lemon Dove, Barred Long-tailed Cuckoo, Black Coucal, Pel's Fishing-Owl, Silvery-cheeked Hornbill, African Broadbill, African Crested-Flycatcher, Marsh Tchagra, Retz's and Chestnut-fronted Helmetshrikes, Bearded Scrub-Robin, African Bush-Warbler, Peters' Twinspot.

Access

Between Beira and Dondo any remnant gallery forest and mangrove may be worth exploring in search of Pel's Fishing-Owl and Mangrove Kingfisher. West of Dondo the road used to pass through thick *Brachystegia* woodland, which used to support African Crested-Flycatcher, Pale Batis, White-chested Alethe and Lesser Seedcracker. Any remaining marshes around Tica, 37 km beyond Dondo, at the Pungwe river crossing, may still support Black Coucal.

DONDO NORTH

Any remnant *Brachystegia* woodland north of Dondo may still support Boehm's Bee-eater, Racket-tailed Roller, Zululand Batis and Locustfinch.

Specialities

Boehm's Bee-eater, Racket-tailed Roller, African Green-Tinkerbird, Zululand Batis, East Coast Akalat*, Stierling's Wren-Warbler, Olive-headed Weaver, Plain-backed Sunbird*.

Others

Barred Long-tailed Cuckoo, Bat-like Spinetail, Swallow-tailed Bee-eater, Silvery-cheeked Hornbill, Green-backed Woodpecker, African Broadbill, Livingstone's Flycatcher, Retz's and Chestnut-fronted Helmetshrikes, Black-and-white Shrike-flycatcher, Southern Hyliota, Locustfinch.

Access

Turn north 4 km northwest of Dondo towards Muanza. Bird any road-side forest between here and Muanza, east along the road to Chunizia (turn east 10 km south of Muanza), and north of Muanza to Inhaminga, Inhamitanga, and Lacerdonia, on the Zambezi river. The forest around Inhaminga and north to Inhamitanga used to be the best.

GORONGOZA NATIONAL PARK

The dry woodland, grassland and seasonal (Oct–Mar) marshes in this huge (3770 sq km) park in central Mozambique may still exist and, if so, still support masses of waterbirds including Lesser Jacana.

Specialities

Lesser Jacana, Collared Palm-Thrush, Stierling's Wren-Warbler.

Others

Goliath and Rufous-bellied Herons, Dwarf Bittern, Bat Hawk, White-headed Vulture, Martial Eagle, Dickinson's Kestrel, Kaffir Rail, African and Black Crakes, Black-and-white Shrike-flycatcher, Southern Hyliota, Black-winged Bishop.

Access

Turn north off the Beira–Mutare (Zimbabwe) road at Vila Machado, 110 km northwest of Beira, towards Andrada. Forty km north of Vila Machado (5 km north of the Pungwe river crossing at Mutiambaba) turn east to the park entrance gate at Bue Maria. This track then leads to Chitengo Camp, beyond which lies a maze of tracks, many of which are impassable from October to March.

Accommodation: Chitengo Camp.

GORONGOZA MOUNTAIN

Any forest which remains on the slopes of this wet, isolated mountain (1863 m (6112 ft)) in central Mozambique may still support Swynnerton's Robin* and Chirinda Apalis, both of which are much more 'accessible' in eastern Zimbabwe. Wooded savanna lies below the forest and montane grassland above it.

Specialities

Buff-spotted Flufftail, African Pitta, Black-fronted Bushshrike, White-chested Alethe, Swynnerton's Robin*, Chirinda Apalis.

Others

Scarce Swift, Silvery-cheeked Hornbill, Green-headed Oriole, Orange Ground-Thrush, Stripe-cheeked Bulbul, Red-faced Crimson-wing, Cabanis' Bunting.

Access

Turn north off the Beira–Mutare road at Inchope, to Andrada, then turn northeast to Gorongosa (also known as Cavalo). One km north of Gorongosa turn west on to a track which leads to a ranch, beyond which used to be a good birding track through forest, leading to the central plateau.

Cholo Alethe* and White-winged Apalis* have been recorded on **Mount Chiperone**, an isolated mountain in west Mozambique, 60 km south of Mount Mulanje in Malawi (p. 228). Green Barbet, Cholo Alethe*, Dapple-throat*, and a race of Bar-throated Apalis known as 'Namuli Apalis', have been recorded in the remote **Namuli Mountains** (2680 m (8793 ft)), in northwest Mozambique.

VILANCULOS

Most of the natural grassland and evergreen forest which used to surround Vilanculos, on Mozambique's east coast, south of Beira, has been turned over to farmland, but remnant patches may still support Zululand Batis and Rudd's Apalis, whilst Crab Plover occurs along the coast.

Specialities

Zululand Batis, Tiny Greenbul, Rudd's Apalis, Olive-headed Weaver, Plain-backed* and Neergaard's* Sunbirds, Lemon-breasted Seedeater.

Others

Shelley's Francolin, Crab Plover, Livingstone's Flycatcher, Bearded Scrub-Robin, Southern Hyliota, Southern Brown-throated Weaver, Black-eared Seedeater.

Access

It used to be possible to fly into Vilanculos where the extensive mudflats offshore, baobab country to the north, the road to Chichocane to the south, and the road inland to the Pambara–Govuro road, used to be worth birding.

PANDA

Although much of the area around Panda, in southeast Mozambique, has been turned over to farmland, there may still be some seasonally flooded grassland and patches of remnant *Brachystegia* woodland worth exploring.

Specialities

Stierling's Wren-Warbler, Olive-headed Weaver, Lemon-breasted Seedeater.

Others

Fasciated Snake-Eagle*, Shelley's Francolin, Mottled and Bat-like Spinetails, Green-backed Woodpecker, African Broadbill, Four-coloured Bushshrike, Retz's and Chestnut-fronted Helmetshrikes, Southern Hyliota.

Access

Previously productive birding areas around Panda were the seasonally flooded grassland (Oct–Mar) between Panda and Maxixe, to the north-east, and the environs of the Inhatouce river, just north of Panda.

INHACA ISLAND

Situated at the seaward side of Maputo Bay in extreme southeast Mozambique, this tiny island (10 km by 6 km) may still support a narrow strip of coastal forest on the eastern dunes. Much of the rest of the island is farmland and scrub, although extensive mudflats lie between the beach and reef, especially along the west coast. Although Rudd's Apalis and Neergaard's Sunbird* are the island's star attractions, seawatching could turn out to be more exciting.

Specialities

Rudd's Apalis, Neergaard's Sunbird*.

Others

Shy and Yellow-nosed Albatrosses, Great-winged and White-chinned Petrels, Wilson's Storm-Petrel, Red-tailed and White-tailed Tropicbirds, Great Frigatebird, Cape Gannet*, Crab Plover, Kelp Gull, Four-coloured Bushshrike, Black-tailed Waxbill, Rosy-throated Longclaw, Purple-banded Sunbird.

Access

Inhaca Island is accessible by ferry from Mozambique's capital, Maputo. Good birding areas in the past included the mudflats and mangroves on the southern and western coasts, especially around Saco da Inhaca Bay and north of the landing jetty. Shorebirds used to roost at Point Rasa in the southwest and on Portuguese Island (accessible by foot on very low tides) off the northwest coast. Seawatching from Cape Inhaca, at the northern tip of the island, has been very exciting between March (the best time for tropicbirds, at the end of the cyclone season) and September.

ADDITIONAL INFORMATION

Books and Papers

Where to Watch Birds in Southern Africa. Berruti, A and Sinclair, I. 1983. Struik, Cape Town. Out of Print.

Addresses

Wildlife Society of Mozambique, c/o Ms Milagre OFN Cezerilo, Director of Forestry and Wildlife, Ministry of Agriculture, Maputo.

Please send all records to Dr Heimo Mikkola, FAO Representative for Malawi, Box 30750, Lilongwe 3, Malawi, who is currently preparing a checklist.

Near-endemics

Stierling's Woodpecker*, Southern Tchagra, Southern Boubou, Olive Bushshrike, Short-tailed, Malawi, Zululand and Pale Batises, White-chested and Cholo* Alethes, Swynnerton's Robin*, East Coast Akalat*, Olive-flanked Robin-Chat, Brown Scrub-Robin, Stripe-cheeked Bulbul, Fischer's and Tiny Greenbuls, Roberts' Prinia, White-winged*, Rudd's and Chirinda Apalises, African Scrub-Warbler, African and Long-billed* Tailorbirds, Kretschmer's Longbill, Dapple-throat*, Lesser Seedcracker, Pink-throated Twinspot, Swee Waxbill, Bertrand's and Olive-headed Weavers, Zanzibar Bishop, Gurney's Sugarbird, Plain-backed*, Uluguru Violet-backed, Eastern Double-collared and Neergaard's* Sunbirds, Lemon-breasted Seedeater.

NAMIBIA

INTRODUCTION

Summary

Thanks to its excellent infrastructure, remarkable landscapes and superb selection of birds and mammals, Namibia has become a very popular birding destination in recent years. Birders contemplating a trip to Botswana or South Africa should remember that many of the southern African specialities, including those whose ranges are centred in the Okavango, can be seen in Namibia.

Size

At 824,292 sq km, Namibia is six times the size of England and slightly larger than Texas.

Getting Around

It is very difficult to get around Namibia without personal transport as public transport is virtually non-existent and birding on foot is not

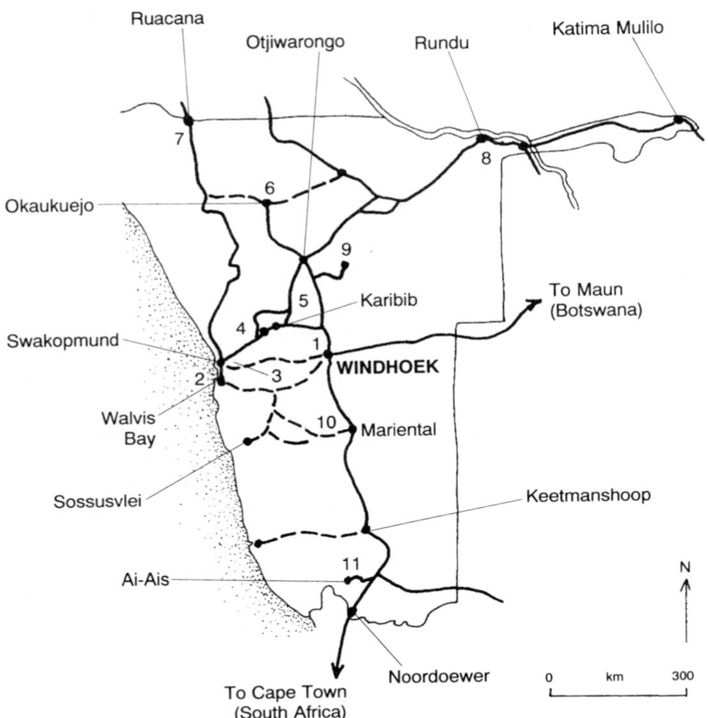

1 Daan Viljoen Reserve
2 Walvis Bay and Swakopmund
3 Namib–Naukluft NP (North)
4 Spitzkop
5 Erongo Mountains
6 Etosha NP
7 Ruacana
8 Caprivi Strip
9 Waterberg Plateau NP
10 Hardap Dam
11 Ai-Ais and Fish River Canyon

allowed in some national parks. Despite the harsh terrain the roads are excellent. All national parks must be entered before sunset and left after sunrise.

Accommodation and Food

There is a good sprinkling of cheap campsites, caravan parks and bungalows, but hotels, guesthouses and lodges are more expensive. Accommodation is often full during the four school holidays (December–January, late March–early April, mid June–mid July, and late September–early October) but can be booked in advance through The Namib Travel Shop, PO Box 6850, Windhoek 9000 (tel: 226174/225178; fax: 33332). Much of the food has a European 'flavour'.

Health and Safety

Immunisation against hepatitis, polio, rabies, typhoid and yellow fever is recommended, as are precautions against malaria, especially if visiting the far north (November to May).

Namibians are very friendly people, but beware of muggers in Windhoek, especially in Independence Avenue.

Climate and Timing

Most of Namibia is hot and dry during the summer (Sep–May), and despite the fact that the northern rainy season (Dec–Mar) falls within this period, this is the best time to visit. November is particularly hot in the north. It can be surprisingly cold in winter (Jun–Aug), especially at night.

Habitats

The cold, nutrient-rich Benguela Current that flows north off Namibia's 1280 km 'Skeleton Coast' is responsible for the Namib Desert, one of the driest in the world. Here plants, including the famous *Welwitschia*, survive on dew and fog, and coastal lagoons support some of the largest concentrations of waterbirds in Africa. The current itself attracts many seabirds, especially during the austral winter (Jun–Oct).

Inland, the dunes and gravel plains of the Namib Desert give way to the central highlands, which run north to south at an average height of 1000–1700 m (3281—5577 ft), and rise to 2610 m (8563 ft). Scrub at the desert edge gives way to bush and mopane woodland, some of which has been turned over to intensive agriculture. In the far east of the country there is another desert, the Kalahari. The Caprivi Strip, in extreme northeast Namibia, is dominated by sand forest, but it is also crossed by the Okavango river, with its associated wetlands and gallery forest.

Conservation

Six threatened and 14 near-threatened species occur in Namibia.

Although not endemic, Namibia is the best place to see the striking White-tailed Shrike

Bird Families

Seven of the ten families endemic to the African mainland are represented in Namibia, and bustards and larks are particularly well represented. In the case of larks, beware of the subtle colour differences within species,which have evolved in line with the slightly different micro-habitats.

Bird Species

A total of 624 species have been recorded in Namibia, 166 fewer than South Africa. Non-endemic specialities and spectacular species include Rufous-bellied Heron, Wattled Crane*, Lesser Jacana, Chestnut-banded Plover, Damara Tern*, Pel's Fishing-Owl and Racket-tailed Roller.

Endemics

Although Dune Lark is the only endemic species in Namibia, there are many near-endemics, which are easier to see here than in neighbouring Angola, Botswana, or South Africa. These include Hartlaub's Francolin, Ludwig's and Ruppell's Bustards, African Oystercatcher*, Rueppell's Parrot, Monteiro's Hornbill, White-tailed Shrike, Rufous-tailed Palm-Thrush, Herero Chat*, Damara Rock-jumper, Bare-cheeked Babbler, Gray's Lark, and Cinderella Waxbill*. In addition, Okavango specialities such as Slaty Egret*, occur in the Caprivi Strip.

Expectations

It is possible to see over 300 species during a comprehensive four-week trip.

DAAN VILJOEN RESERVE

The acacia savanna, woodland and dams within this 40 sq km reserve, near the capital, Windhoek, support a handful of southern African specialities, including the rare Damara Rock-jumper.

Birding on foot is permitted in this reserve.

Specialities

Rosy-faced Lovebird, Monteiro's Hornbill, White-tailed Shrike, Short-toed Rock-Thrush, Black-chested Prinia, Barred Wren-Warbler, Damara Rock-jumper, Bradfield's and Stark's Larks.

Others

African Darter, Maccoa Duck, South African Shelduck, Cape Shoveler, Hamerkop, Orange River and Red-billed Francolins, Three-banded Plover, Namaqua Sandgrouse, Grey Go-away-bird, Swallow-tailed Bee-eater, Rufous-crowned Roller, Common Scimitar-bill, Pied Barbet, Crimson-breasted Gonolek, Pririt Batis, Groundscraper Thrush, Pale-winged Starling, Red-shouldered Glossy-Starling, Mariqua Flycatcher, Mountain Wheatear, Familiar Chat, White-throated Swallow, Yellow-bellied and Burnt-neck Eremomelas, Rufous-vented Warbler, Southern Black-Tit, Ashy Tit, Southern Penduline-Tit, Rufous Sparrow, Green-winged Pytilia, Violet-eared and Black-cheeked Waxbills, Shaft-tailed Whydah, Red-headed Finch, Cape Wagtail, Buffy Pipit, Scaly Weaver, Dusky and Mariqua Sunbirds, White-throated Canary, Lark-like and Cape Buntings.

Other Wildlife

Black-backed jackal, Burchell's zebra, chacma baboon, eland, greater kudu, hartebeest, Hartmann's mountain zebra, springbok, wildebeest.

Access

This reserve is just 24 km west of Windhoek (55 km from the airport). It is signposted from the C28 road to Swakopmund, approximately 15 km west of Windhoek. Bird the one-way 6.4-km track, the two trails (the 3-km 'Wag 'n' Bietjie' Trail, and the 9-km trail) and the dam (best just before dusk). Damara Rock-jumper occurs on steep, rocky and bushy slopes.

Accommodation: Bungalows (B); camping (C).

White-quilled Bustard and a few larks occur at **Karibib Airstrip**, between Windhoek and Walvis Bay, whilst other roadside birds along this route include Ruppell's Bustard, Cream-coloured Courser, Namaqua Sandgrouse, White-tailed Shrike, Chat Flycatcher, Kalahari Scrub-Robin, Tractrac Chat and Spike-heeled and Gray's Larks. The latter lark has been recorded approximately 250 km northeast of Walvis Bay, near the road to Ebony's Siding (signposted).

WALVIS BAY AND SWAKOPMUND

These two towns, 30 km apart, are situated on the virtually unvegetated Atlantic coast, and yet the birding can be fantastic, thanks to coastal lagoons, which attract vast numbers of waterbirds, including the rare Damara Tern*. Inland, within the Namib-Naukluft NP (see next site) the stark but stunning desert supports the near-endemic Gray's Lark.

Specialities

Crowned*, Bank* and Cape Cormorants, African Oystercatcher*, Damara Tern* (Nov–Mar), Black-chested Prinia.

Others

White-chinned Petrel (Apr–Sep), Cape Gannet*, Maccoa Duck, South African Shelduck, Cape Teal, Cape Shoveler, Greater and Lesser*

The rare Damara Tern is a Walvis Bay speciality*

Flamingos, Three-banded, Chestnut-banded, White-fronted and Blacksmith Plovers, Hartlaub's Gull, Antarctic Tern (Apr–Sep), White-backed Mousebird, Pale-winged Starling, Tractrac Chat, Mossie, Cape Wagtail, Dusky Sunbird. (Jackass Penguin* is a rare visitor.)

Other Wildlife

Cape fur seal.

Access

Mornings on the Atlantic coast are often cold and foggy, but the fog usually disperses quite quickly and it soon warms up. The best birding areas are: (1) The **Bird Park**, signposted from 13th Road in Walvis Bay town, complete with observation tower. (2) **Walvis Bay Lagoon**, south of town, accessible via the road to Paaltjies. The lagoon is a good site for Damara Tern*. (3) The **Swakopmund Saltworks**, another good site for Damara Tern*, as well as Chestnut-banded Plover, reached by turning west 6 km north of town. Drive along the track which runs along the eastern edge to the Guano Works. (4) **Swakop Rivermouth**. (5) The **Cape Cross Seal Reserve**, 115 km north of Swakopmund, which is a good place to seawatch.

The best way to see seabirds possibly including Jackass Penguin* is on boat trips, which can be arranged at the restaurant in Long Beach, between Swakopmund and Walvis Bay.

Accommodation: There are plenty of small hotels and 'bed-and-breakfasts' in Walvis Bay and Swakopmund; camping is possible in Walvis Bay.

WALVIS BAY, SWAKOPMUND AND NAMIB–NAUKLUFT NP (NORTH)

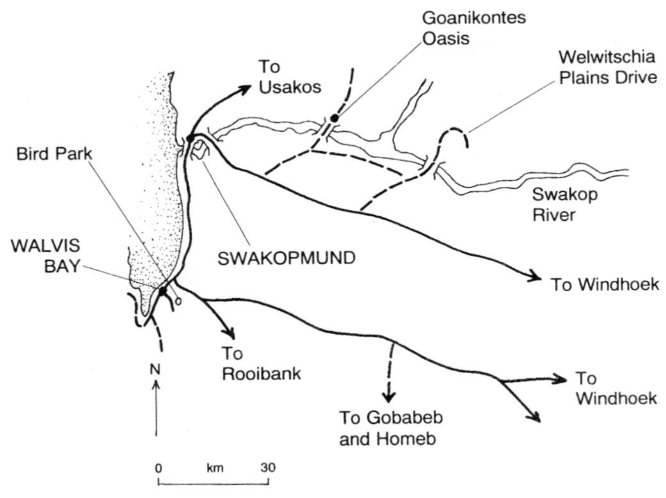

NAMIB–NAUKLUFT NATIONAL PARK (NORTH)

This huge park (49,000 sq km) is the fourth largest in the world. Birds are few and far between in the desert and scrubby riverbeds but include the endemic Dune Lark and near-endemic Gray's Lark, as well as Ludwig's and Ruppell's Bustards.

It is necessary to obtain a permit from the Directorate of Nature Conservation, in Bismarck Street, Swakopmund, or from the Walvis Bay Service Station, 7th Street, Walvis Bay, before entering this park.

Namibia Endemics

Dune Lark.

Specialities

Ludwig's and Ruppell's Bustards, Gray's Lark.

Others

Ostrich, Namaqua Sandgrouse, Cream-coloured Courser, White-backed and Red-faced Mousebirds, Swallow-tailed Bee-eater, Sicklewing and Karoo Chats, Grey-backed Sparrow-Lark, Rufous Sparrow, Mossie, Scaly Weaver, Dusky Sunbird.

Other Wildlife

Aardwolf, cape fox, grey meerkat, oryx (gemsbok), springbok.

Access

The northern tip of this national park is accessible from Walvis Bay and Swakopmund. From Walvis Bay head east on the airport road, then turn south to Rooibank. Just before Rooibank take the track to the right. This leads to some low dunes where the endemic Dune Lark occurs. From Swakopmund head southeast towards Windhoek and turn north on to: (1) The track to Goanikontes Oasis, where White-backed Mousebird occurs. (2) The track to Welwitschia Plains Drive which traverses gravel desert and is famous for a giant *Welwitschia* plant.

Accommodation: Camping only.

The entrance to the middle of Namib–Naukluft NP, famous for the highest sand dunes in the world (300 m (984 ft)), is at **Sesriem**, 55 km south of Solitaire and 102 km north of Maltahohe. The one-way track west from here leads to Sossusvlei.

Accommodation: Sesriem: Camp and lodge, with more choice within 40 km.

SPITZKOP

The dry, boulder-strewn scrub at the base of the granite inselbergs near Usakos, northeast of Swakopmund, supports the near-endemic Herero Chat*.

Specialities

Ludwig's and Ruppell's Bustards, Monteiro's Hornbill, White-tailed Shrike, Short-toed Rock-Thrush, Herero Chat*, Stark's Lark.

Others

Bokmakierie, Pale-winged Starling, Karoo Scrub-Robin, Mountain Wheatear, Tractrac Chat, Layard's Warbler, Sabota, Long-billed and Spike-heeled Larks, Grey-backed Sparrow-Lark, Dusky Sunbird.

Access

25 km southwest of Usakos turn west off the B2 on to the Hentiesbaai road. After 1 km turn north towards Uis. After 28 km turn west on to a track that runs along the base of Spitzkop. From the small settlement take the track towards the base of the mountain, where the tricky Herero Chat* occurs in dry and bushy open gullies.

ERONGO MOUNTAINS

The rocky slopes at the base of these mountains, which are believed to be the oldest on earth, support the near-endemic Hartlaub's Francolin.

Specialities

Hartlaub's Francolin, Rosy-faced Lovebird, Bradfield's Swift.

Others

Bat Hawk, Red-necked Falcon, Burchell's Sandgrouse, White-backed Mousebird, Freckled Nightjar, Lilac-breasted and Rufous-crowned Rollers, Monteiro's Hornbill, Golden-tailed and Bearded Woodpeckers, Pririt Batis, Burchell's Glossy-Starling, Yellow-bellied Eremomela, Southern Black-Tit, White-throated Canary.

Access

The small village of Omaruru, at the base of the mountains, makes a good base for exploring the surrounding slopes, especially the (usually) dry river bed near the village.

Accommodation: Omaruru: Hotel Staebe.

Bare-cheeked Babbler, as well as Jackal Buzzard, Namaqua and Yellow-throated Sandgrouse, Monteiro's Hornbill, Southern Penduline-Tit, Grey-backed Sparrow-Lark and Lark-like Bunting occur at **Khorixas Rest Camp**, near Khorixas. Herero Chat* occurs 40 km to the north, behind the 'Petrified Forest'.

Accommodation: bungalows, camping.

ETOSHA NATIONAL PARK

Etosha in native Namibian means 'Great White Place', a name which reflects the presence of a huge pan in this spectacular park. This shallow depression, which is usually dry and blinding white, is up to 150 km long and 70 km wide. It takes up nearly 25% of the 22,270 sq-km park, which also supports semi-desert, grassy plains and mopane woodland, where many mammals and nearly 400 species of bird have been recorded, including Blue Crane*, Bare-cheeked Babbler and a diverse group of bustards and larks.

There are always some wet springs draining into the pan and a few artificial waterholes, both of which are especially attractive to birds and mammals. The onset of the rains means mammals are harder to find from December onwards, during which period they disperse over a larger area.

Etosha is a very popular national park and some places are very crowded, especially the waterholes. Birding on foot away from the camps and night driving are not permitted.

Specialities

Blue Crane*, Violet Woodhoopoe, White-tailed Shrike, Short-toed Rock-Thrush, Black-chested Prinia, Black-lored Babbler, Southern Pied-Babbler, Bare-cheeked Babbler, Monotonous, Pink-billed and Stark's Larks, Social and Chestnut Weavers.

Others

Ostrich, White-headed Vulture, Bateleur, Pale Chanting-Goshawk, Gabar Goshawk, Martial Eagle, Pygmy Falcon, Greater Kestrel, Red-necked Falcon, Secretary-bird, Swainson's Spurfowl, Kori, Red-crested and White-quilled Bustards, Spotted Thick-knee, Double-banded and Bronze-winged Coursers, Three-banded and Blacksmith Plovers, Crowned Lapwing, Namaqua, Double-banded and Burchell's Sandgrouse, Red-faced Mousebird, Grey Go-away-bird, African and White-faced Scops-Owls, Verreaux's Eagle-Owl, Rufous-cheeked Nightjar, Swallow-tailed Bee-eater, Lilac-breasted Roller, Common Scimitar-bill, Pied Barbet, White-crowned Shrike, Crimson-breasted Gonolek, White Helmetshrike, Pririt Batis, Chat and Mariqua Flycatchers, Kalahari Scrub-Robin, Southern Anteater-Chat, Desert Cisticola, Rufous-eared Warbler, Southern Penduline-Tit, Rufous-naped, Clapper, Fawn-coloured and Spike-heeled Larks, Chestnut-backed and Grey-backed Sparrow-Larks, Rufous Sparrow, Violet-eared and Black-cheeked Waxbills, Red-headed Finch, Cape Wagtail, Scaly Weaver, White-breasted, Dusky and Mariqua Sunbirds, Lark-like Bunting.

Other Wildlife

Bat-eared fox, black rhino, Burchell's zebra, cheetah, Damara dik-dik, elephant, giraffe, greater kudu, hartebeest, honey badger, impala, leopard, lion, oryx (gemsbok), spotted hyena, springbok, steenbok, wildebeest.

Access

From Otjiwarongo take the C38 northwest via Outjo to **Okaukuejo Camp**, at the southern edge of the park. There is a floodlit waterhole here and the camp grounds support Southern Pied-Babbler. East of here is **Halali Camp**, where Violet Woodhoopoe and Bare-cheeked Babbler occur and, further east, **Namutoni Camp**, another excellent birding area. Naturally, all other tracks are worth exploring if time allows.

ETOSHA NP

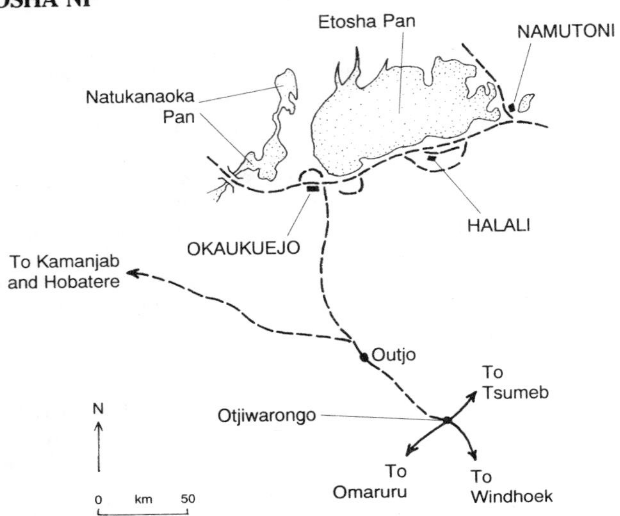

Accommodation: Okaukuejo, Halali, and Namutoni Camps, all of which have bungalows (B), campsites (C), restaurants, petrol, and swimming pools, and are situated near lodges (A). A fourth camp, Otjovasandu, in the western extremity of the park, has been at the planning stage for 15 years. To book in advance contact the Directorate of Tourism.

Hartlaub's Francolin, Bronze-winged Courser, Freckled Nightjar, Violet Woodhoopoe, Bare-cheeked Babbler, and Chestnut Weaver, as well as aarvark and aardwolf, have been recorded in and around **Hobatere Lodge**, between Etosha and Ruacana.

The gallery forest, mopane woodland and savanna near the Kunene river, close to the town of **Ruacana** on the Angola border in northwest Namibia, support a handful of very localised species, including Gabon Boubou, Rufous-tailed Palm-Thrush, Dusky Lark and Cinderella Waxbill*. The best birding area is below the waterfall.

CAPRIVI STRIP

This narrow strip of land in extreme northeast Namibia supports many species not found elsewhere in the country. Here it is possible to see all of the Okavango specialities, such as Slaty Egret*, without the expense of visiting the central Okavango in Botswana (p. 48), as well as Wattled Crane*, Lesser Jacana and Racket-tailed Roller.

Specialities

Slaty Egret*, Wattled Crane*, Lesser Jacana, Coppery-tailed Coucal, Racket-tailed Roller, Bradfield's Hornbill, Green-backed Honeyguide, Gabon Boubou, Sharp-tailed Glossy-Starling, Pearl-breasted Swallow, Chirping Cisticola, Angola Babbler, Dusky Lark, Brown Firefinch.

Others

Ostrich, African Darter, White-backed Duck, African Pygmy-goose, Black and Rufous-bellied Herons, White-backed Night-Heron, Dwarf Bittern (Oct–Mar), Hamerkop, Saddle-billed Stork, Banded Snake-Eagle, Black Goshawk, Swainson's Spurfowl, Black Crake, African Finfoot, Greater Painted-snipe, Spotted Thick-knee, Rock Pratincole (Nov–May), Long-toed and White-headed Lapwings, African Skimmer (Jul–Dec), Double-banded and Burchell's Sandgrouse, Livingstone's Turaco, Pel's Fishing-Owl, African Barred Owlet, Marsh Owl, Pennant-winged Nightjar (Oct–Mar), Giant Kingfisher, Little, Swallow-tailed and Southern Carmine Bee-eaters, Yellow-fronted Tinkerbird, Bennett's Woodpecker, White-breasted Cuckoo-shrike, Souza's Shrike, Retz's Helmetshrike, Red-billed Oxpecker, Pale Flycatcher, Red-capped Robin-Chat, White-headed Black-Chat, Banded Martin, Grey-rumped and Mosque Swallows, Piping Cisticola, African Bush-Warbler, Greater Swamp-Warbler, Greencap Eremomela, Cape Crombec, African Penduline-Tit, Jameson's Firefinch, African Quailfinch, White-breasted and Mariqua Sunbirds.

Other Wildlife

Elephant, hippo, lechwe, Nile crocodile, sable, tsessebe, waterbuck.

Access

Rundu, which is not actually in the Caprivi Strip but supports a similar avifauna, is 450 km east of Etosha NP. Slaty Egret*, Rufous-bellied Heron, Dwarf Bittern, White-backed Duck, African Skimmer, Coppery-tailed Coucal, Marsh Owl, Bradfield's Hornbill, Green-backed Honeyguide, Gabon Boubou, Angola Babbler and Brown Firefinch all occur here, along the shores of the Okavango river and around the fish-ponds between Rundu and Kaisosi, 5 km to the east.

CAPRIVI STRIP (WEST)

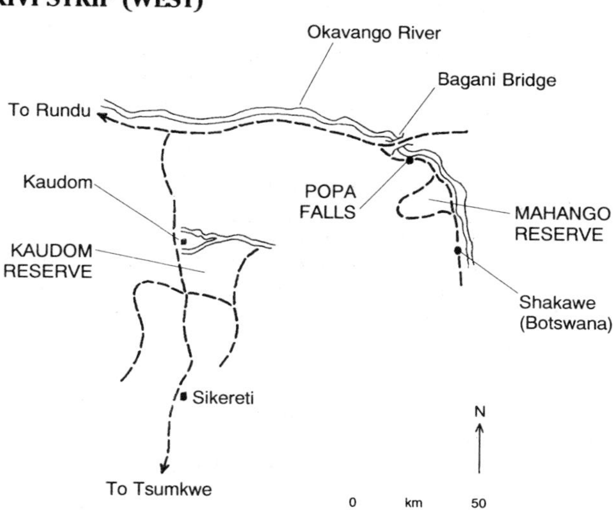

Popa Falls, 210 km east of Rundu, lies near lush gallery forest, papyrus swamps, and rapids where Rock Pratincole (Nov–May), Gabon Boubou, and Brown Firefinch occur. Bird the riverside and trails through forest. At Skimmer Camp, 10 km southeast of Popa Falls, it is possible to hire a boat to look for African Skimmer and Pel's Fishing-Owl.

The entrance to the 250-sq-km **Mahango Reserve** which lies on the Okavango floodplain, is just 15 km south of Popa Falls, along the track to Shakawe in Botswana (see below). In the wetland and woodland here it is possible to see nearly 200 species in a day, including African Pygmy-goose, Slaty Egret*, Rufous-bellied Heron, Saddle-billed Stork, Banded Snake-Eagle, Wattled Crane*, Rock Pratincole (Nov–May), African Skimmer (Jul–Dec), Burchell's Sandgrouse, Coppery-tailed Coucal, Pel's Fishing-Owl, Giant Kingfisher, Little Bee-eater, Racket-tailed Roller, Bradfield's Hornbill, Gabon Boubou, Red-billed Oxpecker, Chirping Cisticola, Angola Babbler and Brown Firefinch. Bird the riverside track (4WD recommended Dec–Mar), especially around the two picnic sites, and side tracks.

Beyond the entrance to Mahango the track south from Popa Falls continues to **Shakawe**. Because Shakawe lies in Botswana, it is necessary to 'check in' with the police. South of this village is Shakawe Fishing Camp and Drotsky's Camp, both of which lie in yet more excellent birding country (Pel's Fishing-Owl etc.).

Much further east along the Caprivi Strip, African Pygmy-goose, Coppery-tailed Coucal, Southern Carmine Bee-eater, Banded Martin and Brown Firefinch occur around **Lianshulu Lodge**. This private lodge lies on the Kwando river, 40 km south of the main road through the Caprivi Strip, approximately 150 km west of Katima Mulilo. The small town of **Katima Mulilo** lies on the banks of the Zambezi river in extreme northeast Namibia. Here the river supports White-headed Lapwing, whilst Livingstone's Turaco occurs in the riparian forest and Lesser Jacana occurs at the sewage farm, just west of town. Twelve km east of town is Maningi Manzi, a good site for African Finfoot and Pel's Fishing-Owl.

Accommodation: Rundu: Kaisosi Safari Lodge (A), 5 km east of Rundu. Popa Falls: Bungalows (C); Ndhovu Lodge (A). Katima Mulilo: Zambezi River Lodge/campsite.

WATERBERG PLATEAU NATIONAL PARK

Topped with deciduous woodland and surrounded by semi-arid acacia savanna, this 405-sq-km park, 100 km southeast of Otjiwarongo in north-central Namibia, supports a number of southern African specialities including Damara Rock-jumper.

Specialities

Hartlaub's Francolin, Rueppell's Parrot, Rosy-faced Lovebird, Bradfield's Swift, Monteiro's and Bradfield's Hornbills, White-tailed Shrike, Short-toed Rock-Thrush, Black-chested Prinia, Damara Rock-jumper, Southern Pied-Babbler.

Others

Coqui Francolin, Swainson's Spurfowl, Grey Go-away-bird, Swallow-tailed Bee-eater, Pied Barbet, White-crowned Shrike, White Helmetshrike, Pririt Batis, Pale-winged Starling, Burchell's Glossy-Starling, Kalahari Scrub-Robin, Southern Anteater-Chat, Black-cheeked Waxbill, White-breasted Sunbird, Cape Bunting . (Cape Griffon* is a rarity here.)

Other Wildlife

Leopard, roan.

Access

Turn east 22 km south of Otjiwarongo off the B1 on to the C22 Okakarara road, then turn north after 41 km on to the 26 km road to the park entrance.

Accommodation: Bernabé de la Bat Camp (bungalows (B)/camping (C)).

HARDAP DAM

This 25-sq-km dam situated on the upper Fish river, 245 km south of Windhoek, is surrounded by savanna, scrub and riparian thickets, which support the localised Kopje Warbler, Sclater's Lark* and Social Weaver.

Specialities

Ludwig's Bustard, Rosy-faced Lovebird, Kopje Warbler, Sclater's Lark*, Social Weaver.

Others

Ostrich, African Darter, African Pygmy-goose, South African Shelduck, African Black Duck, Goliath and Rufous-bellied Herons, Dwarf Bittern, Hamerkop, African Fish-Eagle, Pale Chanting-Goshawk, Pygmy Falcon, Spotted Thick-knee, Three-banded, Chestnut-banded and Blacksmith Plovers, White-backed and Red-faced Mousebirds, Swallow-tailed Bee-eater, Cape Robin-Chat, Karoo Scrub-Robin, Rufous-eared and Fairy Warblers, Ashy Tit, Sabota and Spike-heeled Larks, Rufous Sparrow, Mossie, Red-headed Finch, Shaft-tailed Whydah, Scaly Weaver, Lark-like and Cape Buntings.

Other Wildlife

Greater kudu, hartebeest, oryx (gemsbok), springbok.

Access

The dam is 23 km northwest of Mariental. Turn west off the B1, approximately 20 km north of Mariental (the irrigated fields next to the B1 in this area are worth exploring). A track runs along the east shore and across the dam to a network of further tracks. There are two hiking trails (9 km and 15 km).

Accommodation: Bungalows (A)/camping (C). Mariental: Guglhuft Restaurant.

AI-AIS AND FISH RIVER CANYON

Ranked by some alongside Mount Kilimanjaro and Victoria Falls as one of Africa's most amazing natural wonders, the magnificent Fish River Canyon is 161 km long, up to 27 km wide and 550 m (1805 ft) deep. In world terms, it is second only in size to the Grand Canyon in North America. Although not noted for its birds, it is a good site for the localised Yellow-rumped Eremomela.

Much of this site is accessible only from March to October.

Specialities

Karoo Bustard, Rosy-faced Lovebird, Karoo Chat, Yellow-rumped Eremomela, Karoo Lark.

Others

Ostrich, South African Shelduck, African Fish-Eagle, Three-banded Plover, White-backed Mousebird, Bokmakierie, Karoo Scrub-Robin, Cape Robin-Chat, Pale White-eye, Rufous-eared Warbler, Lark-like Bunting.

Access

Ai-Ais, a hot-springs resort complex at the southern end of the canyon, is 82 km west of the Keetmanshoop–Noordoewer road in south Namibia. It is open only from mid March to October and a special permit is needed to undertake the four-day, 86-km trek along the canyon. Fortunately, Yellow-rumped Eremomela occurs around Ai-Ais.

Accommodation: Ai-Ais (B); campsite (near viewpoint at north end).

ADDITIONAL INFORMATION

Books and Papers

Illustrated Guide to the Birds of Southern Africa. Sinclair, I *et al.* 1993. New Holland.
Popular Checklist of the Birds of Namibia. Williams, A. 1988. Department of Agriculture and Nature Conservation.
Mammals of Southern Africa. Cillie, B. 1989. Frandsen.
Where to watch Birds in Southern Africa. Berruti, A and Sinclair, JC. 1983. Struik.

Addresses

The Namibia Bird Club, Box 67, Windhoek 9000, produces an occasional journal, *Laniturdus*, edited by Joris Komen, Department of Birds, The State Museum of Namibia, Box 1203, Windhoek.

Please send records to The Ornithologist, Ministry of Wildlife, Conservation and Tourism, Private Bag 13306, Windhoek 9000.

SWA-Namibia Information Service, PO Box 2160, Windhoek (for accommodation guides and maps).

The Directorate of Tourism and Nature Conservation, Private Bag 13267, Windhoek 9000 (tel: 061 36975-8).

ENDEMICS (1)

Dune Lark	West/central: Rooibank, Namib Naukluft NP, near Swakopmund

Near-endemics (Central)
Grey Tit, Gray's Lark.

Near-endemics (Extreme northwest)
Rufous-tailed Palm-Thrush, Cinderella Waxbill*.

Near-endemics (Northeast)
Slaty Egret*, Black-cheeked Lovebird, Bradfield's Hornbill, Coppery-tailed Coucal, Black-lored and Angola Babblers, Brown Firefinch.

Near-endemics (North)
Hartlaub's Francolin, Blue Crane*, Ruepell's Parrot, Monteiro's Hornbill, White-tailed Shrike, Herero Chat*, Damara Rock-jumper, Fairy Warbler, Southern Pied-Babbler, Bare-cheeked Babbler.

Near-endemics (Coastal and throughout)
Jackass Penguin*, Crowned*, Bank* and Cape Cormorants, South African Shelduck, Jackal Buzzard, Ludwig's and Ruppell's Bustards, African Oystercatcher*, Hartlaub's Gull, Rosy-faced Lovebird, White-backed Mousebird, Bradfield's Swift, Short-toed Rock-Thrush, Pale-winged Starling, Chat Flycatcher, Mountain Wheatear, Karoo and Tractrac Chats, Red-headed Cisticola, Layard's Warbler, Clapper, Bradfield's, Long-billed, Pink-billed and Stark's Larks, Social Weaver, Dusky Sunbird, White-throated Canary.

Near-endemics (South)
Black Harrier*, Cape Francolin, Karoo Bustard, Karoo Scrub-Robin, Sicklewing Chat, Karoo and White-breasted Prinias, Rufous-eared and Kopje Warblers, Yellow-rumped Eremomela, Karoo and Sclater's* Larks, Black-eared Sparrow-Lark, Southern Double-collared Sunbird, Damara Canary.

NIGER

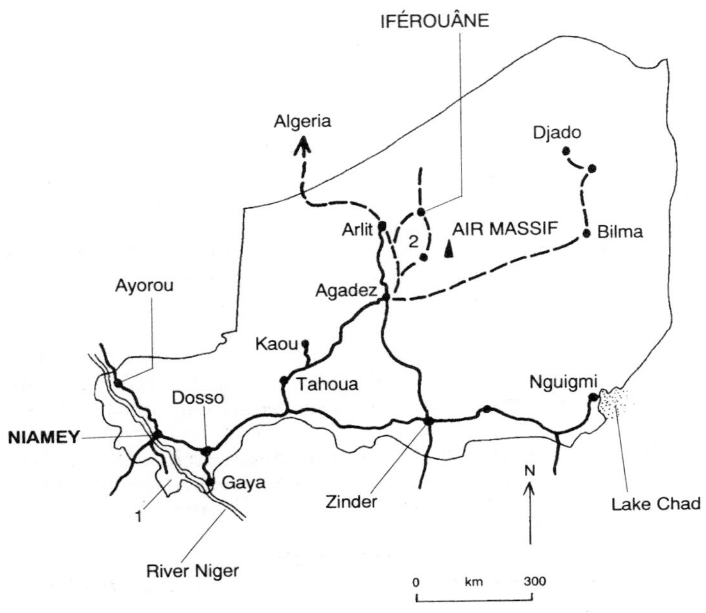

1 W NP
2 Air et Tenere NP

INTRODUCTION

Summary

Despite possessing a relatively good infrastruture for a West African country, and two wild and superb national parks, one alongside the River Niger in the southwest and the other in the southern Sahara, few birders have ventured to Niger. This is probably because most of the best species can be seen more easily elsewhere, but adventurous birders in search of little-known species such as River Prinia* may be tempted to make the trip in the future.

Size

Niger is a big country: at 1,267,080 sq km it is nearly ten times larger than England and twice the size of Texas.

Getting Around

The roads are excellent by African standards, even to Agadez in the Sahara and Lake Chad, and there is a good, relatively cheap bus service. It is also possible to travel along the Niger river between Ayorou and Gaya, but the internal air network is limited and expensive.

Accommodation and Food

Accommodation in Niger is quite expensive, but there are some cheap campsites. The local food is dominated by beans and rice, served with fish near the Niger river.

Health and Safety

Immunisation against hepatitis, meningitis, polio, typhoid and yellow fever is recommended, as are precautions against malaria.

Climate and Timing

Although hot most of the year, it is cooler, and better for birding, between January and April. The Niger river usually floods during February, creating extensive wetlands, but by July it is usually very dry, with extensive sand bars in the river channel. The limited rainy season in the south lasts from July to September. In November the Harmattan wind blows Saharan sand south, making conditions around Agadez and to the north very inhospitable.

Habitats

Niger, for the most part, is a country of sandy and rocky desert, rising to 2000 m (6562 ft) at the Air Massif in the centre of the country, although the Sahel and a narrow band of savanna crosses the south, the River Niger and its associated wetlands dominate the far southwest, and part of Lake Chad crosses the border in the extreme southeast.

Conservation

Niger's 'protected' areas include the spectacular W and Air et Tenere National Parks.

Two threatened and three near-threatened species occur in Niger.

Bird Families

Seven of the ten families endemic to the African mainland are represented in Niger.

Bird Species

A total of 482 species have been recorded in Niger, 90 fewer than in its similar neighbour, Mali. Non-endemic specialities and spectacular species include Black Crowned-Crane, Nubian* and Arabian Bustards, Lesser Jacana, Egyptian Plover, Grey Pratincole, River Prinia*, Kordofan Lark and Sudan Golden-Sparrow.

Endemics

There are no endemics, but some arid-savanna specialities such as Cricket Longtail are present.

W NATIONAL PARK

This park in extreme southwest Niger (2200 sq km) also includes parts of Benin and Burkino Faso. It was established as long ago as 1936 to protect savanna and riverside wetlands, where over 280 species have been recorded, including Arabian Bustard, Lesser Jacana, Egyptian Plover and Grey Pratincole.

The park is closed from June to September, sometimes through to December.

Specialities

Arabian Bustard (Dec–Apr), Lesser Jacana, Egyptian Plover, Grey Pratincole (Mar–May), Sudan Golden-Sparrow (Nov–Apr).

Others

African Darter, African Pygmy-goose (Jul–Aug), Black-headed and Goliath Herons, Hamerkop, African Openbill, Woolly-necked and Saddle-billed Storks, Scissor-tailed Kite (Feb–Apr), White-headed Vulture, Brown and Banded Snake-Eagles, Bateleur, Gabar Goshawk, Grasshopper Buzzard, Martial Eagle, Grey Kestrel, Stone Partridge, Quail-plover, Black Crake, Allen's Gallinule (Mar–Jul), Lesser Moorhen (Mar–Jul), Black Crowned-Crane, Stanley (Nov–Apr) and Black-bellied Bustards, Greater Painted-snipe, Senegal and Spotted Thick-knees, Bronze-winged Courser (Nov–Apr), Rock Pratincole (May–Jul), Black-headed and White-headed Lapwings, African Skimmer (Apr–Aug), Chestnut-bellied (Nov–May) and Four-banded Sandgrouse, Vinaceous Dove, Bruce's Green-Pigeon, Senegal Parrot, Violet Turaco, Western Grey Plantain-eater, Levaillant's and African Cuckoos, Senegal Coucal, White-faced Scops-Owl, Verreaux's Eagle-Owl, Pel's Fishing-Owl, Plain (Apr–Jul), Long-tailed and Standard-winged Nightjars, African Pygmy-Kingfisher, Blue-breasted Kingfisher, Red-throated, Little, Green and Northern Carmine Bee-eaters, Abyssinian Roller, Black Scimitar-bill, Abyssinian Ground-Hornbill, Yellow-fronted Tinkerbird, Bearded Barbet, Fine-spotted Woodpecker, Piapiac, Red-shouldered Cuckoo-shrike, Yellow-billed Shrike, Common Gonolek, White Helmetshrike, Senegal Batis, Purple and Long-tailed Glossy-Starlings, Yellow-billed Oxpecker, Snowy-crowned and White-crowned Robin-Chats, Black Scrub-Robin (Jan–Apr), Northern Anteater-Chat, Pied-winged Swallow (Dec–Mar), Singing Cisticola (Nov–Mar), Oriole Warbler (Dec–Mar), Senegal Eremomela, Chestnut-backed Sparrow-Lark (Oct–Mar), Lavender and Black-rumped Waxbills, Variable Indigobird, Little, Village and Black-headed (Jul–Aug) Weavers, Pygmy and Beautiful Sunbirds, White-rumped Seedeater, Yellow-fronted Canary, Cinnamon-breasted Bunting.

Other Wildlife

Baboon, buffalo, elephant, hippo.

Access

Many species associated with water are present only from October to May. Species restricted to the Niger river area, along the eastern boundary, include Grey Pratincole (Mar–May) and African Skimmer (Apr–Aug). The narrow Mekrou river, which runs through the middle of the park, supports Pel's Fishing-Owl and several Northern Carmine Bee-eater colonies (Jan–Feb). The even narrower Tapoa river, which forms the northern boundary, is also excellent for birds, especially during the dry season (Jan–Feb). Many tracks criss-cross the park and are worth exploring.

Accommodation: Hotel de la Tapoa (A).

Some of the species listed above including Arabian Bustard, Egyptian Plover, Grey Pratincole and African Skimmer, as well as African Finfoot (Sirba river) and the little-known River Prinia*, occur along the length of the Niger River, and may be seen from the roads, or by boat, between Ayorou and Gaya.

Black Crowned-Crane, Little Grey Woodpecker and Sennar Penduline-Tit occur around **Kaou**, some 30 km north of the Tahoua–Agadez road in central Niger, and Kordofan Lark occurs alongside the Tahoua–Agadez road. **Agadez** in north Niger is the gateway to Air et Tenere NP (see below).

AIR ET TENERE NATIONAL PARK

Situated at the southern edge of the Sahara in central Niger, this national park is a true wilderness of rocky mountains, sand and gravel plains and semi-desert, with some vegetated wadis and small, irrigated farms, where the species include Nubian Bustard*, Heuglin's Wheatear and Cricket Longtail.

Specialities

Nubian Bustard*, Sudan Golden-Sparrow.

Others

Ostrich, Cream-coloured Courser, Spotted, Crowned and Lichtenstein's Sandgrouse, Pied Cuckoo, Abyssinian Roller, White-throated Bee-eater, Vieillot's and Yellow-breasted Barbets, Little Grey Woodpecker, Fan-tailed Raven, Black Scrub-Robin, White-tailed and Heuglin's Wheatears, Blackstart, Rock Martin, Desert Cisticola, Cricket Longtail, Yellow-bellied Eremomela, Fulvous Chatterer, Bar-tailed and Desert Larks, Greater Hoopoe-Lark, Desert Sparrow, African Silverbill, Village Indigobird, Vitelline Masked-Weaver, Trumpeter Finch, House Bunting.

Other Wildlife

Addax, dorca gazelle, patas monkey.

Access

All the tracks in this region are obscure and it is easy to get lost, so officially all birders must travel beyond the Agadez–Arlit road with a guide. These can be hired (A) at the tourist office opposite the Post Office in Agadez. Bird the Agadez–Arlit–Iférouâne triangle. The park HQ is at Iferouane.

ADDITIONAL INFORMATION

Books and Papers

Air Faune du Niger: Etat des connaissances en 1986. Giraudoux, P *et al.* *Malimbus* 10:1–143.

Addresses

West African Ornithological Society (WAOS); see p. 413.

NIGERIA

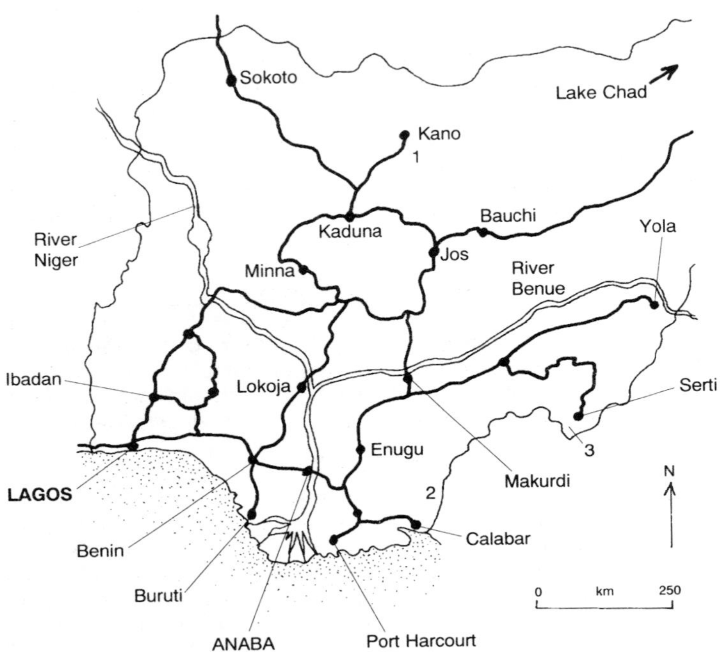

1 Falgore Reserve
2 Cross River (NP)
3 Gashaka–Gumti Reserve

Summary

Although Nigeria has one of the most diverse avifaunas in Africa, and plenty of mammals, including gorillas, no one in their right mind would recommend birders to take a trip to this country, until violence and corruption are stamped out, and the infrastructure is greatly improved. If the authorities would recognise the fact that their country is full of natural wonders, and make it possible for ecotourists to see them, then Nigeria would undoubtedly be a very popular destination.

Size

At 923,768 sq km, Nigeria is seven times larger than England, and 1.3 times the size of Texas.

Getting Around

Travelling around Nigeria by road is dangerous. In the south there are numerous roadblocks, including many illegal ones, especially near towns. However, there is an extensive, cheap, internal air network which could form the basis for transporting potential visitors to the best sites.

Accommodation and Food

There are many excellent hotels in Nigeria, but few of them are near the best birding sites. The extensive missions are more basic, but cheaper. The Nigerians, especially in the south, like beer and spicy hot food.

Health and Safety

Immunisation against hepatitis, meningitis, polio, typhoid and yellow fever is recommended, as are precautions against malaria.

To anyone who has never experienced an overcrowded and overexcited third world city, Lagos, and some of Nigeria's other cities, will seem like hell on earth. Gangs, guns and corruption are present, but such things can be avoided using common sense. Driving alone in the south is definitely not recommended.

Climate and Timing

The short, sparse northern rainy season lasts from July to August. The long southern rainy season lasts from March to October, and during this time it absolutely pours down, especially in May and June. There is little doubt about the best time to visit Nigeria: November to February, especially December, although it is very humid in the south throughout the year.

Habitats

Inland from the mangrove-lined southern coast lies a little remnant lowland rainforest, Guinea and Sudan savannas and the Sahel, with Lake Chad in the extreme northeast. The broad savanna belt is crossed by two huge rivers: the Niger and the Benue. Rugged and remote forested mountains dominate the southeast corner of the country, next to Cameroon.

Conservation

Only 10% of Nigeria's original rainforest remains and the sickening destruction of this rich habitat continues apace. One fifth of all Africans live in Nigeria, and the population growth rate is one of the highest in the world, so the chance of any rainforest being left by the end of the century is slim. The Nigerian Conservation Foundation are making a valiant effort to halt the destruction, but they face an awesome task.

Eight threatened and eleven near-threatened species occur in Nigeria.

Bird Families

Eight of the ten families endemic to the African mainland are represented, and well represented families include kingfishers, bee-eaters, rollers, hornbills, bushshrikes, bulbuls, babblers, weavers and waxbills.

Bird Species

A total of 862 species have been recorded in Nigeria. Non-endemic specialities and spectacular species include Long-tailed Hawk, Egyptian and Forbes' Plovers, Brown-chested Lapwing, Black-headed and Rosy Bee-eaters, Green-breasted Bushshrike*, Red-winged Grey Warbler and Red-faced Pytilia.

Endemics

Surprisingly for such a large country there are only two endemic species in Nigeria: Anambra Waxbill* and Ibadan Malimbe*. However, there are a few near-endemics, including Yellow-breasted Boubou,

Green-breasted Bushshrike*,Grey-necked Rockfowl* and Bannerman's Weaver*, most of which also occur in Cameroon.

Yellow-throated Cuckoo, Great Blue Turaco, Bates' Swift, White-bellied Kingfisher, Blue-throated Roller, Willcock's Honeyguide, Green-backed Woodpecker, Purple-throated Cuckoo-shrike, White-browed Forest-Flycatcher, Forest Robin, Grey-winged Robin-Chat, Puvel's Illadopsis, Capuchin Babbler and Buff-throated Sunbird have been recorded at **Nindam FR**, a few km south of Kagoro in central Nigeria. The Kaduna–Jos road runs through the eastern end of the reserve. A few km south of Nindam FR lies the **Sangi River Reserve**, where Brown-chested Lapwing (Dec–May) has bred in the past.

FALGORE RESERVE

Situated in north/central Nigeria, south of Kano at the southern end of Tiga Lake, this big reserve (920 sq km) supports a typical Guinea savanna avifauna, and the species list is similar to that of Gambian sites.

Specialities

Pale-winged Indigobird.

Others

Hamerkop, Wahlberg's and Martial Eagles, White-throated Francolin, Stone Partridge, Bruce's Green-Pigeon, Violet Turaco, Western Grey Plantain-eater, Red-throated and Northern Carmine Bee-eaters, Abyssinian and Blue-bellied Rollers, Black Scimitar-bill, Vieillot's and Bearded Barbets, Brown-backed Woodpecker, Piapiac, White Helmetshrike, White-fronted Black-Chat, Pied-winged Swallow, Fanti Sawwing, Croaking Cisticola, Yellow-bellied Hyliota, Red-headed Weaver.

Access

Access is very difficult, although it is possible to walk the banks of the Kano river, at least in the dry season (Dec–Mar).

Over 275 species have been recorded in the **Hadejia–Nguru** wetlands, northeast of Kano, an important site for wintering Palearctic waterfowl, and the subject of a conservation project backed by the RSPB.

Fox Kestrel, White-throated Francolin, Forbes' Plover, Black Scimitar-bill, Abyssinian Roller and White-crowned Cliff-Chat have been recorded in **Yankari Reserve**, 100 km east of Bauchi.

Accommodation: Lodge/campsite.

Long-tailed Hawk, Forest Francolin, Yellow-throated Cuckoo, Blue-headed Bee-eater and African Forest-Flycatcher occur at **Okomu FR**, near Benin city, in southwest Nigeria. To the east, alongside the Niger River, the endemic Anambra Waxbill* has recently (1987) been recorded, 0.5 km north of the bridge on the west side of the river at **Anaba**, opposite Onitsha.

CROSS RIVER (NATIONAL PARK)

This proposed park in southeast Nigeria consists of the Okwango (920 sq km) and Oban Hills (2800 sq km) FRs. These reserves abut Korup NP in Cameroon (p. 69), so the avifauna is virtually the same, and includes Blue-headed Bee-eater and Grey-necked Rockfowl*.

Specialities

Blue-headed Bee-eater, Forest Swallow, Green-tailed Bristlebill*, Grey-necked Rockfowl*, Fernando Po Oliveback, Rachel's Malimbe.

Others

White-crested Bittern, Olive Ibis, Long-tailed Hawk, Dusky Long-tailed Cuckoo, Dwarf Kingfisher, Dusky Crested-Flycatcher, Pink-footed Puffback, Chestnut and White-spotted Wattle-eyes, Crossley's Ground-Thrush*, Narrow-tailed Starling, Ussher's and Olivaceous Flycatchers, Mountain Wagtail, Oriole Finch.

Other Wildlife

Drill, gorilla.

Access

The nearest large town, Calabar, is accessible by air from Lagos. Dwarf Kingfisher, Blue-headed Bee-eater and Forest Swallow occur at **Oban Hills FR**, north of Calabar. White-crested Bittern, Long-tailed Hawk and Blue-headed Bee-eater, as well as drill and gorilla, occur in **Okwango FR**, which is east of Obudu. Crossley's Ground-Thrush* and Fernando Po Oliveback have been recorded at **Obudu Cattle Ranch**, next to Okwango FR, where it is possible to stay in chalets, bookable in advance by writing to PO Box 40, Obudu, Cross River State. The rare Grey-necked Rockfowl* seems to be surviving in southeast Nigeria, where in 1987, 94 breeding sites supporting 500–1,000 birds were found.

Green-breasted Bushshrike*, Cameroon Mountain* and Grey-headed* Greenbuls, White-throated Mountain-Babbler*, and Bannerman's Weaver* have been recorded on the **Obudu Plateau**, north of Cross river.

GASHAKA–GUMTI RESERVE

Over 330 species have been recorded in the savanna and montane forest of this huge reserve (7000 sq km), near Serti, in southeast Nigeria. These species, most of which can be seen with considerably more ease in neighbouring Cameroon, include Mountain Robin-Chat, Red-winged Grey Warbler, Red-faced Pytilia and Bannerman's Weaver*.

Specialities

Grey Pratincole, Western Green-Tinkerbird, Yellow-breasted and Mountain Boubous, Mountain and Grey-winged Robin-Chats, Cameroon Mountain Greenbul*, Red-winged Grey Warbler, Red-faced Pytilia, Bannerman's Weaver*, Cameroon Sunbird.

Others

Fox Kestrel, White-throated and Scaly Francolins, White-headed Lapwing, Guinea, Yellow-billed, White-crested and Violet Turacos, Freckled Nightjar, Bar-tailed Trogon, Shining Blue Kingfisher, Blue-breasted Bee-eater, Abyssinian Roller, Elliot's Woodpecker, White-bellied Crested-Flycatcher, Many-coloured Bushshrike, Sooty Chat, White-crowned Cliff-Chat, Spotted Creeper, Mountain and Yellow-throated Greenbuls, Cameroon Olive-Greenbul, Green Longtail, Black-collared and Grey Apalises, Black-capped Woodland-Warbler, Abyssinian Hill-Babbler, Grey-chested Illadopsis, Grey-headed Oliveback, Red-faced Crimson-wing, Brown and Dybowski's Twinspots, Black-crowned Waxbill, Magpie Mannikin, Black-billed and Brown-capped Weavers, Orange-tufted and Northern Double-collared Sunbirds, Thick-billed Seedeater, Oriole Finch.

Other Wildlife

Chimpanzee, crested mona, giant forest hog.

Access

This reserve lies southeast of Serti.

A SELECTED LIST OF SPECIES RECORDED IN NIGERIA

Hartlaub's Duck, Striped Crake, Demoiselle Crane (Dikwa, Lake Chad), Arabian Bustard, Bronze-winged Courser (Zaria), Egyptian Plover, Damara Tern* (Lagos), Grey Parrot, Black, Black-headed and Rosy Bee-eaters, Yellow-breasted Barbet (Lake Chad), African Pitta (Ibadan and Benin), Blue Cuckoo-shrike (Benin), Emin's Shrike (Lake Chad and Benin), Sun Lark (Zaria).

ADDITIONAL INFORMATION

Books and Papers

The Birds of Nigeria (BOU Checklist No 4). Second Edition. Elgood, J. 1994. BOU

Additions to the Avifauna of Nigeria. Ash, J. 1990. *Malimbus* 11:104–115.

The Avifauna of the southern sector of the Gashaka–Gumti Game Reserve. Green, A. 1990. *Malimbus* 12:31–51.

Birds in Falgore Game Reserve. Wilkinson, R and Beecroft, R. 1985. *Malimbus* 7:63–71.

Addresses

Nigerian Conservation Foundation, Box 74638, Victoria Island, Lagos.

Please send unusual records to John Elgood, 16 The Anchorage, 157 Mudeford, Christchurch, Dorset BH23 4AG, UK.

ENDEMICS (2)

Anambra Waxbill*	South: Anaba

Ibadan Malimbe*	Southwest: in the area circumscribed by Ibadan, Ife, Iperu and Ilaro

Near-endemics

Cameroon Pigeon, Bates' Swift, Brown-cheeked Hornbill*, Yellow-breasted Boubou, Green-breasted Bushshrike*, Chestnut-bellied Helmetshrike, Finsch's Flycatcher-Thrush, Mountain Robin-Chat, Mountain Sawwing*, Cameroon Mountain Greenbul*, Cameroon Olive-Greenbul, Grey-headed Greenbul*, Green Longtail, Black-capped Woodland-Warbler, White-throated Mountain-Babbler*, Grey-necked Rockfowl*, Bannerman's Weaver*, Rachel's Malimbe, Cameroon Sunbird.

RWANDA

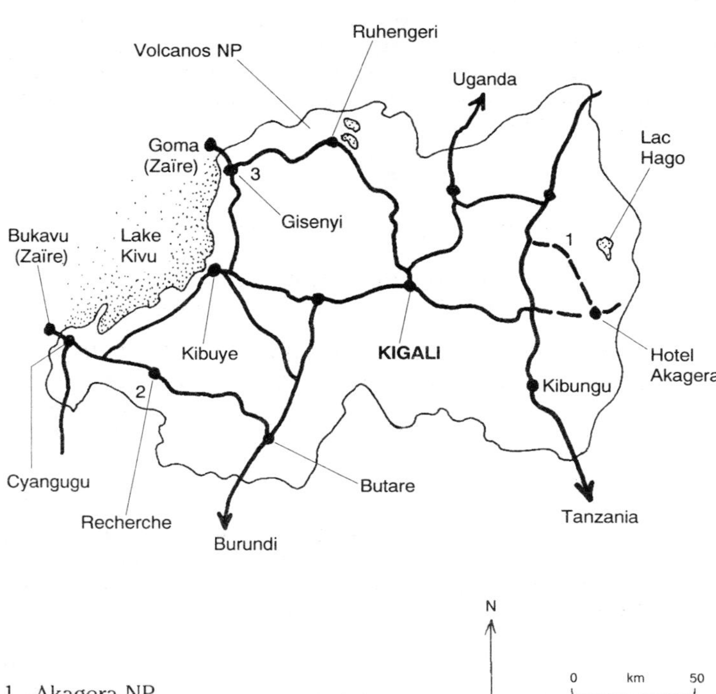

1 Akagera NP
2 Nyungwe FR
3 Gishwati Forest

Summary

Before the horrendous tribal war broke out in 1994, Rwanda was a very popular destination for people in search of birds and gorillas. However, since then it has not been advisable to consider visiting Rwanda, even though the avifauna includes Shoebill* and 25 of the 43 Albertine Rift endemics.

Size

This tiny country (26,338 sq km) is one fifth the size of England, and only a fraction the size of Texas.

Getting Around

The roads were pretty good before the war, and plenty of modern minibuses used them to reach most communities. There also used to be a fairly extensive internal air network.

Accommodation and Food

Rwanda's accommodation and food used to be expensive by African standards. However, budget birders got by on 'campsites and omelettes'.

Health and Safety

Immunisation against hepatitis, polio, typhoid and yellow fever is recommended, as are precautions against malaria and bilharzia. Drinking tap water is not recommended.

Before the war, Rwanda was a perfectly safe place to visit.

Climate and Timing

February and August are the peak times to visit Rwanda, August if the proposed trip also includes Zaïre, although low cloud and mist are a year-round problem at the montane sites. There are two dry seasons: mid May to mid September, and mid December to mid May.

Habitats

Rwanda has been described as a land of misty mountains (rising to over 4000 m (13,123 ft)), big forests and wild swamps. In reality, every inch of land, outside the national parks and forest reserves, used to be under cultivation. Most hillsides are terraced and even roadside verges were used to grow crops, mainly tea.

Conservation

It is distressing to think what might have happened to the national parks and forest reserves during the war. They used to 'protect' what was left of the natural habitat, but it now seems likely that they will have suffered from the conflict, a situation likely to be exacerbated by returning refugees.

Bird Families

Six of the ten families endemic to the African mainland are represented in Rwanda, including Shoebill*. Well represented families include francolins, woodpeckers and sunbirds.

Bird Species

A total of 666 species have been recorded in Rwanda, an amazing total for such a small, land-locked country. Non-endemic specialities and spectacular species include Rufous-bellied Heron, Shoebill* and Brown-chested Lapwing.

Endemics

There are no endemic species in Rwanda, but 25 of the 43 Albertine Rift endemics have been recorded, including Handsome Francolin, Albertine Owlet*, Collared Apalis, Grauer's and Neumann's Warblers, and Red-collared Mountain-Babbler*, as well as other near-endemics such as Red-faced Barbet* and Papyrus Gonolek*.

Expectations

It is possible to see 250 species in a week, and up to 300 in two weeks in Rwanda.

AKAGERA NATIONAL PARK

This park was overrun by rebel forces in 1991 and has since been settled by displaced people. The government also look likely to recommend the park as an area for returning refugees to set up home. However, it used to cover an amazing 10% of Rwanda (2500 sq km), boasting one of the biggest site lists in Africa. Over 500 species have been recorded in the acacia savanna, gallery forest, lakes and huge papyrus swamps including Shoebill* and other localised birds such as Brown-chested Lapwing, Red-faced Barbet* and Papyrus Gonolek*.

Specialities

Shoebill*, Ring-necked and Shelley's Francolins, Red-chested Flufftail, Brown-chested Lapwing (Jul–Dec), Red-faced Barbet*, Papyrus Gonolek*, Carruthers' and Tabora Cisticolas, White-winged Scrub-Warbler, Fan-tailed Grassbird, Short-tailed Pipit, Red-chested Sunbird.

Others

African Darter, African Pygmy-goose, Madagascar Pond-Heron*, Rufous-bellied Heron, Hamerkop, Saddle-billed Stork, White-headed Vulture, Brown Snake Eagle, Gabar Goshawk, Little Sparrowhawk, Wahlberg's and Martial Eagles, Red-winged and Hildebrandt's Francolins, White-spotted Flufftail, Black Crake, African Finfoot, Grey Crowned-Crane, Stanley and Black-bellied Bustards, Bronze-winged and Temminck's Coursers, Three-banded and Caspian Plovers, Long-toed and Senegal Lapwings, Meyer's Parrot, Purple-crested and Ross's Turacos, Bare-faced Go-away-bird, African Scops-Owl, Verreaux's Eagle-Owl, Freckled and Pennant-winged Nightjars, Narina Trogon, Little Bee-eater, Lilac-breasted Roller, Common Scimitar-bill, Yellow-fronted Tinkerbird, Spot-flanked and Double-toothed Barbets, Golden-tailed and Green-backed Woodpeckers, Black Cuckoo-shrike, Souza's Shrike, Marsh Tchagra, Luehder's Bushshrike, Splendid Glossy-Starling, Yellow-billed and Red-billed Oxpeckers, Swamp Flycatcher, Blue-shouldered, Red-capped and Snowy-crowned Robin-Chats, Familiar and Sooty Chats, White-headed Black-Chat, Banded Martin, Grey-rumped and Angola Swallows, White-headed Sawwing, Stout, Croaking, Siffling and Wing-snapping Cisticolas, White-chinned Prinia, Grey Wren-Warbler, Greater Swamp-Warbler, White-winged Black-Tit, Dusky Tit, Rufous-naped and Flappet Larks, Red-billed Quailfinch, Cape Wagtail, Yellow-throated Longclaw, Slender-billed, Black-necked and Black-headed Weavers, Copper Sunbird, Cabanis' Bunting.

Other Wildlife

Baboon, bohor reedbuck, buffalo, Burchell's zebra, eland, elephant, Grant's gazelle, hippo, impala, klipspringer, lion, oribi, red river hog, roan, side-striped jackal, sitatunga, spotted hyena, topi, waterbuck.

Access

The access points used to be Akagera Hotel in the south and Gabiro Guesthouse in the north.

NYUNGWE FOREST RESERVE

Together with the contiguous Kibira NP in north Burundi (p. 59), this is the biggest remaining tract of montane forest in Africa. It lies between 1650 and 2950 m (5413–9679 ft) and covers 970 sq km. Virtually all of the Albertine Rift endemics recorded in Rwanda occur here, as well as White-winged Flufftail* and Kungwe Apalis*.

Specialities

Handsome Francolin, Ruwenzori Turaco, Albertine Owlet*, Dwarf Honeyguide*, White-tailed Blue-Flycatcher, Mountain Boubou, Doherty's and Lagden's* Bushshrikes, Ruwenzori Batis, Kivu Ground-Thrush*, Red-throated Alethe, Yellow-eyed Black-Flycatcher, White-bellied and Archer's Robin-Chats, Black-faced Prinia, Collared, Masked and Kungwe* Apalises, Grauer's Scrub-Warbler*, Evergreen Forest Warbler, Grauer's Warbler, White-browed Crombec, Neumann's Warbler, Red-faced Woodland-Warbler, Ruwenzori Hill-Babbler, Red-collared Mountain-Babbler*, Stripe-breasted Tit, Dusky and Shelley's* Crimson-wings, Strange Weaver, Blue-headed, Stulhmann's, Regal and Purple-breasted Sunbirds.

Others

Mountain Buzzard, Cassin's Hawk-Eagle, African Snipe, African Pigeon, Lemon Dove, Black-billed and Great Blue Turacos, Black and Barred Long-tailed Cuckoos, Bar-tailed Trogon, Cinnamon-chested Bee-eater, White-headed Woodhoopoe, Scaly-throated Honeyguide, Tullberg's, Golden-crowned, Elliot's and Olive Woodpeckers, Dusky and White-bellied Crested-Flycatchers, Black-tailed Oriole, Mackinnon's Shrike, Pink-footed Puffback, Many-coloured Bushshrike, White-tailed Ant-thrush, Stulhmann's, Slender-billed and Sharpe's Starlings, White-starred Robin, Equatorial Akalat, Mountain Greenbul, Grey Apalis, Cinnamon Bracken-Warbler, Black-faced Rufous Warbler, Mountain Warbler, Grey-chested Illadopsis, Red-faced Crimson-wing, Yellow-bellied Waxbill, Black-billed, Forest and Brown-capped Weavers, Northern Double-collared Sunbird, Streaky and Thick-billed Seedeaters, Oriole Finch.

(Congo Bay-Owl*, known from only one specimen taken in 1951 in Zaïre, may have been heard here in 1990.)

Other Wildlife

Angolan colobus, chimpanzee, L'Hoest's monkey, mona monkey, Weyn's duiker.

Access

The Recherche Centre area, 60 km from Cyangugu on the Butare road, used to be the best birding base. There were a number of trails near the centre, including the Red Trail which, because it descended to lower altitudes, was probably the best. Many of the Albertine Rift endemics used to occur near the centre, including Handsome Francolin, Kivu Ground-Thrush* and Red-collared Mountain-Babbler*, whilst Grauer's Scrub-Warbler* was present in the roadside swamps at km 65 and km 99, and Neumann's Warbler at the beginning of the forest along the trail which began 50 m before km 99. The road to Rangiro, which begins 500 m before the centre, was also worth birding.

Accommodation: It used to be possible to stay at Recherche and Cyangugu.

It is only a short distance from Cyangugu to Kahuzi-Biega NP in Zaïre (p. 379).

GISHWATI FOREST

This forest, in northwest Rwanda, supports similar birds to Nyungwe, although there are less Albertine Rift endemics. This is another site which may be settled by returning refugees.

Specialities

Ruwenzori Turaco, Western Green-Tinkerbird, Mountain Boubou, Doherty's Bushshrike, Ruwenzori Batis, Black-faced Prinia, Collared and Masked Apalises, White-browed Crombec, Red-faced Woodland-Warbler, Dusky Crimson-wing, Strange Weaver, Blue-headed, Regal and Purple-breasted Sunbirds.

Others

Cassin's Hawk-Eagle, Black-billed Turaco, Red-chested Cuckoo, White-headed Woodhoopoe, Green-backed, Golden-crowned and Olive Woodpeckers, Black-tailed Oriole, Pink-footed Puffback, Slender-billed Starling, Sooty Flycatcher, White-starred Robin, Equatorial Akalat, Placid Greenbul, Black-throated and Chestnut-throated Apalises, Cinnamon Bracken-Warbler, Mountain Warbler, Red-faced Crimson-wing, Black-bellied Seedcracker, Northern Double-collared Sunbird, Thick-billed Seedeater.

Other Wildlife

L'Hoest's monkey.

Access

The forest is south of the main Ruhengeri–Gisenyi road and is penetrated by a number of tracks. Forest 20 km along the rough Kibuye Track, which leads south 10 km east of Gisenyi, used to be particularly good.

Accommodation: It used to be possible to stay at Gisenyi.

Black Goshawk, Ruwenzori Turaco, Mountain Boubou, White-starred Robin, Archer's Robin-Chat, Collared and Masked Apalises, Mountain Warbler, Strange Weaver, and Blue-headed, Regal and Red-tufted Sunbirds have been recorded in **Volcanos NP**, near Ruhengeri, in the north of the country on the borders with Uganda and Zaïre. This park was made famous by the research project run by Dian Fossey, and it is where everyone used to go to see gorillas in Rwanda. Before the war, it was virtually impossible to obtain permits to look for gorillas during July and August, unless they were booked well in advance. It made sense to obtain permits well in advance from a travel agent or a tour operator in Kigali. Otherwise, it was possible to just turn up at the park HQ in Kinigi, 18 km from Ruhengeri, and hope for a cancellation. Visitors arriving at any other time than July and August used to obtain permits within two days.

It has been reported that the new government recognises the value of gorilla tourism to the country's future economy, and since the gorillas here have survived the war the area may be opened up again.

ADDITIONAL INFORMATION

Addresses

The Association pour la Conservation de la Nature au Rwanda (ACNR), UNR BP 117 Butare, used to publish the *Le Nectar* newsletter and collect all bird records.

Near-endemics (Albertine Rift)

Handsome Francolin, Ruwenzori Turaco, Albertine Owlet*, Ruwenzori Nightjar, Ruwenzori Batis, Kivu Ground-Thrush*, Red-throated Alethe, Yellow-eyed Black-Flycatcher, Archer's Robin-Chat, Collared and Black-faced Apalises, White-winged and Grauer's* Scrub-Warblers, Grauer's and Neumann's Warblers, Red-faced Woodland-Warbler, Red-collared Mountain-Babbler*, Stripe-breasted Tit, Dusky and Shelley's* Crimson-wings, Strange Weaver, Blue-headed, Stuhlmann's, Regal and Purple-breasted Sunbirds. (Congo Bay-Owl* may have been heard at Nyungwe in 1990.)

Near-endemics (others)

Red-faced Barbet*, Dwarf Honeyguide*, Papyrus Gonolek*, Doherty's Bushshrike, White-browed Crombec.

SÃO TOMÉ AND PRINCIPE ISLANDS

INTRODUCTION

These two small islands, which lie 250 km west of Gabon in the Gulf of Guinea, support an amazing 25 endemics, the fourth highest total of endemics for any offshore archipelago or mainland country in the Afrotropical region. Although tourism is in its infancy here, these tropical islands seem set to become a popular destination for birders in the future.

São Tomé and Principe can be reached on regular flights from Portugal and Gabon. The few roads, most of which remain in good condition, were built to service the now abandoned cocoa plantations, leaving the steeper slopes, where primary forest still remains, virtually inaccessible. A few endemics are restricted to such remote areas and a mini-expedition is necessary to catch up with these rare birds. Cheap buses run along the major roads, but accommodation is expensive and scarce away from the major towns.

Immunisation against hepatitis, polio, typhoid and yellow fever is recommended, as are precautions against malaria. The climate is very wet and it is often cloudy, especially in the highlands of southwest São Tomé. However, there is a short dry season, which lasts from June to September, and this is the best time to visit. Fortunately, this dry season coincides with the best time to visit Gabon (p. 139) which, combined with a visit to São Tomé and Principe, would make a very exciting birding trip indeed. The mountains of São Tomé rise to 2024 m (6640 ft), and whilst their upper slopes remain forested, the lower slopes are covered with extensive, neglected cocoa plantations. Fortunately, these plantations were managed in the old-fashioned way, with large native trees kept for shade, and many of the endemics have been able to adapt to this unnatural habitat. However, plans to resurrect the plantations and manage them with modern methods, which does not leave room for native trees, will increase the threats to the islands' nine threatened and three near-threatened species. Promoting tourism seems like a far better way to generate revenue, and save the birds. The thousands of seabirds, which breed on the offshore islets, seem to be safe for now.

Over 120 species have been recorded on the two islands, and no less than 25 are endemic. A week's visit is unlikely to produce many more than 50 to 60 species, but over 20 will probably be endemic.

SÃO TOMÉ

This somewhat cloudy tropical island (45 km by 25 km) is surrounded by palm-fringed beaches and mangrove-lined estuaries.

An incredible 15 species occur only on this island, and a further four are found only here and on Principe.

São Tomé Endemics

São Tomé Olive Pigeon*, São Tomé Green-Pigeon, São Tomé Scops-Owl*, São Tomé Kingfisher, São Tomé Paradise-Flycatcher, São Tomé Oriole*, Newton's Fiscal*, Black-capped Speirops, São Tomé Prinia, Bocage's Longbill*, Giant and São Tomé Weavers, Newton's and São Tomé* Sunbirds, São Tomé Grosbeak*.

São Tomé and Principe Endemics

São Tomé Spinetail, Olivaceous Thrush*, São Tomé White-eye*, Principe Seedeater.

Specialities

São Tomé Pigeon, Golden-backed Bishop*.

Others

White-tailed Tropicbird, Western Reef-Egret, Olive Ibis, Harlequin Quail, Lemon Dove, Red-headed Lovebird, African Emerald Cuckoo, Chestnut-winged Starling, Blue-breasted Cordonbleu, Vitelline Masked-Weaver, Black-winged Bishop, White-winged Widowbird.

Access

It is best to concentrate birding on: (1) The montane forest in the central highlands at **Lagoa Amelia**, accessible via a track to the lip of a volcanic crater (4 hours on foot). A few of the endemics occur here, including São Tomé Olive Pigeon*. (2) The forest bordering **Rio Xufexufe**, on the slopes of the southwestern mountains, accessible via Santo Antonio. Newton's Fiscal*, Bocage's Longbill* and São Tomé Grosbeak*, the three rarest and most localised endemics, occur here. Birding this area will involve camping in treacherous terrain where black cobras are not uncommon.

SÃO TOMÉ

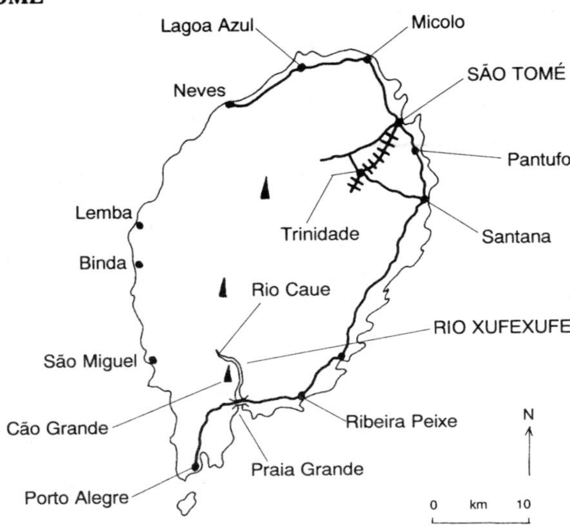

Also bird the northeast lowlands, around Guadalupe for example, where the dry woodland, farmland and mangrove-lined estuaries support São Tomé Spinetail and Golden-backed Bishop* (which otherwise occurs only in coastal Angola).

PRINCIPE

Six species are endemic to this tiny island (17 km by 8 km), 200 km northeast of São Tomé. They are all relatively easy to see with just a little exploration.

Principe Endemics

Principe Kingfisher, Principe Glossy-Starling, Dohrn's Flycatcher, Principe Speirops*, Principe Golden-Weaver, Principe Sunbird.

Principe and São Tomé Endemics

São Tomé Spinetail, Olivaceous Thrush*, São Tomé White-eye*, Principe Seedeater.

Specialities

São Tomé Pigeon.

Others

White-tailed Tropicbird, Olive Ibis, Sooty Tern, Brown and Black Noddies, Lemon Dove, Grey Parrot, Red-headed Lovebird, African Emerald Cuckoo, Blue-breasted Kingfisher, Olive Sunbird.

Access

Bird the track from Santo Antonio up to and above Bela Vista, in the mountains. Islets, including Pedra da Gale off the south coast, support White-tailed Tropicbird, Sooty Tern, and Brown and Black Noddies. Unidentified frigatebirds, which have been recorded around these islets, may well be Ascension Island Frigatebirds*.

PRINCIPE

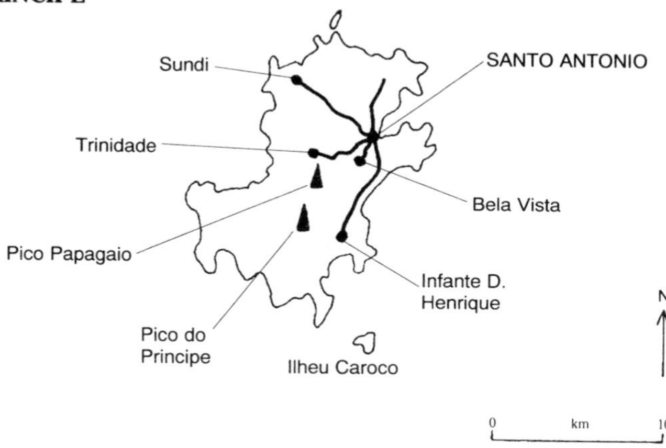

ADDITIONAL INFORMATION

Books and Papers

The Birds of São Tomé and Principe. Jones, P and Tye, A. In prep. BOU.
A Birder's Guide to the Gulf of Guinea Islands of São Tomé and Principe. Sargeant, D. 1992. Available from D Sargeant, Ieplaan 179, 2565 LK Den Haag, The Netherlands.

Addresses

Please send all records to Dr P Jones, ICAPB (Zoology Building), The King's Building, Edinburgh EH9 3JT, UK.

ENDEMICS (25)

São Tomé (15)
São Tomé Olive Pigeon*
São Tomé Green-Pigeon
São Tomé Scops-Owl*
São Tomé Kingfisher
São Tomé Paradise-Flycatcher
São Tomé Oriole*
Newton's Fiscal*
Black-capped Speirops
São Tomé Prinia
Bocage's Longbill*
Giant Weaver
São Tomé Weaver
Newton's Sunbird
São Tomé Sunbird*
São Tomé Grosbeak*

(The form of Olive Ibis on São Tomé is considered by some authorities to be a separate species, and is known as 'Dwarf Olive Ibis'.)

Principe (6)
Principe Kingfisher
Principe Glossy-Starling
Dohrn's Flycatcher
Principe Speirops*
Principe Golden-Weaver
Principe Sunbird

São Tomé and Principe (4)
São Tomé Spinetail
Olivaceous Thrush*
São Tomé White-eye*
Principe Seedeater

Near-endemics

São Tomé Pigeon (also occurs on Annobon Island), Golden-backed Bishop (also occurs in Angola).

SENEGAL

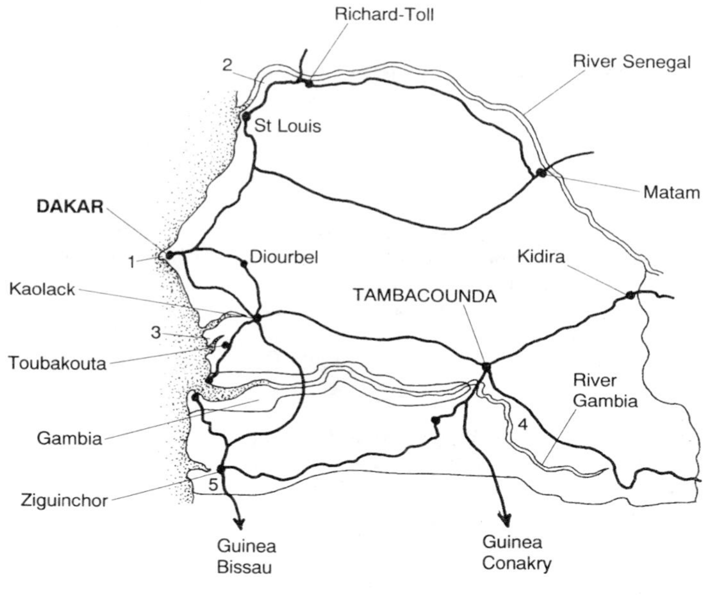

1 Dakar
2 Djoudj NP
3 Saloum Delta NP
4 Niokola Koba NP
5 Basse Casamance NP

N

0 km 100

INTRODUCTION

Summary

Most birders prefer Gambia to Senegal. Most of the spectacular avian attractions, such as Egyptian Plover, occur in both countries, but there are some differences which account for this preference. For example, Arabian Bustard and White-headed Lapwing, which can be seen in Senegal, are both very rare in Gambia, whilst Swallow-tailed Bee-eater and Blue-bellied Roller, which can be seen with some ease in Gambia, could be missed in Senegal. Since Gambia experienced a minor coup in 1994, Senegal, which does support more arid-savanna specialities compared to Gambia, may become more popular, although budget birders will have to camp where there are few, if any, facilities.

Size

At 196,192 sq km, Senegal is 1.5 times the size of England, and one third the size of Texas.

Getting Around

Senegal's roads are amongst the best in West Africa. It is possible to reach most sites in the ubiquitous bush taxis, but Niokola Koba NP, where Egyptian Plover occurs, is difficult to reach without a vehicle, and car-hire is very expensive.

Accommodation and Food

A wide range of accommodation is available, but it is usually expensive. Fortunately for budget birders, it is possible to camp safely away from main towns and villages. The food is excellent, as one would expect in a French colony, although most bush dishes are dominated by rice and fish.

Health and Safety

Immunisation against hepatitis, meningitis, polio, typhoid and yellow fever is recommended, as are precautions against malaria.

Since 1983 there has been sporadic fighting between government forces and Diola separatists in the Casamance region, in south Senegal. It would be wise to check with the Foreign Office before venturing to this part of the country.

Climate and Timing

The short rainy season lasts from July to September (October in the south) when most national parks are closed, and the best time to visit is December to April, although the dusty Saharan wind known as Harmattan can blow strongly at this time.

Habitats

Senegal is a very flat country, which rises to only 500 m (1640 ft). The Atlantic coastline is dotted with important wetlands. Inland there is a wide belt of Sahel in the north, savanna in the south and some gallery forest in the extreme southwest.

Conservation

Senegal's six national parks go some way to protecting the five threatened and six near-threatened species which occur here, although the Basse–Casamance NP has been severely degraded in recent years owing to the local conflict there.

Bird Families

Seven of the ten families endemic to the African mainland are represented in Senegal.

Bird Species

Over 610 species have been recorded in Senegal, only 80 more than Gambia. Non-endemic specialities and spectacular species include a selection of passage seabirds, Red-billed Tropicbird, Black Crowned-Crane, Arabian Bustard, Egyptian Plover, Golden Nightjar, Red-throated Bee-eater, Chestnut-bellied Starling, River Prinia*, Cricket Longtail, Kordofan Lark and Sudan Golden-Sparrow.

Endemics

There are no endemics, but a number of arid-savanna specialities are present.

Expectations

It is possible to see over 250 species in two weeks.

Senegal's capital, **Dakar**, is situated on the Cap Vert peninsula, the most westerly extremity of the African mainland. Seawatching from the golf course (north of Hotel du President) at Pointes des Almadies, 8 km west of Dakar airport, has revealed passing Bulwer's Petrel, Cory's, Sooty and Little Shearwaters, Wilson's and European Storm-Petrels, Cape Gannet*, Brown Booby, Red Phalarope, Audouin's* and Sabine's Gulls and Royal and Bridled Terns, especially in spring (Apr–May) and autumn (Sep–Oct). It is possible to hire sport-fishing boats (A+) in Dakar to get good views of such birds offshore.

Other good birding sites around Dakar include Îles de la Madeleine NP, where Red-billed Tropicbird and Bridled Tern breed (the necessary permits are available from Direction des Parcs Nationaux du Senegal, in Dakar), Hann Beach (gulls and terns), and Malika Lake (shorebirds), near Pikine. A 'black oystercatcher' seen on the coast just south of Dakar in 1970 may have been a Canary Island Oystercatcher*, now believed to be extinct.

Roadside birds between Dakar and St Louis, near Djoudj NP (see below), to the north, include Audouin's Gull*, African Collared-Dove, Chestnut-bellied Starling, Northern Anteater-Chat and Sudan Golden-Sparrow.

DJOUDJ NATIONAL PARK

This huge seasonal wetland (160 sq km) at the mouth of the River Senegal north of Dakar, supports important wintering concentrations of Palearctic waterfowl, shorebirds and passerines, including up to 150,000 Garganey, a million Ruff, and at least a million Sand Martins.

Riverine thickets and semi-desert within and outside the park support a handful of arid-savanna specialities, which are less accessible elsewhere in Africa, including Golden Nightjar, River Prinia*, and Kordofan Lark. Other good birds in this area include Arabian Bustard and Black Crowned-Crane.

The floodwaters normally recede in December, so this is the best time to visit.

Specialities

Arabian Bustard, Golden Nightjar, River Prinia*, Cricket Longtail, Sennar Penduline-Tit, Kordofan Lark, Sudan Golden-Sparrow.

Others

African Darter, Greater and Lesser* Flamingos, Black Heron, Western Reef-Egret, African Fish-Eagle, Red-necked Falcon, Black Crowned-Crane, Greater Painted-snipe, Senegal Thick-knee, Chestnut-bellied Sandgrouse, Blue-naped Mousebird, Long-tailed Nightjar, Malachite Kingfisher, Abyssinian Roller, Little Grey Woodpecker, Senegal Batis, Long-tailed Glossy-Starling, Black Scrub-Robin, Winding Cisticola, Orphean Warbler, Chestnut-backed and Black-crowned Sparrow-Larks, Zebra Waxbill, African Quailfinch, African Silverbill, White-rumped Seedeater.

Other Wildlife

Red patas monkey.

Access

The park is 65 km northeast of St Louis; the entrance track is signposted on the left near the village of Ndiol. There are a number of tracks worth exploring, pirogues for hire and hides overlooking Grand Lac. The Wildfowl and Wetlands Trust runs a major ringing project here, and may be interested to hear from potential volunteers. Golden Nightjar, Little Grey Woodpecker, Cricket Longtail, Sennar Penduline-Tit and Kordofan Lark have been recorded in the arid acacia savanna around the village of **Richard-Toll**, east of the park.

Accommodation: Campement (A), at the park entrance, bookable in advance through the Senegal Tourist Department (tel: 443-2527).

The road south from Dakar to Saloum Delta NP (see below) passes through cultivation and wooded savanna, where Scissor-tailed Kite, Abyssinian Roller, Piapiac and Sudan Golden-Sparrow occur.

SALOUM DELTA NATIONAL PARK

This national park on Senegal's west coast near the Gambian border was set up to protect the maze of mangroves, lagoons and islands at the mouth of the River Saloum. These important wetlands and the surrounding savanna and gallery forest support the scarce White-crested Bittern.

Specialities

Sudan Golden-Sparrow.

Others

African Darter, Western Reef-Egret, Goliath Heron, White-crested Bittern, Palm-nut Vulture, Brown Snake-Eagle, Double-spurred Francolin, Bronze-winged Courser, White-fronted Plover, Royal Tern, Vinaceous Dove, Bruce's Green-Pigeon, Senegal Parrot, Violet Turaco, Western Grey Plantain-eater, Little Bee-eater, Abyssinian Roller, Bearded Barbet, Fine-spotted Woodpecker, Yellow-billed Shrike, Common Gonolek, White Helmetshrike, Brown-throated Wattle-eye, Bronze-tailed Glossy-Starling, Blackcap and Brown Babblers, Lavender Waxbill, Vitelline Masked-Weaver, Mouse-brown Sunbird.

Other Wildlife

Dugong.

Access

It is possible to look for White-crested Bittern by boat (hire from the Keur Saloum Lodge). The Fathala Forest, 16 km south of Toubakouta and 44 km north of the Gambian border, via Missirah, is also worth a look.

Accommodation: Keur Saloum Lodge (A), near the village of Toubakouta; camping.

The town of **Kaolack**, on the River Saloum inland from the delta, is surrounded by wooded savanna which supports Scissor-tailed Kite, Quail-plover, Spotted Thick-knee, Bronze-winged Courser, Blue-naped Mousebird, Green Bee-eater, Black Scimitar-bill, Chestnut-bellied Starling, Black Scrub-Robin and Sudan Golden-Sparrow. The area to the north in the direction of Diourbel has been best in the past.

Accommodation: Hotel Dior (A).

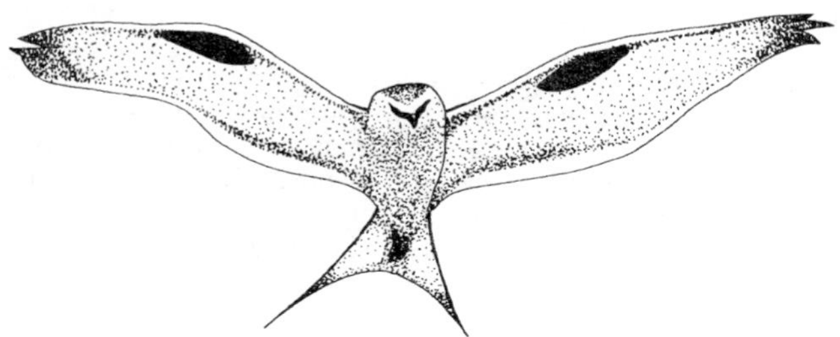

Whilst driving across Senegal it is wise to keep a look out for the superb Scissor-tailed Kite, which resembles a terrestrial tern

The dry woodland alongside the Kaolack–Tambacounda road, 6 km west of Tambacounda, supports Senegal Batis, Yellow Penduline-Tit, Chestnut-crowned Sparrow-Weaver and Brown-rumped Bunting.

Accommodation: Tambacounda: Hotel Asta Kebe (A).

NIOKOLA KOBA NATIONAL PARK

This big park (8130 sq km), south of Tambacounda in southeast Senegal, protects Guinea savanna which lies either side of the River Gambia. Over 330 species have been recorded, and it is possible to see over 200 species in a week, including Egyptian Plover from the lodge bar.

Niokola Koba is open from December to May.

Specialities

Egyptian Plover.

Others

Hamerkop, Hadada Ibis, Saddle-billed Stork, White-headed Vulture, Brown Snake-Eagle, Bateleur, Martial Eagle, Helmeted Guineafowl, Double-spurred Francolin, Stone Partridge, Black Crowned-Crane, Black-bellied Bustard, Greater Painted-snipe, Senegal Thick-knee, White-headed Lapwing, Chestnut-bellied and Four-banded Sandgrouse, Bruce's Green-Pigeon, Violet Turaco, Western Grey Plantain-eater, African Scops-Owl, Long-tailed and Standard-winged Nightjars, Mottled

Spinetail, Blue-breasted Kingfisher, Red-throated, Green and Northern Carmine Bee-eaters, Black Scimitar-bill, Abyssinian Ground-Hornbill, Bearded Barbet, Fine-spotted and Brown-backed Woodpeckers, African Blue-Flycatcher, Common Gonolek, White Helmetshrike, Bronze-tailed Glossy-Starling, Grey Tit-Flycatcher, White-crowned Robin-Chat, Oriole Warbler, Senegal Eremomela, Black-rumped Waxbill, African Quailfinch, Broad-tailed Paradise-Whydah, Vitelline Masked-Weaver, Pygmy Sunbird.

Other Wildlife

Guinea baboon, hartebeest, hippo, honey badger, kob, Nile crocodile, oribi, red-flanked duiker, roan. (Buffalo, elephant and lion are all rare.)

Access

This park is 460 km from Dakar, 80 km south of Tambacounda. It is possible to see Egyptian Plover and White-headed Lapwing from the bar of Simenti Lodge. African Blue-Flycatcher and Oriole Warbler both occur along the short path from Simenti Lodge to the river, as well as some mammals including kob and oribi. The Camp Lion area, to the east, and any other tracks are also worth birding.

Accommodation: Simenti Lodge (A); Camp Lion Campsite (free but no facilities).

If travelling to Gambia from Tambacounda it is worth stopping at **Goulombo Bridge**, where Egyptian Plover and White-headed Lapwing occur.

NIOKOLA KOBA NP

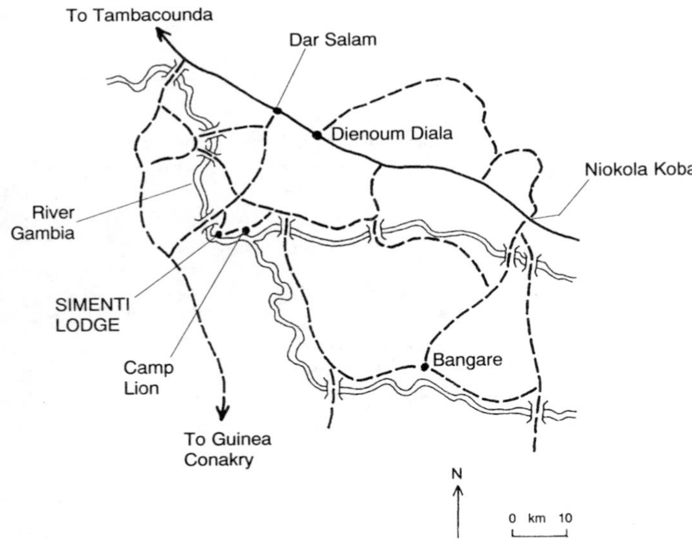

BASSE CASAMANCE NATIONAL PARK

This small park (50 sq km), which lies near the Guinea Bissau border in the heavily populated Casamance region of southwest Senegal, has been badly damaged in recent years owing to the local conflict between the Diola separatists and Government troops. The Guinea savanna, gallery forest and mangrove within the park may still support a good selection of birds, including Yellow-casqued Hornbill*.

Others

African Darter, Palm-nut Vulture, Black Goshawk, Senegal Thick-knee, Senegal Parrot, Guinea Turaco, Blue-breasted Kingfisher, African Pied, Piping and Yellow-casqued* Hornbills, Spotted Honeyguide, Black-headed Paradise-Flycatcher, Red-shouldered Cuckoo-shrike, Brown-throated Wattle-eye, Snowy-crowned Robin-Chat, Little and Slender-billed Greenbuls, Grey-headed Bristlebill, Oriole Warbler, Green Hylia, Yellow-bellied Hyliota, Blackcap and Capuchin Babblers, Chestnut-breasted Negrofinch, Western Bluebill.

Other Wildlife

Blue duiker, mona monkey, red colobus.

Access

This park is 12 km from Oussouye. Bird from the observation platforms (miradors) named Oiseaux, Crocodile, Hippo and Buffle, the Houssiou (2.5 km) and Raphias circuits, and around Ukunum Poste.

Accommodation: Campement (B)/camping (free).

Two 'black oystercatchers' seen on the coast near the Guinea-Bissau border in 1975 may have been Canary Island Oystercatchers*, now believed to be extinct.

ADDITIONAL INFORMATION

Books and Papers

A Field Check-list for the Birds of Senegambia. Rumsey, S and Rodwell, S. 1992. The Wildfowl and Wetlands Trust.
Les Oiseaux de Senegambia. Morel, G and Morel, M. 1990. ORSTOM, Paris.
A Field Guide to the Birds of The Gambia and Southern Senegal. Barlow, C *et al.* In prep. Pica Press.

Addresses

The Wildfowl and Wetlands Trust, Slimbridge, Gloucester GL2 7BT, UK.

SEYCHELLES

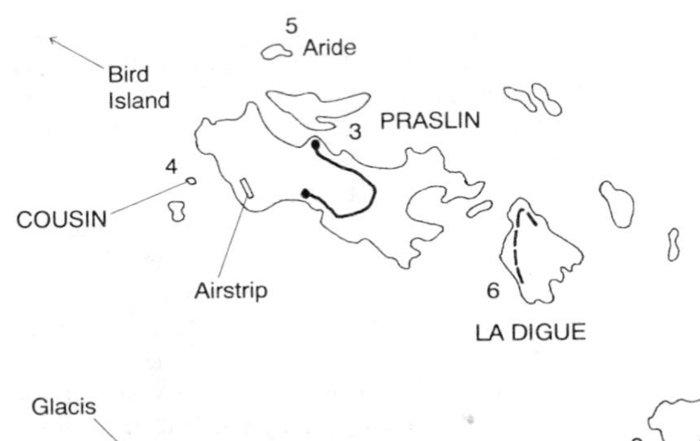

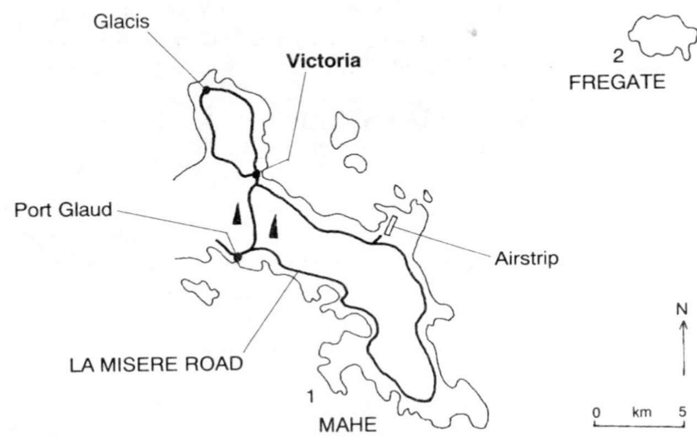

1 Mahe
2 Fregate
3 Praslin
4 Cousin
5 Aride
6 La Digue

INTRODUCTION

Summary

These truly tropical islands, 1500 km east of the African mainland, complete with palm-fringed beaches, have long been a favourite with birders, thanks to their breeding seabirds and eleven endemics. However, birding the Seychelles remains a dream for budget birders because accommodation, food and transport between the individual islands, are all very expensive.

Size

Although only 280 sq km, the 90 islands of the Seychelles form an extensive archipelago.

Getting Around

There are ferries and a good internal flight network connecting the major islands. Buses are available on Mahe and Praslin, and it is possible to hire bikes on the larger islands.

Accommodation and Food

The high price of accommodation and food in the Seychelles is a major drawback to the budget birder. Prices are at their highest during the high seasons: July to August and December to January. Camping is not encouraged.

Health and Safety

Immunisation against hepatitis, polio and typhoid is recommended. The local people are famously friendly and, as one might expect, in such a beautiful part of the world, carefree.

Climate and Timing

July to October is the best time to visit the Seychelles because the seabirds are breeding at this time. The peak time is October, when the southeasterly trade winds are subsiding. When these winds blow hard, some islands are inaccessible. It can be cloudy at any time of the year, and from December to March the northwesterly trade winds bring rain.

Habitats

The palm-fringed beaches and mangroves give way to misty montane forest on the main island, Mahe, but vegetation is limited to citrus orchards, scrub and degraded woodland on most of the other islands, and some are just slabs of rock where thousands of seabirds breed in peace.

Conservation

Eight of the eleven endemics are threatened, thanks to rats, which have decimated bird populations on Mahe and Praslin, cats and deforestation for tourist and private developments. However, various bird conservation organisations around the world are doing their utmost to ensure the continued survival of these extremely rare birds.

Bird Families

None of the 17 endemic Afrotropical families are represented in the Seychelles.

Bird Species

Over 220 species have been recorded on the Seychelles, including many vagrants. Non-endemic specialities and spectacular species include Red-tailed and White-tailed Tropicbirds, Crab Plover, Sooty and Saunders' Terns, Brown and Lesser Noddies and Common White-Tern.

Endemics

Eleven species occur only on the Seychelles: a kestrel, a 'blue' pigeon, a scops-owl, a swiftlet, a paradise-flycatcher, a magpie-robin, a bulbul, a white-eye, a brush-warbler, a fody and a sunbird. Two further species, one of which may now be extinct, are confined to Aldabra. The two other Malagasy endemics occurring on the Seychelles are Madagascar Turtle-Dove and Black Parrot.

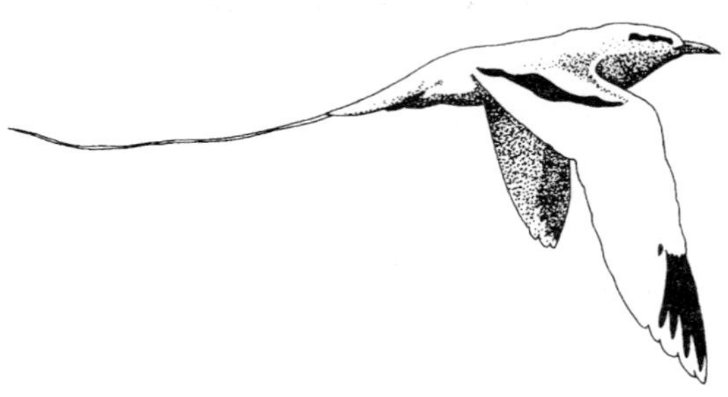

White-tailed Tropicbird graces the truly tropical islands of the Seychelles

MAHE

Mahe is the largest island in the archipelago. Here palm-fringed beaches, mangroves and wet (Oct–Mar) montane forest on the 30 km spine of the island (905 m (2969 ft)), support seven of the eleven endemics including Seychelles Scops-Owl* and Seychelles White-eye*, both of which occur only on this island.

Seychelles Endemics

Seychelles Kestrel*, Seychelles Blue-Pigeon, Seychelles Scops-Owl*, Seychelles Swiftlet*, Seychelles Bulbul, Seychelles White-eye*, Seychelles Sunbird.

Specialities

Madagascar Turtle-Dove, Saunders' Tern.

Others

Wedge-tailed Shearwater, White-tailed Tropicbird, Crab Plover. (Introductions: Zebra Dove, Common Myna and Red Fody.)

Access

Concentrate on the La Misere road for Seychelles Scops-Owl* (the area around the Mission is particularly good), and Seychelles White-eye*, although there may only be less than twenty pairs of the white-eye left. The botanic gardens in Victoria and the mudflats near town are also worth a look.

FREGATE

This small (2 sq km) private island with few inhabitants is covered in citrus orchards, although remnant pockets of native vegetation support one of the world's rarest birds, Seychelles Magpie-Robin*. The population stood at just 46 birds in 1994, although BirdLife International, the RSPB and the island's owner are desperately trying to increase this figure, and a pair were introduced to Aride island in 1994.

Seychelles Endemics

Seychelles Blue-Pigeon, Seychelles Magpie-Robin*, Seychelles Sunbird, Seychelles Fody*.

Specialities

Madagascar Turtle-Dove.

Others

Common White-Tern. (Introductions: Red Fody and giant Aldabra tortoise.)

Access

This island is accessible by air (15 minutes) from Mahe.

PRASLIN

This sparsely populated island supports a selection of endemics, and Black Parrot, which otherwise occurs only on Madagascar and the Comoros.

Seychelles Endemics

Seychelles Kestrel*, Seychelles Blue-Pigeon, Seychelles Swiftlet*, Seychelles Bulbul, Seychelles Sunbird.

Specialities

Black Parrot.

Access

Bird Vallée de Mai NP, where the famous Coco-de-Mer grows. This island is also renowned for spectacular offshore snorkelling.

COUSIN

This low, lightly wooded island, just 1 km wide, is a BirdLife International reserve. It supports one of the two populations of Seychelles Brush-Warbler* (the other population, on Aride, has been introduced), of which only 300–400 remain, but the real highlight is the seabirds.

Seychelles Endemics

Seychelles Brush-Warbler*, Seychelles Fody*.

Others

Wedge-tailed and Audubon's Shearwaters, White-tailed Tropicbird, Bridled Tern, Brown and Lesser Noddies, Common White-Tern.

Access

This island is accessible by boat from Mahe and Praslin on Tuesdays, Thursdays and Fridays.

ARIDE

The lightly vegetated rocky hills of this small island support masses of seabirds, not least 20,000 White-tailed Tropicbirds and 250,000 Sooty Terns.

Seychelles Endemics

Seychelles Blue-Pigeon, Seychelles Sunbird.

Others

Red-tailed and White-tailed Tropicbirds, Great and Lesser Frigatebirds, Roseate, Bridled and Sooty Terns, Brown and Lesser Noddies, Common White-Tern. (Seychelles Magpie-Robin* and Seychelles Brush-Warbler* have been introduced on this island.)

Access

This RSNC reserve is accessible by boat (one hour) from Mahe and Praslin from October to April. A few pairs of Red-tailed Tropicbird and both frigatebirds occur on the far side of the island.

LA DIGUE

La Digue's star bird is the Seychelles Paradise-Flycatcher*, which lives in the vanilla woods and occurs on no other island.

Seychelles Endemics

Seychelles Swiftlet*, Seychelles Paradise-Flycatcher*, Seychelles Sunbird.

Others

Crab Plover, Common Waxbill. (Yellow Bittern also occurs on this island, either as a genuine colonist or as an introduction.)

Access

This island is accessible by boat from Praslin. Seychelles Paradise-Flycatcher* occurs in a reserve reached by ox-cart.

Bird Island, a coral-cay nearly 100 km north of Mahe, supports eight species of tern, including 400,000 Sooty Terns. It is accessible by boat from Mahe and on charter flights.

Two birds are endemic to **Aldabra**: the Aldabra Drongo* and the Aldabra Brush-Warbler*. Since 1977 only two brush-warblers have been recorded (in 1983) and this species may now be extinct. Two species are confined to Aldabra and the Comoros: Comoro Blue-Pigeon and Red-headed Fody. A further six occur only here and on Madagascar: Newton's Kestrel, Cuvier's Rail, Madagascar Coucal (which also occurs on Assumption Island), Madagascar Nightjar, Madagascar Cisticola and Souimanga Sunbird, whereas Madagascar Bulbul and Madagascar White-eye occur on Aldabra, the Comoros and Madagascar. The total species list of 86 also includes Audubon's Shearwater, Red-tailed and White-tailed Tropicbirds, Great and Lesser Frigatebirds, Masked and Red-footed Boobies, Madagascar Pond-Heron*, Black-naped Tern, Brown Noddy and Common White-Tern.

ADDITIONAL INFORMATION

Books and Papers

A Birdwatcher's Guide to the Seychelles. Skerrett, A and Bullock, I. 1992. Prion.

A Guide to the Birds of the Seychelles. Skerrett, A and Bullock, I. In prep.

Addresses

The Seychelles Bird Group, c/o Nature Protection Trust of Seychelles, Box 207 Victoria, Seychelles, publishes *Birdwatch* magazine.

Please send records to Adrian Skerrett, Secretary, Seychelles Bird Records Committee, Box 336, Victoria, Seychelles.

SEYCHELLES ENDEMICS (11)

Seychelles Kestrel*	Mahe, Praslin and Silhouette
Seychelles Blue-Pigeon	Mahe, Fregate, Praslin, and Aride
Seychelles Scops-Owl*	Mahe only
Seychelles Swiftlet*	Mahe, Praslin and La Digue
Seychelles Paradise-Flycatcher*	La Digue only
Seychelles Magpie-Robin*	Fregate only, although a pair was introduced to Aride in 1994
Seychelles Bulbul	Mahe and Praslin
Seychelles White-eye*	Mahe only
Seychelles Brush-Warbler*	Cousin only, although birds have been introduced to Aride and Cousine
Seychelles Fody*	Fregate, Cousin, and Cousine
Seychelles Sunbird	Mahe, Fregate, Praslin, Aride, and La Digue

ALDABRA ENDEMICS (2)

Aldabra Drongo*	Widespread
Aldabra Brush-Warbler*	Probably extinct

Near-endemics

Seychelles, Madagascar and Comoros
Black Parrot.

Seychelles, Aldabra, Madagascar and Comoros
Madagascar Turtle-Dove.

Aldabra and Comoros
Comoro Blue-Pigeon, Red-headed Fody.

Aldabra and Madagascar
Newton's Kestrel, Cuvier's Rail, Madagascar Coucal, Madagascar Nightjar, Madagascar Cisticola, Souimanga Sunbird.

Aldabra, Comoros and Madagascar
Madagascar Bulbul, Madagascar White-eye.

SIERRA LEONE

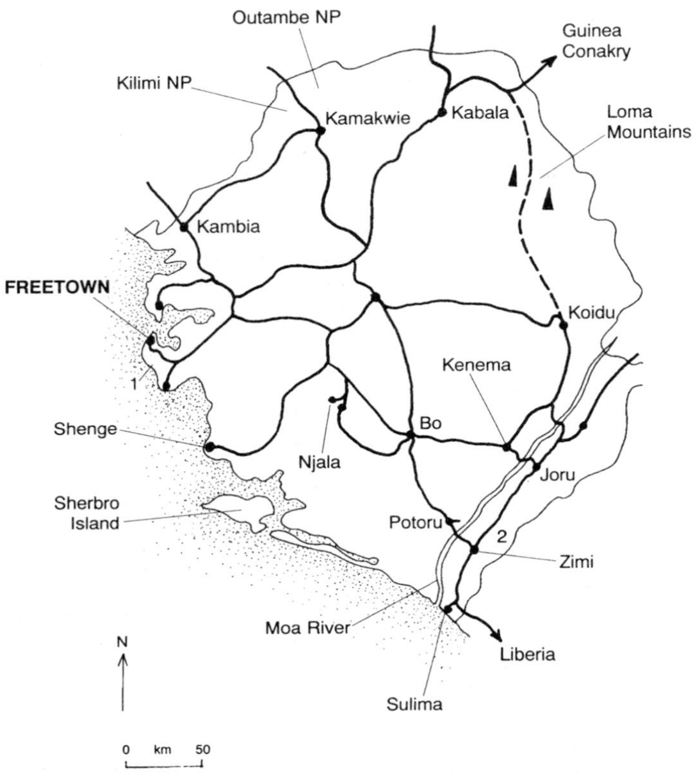

1 Freetown Peninsula
2 Gola FRs

INTRODUCTION

Summary

Few birders have been to this small West African country, for although it supports 15 of the 16 Upper Guinea forest endemics, all of these but one also occur in more accessible Côte D'Ivoire. However, one of these regional endemics, the superb White-necked Rockfowl*, is widespread in Sierra Leone, but localised and difficult to see in Côte D'Ivoire.

Size

At 71,740 sq km, Sierra Leone is approximately half the size of England, and just a tenth the size of Texas.

Getting Around

There are plenty of bush taxis, known locally as 'poda podas', as well as some 'express' buses, but petrol shortages can delay travel in Sierra Leone. During the rainy season (Apr–Nov) some roads are impassable, and at certain times there are also numerous police road blocks.

Accommodation and Food

Out of the capital, Freetown, accommodation and food are scarce but cheap.

Health and Safety

Immunisation against hepatitis, meningitis, polio, typhoid and yellow fever is recommended, as are precautions against malaria.

In 1994 rebel forces engaged in Liberia's civil war were present in east Sierra Leone, making visits to the Gola FRs and Tiwai Island Nature Reserve potentially very risky. There are also sporadic conflicts between the Revolutionary United Front and government troops in various parts of the country. Wandering around Freetown or on the beaches at night is not advisable, although people are, on the whole, very friendly.

Climate and Timing

The long wet season (Apr–Nov) is very wet indeed, and it is hot and humid all year round, especially in March, which unfortunately is the best time to look for White-necked Rockfowl*. Otherwise December and January, when it can also rain, is the best time to visit.

Habitats

The swampy southern coastal plain gives way to cultivated lowlands (dominated by paddies in the west) and savanna in the north. In the east there is a plateau, which rises to 1945 m (6381 ft) at Bintumani Mountain, where remnant blocks of Upper Guinea forest survive.

Conservation

Just 4% of the original 60% forest cover remains, and most of this is confined to the Gola Forest Reserves in the east. Much of the original forest was lost to agriculture and plantations, and even the remaining forests are threatened by logging and hunting, which leaves little hope for the twelve threatened and ten near-threatened species which occur in Sierra Leone, despite the establishment of 30 so-called Forest Reserves.

Bird Families

Since families associated with savanna, such as mousebirds, are absent, only four of the ten families endemic to the African mainland are represented in Sierra Leone.

Bird Species

A total of 622 species have been recorded in Sierra Leone, only 70 fewer than the much bigger Côte D'Ivoire. Non-endemic specialities and spectacular species include Long-tailed Hawk, Forbes' Plover, Chocolate-backed Kingfisher, Black and Blue-headed Bee-eaters, Red-cheeked Wattle-eye and Jameson's Antpecker.

Endemics

There are no endemics, but 15 of the 16 Upper Guinea endemics are present, the best total for any country within this region. Only Liberian Greenbul*, which is endemic to Liberia, is absent, and those present include White-breasted Guineafowl*, Ghana Cuckoo-shrike*, Turati's Bushshrike*, Liberian Black-Flycatcher*, White-necked Rockfowl* and Ballman's Malimbe*.

FREETOWN PENINSULA

The forested hills of this peninsula, which lie less than 5 km away from Freetown, Sierra Leone's bustling capital, support White-necked Rockfowl*.

Specialities

White-necked Rockfowl*.

Others

Western Reef-Egret, Palm-nut Vulture, African Goshawk, Royal Tern, Red-headed Lovebird, Western Grey Plantain-eater, Narina Trogon, White-throated Bee-eater, African Pied Hornbill, Yellow-throated and Yellow-rumped Tinkerbirds, Black-headed Paradise-Flycatcher, Black-and-white Shrike-flycatcher, Ussher's Flycatcher, Snowy-crowned Robin-Chat, Pied-winged Swallow, Square-tailed and Fanti Sawwings, Honeyguide and Simple Greenbuls, Grey-headed Bristlebill, Oriole Warbler, Green Hylia, Chestnut-breasted Negrofinch, Grey-headed Oliveback, Crimson Seedcracker, Western Bluebill, Black-and-white Mannikin, Black-necked and Vieillot's Black Weavers, Black-winged Bishop, Mouse-brown and Johanna's Sunbirds.

Access

The best birding areas are: (1) The forested streams and riverbeds, which are usually dry in March and April, where the elusive White-necked Rockfowl* occurs. (2) Cape Sierra (Oriole Warbler). (3) Aberdeen Creek, an extensive area of mudflats and mangrove, accessible via the grounds of Le Lagoon Bleu at the west end of Aberdeen Bridge, or Paddy's Bar at the north end of Lumley Beach (Mouse-brown Sunbird). (4) The Golf Club and its surrounding mangroves and wetlands, 3 km southeast of Cape Sierra (Pied-winged Swallow). (5) Fourah Bay College Campus, on the edge of some secondary forest on Mount Aureol, south of the city centre. The Botanical Gardens near here are particularly good (ask for permission to enter) and support Narina Trogon, Grey-headed Bristlebill and Western Bluebill. (6) The Regent/Leicester area. (7) Guma Dam, some 20 km from Freetown, which is surrounded by secondary forest. To visit, permission is needed from the Guma Dam Office (Building), Lamina Sankoh Street, opposite the French embassy in Freetown. Bird the 6-km track from the check-point up to the dam.

Turati's Bushshrike*, as well as Forbes' Plover (Jan–Feb), Grey-headed Oliveback (May–Oct) and Dybowski's Twinspot have been recorded in the grounds of **Njala University**, and the surrounding fields and scrub. This university is 205 km east of Freetown and includes an agricultural research station next to the Taia river.

GOLA FOREST RESERVES

These three reserves (in two forest blocks covering 748 sq km) in east Sierra Leone constitute one of the most important areas of Upper Guinea forest in Africa. They have all been selectively logged, but over 270 species have been recorded, including 12 of the 16 Upper Guinea Forest endemics, as well as Yellow-footed Honeyguide*, Forest Scrub-Robin and Jameson's Antpecker.

Specialities

White-breasted Guineafowl*, Yellow-throated Cuckoo, Rufous Fishing-Owl*, Red-chested Owlet, Black Spinetail, Brown-cheeked Hornbill*, Yellow-footed Honeyguide*, Little Green Woodpecker, African Pitta, Ghana Cuckoo-shrike*, Red-cheeked Wattle-eye, Finsch's Flycatcher-Thrush, Grey Ground-Thrush, Copper-tailed Glossy-Starling*, Liberian Black-Flycatcher*, Forest Scrub-Robin, Green-tailed Bristlebill*, Yellow-bearded Greenbul*, Sharpe's Apalis, Black-capped Rufous Warbler*, Rufous-winged Illadopsis*, White-necked Rockfowl*, Jameson's Antpecker, Ballman's Malimbe*.

Others

White-crested Bittern, Palm-nut Vulture, Long-tailed Hawk, Ayres' and Cassin's Hawk-Eagles, Forest Francolin, White-spotted Flufftail, Nkulengu and Grey-throated Rails, African Finfoot, Grey Parrot, Yellow-billed and Great Blue Turacos, Thick-billed Cuckoo, Dusky Long-tailed and Olive Long-tailed Cuckoos, African Emerald Cuckoo, Black-throated Coucal, Fraser's, Shelley's and Akun Eagle-Owls, Standard-winged Nightjar, Narina Trogon, Shining Blue, White-bellied, Dwarf, Chocolate-backed and Blue-breasted Kingfishers, Black, Blue-headed and White-throated Bee-eaters, Blue-throated Roller, White-crested, Black Dwarf, Red-billed Dwarf, Piping, Black-casqued and Yellow-casqued* Hornbills, Naked-faced and Bristle-nosed Barbets, Speckled and Yellow-throated Tinkerbirds, Hairy-breasted and Yellow-billed Barbets, Lyre-tailed and Cassin's Honeyguides, Melancholy and Fire-bellied Woodpeckers, Rufous-sided Broadbill, Chestnut-capped Flycatcher, Blue-headed Crested-Flycatcher, Black-winged Oriole, Blue Cuckoo-shrike, Large-billed Puffback, Many-coloured and Fiery-breasted Bushshrikes, African and Black-and-white Shrike-flycatchers, Chestnut and Yellow-bellied Wattle-eyes, Brown-chested and White-tailed Alethes, African and White-browed Forest-Flycatchers, Ussher's, Olivaceous and Tessman's Flycatchers, Forest Robin, Lowland Akalat, Yelllow-whiskered Bulbul, Spotted, Simple, Swamp, Baumann's* and White-throated Greenbuls, Grey-headed Bristlebill, Western Bearded Greenbul, Kemp's and Grey Longbills, Green Hylia, Violet-backed Hyliota, Blackcap, Puvel's and Pale-breasted Illadopsises, Dusky Tit, Tit-hylia, White-breasted and Chestnut-breasted Negrofinches, Crimson Seedcracker, Yellow-mantled Weaver, Red-vented, Gray's, Crested and Red-headed Malimbes, Black-winged Bishop, Scarlet-tufted, Blue-throated Brown, Buff-throated, Tiny and Johanna's Sunbirds.

Other Wildlife

Bongo, chimpanzee, Jentink's duiker, pygmy hippo, red colobus, western black-and-white colobus, zebra duiker.

Access

In Gola North, bird the Mogbai, Madina and Lalehun areas, in Gola East, bird around Wemago on the Njama–Tolo path, and in Gola West, bird the paths in Nyayama Forest.

The **Tiwai Island NR**, a 12-sq-km island with secondary forest, in the Moa river near Bo, is probably excellent for birds, since it is just 6 km upstream from the Gola West FR. There is a tented camp here but it is very difficult reach without a vehicle.

Rufous Fishing-Owl*, Sierra Leone Prinia* and White-necked Rockfowl* have been recorded on **Mount Loma** in the northeast, and White-necked Rockfowl* also occurs at **Kambui Hills FR**, northwest of the Gola FRs (ask local hunters to act as guides).

The black-and-yellow Ballman's Malimbe is one of Gola's many wonderful birds*

ADDITIONAL INFORMATION

Books and Papers

The Birds of Sierra Leone. Field, G. In prep. BOU.

Addresses

Conservation Society of Sierra Leone (CSSL), 4 Sanders Street, Box 1292, Freetown.

West African Ornithological Society (WAOS); see p. 413.

Please send all records to CSSL and G Field, 37 Milton Grove, New Milton, Hampshire BH25 6HB, UK.

Near-endemics (Upper Guinea)

White-breasted Guineafowl*, Rufous Fishing-Owl*, Little Green Woodpecker, Ghana Cuckoo-shrike*, Turati's Bushshrike*, Iris and Copper-tailed Glossy-Starlings*, Liberian Black-Flycatcher*, Yellow-bearded Greenbul*, Sierra Leone Prinia*, Sharpe's Apalis, Black-capped Rufous Warbler*, Rufous-winged Illadopsis*, White-necked Rockfowl*, Ballman's Malimbe*.

Near-endemics (Upper Guinea and Nigeria)

Brown-cheeked Hornbill*, Chestnut-bellied Helmetshrike, Finsch's Flycatcher-Thrush.

SOCOTRA ISLAND

Politically part of Yemen, this remote, rustic island (110 km x 30 km), situated off the northeastern tip of Somalia, is more African than Arabian. Six species are endemic to Socotra, and a few more are near-endemic, so it is a potential birding hotspot. However, the presence of human cave-dwellers reflects the fact that Socotra is still one of the least 'developed' places on earth, and getting there is very difficult, especially since the recent conflict in Yemen, the only country from which to reach Socotra.

There are *no* roads, only tracks, and although it is theoretically possible to hire an expensive jeep, the only definite means of transport is limited to the local trucks and porters. Since there is only one place to stay, in Hadibu, birding this island involves a major camping expedition. However, it is possible to see most of the attractions on one-day trips from Hadibu. Even food is thin on the ground and vegetables are rarer than most of the birds. Another logistical problem is the variation in the spelling of place names.

Many of Socotra's plants are unique, and form extraordinary habitats which include evergreen and succulent bushland in the montane interior. Otherwise, there are some areas of mangroves around the coast, semi-desert coastal plains and wooded wadis. None of these habitats, all of which are heavily degraded, are protected.

Around 110 species have been recorded on Socotra, including six endemics (listed below), as well as Jouanin's Petrel (Ra's Momi), Socotra Cormorant*, Cream-coloured Courser (Noged Plain), Somali Starling and Golden-winged Grosbeak (Wadi Ayhaft and Hamaderoh Plateau).

ADDITIONAL INFORMATION

Addresses

The Ornithological Society of the Middle East (OSME), c/o The Lodge, Sandy, Beds, SG19 2DL, UK, publishes an excellent biannual journal, *Sandgrouse*, which includes information on Socotra.

Please send records to Guy Kirwan at the OSME address above.

ENDEMICS (6)

Socotra Starling*	Wadi Ayhaft, Ras Hebaq, Shidadah
Socotra Cisticola	Wadi Ayhaft, Jabal Jef, Hamaderoh plateau
Island Cisticola*	Noged Plain and the dunes near the airport
Socotra Sparrow	Noged Plain, Shidadah, Hamaderoh Plateau, Di-Ishal
Socotra Sunbird	Wadi Ayhaft, Jabal Jef, Shidadah, Hamaderoh Plateau
Socotra Bunting*	Rookib Hills, Hajhir Mountains

Near-endemics

Somali Starling, Golden-winged Grosbeak. (Forbes-Watson's Swift, which occurs at Jabal Jef and in the Hajhir Mountains, also occurs on mainland Africa (eg. the Kenyan coast).)

SOMALIA

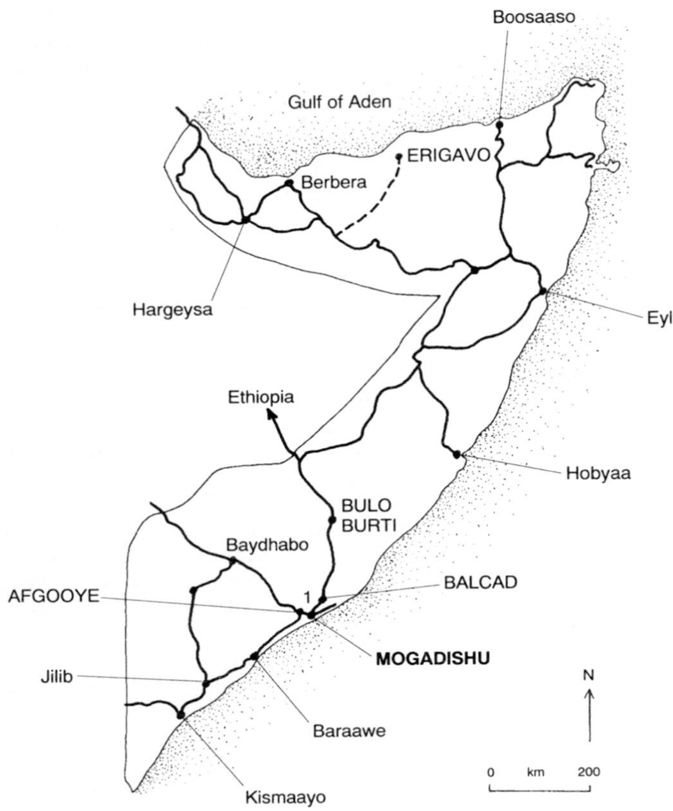

1 Mogadishu Area

INTRODUCTION

Summary

If Somalia were free from political strife and possessed a good infrastrucure it would be a popular birding destination, thanks to its fine selection of birds, which includes many northeast African specialities and ten endemics. Meanwhile, birders can only live in hope that one day they will be able to enjoy a birding trip to this little known country.

Size

At 637,657 sq km, Somalia is five times larger than England and almost as large as Texas.

Getting Around

There are few roads, but most of the numerous tracks are passable with some ease from January to March. A 4WD is recommended at other times of the year and for an extensive trip. Buses cover most of the south, but are few and far between in the north. The limited internal air network serves Hargeysa and Berbera in the north, and Kismaayo in the south.

Accommodation and Food

Accommodation is rare away from Mogadishu and Kisimaayo. Rice and pasta, sometimes with sheep or goat, and washed down with copious amounts of chai, dominate the diet.

Health and Safety

Immunisation against hepatitis, polio, smallpox, typhoid and yellow fever is recommended, as are all precautions against malaria.

Climate and Timing

It is hot and humid during the two northern rainy seasons, which in normal years last from April to June and October to November, and during the southern rainy season, which lasts from July to September. January to March is the best time to visit.

Habitats

The 3300-km-long coastline is mainly rocky but also has plenty of beaches. There are mountains inland from the northern coast, but the only two perennial rivers, the Shebelle and Juba, originate in the Ethiopian highlands and flow southeast through the southern half of the country. There is plenty of rather parched savanna, especially south of Mogadishu, but the land becomes increasingly arid to the north. Owing to the desert-like terrain, farmland is rare north of Mogadishu, and the people survive with herds of sheep and goats. South of the capital, there are corn fields and banana plantations on the fertile coastal plain, which stretches north from Kenya.

Conservation

In recent decades, increasing numbers of cattle have accelerated desertification in the north and degraded or totally destroyed large areas of savanna in the south. Together with hunting and poaching, cattle grazing has led to the localisation of many birds and large mammals. The unique gallery forest of the south, along the lower Juba river, has also been severely depleted, especially since the mid 1980s. With many other habitats being destroyed, the eight threatened and ten near-threatened species which occur in Somalia, are cause for particular concern.

Bird Families

Seven of the ten families endemic to the African mainland are represented in Somalia, and well represented families include bustards and larks.

Bird Species

A total of 649 species have been recorded in Somalia. Non-endemic specialities and spectacular species include Vulturine Guineafowl, Crab Plover, Madagascar Pratincole, Mangrove Kingfisher and Madagascar Bee-eater.

Endemics

Somalia boasts ten endemics, a generous helping for a mainland African country. These include a boubou, six larks and a linnet. There are also plenty of near-endemics, including Little Brown Bustard*, Fischer's Turaco*, Somali Bee-eater, Mombasa Woodpecker, Malindi Pipit* and Golden-winged Grosbeak.

MOGADISHU AREA

Over 370 species have been recorded within a 100 km radius of Somalia's capital, including three of the six endemic larks, Vulturine Guineafowl and Mangrove Kingfisher.

Endemics

Somali Long-billed Lark, Lesser Hoopoe-Lark, Obbia Lark*.

Specialities

Vulturine Guineafowl, Madagascar Pratincole, White-headed Mousebird, Mangrove Kingfisher, Somali Fiscal, Fischer's and Golden-breasted Starlings, White-breasted White-eye, Somali Crombec, Scaly Babbler, Golden Palm and Salvadori's Weavers, Fire-fronted Bishop, Kenya Violet-backed Sunbird.

Others

African Darter, Goliath Heron, Dwarf Bittern, Hamerkop, Hadada Ibis, African Openbill, Saddle-billed Stork, Bateleur, Gabar Goshawk, Martial Eagle, Pygmy Falcon, Crested Francolin, Harlequin Quail, Black Crake, Allen's Gallinule, Buff-crested and Hartlaub's Bustards, Crab Plover, Water and Spotted Thick-knees, Cream-coloured Courser, White-fronted Plover, Black-headed and Crowned Lapwings, Sooty Tern, Black-faced Sandgrouse, Orange-bellied Parrot, Blue-naped Mousebird, White-bellied Go-away-bird, Pied Cuckoo, Yellowbill, Little, Madagascar and Northern Carmine Bee-eaters, Lilac-breasted and Rufous-crowned Rollers, Abyssinian Scimitar-bill, Von der Decken's Hornbill, D'Arnaud's Barbet, Nubian Woodpecker, White-rumped Shrike, Slate-coloured Boubou, Superb Starling, Red-billed Oxpecker, Ethiopian Swallow, Sombre Greenbul, Northern Brownbul, Purple Grenadier, African Silverbill, Cut-throat, Steel-blue and Straw-tailed Whydahs, Golden Pipit, Black-headed, Chestnut and Grosbeak Weavers, Fan-tailed Widowbird, Purple-banded Sunbird, White-bellied Canary.

Other Wildlife

Speke's gazelle.

Access

Somali Long-billed Lark, Lesser Hoopoe-Lark and Obbia Lark*, as well as Cream-coloured Courser, White-headed Mousebird, and Somali Fiscal occur alongside the 38-km road northeast from Mogadishu to the **Maahay Peninsula**. Obbia Lark* also occurs in the grassy dunes alongside the 40-km coast road south from Mogadishu to **Dhanaane**. The beaches, lagoons, acacia scrub and farmland alongside this road also support Pygmy Falcon, Crab Plover, and Spotted Thick-knee, whilst

Sooty Tern may be seen offshore. To return to Mogadishu on an inland route, thus completing a circuit of 110 km, turn west 1.5 km south of Dhanaane and head for the Shalamboot–Afgooye road. Turn north on reaching this road and return to Mogadishu via the farm and bushland around **Afgooye**, which supports White-headed Mousebird. Alternatively, turn south on reaching the Shalamboot–Afgooye road. Five km north of Shalamboot turn west on to the track to Jannale. This track passes through marshes where Black Crake, Allen's Gallinule and Golden Palm Weaver occur. From Afgooye it is possible to reach Aw Dheegle, to the southwest, via both banks of the Shebelle river. Madagascar Pratincole, Slate-coloured Boubou, Golden Palm Weaver, Fire-fronted Bishop and Steel-blue Whydah have been recorded on this loop. It is also possible to reach Balcad to the north via both banks of the Shebelle river, and birding this loop may also be worthwhile.

Nearly 200 species have been recorded in **Balcad NR**, including Hartlaub's Bustard, Yellowbill, Von der Decken's Hornbill, Fischer's Starling, Northern Brownbul, Somali Crombec, Scaly Babbler and Salvadori's Weaver. This 190-ha reserve, which supports savanna and remnant gallery forest on the east bank of the Shebelle river, is managed by the Somali Ecological Society. Turn west 35 km north of Mogadishu, 2 km south of Balcad town. There is a Field Centre here, complete with a dormitory and cooking facilities, and camping is also allowed.

African Darter, Dwarf Bittern, Saddle-billed Stork, Madagascar Pratincole, Orange-bellied Parrot, Golden-breasted Starling and Ethiopian Swallow occur around the 108-sq-km **Xawadley Reservoir**, 38 km northeast of Balcad. The easiest way to reach the reservoir is to turn east opposite the Somaltex factory in Balcad. This road to the dam passes through farmland where Saddle-billed Stork and Pygmy Falcon occur. The tricky, but more interesting route, is to turn east 200 m south of the Balcad NR entrance. After 14.5 km turn north on to a track which passes through acacia scrub where Buff-crested Bustard and Kenya Violet-backed Sunbird occur. This track meets the road between Balcad and the reservoir after 11.5 km. Turn east here. At the reservoir it is normally possible to drive along the dam, which is an excellent vantage point.

The long sandy beaches to the south of **Baraawe**, 260 km southwest of Mogadishu, support Crab Plover and Sooty Gull, whilst White-cheeked Tern may be seen offshore. Vulturine Guineafowl and Somali Fiscal occur in the acacia scrub above Baraawe town. The rice-growing areas of Fanooue, 360 km southwest of Mogadishu, and Mogaambo, 410 km southwest of Mogadishu, near Kisimaayo, may be worth exploring. The Juba river forests (eg. **Barako** and **Shoonto FRs**, near Caanoole, north of Kisimaayo), used to support similar species to those found in the coastal forest of Kenya (p. 194), but these forests have been disappearing fast since the mid 1980s, and there may be none left by the time any birders ever get to visit Somalia.

In extreme north Somalia, the degraded juniper woodland in the **Daalo FR**, just west of Erigavo, supports the endemic Warsangli Linnet*, whilst the endemic Somali Pigeon* occurs on the sparsely wooded, stony coastal plains below Daalo FR.

ADDITIONAL INFORMATION

Books and Papers

Birds of Somalia: Their habitat, status and distribution (*Scopus* Special Supplement No 1). Ash, J and Miskell, J. 1983. EAOS.
Changes to the Somalia Check-list. Ash, J. 1993. *Scopus* 17:26–31.

Addresses

The Somali Ecological Society needs support and has some details on birding possibilities. Contact John Leefe OBE, The Spinney, Clipsham Road, Stretton, nr Oakham, Leics, LE15 7QS, UK, or Dr Talib Ali, FAO Rep. in Somalia, c/o FAO Rep. in Kenya, Box 30470, Nairobi, Kenya.

Please send records to Dr John Ash, Paysanne, Godshill Wood, Fordingbridge, Hants, UK.

ENDEMICS (10)

Archer's Buzzard	North: highlands
Somali Pigeon*	North: below Daalo FR
Bulo Burti Boubou*	Central: known from only one specimen, captured in the hospital grounds at Bulo Burti in 1989, and released nearby, in 1990
Somali Long-billed Lark	Southeast: near Mogadishu
Ash's Lark*	South: coastal plains north of Uarsciek
Somali Lark	North: grassy plains
Archer's Lark*	Northwest: west of Hargeysa. Not seen since 1955
Lesser Hoopoe-Lark	Southeast: near Mogadishu
Obbia Lark*	Southeast: near Mogadishu
Warsangli Linnet*	North: Daalo FR

Near-endemics (North)

Somali Starling, Sombre Chat*, Abyssinian and Blanford's Larks, Arabian Golden-Sparrow, Brown-rumped Seedeater, Golden-winged Grosbeak.

Near-endemics (General)

Chestnut-naped Francolin, Heuglin's and Little Brown* Bustards, White-winged Collared-Dove*, Somali Bee-eater, Black-billed Woodhoopoe, Red-naped Bushshrike, Somali Wheatear, Brown-tailed Apalis, Short-billed* and Somali Crombecs, Collared and Gillett's Larks, Somali and Swainson's Sparrows, Golden Palm and Salvadori's Weavers, Abyssinian Grosbeak-Canary.

Near-endemics (South)

White-headed Mousebird, Fischer's Turaco*, Mombasa Woodpecker, Yellow Flycatcher, Long-tailed Fiscal, Fischer's Starling, Pangani Longclaw, Malindi Pipit*, Donaldson-Smith's Sparrow-Weaver, Fire-fronted Bishop, Violet-breasted Sunbird.

SOUTH AFRICA (INCLUDING LESOTHO AND SWAZILAND)

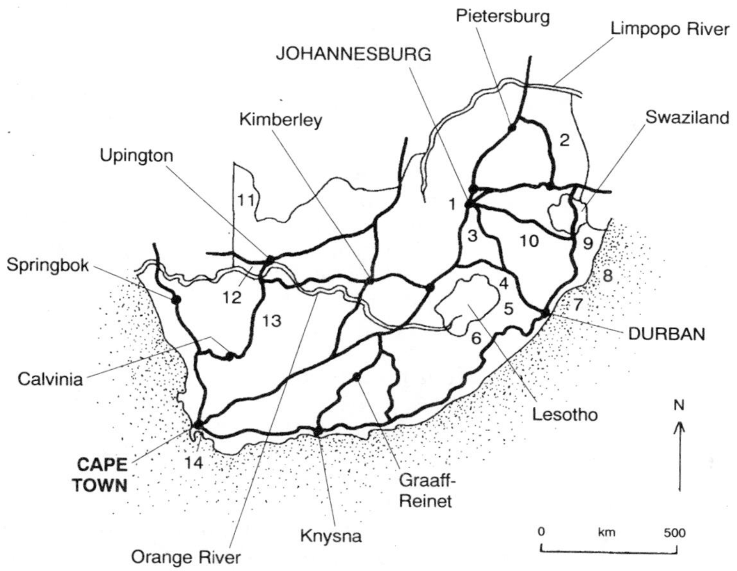

1	Johannesburg	8	St Lucia Lagoon
2	Kruger NP	9	Mkuzi Reserve
3	Suikerbosrand	10	Wakkerstroom
4	Giants Castle Reserve	11	Kalahari Gemsbok NP
5	Sani Pass	12	Upington to Augrabies Falls NP
6	Matatiele	13	Bushmanland
7	Mtunzini and Umlalazi NR	14	Cape Town

INTRODUCTION

Summary

The world rejoiced when apartheid ended in April 1994, and although many birders sampled the avian delights of South Africa before, it seems likely that even more will do so in the future. Although no where near as rich in terms of sheer variety as East Africa, the southern third of the continent boasts well over 100 endemics, and many of these can be seen in South Africa. As well as a superb selection of mammals, South Africa also boasts 34 endemic birds, the highest number for a mainland African country.

Size

At 1,184,827 sq km, South Africa is ten times larger than England, and twice the size of Texas, so distances are big. For example, it is 1600 km from Johannesburg in the north to Cape Town in the south.

Getting Around

The roads are excellent and even many of the tracks are well maintained, although some may be impassable during the wet season (Apr–Sep). Public transport seems to be limited to the major routes, and since it is not possible to bird on foot in most of the national parks, it makes sense to hire a vehicle in South Africa. There is a good internal air network.

Accommodation and Food

Most types of budget accommodation, including campsites, have excellent facilities, including special fireplaces and fuel: barbecues (braais) are very popular. There are also plenty of hotels and lodges, but it is wise to book these in advance, via the National Parks Board, during the school holidays, which fall in January, April, July, September and December.

Health and Safety

Immunisation against hepatitis, polio, typhoid and yellow fever is recommended, as are precautions against malaria.

Climate and Timing

The southern Cape enjoys a Mediterranean-like climate, with hot, somewhat humid summers (Oct–Mar), and cool, wet winters (Apr–Sep). The best time to visit South Africa is October, during the austral spring, when resident birds are breeding, intra-African migrants are returning south, and Proteas, the foodplant for some of the cape endemics, are still in bloom.

Habitats

The mountains of the Cape support Mediterranean-like maquis, known as fynbos. This remarkable habitat, which supports a number of endemic birds, has more plant species per square metre than any other habitat on earth. Offshore, the turbulence caused by the meeting of the Atlantic and Indian Oceans off the Cape of Good Hope attracts many seabirds. The semi-desert shrublands of the karoo lie north of the Cape, and south of the Orange river. This moon-like landscape with red sand dunes gives way to arid savanna to the north and moist savanna to the east. In the east, the misty Drakensburg Mountains, which run north to south parallel to the coast, support rolling, montane grassland and forest. Along the east coast there is a string of mangrove-lined estuaries and lagoons, as well as remnant pockets of lowland forest.

Conservation

The South African authorities are aware that ecotourism is a more effective way of generating sustainable economic growth than many other activities, some of which provide only short-term gain and harm the natural environment. However, indigenous people, such as the Zulus, are even more aware that much of their land was confiscated during the 1960s and 1970s for nature conservation and ecotourism. ANC policy is to compensate people who have lost land, to involve them in the future management of the national parks and nature reserves, and grant them their fair share of the benefits. Whilst this is a commendable aim, conflicts loom large since many areas are not government-owned and remain in private hands.

Future competition for space between people, birds and mammals is another huge hurdle the new government has to face. The solution put forward by the South African Wildlife Trust to make the animals pay for their conservation through what amounts to 'cattle ranching' leaves something to be desired.

Sixteen threatened and 30 near-threatened species occur in South Africa.

Bird Families

Eight of the ten families endemic to mainland Africa are represented in South Africa, including sugarbirds. Well represented families include raptors, francolins, bustards, larks and pipits.

Bird Species

Over 790 species have been recorded in South Africa, nearly 300 fewer than Kenya. Non-endemic specialities and spectacular species include a selection of seabirds, Cape Griffon*, Wattled Crane*, Lesser Jacana, Black-winged Lapwing, Mangrove Kingfisher, Cape Batis and Spotted Ground-Thrush*.

Endemics

Thirty-four species occur only in South Africa. They include Bald Ibis*, Black Bustard, Ground Woodpecker*, Cape* and Orange-breasted* Rock-jumpers, Bush Blackcap*, Rudd's*, Ferruginous, Botha's* and Large-billed Larks and Cape Sugarbird.

Species confined to southern Africa, which are more likely to be found in South Africa than Namibia, Botswana or Zimbabwe, include Jackass Penguin*, Black Harrier*, Jackal Buzzard, Karoo Bustard, Southern Tchagra, Southern Boubou, Zululand Batis, Rudd's Apalis and Swee Waxbill.

Expectations

It is possible to see 400 species during a three-week trip, if both the north and south are covered.

JOHANNESBURG NORTHEAST TO KRUGER NATIONAL PARK

JOHANNESBURG

The wetlands created as a result of gold mining in the vicinity of South Africa's biggest city support a few endemics and Blue Crane*.

South Africa Endemics

African Pied Starling, Cape Weaver, Greater Double-collared Sunbird.

Specialities

Jackal Buzzard, Blue Crane*, Fiscal Flycatcher, Fairy Warbler.

Others

Ostrich, Maccoa Duck, Cape Shoveler, Greater and Lesser* Flamingos, Hadada Ibis, Verreaux's Eagle, Black Crake, African Snipe, Three-banded Plover, Tinkling Cisticola, Lesser Swamp-Warbler, Zebra Waxbill, African Quailfinch, Red-headed Finch, Cape Wagtail, Cape Longclaw, Southern Masked-Weaver, Red Bishop, Long-tailed Widowbird.

Access

Verreaux's Eagle and Greater Double-collared Sunbird occur in the Witwatersrand National Botanical Garden just outside Johannesburg, in the Roodepoort district west of the city. Leeupan Rubbish Tip near Benoni, east of town, Leeupan Pan 5 km south of Benoni, and Rolfes Pan, off the R21 to Boksburg near Jan Smuts Airport, are also good birding sites. Blue Crane* and many other waterbirds occur at the small (95 ha) but excellent **Rondebult Bird Sanctuary**, where there are eight hides. The reserve is signposted from the N3 and lies just south of the R554 to Brakpan. Contact Witwatersrand Bird Club for more details. Another good site near Johannesburg is Suikerbosrand NR (p. 321).

Accommodation: Balalaika Hotel (A).

Between Johannesburg and Kruger NP, the wet grassland around **Dullstroom**, near Belfast on the N4, supports Bald Ibis*, the rare Striped and White-winged* Flufftails, Wattled* and Blue* Cranes, Grey Crowned-Crane and Stanley Bustard. Turn north at Belfast and bird the roads east and north of Dullstroom as far as Kruisfontein and the Steenkampsberg Pass. Bald Ibis* also occurs at the **Waterval-Boven** gorge. Approximately 4 km east of Waterval-Boven town, east of the tunnel, pull into the car park on the left for a view over the gorge. There is a trail to a waterfall from here, where you can gain better views of the gorge.

KRUGER NATIONAL PARK

This huge park is 350 km long, 60 km wide and nearly 2 million ha in extent. It is situated in far northeast South Africa in acacia savanna country. Nearly 500 species have been recorded including Cape Griffon*, although there are no South African endemics here and most of the birds are widespread in Africa. The huge numbers of mammals are Kruger's star attraction; as a result, this park is often overcrowded, especially in the south.

Apart from December and January, night-drives are not allowed, all visitors and their vehicles must be in camp before sunset, and no one must leave camp before sunrise. Birding on foot is permitted only within camp grounds and a few picnic areas. These are strict rules.

Specialities

Cape Griffon*, Magpie Shrike, Pale White-eye, Stierling's Wren-Warbler, Monotonous Lark, Pink-throated Twinspot, Swee Waxbill, Bush Pipit.

Others

Ostrich, African Darter, White-backed Duck, Goliath Heron, White-backed Night-Heron, Hamerkop, Woolly-necked and Saddle-billed Storks, African Cuckoo-Falcon, Bat Hawk, White-headed Vulture, Brown Snake-Eagle, Bateleur, Martial Eagle, Crowned Hawk-Eagle, Secretary-bird, Dickinson's Kestrel, Crested Guineafowl, Crested and Natal Francolins, Swainson's Spurfowl, African Finfoot, Kori and Red-crested Bustards, Water and Spotted Thick-knees, Temminck's Courser, Three-banded and Blacksmith Plovers, White-headed and Crowned Lapwings, Brown-headed Parrot, Red-faced Mousebird, Purple-crested Turaco, Grey Go-away-bird, African Scops-Owl, Pel's Fishing-Owl, Bat-like Spinetail Brown-hooded Kingfisher, White-fronted, Little and Southern Carmine Bee-eaters, Lilac-breasted Roller, Common Scimitar-bill, Southern Ground-Hornbill, Yellow-rumped Tinkerbird, Pied, Black-collared and Crested Barbets, African Crested-Flycatcher, White Helmetshrike, Kurrichane Thrush, Red-shouldered and Burchell's Glossy-Starlings, Red-billed Oxpecker, White-throated and Red-capped Robin-Chats, Red-backed Scrub-Robin, White-headed Black-Chat, Pearl-breasted Swallow, Terrestrial Brownbul, Yellow-streaked Bulbul, Tinkling and Piping Cisticolas, Greencap and Burnt-neck Eremomelas, Arrow-marked Babbler, Southern Black-Tit, Sabota Lark, Black-and-white Mannikin, Variable and Purple Indigobirds, Eastern Paradise-Whydah, Cape Wagtail, Yellow-throated Longclaw, Lesser Masked and Spectacled Weavers, White-breasted and Mariqua Sunbirds.

Other Wildlife

Black-backed jackal, buffalo, Burchell's zebra, cheetah, civet, eland, elephant, giraffe, hippo, hunting dog, impala, klipspringer, leopard, lion, nyala, roan, sable, spotted hyena, wildebeest.

Access

Kruger NP is accessible by air via the airfield at **Skukuza**. There is a 2000-km road and track network, some 20 camps and many dams. In the south, the best birding areas are **Skukuza Camp** and the **Lower Sabie** area (African Finfoot, White-headed Lapwing), east of Skukuza. White-backed Night-Heron and Pel's Fishing-Owl have been recorded alongside **Olifants Trail** near Letaba in the centre of the park. The northern end of the park, north of Letaba, is often drought-stricken and birdless, but Pafuri near the River Luvuvhu is a good site for White-headed Lapwing.

Accommodation: Some 20 camps include the conveniently situated Berg en Daal campsite (southern end), Lower Sabie (A) (south), Olifants (A) (centre), and Punda Maria (A) (north). Book through National Parks Board.

The localised and rare Short-clawed Lark* occurs near **Pietersburg**. From the N1 in town take the N71 signposted to Tzaneen and search the area of sparse acacias near the junction with the R37. The **Nyl Floodplain**, two hours drive north of Johannesburg, supports spectac-

KRUGER NP

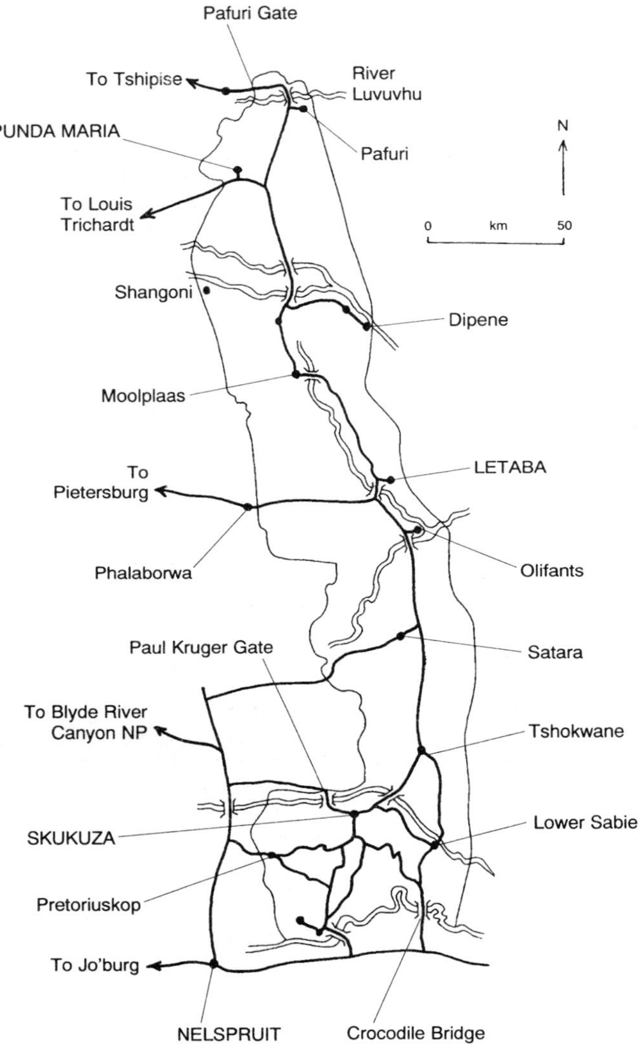

ular numbers of breeding waterbirds when flooded. These include White-backed Duck, African Pygmy-goose, Black and Rufous-bellied Herons, Dwarf Bittern, Red-chested Flufftail, Kaffir Rail, African Crake, Allen's Gallinule and Lesser Moorhen. Turn east off the N1 northeast of Pretoria, 11 km south of Naboomspruit. The Nylsvley entrance is on the left 8 km along here. Alternatively, turn east on to the R519, just south of Naboomspruit, towards Roedtan. The entrance to Mosdene Private NR is on the left 3 km along here.

JOHANNESBURG SOUTH TO DURBAN

SUIKERBOSRAND NATURE RESERVE

This reserve, 40 km south of Johannesburg, supports an excellent selection of grassland birds, including a few endemics.

South Africa Endemics

Ground Woodpecker*, Sentinel Rock-Thrush (Apr–Sep), African Pied Starling, Cape Weaver.

Specialities

Black Harrier*, Jackal Buzzard, Southern Boubou, Bokmakierie, Cape Rock-Thrush, Fiscal Flycatcher, Cape Robin-Chat, Pink-billed Lark.

Others

Orange River Francolin, African Pigeon, Red-faced Mousebird, Black-collared Barbet, Kalahari Scrub-Robin, Mountain Wheatear, Familiar Chat, Southern Anteater-Chat, South African Swallow, Black-fronted Bulbul, Ashy Tit, Long-billed and Spike-heeled Larks, Mossie, Cape Wagtail, Cape Longclaw, Yellow-crowned Bishop, Red-collared Widowbird, Red-headed Finch.

Other Wildlife

Eland, hartebeest, springbok, wildebeest.

Access

Head east out of Johannesburg on the M2, then south on the N3 towards Durban. After 37 km turn off in response to the 'Kliprivier' sign, and after a few km turn left in response to the reserve sign. Bird the 60-km circular drive. It is only possible to bird on foot at the Holhoek picnic site.

The **Giants Castle Reserve** is an excellent birding site near the N3 between Johannesburg and Durban. Forested valleys and grassland

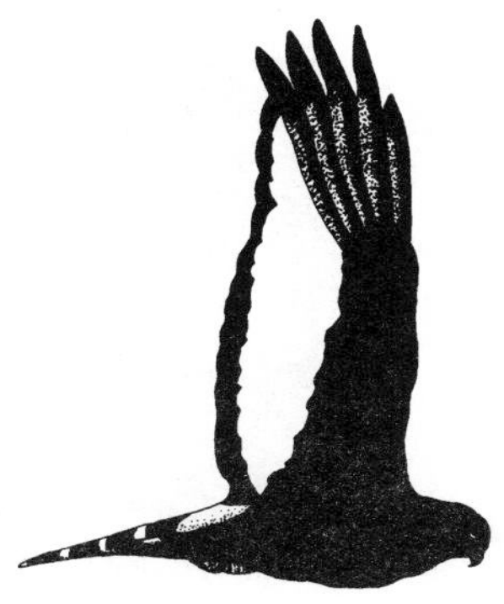

The impressive Black Harrier is one of a fine selection of raptors present in Giants Castle Reserve*

here support Lammergeier, Cape Griffon*, Black Harrier*, Jackal Buzzard, Horus Swift, Ground Woodpecker*, Southern Boubou, Cape Batis, Orange-breasted Rock-jumper*, Bush Blackcap*, Lazy Cisticola, Yellow-breasted Pipit*, Short-tailed Pipit (on grassy slopes to the left on approaching the gate), Gurney's Sugarbird, Greater Double-collared and Malachite Sunbirds and Drakensburg Siskin*. The reserve is 60 km from Eastcourt and/or Mooirivier and is well signposted.

Accommodation: Camp/campsite.

SANI PASS

The lakes, marshes, grassland, scrub and forest of the Drakensburg Mountains support a number of localised endemics, and the high Sani Pass (2800 m (9186 ft)) on the border between Natal and Lesotho, 125 km west of Pietermaritzburg, is one of the best sites to look for these scarce birds, especially Buff-streaked Chat*, Drakensburg Prinia and Forest Canary.

South Africa Endemics

Bald Ibis*, Grey-wing Francolin, Knysna Turaco, Ground Woodpecker*, Sentinel Rock-Thrush, Orange-breasted Rock-jumper*, Buff-streaked Chat*, Drakensburg Prinia, Bush Blackcap*, Yellow-breasted*, Yellow-tufted and Mountain* Pipits, Cape Weaver, Forest Canary, Drakensburg Siskin*.

Specialities

Cape Griffon*, Jackal Buzzard, Wattled* and Blue* Cranes, Black-winged Lapwing, Cape Batis, Cape Rock-Thrush, Sicklewing Chat, African Scrub-Warbler, Swee Waxbill, Gurney's Sugarbird.

Others

Hadada Ibis, Lammergeier, Rufous-chested Sparrowhawk, Swainson's Spurfowl, Grey Crowned-Crane, Stanley Bustard, Olive Woodpecker,

Buff-streaked Chat is one of a number of localised South African endemics occurring at Sani Pass*

Red-winged Starling, Chorister Robin-Chat, Lazy and Wailing Cisticolas, Bar-throated Apalis, Cape Longclaw, Fan-tailed, Red-collared and Long-tailed Widowbirds.

Other Wildlife

Blesbok, eland, mountain reedbuck, oribi, wildebeest.

Access

Bird all elevations alongside the road between Goodhope and Sani Pass, and beyond to the Kotisephola Pass in Lesotho, *en route* to Makhotlong.

Accommodation: Mooirivier, Nottingham Road.

DURBAN SOUTH TO MATATIELE

The Natal Bird Club, c/o SAOS, organise pelagic trips from **Durban**, which often produce some very exciting seabirds.

Knysna Turaco and Knysna Woodpecker* occur in the forested **Oribi Gorge NR**, near Port Shepstone, as well as Buff-spotted Flufftail, Narina Trogon, Half-collared Kingfisher, White-starred Robin, Brown Scrub-Robin and Cape Rock-Thrush. From Port Shepstone head west towards Harding, and follow the signposts after 20 km. Bird the camp gardens, the cliff viewpoint in front of the camp (Knysna Turaco), and the road down into the gorge where dry forest supports Knysna Woodpecker*.

Accommodation: Camp, bookable through the Natal Parks Board.

Naude's Nek Pass, near the town of **Matatiele** inland from Port Shepstone near the Lesotho border, is an excellent site for Jackal Buzzard, Grey-winged Francolin, Ground Woodpecker*, Sentinel Rock-Thrush, Orange-breasted Rock-jumper*, Sicklewing Chat, Mountain Pipit*, Malachite Sunbird and Drakensburg Siskin*. Out of Matatiele the road to Mount Fletcher becomes a rough track. Just after Mount Fletcher turn right and continue through Lower Pitseng up to Naude's Nek Pass to bird the boulder slopes and grassland. Blue Crane*, Rudd's Lark* and Gurney's Sugarbird also occur in the Matatiele area.

DURBAN NORTH TO WAKKERSTROOM

MTUNZINI and UMLALAZI NATURE RESERVE

The village of Mtunzini, 140 km north of Durban, lies near the mangrove-lined Umlalazi estuary and an excellent remnant dune forest, where Mangrove Kingfisher and Spotted Ground-Thrush* occur.

Specialities

Mangrove Kingfisher (Apr–Sep), Southern Boubou, Spotted Ground-Thrush* (Apr–Sep), Pale White-eye.

Others

Goliath Heron, Woolly-necked Stork, Palm-nut Vulture, Crowned Hawk-Eagle, African Finfoot, Purple-crested Turaco, Yellowbill, Pel's Fishing-Owl, Narina Trogon, Trumpeter Hornbill, White-eared Barbet, African Crested-Flycatcher, Black-bellied Glossy-Starling, Red-capped Robin-Chat, Yellow-bellied Greenbul, Cape Wagtail, Green-backed Twinspot, Black-tailed Waxbill, Mouse-coloured Sunbird.

Access

Mtunzini and the adjacent **Umlalazi NR** are 5 km east of the N2, 40 km south of Richards Bay. The best birding areas are the area around the car park at the Umlalazi river estuary, the Mangrove Trail (African Finfoot and Mangrove Kingfisher), the Siyayi Dune Forest Trail (Spotted Ground-Thrush*), and the footbridge over the Siyayi river (African Finfoot).

Accommodation: Hotel, cottages, bungalows, huts, campsite.

The 2380-ha **Ngoye Forest**, near Eshowe north of Durban, is usually accessible only with a permit (contact the Natal Bird Club for details) and a 4WD. Delegorgue's Pigeon, Black Cuckoo, Narina Trogon, Dwarf Kingfisher, Green Barbet, Spotted Ground-Thrush* and Brown Scrub-Robin occur here. Turn west off the N2, 12 km north of Mtunzini, then turn right after 4.6 km, turn right again after a further 5 km, and then left after another 1km (the forest is 11 km from the N2).

SAINT LUCIA LAGOON

This huge (325 sq km), shallow coastal lagoon supports important breeding concentrations of waterbirds, notably pelicans, flamingos and Caspian Terns. The surrounding dense coastal forest is equally important as it supports such scarce and localised birds as Zululand Batis.

South Africa Endemics

Knysna Turaco.

Specialities

Red-chested Flufftail, Lesser Jacana, Mangrove Kingfisher (Apr–Sep), Zululand Batis, Spotted Ground-Thrush* (Apr–Sep), Brown Scrub-Robin, Rudd's Apalis, Short-tailed Pipit, Neergaard's Sunbird*, Lemon-breasted Seedeater.

Others

White-backed Duck, African Pygmy-goose, Woolly-necked and Saddle-billed Storks, African Cuckoo-Falcon, Bat Hawk, Fasciated Snake-Eagle*, Black Crake, Water Thick-knee, African Pigeon, Lemon and Tambourine Doves, Livingstone's Turaco, Yellowbill, African Wood-Owl, Swamp Nightjar, Brown-hooded Kingfisher, Crowned Hornbill, White-eared Barbet, Yellow-rumped Tinkerbird, African Broadbill, African Crested-Flycatcher, Olive and Four-coloured Bushshrikes, Black-bellied Glossy-Starling, Bearded Scrub-Robin, Red-capped Robin-Chat, Black Sawwing, Sombre Greenbul, Terrestrial Brownbul, Croaking Cisticola, Green-backed Twinspot, Black-and-white Mannikin, Rosy-throated Longclaw, Forest Weaver, Grosbeak Weaver, Mouse-coloured Sunbird.

Other Wildlife

Hippo, Nile crocodile.

Access

To bird the east side of the lagoon, where Zululand Batis occurs, turn east off the N2 to Mtubatuba and St Lucia village. The batis occurs around the campsite at Cape Vidal, 30 km north of St Lucia. To bird the west side of the lagoon turn east off the N2, 25 km north of the Mtubatuba turning. There are two trails worth birding at Charter's Creek, 13 km east of the N2: the 5-km Umkhumbe Trail and the 7-km Isikhova Trail.

Accommodation: Mtubatuba: Sundowner Hotel (A). Charter's Creek: Cabins (B), bookable throught the Natal Parks Board.

MKUZI RESERVE

Over 400 species have been recorded in Mkuzi Reserve's wide range of habitats, which include acacia savanna, gallery forest dominated by fig trees, and pans. Notable species usually present include Rudd's Apalis and Pink-throated Twinspot.

Specialities

Lesser Jacana, Red-fronted Tinkerbird, Southern Tchagra, Southern Boubou, Rudd's Apalis, Stierling's Wren-Warbler, Bush Pipit, Pink-throated Twinspot, Neergaard's Sunbird*.

Others

African Darter, African Pygmy-goose, Cape Shoveler, Hamerkop, African Cuckoo-Falcon, Fasciated Snake-Eagle*, Bateleur, Ovampo Sparrowhawk, Secretary-bird, Crested Guineafowl, Crested Francolin, Black-rumped Buttonquail, Three-banded and Blacksmith Plovers, Red-faced Mousebird, Purple-crested Turaco, Grey Go-away-bird, Klaas' Cuckoo, Yellowbill, Pel's Fishing-Owl, African Wood Owl, Fiery-necked Nightjar, Narina Trogon, Brown-hooded Kingfisher, White-fronted and Little Bee-eaters, Lilac-breasted Roller, Common Scimitar-bill, Trumpeter Hornbill, Yellow-rumped Tinkerbird, Black-collared Barbet, Scaly-throated Honeyguide, Golden-tailed Woodpecker, African Broadbill, African Crested-Flycatcher, Grey Cuckoo-shrike, Four-coloured Bushshrike, Black-bellied Glossy-Starling, Chorister Robin-Chat, Red-backed Scrub-Robin, Yellow-bellied Greenbul, Terrestrial Brownbul, Red-faced, Croaking and Piping Cisticolas, Greencap and Burnt-neck Eremomelas, Southern Black-Tit, Sabota Lark, Black-tailed Waxbill, Eastern Paradise-Whydah, Cape Wagtail, Lesser Masked Weaver, African Golden-Weaver, White-breasted and Purple-banded Sunbirds.

Other Wildlife

Black rhino, Burchell's zebra, giraffe, greater kudu, hippo, impala, leopard, nyala, reedbuck, steenbok, white rhino, wildebeest.

Access

This reserve is signposted from Mkuzi, just off the N2, 32 km north of Hluhluwe. Ensumo Pan, when wet, is excellent and is viewable from two hides. Pel's Fishing-Owl occurs in the riverine forest below Emantuma Camp on the Mkuzi river and in the forest near Ensumo Pan. Rudd's Apalis, Pink-throated Twinspot and Neergaard's Sunbird* occur in the sand forest around Kumasinga Hide, and African Broadbill occurs in the sand forest around Kubube Hide. Both of these hides overlook small pans. African Crested-Flycatcher occurs along the excellent 3-km-long Fig Forest Trail. Guided walks to restricted areas and night-drives can be arranged.

Accommodation: Cottages (A), bungalows (A), huts (B), campsite, bookable through Natal Parks Board. Mkuzi town: Ghost Mountain Inn.

Many of the birds listed for Mkuzi also occur in **Ndumu Reserve**, much further north near the Mozambique border. It is crucial to book a visit to this reserve in advance, through the KwaZulu Bureau of Natural Resources (tel: 0331 94-6698). The reserve is signposted from Ndumu, on the Jozini–Kwangwanase road. Pel's Fishing-Owl and Black-and-white Shrike-flycatcher occur in the gallery forest, whilst sand forest near the River Pongolo at the eastern end of the park supports Rudd's Apalis and Neergaard's Sunbird*.

MKUZI RESERVE

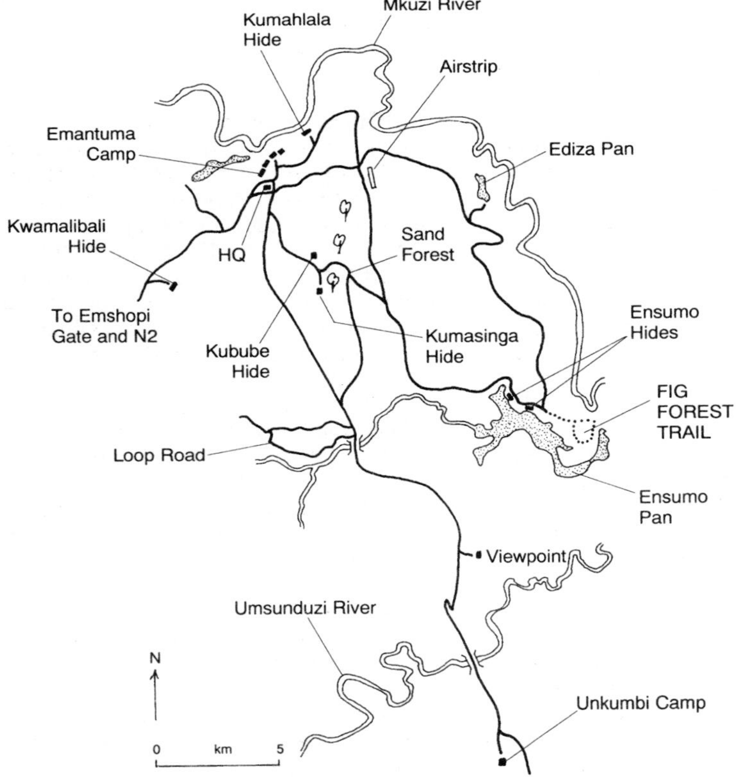

Rudd's Apalis, a bird which occurs only in northeast South Africa and south Mozambique, is regularly seen at Mkuzi

WAKKERSTROOM

The montane grassland around Wakkerstroom, in the northern Drakensburg Mountains, supports a number of rare and localised endemics, not least Blue Bustard* and Botha's Lark*, as well as Wattled* and Blue* Cranes and African Grass-Owl.

South Africa Endemics

Bald Ibis*, Grey-winged Francolin, Blue Bustard*, Ground Woodpecker*, Sentinel Rock-Thrush, Buff-streaked Chat*, Bush Blackcap*, Rudd's* and Botha's* Larks, Yellow-breasted* and Yellow-tufted Pipits.

Specialities

Black Harrier*, Red-chested and White-winged* Flufftails, Wattled* and Blue* Cranes, Black-winged Lapwing, African Grass-Owl, Cloud Cisticola, Latakoo and Pink-billed Larks, Short-tailed Pipit.

Others

Maccoa Duck, Secretary-bird, Kaffir Rail, Grey Crowned-Crane, Stanley Bustard, African Snipe, Marsh Owl, Purple-crested Turaco, Olive Bushshrike, Chorister Robin-Chat, Mountain Wheatear, Southern Anteater-Chat, South African Swallow, Wing-snapping Cisticola, African Yellow Warbler, Long-billed and Spike-heeled Larks, African Quailfinch, Cape Longclaw, Long-tailed Widowbird, Cape Bunting.

Access

Turn south off the N2 at Piet Retief on to the R543, and, once at Wakkerstroom bird the circular drives around the town. Rudd's Lark* prefers short grass at the water's edge, and Botha's Lark* prefers short grass on the upper stony slopes. Bald Ibis* roost in the willows at the 650-ha Wakkerstroom Natural Heritage Association (WNHA) Reserve, just outside town.

Accommodation: Weaver's Nest Lodge (run by birders for birders), campsite (adjacent to Martins Dam).

Blue Bustard*, African Grass-Owl, and Rudd's* and Botha's* Larks also occur around **Amersfoort**, north of Wakkerstroom.

JOHANNESBURG SOUTHWEST TO CAPE TOWN

The remote **Kalahari Gemsbok NP**, between the borders of Namibia and Botswana, lies at the southern edge of the Kalahari Desert. Here, the red dunes, grassy plains and wooded riversides support a handful of southern African specialities, including Ludwig's, Red-crested and White-quilled Bustards, Kalahari Scrub-Robin, Southern Pied-Babbler, lots of larks such as Monotonous, Clapper, Pink-billed and Sclater's*, and a fine selection of mammals, including cheetah, lion and oryx. This national park is 320 km north of Upington.

Accommodation: Lodge.

UPINGTON TO AUGRABIES FALLS NATIONAL PARK

The narrow strip of pools, gallery forest and cultivation alongside the Orange river, which runs through an otherwise arid landscape of semi-desert karoo scrub, support a fine selection of southern African specialities, including White-breasted Prinia.

Specialities

Ludwig's Bustard, Rosy-faced Lovebird, Bradfield's Swift, Karoo Scrub-Robin, Red-headed Cisticola, White-breasted Prinia, Rufous-eared, Kopje, Fairy and Layard's Warblers.

Others

African Darter, South African Shelduck, African Black Duck, Hamerkop, Pale Chanting-Goshawk, Verreaux's Eagle, Greater Kestrel, Kori Bustard, Double-banded Sandgrouse, White-backed and Red-faced Mousebirds, African Swift, Swallow-tailed Bee-eater, Pied Barbet, Pririt Batis, Pale-winged Starling, Familiar Chat, Mariqua Flycatcher, White-throated Swallow, Black-chested Prinia, Rufous-vented Warbler, Southern Penduline-Tit, Rufous Sparrow, Cape Wagtail, Red Bishop, Dusky Sunbird, White-throated Canary.

Other Wildlife

Black rhino, chacma baboon, greater kudu, springbok, steenbok.

Access

Augrabies Falls NP is 39 km northwest of Kakamas. Turn north 8 km west of Kakamas off the road to Pofadder. There is a small road network and hiking trails with overnight huts.

Accommodation: Augrabies Falls NP: Lodge (A)/campsite, bookable through the National Parks Board.

BUSHMANLAND

'Larksville' would be an apt alternative name for this huge area of flat-topped mountains, scree, boulders, gravel plains, red sand dunes and wooded wadis. At least twelve species of lark occur here, including the rare Ferruginous Lark*, as well as other South African endemics such as Black Bustard. Breeding European Bee-eaters make a mockery of this species' name and lend weight to the arguments of those of us who think the old Russian name of 'Golden Bee-eater' would be much more appropriate.

Bushmanland is best in the austral spring (Sept–Dec) when, in good years, a mass of flowers create a splendid place in which to go birding.

South Africa Endemics

Black Bustard, Ground Woodpecker*, Ferruginous* and Large-billed Larks, Black-headed Canary.

Specialities

Ludwig's and Karoo Bustards, Short-toed Rock-Thrush, Karoo Scrub-Robin, Karoo and Tractrac Chats, White-breasted Prinia, Rufous-eared, Kopje and Fairy Warblers, Yellow-rumped Eremomela, Grey Tit, Karoo Lark, Black-eared Sparrow-Lark, Pink-billed, Sclater's* and Stark's Larks, Social Weaver.

Others

Pale Chanting-Goshawk, Pygmy Falcon, Greater Kestrel, Cream-coloured Courser, Namaqua Sandgrouse, Cape Eagle-Owl, Rufous-cheeked Nightjar, European Bee-eater (Sep–Nov), Pied Barbet, Chat Flycatcher, Mountain Wheatear, Southern Anteater-Chat, South African Swallow, Yellow-bellied Eremomela, Clapper, Long-billed and Spike-heeled Larks, Chestnut-backed and Grey-backed Sparrow-Larks, Mossie, Scaly Weaver, Dusky Sunbird, White-throated Canary, Lark-like Bunting.

Other Wildlife

Aardwolf, bat-eared fox, zorilla.

The intricate markings of the Scaly Weaver provide a nice distraction whilst looking for the more sombre larks in Bushmanland

Access

The whole area encircled by the roads between Calvinia, Springbok, Pofadder, and Kenhardt is worth exploring. Previously productive spots include the area around Pofadder, Goegap Provincial NR, 12 km south-east of Springbok off the R355 to Gamoep, and the area around **Brandvlei**, where there are also a few pans, on the Calvinia–Kenhardt road. Much of the area is private land so it is wise to stick to the roads and tracks. Kenhardt, Brandvlei and Vanwyksvlei are all approximately 140 km from each other.

Accommodation: Calvinia, Pofadder, Kenhardt, Brandvlei, Vanwyksvlei.

Black Harrier*, Grey-winged and Cape Francolins, Karoo Bustard, Rufous-cheeked Nightjar, Horus Swift, Sicklewing and Karoo Chats, Karoo and White-breasted Prinias, Rufous-eared and Kopje Warblers, Victorin's Scrub-Warbler, Fairy Warbler, Yellow-rumped Eremomela, Karoo Lark, Cape Siskin*, Black-headed Canary and Cape Bunting occur alongside the **Calvinia–Ceres Road**, south of Calvinia.

The seabird colony on the edge of **Lambert's Bay** (Map p. 332) fishing village, 65 km west of Clanwilliam, contains a few Jackass Penguins* and thousands of Cape Gannets*, whilst Crowned*, Bank* and Cape Cormorants and Hartlaub's Gull also occur here. In Lambert's Bay follow signs for the Marine Hotel, park and walk down through the fish factory to a breakwater, which leads to the island where the seabird colony is located. Ground Woodpecker* and Layard's Warbler occur at the **Heerenlogment Caves**, a popular tourist site near Lambert's Bay. Karoo Lark occurs in the semi-desert surrounding **Elands Bay**, to the south via Leipoldtville. Other good birding spots in the vicinity of Clanwilliam (approximately 235 km north of Cape Town) include

BUSHMANLAND

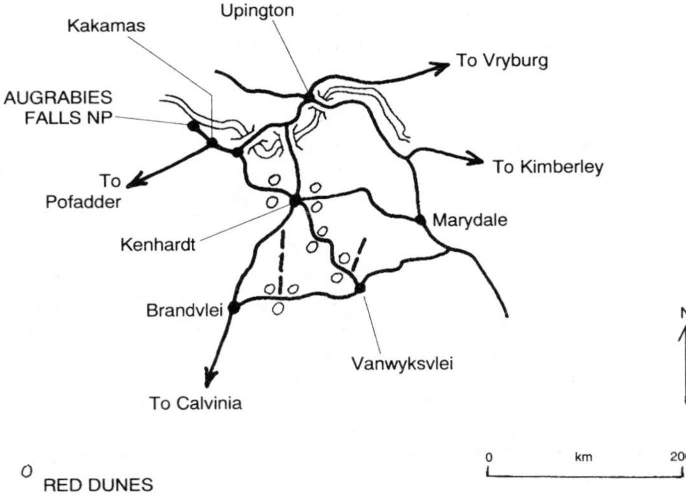

Kransvlei Poort is a narrow canyon 10 km southeast of Clanwilliam (via the N7), where Cape Francolin, Cape Batis, Cape Sugarbird, Cape Canary, White-winged Seedeater* and Cape Siskin* occur.

Accommodation: Clanwilliam Dam Resort (A), bookable through The Town Clerk, Private Bag X2, Clanwilliam 8135, Cape Province (tel: 02682-215).

One hundred and ten km north of Cape Town, the coastal islands, lagoons and saltmarshes around **Langebaan** (Map p. 332) support Jackass Penguin*, Cape Gannet*, Crowned*, Bank* and Cape Cormorants, Black Harrier*, African Oystercatcher*, Chestnut-banded Plover, Marsh Owl, African Bush-Warbler and Cape Weaver. The best birding areas are around Saldanha Bay and alongside the road south of Langebaan.

Accommodation: Langebaan Lodge, bookable through the National Parks Board.

CAPE TOWN

Landbirds are few and far between at the southern tip of the African continent, but most of those present are endemic. They include the superb Cape Rock-jumper*, Knysna Scrub-Warbler, Cape Sugarbird and Orange-breasted Sunbird. The seabirds are equally exciting.

South Africa Endemics

Hottentot Buttonquail, Ground Woodpecker*, Sentinel Rock-Thrush, Cape Rock-jumper*, Cape Bulbul, Knysna and Victorin's Scrub-Warblers, Cape Weaver, Cape Sugarbird, Orange-breasted Sunbird, White-winged Seedeater*, Cape Siskin*.

Specialities

African Oystercatcher*, Cape Francolin, Southern Boubou, Bokmakierie, Cape Batis, Fiscal Flycatcher, Red-headed Cisticola, Karoo Prinia, Cape Canary.

Others

Black-browed and Shy Albatrosses, White-chinned Petrel, Cape Shoveler, Black Crake, Greater Painted-snipe, Antarctic Tern, Pied Barbet, Cape Robin-Chat, Cape Grassbird, Yellow Bishop.

Access

There are a number of excellent birding areas in and around Cape Town. They include: (1) The **Harold Porter Botanical Gardens**, where Southern Boubou, Victorin's Scrub-Warbler, Cape Sugarbird, Orange-breasted Sunbird, Cape Canary and Cape Siskin* occur. (2) The **Kirstenbosch Botanical Gardens** near the base of Table Mountain, 13 km from the city centre. This is probably the best site for Knysna Scrub-Warbler, and good for Bokmakierie, Cape Batis, Cape Grassbird, Cape Sugarbird and Orange-breasted Sunbird. The best time to visit Cape Town's botanical gardens is from August to October, when the Proteas are in bloom. (3) The **Rondevlei NR** (open 08.00–17.00 daily), 25 km south of town, which is a good site for Cape Shoveler and Greater Painted-snipe. Head east on the N2, south on the M5 and southeast on Victoria Road. There is a trail here with hides and towers. (4) The **Cape of Good Hope NR**, 40 km south of town, where fynbos supports similar birds to Helderberg NR (see opposite), as well as Hottentot Buttonquail, Ground Woodpecker*, Sentinel Rock-Thrush, and Red-headed Cisticola. This is also a good site for African Oystercatcher*, and seawatching has produced Light-mantled Albatross in favourable weather conditions. (5) If desperate, the **Moville Point Sewage Outfall** is a good place for Jackass Penguin* and Sabine's Gull (Nov–Mar).

CAPE TOWN AREA

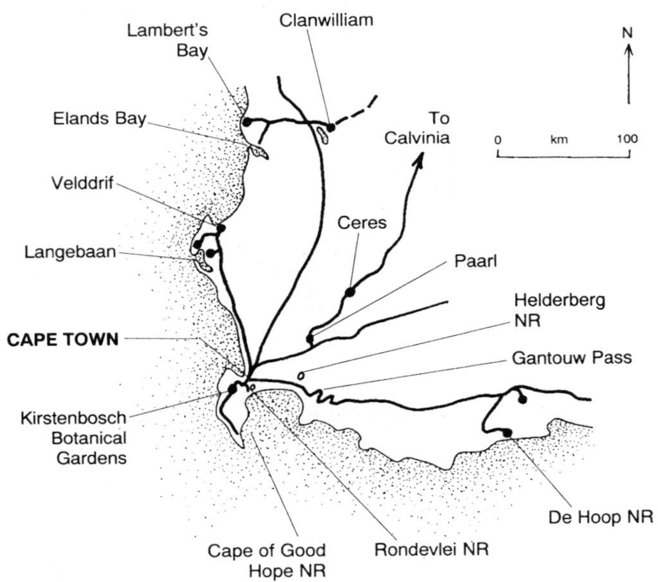

Pelagic trips off Cape Town are one of South Africa's ornithological highlights. Deep-sea tuna-fishing and sport-fishing boats can be hired to visit the trawling grounds, 40–60 km west of Cape Town, which are usually packed with seabirds. Hout Bay, 20 km south of Cape Town is the best place to ask, and the austral winter (Apr–Sep) is the best time to go. Better still, contact the Cape Bird Club, Box 5033, Cape Town 8000 for details of their organised charters. Situated in the cold Benguela Current, the trawlers act as a magnet for masses of seabirds, especially albatrosses, and species present include Jackass Penguin*, Wandering*, Shy, Grey-headed* and Yellow-nosed Albatrosses, Antarctic and Hall's* Giant Petrels, Southern Fulmar, Cape, Great-winged and Soft-plumaged Petrels, Broad-billed Prion, White-chinned Petrel, Black-bellied Storm-Petrel, Cape Gannet*, Sabine's Gull, Southern Skua, and various rarities. From the mainland the **Cape of**

Good Hope, 50 km south of Cape Town, is the best seawatching point, especially in strong northwesterlies and southwesterlies. Take the track to the right on the 'saddle' above the car park.

Cape Rock-jumper*, Fiscal Flycatcher, Victorin's Scrub-Warbler, Cape Weaver, Cape Sugarbird, Orange-breasted Sunbird, White-winged Seedeater* and Cape Siskin* occur in **Helderberg NR** east of Cape Town. Head east on the N2 and take the first exit to Somerset West town. In town turn left and follow the reserve signs. Bird the botanical gardens and trails up from there. Ground Woodpecker*, Cape Rock-jumper*, Victorin's Scrub-Warbler, and Cape Siskin* occur at **Gantouw Pass**, where the N2 crosses the mountains east of Cape Town. One km beyond the pass park at the gate on the north side of the road, opposite the track south to Steenbras Dam, and walk through the pine and eucalypt plantation. Then take the track left, cross the railway line and turn right. After the power lines turn left and follow the track to a T-junction. Continue straight on the small path (with the power lines still on the left) to the pass where Cape Rock-jumper* occurs.

The superb Cape Rock-jumper is one of the specialities of the Cape Town area*

The 18,000 ha of fynbos, brackish lagoons and coastline in **De Hoop NR** support Black Harrier*, Jackal Buzzard, Grey-winged and Cape Francolins, the endemic Hottentot Buttonquail, Blue Crane*, Damara Tern*, Knysna Woodpecker, and Southern Tchagra. Turn south 2 km west of Wydgelee (38 km northeast of Bredasdorp) on to the road which runs through the reserve to the coast, where southern right whale can be seen offshore from Koppie Alleen, a good site for African Oystercatcher*.

Much further east along the N2, the estuary, fynbos and temperate forest around the small town of **Knysna** support Knysna Woodpecker*, Knysna and Victorin's Scrub-Warblers, Cape Sugarbird and Forest Canary. The best site is probably **Goukamma NR**, reached by turning south off the N2, 12 km west of Knysna, on to the Buffels Bay road. The reserve entrance is on the right 6 km along here. Turn right beyond the entrance, through the picnic area to a gate. The track from here leads to a swing-bridge across the river to forest on the far side. Bird the trail to the right.

ADDITIONAL INFORMATION

Books and Papers

Illustrated Guide to the Birds of Southern Africa. Sinclair, I *et al.* 1993. New Holland.
Top Birding Spots in Southern Africa. Chittenden, H. 1992. Southern.
Mammals of Southern Africa. Cillie, B. 1989. Frandsen.

Addresses

The Southern African Ornithological Society (SAOS), Box 84394 Greenside, Johannesburg 2034, publishes a quarterly journal, *Ostrich*, and magazine, *Birding in Southern Africa*.

There are a number of other regional and local clubs and societies, which can be contacted via the SAOS.

All unusual records should be sent to The Chairman, Southern African Rarities Committee, SAOS.

Witwatersrand Bird Club, Box 72091 Parkview, Johannesburg 2122.

The Natal Bird Club, PO Box 1218, Durban 4000, assists African Bird Club members with enquiries regarding potential trips to South Africa.

National Parks Board, PO Box 787, Pretoria 0001, Transvaal (tel: 012-343-1991).

Natal Parks Board, PO Box 662, Pietermaritzburg 3200, Natal (tel: 0331-47-1981).

ENDEMICS (34)

Bald Ibis*	Northeast/east: widespread
Grey-winged Francolin	Widespread
Hottentot Buttonquail	South: De Hoop NR, Cape of Good Hope NR
Black Bustard	Southwest: Bushmanland
Blue Bustard*	Northeast: Wakkerstroom, Amersfoort
Knysna Turaco	Northeast/east: widespread
Knysna Woodpecker*	East/south: Oribi Gorge, De Hoop NR, Knysna
Ground Woodpecker*	Widespread
Sentinel Rock-Thrush	Widespread
Cape Rock-jumper*	South: Helderberg NR, Gantouw Pass
Orange-breasted Rock-jumper*	East: Sani Pass, Giant's Castle Reserve, Matatiele
African Pied Starling	North: Johannesburg, Suikerbosrand
Buff-streaked Chat*	Northeast/east: Sani Pass, Wakkerstroom
Drakensburg Prinia	East: Sani Pass
Knysna Scrub-Warbler	South: Cape Town, Knysna
Victorin's Scrub-Warbler	South: Calvinia–Ceres road, Cape Town, Knysna
Cape Bulbul	South: widespread
Bush Blackcap*	Northeast/east: Sani Pass, Giant's Castle Reserve, Wakkerstroom
Ferruginous Lark*	Southwest: Bushmanland

Rudd's Lark*	Northeast/east: Matatiele, Wakkerstroom, Amersfoort
Botha's Lark*	Northeast: Wakkerstroom, Amersfoort
Large-billed Lark	Southwest: Bushmanland
Yellow-breasted Pipit*	Northeast/east: Sani Pass, Giant's Castle, Wakkerstroom
Yellow-tufted Pipit	Northeast/east: Sani Pass, Wakkerstroom
Mountain Pipit*	East: Sani Pass, Matatiele
Cape Weaver	Widespread
Cape Sugarbird	South: Kransvlei Poort, Cape Town, Knysna
Orange-breasted Sunbird	South: Cape Town
Greater Double-collared Sunbird	North/east: Johannesburg, Giant's Castle Reserve
Forest Canary	East/south: Sani Pass, Knysna
Black-headed Canary	Southwest: Bushmanland, Calvinia–Ceres road
White-winged Seedeater*	South: Kransvlei Poort, Helderberg NR
Cape Siskin*	South: widespread
Drakensburg Siskin*	East: Sani Pass, Giant's Castle Reserve, Matatiele

Near-endemics (Southwest)

Jackass Penguin*, Crowned*, Bank* and Cape Cormorants, South African Shelduck, Black Harrier*, Cape Francolin, Blue Crane*, Ludwig's and Karoo Bustards, African Oystercatcher*, Hartlaub's Gull, Rosy-faced Lovebird, Bradfield's Swift, Southern Tchagra, Southern Boubou, Short-toed Rock-Thrush, Karoo Scrub-Robin, Sicklewing, Karoo and Tractrac Chats, Karoo Scrub-Robin, Red-headed Cisticola, Karoo and White-breasted Prinias, Rufous-eared, Kopje and Fairy Warblers, Yellow-rumped Eremomela, Layard's Warbler, Grey Tit, Monotonous, Bradfield's and Karoo Larks, Black-eared Sparrow-Lark, Pink-billed, Sclater's* and Stark's Larks, Social Weaver, Southern Double-collared Sunbird, Damara Canary.

Near-endemics (North/Central)

Transvaal Rock-Thrush, Latakoo and Short-clawed* Larks.

Near-endemics (East/Northeast)

Zululand Batis, Brown Scrub-Robin, Rudd's Apalis, African Scrub-Warbler, Pink-throated Twinspot, Swee Waxbill, Gurney's Sugarbird, Neergaard's Sunbird*, Lemon-breasted Seedeater.

Near-endemics (Throughout)

Jackal Buzzard, Bokmakierie, Cape Rock-Thrush, Fiscal Flycatcher, Pale White-eye, Cape Canary.

SUDAN

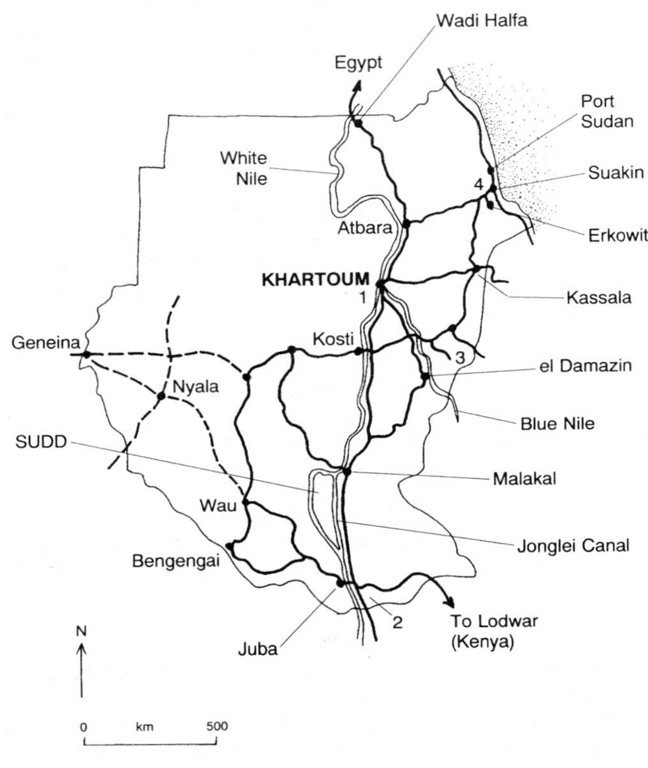

1 Khartoum
2 Immatong Mountains
3 Dinder NP
4 Port Sudan and Suakin

INTRODUCTION

Summary

Sudan's continuing civil war has seriously affected access to the country's most interesting birding areas, including the Sudd and its Shoebills*. However, Khartoum, where Egyptian Plovers are still quite common, would make an interesting stopover *en route* to the more popular countries further south.

Size

At 2,505,813 sq km, Sudan is Africa's largest country. It is twenty times the size of England, and nearly four times the size of Texas.

Getting Around

Sudan is a very difficult country to get around. Roads are few and far between, but the main routes, such as Khartoum–Kassala–Port Sudan and Khartoum–Kosti, are served by public transport including a slow train network which also reaches Wadi Halfa on the Egyptian border.

Travel permits (available in major towns) are needed to visit anywhere in Sudan. Up to 1994 at least, permits were still not being issued to travel to the Sudd, owing to the presence of the Sudanese People's Liberation Movement (SPLM). Occasional flights do go to Juba, at the south end of the Sudd, despite the fact that at least one plane has been shot down by the SPLM.

Accommodation and Food

There are hotels in Khartoum and Kassala, but these are often full. Away from the main towns there is little accommodation to choose from. Bean stew is the staple diet, although fish is available along the White and Blue Nile rivers. Alcohol is illegal, so there is little chance of a cold beer at the end of a day's birding in Sudan.

Health and Safety

Immunisation against hepatitis, meningitis, polio, typhoid and yellow fever is recommended, as are precautions against malaria.

The Sudanese are exceptionally friendly.

Climate and Timing

For the most part, Sudan is an unrelentingly hot, dry and dusty country. If it rains at all it usually does so in the far south between June and September.

Habitats

North Sudan lies in the Nubian region, at the southeastern corner of the Sahara. South of Khartoum, which lies at the relatively fertile confluence of the White and Blue Nile rivers, the desert gives way to semi-desert, sparsely vegetated savanna, the vast swamps of the Sudd and, in the extreme south, the forested Immatong Mountains.

Conservation

There are thirteen national parks and reserves in Sudan, but only one, Dinder NP, merits anything like 'protected' status.

Nine threatened and eight near-threatened species occur in Sudan.

Bird Families

Eight of the ten families endemic to the African mainland are represented in Sudan, including Shoebill*. Well represented families include bustards and nightjars.

Bird Species

A total of 938 species have been recorded in Sudan, the fifth highest country list in Africa. Although Sudan supports over 500 more species than Egypt to the north, its list is still 50 short of Uganda's to the south, despite the fact that Uganda is only one tenth its size. Non-endemic specialities and spectacular species include Shoebill*, Black Crowned-Crane, Arabian Bustard, Lesser Jacana, Egyptian Plover, Pharaoh Eagle-Owl, Jameson's Wattle-eye and Sudan Golden-Sparrow.

Endemics

Despite its immense size only two birds are endemic to Sudan: Red Sea Swallow*, which is known from only a single specimen, and Cinnamon Weaver. Near-endemics include Heuglin's Francolin and Cretzschmar's Babbler.

Expectations

It is possible to see up to 250 species during a three-week trip to south Sudan.

KHARTOUM

Sudan's capital lies at the confluence of the White and Blue Niles, in the centre of the country. Thanks to these two rivers and the fertile land between them, it is possible to see a fine selection of birds in the vicinity of Sudan's capital, including Egyptian Plover, Pharaoh Eagle-Owl, Cricket Longtail and the near-endemic Cretzschmar's Babbler.

Specialities

Lesser Jacana (Aug), Egyptian Plover (Aug–Feb), Pharaoh Eagle-Owl, Cretzschmar's Babbler, Sudan Golden-Sparrow.

Others

Black-headed Heron, Abdim's Stork, Lesser Spotted Eagle, Spotted Thick-knee, Caspian Plover (Nov–Mar), African Skimmer, Chestnut-bellied Sandgrouse, Blue-naped Mousebird, Long-tailed Nightjar (Sep–Mar), Little, White-throated and Green Bee-eaters, Abyssinian Roller, Masked Shrike (Nov–Mar), Black-headed Gonolek, Black Scrub-Robin, Isabelline and Heuglin's Wheatears, Ethiopian Swallow, Graceful Prinia, Cricket Longtail, Chestnut-backed Sparrow-Lark, Desert Lark, Greater Hoopoe-Lark, Crimson-rumped Waxbill, African Silverbill, Little Weaver, Northern and Vitelline Masked-Weavers, Pygmy and Beautiful Sunbirds, White-rumped Seedeater.

Access

There are plenty of places to go birding in and around Khartoum. These include: (1) The farmland between the Blue Nile and Burrie Bridge, accessible via the riverside path (Abyssinian Roller). Do not show binoculars near the police college immediately after the Burrie Bridge. (2) The Omdurman Bridge (African Skimmer), which is best in early morning and late evening. (3) The Sunt (acacia) Forest (5 sq km), which can be reached by walking south along the White Nile (Cretzschmar's Babbler). (4) Tuti Island, which is situated in the confluence (Lesser Jacana (Aug), Black Scrub-Robin, Heuglin's Wheatear and Cretzschmar's Babbler). Further afield (5) The Jebel Aulia Dam (Spotted Thick-knee, in acacias on west side of dam), which lies south of the city past Gordon's Tree and the Satellite Station. (6) Es Seleina, south of the city via Wad Medani. (7) Jebel Silietat (Cricket Longtail, Desert Lark, and Greater Hoopoe-Lark), north of the city via Kadarou. To reach this excellent area, turn right near the railway station beyond Kadarou, on to a track which crosses the railway line and passes through scattered settlements before reaching an area of irrigation spills.

KHARTOUM

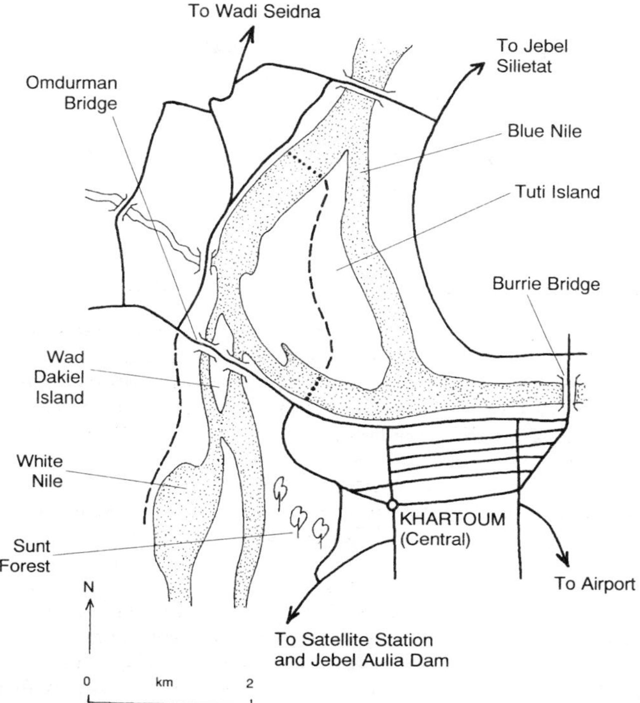

Species recorded around **Kosti**, a few hundred km south of Khartoum, include Black Crake, Lesser Jacana, Greater Painted-snipe, Caspian Plover, Long-toed and White-tailed Lapwings, Piapiac, Black-headed Gonolek, Black Scrub-Robin, Cricket Longtail and Sudan Golden-Sparrow. Abba Island, north of town (accessible by ferry), and the swamps south of town, are probably the best areas. It used to be possible to travel south from Kosti along the **White Nile** via Lake No through the Sudd to Juba, the access point for the Immatong Mountains (see below). This lengthy boat trip has produced birds such as African Darter, Shoebill* (especially along the Lake No stretch), Saddle-billed Stork, Black Crowned-Crane, African Skimmer, Abyssinian Roller and Marsh Tchagra. During the early 1980s, the impact assessment work on the Jonglei Canal suggested there were up to 10,000 Shoebills* in the Sudd. The subsequent construction of the canal has probably led to a decline but the Sudd remains one of the Shoebill's* major strongholds.

IMMATONG MOUNTAINS

The forested Immatong Mountains, in extreme south Sudan near Juba, support an avifauna akin to the forests of Uganda and western Kenya.

Specialities

Heuglin's Francolin, White-crested Turaco, Jameson's Wattle-eye.

Others

African Black Duck, Black Goshawk, Mountain Buzzard, Crowned Hawk-Eagle, Crested Guineafowl, Scaly Francolin, Black-billed and Great Blue Turacos, Black and African Emerald Cuckoos, Narina Trogon, Cinnamon-chested and White-throated Bee-eaters, White-headed Woodhoopoe, Black-and-white-casqued Hornbill, Grey-throated and Yellow-billed Barbets, African Blue-Flycatcher, Black-winged Oriole, Black, Purple-throated and Red-shouldered Cuckoo-shrikes, Pink-footed Puffback, Luehder's Bushshrike, Chestnut Wattle-eye, Waller's and Sharpe's Starlings, White-starred Robin, Equatorial Akalat, Grey-winged, Red-capped and Snowy-headed Robin-Chats, White-headed Sawwing, Slender-billed, Honeyguide, Joyful and White-throated Greenbuls, Toro Olive-Greenbul, White-chinned Prinia, Black-collared, Black-throated and Grey Apalises, Cinnamon Bracken-Warbler, Mountain Warbler, Rufous-crowned Eremomela, Brown Woodland-Warbler, Yellow-bellied Hyliota, Brown Illadopsis, Abyssinian Hill-Babbler, White-bellied and Dusky Tits, Abyssinian Crimson-wing, Red-headed Bluebill, Dybowski's Twinspot, Black-crowned Waxbill, Black-billed, Forest and Brown-capped Weavers, Red-headed Malimbe, Yellow Bishop, Northern Double-collared, Copper and Tacazze Sunbirds, Streaky Seedeater, Oriole Finch, Cabanis' Bunting.

Access

Previously productive spots southeast of Juba have included: (1) The forest tracks at Gilo, near Katire, accessible by road from Torit, or by foot from Upper Talanga. (2) The Upper Talanga area, where Grey-winged Robin-Chat has been recorded in the forest below the waterfall. (3) Lotti Forest, where Heuglin's Francolin has been recorded in the open country to the north of Lerwa Mission.

Stone Partridge, Black Scimitar-bill, and Brown-rumped Bunting occur in **Nimule NP**, just north of Nimule on the Uganda border. Chocolate-backed Kingfisher, Black-headed Bee-eater and Red-bellied Malimbe have been recorded at **Bengengai** in south Sudan.

Southeast of Khartoum, there are plenty of good birds along the Blue Nile. Lesser Jacana, Egyptian and Caspian Plovers, Horus Swift, Red-throated and Northern Carmine Bee-eaters and Golden-tailed Woodpecker occur around **Singa**, and Lesser Jacana, Egyptian Plover, White-tailed Lapwing, Abyssinian Roller, Red-throated and Northern Carmine Bee-eaters, Yellow-breasted Barbet and Snowy-crowned Robin-Chat occur around **el Damazin**, the town at the northern end of Lake Roseires on the Ethiopian border.

DINDER NATIONAL PARK

This big park, on the Ethiopian border southeast of Khartoum, 'protects' palm savanna and seasonal marshes where Arabian Bustard and Cretzschmar's Babbler occur.

Getting to Dinder NP is very difficult without a vehicle.

Specialities

Arabian Bustard, Lesser Jacana, White-rumped and Cretzschmar's Babblers, Sennar Penduline-Tit, Red-chested Sunbird.

Others

Ostrich, African Pygmy-goose, Goliath Heron, Hamerkop, Saddle-billed Stork, Bateleur, Gabar Goshawk, Verreaux's and Martial Eagles, Clapperton's Francolin, Senegal Thick-knee, Chestnut-bellied Sandgrouse, Black-billed Wood-Dove, Red-throated, Little and Northern Carmine Bee-eaters, Abyssinian Roller, Black Scimitar-bill, Abyssinian Ground-Hornbill, Vieillot's Barbet, Black-crowned Tchagra, Black-headed Gonolek, Rueppell's Glossy-Starling, Ethiopian Swallow, Upcher's (Nov–Mar) and Orphean (Nov–Mar) Warblers, Crimson-rumped Waxbill, Beautiful Sunbird.

Access

Guides are compulsory and must be contacted at the Park HQ in the village of Dinder, 165 km west of the park. Upcher's Warbler and Sennar Penduline-Tit occur around Dinder village. In the park bird the various tracks from the HQ, especially those around Lake Grerisa.

Scissor-tailed Kite, Fox Kestrel, Black-headed Lapwing, Bruce's Green-Pigeon, Green Bee-eater, Yellow-breasted Barbet, Fan-tailed Raven, Yellow-billed Oxpecker, Black Scrub-Robin, Red-faced Apalis, Sudan Golden-Sparrow, Shining Sunbird and House Bunting have been recorded in the farmland around **Kassala**, a small town in east Sudan at the base of the hills (900 m (2953 ft)) on the Ethiopian border.

Brown Booby, Greater Flamingo, Western Reef-Egret, Cream-coloured Courser, White-eyed* and Sooty Gulls, Great Crested-Tern, Chestnut-bellied and Spotted Sandgrouse, Red-tailed Wheatear, Black-crowned Sparrow-Lark, Greater Hoopoe-Lark, Sudan Golden-Sparrow, Rueppell's Weaver, and Cretzschmar's Bunting (Nov–Mar) occur around **Port Sudan and Suakin**, on Sudan's Red Sea coast. Some of these species, as well as Sand Partridge, Demoiselle Crane (Sinkat) (Nov–Mar), Yellow-breasted Barbet, Fan-tailed Raven, Rosy-patched Bushshrike, Grey-headed Batis, Black Scrub-Robin, Brown-tailed Chat, Blackstart, White-breasted White-eye, Red-faced Apalis, Red Sea and Menetrie's (Nov– Mar) Warblers, Fulvous Chatterer, Desert Lark, Shining Sunbird and House Bunting, occur around **Erkowit** and **Sinkat** south of Port Sudan.Cinereous Bunting* occurs in the hills bordering the Red Sea north of Port Sudan, at least as a migrant, and possibly as a winter visitor (Nov–Mar).

In 1984, a Red Sea Swallow* was found dead at Sanganeb Lighthouse northeast of Port Sudan. To this day, this species is known from only this single specimen, no birds having ever been seen in the wild. It may have originated in Sudan's coastal hills, although unidentified swallows have recently been seen in Ethiopia.

ADDITIONAL INFORMATION

Books and Papers

Birds of South Sudan (*Scopus* Special Supplement No 3). Nikolaus, G. 1989. EAOS.

Distribution Atlas of Sudan's Birds with Notes on Habitat and Status. Nikolaus, G. 1987. *Bonner Zool. Monogrn.* 25:1–322.

Addresses

Please send records to Gerhard Nikolaus, Bossenbuttel 4, D-27637 Spieka, Germany.

ENDEMICS (2)

Red Sea Swallow*	East: known from only one specimen, found dead near Port Sudan in 1984
Cinnamon Weaver	South: alongside the Niles south of Khartoum

Near-endemics (South/Southwest)

Schlegel's and Heuglin's Francolins, Niam-Niam Parrot, Jackson's Hornbill, Mangbettu Sawwing, Mongalla Cisticola, Dusky Babbler.

Near-endemics (East)

Erckell's Francolin, White-cheeked Turaco, Black-throated Firefinch, Abyssinian Waxbill.

Near-endemics (Central)

White-rumped Babbler, Cretzschmar's Babbler.

TANZANIA

INTRODUCTION

Summary

Tanzania used to have a reputation for bumbling bureaucracy and fuel shortages, but since the early 1990s the situation has improved greatly. However, whilst the famous sites in the north such as the Serengeti and the Ngorongoro Crater are on a par with Kenya as far as accessibility is concerned, looking for the rarer endemics and the many specialities of the central mountain ranges, and exploring the much wilder national parks of the south, still requires patience, energy and an expensive 4WD. Nevertheless, those who like logistical problems will probably enjoy Tanzania.

Size

At 939,762 sq km, Tanzania is seven times the size of England, and a little larger than Texas.

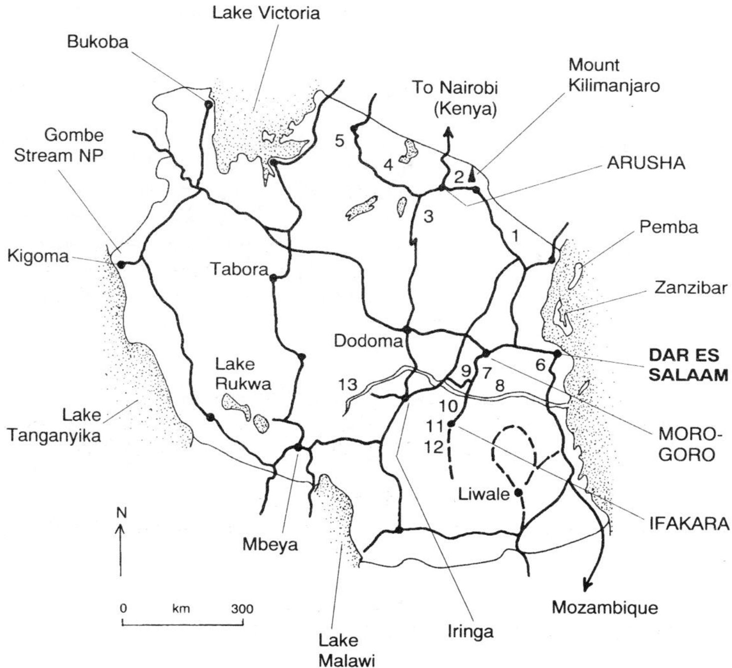

1	Usambara Mountains	8	Selous Reserve
2	Arusha	9	Mikumi NP
3	Tarangire NP	10	Mwanihana
4	Ngorongoro Crater	11	Ifakara
5	Serengeti NP	12	Chita Forest
6	Pugu FR	13	Ruaha NP
7	Uluguru Mountains		

Getting Around

Birders in search of Tanzania's best birds with little time to spare will need an expensive 4WD. Those with more time will find a fairly reliable, cheap internal air network which reaches most national parks, an excellent bus network and railways which connect some of the major towns.

It is relatively expensive (B) to enter all the national parks.

Accommodation and Food

There is a wide range of accommodation available in most places, and these generally serve reasonable food. Camping in national parks is expensive (A) but not as expensive as the luxurious lodges. The staple diet comprises beans and maize-meal, although there is some good seafood along the coast.

Health and Safety

Immunisation against hepatitis, polio, rabies, typhoid and yellow fever is recommended, as are precautions against malaria.

Beware of petty thieves in the larger towns, tsetse flies in the 'bush', and chilly nights in the highlands.

Climate and Timing

The coast and the three offshore islands, Zanzibar, Pemba and Mafia, are hot and humid all year round, especially from January to March. It is very wet from April to June, and the two dry seasons which last from January to March and July to November, are the best times to visit.

Habitats

Most of Tanzania lies on a highland plateau dominated by dry savanna. There are also many lakes, swamps and a number of isolated mountain ranges, which rise to a peak of 5894 m (19,337 ft) at Mount Kilimanjaro in the extreme northeast. These mountains support remnant forest, and forest also survives in some places along the east coast.

Conservation

Over a quarter (26%) of Tanzania's land lies within the many national parks. However, the coastal and montane forests of the east, which support many of the rarest and most localised birds, are still under serious threat from logging, kaolin extraction, agriculture and the felling of trees for fuel and timber. As a result, there are more threatened and near-threatened species (a total of 52) in Tanzania than in any other African country, archipelago or island.

Bird Families

Eight of the ten families endemic to the African mainland are represented in Tanzania. Well represented families include 'raptors', plovers, parrots, turacos, bee-eaters, barbets, starlings, pipits, weavers and sunbirds.

Bird Species

A total of 1038 species have been recorded in Tanzania, the third highest total in Africa, just 56 fewer than Zaïre and 40 fewer than Kenya. Non-endemic specialities and spectacular species include Shoebill*, Lesser Jacana, Crab Plover, Madagascar Pratincole, Boehm's Bee-eater and Racket-tailed Roller.

Endemics

Twenty species including two on Pemba Island are found only in Tanzania. These include Udzungwa Forest-partridge*, which was described only in 1991, Uluguru Bushshrike*, Usambara Akalat*, Mrs Moreau's Warbler*, and Rufous-winged Sunbird*. There are also many near-endemics, including Pale Batis, Swynnerton's Robin*, White-winged Apalis*, African and Long-billed* Tailorbirds, Spot-throat, Dapple-throat*, Lesser Seedcracker, Sokoke Pipit* and Amani Sunbird*.

Expectations

It is possible to see up to 400 species during a three week trip to the north, and over 550 on a longer trip that includes the north, centre and east.

The **Africana** Holiday complex, 24 km north of Dar es Salaam, lies near coastal mudflats, saltpans, marshes and scrub, where Madagascar Pond-Heron* (Apr–Sep), Crab Plover, Madagascar Pratincole (Apr–Sep), Sombre Greenbul and Purple-banded Sunbird occur.

DAR ES SALAAM NORTH AND WEST TO THE SERENGETI

Black-backed Puffback, Short-tailed Batis, Orange Ground-Thrush, Kretschmer's Longbill and Sokoke Pipit* occur in coastal **Kiono Forest**, 20 km southwest of Sadani, north of Dar Es Salaam. This forest is accessible only with a vehicle.

USAMBARA MOUNTAINS

These mountains in northeast Tanzania are separated in to the East Usambaras (1500 m (4921 ft)) and the West Usambaras (2250 m (7382 ft)), by the Lwengera Valley. The forested slopes of these two mountain blocks support many restricted-range specialities, such as Sokoke Scops-Owl* and Long-billed Tailorbird*, and four endemics, one of which, Usambara Akalat*, occurs only here.

There are eleven montane and five lowland forest reserves in the East Usambaras alone, and many of the specialities are either found in the montane or lowland areas, not both, so birders will need to visit at least three of these reserves in order to have a chance of seeing all the Usambara specialities.

Tanzania Endemics

Usambara Eagle-Owl*, Usambara Akalat*, Usambara Weaver*, Banded Sunbird*.

Specialities

Buff-spotted Flufftail, Fischer's* and Hartlaub's Turacos, Sokoke Scops-Owl*, Moustached Green-Tinkerbird, Fuelleborn's Boubou, Black-fronted Bushshrike, Short-tailed Batis, White-chested Alethe, Swynnerton's Robin*, East Coast Akalat*, Kenrick's Starling, Stripe-cheeked Bulbul, Tiny Greenbul, Evergreen Forest Warbler, African and Long-billed* Tailorbirds, Spot-throat, Dapple-throat*, Plain-backed, Uluguru Violet-backed and Amani* Sunbirds.

Others

Olive Ibis, Fasciated Snake-Eagle*, Mountain Buzzard, Crowned Hawk-Eagle, Barred Long-tailed Cuckoo, African Emerald Cuckoo, African Wood-Owl, Montane Nightjar, Mottled and Bat-like Spinetails, Bar-tailed Trogon, Half-collared Kingfisher, Cinnamon-chested Bee-eater, Silvery-cheeked Hornbill, African Green-Tinkerbird, Olive Woodpecker, African Broadbill, Dusky and White-tailed Crested-Flycatchers, Green-headed Oriole, Grey Cuckoo-shrike, Orange Ground-Thrush, Waller's and Sharpe's Starlings, Black-bellied Glossy-Starling, White-starred Robin, Shelley's, Little, Mountain and Placid Greenbuls, Yellow-streaked Bulbul, Red-faced Cisticola, Bar-throated and Black-headed Apalises, African Bush-Warbler, Yellow-throated Wood-Warbler, Pale-breasted Illadopsis, Abyssinian Hill-Babbler, Black-and-white Mannikin, Forest Weaver, Olive Sunbird, Oriole Finch.

Access

The best way to find the sites in the Usambara Mountains is with 1:50000 maps, available from the Lands Office in Dar es Salaam. The specialities, Moustached Green-Tinkerbird, Long-billed Tailorbird*, Dapple-throat*, and Uluguru Violet-backed and Amani* Sunbirds occur in the **Amani FRs** in the East Usambaras. Usambara Eagle-Owl* occurs in the lowland **Kambai FR**, also in the East Usambaras. The endemic Usambara Akalat* and Spot-throat occur in **Mazumbai FR**, near Lushoto in the West Usambaras. The University of Morogoro runs a research station here, and there is a good trail. Usambara Weaver* has been recorded at Mount Nilo in the **Lutindi FR**.

The rare and local Rufous Short-toed Lark, an isolated population of Spike-heeled Larks, and Taveta Golden-Weaver occur around **Arusha**, the gateway to the Serengeti, Ngorongoro Crater, Lake Manyara and Tarangire NPs. Maccoa Duck, Hartlaub's Turaco, African Emerald Cuckoo, Narina Trogon, Brown-breasted Barbet, Abbott's Starling*, Grey-olive Greenbul and Jackson's Widowbird* occur in **Arusha NP**, where there is acacia savanna and montane forest on the slopes of the Ngurdoto Crater. Hartlaub's Turaco, Narina Trogon, Four-coloured Bushshrike, Abbott's Starling*, Cinnamon Bracken-Warbler, and Golden-winged and Malachite Sunbirds all occur in **Kilimanjaro NP**, and may be seen on the three-day trek to the summit.

TARANGIRE NATIONAL PARK

The acacia savanna and marshes alongside the Tarangire river in this park (2600 sq km) supports three endemics.

Tanzania Endemics

Ashy Starling, Yellow-collared Lovebird, Rufous-tailed Weaver.

Specialities

Magpie Shrike, Northern Pied-Babbler, Pangani Longclaw.

Others

Ostrich, Saddle-billed Stork, White-headed Vulture, African Hawk-Eagle, Martial Eagle, Pygmy Falcon, Crested Francolin, Double-banded Courser, Senegal Lapwing, Black-faced Sandgrouse, Meyer's and Orange-bellied Parrots, Bare-faced Go-away-bird, Slender-tailed Nightjar, Lilac-breasted Roller, Spot-flanked, White-headed and D'Arnaud's Barbets, Yellow-billed and Red-billed Oxpeckers, Spotted Morning-Thrush, Mosque Swallow, Yellow-breasted Apalis.

Other Wildlife

Buffalo, Burchell's zebra, gerenuk, eland, elephant, giraffe, impala, leopard, lion, oryx.

Accommodation: Lodge/tented camp (A+).

The small **Lake Manyara NP** (318 sq km), which is situated alongside the northern and western shores of a soda lake, is famous for its tree-climbing lions, whilst birds present include Greater and Lesser* Flamingos, Black Heron, Ayre's Hawk-Eagle, Water and Spotted Thick-knees, Three-banded Courser, Chestnut-banded Plover and Red-winged Starling.

NGORONGORO CRATER

This huge volcanic crater, which is 16 km wide and 600 m deep, is one of earth's most amazing natural wonders and, understandably, an extremely popular destination for tourists from around the world. The crater *contains* 30,000 large mammals and a fine selection of birds. Some species such as the endemic Rufous-tailed Weaver occur in the acacia savanna at the bottom of the crater, whilst others, such as Brown-headed Apalis, are present in the montane forest around its rim.

It is possible to descend into the crater only with a 4WD.

Tanzania Endemics

Rufous-tailed Weaver.

Specialities

Black-winged Lapwing, Yellow-throated Sandgrouse, Schalow's Turaco, Kenrick's Starling, Broad-ringed White-eye, Hunter's Cisticola, Brown-headed Apalis, Jackson's Widowbird*, Eastern Double-collared, Tacazze and Golden-winged Sunbirds.

Others

Ostrich, Greater and Lesser* Flamingos, Hadada Ibis, Abdim's and Saddle-billed Storks, Verreaux's Eagle, Secretary-bird, Grey Crowned-Crane, Kori and Black-bellied Bustards, Chestnut-banded and Caspian (Nov–Mar) Plovers, African Pigeon, Dusky Turtle-Dove, Ross's Turaco, Verreaux's Eagle-Owl, Lilac-breasted Roller, Trumpeter Hornbill, Brown-backed Woodpecker, Rueppell's Robin-Chat, Northern Anteater-Chat, Banded Martin, Grey-rumped Swallow, Mountain Greenbul, Winding and Pectoral-patch Cisticolas, Grey-capped Warbler, Brown Warbler, Rufous-naped Lark, Yellow-bellied Waxbill, Rosy-throated Longclaw, Speke's Weaver, Bronze Sunbird, Streaky and Thick-billed Seedeaters.

Other Wildlife

Bat-eared fox, black rhino, buffalo, Burchell's zebra, cheetah, eland, elephant, giraffe, Grant's gazelle, hippo, leopard, lion, spotted hyena, wildebeest.

Access

Bird the base of the crater and alongside the road which runs along the rim.

Accommodation: Usiwara Guesthouse (C); Ngorongoro Rhino Lodge (B) (camping also); Ngorongoro Crater Lodge (B); Ngorongoro Wildlife Lodge (A); Simba Campsite (A).

Huge **Lake Natron** (900 sq km), north of Ngorongoro, is remote, inhospitable and very difficult to access. It supports East Africa's only regular breeding colony of Lesser Flamingos* (up to half a million individuals), as well as Chestnut-banded Plover.

The snake-eating Secretary-bird stalks the plains of the Ngorongoro Crater

SERENGETI NATIONAL PARK

In November, over a million large mammals, together with their predators, usually move into this huge park (14,763 sq km) to breed. Even the most fanatical birder will find it hard to ignore this incredible phenomenon, despite the presence of three Tanzanian endemics and a handful of localised species, including Usambiro Barbet, Red-throated Tit* and Athi Short-toed Lark.

The Serengeti is contiguous with the Kenyan Masai Mara to the north (p. 185).

Tanzania Endemics

Grey-breasted Spurfowl, Fischer's Lovebird*, Rufous-tailed Weaver.

Specialities

Black-winged Lapwing, Yellow-throated Sandgrouse, Usambiro Barbet, Magpie Shrike, Hildebrandt's Starling, Silverbird, Red-throated Tit*, Athi Short-toed and Short-tailed Larks.

Others

Saddle-billed Stork, White-headed Vulture, Brown Snake-Eagle, Pygmy Falcon, Greater Kestrel, Coqui Francolin, White-bellied Bustard, Spotted Thick-knee, Three-banded and Temminck's Coursers, Chestnut-banded and Caspian (Nov–Mar) Plovers, Chestnut-bellied Sandgrouse, White-bellied Go-away-bird, Pied and African Cuckoos, Black Coucal, Abyssinian Scimitar-bill, Von der Decken's Hornbill, Red-fronted Barbet, Taita Fiscal, Yellow-billed and Red-billed Oxpeckers, Buff-bellied and Banded Warblers, Fawn-coloured Lark, Fischer's Sparrow-Lark, Rufous Sparrow, Blue-capped Cordonbleu, Purple Grenadier, Black-cheeked Waxbill, Speckle-fronted Weaver, Beautiful Sunbird.

Other Wildlife

Bat-eared fox, Burchell's zebra, cheetah, eland, giraffe, Grant's gazelle, hartebeeste, hunting dog, impala, Kirk's dik-dik, leopard, lion, rock hyrax, serval, spotted hyena, topi, wildebeest.

Access

Grey-breasted Spurfowl, Fischer's Lovebird* and Rufous-tailed Weaver occur around **Ndutu Lodge** on the edge of the plains, as well as Silverbird, Red-throated Tit* and Short-tailed Lark. Nearby Lake Lagarja supports Chestnut-banded Plover. The **Seronera** area supports Usambiro Barbet and Magpie Shrike.

Accommodation: Seronera Lodge (A)/hostel/campsite (C); Lobo Wildlife Lodge (A); Ndutu Lodge.

DAR ES SALAAM WEST TO RUAHA NATIONAL PARK

PUGU FOREST RESERVE

The small area of montane forest (10 sq km) on the Pugu Hills (305 m (1001 ft)) near Dar es Salaam supports a number of specialities including African Pitta and Lesser Seedcracker.

Parts of this reserve are permanently closed owing to the presence of a military camp.

Specialities

Fischer's Turaco*, Mombasa Woodpecker, African Pitta (Apr–May), Yellow Flycatcher, Short-tailed Batis, Spotted Ground-Thrush* (Apr–May), East Coast Akalat*, Lesser Seedcracker, Sokoke Pipit*, Plain-backed* and Uluguru Violet-backed Sunbirds.

Others

Fasciated Snake-Eagle*, Yellowbill, Trumpeter Hornbill, Green-backed Woodpecker, African Broadbill, Four-coloured Bushshrike, Chestnut-fronted Helmetshrike, Sombre Greenbul, Pale-breasted Illadopsis, Peters' Twinspot, Mouse-coloured Sunbird.

Access

This forest reserve is 15 km south of Pande and much easier to find with a 1:50000 map, available from the Lands Office in Dar es Salaam.

ULUGURU MOUNTAINS

This isolated mountain range (50 km by 20 km, 2668 m (8753 ft)) just south of Morogoro supports a lowland forest avifauna similar to that of coastal Kenya and Tanzania, and a montane forest avifauna similar to that of the Usambara Mountains (p. 345). Five endemics are present, two of which occur only here, Uluguru Bushshrike* and Loveridge's Sunbird*, as well as specialities such as Sharpe's Akalat, White-winged* and Chapin's Apalises and Lesser Seedcracker.

Tanzania Endemics

Uluguru Bushshrike*, Mrs Moreau's Warbler*, Usambara Weaver*, Loveridge's Sunbird*.

Specialities

Green Barbet, Moustached Green-Tinkerbird, Yellow Flycatcher, Fuelleborn's Boubou, Black-fronted Bushshrike, White-chested Alethe, Kenrick's Starling, Sharpe's Akalat, Olive-flanked Robin-Chat, Stripe-cheeked Bulbul, White-winged* and Chapin's Apalises, Evergreen Forest Warbler, African Tailorbird, Kretschmer's Longbill, Spot-throat, Lesser Seedcracker, Bertrand's Weaver, Uluguru Violet-backed Sunbird.

Others

Fasciated Snake-Eagle*, Mountain Buzzard, Lemon Dove, Livingstone's Turaco, Barred Long-tailed Cuckoo, African Wood-Owl, Narina and Bar-tailed Trogons, Olive Woodpecker, White-tailed Crested-Flycatcher, Green-headed Oriole, Purple-throated Cuckoo-shrike, Black-and-white Shrike-flycatcher, Red-tailed Ant-Thrush, Orange Ground-Thrush, Waller's Starling, White-starred Robin, Red-capped Robin-Chat, Shelley's and Mountain Greenbuls, Bar-throated and Black-headed Apalises, Yellow-throated Wood-Warbler, Abyssinian Hill-Babbler, Red-faced Crimson-wing, Peters' Twinspot, Mountain Wagtail, Oriole Finch.

Access

The montane forest is accessible only with a 4WD or via a half-day walk from Morogoro. Uluguru Bushshrike* occurs in **Uluguru North FR**. The lowland forest at **Kimboza** is easily accessible, and although the birds of Uluguru are little known, it seems at least some montane species are altitudinal migrants so may be present in Kimboza during July to September.

SELOUS RESERVE

This reserve is the biggest in the world (54,600 sq km) and one of earth's last true wildernesses. Mammals and the 'wild' factor are the highlights here, although good birds include Boehm's Bee-eater.

The lodges and campsites are closed during the wet season (Apr–Jun). Although most visitors fly in and take walking safaris, or make use of the reserve's on-site vehicles, serious birders will need a 4WD. All these options are expensive.

Specialities

Lesser Jacana, Boehm's Bee-eater.

Others

African Darter, Palm-nut Vulture, Martial Eagle, Dickinson's Kestrel, Greater Painted-snipe, Spotted Thick-knee, Bronze-winged Courser,

Three-banded Plover, White-headed Lapwing, African Skimmer, Brown-headed Parrot, White-bellied Go-away-bird, Pel's Fishing-Owl, Bat-like Spinetail, White-fronted Bee-eater, Lilac-breasted Roller, Von der Decken's Hornbill, Southern Ground-Hornbill, Brown-crowned Tchagra, Yellow-billed Oxpecker, Bearded Scrub-Robin, Flappet Lark, African Golden-Weaver, Mariqua Sunbird.

Other Wildlife

Buffalo, Burchell's zebra, bush baby, elephant, giraffe, greater kudu, hartebeeste, hippo, hunting dog, impala, lion, spotted hyena, wildebeest.

Access

Boehm's Bee-eater occurs around the Rufiji River Camp, and Lesser Jacana on Lake Tagalala. It is possible to take boat trips on the river where White-headed Lapwing, African Skimmer and Pel's Fishing-Owl occur.

Accommodation: Rufiji River Camp (A); Mbuyu Camp (A); Beho Beho Camp (A); Lake Tagalala campsite.

MIKUMI NATIONAL PARK

The 3000 sq km of savanna, gallery forest, and miombo woodland in this national park, some 300 km west of Dar es Salaam, support a few miombo specialities, such as Racket-tailed Roller and Shelley's Sunbird, which are at the northern limit of their ranges here.

Specialities

Boehm's Bee-eater, Racket-tailed Roller, Pale-billed Hornbill, Magpie Shrike, Miombo Rock-Thrush, Cinnamon-breasted Tit, Shelley's Sunbird.

Others

Gabar Goshawk, Wahlberg's Eagle, Dickinson's Kestrel, Secretary-bird, Grey Crowned-Crane, Black-bellied Bustard, Blacksmith Plover, Crowned Lapwing, Purple-crested Turaco, Levaillant's Cuckoo, Black Coucal, Verreaux's Eagle-Owl, African Barred Owlet, Mottled Swift, Little and Swallow-tailed Bee-eaters, Southern Ground-Hornbill, Red-fronted Tinkerbird, Bennett's Woodpecker, Brown-crowned Tchagra, Southern Blue-eared Glossy-Starling, Superb Starling, Spotted Morning-Thrush, White-headed Black-Chat, Siffling Cisticola, Barred Wren-Warbler, Moustached Grass-Warbler, Greencap Eremomela, Southern Hyliota, Flappet Lark, Orange-winged and Green-winged Pytilias, Broad-tailed Paradise-Whydah, Parasitic Weaver.

Other Wildlife

Baboon, buffalo, Burchell's zebra, cheetah, eland, elephant, giraffe, greater kudu, hartebeeste, hippo, hunting dog, impala, leopard, lion, sable, wildebeest.

Access

The best birding areas are west of the main road through the national park, the Mwanambogo Dam, and the miombo woodland to the south (where tsetse flies can be a problem).

Accommodation: Mikumi Wildlife Lodge (with waterhole) (A); Mikumi Wildlife Camp (A); campsite (take supplies).

The Udzungwa Forest-partridge* (*Xenoperdix udzungwensis*) was discovered near Udekwa in the western **Udzungwa Mountains NP** in 1991. These mountains, which measure some 200 km north to south and rise to 2576 m (8451 ft) at Mount Luhombero in the north, also support six other Tanzanian endemics: Iringa Akalat*, Mrs Moreau's Warbler*, Usambara Weaver*, Banded* and Rufous-winged* Sunbirds and Kipengere Seedeater*, as well as Swynnerton's Robin*, White-winged Apalis*, Dapple-throat* and Uluguru Violet-backed and Amani* Sunbirds. Adventurous birders should explore the richer eastern forest at Mwanihana and Chita (see below), and the western forest at Udekwa, Luhombero, Dabaga, Kibogo and Mufindi. **West Kilombero FR**, accessible from Udekwa (east to the Ndundulu Range, and south to the Nyumbanitu Range), supports the partridge, which is rare, as well as Iringa Akalat*, Olive-flanked Robin-Chat, White-winged Apalis*, Spot-throat, Dapple-throat*, Usambara Weaver* and Amani*, Banded* and Rufous-winged* Sunbirds.

MIKUMI NP

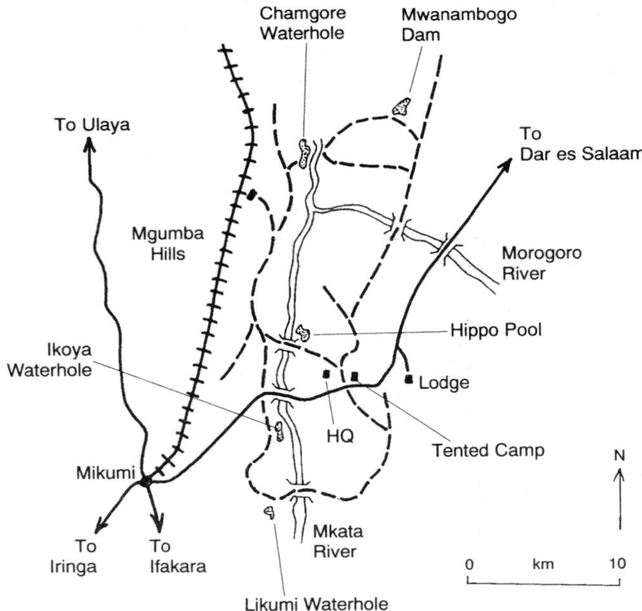

UDZUNGWA MOUNTAINS

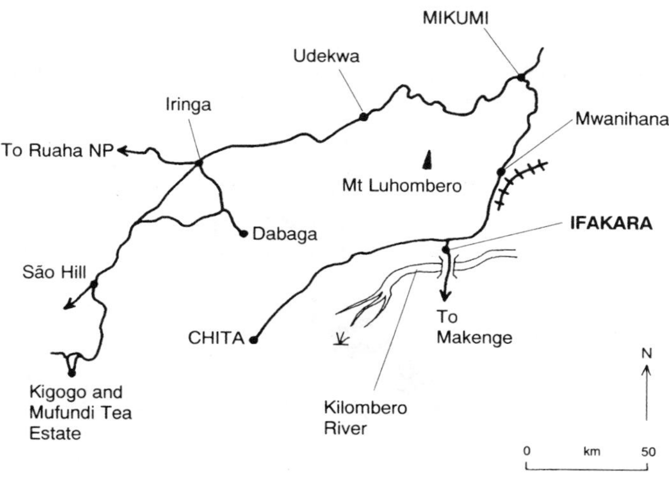

MWANIHANA

Situated in the northern Udzungwa Mountains NP on the wet east scarp, the lush forest near Mwanihana, between Mikumi NP and Ifakara, supports the rare endemic Rufous-winged Sunbird*, which was discovered here in 1981, as well as a long list of specialities which include Pale Batis, Swynnerton's Robin*, White-winged Apalis* and Dapple-throat*.

Tanzania Endemics

Mrs Moreau's Warbler*, Usambara Weaver*, Banded* and Rufous-winged* Sunbirds.

Specialities

Green Barbet, Moustached Green-Tinkerbird, Pallid Honeyguide, Fuelleborn's Boubou, Black-fronted Bushshrike, Short-tailed and Pale Batises, White-chested Alethe, Kenrick's Starling, Swynnerton's Robin*, Sharpe's Akalat, Stripe-cheeked Bulbul, White-winged*, Chapin's and Brown-headed Apalises, Evergreen Forest Warbler, Kretschmer's Longbill, Spot-throat, Dapple-throat*, Uluguru Violet-backed Sunbird.

Others

Palm-nut Vulture, Fasciated Snake-Eagle*, Black Goshawk, Mountain Buzzard, Crowned Hawk-Eagle, Crested Guineafowl, Livingstone's Turaco, Barred Long-tailed Cuckoo, African Barred Owlet, Narina and Bar-tailed Trogons, Half-collared Kingfisher, Swallow-tailed Bee-eater, White-eared and Black-collared Barbets, Olive Woodpecker, African Broadbill, Livingstone's Flycatcher, White-tailed Crested-Flycatcher, Green-headed Oriole, Black-backed Puffback, Retz's and Chestnut-fronted Helmetshrikes, Black-and-white Shrike-flycatcher, Orange Ground-Thrush, Waller's Starling, White-starred Robin, Red-capped Robin-Chat, Bearded Scrub-Robin, Shelley's, Mountain and Yellow-bellied Greenbuls, Yellow-streaked Bulbul, Black-headed Apalis, Yellow-throated Wood-Warbler, Red-faced Crimson-wing, Peters' Twinspot.

Access

Rufous-winged Sunbird occurs in the forest surrounding the waterfall at Sanje.

Pale Batis is one of many localised species at Mwanihana

IFAKARA

This town lies on the Kilombero river floodplain, which forms part of Kibasira Swamp, the type-locality of the endemic Kilombero Weaver*.

Tanzania Endemics

Kilombero Weaver*.

Others

African Darter, Black and Rufous-bellied Herons, Black Crake, Three-banded Plover, Long-toed and White-headed Lapwings, White-fronted Bee-eater, Anchieta's Tchagra, Spotted Morning-Thrush, African Bush-Warbler, African Reed-Warbler, Arrow-marked Babbler, Zebra Waxbill, African Golden-Weaver.

(Two potential new species of cisticola, provisionally called 'Melodious' and 'Kilombero', were trapped here in 1986; both are common.)

Access

Bird from the raised causeway just south of town, west of the Kivukoni Ferry.

Accommodation: Mission.

CHITA FOREST

Situated in the southern Udzungwa Mountains NP, on the wet east scarp, this forest is not as rich as Mwanihana, but species occuring here and not there include the endemic Iringa Akalat* and Olive-flanked Robin-Chat.

Tanzania Endemics

Iringa Akalat*, Usambara Weaver*, Kipengere Seedeater.

Specialities

Green Barbet, Moustached Green-Tinkerbird, Fuelleborn's Boubou, Black-fronted Bushshrike, Short-tailed Batis, White-chested Alethe, Kenrick's Starling, Swynnerton's Robin*, Sharpe's Akalat, Olive-flanked Robin-Chat, Stripe-cheeked Bulbul, White-winged*, Chapin's and Brown-headed Apalises, Evergreen Forest Warbler, African Tailorbird, Spot-throat, Dapple-throat*, Uluguru Violet-backed Sunbird.

Others

Mountain Buzzard, Crowned Hawk-Eagle, Livingstone's Turaco, Barred Long-tailed Cuckoo, Narina and Bar-tailed Trogons, Half-collared Kingfisher, Olive Woodpecker, African Broadbill, White-tailed Crested Flycatcher, Black-backed Puffback, Orange Ground-Thrush, Waller's Starling, White-starred Robin, Red-capped Robin-Chat, Shelley's and Mountain Greenbuls, Yellow-streaked Bulbul, Yellow-throated Wood-Warbler, Pale-breasted Illadopsis, Abyssinian Hill-Babbler and Red-faced Crimson-wing.

Access

The forest is accessible from Chita, southwest of Ifakara.

RUAHA NATIONAL PARK

This big park (29,115 sq km) in west-central Tanzania, 130 km west of Iringa, supports the endemic Ashy Starling and Racket-tailed Roller.

The best time to visit Ruaha NP is between July and December, and even then a 4WD is recommended.

Tanzania Endemics

Ashy Starling, Yellow-collared Lovebird.

Specialities

Racket-tailed Roller, Magpie Shrike.

Others

Ostrich, White-backed Night-Heron, Saddle-billed Stork, Martial Eagle, Grey Crowned-Crane, Buff-crested Bustard, White-headed Lapwing, African Skimmer, Black-faced Sandgrouse, Meyer's Parrot, Bare-faced Go-away-bird, Verreaux's Eagle-Owl, Von der Decken's Hornbill, Spot-flanked Barbet, Superb Starling, Yellow-billed and Red-billed Oxpeckers, White-headed Black-Chat, Fischer's Sparrow-Lark.

Other Wildlife

Buffalo, Burchell's zebra, eland, elephant, giraffe, Grant's gazelle, greater kudu, hartebeeste, hippo, impala, Kirk's dik-dik, leopard, lion, roan, rock hyrax, sable.

Access

It is possible to fly into Ruaha NP from Dar es Salaam or Kilimanjaro. The park HQ is at Msembe, 130 km west of Iringa. White-backed Night-Heron occurs alongside the river by the Ibuguziwa Ferry crossing, 8 km from the park boundary. Bird all tracks, especially those along the Magusi Sand and Great Ruaha rivers.

Accommodation: Ruaha River Camp; Msembe Camp (bandas); Mwagusi Camp.

White-headed Lapwings can be seen along the sandy rivers of Ruaha NP

Adventurous birders may wish to consider visiting **Gombe Stream NP** and **Mahale Mountains NP**, both of which lie on the shores of Lake Tanganyika in west Tanzania, and were set up to protect chimpanzees. The montane forest, grassland and extensive tracts of bamboo in the latter park could yield some very interesting birds indeed. To the south, the plateau near Lake Malawi in southwest Tanzania, known as the **Southern Highlands** (2961 m (9715 ft)), may also be worth birding. Remnant patches of montane forest on this plateau support three endemics: Uhehe Fiscal, Iringa Akalat* and Kipengere Seedeater*. It is also possible to search for Shoebill* in southwest Tanzania, in the remote **Moyowosi-Kigosi Swamp**, where the population of this odd bird was estimated at 2,500 in 1990.

There are also a few interesting sites south of Dar es Salaam, although these are difficult to get to, and the birds all occur at other, more accessible, sites. Boehm's Bee-eater (Aug–Sep), African Pitta (Oct–Nov), Kretschmer's Longbill, Sokoke Pipit* and Lesser Seedcracker occur in **Vikundu FR**, 17 km south of Dar es Salaam. African Pitta (Jan–Mar) and Kretschmer's Longbill occur in **Kiwengoma Forest**, 25 km southeast of Utete, further south of Dar Es Salaam. African Pitta (December at least) also occurs in **Rondo Forest**, 77 km west of Lindi in southeast Tanzania, as well as Green Barbet, Livingstone's Flycatcher and East Coast Akalat*.

ADDITIONAL INFORMATION

Books and Papers

A Field Guide to the Birds of East Africa. Williams, J. 1980. HarperCollins.
The Birds of Zanzibar and Pemba. Pakenham, R. 1979. BOU
Guide to Tanzania. Briggs, P. 1993. Bradt.
Birds of Kenya and Northern Tanzania. Zimmerman, D *et al.* In prep. Helm.

Addresses

The Wildlife Conservation Society of Tanzania, Box 70919 Dar es Salaam, produces a regular newsletter called *Miombo.*

Please send all records to the Tanzania Bird Atlas Project, Box 23404, Dar es Salaam.

Tanzania Tourist Corporation (TTC), PO Box 2485, Maktaba St., Dar es Salaam.

Tanzania National Parks Authority (TANAPA), PO Box 3134, Arusha (tel: 3471).

ENDEMICS (20)

Udzungwa Forest-partridge*	Central: West Kilombero FR
Grey-breasted Spurfowl	North: Serengeti
Fischer's Lovebird*	North: Serengeti
Yellow-collared Lovebird	North/central: Tarangire and Ruaha NPs
Usambara Eagle-Owl*	Northeast/central: Usambara and Uluguru Mountains
Uhehe Fiscal	South: southern Highlands
Uluguru Bushshrike*	Central: Uluguru Mountains
Reichenow's Batis	Southeast: coastal lowlands
Usambara Akalat*	Northeast: West Usambara Mountains
Iringa Akalat*	Central/south: West Kilombero FR, Chita and Southern Highlands
Ashy Starling	North/central: Tarangire and Ruaha NPs
Mrs. Moreau's Warbler*	Central: Uluguru Mountains and Mwanihana
Rufous-tailed Weaver	North: Ngorongoro Crater, Serengeti, Tarangire NP
Kilombero Weaver*	Central: Ifakara
Tanzania Masked-Weaver	Southwest: swamps
Usambara Weaver*	Northeast/central: Usambara, Uluguru and Udzungwa Mountains
Banded Sunbird*	Northeast/central: Usambara Mountains, West Kilombero FR and Mwanihana
Loveridge's Sunbird*	Central: Uluguru Mountains
Rufous-winged Sunbird*	Central: West Kilombero FR and Mwanihana
Kipengere Seedeater*	Central/south: Udzungwa Mountains (Chita Forest) and Southern Highlands

PEMBA ISLAND (2)

Pemba Green-Pigeon*	Pemba Island: lowlands
Pemba White-eye*	Pemba Island: forest

(Violet-breasted Sunbird has also been recorded in south Somalia and northeast Tanzania.)

Near-endemics (North)

White-headed Mousebird, Hartlaub's Turaco, Usambiro Barbet, Long-tailed Fiscal, Grey-crested Helmetshrike*, Hildebrandt's, Abbott's* and Fischer's Starlings, Moorland Chat, Broad-ringed White-eye, Chubb's and Hunter's Cisticolas, Karamoja Apalis*, Scaly Chatterer, Scaly Babbler, Sharpe's and Northern Pied-Babblers, Red-throated Tit*, Buff-bellied Penduline-Tit, Athi Short-toed Lark, Swahili Sparrow, Pangani Longclaw, Taveta Golden-Weaver, Fire-fronted Bishop, Jackson's Widowbird*, Golden-winged and Violet-breasted (also on Pemba Island) Sunbirds, Kenya Grosbeak-Canary.

Near-endemics (Northeast, central montane and Coastal forests)

Fischer's Turaco*, Sokoke Scops-Owl*, Scheffler's Owlet, Mombasa Woodpecker, Yellow Flycatcher, Fuelleborn's Boubou, Short-tailed and Pale Batises, White-chested Alethe, Kenrick's Starling, Swynnerton's Robin*, Sharpe's and East Coast* Akalats, Olive-flanked Robin-Chat, Stripe-cheeked Bulbul, Fischer's and Tiny Greenbuls, White-winged*, Chapin's and Brown-headed Apalises, African and Long-billed* Tailorbirds, Kretschmar's Longbill, Spot-throat, Dapple-throat*, Lesser Seedcracker, Sokoke Pipit*, Bertrand's Weaver, Zanzibar Bishop, Plain-backed*, Uluguru Violet-backed, Amani* and Eastern Double-collared Sunbirds.

Near-endemics (South)

Miombo Barbet, Stierling's Woodpecker*, Babbling Starling, Sharpe's Greenbul, Black-lored and Churring* Cisticolas, Olive-headed Weaver, Buff-shouldered Widowbird, Oustalet's Sunbird, Yellow-browed Seedeater.

Near-endemics (West)

Red-faced Barbet*, Kungwe Apalis*, Laura's Wood-Warbler.

Near-endemics (Pemba, Comoros and Madagascar)

Malagasy Scops-Owl (some authorities regard this as a full species: Pemba Scops-Owl).

TOGO

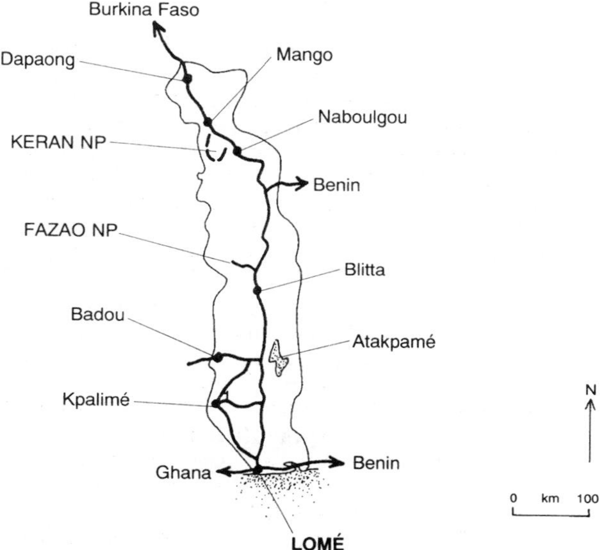

1 Southwest Plateau

INTRODUCTION

Tiny Togo lies in the 'Dahomey Gap', the area of savanna which separates the Upper Guinea forests to the west from the Lower Guinea forests of Nigeria and the Congo Basin to the east. Only one of the Upper Guinea endemics is present. Political instability in the early 1990s has led to some safety problems in Togo, and birders should check the situation before considering a visit.

Togo (56,785 sq km) is less than half the size of England, and one twelfth the size of Texas. By West African standards, Togo has an excellent infrastructure, with good roads, private taxis, and basic, but fairly priced accommodation and food. The only drawbacks are expensive car-hire, malaria and the usual assortment of diseases for which immunisations are recommended. The long but sparse rains usually last from March to November, with a break in August, but they rarely cause transport problems. The lagoons of the coast give way to a fertile plateau in the west, where coffee, cocoa, fruit and palm plantations cover most of the slopes. Much of the rest of the country comprises degraded savanna, although small patches of forest remain along the border with Ghana. Five near-threatened species have been recorded in Togo, but three of these are forest birds and may now be extremely rare.

A total of 622 species have been recorded in Togo, only 100 fewer than Ghana its western neighbour, which is four times larger. Non-endemic specialities and spectacular species include Long-tailed Hawk, Black Crowned-Crane, Egyptian and Forbes' Plovers and Damara Tern*. There are no endemics and only two near-endemics: Chestnut-bellied Helmetshrike and Rufous-winged Illadopsis*.

White-fronted Plover, and Royal and Damara* (Oct–Nov) Terns have been recorded near the capital, **Lomé**, on the south coast. It used to be possible to see these birds between the Sara-Kawa Hotel and the port, but this is now the haunt of muggers and may be too dangerous to visit. The best birding site accessible by taxi from Lome used to be the lower Sio river near Dhagble.

SOUTHWEST PLATEAU

The fertile upland plateau of southwest Togo, near the border with Ghana, supports remnant Upper Guinea forest amongst the numerous coffee and cocoa plantations, where Long-tailed Hawk and Chestnut-bellied Helmetshrike occur.

Specialities

Chestnut-bellied Helmetshrike.

Others

Long-tailed Hawk, Guinea Turaco, Black-throated Coucal, Shining Blue and Blue-breasted Kingfishers, White-throated Bee-eater, Blue-throated Roller, Hairy-breasted and Yellow-billed Barbets, Melancholy and Fire-bellied Woodpeckers, Black-winged Oriole, African Shrike-flycatcher, Little and Honeyguide Greenbuls, Whistling Cisticola, Rufous-crowned Eremomela, Green Crombec, White-shouldered Black-Tit, Yellow-mantled and Red-headed Weavers, Buff-throated Sunbirds.

Access

This area used to be easily accessible, and the best birding areas were the **Misahohe Forest**, near Kpalime, around **Badou**, **Aledjo Forest**, north of Badou, and the area around **Djodji** (Long-tailed Hawk and Chestnut-bellied Helmetshrike).

In north Togo, previously productive birding areas included the **Landa Pozanda Rapids**, 2 km upstream from Kara (Rock Pratincole/May–Sep); **Keran NP**, now largely destroyed except around the HQ/Lodge at Naboulgou, which is on Route 1 south of Mango (Black Crowned-Crane, Narina Trogon, Red-throated Bee-eater); the **Oti Valley** upstream from Mango; **Domaine Gravillou**, an area of paddies 4 km north of Mango (African Pygmy-goose, Black Crowned-Crane, Northern Carmine Bee-eater); and **Tantigou**, 5 km northeast of Dapaong, the best area in Togo for waterfowl, and a good site for Red-necked Falcon.

A SELECTED LIST OF SPECIES RECORDED IN TOGO

White-backed Night-Heron, White-crested Bittern, Hamerkop, Scissor-tailed Kite, Secretary-bird, Fox Kestrel, Ahanta Francolin, Red-chested Flufftail, Nkulengu Rail, African Finfoot, Egyptian (Lama-Kara) and

Forbes' Plovers, Grey Parrot, Great Blue Turaco (Lando-Mono), Dusky Long-tailed and Yellow-throated Cuckoos, Black Coucal (Lama-Kara), White-bellied Kingfisher, Black, Swallow-tailed and Rosy Bee-eaters, Abyssinian and Blue-bellied Rollers, White-crested and Piping Hornbills, Naked-faced and Bristle-nosed Barbets, Willcock's and Wahlberg's Honeyguides, African Pitta, Rufous-sided Broadbill, Piapiac, Blue Cuckoo-shrike, Many-coloured Bushshrike, Red-cheeked Wattle-eye, White-tailed Alethe, Chestnut-winged Starling, Bronze-tailed Glossy-Starling, Cassin's Flycatcher, Forest Robin, Pied-winged and Preuss' Swallows, Baumann's Greenbul*, Grey-headed Bristlebill, Siffling, Rufous and Black-necked Cisticolas, Grey Longbill, Rufous-winged Illadopsis*, Capuchin Babbler, Sun Lark, Grey-headed Oliveback, Baka and Pale-winged Indigobirds, Togo Paradise-Whydah, Orange Weaver, Scarlet-tufted and Johanna's Sunbirds.

ADDITIONAL INFORMATION

Books and Papers

The Birds of Togo. Cheke, R and Walsh F. In prep. BOU.

Near-endemics (Upper Guinea)

Rufous-winged Illadopsis*.

Near-endemics (Upper Guinea and Nigeria)

Chestnut-bellied Helmetshrike.

TUNISIA

INTRODUCTION

Summary

Although Tunisia is not as rich in avian terms as Morocco, it supports most of the North African specialities, including Moussier's Redstart, and still attracts the occasional Slender-billed Curlew*. A short trip is worth considering, especially for birders who have been to Morocco and missed a couple of 'target' species.

Size

At 163,610 sq km, Tunisia is a little larger than England, and one quarter the size of Texas.

Getting Around

Although cheap buses reach most places, serious birders with limited time are advised to hire a car.

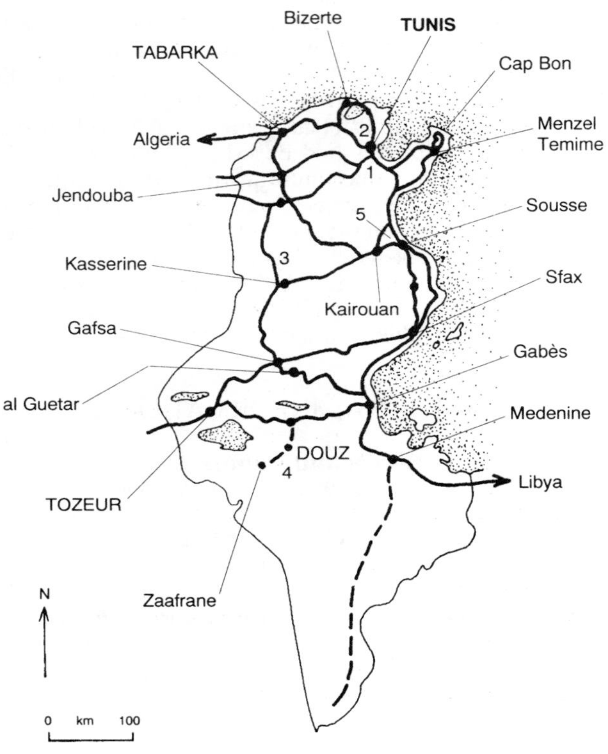

1 Tunis
2 Lake Ichkeul
3 Tabarka to Tozeur
4 Douz
5 Lake Kelbia

Accommodation and Food

Accommodation is basic but cheap away from the major resort areas such as Tunis and Sousse. The food is fine, especially fish.

Health and Safety

Immunisation against hepatitis, polio, typhoid and yellow fever is recommended.

Climate and Timing

The winter (Nov–Mar) is usually wet and mild in the north; summers (Apr–Sep) are hot and dry throughout, especially in the south. Spring, autumn and winter are all good times to go.

Habitats
Green coastal plains and mountains clad with cork-oak woods in the north give way to plains dotted with salty pans (chotts) and the arid, rocky semi-desert of the south, at the northern edge of the Sahara. A string of coastal lagoons along the north and east coasts support important numbers of Palearctic wildfowl.

Conservation
Six threatened and three near-threatened species occur in Tunisia, and this country is of particular importance for White-headed Duck* and Marbled Teal*.

Bird Families
None of the families endemic to Africa are represented in Tunisia.

Bird Species
A total of 353 species have been recorded in Tunisia, over 100 fewer than Morocco. Non-endemic specialities and spectacular species include White-headed Duck*, Marbled Teal*, Barbary Partridge, Slender-billed Curlew* (rare), Cream-coloured Courser, Audouin's Gull*, Red-necked and Egyptian Nightjars and Desert Sparrow.

Endemics
There are no endemics, but there are three near-endemics: Levaillant's Woodpecker, Moussier's Redstart and Tristram's Warbler.

Expectations
It is possible to see 140 species during a two-week trip.

TUNIS

Some excellent species occur around the capital Tunis, in the north of the country, including White-headed Duck* and Moussier's Redstart.

Specialities
White-headed Duck*, Moussier's Redstart.

Others
Greater Flamingo, Bonelli's Eagle, Barbary Falcon, Barbary Partridge, Laughing Dove, Black-crowned Tchagra, Spotless Starling, Thekla Lark, Rock Petronia, Rock Bunting.

Access
White-headed Duck* occurs on the small lake northwest of Menzel Temime on **Cap Bon**, east of Tunis, and on Sidi Jdidi near Hammamet. Barbary Partridge and Black-crowned Tchagra also occur on Cap Bon. **Lake Tunis**, north of the port *en route* to Carthage, supports Greater Flamingo. The track south of **Zaghouan**, south of Tunis off the C133, ascends a valley where Barbary Partridge and Moussier's Redstart occur.

LAKE ICHKEUL

This huge lake near the northern Mediterranean coast, a few km south of Bizerte, is an important refuelling stop for Palearctic migrants, especially in spring, and a major wintering ground for waterfowl. During the summer much of the lake usually dries up, although White-headed Duck* and Marbled Teal* may both be present at this time.

Specialities

White-headed Duck*, Marbled Teal*, Moussier's Redstart.

Others

Cory's Shearwater, Greater Flamingo, Long-legged Buzzard (Nov–Mar), Eleonora's (Oct–Nov), Lanner and Barbary (Nov–Mar) Falcons, Barbary Partridge, Purple Swamphen, Audouin's Gull*, Lesser Short-toed and Thekla Larks, Spanish Sparrow.

(A Slender-billed Curlew* was reported from here in November 1991, and two were reported in December 1993.)

Access

Bird from the road that fringes the northern and eastern sides, and alongside the road up Djebel Ichkeul (Moussier's Redstart). Audouin's Gull* occurs in Bizerte harbour. Barbary Partridge occurs on **Cap Blanc**, north of Bizerte, which is a good place from which to seawatch.

Accommodation: Bizerte.

TABARKA TO TOZEUR

The road south from Tabarka, a coastal resort on the north Mediterranean coast, to Tozeur at the northern edge of the Sahara, passes through oak woods, pine forest and stony semi-desert, each of which supports a characteristic avifauna.

Specialities

Levaillant's Woodpecker, Tristram's Warbler.

Others

Long-legged Buzzard, Cream-coloured Courser, Red-necked Nightjar, Black, Mourning and Red-rumped Wheatears, Streaked Scrub-Warbler, Orphean Warbler, Bar-tailed and Desert Larks, Greater Hoopoe-Lark, Trumpeter Finch, House Bunting.

Access

Levaillant's Woodpecker occurs in the oak woods alongside the P17 between Ain Draham and Jendouba. Much further south, turn west 15 km south of **Kasserine** towards Djebel Chambi. Take the right fork after the river (usually dry) up to the dwarf pine forest, where Red-necked Nightjar, Black Wheatear and Tristram's Warbler occur. Further south still, turn west 62 km north of **Gafsa** on to a track which passes through stony desert (Desert Lark and Trumpeter Finch) to a gorge which is only accessible on foot (Black Wheatear and House Bunting). Near Gafsa, the hills east of al Guetar on the P15 support Mourning and Red-rumped Wheatears. Roadside birds between Gafsa and **Tozeur** include Cream-coloured Courser. The surrounds of Tozeur oasis are also worth birding.

DOUZ

It is best to visit this desert backwater in south Tunisia in winter, when it is capable of producing some of the best birding the country can offer thanks to birds such as Egyptian Nightjar, Moussier's Redstart and the delightful Desert Sparrow.

Specialities

Marbled Teal*, Moussier's Redstart (Nov–Mar), Tristram's Warbler (Nov–Mar), Desert Sparrow.

Others

Ruddy Shelduck, Glossy Ibis, Egyptian Nightjar, Brown-necked Raven, Streaked Scrub-Warbler, Desert Warbler, Fulvous Chatterer, Greater Hoopoe-Lark, Spanish Sparrow, House Bunting.

Access

Egyptian Nightjar occurs around the marsh west of Douz, behind the barracks and rubbish dump. The 4-km track south from the Hotel des Roses Sable in Douz leads to the El Hessai oasis, which lies to the west of the track. Desert Sparrow, which is often with Spanish Sparrows, occurs in the dunes surrounding this oasis. The road southwest from Douz to Sabria passes tamarisk scrub and pools where Marbled Teal*, Fulvous Chatterer and House Bunting occur. The areas south of Sabria and the Douz–Gabès road, to the east of Douz, are also worth exploring for desert species. Marbled Teal* also occurs on the lakes between Douz and El Nouail and Douz and El Fouar (400 on these two lakes in January 1994, and 755 in the Douz area up to April 1994).

Accommodation: Hotel des Roses Sable.

The oases and desert around the town of **Tatahouine**, 50 km south of Medenine, in southeast Tunisia, support Streaked Scrub-Warbler, Tristram's Warbler, Desert Lark, Greater Hoopoe-Lark, and Temminck's Lark. Bird the track which leads east 23.5 km north of Tatahouine for larks, and the Oued Dekouk, 25 km south of Tatahouine on the GP19, for warblers.

There are a number of excellent coastal lagoons along the east Mediterranean coast between Gabes, in the southeast, and Tunis in the north, including the internationally important **Lake Kelbia**, 35 km north of Sousse. When wet, this lagoon may support White-headed Duck*, Greater Flamingo, Purple Swamphen and Common Crane. To reach the northwest corner, the best access point near the junction of the GP2 and MC48, head north from Sousse, then turn west towards Kebira on the MC48. Cream-coloured Courser, Black-bellied Sandgrouse, Marmora's Warbler and Thekla Lark have also been recorded here.

Slender-billed Curlew* has been reported from the **Kairouan** area in northeast Tunisia in January 1974, January 1977, Nov–Dec 1986 and November 1992 (at Metbassta, 15 km to the north of Kairouan).

ADDITIONAL INFORMATION

Books

Birds of Tunisia, An Annotated Checklist and a Field Guide to Birdwatching. Thomson, P and Jacobsen, P. 1979. Jelling Alps, Copenhagen, Denmark.

Addresses

Les Amis des Oiseaux, Faculte des Sciences, Campus Universitaire, 1060 Tunis Belvedere, Tunisia.

Near-endemics

Levaillant's Woodpecker, Moussier's Redstart, Tristram's Warbler.

UGANDA

INTRODUCTION

Summary

In terms of size, Uganda is the richest country for birds in Africa. With an excellent infrastructure, a great diversity of wetland, savanna and forest birds, including 29 of the 43 Albertine Rift endemics, as well as gorillas and chimpanzees, Uganda could soon rival Kenya as the most popular destination on the continent. After the end of many years of brutal dictatorship, ecotourism is being positively encouraged.

Size

At 236,578 sq km, Uganda is twice the size of England, and one third the size of Texas.

Getting Around

Uganda has reasonable road and bus networks, although many roads are unsurfaced. There are no internal scheduled flights.

Accommodation and Food

There is a wide variety of accommodation available, from expensive lodges to cheap, basic hotels and guesthouses, as well as campsites in the main national parks. The local diet is dominated by sweet potatoes and fish.

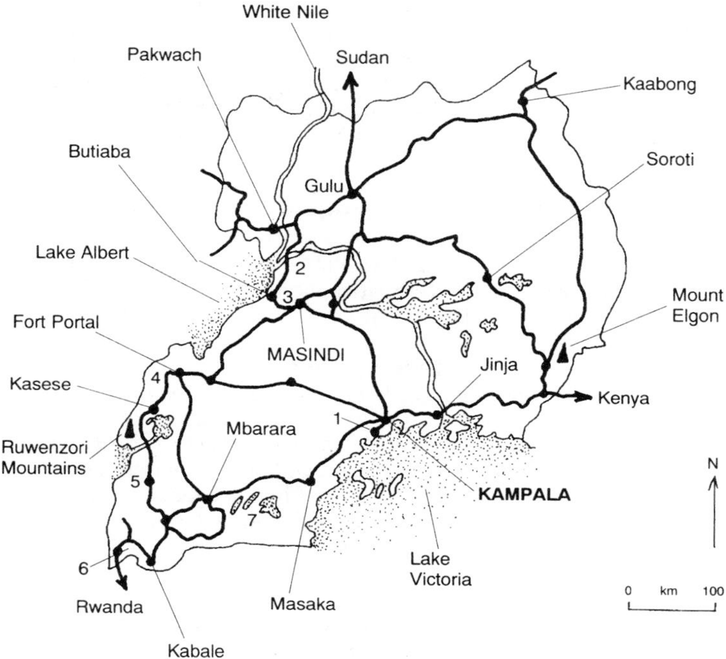

1 Entebbe
2 Kabalega Falls NP
3 Budongo Forest
4 Kibale Forest NP
5 Ruwenzori NP
6 Inpenetrable (Bwindi) Forest NP
7 Lake Mburo NP

Health and Safety

Immunisation against hepatitis, meningitis, polio, typhoid and yellow fever is recommended, as are precautions against malaria. Also beware of bilharzia.

Ecotourism is being encouraged, but there are still armed holdups of vehicles on public roads.

Climate and Timing

Uganda has two dry seasons: December to March and June to September, both of which are good times to visit. However, June to September, especially September, when Brown-chested Lapwing is possible, is the best time.

Habitats

For such a small country Uganda has a great diversity of habitats, with savanna, lowland forest and wetland, inbetween montane forest and grassland of the Ruwenzori Mountains in the west, and Mount Elgon in the east.

Conservation

Many large animals and much habitat was destroyed by Amin's and Okello's troops, but the new government is making a brave effort to restore Uganda's deserved reputation as an outstanding ecotourist's destination. There are now ten national parks, which will help to protect the ten threatened and 19 near-threatened species which occur there.

Bird Families

Eight of the ten families endemic to the African mainland are represented in Uganda, including Shoebill*. Well represented families include francolins, turacos, bee-eaters, hornbills, honeyguides, greenbuls, weavers and sunbirds.

Bird Species

A remarkable 992 species have been recorded in Uganda, the fourth highest total for an African country. Although Uganda is less than half the size of Kenya it supports nearly as many species (just 86 fewer). Non-endemic specialities and spectacular species include Shoebill*, Lesser Jacana, Brown-chested Lapwing, Chocolate-backed Kingfisher, Black and Blue-breasted Bee-eaters, Blue-throated Roller, Jameson's Wattle-eye and Woodhouse's Antpecker.

Endemics

Two species are endemic to Uganda: Kibale Ground-Thrush*, which is known only from two specimens collected in 1966, and Fox's Weaver*. Many near-endemics, including 29 of the 43 Albertine Rift endemics, also occur here, including Kivu* and Oberlander's* Ground-Thrushes.

Expectations

Well prepared energetic birders may see 500 species during a three-week trip.

ENTEBBE

The lakeside vegetation, botanical gardens, scrub and marshes surrounding Entebbe, 24 km south of Kampala on the shores of Lake Victoria, support Lesser Jacana, Blue-breasted Bee-eater and the localised Red-chested Sunbird.

Specialities

Lesser Jacana, Red-chested Sunbird.

Others

African Pygmy-goose, Hamerkop, Hadada Ibis, Palm-nut Vulture, Grey Crowned-Crane, Rock Pratincole, Long-toed Lapwing, Grey Parrot, Red-headed Lovebird, Ross's Turaco, Eastern Grey Plantain-eater, Great Blue Turaco, African Pygmy-Kingfisher, Blue-breasted and White-throated Bee-eaters, African Pied and Black-and-white-casqued Hornbills, Double-toothed Barbet, Marsh Tchagra, Black-headed Gonolek, Black-and-white Shrike-flycatcher, Splendid and Rueppell's Glossy-Starlings, Swamp Flycatcher, Banded Martin, Angola Swallow,

Red-faced Cisticola, White-chinned Prinia, Greater Swamp-Warbler, Black-crowned Waxbill, Slender-billed, Orange, Northern Brown-throated, Vieillot's Black and Black-headed Weavers, Fan-tailed Widowbird, Olive-bellied Sunbird.

Other Wildlife

Spot-necked otter.

Access

The best birding areas are the Nsamizi area where it is possible to hire boats to explore Lake Victoria, the Botanical Gardens (Great Blue Turaco), the area around the Yacht Club, the zoo, and Bogo Forest, on the lakeshore 30 km southeast of Lugazi.

Accommodation: Lake Victoria Hotel.

Scrub and grassland near the capital, **Kampala**, support White-crested Turaco and Speckle-breasted Woodpecker. The golf course is a particularly good spot.

Accommodation: Athina Club; Fairway Hotel.

Grey-capped Warbler, White-collared Oliveback, Northern Brown-throated Weaver and Papyrus Canary have been recorded at Namulonge Agricultural Research Station, 30 km northeast of Kampala, and Weyns' Weaver occurs in Mpanga Forest, 35 km west of Kampala.

KABALEGA FALLS NATIONAL PARK

The major tourist attraction in this big national park (3900 sq km) in west Uganda, is Kabalega Falls, a spectacular drop in the White Nile. Below the falls, in the papryus beds lining the Nile, it is possible to see the park's major avian attraction: Shoebill*.

There are plenty of good birds in the rest of the park, which is mainly savanna, including Heuglin's Francolin and Red-throated Bee-eater.

Specialities

Shoebill*, Heuglin's Francolin, Emin's Shrike, Black-headed Batis, Silverbird, Carruthers' Cisticola.

Others

African Darter, Goliath Heron, Saddle-billed Stork, Bat Hawk, Bateleur, Harlequin and Blue Quails, Black Crake, African Finfoot, Stanley Bustard, Senegal and Spotted Thick-knees, Rock Pratincole, Bronze-winged and Temminck's Coursers, Long-toed Lapwing, African Skimmer, Vinaceous Dove, Bruce's Green-Pigeon, Ross's Turaco, Black Coucal, Marsh Owl, Plain, Standard-winged and Pennant-winged Nightjars, Giant Kingfisher, Red-throated and Swallow-tailed Bee-eaters, Abyssinian Roller, Abyssinian Ground-Hornbill, Piapiac, Marsh Tchagra, Black-headed Gonolek, Yellow-billed Oxpecker, Sooty Chat, Banded Martin, Siffling Cisticola, Lesser Swamp-Warbler, Brown Twinspot, White-winged Widowbird, Beautiful Sunbird, White-rumped Seedeater.

Other Wildlife

Buffalo, elephant, giraffe, hippo, kob, lion, Nile crocodile, olive baboon.

Access

Bush taxis can be hired in Masindi to get to this park. It is a short walk from Paraa to the river, from where the falls are 11 km upstream. Look for Shoebill* in the papyrus swamps just below the falls. This strange looking bird also occurs downstream from Paraa.

Accommodation: NP: Paraa Bandas/camping (take own food); Rabongo Bungalows, Chobe Safari Lodge; Inns of Uganda. Masindi: Masindi Hotel.

BUDONGO FOREST

This small (435 sq km), easily accessible forest near Masindi supports some localised birds, including Nahan's Francolin, Ituri Batis and Jameson's Wattle-eye.

Specialities

Nahan's Francolin*, Buff-spotted Flufftail, Ituri Batis, Jameson's Wattle-eye, Uganda Wood-Warbler, Grey-headed Sunbird.

Others

Cassin's Hawk-Eagle, White-spotted Flufftail, Afep Pigeon, Dusky Long-tailed Cuckoo, Black-shouldered Nightjar, Narina Trogon, Dwarf, Chocolate-backed and Blue-breasted Kingfishers, White-throated Bee-eater, White-thighed Hornbill, Yellow-throated Tinkerbird, Yellow-spotted Barbet, Willcock's Honeyguide, Golden-crowned Woodpecker, Chestnut-capped Flycatcher, African Shrike-flycatcher, Chestnut Wattle-eye, Rufous Flycatcher-Thrush, Red-tailed Ant-thrush, Narrow-tailed Starling, African Forest-Flycatcher, Sooty and Cassin's Flycatchers, Grey-throated Tit-Flycatcher, Blue-shouldered Robin-Chat, White-headed Sawwing, Little, Spotted and Red-tailed Greenbuls, Black-capped Apalis, Yellow-browed and Olive-green Camaropteras, Lemon-bellied Crombec, Yellow and Grey Longbills, Green Hylia, Pale-breasted Illadopsis, Grey-headed Oliveback, Red-headed Bluebill, Weyns' Weaver, Crested Malimbe.

Other Wildlife

Black-and-white colobus, blue monkey, chimpanzee, olive baboon, red-tailed monkey.

Access

The forest is northwest of Masindi. Bird the entrance track, known as the 'Royal Mile', on the Sawmills road.

Accommodation: Masindi: Masindi Hotel.

Swamps between Masindi and Fort Portal support White-winged Scrub-Warbler and Papyrus Canary.

KIBALE FOREST NATIONAL PARK

This national park, near Fort Portal in west Uganda is one of the few places in Africa where there is a good chance of seeing chimpanzees. Over 300 bird species have also been recorded, including Blue-throated Roller and Woodhouse's Antpecker.

Specialities

White-winged Scrub-Warbler, Uganda Wood-Warbler.

Others

Black Goshawk, Crowned Hawk-Eagle, Afep Pigeon, Grey Parrot, Black-billed and Great Blue Turacos, Olive Long-tailed Cuckoo, African Wood-Owl, Scarce Swift, Narina Trogon, Chocolate-backed Kingfisher, Blue-throated Roller, White-headed Woodhoopoe, Speckled Tinkerbird, Brown-eared and Elliot's Woodpeckers, Cassin's Honeyguide, African Shrike-flycatcher, Chestnut Wattle-eye, Rufous Flycatcher-Thrush, Brown-chested Alethe, Cassin's Flycatcher, Grey-throated Tit-Flycatcher, Equatorial Akalat, Blue-shouldered Robin-Chat, White-headed Sawwing, Honeyguide and Joyful Greenbuls, Black-throated and Buff-throated Apalises, Green Crombec, Scaly-breasted Illadopsis, Dusky Tit, Woodhouse's Antpecker, White-breasted and Chestnut-breasted Negrofinches, Black-necked, Yellow-mantled and Grosbeak Weavers, Blue-throated Brown, Northern Double-collared and Superb Sunbirds.

(This is also the only known locality for the endemic Kibale Ground-Thrush*, two specimens of which were collected here in 1966. However, despite extensive searches this species has never been seen since.)

Other Wildlife

Black-and-white colobus, chimpanzee, grey-cheeked mangabey, L'Hoest's monkey, red colobus, red-tailed monkey.

Access

Bird the main track from Kanyanchu Camp. A number of trails lead off from here and are also worth exploring, especially Trail B.

White-headed Woodhoopoe is one of many excellent birds present in Kibale Forest

Accommodation: National Park: Kanyanchu Camp. Fort Portal: Mountains of the Moon Hotel.

Over 400 species have been recorded in **Semliki (Bwamba) Forest NP** (220 sq km) on the east bank of the Semliki river northwest of Fort Portal, near Bundibugyo, including Nkulengu Rail, White-naped Pigeon*, Yellow-throated Cuckoo, Pel's Fishing-Owl, Chestnut Owlet, White-bellied Kingfisher, Lyre-tailed Honeyguide, Rufous-sided Broadbill, Oberlander's Ground-Thrush*, Scaly-breasted Illadopsis, Capuchin Babbler and Black-bellied Seedcracker.

Carruthers' Cisticola, White-winged Scrub-Warbler and Papyrus Canary occur in roadside swamps between Fort Portal, Pachwa and Kynjojo.

RUWENZORI NATIONAL PARK

This relatively small park (2000 sq km) protects the Ruwenzori Mountain, gallery forest, savanna and wetlands, and boasts the biggest site list in Africa. By 1992 an amazing 535 species had been recorded including the rarely encountered Brown-chested Lapwing and Papyrus Gonolek*.

Specialities

Brown-chested Lapwing (Sep), Papyrus Gonolek*, Carruthers' Cisiticola.

Others

African Pygmy-goose, Goliath Heron, White-headed Vulture, Bateleur, Martial and Long-crested Eagles, Blue Quail, Black-rumped Buttonquail, White-spotted Flufftail, African Crake, Water Thick-knee, Temminck's Courser, Long-toed and Senegal Lapwings, African Skimmer, Red-headed Lovebird, Ross's Turaco, Verreaux's Eagle-Owl, Swamp Nightjar, Little, Blue-breasted and White-throated Bee-eaters, Marsh Tchagra, Black-headed Gonolek, Stout, Croaking and Wing-snapping Cisticolas, Grey-capped Warbler, Rufous-naped and Flappet Larks, Yellow-throated Longclaw, Slender-billed Weaver, White-winged Widowbird, Copper and Mariqua Sunbirds.

Other Wildlife

Black-and-white colobus, buffalo, elephant, giant forest hog, hippo, kob, leopard, lion, red-tailed monkey, spotted hyena, topi.

Access

Boat trips along the Kazinga Channel (between Lake George and Lake Edward) from Mweya Lodge to the Chambura river, where it is possible to walk up to a gorge, are recommended. Otherwise, good birding areas include the Crater Circuit and the Lake George, Hamukunga and Kasenyi areas.

Accommodation: National Park: Mweya Lodge Hostel/camping (C); Ishasha Camp (extreme south).

IMPENETRABLE (BWINDI) FOREST NATIONAL PARK

The forest in this small park (321 sq km), lying between 1160 m (3806 ft) and 2650 m (8694 ft) near Kabale in southwest Uganda, supports over 30% (300) of the world population of 'mountain' gorillas, and some very special birds, notably Lagden's Bushshrike* and Neumann's Warbler. Over 330 species have been recorded, including 23 of the 43 Albertine Rift endemics and 69 of the 77 montane forest species of the same region. Any serious birder visiting Uganda should plan to spend at least a few days here.

Specialities

Handsome Francolin, Red-chested Flufftail, Ruwenzori Turaco, Red-chested Owlet, Ruwenzori Nightjar, Western Green-Tinkerbird, Dwarf Honeyguide*, White-tailed Blue-Flycatcher, Mountain Boubou, Black-fronted, Doherty's and Lagden's* Bushshrikes, Ruwenzori Batis, Kivu* and Oberlander's* Ground-Thrushes, Red-throated Alethe, Yellow-eyed Black-Flycatcher, Chapin's Flycatcher*, White-bellied and Archer's Robin-Chats, Shelley's and Cabanis' Greenbuls, Chubb's and Carruthers' Cisticolas, Collared and Masked Apalises, Grauer's Scrub-Warbler*, Evergreen Forest Warbler, Grauer's Warbler, White-browed Crombec, Neumann's Warbler, Red-faced Woodland-Warbler, Stripe-breasted Tit, White-collared Oliveback, Dusky and Shelley's* Crimson-wings, Strange Weaver, Grey-headed, Blue-headed, Regal and Purple-breasted Sunbirds.

Others

Rufous-chested Sparrowhawk, Black Goshawk, Mountain Buzzard, Ayre's Hawk-Eagle, Scaly Francolin, African Pigeon, Lemon Dove, Brown-necked Parrot, Black-billed and Great Blue Turacos, Black, Dusky Long-tailed, Barred Long-tailed and African Emerald Cuckoos, Fraser's Eagle-Owl, Horus Swift, Narina and Bar-tailed Trogons, Blue-breasted Kingfisher, Black and Cinnamon-chested Bee-eaters, Blue-throated Roller, White-headed Woodhoopoe, Black-and-white-casqued and White-thighed Hornbills, Grey-throated and Yellow-billed Barbets, Scaly-throated Honeyguide, Tullberg's, Elliot's and Olive Woodpeckers, African Broadbill, Dusky, White-bellied and White-tailed Crested-Flycatchers, Black-tailed Oriole, Petit's and Purple-throated Cuckoo-shrikes, Mackinnon's Shrike, Pink-footed Puffback, Grey-green Bushshrike, Black-and-white Shrike-flycatcher, Rufous Flycatcher-Thrush, Stuhlmann's, Narrow-tailed, Waller's, Slender-billed and Sharpe's Starlings, Dusky-blue Flycatcher, Grey-throated Tit-Flycatcher, White-starred Robin, Equatorial Akalat, Snowy-crowned Robin-Chat, Black Sawwing, Mountain and Red-tailed Greenbuls, White-chinned and Black-faced Prinias, Black-throated and Chestnut-throated Apalises, Grey-capped Warbler, Cinnamon Bracken-Warbler, Mountain Warbler, Brown Woodland-Warbler, Brown and Grey-chested Illadopsises, Dusky Tit, Woodhouse's Antpecker, White-breasted Negrofinch, Red-faced Crimson-wing, Yellow-bellied and Black-headed Waxbills, Cape and Mountain Wagtails, Black-billed and Brown-capped Weavers, Yellow Bishop, Northern Double-collared Sunbird, Thick-billed Seedeater, Oriole Finch.

(Schouteden's Swift*, otherwise endemic to Zaïre, has also been reported here, and other records include Grauer's Broadbill*.)

Other Wildlife

Black-and-white colobus, blue monkey, chimpanzee, gorilla, L'Hoest's monkey, red-tailed monkey.

It is important to bird both the montane forest around **Ruhija** (2438 m (8000 ft)) and the lowland forest around **Buhoma**. Most of the Albertine Rift endemics occur around Ruhija, which is 50 km from Kabale via Rutenga, including Shelley's Crimson-wing* and Regal Sunbird, as well as Red-chested Flufftail, Doherty's Bushshrike and Oriole Finch. From here, it is also possible to walk (3–4 hours, best with guide) to Mubwindi Swamp, a papyrus marsh where Grauer's Scrub-Warbler* occurs. There is an excellent trail at Buhoma where the major attractions, apart from Gorillas, include Black Bee-eater, Kivu Ground-Thrush* and Purple-breasted Sunbird.

Accommodation: Kabale: Highland Hotel (B). Ruhija: Research Station Guesthouse/camping (take food). Buhoma: Tented Camp.

The short-tailed Neumann's Warbler, an Albertine Rift endemic which occurs in the Impenetrable Forest, has a striking head pattern

LAKE MBURO NATIONAL PARK

The papyrus beds, woodland and savanna within this park, between Kabale and Kampala, support Brown-chested Lapwing and Papyrus Gonolek*.

Specialities

Brown-chested Lapwing (Sep), Papyrus Gonolek*.

Others

Saddle-billed Stork, Wahlberg's Eagle, Black-rumped Buttonquail, Grey Crowned-Crane, Three-banded Plover, Senegal Lapwing, Meyer's Parrot, Bare-faced Go-away-bird, Lilac-breasted Roller, Yellow-fronted Tinkerbird, Marsh Tchagra, Swamp Flycatcher, Rufous-chested Swallow, Grey-capped Warbler, Fawn-breasted Waxbill, Yellow-throated Longclaw, Holub's Golden-Weaver, Golden-backed Weaver, White-winged Widowbird.

Other Wildlife

Bohor reedbuck, buffalo, Burchell's zebra, hippo, impala, klipspringer, oribi, topi.

Accommodation: National Park: Rwonyo Restcamp. Mbarara: Lake View Hotel.

ADDITIONAL INFORMATION

Books and Papers

A Field Guide to the Birds of East Africa. Williams, J. 1980. HarperCollins.
Birds of the Kampala Area (*Scopus* Special Supplement No 2). Carswell, M. 1986. EAOS.
Birds of Kenya and Northern Tanzania. Zimmerman, D *et al.* In prep. Helm.

Addresses

East African Natural History Society (EANHS), Box 44486, Nairobi, Kenya.
Please send records to The Data Manager, National Biodiversity Data Bank, PO Box 10066, Kampala.

ENDEMICS (2)

Kibale Ground-Thrush*	West: known from only two specimens collected near Fort Portal, in Kibale Forest in 1966, and not recorded since, despite extensive searches
Fox's Weaver*	Central: swamps around Lake Kyoga

Near-endemics (Albertine Rift)

Nahan's* and Handsome Francolins, Ruwenzori Turaco, Ruwenzori Nightjar, Grauer's Broadbill* (one specimen 1967), Ruwenzori Batis, Grauer's Cuckoo-shrike*, Kivu* and Oberlander's* Ground-Thrushes, Red-throated Alethe, Yellow-eyed Black-Flycatcher, Archer's Robin-Chat, Sassi's Greenbul* (one record), Collared and Black-faced Apalises, White-winged and Grauer's* Scrub-Warblers, Grauer's and Neumann's Warblers, Red-faced Woodland-Warbler, Stripe-breasted Tit, Dusky and Shelley's* Crimson-wings, Grant's Bluebill, Strange Weaver, Grey-headed, Blue-headed, Regal and Purple-breasted Sunbirds.

Near-endemics (West/Southwest)

Red-faced Barbet*, Dwarf Honeyguide*, Doherty's Bushshrike, Papyrus Gonolek*, Chapin's Flycatcher*, Turner's Eremomela* (one record), White-browed Crombec, Uganda Wood-Warbler, Papyrus Canary.

Near-endemics (North)

Mongalla Cisticola, Karamoja Apalis*.

Near-endemics (East)

Moorland and Jackson's Francolins, Hartlaub's Turaco, Lynes' Cisticola, Sharpe's Pied-Babbler, Golden-winged Sunbird.

ZAÏRE

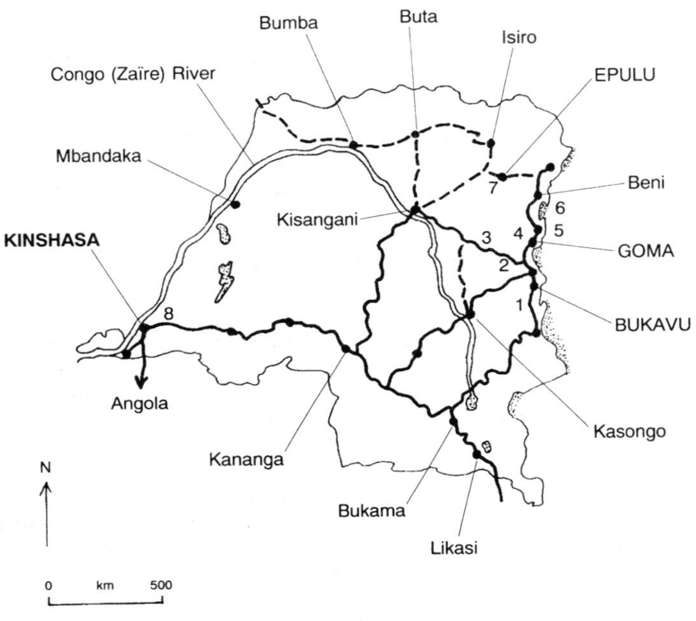

1 Itombwe Mountains
2 Kahuzi–Biega NP
3 Irangi and Itebero
4 Goma-Kibumba
5 Rumangabo
6 Djomba
7 Ituri Forest
8 Lac Ma Valle

INTRODUCTION

Summary

Zaïre is Africa's Amazonia, where vast expanses of remote lowland rainforest still exist. Although the greater part of this wonderful wilderness is still largely inaccessible, it is possible to see some of its avian inhabitants in extreme east Zaïre, which just happens to be where all 43 of the Albertine Rift endemics and most of Zaïre's endemics occur as well. However, the mass influx of Rwandan refugees in 1994 may have affected travel to this exciting part of Africa.

Size

At 2,345,409 sq km, this huge country is 18 times larger than England, and 3.4 times the size of Texas.

Getting Around

Apart from in the extreme east, the only means of getting around most of Zaïre is via the Congo river and its tributaries. The Congo is navigable for 1734 km, from Kinshasa in the west to Kisangani in the east and a boat trip between these two cities takes nearly two weeks. Between Kisangani and the extreme east the roads can be appalling, especially during the rains (Oct–May), although the situation is improving. The extreme east is accessible by air from east African countries and once there getting to the major birding sites is fairly easy.

Accommodation and Food

Accommodation is rare outside the main towns, and hotels, where available, are expensive. Chicken, yams and fish are usually available, at least on the major routes.

Health and Safety

Immunisation against hepatitis, polio, typhoid and yellow fever is recommended, as are precautions against malaria.

Zaïre is a politically unstable country and the west is particularly prone to civil and military unrest, so it is not currently advisable to visit Kinshasa and its environs. Millions of Rwandan refugees sought sanctuary in the extreme east in 1994, and this may lead to problems travelling there.

Climate and Timing

In the extreme east the driest part of the year is from June to September (August is the peak time to visit), although it is very humid all year round.

Habitats

Over one million sq km of virtually untouched lowland rainforest is still thought to exist in Zaïre. Only huge rivers and patches of savanna break the canopy, which would otherwise stretch across the whole of the country. In the extreme east this great forest gives way to montane forest. In north Zaïre the forest is replaced with savanna and, in the south, with savanna and miombo woodland.

Conservation

The great forest of Zaïre has survived until now because much of it remains remote and inaccessible, but there is no doubt that the logging companies of the world have their eyes on it, and if any of the forest survives well into the 21st Century many people will be greatly surprised.

This forest is of immense value as a sustainable natural resource to a country with crippling debts, and the government, recognising this, have stated ambitious plans to double the extent of 'protected' areas, from the existing 7% to 12–15% of the country's land surface. However, many so-called protected areas are little more than 'lines-on-a-map' and badly under resourced. Zaïre's 26 threatened and 19 near-threatened species, like the country itself, face an uncertain future.

Bird Families

Seven of the ten families endemic to mainland Africa are represented in Zaïre, including Shoebill*. Well represented families include francolins, turacos, bee-eaters, barbets, swallows, bulbuls, babblers and weavers.

Bird Species

More species have been recorded in Zaïre than any other African country, although the total of 1,094 is just 16 higher than Kenya's, a country which is one quarter the size. However, much of Zaïre awaits thorough ornithological investigation and its list is likely to grow steadily if this ever takes place. Non-endemic specialities and spectacular species include Hartlaub's Duck, Long-tailed Hawk, Bare-cheeked Trogon, Chocolate-backed Kingfisher and Jameson's Antpecker.

Endemics

Eighteen species occur only in Zaïre, including Congo Peacock*, Bedford's Paradise-Flycatcher*, Golden-naped Weaver* and Yellow-legged Malimbe*. All 43 Albertine Rift endemics are present, including Nahan's Francolin*, Grauer's Broadbill*, Oberlander's Ground-Thrush*, Sassi's Greenbul*, Neumann's Warbler and Grant's Bluebill. Other near-endemics include Turner's Eremomela*.

The forest of eastern Zaïre supports many spectacular birds, including the beautiful Masked Apalis

The pleasant town of **Bukavu**, on the shore of Lake Kivu, is the gateway to the forests of extreme east Zaïre (map p. 382). It is necessary to book trips to nearby Kahuzi-Biega NP in advance, at the Institut Zairois pour la Conservation de la Nature (IZCN), 185 Av. du President Mobuto, in Bukavu.

The remote **Itombwe Mountains**, south of Bukavu, run north to south on the west side of Lake Tanganyika and rise to 3475 m (11,401 ft) at Mount Mohi. Of the eight endemics recorded here, four have never been seen for definite anywhere else. These are Congo Bay-Owl*, Prigogine's Nightjar*, Schouteden's Swift*, and Itombwe Flycatcher. The four other endemics which occur on or around these mountains are Congo Peacock*, Bedford's Paradise-Flycatcher*, Chapin's Mountain-Babbler* and Rockefeller's Sunbird*, whilst the forest also supports White-naped Pigeon*, Albertine Owlet*, Dwarf Honeyguide*, Grauer's Broadbill*, Kivu* and Oberlander's* Ground-Thrushes, Chapin's Flycatcher*, Sassi's Greenbul*, Red-collared Mountain-Babbler*, and Shelley's Crimson-wing*. Unfortunately, birding these forests would be virtually impossible without mounting a full-scale expedition, although birders who get as far as the mining centre of Kamituga may find some very mysterious species in the vicinity.

The endemic Kabobo Apalis* is confined to **Mount Kabobo**, an isolated mountain south of the Itombwe Mountains. Further south still, in southeast Zaïre, are the **Marungu Highlands**, the only known locality of the endemic Prigogine's Sunbird*, which occurs in riparian forest.

KAHUZI-BIEGA NATIONAL PARK

This big park (7000 sq km), northwest of Bukavu, protects misty montane forest with large areas of giant bamboo, and lies between 1800 m (5906 ft) and 3300 m (10,827 ft). Five endemics occur here, including the rare and localised Yellow-crested Helmetshrike*, as well as many Albertine Rift endemics, which include Grauer's Broadbill*. The almost mystical Congo Peacock* is not likely to be seen, but it has been recorded in the past.

This park is where most tourists are taken to look for gorillas so it can be quite busy during the driest part of the year, from June to August.

Zaïre Endemics

Congo Peacock*, Bedford's Paradise-Flycatcher*, Yellow-crested Helmetshrike*, Chapin's Mountain-Babbler*, Rockefeller's Sunbird*.

Specialities

Handsome Francolin, White-naped Pigeon*, Ruwenzori Turaco, Dwarf Honeyguide*, Grauer's Broadbill*, Ruwenzori Batis, Kivu Ground-Thrush*, Red-throated Alethe, Sassi's Greenbul*, Masked Apalis, Grauer's Scrub-Warbler*, Red-faced Woodland-Warbler, Red-collared Mountain-Babbler*, Shelley's Crimson-wing*, Regal and Purple-breasted Sunbirds.

Others

Barred Long-tailed Cuckoo, Olive Woodpecker, Black-tailed Oriole, Grey and Black Cuckoo-shrikes, Equatorial Akalat, Chestnut-throated Apalis.

Other Wildlife

Gorilla, L'Hoest's monkey, owl-faced monkey.

Access

To reach this national park head north from Bukavu and turn west after 25 km. From here it is 17 km to the Tschivanga Gate at 1900 m (6234 ft). From here the road northwest runs for 20 km through superb forest. Grauer's Scrub-Warbler* occurs in the swamp on the south side of the road, just after it reaches the end of the park. There are also a few trails leading from the cabin at Tschivanga Gate. The one following the water pipe has been the best in the past. It is possible to ascend Mount Kahuzi with a guide, and this may be the only way to see the rare Rockefeller's Sunbird*.

Accommodation: Cabin at Tschivanga (take food).

IRANGI and ITEBERO

The most accessible lowland rainforest in Zaïre is at Irangi (800–900 m (2625–2953 ft)), and anyone who manages to spend some time birding here may see a lot of rarely seen species, including Sladen's Barbet, Oriole Cuckoo-shrike, Ituri Batis and Grant's Bluebill.

Zaïre Endemics

Bedford's Paradise-Flycatcher*, Yellow-crested Helmetshrike*.

Specialities

Hartlaub's Duck, Spot-breasted Ibis, Black Guineafowl, Bates' Swift, Bare-cheeked Trogon, Sladen's Barbet, Oriole Cuckoo-shrike, Ituri Batis, Toro Olive-Greenbul, Uganda Wood-Warbler, Forest Penduline-Tit, Jameson's Antpecker, Grant's Bluebill, Grey-headed Sunbird.

Others

Bat Hawk, Palm-nut Vulture, Congo Serpent-Eagle, Chestnut-flanked Sparrowhawk, Long-tailed Hawk, Cassin's Hawk-Eagle, White-spotted Flufftail, Nkulengu Rail, Afep Pigeon, Grey Parrot, Black-billed and Great Blue Turacos, Olive Long-tailed Cuckoo, Yellowbill, Black-throated Coucal, Akun Eagle-Owl, African Wood-Owl, Scarce Swift, Shining Blue, Dwarf, White-bellied, Chocolate-backed and Blue-breasted Kingfishers, Blue-throated Roller, White-crested, Black Dwarf, Red-billed Dwarf, African Pied, Piping, White-thighed and Black-casqued Hornbills, Grey-throated Barbet, Red-rumped and Yellow-throated Tinkerbirds, Yellow-spotted and Hairy-breasted Barbets, Willcock's and Cassin's Honeyguides, African Piculet, Brown-eared and Elliot's Woodpeckers, Rufous-sided Broadbill, Chestnut-capped Flycatcher, Dusky and Blue-headed Crested-Flycatchers, Black-winged Oriole, Blue and Black Cuckoo-shrikes, Red-eyed Puffback, Sooty Boubou, African and Black-and-white Shrike-flycatchers, Chestnut and White-spotted Wattle-eyes, Rufous Flycatcher-Thrush, Fire-crested Alethe, Chestnut-winged Starling, African Forest-Flycatcher, Sooty, Olivaceous, Little Grey, Yellow-footed, and Cassin's Flycatchers, Grey-throated Tit-Flycatcher, Forest Robin, Angola and White-throated Blue Swallows, Square-tailed Sawwing, Little, Ansorge's, Plain, Honeyguide, Spotted, Simple, White-throated, Eastern Bearded and Red-tailed Greenbuls, Whistling and Chattering Cisticolas, Black-capped, Buff-throated and Gosling's Apalises, Yellow-browed and Olive-green Camaropteras, Green and Lemon-bellied Crombecs, Yellow Longbill, Green Hylia, Pale-breasted and Brown Illadopsises, Capuchin Babbler, Dusky Tit, Tit-hylia, Woodhouse's Antpecker, Pale-fronted Negrofinch, Black-bellied Seedcracker, Black-crowned and Black-headed Waxbills, Magpie Mannikin, Yellow-mantled and Maxwell's Black Weavers, Red-crowned, Gray's, Crested and Red-headed Malimbes, Bates', Blue-throated Brown, Tiny and Superb Sunbirds.

Access

Irangi is accessible via a good road from Bukavu. Look out for the 'CSRN Irangi Station de Recherches' sign, on the right after a river crossing. Bird the roadside, the riverside and trails in the forest across the River Lwana, reached via a bamboo bridge. Itebero is nearby. An all-black, big 'spinetail' swift, thought to be a new species, has been seen here on a few occasions in recent years.

Accommodation: Lodge (A) bookable (in French) through Ndumbo-Kirundu, Responsable de Reserve Naturelle d'Irangi, CSRN a Irangi, DS Bukavu/Irangi.

Birders intending to visit Djomba (p. 383) should book accommodation and guided walks (for gorillas) at the IZCN office next to the commercial bank in **Goma**.

GOMA-KIBUMBA

The forest alongside the track north of Goma, to Kibumba, supports a number of specialities, but most of these birds are easier to find at Djomba (p. 383).

Specialities

White-tailed Blue-Flycatcher, Ruwenzori Batis, Yellow-eyed Black-Flycatcher, Archer's Robin-Chat, Collared and Masked Apalises, White-browed Crombec, Red-faced Woodland-Warbler, Strange Weaver, Regal Sunbird.

Others

Black-billed Turaco, Narina Trogon, Black-tailed Oriole, Grey Cuckoo-shrike, Luehder's Bushshrike, Stuhlmann's Starling, Yellow-whiskered Bulbul, Mountain Greenbul, Chubb's Cisticola, Black-throated and Chestnut-throated Apalises, Cinnamon Bracken-Warbler, Red-headed Bluebill, Brown-capped Weaver, Northern Double-collared Sunbird.

Access

The only track north from Goma goes past the airport and across a lava field before ascending from 1450 m (4757 ft) to 2000 m (6562 ft). After the vegetable market on the right-hand side of the road in Kibumba (20 km north of Goma) the track enters montane forest, which is actually within Virunga NP. Archer's Robin-Chat, Collared Apalis and Regal Sunbird occur at the higher altitudes.

RUMANGABO

The forest near the Virunga NP HQ at Rumangabo (1600 m (5249 ft)) has not been burnt by recent lava flows and supports more species than most forests in this area. It is particularly good for frugivores (including Western Green-Tinkerbird) thanks to the large number of fig trees.

Specialities

Western Green-Tinkerbird, White-tailed Blue-Flycatcher, Ruwenzori Batis, White-browed Crombec, White-collared Oliveback.

Others

Bat Hawk, Black Goshawk, Crested Guineafowl, Black-billed, Ross's and Great Blue Turacos, Yellowbill, Cinnamon-chested Bee-eater, White-headed Woodhoopoe, Black-and-white-casqued Hornbill, Grey-throated, Hairy-breasted, Double-toothed and Yellow-billed Barbets, Cassin's Honeyguide, Speckle-breasted Woodpecker, Black-tailed Oriole, Petit's and Black Cuckoo-shrikes, Mackinnon's Shrike, Pink-footed Puffback, Luehder's and Grey-green Bushshrikes, Stuhlmann's, Narrow-tailed, Slender-billed and Sharpe's Starlings, Equatorial Akalat, Snowy-crowned Robin-Chat, Shelley's, Little, Mountain, Honeyguide and Yellow-throated Greenbuls, Chubb's Cisticola, Black-throated Apalis, Grey-capped Warbler, Green Hylia, Red-headed Bluebill, Black-necked, Black-billed, Vieillot's Black, Forest and Brown-capped Weavers, Blue-throated Brown and Northern Double-collared Sunbirds.

Access

Rumangabo is 44 km north of Goma. The forest on the left-hand side of the road, just before Virunga NP HQ, reached by turning right at the monument, is best. This road connects with the main road to Djomba.

The 65 km road from **Rumangabo** to **Djomba** (4WD recommended) descends from Rumangabo and passes a coffee plantation. Cinnamon-chested Bee-eater occurs around the pool on the left, 2 km from

EAST ZAÏRE

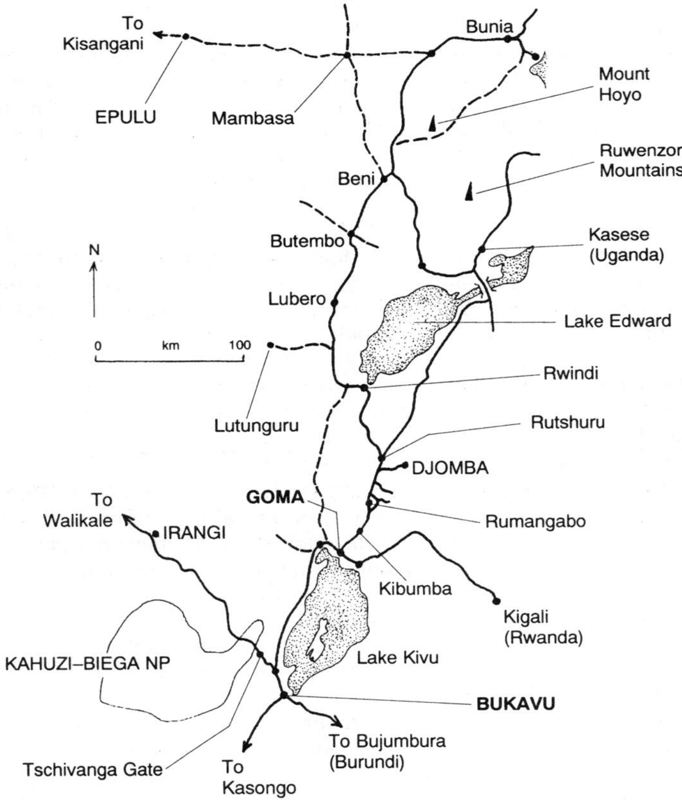

Rumangabo. Black Bishop occurs in the fields alongside the start of the track to the right, 25 km from Rumangabo and signposted 'Chutes de Rutshuru.' This track leads to some falls surrounded by forest where Great Blue Turaco and Green Crombec occur. Back on the Rumangabo–Djomba road continue for 10 km to the bridge over the Rutshuru river, a good site for White-throated Bee-eater. Three to four km from here turn right in response to the 'Visites aux Gorilles' sign. Narrow-tailed Starling occurs along this stretch of road. Papyrus Gonolek* has been seen from the bridge just past the 'Rwangbu Hospital' sign, after 17 km. From here follow the 'Gorilles' signs for another 9 km, after which it is necessary to leave any vehicles (minders available), and walk (with porters if required) up a steep slope for 40 minutes to reach the cabins at Djomba (remember to book in advance in Goma).

DJOMBA

Djomba forest supports a fine selection of Albertine Rift endemics, although the main attraction is the gorillas.

It is necessary to book accommodation and guided walks (for gorillas) in advance, at the IZCN office next to the commercial bank in Goma.

Specialities

Handsome Francolin, Ruwenzori Turaco, Ruwenzori Nightjar, Western Green-Tinkerbird, White-tailed Blue-Flycatcher, Mountain Boubou, Doherty's and Lagden's* Bushshrikes, Ruwenzori Batis, Red-throated Alethe, Archer's Robin-Chat, Collared and Masked Apalises, White-browed Crombec, Red-faced Woodland-Warbler, Stripe-breasted Tit, Dusky Crimson-wing, Strange Weaver, Blue-headed and Regal Sunbirds.

Others

Rufous-chested Sparrowhawk, Black Goshawk, African Snipe, Brown-necked Parrot, Black-billed Turaco, Narina Trogon, Cinnamon-chested Bee-eater, White-headed Woodhoopoe, Grey-throated and Yellow-billed Barbets, Olive Woodpecker, White-tailed Crested-Flycatcher, Black-tailed Oriole, Black Cuckoo-shrike, Mackinnon's Shrike, Waller's, Slender-billed and Sharpe's Starlings, White-starred Robin, Angola Swallow, Black Sawwing, Yellow-whiskered Bulbul, Mountain Greenbul, Chubb's Cisticola, Chestnut-throated Apalis, Cinnamon Bracken-Warbler, Black-faced Rufous Warbler, Abyssinian Hill-Babbler, Grey-chested Illadopsis, Red-faced Crimson-wing, Black-headed Waxbill, Black-and-white Mannikin, Holub's Golden-Weaver, Brown-capped Weaver, Northern Double-collared Sunbird, Thick-billed Seedeater.

Other Wildlife

Golden monkey, gorilla.

Access

Bird: (1) The trail on the right behind the cabins. (2) The Sabyinyo Trail (with guide), along which Ruwenzori Turaco occurs (in the bamboo belt).

Accommodation: Cabins (take own food).

ITURI FOREST

This huge forest (65,000 sq km) is one of the richest avian habitats in Africa, and home to Mbuti pygmies. Over 400 species have been recorded, including three rare endemics which are found only here: Neumann's Coucal*, Golden-naped Weaver* and Yellow-legged Malimbe*. Even seeing all three could be overshadowed by the sight of an okapi, although seeing one of these elusive beasts is as likely as seeing a Congo Peacock*. In other words, a very remote possibility indeed.

Zaïre Endemics

Congo Peacock*, Neumann's Coucal*, Golden-naped Weaver*, Yellow-legged Malimbe*.

Specialities

Black Guineafowl, Nahan's Francolin, White-naped Pigeon*, Sassi's Greenbul*, Turner's Eremomela*, Jameson's Antpecker, Grant's Bluebill.

Others

Rock Pratincole, Black Cuckoo, Blue-headed Bee-eater, White-crested, Red-billed Dwarf, African Pied and White-thighed Hornbills, Yellow-throated Tinkerbird, Hairy-breasted and Yellow-billed Barbets, Spotted and Lyre-tailed Honeyguides, Brown-eared, Gabon and Elliot's Woodpeckers, Red-eyed Puffback, African and Black-and-white Shrike-flycatchers, Chestnut and Yellow-bellied Wattle-eyes, Rufous Flycatcher-Thrush, Brown-chested and Fire-crested Alethes, African Forest-Flycatcher, Sooty, Olivaceous and Yellow-footed Flycatchers, Grey-throated Tit-Flycatcher, Forest Robin, Little, Grey, Ansorge's, Spotted, Simple and Xavier's Greenbuls, Yellow-throated Nicator, Pale-breasted Illadopsis, Dusky Tit, Yellow-mantled Weaver, Gray's and Crested Malimbes.

Other Wildlife

Aquatic civet, elephant, leopard, okapi and 13 species of primate including owl-faced Monkey.

Access

Without a light aircraft or lots of time this forest is only readily accessible at **Epulu**. Golden-naped Weaver* occurs in the forest around this small settlement, where tourists converge to visit the local pygmies, on the rough road north of Beni. The IZCN HQ is also here. Bird the roadside, the gardens (take the path off the main road in the middle of town), and the two trails near the house by the river behind the main road. Yellow-legged Malimbe* has been recorded rarely in the Okapi Faunal Reserve.

Accommodation: Epulu: Basic hotel.

The eastern part of Ituri Forest is especially bird-rich, and anyone who is able to get up Mount Hoyo (previous trails are overgrown) may see some very rare and little known species. Mount Hoyo is 13 km off the Beni–Bunia road, near Komanda.

The incredibly rare Congo Peacock* was filmed in forest approximately four days (on motorcycle and foot) southwest of Epulu, in September 1993.

Bedford's Paradise-Flycatcher*, Grauer's Cuckoo-shrike* and Prigogine's Greenbul* were all recorded in **Djugu Forest**, 250 km northeast of Beni, in 1994. This forest lies on the **Lendu Plateau** west of Lake Albert in extreme northeast Zaïre, and previous records from here include the endemic Chapin's Mountain-Babbler*, as well as White-naped Pigeon* and Chapin's Flycatcher*.

Egyptian Plover, Pel's Fishing-Owl, Emin's Shrike, Rufous-rumped Lark and Red-winged Pytilia have recently been recorded in **Garamba NP**, in extreme northeast Zaïre.

LAC MA VALLE

This artificial lake, 25 km from the centre of Kinshasa in west Zaïre, may still be surrounded by forest and scrub, which used to support some excellent birds, including Black-headed Bee-eater and Perrin's Bushshrike.

Specialities

Black-headed Bee-eater, Perrin's Bushshrike, Forest Scrub-Robin, Black-tailed Waxbill.

Others

African Cuckoo-Falcon, Red-thighed Sparrowhawk, Senegal Lapwing, Red-headed Lovebird, Black-billed Turaco, African Emerald Cuckoo, Yellowbill, Black-shouldered Nightjar, Shining Blue, Brown-hooded and Giant Kingfishers, Black Bee-eater, African Pied Hornbill, Yellow-throated Tinkerbird, Thick-billed and Cassin's Honeyguides, Red-eyed and Large-billed Puffbacks, Brown-crowned Tchagra, Sooty Boubou, Black-and-white Shrike-flycatcher, Black-headed Batis, Blue-headed Crested-Flycatcher, Rufous Flycatcher-Thrush, White-tailed Ant-thrush, Snowy-crowned Robin-Chat, White-throated Blue Swallow, Little and Ansorge's Greenbuls, Yellow-whiskered Bulbul, Honeyguide, Simple and Yellow-necked Greenbuls, Yellow-throated Nicator, Siffling Cisticola, Buff-throated Apalis, Moustached Grass-Warbler, Green Crombec, Grey Longbill, Green Hylia, Brown Illadopsis, White-breasted and Chestnut-breasted Negrofinches, Brown Twinspot, Black-necked Weaver, Blue-throated Brown and Copper Sunbirds.

Access

Black-headed Bee-eater and Perrin's Bushshrike may still occur in any remnant forest patches near the lake. The best area used to be accessible by turning left just before the gate across the road to the lake, and left again after 300 m on to a track. The hill to the right of this track used to be worth birding. Otherwise, a trail encircles the lake where Shining Blue Kingfisher occurs.

ADDITIONAL INFORMATION

Books and Papers

Les Oiseaux de Zaïre. Lippens, L and Wille, H. 1976. Belgium. Edition Lanoo Tielt.

ENDEMICS (18)

Congo Peacock*	East: very rare, Itombwe Mountains, Kahuzi-Biega NP and Ituri Forest
Congo Bay-Owl*	East: known only definitely from a specimen taken in 1951 in the Itombwe Mountains, despite extensive searches since, although this species may have been heard in Nyungwe Forest, Rwanda, in 1990
Neumann's Coucal*	East: Ituri Forest
Prigogine's Nightjar*	East: known only from a single specimen collected in 1955, in the Itombwe Mountains
Schouteden's Swift*	East: known only from a handful of records from near the Itombwe Mountains
Bedford's Paradise-Flycatcher*	East: widespread
Yellow-crested Helmetshrike*	East: Kahuzi-Biega NP
Itombwe Flycatcher	East: Itombwe Mountains
Prigogine's Greenbul*	East: Djuga Forest, Lendu Plateau
Kabobo Apalis*	East: Mount Kabobo
Chapin's Crombec	Northeast: montane forest
Chapin's Mountain-Babbler*	East: widespread
Black-faced Waxbill*	South: Lualaba river and Lake Upemba areas
Ruwet's Masked-Weaver*	South: Lake Lufira swamps (near Likasi)
Golden-naped Weaver*	East: Ituri Forest
Yellow-legged Malimbe*	East: Ituri Forest
Prigogine's Sunbird*	Southeast: Marungu Highlands
Rockefeller's Sunbird*	East: Itombwe Mountains and Kahuzi-Biega NP

Near-endemics (Albertine Rift)

Nahan's* and Handsome Francolins, Ruwenzori Turaco, Albertine Owlet*, Ruwenzori Nightjar, Grauer's Broadbill*, Ruwenzori Batis, Grauer's Cuckoo-shrike*, Kivu* and Oberlander's* Ground-Thrushes, Red-throated Alethe, Yellow-eyed Black-Flycatcher, Archer's Robin-Chat, Sassi's Greenbul*, Collared and Black-faced Apalises, White-winged and Grauer's* Scrub-Warblers, Grauer's and Neumann's Warblers, Red-faced Woodland-Warbler, Red-collared Mountain-Babbler*, Stripe-breasted Tit, Dusky and Shelley's* Crimson-wings, Grant's Bluebill, Strange Weaver, Grey-headed, Blue-headed, Stuhlmann's, Regal and Purple-breasted Sunbirds.

Near-endemics (East)

Dwarf Honeyguide*, Doherty's Bushshrike, Papyrus Gonolek*, Chapin's Flycatcher*, Turner's Eremomela*, White-browed Crombec, Uganda Wood-Warbler, Papyrus Canary.

Near-endemics (Northeast)

Mangbettu Sawwing, Dusky Babbler.

Near-endemics (West and South)

Perrin's Bushshrike, Boulton's and Angola Batises, Bocage's Akalat, White-headed Robin-Chat*, African River-Martin, Congo and Brazza's Martins, Black-and-rufous Swallow, Sjostedt's and Pale-olive Greenbuls, Lepe, Bubbling and Slender-tailed Cisiticolas, Kungwe Apalis*, Salvadori's and Black-necked Eremomelas, Laura's Wood-Warbler, Angola Lark, Pale-billed Firefinch, Grimwood's Longclaw*, Black-chinned*, Loango* and Bocage's Weavers, Katanga Masked-Weaver, Bar-winged and Bob-tailed Weavers, Bannerman's, Bocage's and Congo Sunbirds.

ZAMBIA

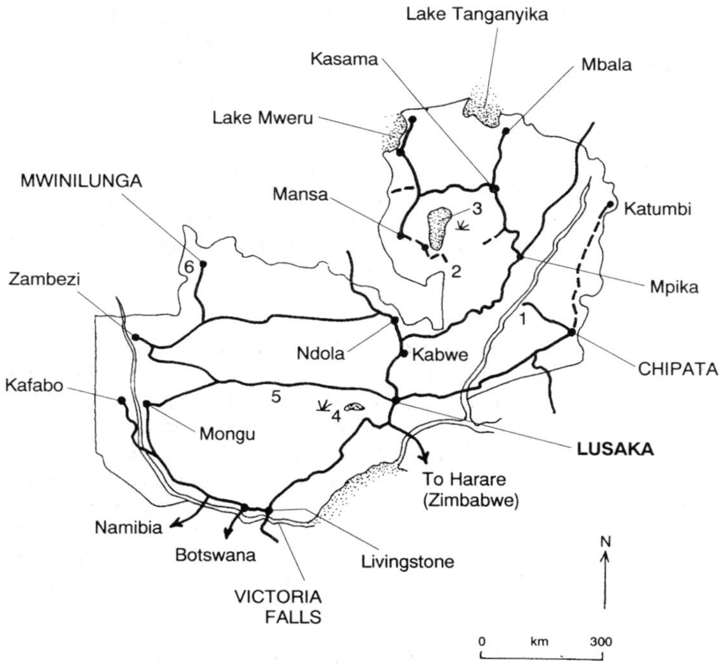

1	South Luangwa NP	4	Lochinvar Reserve
2	Kasanka NP	5	Kafue NP
3	Bangweulu Swamp	6	Mwinilunga District

INTRODUCTION

Summary

Zambia supports one of the best selections of large mammals in Africa as well as some splendid birds, which include Shoebill* and a handful of species otherwise confined to Angola and Zaïre; and yet, compared to East and southern Africa, it attracts relatively few tourists or birders. This is because it is a difficult country to cover thoroughly in a short time without a 4WD. However, it is possible to visit (with some ease) one of the best parts of Zambia, the Luangwa Valley, from adjacent Malawi.

Size

At 752,614 sq km, Zambia is six times larger than England, and roughly the same size as Texas.

Getting Around

Most of the roads in Zambia are unsurfaced, creating problems for birders without 4WDs, although the Lusaka–Chipata–Luangwa Valley road is an exception. Some of the roads, especially around the capital, Lusaka, have road blocks, and the people stationed at these are not always friendly. There are plenty of buses, but they do not reach all of the best birding sites. There is a good internal flight network.

Crossing the Zambia–Malawi border near Chipata can be a slow process, although having the compulsory cholera and yellow fever certificates and passports ready may speed up proceedings.

Some national parks and reserves are open only during the dry season (Jun–Oct).

Accommodation and Food

National Park lodges and tented camps are expensive and, unfortunately, the cheaper government resthouses are mostly situated in towns (eg. Chipata). Budget birders will have to camp in Zambia.

Health and Safety

Immunisation against hepatitis, polio, typhoid and yellow fever is recommended, as are precautions against malaria.

A few unfortunate travellers have been arrested 'for no apparent reason' by the army and police who, before apartheid at least, seemed to hold a serious grudge against certain people with South African stamps in their passport. Walking around Lusaka at night is not recommended but, on the whole, Zambian people are extremely friendly.

Climate and Timing

The dry season, June to October, is the best time to visit Zambia, although October is much hotter than June. The rains usually last from November to May and at this time some areas are inaccessible, even with a 4WD. Owing to the country's relatively high altitude, it is usually cool at night, although this is not the case in the lower Luangwa and Zambezi Valleys.

Habitats

Zambia lies on a primarily flat plateau (900 m (2953 ft)–1500 m (4921 ft)), dotted with lakes, vast marshes, woodland and savanna. The Zambezi river runs along most of the country's southern border with Zimbabwe, and the Victoria Falls are situated here.

Conservation

Ten threatened and eight near-threatened species occur in Zambia.

Bird Families

Seven of the ten families endemic to the African mainland are represented in Zambia, including Shoebill*.

Bird Species

A total of 737 species have been recorded in Zambia. Non-endemic specialities and spectacular species include Shoebill*, Wattled Crane*, Boehm's Bee-eater and Racket-tailed Roller.

Endemics

Although there is only one endemic, Chaplin's Barbet*, there are a few near-endemics, which include such little known birds as Black-and-rufous Swallow, Bamboo Scrub-Warbler, Laura's Wood-Warbler and Grimwood's Longclaw*.

African Swift, Lilac-breasted Roller and Blue-breasted Cordonbleu occur in Zambia's sprawling capital, **Lusaka**. Nearby, Cabanis' Greenbul and Buffy Pipit occur at the Dutch Farm, 15 km northwest of Lusaka; Wattled Crane* occurs at the ANC Farm, where there is an artificial lake, 30 km northeast of Lusaka, and Slaty Egret* has been recorded on dams at Huntley Farm in the Chisamba area, off the Lusaka–Kabwe road, north of Lusaka. Since these are sensitive private sites it is wise to contact the Zambian Ornithological Society (ZOS) for more details before visiting them.

Boehm's Bee-eater, as well as Hamerkop, Red-winged Starling, Familiar Chat, Wailing Cisticola, Striped Pipit, Yellow Bishop and White-winged Widowbird, have been recorded around **Nyanje**, which lies in an area of low rocky hills, 6 km from the Mozambique border, in east Zambia.

SOUTH LUANGWA NATIONAL PARK

This large national park (9050 sq km) lies between the Mchinga Escarpment to the west and the ever changing Luangwa river to the east, in a landscape dominated by savanna and miombo and mopane woodland. This superb wilderness supports one of the most impressive selections of large mammals in Africa, as well as many birds, including Southern Carmine Bee-eater and Racket-tailed Roller.

Much of this park is inaccessible even with 4WD during the wet season (Nov–Apr), although at least one lodge may be open all year round.

Specialities

Racket-tailed Roller, Meves' Glossy-Starling.

Others

African Darter, Goliath Heron, Hamerkop, Hadada Ibis, Saddle-billed Stork, White-headed Vulture, Bateleur, Little Sparrowhawk, Martial Eagle, Swainson's Spurfowl, Grey Crowned-Crane, Greater Painted-snipe, Water Thick-knee, Bronze-winged and Three-banded Coursers,

Three-banded and White-fronted Plovers, Long-toed Lapwing, Blacksmith Plover, White-headed Lapwing, African Skimmer, Double-banded Sandgrouse, Meyer's Parrot, Lilian's Lovebird, Grey Go-away-bird, Black Coucal, African Scops-Owl, Verreaux's Eagle-Owl, Pel's Fishing-Owl, Brown-hooded Kingfisher, White-fronted, Little and Southern Carmine Bee-eaters, Lilac-breasted Roller, Common Scimitar-bill, Crowned Hornbill, Southern Ground-Hornbill, Crested Barbet, White-breasted Cuckoo-shrike, White and Retz's Helmetshrikes, Yellow-billed and Red-billed Oxpeckers, Yellow-bellied Eremomela, Arrow-marked Babbler, Jameson's Firefinch, Blue-breasted Cordonbleu, Black-tailed Waxbill, White-breasted Sunbird, Brimstone Canary.

Other Wildlife

Buffalo, Burchell's zebra, chacma baboon, eland, elephant, four-toed elephant shrew, giraffe, greater kudu, hippo, hunting dog, klipspringer, kob, leopard, lion, Nile crocodile, porcupine, puku, spotted hyena.

Access

This national park is accessible on good roads from Lusaka (a distance of 522 km) and Malawi (six hours from Lilongwe). The main camp, Mfuwe, is 130 km northwest of Chipata, on the Zambia/Malawi border. It is also possible to fly into Mfuwe. There are a number of tracks worth exploring, especially those near the river. Racket-tailed Roller occurs around Kapani Lodge. Organised dawn and night safaris (A) can be arranged at Mfuwe Lodge.

SOUTH LUANGWA NP

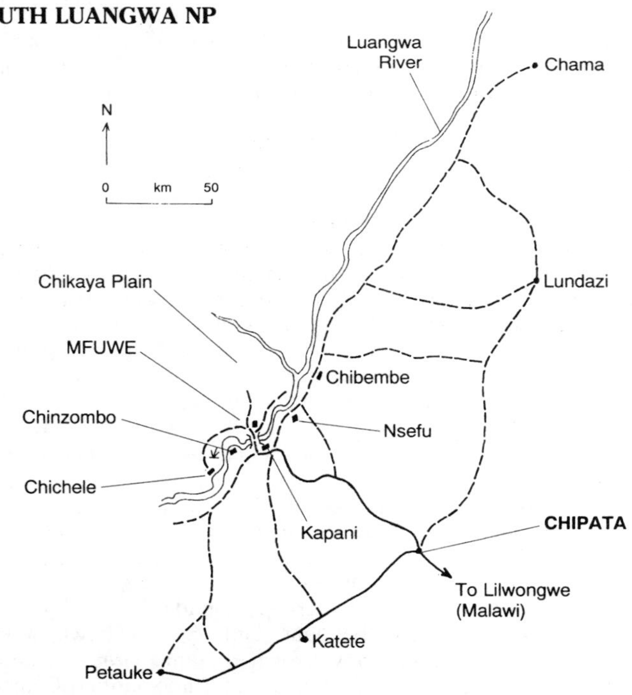

Accommodation: Tented Camps: Nkwali, Tena Tena, Kakuli, and Mchenja. Lodges: Mfuwe, James Schultz (self-catering (B)), Kapani (A). Camping: Crocodile Camp. Whilst most camps are closed from November to April, Mfuwe may now be open all year round.

There are three other national parks in the Luangwa Valley, but there are no tracks in the remote **North Luangwa NP**, which is only accessible on organised walking safaris. There are some good lagoons in the small **Luambe NP**, which is accessible via tracks, and the higher **Lukusuzi NP**, to the east, is also accessible via rough tracks.

African Pygmy-goose, Wattled Crane*, Pel's Fishing-Owl, Half-collared Kingfisher, Anchieta's and Black-backed Barbets, and Anchieta's Sunbird occur in the small **Kasanka NP**, at the southeast corner of the Bangweulu Swamp in north Zambia.

BANGWEULU SWAMP

This huge papyrus swamp in north Zambia supports one of the country's major avian attractions, Shoebill*. Whilst looking for this bizarre bird it is also possible to see Wattled Crane*, Blue-breasted Bee-eater and African Pitta.

Specialities

Shoebill*, Wattled Crane*, Coppery-tailed Coucal, African Pitta, Angola Babbler.

Others

Long-toed Lapwing, Blue-breasted Bee-eater, Copper Sunbird.

Other Wildlife

Black lechwe, buffalo, elephant, oribi, sitatunga, tsessebe.

Access

The best way to get to the Bangweulu Swamp is to fly from Lusaka, although it is also possible to reach the area by road, via Chiundaponde and Muwele School to Chikuni, where there is a resthouse and boats can be hired to look for Shoebill*.

LOCHINVAR RESERVE

Over 400 species have been recorded in this small reserve on the floodplain of the Kafue river in south Zambia. Huge numbers of waterbirds are present when the water levels are right, and recent counts have included 58,000 Fulvous Whistling-Ducks, 14,000 Ruff and 1,400 Black Herons. Passerines include the brilliant Locustfinch.

Specialities

Wattled Crane*, Yellow-throated Sandgrouse, Coppery-tailed Coucal, Angola Babbler.

Others

Fulvous Whistling-Duck, Black Heron, Saddle-billed Stork, Greater Painted-snipe, Caspian Plover (Nov–Mar), Long-toed Lapwing, Marsh Owl, Sooty Chat, Peters' Twinspot, Locustfinch, Rosy-throated Longclaw.

Other Wildlife

Burchell's zebra, red lechwe, wildebeest.

Access

Contact the ZOS for more details of this site.

KAFUE NATIONAL PARK

The grassy savanna, gallery forest and seasonally flooded wetlands of this massive park (22,000 sq km) in south Zambia support the endemic Chaplin's Barbet, as well as Wattled Crane*, Boehm's Bee-eater and Racket-tailed Roller.

Zambia Endemics

Chaplin's Barbet.

Specialities

Wattled Crane*, Boehm's Bee-eater, Racket-tailed Roller, Collared Palm-Thrush.

Others

White-backed Night-Heron, Woolly-necked Stork, African Hawk-Eagle, Allen's Gallinule, African Finfoot, African Skimmer, Ross's Turaco, African Barred Owlet, Rufous-cheeked, Square-tailed and Pennant-winged Nightjars, Red-backed Scrub-Robin, Striped Pipit.

Other Wildlife

Elephant, greater kudu, lechwe, lion, puku, roan, sable.

Access

Nalusanga Gate, at the eastern edge of the park, is 237 km west of Lusaka by surfaced road. Dumdumwenze Gate, at the southern edge, is 200 km north of Livingstone. The road west from Lusaka to the Nalusanga Gate passes the entrance track to Blue Lagoon NP (where the endemic Chaplin's Barbet* occurs), before entering excellent miombo woodland after Mumbwa. Wattled Crane*, Boehm's Bee-eater and Racket-tailed Roller occur around Lufupa Camp, which lies at the confluence of the Lufupa and Kafue rivers. African Finfoot occurs on these rivers, and it is possible to hire boats to look for this secretive species. Also bird the plains to the north, but beware of the heat and tsetse flies.

Accommodation: Lufupa Camp; David Shepherd Lodge (C); Kafwala Camp (C) (take own food).

The **Victoria Falls** (p. 403) are 7 km south of Livingstone, which is 200 km south of Kafue NP.

Chaplin's Barbet, the only Zambian endemic, occurs in Kafue and Blue Lagoon National Parks*

MWINILUNGA DISTRICT

This remote region of lowland forest, marsh and grassland in extreme northwest Zambia, supports a number of restricted-range specialities, most of which are virtually impossible to see elsewhere in Africa, owing to various travel difficulties in politically unstable countries.

Specialities

Forbes' Plover, Anchieta's Barbet, Anchieta's Tchagra, Perrin's Bushshrike, Black-and-rufous Swallow, Black-collared Bulbul, Cloud-scraping Cisticola, Bamboo Scrub-Warbler, Salvadori's Eremomela, Laura's Wood-Warbler, Thrush Babbler, Angola Lark, Grimwood's Longclaw*, Bocage's Weaver, Bates' Sunbird.

Others

Rock Pratincole, Afep Pigeon, Olive Long-tailed Cuckoo, Blue-breasted Kingfisher, Brown-eared Woodpecker, Rufous Flycatcher-Thrush, Sooty and Cassin's Flycatchers.

Access

The town of Mwinilunga lies near the Angola and Zaïre borders. Birders intending to visit this sensitive area are advised to contact the ZOS before doing so. Black-and-rufous Swallow, Cloud-scraping Cisticola, Angola Lark and Grimwood's Longclaw* occur on the **Chitunta Plain**, Bocage's Weaver along the **Luakela Stream**, Anchieta's Tchagra, Black-collared Bulbul, Salvadori's Eremomela and Thrush Babbler in **Kafweko Forest**, near the Angolan border, Bamboo Scrub-Warbler along the **Kamukundu Stream**, near the Zaïre border, and Perrin's Bushshrike 200 km to the south.

For sites in northeast Zambia see Malawi (p. 224).

ADDITIONAL INFORMATION

Books and Papers

Common Birds of Zambia. ZOS, 1990. ZOS.

Addresses

The Zambian Ornithological Society (ZOS), PO Box 33944, Lusaka, publishes a newsletter which is edited by Carl Beel, Kasama Boys Secondary School, Box 410235, Kasama. Please send all records here.

Wildlife Conservation Society, Box 30255, Lusaka.

ENDEMICS (1)

Chaplin's Barbet	West: Kafue and Blue Lagoon NPs

Near-endemics (General)

Coppery-tailed Coucal, Bocage's Akalat, Black-necked Eremomela, Angola Babbler, Oustalet's Sunbird.

Near-endemics (Northwest)

Perrin's Bushshrike, Boulton's Batis, Black-and-rufous Swallow, Slender-tailed Cisticola, Salvadori's Eremomela, Laura's Wood-Warbler, Angola Lark, Grimwood's Longclaw*, Bocage's Weaver, Bannerman's Sunbird.

Near-endemics (South)

Slaty Egret*, Black-cheeked Lovebird*, Brown Firefinch.

Near-endemics (North)

Katanga Masked-Weaver, Bar-winged Weaver.

Near-endemics (Northeast)

Fuelleborn's Boubou, Malawi Batis, Babbling Starling, Black-lored and Churring* Cisticolas, Chapin's Apalis, Buff-shouldered Widowbird.

ZIMBABWE

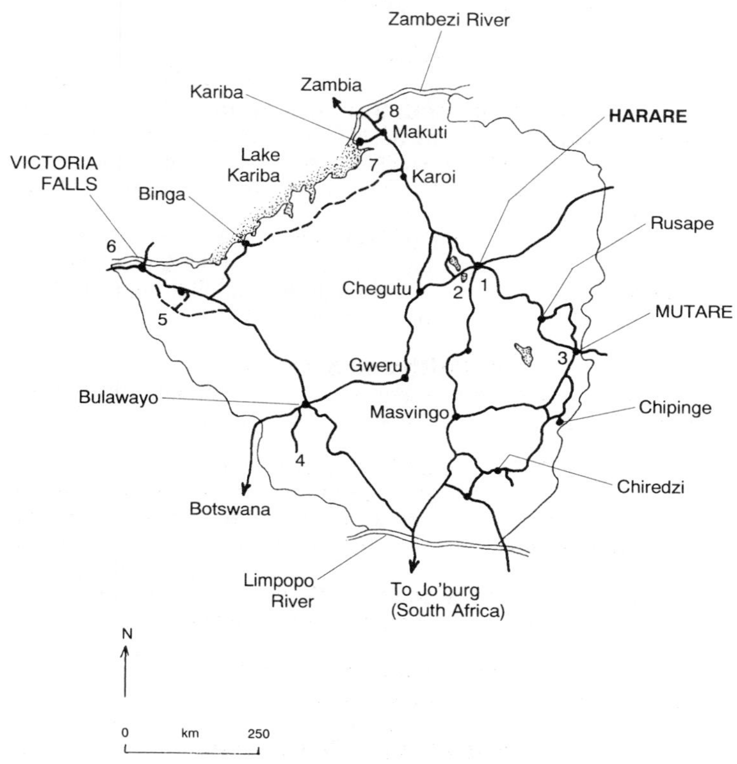

1 Harare
2 Lake Mcilwaine
3 Vumba Mountains
4 Rhodes Matopos NP
5 Hwange NP
6 Victoria Falls and Zambezi NP
7 Lake Kariba
8 Mana Pools NP

INTRODUCTION

Summary

Zimbabwe does not support as many species as the East African countries or South Africa, but its modern infrastructure, plentiful mammals and avian specialities, which include Taita Falcon* and African Pitta, make it a worthy destination, especially for experienced African birders in search of somewhere new.

Size

At 390,624 sq km, Zimbabwe is three times as large as England and around half the size of Texas.

Getting Around

A traffic-free modern road network makes travelling around Zimbabwe by car a delight. With considerable patience and time it would be possible to reach most birding sites by bus, but they are few and far between off the main routes. Cheap trains serve most cities, but they are slow and need to be booked well in advance. There is a good internal air network.

Accommodation and Food

Hotels and lodges are expensive. However, there are many cheap campsites and caravan parks which are often located at remote, beautiful sites, in the national parks. They are clean and well run, but not always entirely safe, thanks to roaming elephants and lions. It is advisable to book all accommodation well in advance, especially during the school holidays (April–mid May, mid August to mid September, and mid December to mid January), through the National Parks Booking Office. The food is excellent and reasonably priced.

Health and Safety

Immunisation against hepatitis, polio, rabies, typhoid and yellow fever is recommended, as are precautions against malaria.

Zimbabwe is a very friendly country.

Climate and Timing

Zimbabwe enjoys a healthy climate. October to November, at the start of the wet season, and January to February, when the birds are breeding, are the best times to visit, although January is the wettest month. The wet season ends in March and it is dry from April to October, June being the coolest month and October the hottest.

Habitats

Most of this land-locked country lies on a plateau between the Zambezi river to the west and north and the Limpopo river to the south. Much of this plateau (1200 m–1600 m (3937–5249 ft)) is still covered in savanna and miombo woodland. To the east, on the border with Mozambique, lie the Vumba Mountains, which rise to 2592 m (8504 ft) at Mount Inyangani. Remnant patches of lush montane forest are scattered across these mountains. To the west there is acacia savanna and the eastern extremity of the Kalahari Desert. There are no natural lakes in Zimbabwe but plenty of waterholes and rivers with man-made dams, one of which has formed the huge Lake Kariba, which runs along the country's border with Zambia in the northwest. Finally, one of Zimbabwe's major tourist attractions, the Victoria Falls, is in the southwest.

Conservation

Much of the montane forest in the Vumba Mountains has been lost to agriculture, but Zimbabwe has a pretty good record as far as conservation goes and, currently, over 10% of the land is designated as 'protected'.

Seven threatened and six near-threatened species occur in Zimbabwe.

Bird Families

Eight of the ten families endemic to the African mainland are represented in Zimbabwe, including sugarbirds.

Bird Species

A total of 648 species have been recorded in Zimbabwe. Non-endemic specialities and spectacular species include Cape Griffon*, Taita Falcon*, African Finfoot, Lesser Jacana, Racket-tailed Roller, African Pitta and Collared Palm-Thrush.

Endemics

There are no endemic birds in Zimbabwe, but near-endemics include Swynnerton's Robin*, Boulder Chat, Roberts' Prinia, Chirinda Apalis, Brown Firefinch and Gurney's Sugarbird.

Expectations

It is possible to see 400 species on an extensive three-week trip.

Birders who do not book accomodation prior to arriving in Zimbabwe are advised to do so at the Department of National Parks and Wildlife in the capital, **Harare**, before dashing off to look for the birds.

There are a number of excellent birding sites near Harare. These include: (1) **Mukuvisi Reserve**, which is 3.5 km from the city centre. Head east along Robert Mugabe Road and turn south on to Glenora Avenue. The entrance is 100 m along here. Birds occurring outside the fenced area, especially to the south of the reserve office, include Bennett's Woodpecker, Miombo Rock-Thrush, Spotted Creeper, Stierling's Wren-Warbler and Miombo Sunbird. (2) **Cleveland Dam**, which is 8 km east of the city centre, on the Mutare road. Spotted Creeper as well as African Pygmy-goose occur at and around the dam. (3) The **Botanical Gardens**, 4 km north of the city along the 5th street extension, where Red-faced Mousebird, Purple-crested Turaco, African Pygmy-Kingfisher, Black-collared Barbet, White-throated Robin-Chat and Miombo Sunbird occur. (4) **Christon Bank Estate NR**, 22 km northwest of Harare on the Mazoe road, where the speciality is Boulder Chat. (5) **Lake Robertson (Darwendale Dam)**, 30 km south of Harare, where African Pygmy-goose, Black Heron, Lesser Jacana, White-throated Swallow, African Quailfinch, and Parasitic Weaver occur. Turn northwest off the Chegutu road 31 km southwest of Harare in response to the 'Porta Road' signpost. Bird the bay on the south side of the road after 5 km. Turn south 6 km further on and bird the bay to the east of the road, a good site for Parasitic Weaver. (6) The **Lake Chiputi** area, where African Barred Owlet, Pennant-winged Nightjar (Nov–Apr), Spotted Creeper, Miombo Tit and Miombo Sunbird occur in the miombo woodland. Flooded grassland around here and elsewhere near Harare supports Dwarf Bittern, Streaky-breasted Flufftail, African, Corn* and Striped Crakes, Black Coucal, African Quailfinch, Locustfinch, Cape and Rosy-throated Longclaws and Parasitic Weaver.

African Pitta as well as Thick-billed and Barred Long-tailed Cuckoos, African Broadbill, Livingstone's Flycatcher and the little known Dusky Lark occur near the small town of **Guruve**, northwest of Harare. Bird the wooded valleys near Mushumbi Pools at dawn and between December and March for the best results.

Accommodation: Guruve.

LAKE MCILWAINE

This lake, near the Bulawayo road southwest of Harare, is surrounded by marshes, miombo woodland, and kopjes, where the fine array of birds include Boulder Chat, Pearl-breasted Swallow and Stierling's Wren-Warbler.

Specialities

Boulder Chat, Pearl-breasted Swallow, Stierling's Wren-Warbler, Miombo Tit, Miombo Sunbird.

Others

Ostrich, African Darter, Maccoa and Arican Black Ducks, Goliath Heron, Hamerkop, Coqui Francolin, Kaffir Rail, Water Thick-knee, Red-faced Mousebird, Grey Go-away-bird, African Scops-Owl, Fiery-necked Nightjar, Brown-hooded Kingfisher, Lilac-breasted Roller, Common Scimitar-bill, Whyte's Barbet, Yellow-fronted Tinkerbird, Bennett's Woodpecker, White-breasted Cuckoo-shrike, White Helmetshrike, Groundscraper Thrush, Lesser Blue-eared Glossy-Starling, White-throated Robin-Chat, Spotted Creeper, Grey-rumped Swallow, Red-faced, Lazy and Tinkling Cisticolas, African Bush-Warbler, Lesser Swamp-Warbler, Greencap Eremomela, Cape Crombec, Southern Hyliota, Southern Black-Tit, Southern Penduline-Tit, Rufous-naped Lark, Blue-breasted Cordonbleu, Yellow-throated Longclaw, Striped Pipit, Lesser Masked Weaver, Southern Masked-Weaver, Red-headed Weaver, Yellow Bishop, White-winged Widowbird, Western Violet-backed, Amethyst and White-breasted Sunbirds.

Other Wildlife

Buffalo, Burchell's zebra, eland, giraffe, sassaby, white rhino, wildebeest.

Access

Take the Bulawayo road southwest from Harare and turn east in response to the 'Lake Mcilwaine Upper Reaches' sign. From here head to the Msasa campsite, the base for exploring the northern end of the lake. To bird the south end of the lake it is necessary to return to the Bulawayo road and continue south for 33 km to the turning east, just south of the Hunyani Bridge. Here, the picnic areas and Bushman's Point, where it is possible to bird on foot, are the best birding areas.

Accommodation: Msasa Campsite.

VUMBA MOUNTAINS

Situated on the border with Mozambique, just south of Mutare in east Zimbabwe, the remnant montane forest, grassy slopes and gardens of the Vumba Mountains support three very localised species: Swynnerton's Robin*, Roberts' Prinia and Chirinda Apalis, as well as the superb Four-coloured Bushshrike, Spotted Ground-Thrush* and Gurney's Sugarbird.

Specialities

Buff-spotted Flufftail, Black-fronted Bushshrike, Spotted Ground-Thrush*, Swynnerton's Robin*, Stripe-cheeked Bulbul, Roberts' Prinia, Chirinda Apalis, African Scrub-Warbler, Gurney's Sugarbird.

Others

Augur Buzzard, Long-crested Eagle, Shelley's Francolin, African and Delegorgue's Pigeons, Lemon and Tambourine Doves, Livingstone's Turaco, African Wood-Owl, Scarce Swift, Narina Trogon, Trumpeter and Silvery-cheeked Hornbills, White-eared and Whyte's Barbets, Yellow-rumped Tinkerbird, Scaly-throated, Green-backed and Wahlberg's Honeyguides, White-tailed Crested-Flycatcher, Olive and Four-coloured Bushshrikes, Cape Batis, Orange Ground-Thrush, White-starred Robin (Sep-Feb), Cape, White-browed and Red-capped Robin-Chats, Eastern Sawwing, Yellow-streaked Bulbul, Singing and Wailing Cisticolas, Bar-throated Apalis, Cape Grassbird, African Yellow Warbler, Red-faced Crombec, Yellow-throated Wood-Warbler, Red-faced Crimson-wing, Peters' Twinspot, Black-tailed and Yellow-bellied Waxbills, Black-and-white Mannikin, Forest and Grosbeak Weavers, Yellow Bishop, Yellow-shouldered Widowbird, Western Violet-backed, Bronze and Malachite Sunbirds, Cape and Brimstone Canaries, Streaky-headed Seedeater, Cabanis' Bunting.

Other Wildlife

Samango monkey, white-throated guenon.

Access

Head southeast out of Mutare on the Vumba road and bird: (1) The **Seldomseen** Field Study Centre area, reached by turning north after 24.5 km on to the Nyamheni Track. From here turn left after 800 m on to a steep track signposted 'Seldomseen' and 'Twinstreams'. Around the cottages there are forest trails where Four-coloured Bushshrike occurs, whilst the grassy slopes below Seldomseen support Gurney's Sugarbird. (2) **Bunga Forest** Botanical Reserve, through which the Vumba road passes. (3) **Vumba Botanical Gardens**, 32 km from Mutare. Swynnerton's Robin* is present in all three of these areas. The area around the White Horse Inn, reached by turning left on to Essex Road

*Zimbabwe's Vumba Mountains support the localised Swynnerton's Robin**

VUMBA MOUNTAINS

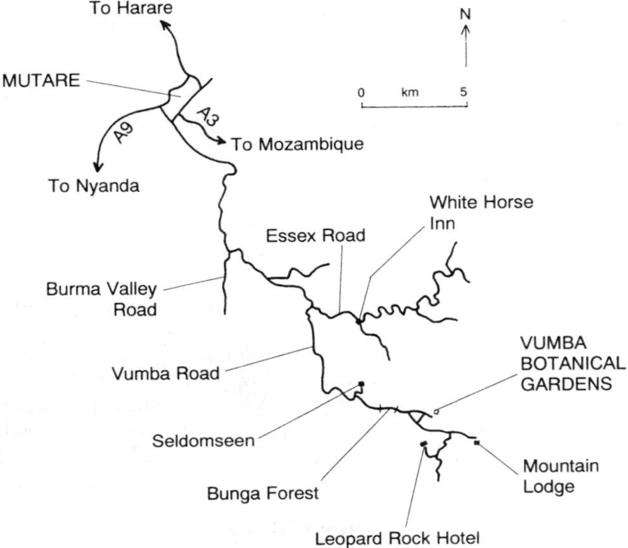

before the turning to Seldomseen, is also a good spot. Peters' Twinspot occurs here, by the road and along the short trail behind the Inn.

Accommodation: Youth Hostel Campsite (C); Seldomseem Cottages (bookable through PO Box 812, Mutare (tel: 2021 5125); Twinstreams Cottages; White Horse Inn. The cottages and inn are all expensive and often full, especially at weekends.

Swynnerton's Robin*, Roberts' Prinia and Chrinda Apalis also occur in the **Chirinda Forest**, 33 km south of Chipinge, in the southern extremity of the Vumba Mountains, and in **Chimanimani NP**, 21 km from Chimanimani, near the Mozambique border, where Pel's Fishing-Owl, Barred Long-tailed Cuckoo, Black-and-white Shrike-flycatcher, Zululand Batis, Tiny Greenbul, Gurney's Sugarbird and Plain-backed Sunbird also occur.

Crowned Hawk-Eagle, Water Thick-knee, White-headed and Black-winged Lapwings, Barred Long-tailed Cuckoo, Pel's Fishing-Owl, Narina Trogon and Retz's Helmetshrike have been recorded in the remote **Gona-Re-Zhou NP**, in southeast Zimbabwe. A 4WD vehicle is recommended here and the park is open only from April to October. Turn south 18 km east of Chiredzi. It is 32 km from here to the park office at Chipindi Pools Campsite on the River Lundi, 10 km from the park entrance. Black-winged Lapwing has been seen around the **Masayana Dam**.

Accommodation: Chipindi Pools campsite (beware of elephants).

RHODES MATOPOS NATIONAL PARK

This park, 50 km south of Bulawayo in southern Zimbabwe, is famous for its rock art and Verreaux's Eagles, but it also protects miombo woodland, grassland and granite kopjes where Boulder Chat and the localised Latakoo Lark occur.

Specialities

Boulder Chat, Latakoo Lark, Miombo Sunbird.

Others

Verreaux's Eagle, Natal Francolin, Freckled Nightjar, Red-faced Mousebird, Purple-crested Turaco, Cape Eagle Owl, Pied and Black-collared Barbets, Yellow-billed Oxpecker, White-throated Robin-Chat, Familiar Chat, Lazy, Tinkling and Piping Cisticolas, Burnt-neck Eremomela, Yellow Bishop, Cape Bunting.

Other Wildlife

Four-toed elephant shrew, giraffe, klipspringer, sable, white rhino, wildebeest.

Access

Bird around the Maleme Dam campsite, 21 km from the entrance, and the Whovi Wild Area.

Accommodation: Four campsites, some with chalets, including one at Maleme Dam.

The **Tshabalala Sanctuary** (12 sq km) is just off the road to Rhodes Matopos NP, 10 km southwest of Bulawayo. It is possible to bird the acacia savanna on foot here (a rare treat in Zimbabwe) in search of Secretary-bird, Spotted Thick-knee, Three-banded and Temminck's Coursers, Crimson-breasted Gonolek, Sabota Lark, African Quailfinch and Scaly Weaver.

HWANGE NATIONAL PARK

This huge park (14,650 sq km) in southwest Zimbabwe is situated at the easternmost edge of the Kalahari Desert, where the open savanna, pans, mopane woodland, granite kopjes and waterholes attract a great variety of large mammals and birds. Over 400 species have been recorded, including Cape Griffon* and Racket-tailed Roller.

Specialities

Cape Griffon*, Racket-tailed Roller, Bradfield's Hornbill, Magpie Shrike, Southern Pied-Babbler, Monotonous Lark.

Others

Ostrich, Saddle-billed Stork, White-headed Vulture, Bat Hawk, Brown Snake-Eagle, Ovampo Sparrowhawk, Martial Eagle, Secretary-bird, Natal and Red-billed Francolins, Swainson's Spurfowl, Kori and Red-crested Bustards, Three-banded and Temminck's Coursers, Crowned

Lapwing, African Skimmer, Double-banded and Burchell's Sandgrouse, Meyer's Parrot, Red-faced Mousebird, African Scops Owl, Spotted Eagle-Owl, Rufous-cheeked and Freckled Nightjars, Swallow-tailed and Southern Carmine (Aug–Mar) Bee-eaters, Common Scimitar-bill, Southern Ground-Hornbill, Pied Barbet, White-crowned Shrike, Crimson-breasted Gonolek, Retz's Helmetshrike, Groundscraper Thrush, Red-shouldered Glossy-Starling, Yellow-billed Oxpecker, Pale and Mariqua Flycatchers, Capped Wheatear, White-headed Black-Chat, Rufous-chested Swallow, Yellow-bellied and Burnt-neck Eremomelas, Rufous-vented Warbler, Ashy Tit, Flappet and Fawn-coloured Larks, Chestnut-backed Sparrow-Lark, Yellow-throated Petronia, Cape Wagtail, Striped Pipit, Violet-eared and Black-cheeked Waxbills, Shaft-tailed Whydah, Scaly Weaver, Holub's Golden-Weaver, Mariqua Sunbird.

(White-backed Duck, African Pygmy-goose, Dwarf Bittern, Striped Crake and Lesser Jacana are all possible when the pans are full.)

Other Wildlife

Buffalo, Burchell's zebra, cheetah, eland, elephant, giraffe, greater kudu, hippo, honey badger, hunting dog, impala, leopard, lion, porcupine, roan, rock dassie, sable, spotted hyena, spring hare, steinbok, waterbuck, white rhino, wildebeest.

Access

Hwange NP is 130 km east of Victoria Falls and 265 km northwest of Bulawayo. The whole park is worth birding, but the best spots include: (1) **Baikiaea Forest** alongside the entrance road to the Main Camp (Racket-tailed Roller). (2) The grounds and surrounds of **Safari Lodge**, 10 km from the main Bulawayo–Victoria Falls road. (3) The area around the **Main Camp** (290 km northwest of Bulawayo (25 km from main Bulawayo–Victoria Falls road)), especially to the north (only pos-

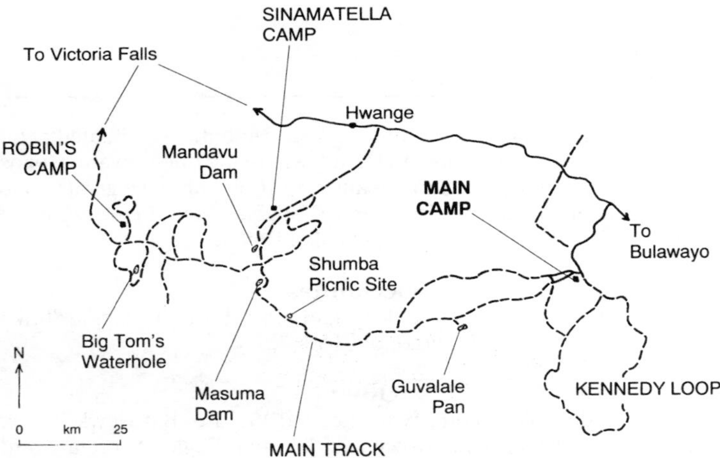

sible on organised walking safaris). Also near here, it is worth birding the pan area 2–4 km to the west, and the Kennedy Loop to the south, where Three-banded Courser, Bradfield's Hornbill and Southern Pied-Babbler occur. (4) The **Main Track** from the Main Camp to Sinamatella and Robin's Camps, via the Shumba picnic site (70 km west of Main Camp). Cape Griffon*, Double-banded and Burchell's Sandgrouse, Mariqua Flycatcher, Fawn-coloured Lark, Striped Pipit and Violet-eared Waxbill occur along this route, and Saddle-billed Stork, Bat Hawk, African Skimmer and Cape Wagtail occur at Mandavu Dam, near Sinamatella Camp. (5) **Big Tom's Waterhole**, near Robin's Camp.

Accommodation: Main Camp: Lodge/chalets (C)/campsite (C) (book well in advance). Robin's Camp: Remote chalets (C)/campsite (C) (take own food/closed Dec–Apr). Sinamatella Camp: Chalets (C)/campsite (C), on ridge overlooking plains.

VICTORIA FALLS and ZAMBEZI NATIONAL PARK

Known in African as Mosi-O-Tunya, which means 'smoke that thunders', the spectacular setting of the Victoria Falls is the most easily accessible site in Africa where it is possible to see the very rare Taita Falcon*. The Zambezi river upstream from the falls is also one of the most reliable places on the continent for African Finfoot, whilst other attractions include White-backed Night-Heron, Rock Pratincole and Collared Palm-Thrush.

Some birders may also consider looking at the falls for a while since it is possible to see species including the localised Brown Firefinch. Here this bird occurs in the luxuriant forest which thrives on the spray from the 1700 m wide and 70–110 m high waterfall.

Specialities

Taita Falcon, Collared Palm-Thrush, Monotonous Lark, Brown Firefinch.

Others

Rufous-bellied Heron, White-backed Night-Heron, Little Sparrowhawk, Verreaux's Eagle, Dickinson's Kestrel, Natal and Red-billed Francolins,

African Finfoot is found throughout the African continent, but the Victoria Falls area is one of the most reliable places to see this very special bird

Swainson's Spurfowl, African Finfoot, Black-bellied Bustard, Rock Pratincole (Jul-Dec), White-headed and Crowned Lapwings, African Skimmer, Red-faced Mousebird, Purple-crested Turaco, African Wood Owl, African Swift, Half-collared and Giant Kingfishers, White-fronted Bee-eater, Trumpeter Hornbill, Red-winged Starling, Bearded Scrub-Robin, Capped Wheatear, White-throated Swallow, Yellow-bellied Greenbul, Terrestrial Brownbul, African Reed-Warbler, Lesser Swamp-Warbler, Greencap Eremomela, Southern Black-Tit, Sabota Lark, Buffy Pipit, Spectacled Weaver, Holub's Golden-Weaver.

Other Wildlife

Hippo, klipspringer, sable.

Access

The best birding areas include: (1) The **Falls Forest**. (2) The **'Taita Falcon* Cliff'**, reached by following the trail from the Victoria Falls Hotel. Scan the cliffs and remember Peregrine Falcon is also present. (3) The **River Trail**, which runs west of the fenced-off falls area, 4 km upstream to the A'Zambezi River Lodge. Collared Palm-Thrush occurs along here and Rock Pratincoles (Jul–Dec) may be seen on the river. (4) The **Zambezi River**, which can be birded from boats, hired at the

VICTORIA FALLS

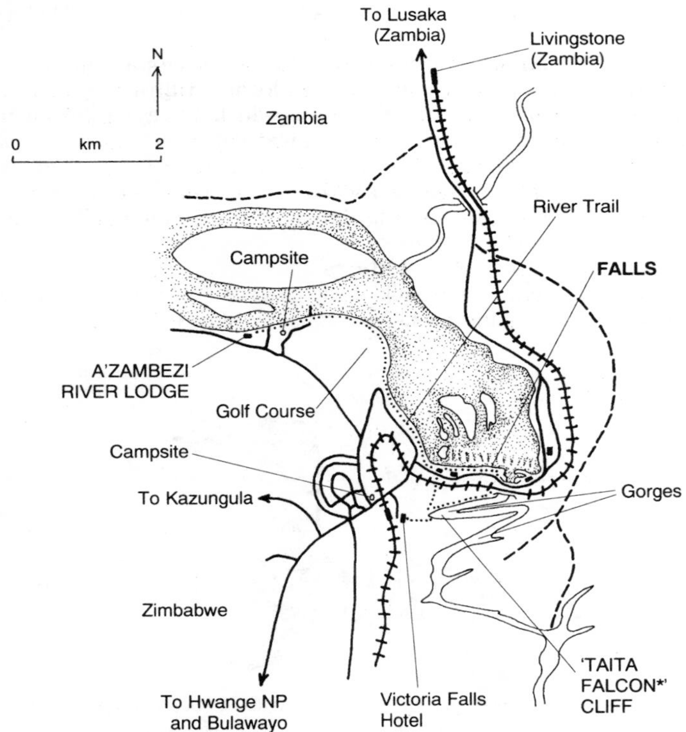

ZAMBEZI NP

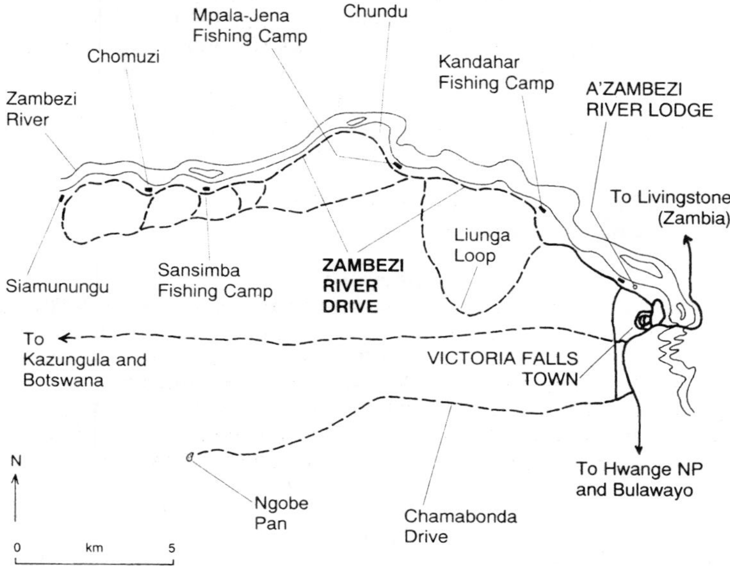

A'Zambezi River Lodge. Rufous-bellied Heron, White-backed Night-Heron, African Finfoot, White-headed Lapwing and African Skimmer all occur along the river and are best seen by boat, although African Finfoot may sometimes be seen on the river from the A'Zambezi River Lodge itself. (5) **Zambezi NP**, which begins west of the A'Zambezi River Lodge. A number of tracks pass through the plains and woodlands in this park, and it is possible to bird on foot at a number of riverside stops along the Zambezi River Drive. White-headed Lapwing, African Skimmer and Collared Palm-Thrush occur along here. Dickinson's Kestrel, Monotonous and Sabota Larks and Buffy Pipit have been recorded along Chamabonda Drive, south of Zambezi River Drive.

Accommodation: A'Zambezi River Lodge (A)/campsite (C) (good birding/African Wood Owl); Victoria Falls Rest Camp/caravan park/cottages (B–C)/chalets (B–C)/hostel (C)/camping (C)); Victoria Falls Hotel (A).

The private **Imbalala Lodge** is 70 km west of Victoria Falls, just off the Kazungula road to Botswana. It is usually possible to stay here (A+) only with a prior booking through the office in Victoria Falls (opposite the Tourist Information Office). However, when it is not full it may be possible to negotiate a lower rate, and it is worth trying because Slaty Egret* and Angola Babbler occur here, as well as African Pygmy-goose, Rufous-bellied Heron, Lesser Jacana, and Greater Painted-snipe. The turn-off to the lodge is 1 km before the Botswana border.

It is possible to visit **Matusadona NP** or, without a 4WD, its entrance road, *en route* from Harare to Kariba and/or Mana Pools. A 4WD is recommended within the park, even in the dry season. To bird the entrance road turn west 170 km northwest of Harare, 8 km northwest of Karoi. The woodland 73 km along this road supports Racket-tailed Roller. Further on, Half-collared Kingfisher occurs at the Sanyati River Crossing, from where it is 60 km to the turning (north) to the park.

LAKE KARIBA

The shoreline, grassland and thickets around this huge, 260-km-long artificial lake in northwest Zimbabwe support some excellent birds, including African Pitta.

Specialities

African Pitta (Nov–Mar), Meves' Glossy-Starling.

Others

Black and Goliath Herons, Hamerkop, Saddle-billed Stork, White-headed Vulture, Bateleur, Ovampo Sparrowhawk, Ayre's Hawk-Eagle, Dickinson's Kestrel, Crested and Natal Francolins, African Finfoot, Stanley Bustard, Greater Painted-snipe, African Snipe, Temminck's Courser, Rock Pratincole (Jul–Dec), White-headed Lapwing, Double-banded Sandgrouse, African Scops-Owl, Marsh Owl, Horus Swift, Swallow-tailed and Southern Carmine Bee-eaters, Crowned Hornbill, Southern Ground-Hornbill, Groundscraper Thrush, Red-billed Oxpecker, White-headed Black-Chat, Eastern Nicator, Desert Cisticola, African Bush-Warbler, Village Indigobird, Rosy-throated Longclaw, Lesser Masked Weaver. (Fuelleborn's Longclaw has been reported here.)

Other Wildlife

Buffalo, elephant, greater kudu, hippo, lion.

Access

To reach the area around Kariba town, turn west 250 km northwest of Harare at Makuti. The Nyanana campsite, on the lakeshore, is on the left of the Kariba road, 20 km before Kariba town and 50 km from Makuti. This is a good site for Black Heron, Saddle-billed Stork, Greater Painted-snipe, African Snipe and African Scops-Owl. Kariba Dam is a good site for Rock Pratincole and Horus Swift; African Finfoot occurs in the Sanyati Gorge, and African Pitta has been recorded in the thickets near Kariba town.

MANA POOLS NATIONAL PARK

This park in northwest Zimbabwe, next to the Zambezi river, is very, very popular. The attraction is the freedom to roam on foot despite the presence of several dangerous mammals including buffalo, elephant and lion. Those who relish the thought of some 'real' birding on foot in the bush will also be attracted by the presence of White-fronted Bee-eater, Racket-tailed Roller and Shelley's Sunbird.

This national park is open from May to October, and usually full in August and September at least, so it is essential to book in advance with the National Parks Booking Office.

Specialities

Racket-tailed Roller, Shelley's Sunbird.

Others

Rufous-bellied Heron, Saddle-billed Stork, Ayres' Hawk-Eagle, Secretary-bird, Crested Guineafowl, Water Thick-knee, Bronze-winged Courser, White-fronted and Blacksmith Plovers, White-headed Lapwing, African Skimmer, Lilian's Lovebird, Pel's Fishing-Owl, White-fronted and Southern Carmine Bee-eaters, Southern Ground-Hornbill, Common Scimitar-bill, Holub's Golden-Weaver.

Other Wildlife

Buffalo, eland, elephant, greater kudu, hippo, lion, Nile crocodile.

Access

A few km west of the National Parks Office at Marangora (where it is necessary to get a permit), turn north. The first campsite is 70 km from here.

Accommodation: Two Lodges (B); camping (C) (take own food).

ADDITIONAL INFORMATION

Books and Papers

Illustrated Guide to the Birds of Southern Africa. Sinclair, I *et al.* 1993. New Holland.
Where to Watch Birds in Southern Africa. Berruti, A and Sinclair, I. 1983. Struik.

Addresses

Ornithological Society of Zimbabwe, Box 8382 Causeway, Harare, Zimbabwe. This society publishes a quarterly journal, *Honeyguide*.

Please send general records to Tony Tree, Chiranwoo Farm, Box 61 Darwendale, and rarity records to Dr Kit Hustler, Department of Ornithology, Natural History Museum of Zimbabwe, Box 240 Bulawayo.

National Parks Booking Office, 93 B Stanley Avenue, PO Box 8151 Causeway, Harare (tel: 706 077).

Near-endemics (East)

Zululand and Pale Batises, Swynnerton's Robin*, Roberts' Prinia, Chirinda Apalis, African Scrub-Warbler, Gurney's Sugarbird.

Near-endemics (Southeast)

Lemon-breasted Seedeater.

Near-endemics (South)

Latakoo Lark, Swee Waxbill.

Near-endemics (Southwest)

Slaty Egret*, Coppery-tailed Coucal, Angola Babbler, Brown Firefinch.

ISLANDS AROUND AFRICA

ASCENSION

This island in the mid Atlantic supports 16 resident species, including the endemic Ascension Island Frigatebird* (unidentified frigatebirds off São Tomé and Principe islands may well be this species). Although the frigatebirds breed only on Boatswainbird Islet, they can be seen all round Ascension, harrying the other seabirds, which include Band-rumped Storm-Petrel, Red-billed and White-tailed Tropicbirds, Masked, Red-footed and Brown Boobies, Sooty Tern, Brown and Black Noddies and Common White-Tern. A further 40 species are regarded as vagrants.

There are relatively few birds on the main island thanks to the thoughtless introduction of cats and the accidental introduction of rats, which are believed to eat many thousands of Sooty Terns every year.

ADDITIONAL INFORMATION

Books and Papers

The Birds of St Helena and Ascension Islands. Kieser, J. 1979. *Bokmakierie* 31:40–43.

The Birds of Ascension Island. Simmons, K. In prep. BOU.

Addresses

Please send all records to Dr K Simmons, BOU, The Natural History Museum, Tring, Herts, HP23 6AP, UK.

ST HELENA

This island, 2800 km west of Angola, supports the endemic St Helena Plover*, whose current population (1993) stands at around 300 (and falling fast). There are also plenty of seabirds here, including Band-rumped Storm-Petrel, Red-billed Tropicbird, Sooty Tern, Brown and Black Noddies, and Common White-Tern. A total of 99 species has been recorded.

ADDITIONAL INFORMATION

Books and Papers

The Birds of St Helena and Ascension Islands. Kieser, J. 1979. *Bokmakierie* 31:40–43.

A Note on the Avifauna of St Helena. Den Hartog, J. 1984. *Bull. BOC* 104:91–95.

The Birds of St Helena. Rowlands, B *et al.* In prep. BOU.

Addresses

Please send all records to Commander M Casement, Dene Cottage, West Harting, Petersfield, Hants, GU31 5PA, UK.

THE TRISTAN DA CUNHA GROUP and GOUGH ISLAND

These islands lie southwest of the Cape of Good Hope. Six endemics are present, and are listed below:

Inaccessible Rail*	This flightless rail occurs only on Inaccessible Island
Tristan Moorhen*	This flightless rail is native to Gough Island, although it has been introduced to Tristan Island
Tristan Thrush*	Inaccessible, Nightingale and Tristan Islands
Gough Island Finch*	Gough Island
Nightingale Finch*	Inaccessible and Nightingale Islands
Wilkins' Finch*	Inaccessible and Nightingale Islands

Photographs of these endemic birds appear in *Ian Sinclair's Field Guide to the Birds of Southern Africa*. Second revised edition. 1987. HarperCollins.

These islands, especially Gough, also support some of the world's most important seabird colonies. The following species breed: Rockhopper Penguin, Wandering*, Yellow-nosed and Sooty* Albatrosses, Kerguelen, Great-winged, Soft-plumaged and Atlantic* Petrels, Broad-billed Prion, White-chinned and Grey Petrels, Great and Little Shearwaters, Grey-backed, White-faced and White-bellied Storm-Petrels, Common Diving-Petrel and Antarctic Tern.

ADDITIONAL INFORMATION

Books and Papers

Aspects of the ornithology of the Tristan da Cunha Group and Gough Island. Richardson, M. 1984. *Cormorant* 112:122–201.

Addresses

The birds of the Tristan da Cunha Group, St Helena and Ascension are dealt with in the biannual bulletin of the African Seabird Group, entitled *Marine Ornithology*, edited by Dr J Cooper, Percy Fitzpatrick Institute of African Ornithology, University of Cape Town, Rondebosch 7700, South Africa. The African Seabird Group can be contacted at Box 34113, Rhodes Gift 7707, South Africa.

Southern African Ornithological Society, Box 84394, Greenside, Johannesburg 2034, South Africa.

Ocean Adventures were offering a rare opportunity to visit Gough, Tristan da Cunha, St Helena, Ascension, Cape Verde, Canary and Madeira Islands on a cruise lasting 51 days, from March to May 1995, and this may be repeated in the future.

BOUVET ISLAND

This island lies south of Gough Island, midway between Africa and Antarctica. Chinstrap Penguin and Snow Petrel breed here.

THE 'SOUTHERN ARC'

The string of islands which lie in an arc between Africa and Antarctica, to the southeast of the Cape of Good Hope, include Marion, Prince Edward, Crozet, Kerguelen, Heard and McDonald Islands. Many seabirds breed on these islands including the rare Kerguelen Tern*, which is endemic. Other species include King, Gentoo and Macaroni Penguins, Grey-headed* and Light-mantled Albatrosses, Cape, White-headed and Blue Petrels, Black-bellied Storm-Petrel, South Georgia Diving-Petrel, Imperial Shag (Marion Island only), and Black-faced Sheathbill.

ADDITIONAL INFORMATION

Books and Papers

Rare Bird Sightings at the Prince Edward Islands. December 1983 to May 1987. Gartshore, N. 1987. *Cormorant* 15:48–58.

AMSTERDAM ISLAND

This remote island lying east-southeast of the Cape of Good Hope supports one of the rarest birds in the world: there are around 70 Amsterdam Island Albatrosses* left. Other seabirds present on Amsterdam Island include Wandering*, Yellow-nosed and Sooty* Albatrosses, Broad-billed Prion and Antarctic Tern.

REQUEST

If you would like to contribute to the second edition of this guide, please send details of any errors or changes to the site details and species lists included in this edition, and information on any new sites you feel deserve inclusion, to:

Nigel Wheatley, c/o Christopher Helm (Publishers) Limited, 35 Bedford Row, London WC1R 4JH, UK.

It would be extremely helpful if information could be submitted in the following format:

1 A summary of the site's position (in relation to the nearest city, town or village), altitude, access arrangements, habitats, number of species recorded (if known), best species, best time to visit, and its richness compared with other sites.
2 A species list, preferably using the names and taxonomic order in Clements' *Check List* and supplements.
3 Details of how to get to the site and where to bird once there, with information on trails etc.
4 A map complete with scale and compass point.
5 Any addresses to write to for permits etc.
6 Any details of accommodation.

Any information on the following species would also be very useful:

Taita Falcon*, Chestnut-headed Flufftail, Striped Crake, Savile's Bustard, Brown-chested Lapwing, Niam-Niam Parrot, Black-cheeked Lovebird*, African Grass-Owl, Maned Owl, Sombre Nightjar, Reichenow's Woodpecker, African Pitta, Green-breasted Pitta, Oriole Cuckoo-shrike, Uhehe Fiscal, Red-naped Bushshrike, Grey-crested Helmetshrike*, *Verreaux's Batis*, Black-eared Ground-Thrush, Grey Ground-Thrush, Babbling Starling, Shari's Sawwing, Fan-tailed Grassbird, Forest Penduline-Tit, Buff-bellied Penduline-Tit, Rusty Lark, Locustfinch, Violet-breasted Sunbird and Reichard's Seedeater.

I would be extremely grateful if you could also include a statement outlining your permission to use your information in the next edition and, finally, your name and address, so that you can be acknowledged appropriately.

I would like to take this opportunity to thank you in anticipation of your help. The usefulness of the next edition depends on your efforts.

CALENDAR

The following is a brief summary of the best countries and regions to visit according to the time of the year. This calendar is aimed to help those birders, such as teachers, who have set holidays, to choose the best destination. Alternatively, if there are birders out there fortunate enough to have a year to go birding in Africa, then following this schedule could produce the best birding and the most birds. If anyone tries this, please let me know how they get on. Better still, if there is a willing sponsor out there, contact me immediately.

Were such a dream to come true why not try the following route: beginning in January spend the first half of the month in Morocco and the second half in Senegal and Gambia, move south to Côte D'Ivoire for two weeks in February, and on to Cameroon until mid March, then fly across to Ethiopia for April. In late April wind down a little with some leisurely birding in Egypt, then return to some serious stuff, with May in Uganda and June in Kenya, before taking a second breather on the Seychelles in early July, catching up with the endemics (and the first six months' notes). In mid July move to Malawi, then Zambia, and on to Gabon for August, with São Tomé and Principe thrown in at the end of the month. In early September head for eastern Zaïre, and after a couple of weeks, turn south again, this time to Namibia, before moving on to South Africa for the whole of October. Madagascar makes sense in November, followed by a brief sojourn on Mauritius and Réunion before the final push — Tanzania in early December and Kenya again to complete what would undoubtedly be a fantastic birding year.

JANUARY: Cameroon, Côte D'Ivoire, Gambia, Ethiopia, Kenya, Morocco, Namibia, Senegal, Tanzania, Zimbabwe.
FEBRUARY: Botswana, Cameroon, Côte D'Ivoire, Gambia, Morocco, Senegal, South Africa, Tanzania, Uganda, Zimbabwe.
MARCH: Botswana, Cameroon, Ethiopia, Kenya, Tanzania, Zambia.
APRIL: Egypt, Morocco.
MAY: Morocco, Namibia, Uganda, South Africa.
JUNE: Canary Islands, Kenya, São Tomé and Principe.
JULY: Kenya, Malawi, Seychelles, Uganda, Zambia.
AUGUST: Botswana, Canary Islands, Gabon, Kenya, Malawi, Namibia, São Tomé and Principe, Uganda, Zambia, Zimbabwe.
SEPTEMBER: Mauritius, Kenya, Namibia, Réunion, Seychelles, South Africa, Zaïre, Zambia.
OCTOBER: Botswana, Kenya, Madagascar, Malawi, Uganda, Seychelles, South Africa, Zaïre.
NOVEMBER: Ethiopia, Gambia, Kenya, Madagascar, Malawi, Mauritius, Namibia, Réunion, Zimbabwe.
DECEMBER: Cameroon, Côte D'Ivoire, Ethiopia, Gambia, Kenya, Morocco, Senegal.

USEFUL ADDRESSES

Clubs and Societies

The African Bird Club (ABC): This club was formed in 1994 with the aim of providing a worldwide focus for African ornithology, and encouraging an interest in the conservation of the birds of the region. Membership costs £12 per year and benefits include receipt of a bi-annual bulletin. **Join now** by writing to The Membership Secretary, African Bird Club, c/o BirdLife International, Wellbrook Court, Girton Road, Cambridge CB3 0NA, UK.

The Ornithlogical Society of the Middle East (OSME): C/o The Lodge, Sandy, Beds SG19 2DL, UK, publishes a bulletin and the *Sandgrouse* journal, both of which cover Egypt, Djibouti and Socotra.

The West African Ornithological Society (WAOS): C/o 1 Fishers Heron, East Mills, Fordingbridge, Hants SP6 2JR, UK, publishes the *Malimbus* journal, a source for much information on the more obscure countries of the continent.

The East African Natural History Society (EANHS): Box 44486, Nairobi, Kenya, publishes a bulletin and the *Scopus* journal.

The Southern African Ornithological Society (SAOS): Box 84394, Greenside, Johannesburg 2034, South Africa, publishes a quarterly newsletter and the *Ostrich* journal, and has many affiliated clubs.

The African Seabird Group: Box 34113, Rhodes Gift 7707, South Africa, and **Royal Navy Bird-watching Society**, which publishes the *Marine Ornithology* journal.

Trip Reports

Dutch Birding Travel Report Service: PO Box 737, 9700 AS Groningen, The Netherlands (tel: 3150145925; fax: 3150144717). To obtain a copy of the catalogue which lists a very extensive selection of reports, covering most African countries, send £3 or $5.

Foreign Birdwatching Reports and Information Service (FBRIS) (Organised and owned by Steve Whitehouse): 5 Stanway Close, Blackpole, Worcester WR4 9XL, UK (tel: 01905 454541). To obtain a copy of the catalogue which lists 400 reports from around the world, send £1.

Tour Companies

Birding: Periteau House, Winchelsea, East Sussex TN36 4EA, UK (tel: 0797 223223; fax: 0797 222911).

Birdquest (and Ocean Adventures): Two Jays, Kemple End, Birdy Brow, Stonyhurst, Lancashire BB6 9QY, UK. (tel: 0254 826317; fax: 0254 826780; telex: 635159 BIRDQ).

Caledonian Wildlife: 30 Culduthel Road, Inverness IV2 4AP, UK (tel: 01463 710017; fax: 01463 233130).

Cygnus Wildlife Holidays: 57 Fore Street, Kingsbridge, Devon TQ7 1PG, UK (tel: 0548 856178; fax: 0548 857537; telex: 45795 WSTTLX G).

Field Guides: P.O. Box 160723, Austin, Texas 78716-0723, USA (tel: 512 327 4953; fax: 512 327 9231).

Naturetrek: Chautara, Bighton, nr. Alresford, Hampshire SO24 9RB, UK (tel: 0962 733051; fax: 0962 733368).

Ornitholodays: 1 Victoria Drive, Bognor Regis, West Sussex PO21 2PW, UK (tel: 0243 821230; fax: 0243 829574).

Sunbird/Wings: P.O. Box 76, Sandy, Beds SG19 1DF, UK (tel: 0767 682969) and P.O. Box 31930, Tucson, Arizona 85751, USA (tel: 602 749 1967; fax: 602 749 3175).

Travel Agents

Wildwings: International House, Bank Road, Bristol BS15 2LX, UK (tel: 0117 984 8040; fax: 0117 967 4444). This company also organises its own tours.

USEFUL GENERAL BOOKS

Regional Field Guides

A number of field guides, including at least two for East Africa and one for West Africa, are currently in preparation. Check with book distributors and shops for the latest information, but the provisional titles of these books are:

A Field Guide to the Birds of East Africa. Stevenson, T *et al.*
Birds of Kenya and Northern Tanzania. Zimmerman, D, Turner, D and Pearson, D. Helm.
The Birds of West Africa: An Identification Guide. Robertson, I, Demey, R and Borrow, N. Helm.

The following regional field guides are in print:

A Field Guide to the Birds of East Africa. Williams, J and Arlott, N. 1980. HarperCollins.
A Field Guide to the Birds of West Africa. Serle, W and Morel, G. 1977. HarperCollins.
Birds of East Africa: Collins Illustrated Checklist. van Perlo, B. 1995. HarperCollins.
Birds of Europe with North Africa and the Middle East. Jonsson, L. 1992. Helm.
Birds of Southern Africa. 1991 update. Newman, K. 1991. HarperCollins.
Birds of the Middle East and North Africa. Hollom, P. 1988. Poyser.
Ian Sinclair's Field Guide to the Birds of Southern Africa (photographic). Sinclair, I. 1987. HarperCollins.
Illustrated Guide to the Birds of Southern Africa. Sinclair, I *et al.* 1993. New Holland.
Southern African Birds: The Essential Guide. Sinclair, I. In prep.

Regional Birding Site Guides

Top Birding Spots in Southern Africa. Chittenden, H. 1992. Southern.

Handbooks and Reference Works

A Handbook to the Swallows and Martins of the World. Turner, A and Rose, C. 1989. Helm.
Birds of Eastern and North-eastern Africa (Volumes 1 and 2). Mackworth-Praed, C and Grant, C. 1957/1960. Longman.
Birds of the Southern Third of Africa (Volumes 1 and 2). Mackworth-Praed, C and Grant, C. 1962/1963. Longman.
Birds of West-central and Western Africa (Volumes 1 and 2). Mackworth-Praed, C and Grant, C. 1970/1973. Longman.
Hamlyn Photographic Guide to the Waders of the World. Rosair, D. 1995. Hamlyn.
Handbook of the Birds of the World (Volumes 1 and 2). del Hoyo *et al.* 1992 and 1995 and continuing. Lynx.
Kingfishers, Bee-eaters and Rollers. Fry, C, Fry, K and Harris, A. 1992. Helm.
Pittas, Broadbills and Asities. Lambert, F. In prep. Pica Press.

Seabirds. Harrison, P. 1985. Helm
Shorebirds. Hayman, P, Marchant, J and Prater, T. 1986. Helm.
Swifts. Chantler, P. 1995. Pica Press.
The Birds of Africa (Volumes 1–4). Brown, L, Fry, H, Keith, S, Urban, E and Newman, K. 1982–1992 and continuing. Academic Press.
The Herons Handbook. Hancock, J and Kushlan, J. 1984. Helm.
The Hornbills. Kemp, A. 1995. OUP.
Tits, Nuthatches and Treecreepers. Harrap, S and Quinn, D. 1995. Helm.
Wildfowl. Madge, S and Burn, H. 1988. Helm.
Woodpeckers. Winkler, H. 1995. Pica Press.

Lists, Distribution and Conservation

A Contribution to the Distribution and Taxonomy of Afrotropical and Malagasy birds. Dowsett, R and Dowsett-Lemaire, F. 1993. *Tauraco Research Report* No 5.
Birds of the World: A Check List. Clements, J. 1991. Ibis.
Birds of the World: A Check List: Supplement No 1. Clements, J. 1992. Ibis.
Birds of the World: A Check List: Supplement No 2. Clements, J. 1993. Ibis.
Birds to Watch 2: The World List of Threatened Birds. Collar, N, Crosby, M and Stattersfield, A. 1994. BirdLife International.
Checklist of Birds of the Afrotropical and Malagasy Regions. Dowsett, R and Forbes-Watson, A. 1993. Tauraco Press.
Putting Biodiversity on the Map. Birdlife International. 1992.
Rare Birds of the World. Mountfort, G. 1988. HarperCollins.
Threatened Birds of Africa and Related Islands. Collar, N and Stuart, S. 1985. ICBP/IUCN.

For a comprehensive list of books, etc. on African birds contact: Natural History Book Service Ltd, 2–3 Wills Road, Totnes, Devon TQ9 5XN, UK (tel: 01803 865913, fax: 01803 865280).

Travel

Africa on a Shoestring. Crowther, G. Annual. Lonely Planet. (A number of African regions are also covered by Lonely Planet guides.)
West Africa: The Rough Guide. Hudgens, J and Trillo, R. Annual. Rough Guides. (A number of single African countries are also covered by the Rough Guides.)

Learn the calls and songs before you go, from the recordings held by **WildSounds**, Dept. ABC2, Cross Street, Salthouse, Norfolk NR25 7XH, UK (tel/fax: 01263 741100).

BIRD NAMES WHICH DIFFER BETWEEN *CLEMENTS* AND SOUTHERN AFRICAN FIELD GUIDES

Only name differences which are not immediately obvious are given.

Name used by *Clements*	**Name used by field guides**	**Latin name**
African Cuckoo-Falcon	Cuckoo Hawk	*Aviceda cuculoides*
Fasciated Snake-Eagle	Southern Banded Snake Eagle	*Circaetus fasciolatus*
African Harrier-Hawk	Gymnogene	*Polyboroides typus*
Shikra	Little Banded Goshawk	*Accipiter badius*
Verreaux's Eagle	Black Eagle	*Aquila verreauxii*
Eurasian Kestrel	Rock Kestrel	*Falco tinnunculus*
Amur Falcon	Eastern Red-footed Falcon	*Falco amurensis*
Small Buttonquail	Kurrichane Buttonquail	*Turnix sylvatica*
White-quilled Bustard	Northern Black Korhaan	*Eupodotis afroides*
Black Bustard	Southern Black Korhaan	*Eupodotis afra*
Senegal Lapwing	Lesser Black-winged Plover	*Vanellus lugubris*
Speckled Pigeon	Rock Pigeon	*Columba guinea*
African Pigeon	Rameron Pigeon	*Columba arquatrix*
Lemon Dove	Cinnamon Dove	*Aplopelia larvata*
Ring-necked Dove	Cape Turtle Dove	*Streptopelia capicola*
Brown-necked Parrot	Cape Parrot	*Poicephalus robustus*
Levaillant's Cuckoo	Striped Cuckoo	*Clamator levaillantii*
Pied Cuckoo	Jacobin Cuckoo	*Clamator jacobinus*
Yellowbill	Green Coucal	*Ceuthmochares aereus*
Verreaux's Eagle-Owl	Giant Eagle Owl	*Bubo lacteus*
African Barred Owlet	Barred Owl	*Glaucidium capense*
Square-tailed Nightjar	Mozambique Nightjar	*Caprimulgus fossii*
Swamp Nightjar	Natal Nightjar	*Caprimulgus natalensis*
African Swift	Black Swift	*Apus barbatus*
Bat-like Swift	Bohm's Spinetail	*Neafrapus boehmi*
Madagascar Bee-eater	Olive Bee-eater	*Merops superciliosus*
Rufous-crowned Roller	Purple Roller	*Coracias naevia*
African Green-Tinkerbird	Green Tinker Barbet	*Pogoniulus simplex*
Yellow-rumped Tinkerbird	Golden-rumped Tinker Barbet	*Pogoniulus bilineatus*
Pallid Honeyguide	Eastern Honeyguide	*Indicator meliphilus*
Green-backed Honeyguide	Slender-billed Honeyguide	*Indicator zambesiae*
Wahlberg's Honeyguide	Sharp-billed Honeyguide	*Indicator regulus*
Green-backed Woodpecker	Little Spotted Woodpecker	*Campethera cailliautii*
African Crested-Flycatcher	Blue-mantled Flycatcher	*Trochocercus cyanomelas*
Magpie Shrike	Long-tailed Shrike	*Corvinella melanoleuca*
Brown-crowned Tchagra	Three-streaked Tchagra	*Tchagra australis*
Four-coloured Bushshrike	Gorgeous Bushshrike	*Telophorus quadricolor*
Gabon Boubou	Swamp Boubou	*Laniarius bicolor*
Retz's Helmetshrike	Red-billed Helmetshrike	*Prionops retzii*
Black-and-white Shrike-flycatcher	Vanga Flycatcher	*Bias musicus*
Zululand Batis	Woodwards' Batis	*Batis fratrum*
Pale Batis	Mozambique Batis	*Batis soror*
Black-throated Wattle-eye	Wattle-eyed Flycatcher	*Platysteira peltata*
Red-shouldered Glossy-Starling	Glossy Starling	*Lamprotornis nitens*
Meves' Glossy-Starling	Long-tailed Starling	*Lamprotornis mevesii*
Violet-backed Starling	Plum-coloured Starling	*Cinnyricinclus leucogaster*
Ashy Flycatcher	Blue-grey Flycatcher	*Muscicapa caerulescens*
Pale Flycatcher	Mouse-coloured Flycatcher	*Melaenornis pallidus*
Grey Tit-Flycatcher	Fan-tailed Flycatcher	*Myioparus plumbeus*
White-headed Black-Chat	Arnot's Chat	*Thamnolaea arnoti*
Red-capped Robin-Chat	Natal Robin	*Cossypha natalensis*
White-browed Robin-Chat	Heuglin's Robin	*Cossypha heuglini*
White-throated Robin-Chat	African White-throated Robin	*Cossypha humeralis*
Red-backed Scrub-Robin	White-browed Robin	*Erythropygia leucophrys*
East Coast Akalat	Gunning's Robin	*Sheppardia gunningi*
Plain Martin	Brown-throated Martin	*Riparia paludicola*
Black-fronted Bulbul	Red-eyed Bulbul	*Pycnonotus nigricans*
Common Bulbul	Black-eyed Bulbul	*Pycnonotus barbatus*
Tiny Greenbul	Slender Bulbul	*Phyllastrephus debilis*
Eastern Nicator	Yellow-spotted Nicator	*Nicator gularis*

Bird Names which Differ Between *Clements* and Southern African Field Giudes

Pale White-eye	Cape White-eye	*Zosterops pallidus*
Wing-snapping Cisticola	Ayres' Cisticola	*Cisticola ayresii*
Pectoral-patch Cisticola	Pale-crowned Cisticola	*Cisticola brunnescens*
Siffling Cisticola	Short-winged Cisticola	*Cisticola brachyptera*
Piping Cisticola	Neddicky	*Cisticola fulvicapilla*
Red-headed Cisticola	Grey-backed Cisticola	*Cisticola subruficappila*
Grey Cisticola	Tinkling Cisticola	*Cisticola rufilata*
Winding Cisticola	Black-backed Cisticola	*Cisticola galactotes*
Tinkling Cisticola	Levaillant's Cisticola	*Cisticoal tinniens*
White-breasted Prinia	Namaqua Prinia	*Prinia substriata*
Karoo Prinia	Spotted Prinia	*Prinia maculosa*
Damara Rock-jumper	Rockrunner	*Achaetops pycnopygius*
Kopje Warbler	Cinnamon-breasted Warbler	*Euryptila subcinnamomea*
Stierling's Wren-Warbler	Stierling's Barred Warbler	*Camaroptera stierlingi*
Barred Wren-Warbler	African Barred Warbler	*Camaroptera fasciolata*
African Scrub-Warbler	Barratt's Warbler	*Bradypterus barratti*
African Bush-Warbler	African Sedge Warbler	*Bradypterus baboecala*
Lesser Swamp-Warbler	Cape Reed Warbler	*Acrocephalus gracilirostris*
African Reed-Warbler	African Marsh Warbler	*Acrocephalus baeticatus*
Moustached Grass-Warbler	African Moustached Warbler	*Melocichla mentalis*
Fan-tailed Grassbird	Broad-tailed Warbler	*Schoenicola brevirostris*
Cape Crombec	Long-billed Crombec	*Sylvietta rufescens*
Yellow-rumped Eremomela	Karoo Eremomela	*Eremomela gregalis*
Layard's Warbler	Layard's Tit Babbler	*Parisoma (Sylvia) layardi*
Rufous-vented Warbler	Tit Babbler	*Parisoma (Sylvia) subcaeruleum*
Southern Hyliota	Mashona Hyliota	*Hyliota australis*
Angola Babbler	Hartlaub's Babbler	*Turdoides hartlaubii*
Miombo Tit	Northern Grey Tit	*Parus griseiventris*
African Penduline-Tit	Grey Penduline-Tit	*Anthoscopus caroli*
Southern Penduline-Tit	Cape Penduline-Tit	*Anthoscopus minutus*
Latakoo Lark	Melodious Lark	*Mirafra cheniana*
Ferruginous Lark	Red Lark	*Certhilauda burra*
Large-billed Lark	Thick-billed Lark	*Galerida magnirostris*
Rufous Sparrow	Great Sparrow	*Passer motitensis*
Mossie	Cape Sparrow	*Passer melanurus*
Peters' Twinspot	Red-throated Twinspot	*Hypargos niveoguttatus*
Lesser Seedcracker	Nyasa Seedcracker	*Pyrenestes minor*
Black-tailed Waxbill	Grey Waxbill	*Estrilda perreini*
Yellow-bellied Waxbill	East African Swee	*Estrilda quartinia*
Zebra Waxbill	Orange-breasted Waxbill	*Sporaeginthus subflavus*
Blue-breasted Cordonbleu	Blue Waxbill	*Uraeginthus angolensis*
Green-winged Pytilia	Melba Finch	*Pytilia melba*
Orange-winged Pytilia	Golden-backed Pytilia	*Pytilia afra*
Black-and-white Mannikin	Red-backed Mannikin	*Spermestes bicolor*
Magpie Mannikin	Pied Mannikin	*Spermestes fringilloides*
Variable Indigobird	Black Widowfinch	*Vidua funerea*
Purple Indigobird	Purple Widowfinch	*Vidua purpurascens*
Village Indigobird	Steel-blue Widowfinch	*Vidua chalybeata*
Mountain Wagtail	Long-tailed Wagtail	*Motacilla clara*
African Pipit	Grassveld Pipit	*Anthus cinnamomeus*
Yellow-tufted Pipit	Rock Pipit	*Anthus crenatus*
Cape Longclaw	Orange-throated Longclaw	*Macronyx capensis*
Rosy-throated Longclaw	Pink-throated Longclaw	*Macronyx ameliae*
Scaly Weaver	Scaly-feathered Finch	*Sporopipes squamifrons*
Village Weaver	Spotted-backed Weaver	*Ploceus cucullatus*
African Golden-Weaver	Yellow Weaver	*Ploceus subaureus*
Grosbeak Weaver	Thick-billed Weaver	*Amblyospiza albifrons*
Parasitic Weaver	Cuckoo Finch	*Anomalospiza imberbis*
Black-winged Bishop	Fire-crowned Bishop	*Euplectes hordeaceus*
Yellow-crowned Bishop	Golden Bishop	*Euplectes afer*
Yellow Bishop	Yellow-rumped Widow	*Euplectes capensis*
Fan-tailed Widowbird	Red-shouldered Widow	*Euplectes axillaris*
Yellow-shouldered Widowbird	Yellow-backed Widow	*Euplectes macrourus*
Amethyst Sunbird	Black Sunbird	*Nectarinia amethystina*
Mouse-coloured Sunbird	Grey Sunbird	*Nectarinia veroxii*
Plain-backed Sunbird	Blue-throated Sunbird	*Anthreptes reichenowi*
Variable Sunbird	Yellow-bellied Sunbird	*Nectarinia venusta*
Brimstone Canary	Bully Canary	*Serinus sulphuratus*
Yellow-fronted Canary	Yellow-eyed Canary	*Serinus mozambicus*
Lemon-breasted Seedeater	Lemon-breasted Canary	*Serinus citrinipectus*
Southern Yellow-rumped Seedeater	Black-throated Canary	*Serinus atrogularis*
White-winged Seedeater	Protea Canary	*Serinus leucopterus*
Streaky-headed Seedeater	Streaky-headed Canary	*Serinus gularis*
Black-eared Seedeater	Black-eared Canary	*Serinus mennelli*
Cinnamon-breasted Bunting	Rock Bunting	*Emberiza tahapisi*

INDEX TO SPECIES